Sydney V. Jackson

REASON AND RESPONSIBILITY

REASON AND RESPONSIBILITY

READINGS IN SOME BASIC PROBLEMS OF PHILOSOPHY

edited by

Joel Feinberg

Princeton University

DICKENSON PUBLISHING COMPANY, INC., BELMONT, CALIFORNIA

Second Printing, August 1966

L. C. Cat. Card No.: 65-21115
Printed in the United States of America

PREFACE

The conviction underlying this volume is that for the purpose of introducing the modern college student to philosophy it is far preferable to have a small number of representative problems examined in great detail than to have a "little bit of everything," with each "branch" of philosophy, each major "ism," and each major historical period represented with scrupulous impartiality, even though the articles may have little relevance to one another. I have selected articles from both classical and contemporary sources on such topics as religion, knowledge, mind, explanation, responsibility, duty, and selfishness. The problems under these headings that concern philosophers are not mere idle riddles, but rather questions of vital interest to any reflective person. Each set of problems is plumbed in considerable depth in essays expressing different, and often opposing, views. My hope is that exposure to this argumentative give and take will encourage the student to take part in the process himself, and develop through practice his powers of philosophical reasoning.

In selecting materials, I have benefited from the advice, positive and negative, of several anonymous readers selected by the publisher, and from the following: Professors Paul Benacerraf and Richard Rorty of Princeton University, Nelson Pike of Cornell University, Wesley Salmon of Indiana University, and James M. Smith of Fresno State College, California. The selection from Freud was first called to my attention by Melissa Feinberg. To my wife I am grateful for her labors in typing and editing, and her sage counsel.

Joel Feinberg

CONTENTS

PART 2 HUMAN KNOWLEDGE: ITS GROUNDS AND LIMITS

PART 3 MIND AND ITS PLACE IN NATURE

PART 6 SELF-LOVE AND THE CLAIMS OF MORALITY

REASON AND RESPONSIBILITY

PART 1 REASON AND

What can reason tell us about such vast topics as the creation of the universe and the existence and nature of God? Most of us have beliefs about these matters—beliefs derived from religious authorities or based on faith; but is there any way that these beliefs can be demonstrated to be reasonable or unreasonable? This question provides the unifying theme for the readings in Part One.

Traditional arguments for the existence of God are often divided into two groups: those that are a posteriori (based on experience) and those that are a priori (independent of experience). In fact, however, only one type of argument has ever purported to be *wholly* a priori; namely, the Ontological Argument, invented by St. Anselm in the eleventh century, and defended in one form or another by Descartes, Spinoza, and Leibniz in the seventeenth century. (For Descartes's version of the argument, see his fifth Meditation, p. 103). The argument purports to show that the very concept of God (or definition of the word "God") entails that God must exist. If the argument is correct, any rational being possessed of the idea of God, even if he has no knowledge whatever of the kind derived from sense experience, would have conclusive rational grounds for believing that God exists. Other arguments for God's existence are often called a priori, but these always contain at least one premise that asserts some simple experiential fact. This is true, for example, of the various versions of the Cosmological Argument, of which the first three of St. Thomas Aquinas's "five ways" are examples. Aquinas begins each argument by citing a familiar fact of experience: some things are in motion, there are causes and effects, things are generated and corrupted; he then attempts to show that this fact can be explained *only* by the existence of God, since alternative explanations lead to logical absurdities.

Both the ontological and cosmological arguments are *deductive* in form; that is, they purport to demonstrate that if their premises are true then their conclusions *must necessarily* be true. The argument a posteriori, on the other hand, is more modest. It argues not that its conclusion follows necessarily from its premises, but

RELIGIOUS FAITH

only that its premises establish a *probability* that the conclusion is true. It is therefore what logicians call an *inductive argument*. The famous Argument from Design, which is given a classic formulation by Cleanthes in Hume's *Dialogues,* has this form. More precisely, it is an argument by analogy, with the form:

1. *a, b, c,* and *d* all have properties *P* and *Q*.
2. *a, b,* and *c* all have property *R* as well.
3. Therefore, *d* has property *R* too (probably).

The closer the similarity between *d* and *a, b,* and *c,* the more probable is the conclusion. Cleanthes' argument can be rendered as follows:

1. Boats, houses, watches, and the whole experienced world all have such properties as "mutual adjustment of parts to whole" and "curious adapting of ends to means."
2. Boats, houses, and watches all have the further property of having been produced by design.
3. Therefore, it is probable that the universe also has this further property, that it too was produced by design.

The conclusion of this argument, that a designer of the world exists, has the same logical role as a scientific hypothesis designed to explain the facts of experience, and must be accepted or rejected according to whether it meets the criteria of adequacy by which hypotheses are appraised in science and in everyday life.

The case against the Argument from Design is put with great force and ingenuity by Philo, probably speaking for Hume himself. The analogies cited by the argument, he claims, are weak, partly because we know only one small part of the universe and cannot with confidence infer from it the nature of the whole. Moreover, he argues, there are other equally plausible ways of accounting for the observed order in the world. One of these alternative explanations, called by Philo in Part VII the "Epicurean Hypothesis," bears striking resemblance to the Darwinian theory that biological adaptations are the result of chance variations and the survival of the fittest. In Parts X and XI occurs one of the most famous discussions of "the problem of evil," so central to religious belief. Here Philo concedes that *if* the existence of God has already been established by some a priori argument, then perhaps one can account for the appearance of evil in the world; but he goes on to argue that one cannot infer the existence of an all-good and all-powerful being *from* the appearance of evil; that is, the former can hardly be an *explanation* of the latter.

Many contemporary philosophers have argued that the interpretation of theological doctrines as larger scientific hypotheses is fundamentally misguided. According to these writers, there is at least one crucial difference between the two: Scientific hypotheses are in principle *falsifiable*. We can at least conceive of an experience that we would count as evidence against Newton's laws, but the true believer's faith is compatible with anything that might happen. The American free-thinker, Robert G. Ingersoll, used to challenge God to strike him dead (as a kind of crucial experiment) and then cite his survival as proof of God's nonexistence. It is doubtful that any but the most childlike faith was ever destroyed by "evidence" like this. The sophisticated believer would have ready explanations at hand. Even for more embarrassing occurrences, say those involving great suffering, he would have explanations: God is testing us, or punishing sinners, or perhaps it is just that God's ways are mysterious. No conceivable worldly disaster would render God's existence, to the truly committed, less than probable. Still, it has been urged, a doctrine that is consistent with everything possible can *explain* nothing actual. In the selection from a symposium on theology and falsification, the contemporary British philosopher Antony Flew challenges his fellow symposiasts to describe any conceivable occurrence that they would accept as evidence against the existence of a loving God. His challenge is met in quite different ways. R. M. Hare rejects the view that religious doctrines are explanatory assertions, yet argues that they are no worse for that; his Oxford colleague Basil Mitchell, on the other hand, would allow the fact of pain to count against—but not decisively against—Christian doctrine.

What if it should turn out (as many philosophers now believe) that all traditional arguments for the existence of God, a priori and a posteriori, are defective, or at least inconclusive? Would it follow that religious belief is unreasonable? William James, in the selection from *The Varieties of Religious Experience,* discusses various accounts of mystic experiences that are literally indescribable, in which there is allegedly a direct experience of God—an experience so vivid and intense that, while under its influence, one cannot doubt its authenticity. To a person subject to such experiences, the rationalistic philosopher's talk of proofs and hypotheses must seem totally irrelevant. Yet how is he to know that his prized experiences are not illusory unless he reasons about the matter? This William James does for him. Mystic experiences "have the right to be absolutely authoritative over the individuals [and only those individuals] to whom they come," he concludes, a result partly opposed to that of Bertrand Russell's later essay on the subject. Sigmund Freud's analysis of the "oceanic consciousness" is included as a specimen example of a psychological explanation of mystic phenomena. The crucial question for the philosopher is whether or not such explanations "explain away" the beliefs of the mystics by undermining their "authority." The essay of

Huston Smith discusses this and related problems in the light of recent experiments with "consciousness-expanding" drugs.

Mystical experiences, while having nothing to do with argument, might nevertheless be considered a kind of "evidence" for their attendant beliefs. The question posed by William James in the final selection in this section, however, is whether beliefs based on *no evidence whatever* can nevertheless be, in some circumstances, reasonable. His ingenious essay answers this question in a cautious affirmative. The careful reader might well ask himself, however, whether James's strict conditions for the proper exercise of "the will to believe" are in fact ever satisfied. If there is one thing that William James, the twentieth-century Protestant, has in common with Blaise Pascal, the seventeenth-century Catholic, it is the conviction that the primary function of religious belief is not simply to allay philosophical curiosity about things. Both are aware that, to many, religious belief is a vital practical need, and each in his own way urges that this be taken into account when the reasonableness of belief is assessed.

SAINT ANSELM

The Ontological Argument, from *Proslogium**

CHAPTER II

Truly there is a God, although the fool hath said in his heart, There is no God.

And so, Lord, do thou, who dost give understanding to faith, give me, so far as thou knowest it to be profitable, to understand that thou art as we believe; and that thou art that which we believe. And, indeed, we believe that thou art a being than which nothing greater can be conceived. Or is there no such nature, since the fool hath said in his heart, there is no God? (Psalms xiv. 1). But, at any rate, this very fool, when he hears of this being of which I speak—a being than which nothing greater can be conceived—understands what he hears, and what he understands is in his understanding; although he does not understand it to exist.

For, it is one thing for an object to be in the understanding, and another to understand that the object exists. When a painter first conceives of what he will afterwards perform, he has it in his understanding, but he does not yet understand it to be, because he has not yet performed it. But after he has made the painting, he both has it in his understanding, and he understands that it exists, because he has made it.

Hence, even the fool is convinced that something exists in the understanding, at least, than which nothing greater can be conceived. For, when he hears of this, he understands it. And whatever is understood, exists in the understanding. And assuredly that, than which nothing greater can be conceived, cannot exist in the understanding alone. For, suppose it exists in the understanding alone: then it can be conceived to exist in reality; which is greater.

Therefore, if that, than which nothing greater can be conceived, exists in the understanding alone, the very being, than which nothing greater can be conceived, is one, than which a greater can be conceived. But obviously this is impossible. Hence, there is no doubt that there exists a being, than which nothing greater can be conceived, and it exists both in the understanding and in reality.

CHAPTER III

God cannot be conceived not to exist.—God is that, than which nothing greater can be conceived. —That which can be conceived not to exist is not God.

And it assuredly exists so truly, that it cannot be conceived not to exist. For, it is possible to conceive of a being which cannot be conceived not to exist; and this is greater than one which can be conceived not to exist. Hence, if that, than which nothing greater can be conceived, can be conceived not to exist, it is not that than which nothing greater can be conceived. But this is an irreconcilable contradiction. There is, then, so truly a being than which nothing greater can be conceived to exist, that it cannot even be conceived not to exist; and this being thou art, O Lord, our God.

So truly, therefore, dost thou exist, O Lord, my God, that thou canst not be conceived not to exist; and rightly. For, if a mind could conceive of a being better than thee, the creature would rise above the Creator; and this is most absurd. And, indeed, whatever else there is, except thee alone, can be conceived not to exist. To thee alone, therefore, it belongs to exist more truly than all other beings, and hence in a higher

* From *St. Anselm: Basic Writings,* trans. S. N. Deane, with an Introduction by Charles Hartshorne (La Salle, Ill.: Open Court, 1961). Reprinted by permission of the publisher.

degree than all others. For, whatever else exists does not exist so truly, and hence in a less degree it belongs to it to exist. Why, then, has the fool said in his heart, there is no God (Psalms xiv. I), since it is so evident, to a rational mind, that thou dost exist in the highest degree of all? Why, except that he is dull and a fool?

CHAPTER IV

How the fool has said in his heart what cannot be conceived.—A thing may be conceived in two ways: (1) when the word signifying it is conceived; (2) when the thing itself is understood. As far as the word goes, God can be conceived not to exist; in reality he cannot.

But how has the fool said in his heart what he could not conceive; or how is it that he could not conceive what he said in his heart? since it is the same to say in the heart, and to conceive.

But, if really, nay, since really, he both conceived, because he said in his heart; and did not say in his heart, because he could not conceive; there is more than one way in which a thing is said in the heart or conceived. For, in one sense, an object is conceived, when the word signifying it is conceived; and in another, when the very entity, which the object is, is understood.

In the former sense, then, God can be conceived not to exist; but in the latter, not at all. For no one who understands what fire and water are can conceive fire to be water, in accordance with the nature of the facts themselves, although this is possible according to the words. So, then, no one who understands what God is can conceive that God does not exist; although he says these words in his heart, either without any, or with some foreign, signification. For, God is that than which a greater cannot be conceived. And he who thoroughly understands this, assuredly understands that this being so truly exists, that not even in concept can it be non-existent. Therefore, he who understands that God so exists, cannot conceive that he does not exist.

I thank thee, gracious Lord, I thank thee; because what I formerly believed by thy bounty, I now so understand by thine illumination, that if I were unwilling to believe that thou dost exist, I should not be able not to understand this to be true.

CHAPTER V

God is whatever it is better to be than not to be; and he, as the only self-existent being, creates all things from nothing.

What art thou, then, Lord God, than whom nothing greater can be conceived? But what art thou, except that which, as the highest of all beings, alone exists through itself, and creates all other things from nothing? For, whatever is not this is less than a thing which can be conceived of. But this cannot be conceived of thee. What good, therefore, does the supreme Good lack, through which every good is? Therefore, thou art just, truthful, blessed, and whatever it is better to be than not to be. For it is better to be just than not just; better to be blessed than not blessed.

SAINT THOMAS AQUINAS

The Five Ways, from *Summa Theologica**

[Part I, Question 2, Article 3]

The existence of God can be proved in five ways.

The first and more manifest way is the argument from motion. It is certain, and evident to our senses, that in the world some things are in motion. Now whatever is moved is moved by another, for nothing can be moved except it is in

* From *The Basic Writings of Saint Thomas Aquinas*, ed. Anton C. Pegis (New York: Random House, London: Burns & Oates, 1945), pp. 22–23.

potentiality to that towards which it is moved; whereas a thing moves inasmuch as it is in act. For motion is nothing else than the reduction of something from potentiality to actuality. But nothing can be reduced from potentiality to actuality, except by something in a state of actuality. Thus that which is actually hot, as fire, makes wood, which is potentially hot, to be actually hot, and thereby moves and changes it. Now it is not possible that the same thing should be at once in actuality and potentiality in the same respect, but only in different respects. For what is actually hot cannot simultaneously be potentially hot; but it is simultaneously potentially cold. It is therefore impossible that in the same respect and in the same way a thing should be both mover and moved, *i.e.*, that it should move itself. Therefore, whatever is moved must be moved by another. If that by which it is moved be itself moved, then this also must needs be moved by another, and that by another again. But this cannot go on to infinity, because then there would be no first mover, and, consequently, no other mover, seeing that subsequent movers move only inasmuch as they are moved by the first mover; as the staff moves only because it is moved by the hand. Therefore it is necessary to arrive at a first mover, moved by no other; and this everyone understands to be God.

The second way is from the nature of efficient cause. In the world of sensible things we find there is an order of efficient causes. There is no case known (neither is it, indeed, possible) in which a thing is found to be the efficient cause of itself; for so it would be prior to itself, which is impossible. Now in efficient causes it is not possible to go on to infinity, because in all efficient causes following in order, the first is the cause of the intermediate cause, and the intermediate is the cause of the ultimate cause, whether the intermediate cause be several, or one only. Now to take away the cause is to take away the effect. Therefore, if there be no first cause among efficient causes, there will be no ultimate, nor any intermediate, cause. But if in efficient causes it is possible to go on to infinity, there will be no first efficient cause, neither will there be an ultimate effect, nor any intermediate efficient causes; all of which is plainly false. Therefore it is necessary to admit a first efficient cause, to which everyone gives the name of God.

The third way is taken from possibility and necessity, and runs thus. We find in nature things that are possible to be and not to be, since they are found to be generated, and to be corrupted, and consequently, it is possible for them to be and not to be. But it is impossible for these always to exist, for that which can not-be at some time is not. Therefore, if everything can not-be, then at one time there was nothing in existence. Now if this were true, even now there would be nothing in existence, because that which does not exist begins to exist only through something already existing. Therefore, if at one time nothing was in existence, it would have been impossible for anything to have begun to exist; and thus even now nothing would be in existence—which is absurd. Therefore, not all beings are merely possible, but there must exist something the existence of which is necessary. But every necessary thing either has its necessity caused by another, or not. Now it is impossible to go on to infinity in necessary things which have their necessity caused by another, as has been already proved in regard to efficient causes. Therefore we cannot but admit the existence of some being having of itself its own necessity, and not receiving it from another, but rather causing in others their necessity. This all men speak of as God.

The fourth way is taken from the gradation to be found in things. Among beings there are some more and some less good, true, noble, and the like. But *more* and *less* are predicated of different things according as they resemble in their different ways something which is the maximum, as a thing is said to be hotter according as it more nearly resembles that which is hottest; so that there is something which is truest, something best, something noblest, and, consequently, something which is most being, for those things that are greatest in truth are greatest in being, as it is written in *Metaph.* ii.[1] Now the maximum in any genus is the cause of all in that genus, as fire, which is the maximum of heat, is the cause of all hot things, as is said in the same book.[2] Therefore there must also be something which is to all beings the cause of their being, goodness, and every other perfection; and this we call God.

[1] [Aquinas refers here to Aristotle's *Metaphysics,* Ia 1(993b30).]

[2] [*Metaphysics,* Ia1 (993b25).]

The fifth way is taken from the governance of the world. We see that things which lack knowledge, such as natural bodies, act for an end, and this is evident from their acting always, or nearly always, in the same way, so as to obtain the best result. Hence it is plain that they achieve their end, not fortuitously, but designedly. Now whatever lacks knowledge cannot move towards an end, unless it be directed by some being endowed with knowledge and intelligence; as the arrow is directed by the archer. Therefore some intelligent being exists by whom all natural things are directed to their end; and this being we call God.

F. C. COPLESTON

On St. Thomas's Proofs*

Aquinas did not, of course, deny that people can come to know that God exists by other ways than by philosophic reflection. Nor did he ever assert that the belief of most people who accept the proposition that God exists is the result of their having elaborated metaphysical arguments for themselves or of their having thought through the metaphysical arguments developed by others. Nor did he confuse a purely intellectual assent to the conclusion of such a metaphysical argument with a living Christian faith in and love of God. But he did think that reflection on quite familiar features of the world affords ample evidence of God's existence. The reflection itself, sustained and developed at the metaphysical level, is difficult, and he explicitly recognized and acknowledged its difficulty: he certainly did not consider that everyone is capable of sustained metaphysical reflection. At the same time the empirical facts on which this reflection is based were for him quite familiar facts. In order to see the relation of finite things to the being on which they depend we are not required to pursue scientific research, discovering hitherto unknown empirical facts. Nor does the metaphysician discover God in a manner analogous to the explorer who suddenly comes upon a hitherto unknown island or flower. It is attention and reflection which are required rather than research or exploration.

What, then, are the familiar facts which for Aquinas imply the existence of God? Mention of them can be found in the famous 'five ways' of proving God's existence, which are outlined in the *Summa theologica* (Ia, 2, 3). In the first way Aquinas begins by saying that 'it is certain, and it is clear from sense-experience, that some things in this world are moved'. It must be remembered that he, like Aristotle, understands the term 'motion' in the broad sense of change, reduction from a state of potentiality to one of act; he does not refer exclusively to local motion. In the second way he starts with the remark that 'we find in material things an order of efficient causes'. In other words, in our experience of things and of their relations to one another we are aware of efficient causality. Thus while in the first way he begins with the fact that some things are in motion or in a state of change, the second way is based upon the fact that some things act upon other things, as efficient causes. In the third way he starts by stating that 'we find among things some which are capable of existing or not existing, since we find that some things come into being and pass away'. In other words, we perceive that some things are corruptible or perishable. In the fourth proof he observes that 'we find in things that some are more or less good and true and noble and so on (than others)'. Finally in

* From F. C. Copleston, *Aquinas* (Harmondsworth: Penguin Books Ltd., 1955), pp. 110–122. Reprinted by permission of the author and publisher.

the fifth way he says: 'we see that some things which lack knowledge, namely natural bodies, act for an end, which is clear from the fact that they always or in most cases act in the same way, in order to attain what is best.'

There is, I think, little difficulty in accepting as empirical facts the starting-points of the first three ways. For nobody really doubts that some things are acted upon and changed or 'moved', that some things act on others, and that some things are perishable. Each of us is aware, for example, that he is acted upon and changed, that he sometimes acts as an efficient cause, and that he is perishable. Even if anyone were to cavil at the assertion that he is aware that he himself was born and will die, he knows very well that some other people were born and have died. But the starting-points of the two final arguments may cause some difficulty. The proposition that there are different grades of perfections in things stands in need of a much more thorough analysis than Aquinas accords it in his brief outline of the fourth way. For the schematic outlining of the five proofs was designed, not to satisfy the critical minds of mature philosophers, but as introductory material for 'novices' in the study of theology. And in any case Aquinas could naturally take for granted in the thirteenth century ideas which were familiar to his contemporaries and which had not yet been subjected to the radical criticism to which they were later subjected. At the same time there is not very much difficulty in understanding the sort of thing which was meant. We are all accustomed to think and speak as though, for example, there were different degrees of intelligence and intellectual capacity. In order to estimate the different degrees we need, it is true, standards or fixed points of reference; but, given these points of reference, we are all accustomed to make statements which imply different grades of perfections. And though these statements stand in need of close analysis, they refer to something which falls within ordinary experience and finds expression in ordinary language. As for the fifth way, the modern reader may find great difficulty in seeing what is meant if he confines his attention to the relevant passage in the *Summa theologica.* But if he looks at the *Summa contra Gentiles* (1, 13) he will find Aquinas saying that we see things of different natures co-operating in the production and maintenance of a relatively stable order or system. When Aqunias says that we see purely material things acting for an end, he does not mean to say that they act in a manner analogous to that in which human beings consciously act for definite purposes. Indeed, the point of the argument is that they do not do so. He means that different kinds of things, like fire and water, the behaviour of which is determined by their several 'forms', co-operate, not consciously but as a matter of fact, in such a way that there is a relatively stable order or system. And here again, though much more would need to be said in a full discussion of the matter, the basic idea is nothing particularly extraordinary nor is it contrary to our ordinary experience and expectations.

It is to be noted also that Aquinas speaks with considerable restraint: he avoids sweeping generalizations. Thus in the first argument he does not say that all material things are 'moved' but that we see that some things in this world are moved or changed. In the third argument he does not state that all finite things are contingent but that we are aware that some things come into being and pass away. And in the fifth argument he does not say that there is an invariable world-order or system but that we see natural bodies acting always or in most cases in the same ways. The difficulty, therefore, which may be experienced in regard to Aquinas' proofs of God's existence concerns not so much the empirical facts or alleged empirical facts with which he starts as in seeing that these facts imply God's existence.

Perhaps a word should be said at once about this idea of 'implication'. As a matter of fact Aquinas does not use the word when talking about the five ways: he speaks of 'proof' and of 'demonstration'. And by 'demonstration' he means in this context what he calls *demonstratio quia* (*S.T.*, I*a*, 2, 2), namely a causal proof of God's existence, proceeding from the affirmation of some empirical fact, for example that there are things which change, to the affirmation of a transcendent cause. It is, indeed, his second proof which is strictly the causal argument, in the sense that it deals explicitly with the order of efficient causality; but in every proof the idea of ontological dependence on a transcendent cause appears in some form or other. Aquinas' conviction was that a full understanding of the empirical facts which are selected for consideration in the five ways involves seeing the dependence of these facts on a transcendent cause. The existence of things which change, for instance, is, in his opinion, not self-explanatory: it can be rendered intelligible only if seen as dependent on a transcendent cause, a cause, that is to say, which does not itself belong to the order of changing things.

This may suggest to the modern reader that Aquinas was concerned with causal explanation in the sense that he was concerned with framing an empirical hypothesis to explain certain facts. But he did not regard the proposition affirming God's existence as a causal hypothesis in the sense of being in principle revisable, as a hypothesis, that is to say, which might conceivably have to be revised in the light of fresh empirical data or which might be supplanted by a more economical hypothesis. This point can perhaps be seen most clearly in the case of his third argument, which is based on the fact that there are things which come into being and pass away. In Aquinas' opinion no fresh scientific knowledge about the physical constitution of such things could affect the validity of the argument. He did not look on a 'demonstration' of God's existence as an empirical hypothesis in the sense in which the electronic theory, for example, is said to be an empirical hypothesis. It is, of course, open to anyone to say that in his own opinion cosmological arguments in favour of God's existence are in fact analogous to the empirical hypotheses of the sciences and that they have a predictive function; but it does not follow that this interpretation can legitimately be ascribed to Aquinas. We should not be misled by the illustrations which he sometimes offers from contemporary scientific theory. For these are mere illustrations to elucidate a point in terms easily understandable by his readers: they are not meant to indicate that the proofs of God's existence were for him empirical hypotheses in the modern sense of the term.

Does this mean, therefore, that Aquinas regarded the existence of God as being logically entailed by facts such as change or coming into being and passing away? He did not, of course, regard the proposition 'there are things which come into being and pass away' as logically entailing the proposition 'there is an absolutely necessary or independent being' in the sense that affirmation of the one proposition and denial of the other involves one in a verbal or formal linguistic contradiction. But he thought that metaphysical analysis of what it objectively means to be a thing which comes into being and passes away shows that such a thing must depend existentially on an absolutely necessary being. And he thought that metaphysical analysis of what it objectively means to be a changing thing shows that such a thing depends on a supreme unmoved mover. It follows that for Aquinas one is involved in a contradiction if one affirms the propositions 'there are things which come into being and pass away' and 'there are things which change' and at the same time denies the propositions 'there is an absolutely necessary being' and 'there is a supreme unmoved mover'. But the contradiction can be made apparent only by means of metaphysical analysis. And the entailment in question is fundamentally an ontological or causal entailment.

Not a few philosophers (certainly all 'empiricists') would presumably comment that if this represents Aquinas' real mind it is clear that he confused the causal relation with logical entailment. But it should be remembered that though Aquinas was convinced that the proposition stating that everything which begins to exist has *a* cause is absolutely certain he did not think that the existence of any finite thing entails the existence of any other finite thing in the sense that the existence of any finite thing can be said to entail the existence of God. In theological language, if we once admit that there is an omnipotent Creator, we can say that He could create and maintain in existence any finite thing without the existence of any other finite thing. But it does not follow that there can be any finite thing without God. In other words, Aquinas is not bound to produce other instances of the ontological entailment which he asserts between the existence of finite things and God. Though the relation of creatures to God is analogous in some way to the relation of causal dependence of one finite thing on another, the former relation is, if we consider it as such, unique. Aquinas was not confusing causal relations in general with logical entailments: he was asserting a unique relation between finite things and the transfinite transcendent cause on which they depend.

It is worth emphasizing perhaps that it does not necessarily follow from Aquinas' view that a metaphysical approach to God's existence is an easy matter. It is true that he was confident of the power of the human reason to attain knowledge of God's existence; and he did not regard his arguments as standing in need of support from rhetoric or emotional appeal. And in the *Summa theologica,* where he is writing for 'novices' in theology, he states the arguments in a bald and perhaps disconcertingly impersonal manner. But we cannot legitimately conclude that he thought it easy for a man to come to the knowledge of God's existence by philosophic reflection alone. Indeed, he makes an explicit statement to the opposite effect. He was well aware that in human life other factors besides metaphysical reflection exercise a great influence. Moreover, he would obviously agree that it is always possible to stop the process of reflection at a particular point. For Aquinas every being, in so far as it is or has being, is intelligible. But we can consider things from different points of view or under different aspects. For example, I might consider coming-into-being and passing-away simply in regard to definite instances and from a subjective point of view. It grieves me to think that someone I love will probably die before me and leave, as we say, a gap in my life. Or it grieves me to think that I shall die and be unable to complete the work which I have undertaken. Or I might consider coming-into-being and passing-away from some scientific point of view. What are the finite phenomenal causes of organic decay or of the generation of an organism? But I can also consider coming-into-being and passing-away purely as such and objectively, adopting a metaphysical point of view and directing my attention to the sort of being, considered as such, which is capable of coming into being and passing away. Nobody can compel me to adopt this point of view. If I am determined to remain on the level of, say, some particular science, I remain there; and that is that. Metaphysical reflections will have no meaning for me. But the metaphysical point of view is a possible point of view, and metaphysical reflection belongs to a full understanding of things so far as this is possible for a finite mind. And if I do adopt this point of view and maintain it in sustained reflection, an existential relation of dependence, Aquinas was convinced, should become clear to me which will not become clear to me if I remain on a different level of reflection. But just as extraneous factors (such as the influence of the general outlook promoted by a technical civilization) may help to produce my decision to remain on a non-metaphysical level of reflection, so also can extraneous factors influence my reflections on the metaphysical level. It seems to me quite wrong to suggest that Aquinas did not regard metaphysical reflection as a possible way of becoming aware of God's existence and that he looked on it, as some writers have suggested, as being simply a rational justification of an assurance which is necessarily attained in some other way. For if it constitutes a rational justification at all, it must, I think, be a possible way of becoming aware of God's existence. But it does not necessarily follow, of course, that it is an easy way or a common way.

After these general remarks I turn to Aquinas' five proofs of the existence of God. In the first proof he argues that 'motion' or change means the reduction of a thing from a state of potentiality to one of act, and that a thing cannot be reduced from potentiality to act except under the influence of an agent already in act. In this sense 'everything which is moved must be moved by another'. He argues finally that in order to avoid an infinite regress in the chain of movers, the existence of a first unmoved mover must be admitted. 'And all understand that this is God.'

A statement like 'all understand that this is God' or 'all call this (being) God' occurs at the end of each proof, and I postpone consideration of it for the moment. As for the ruling out of an infinite regress, I shall explain what Aquinas means to reject after outlining the second proof, which is similar in structure to the first.

Whereas in the first proof Aquinas considers things as being acted upon, as being changed or 'moved', in the second he considers them as active agents, as efficient causes. He argues that there is a hierarchy of efficient causes, a subordinate cause being dependent on the cause above it in the hierarchy. He then proceeds, after excluding the hypothesis of an infinite regress, to draw the conclusion that there must be a first efficient cause, 'which all call God'.

Now, it is obviously impossible to discuss these arguments profitably unless they are first understood. And misunderstanding of them is only too easy, since the terms and phrases used are either unfamiliar or liable to be taken in a sense other than the sense intended. In the first place it is essential to understand that in the first argument Aquinas supposes that movement or change is dependent on a 'mover' acting here and now, and that in the second argument he supposes that there are efficient causes in the world which even in their causal activity are here and now dependent on the causal activity of other causes. That is why I have spoken of a 'hierarchy' rather than of a 'series'. What he is thinking of can be illustrated in this way. A son is dependent on his father, in the sense that he would not have existed except for the causal activity of his father. But when the son acts for himself, he is not dependent here and now on his father. But he is dependent here and now on other factors. Without the activity of the air, for instance, he could not himself act, and the life-preserving activity of the air is itself dependent here and now on other factors, and they in turn on other factors. I do not say that this illustration is in all respects adequate for the purpose; but it at least illustrates the fact that when Aquinas talks about an 'order' of efficient causes he is not thinking of a series stretching back into the past, but of a hierarchy of causes, in which a subordinate member is here and now dependent on the causal activity of a higher member. If I wind up my watch at night, it then proceeds to work without further interference on my part. But the activity of the pen tracing these words on the page is here and now dependent on the activity of my hand, which in turn is here and now dependent on other factors.

The meaning of the rejection of an infinite regress should now be clear. Aquinas is not rejecting the possibility of an infinite series as such. We have already seen that he did not think that anyone had ever succeeded in showing the impossibility of an infinite series of events stretching back into the past. Therefore he does not mean to rule out the possibility of an infinite series of causes and effects, in which a given member depended on the preceding member, say X on Y, but does not, once it exists, depend here and now on the present causal activity of the preceding member. We have to imagine, not a lineal or horizontal series, so to speak, but a vertical hierarchy, in which a lower member depends here and now on the present causal activity of the member above it. It is the latter type of series, if prolonged to infinity, which Aquinas rejects. And he rejects it on the ground that unless there is a 'first' member, a mover which is not itself moved or a cause which does not itself depend on the causal activity of a higher cause, it is not possible to explain the 'motion' or the causal activity of the lowest member. His point of view is this. Suppress the first unmoved mover and there is no motion or change here and now. Suppress the first efficient cause and there is no causal activity here and now. If therefore we find that some things in the world are changed, there must be a first unmoved mover. And if there are efficient causes in the world, there must be a first efficient, and completely nondependent cause. The word 'first' does not mean first in the temporal order, but supreme or first in the ontological order.

A remark on the word 'cause' is here in place. What precisely Aquinas would have said to the David Humes either of the fourteenth century or of the modern era it is obviously impossible to say. But it is clear that he believed in real causal efficacy and real causal relations. He was aware, of course, that causal efficacy is not the object of vision in the sense in which patches of colours are objects of vision; but the human being, he considered, is aware of real causal relations and if we understand 'perception' as involving the cooperation of sense and intellect, we can be said to 'perceive' causality. And presumably he would have said that the sufficiency of a phenomenalistic interpretation of causality for purposes of physical science proves nothing against the validity of a metaphysical notion of causality. It is obviously possible to dispute whether his analyses of change or 'motion' and of efficient causality are valid or invalid and whether there is such a thing as a hierarchy of causes. And our opinion about the validity or invalidity of his arguments for the existence of God will depend very largely on our answers to these questions. But mention of the mathematical infinite series is irrelevant to a discussion of his arguments. And it is this point which I have been trying to make clear.

In the third proof Aquinas starts from the fact that some things come into being and perish, and he concludes from this that it is possible for them to exist or not to exist: they do not exist 'necessarily'. He then argues that it is impossible for things which are of this kind to exist always; for 'that which is capable of not existing, at some time does not exist'. If all things were of this kind, at some time there would be nothing. Aquinas is clearly supposing for the sake of argument the hypothesis of infinite time, and his proof is designed to cover this hypothesis. He does not say that infinite time is impossible: what he says is that if time is infinite and if all things are capable of not existing, this potentiality would inevitably be fulfilled in infinite time. There would then be nothing. And if there had ever been nothing, nothing would now exist. For no thing can bring itself into existence. But it is clear as a matter of fact that there are things. Therefore it can never have been true to say that there was literally no thing. Therefore it is impossible that all things should be capable of existing or not existing. There must, then, be some necessary being. But perhaps it is necessary in the sense that it must exist if something else exists; that is to say, its necessity may be hypothetical. We cannot, however, proceed to infinity in the series or hierarchy of necessary beings. If we do so, we do not explain the presence here and now of beings capable of existing or not existing. Therefore we must affirm the existence of a being which is absolutely necessary (*per se neccessarium*) and completely independent. 'And all call this being *God*.'

This argument may appear to be quite unnecessarily complicated and obscure. But it has to be seen in its historical context. As already mentioned, Aquinas designed his argument in such a way as to be independent of the question whether or not the world existed from eternity. He wanted to show that on either hypothesis there must be a necessary being. As for the introduction of hypothetical necessary beings, he wanted to show that even if there are such beings, perhaps within the universe, which are not corruptible in the sense in which a flower is corruptible, there must still be an absolutely independent being. Finally, in regard to terminology, Aquinas uses the common medieval expression 'necessary being'. He does not actually use the term 'contingent being' in the argument and talks instead about 'possible' beings; but it comes to the same thing. And though the words 'contingent' and 'necessary' are now applied to propositions rather than to beings, I have retained Aquinas' mode of speaking. Whether one accepts the argument or not, I do not think that there is any insuperable difficulty in understanding the line of thought.

The fourth argument is admittedly difficult to grasp. Aquinas argues that there are degrees of perfections in things. Different kinds of finite things possess different perfections in diverse limited degrees. He then argues not only that if there are different degrees of a perfection like goodness there is a supreme good to which other good things approximate but also that all limited degrees of goodness are caused by the supreme good. And since goodness is a convertible term with being, a thing being good in so far as it has being, the supreme good is the supreme being and the cause of being in all other things. 'Therefore there is something which is the cause of the being and goodness and of every perfection in all other things; and this we call *God*.'

Aquinas refers to some remarks of Aristotle in the *Metaphysics;* but this argument puts one in mind at once of Plato's *Symposium* and *Republic.* And the Platonic doctrine of participation seems to be involved. Aquinas was not immediately acquainted with either work, but the Platonic line of thought was familiar to him from other writers. And it has not disappeared from philosophy. Indeed, some of those theists who reject or doubt the validity of the 'cosmological' arguments seem to feel a marked attraction for some variety of the fourth way, arguing that in the recognition of objective values we implicitly recognize God as the supreme value. But if the line of thought represented by the fourth way is to mean anything to the average modern reader, it has to be presented in a rather different manner from that in which it is expressed by Aquinas who was able to assume in his readers ideas and points of view which can no longer be presupposed.

Finally, the fifth proof, if we take its statement in the *Summa theologica* together with that in the *Summa contra Gentiles,* can be expressed more or less as follows. The activity and behaviour of each thing is determined by its form. But we observe material things of very different types co-operating in such a way as to produce and maintain a relatively stable world-order or system. They achieve an 'end', the production and maintenance of a cosmic order. But non-intelligent material things certainly do not co-operate consciously in view of a purpose. If it is said that they co-operate in the realization of an end or purpose, this does not mean that they intend the realization of this order in a manner analogous to that in which a man can act consciously with a view to the achievement of a purpose. Nor, when Aquinas talks about operating 'for an end' in this connexion, is he thinking of the utility of certain things to the human race. He is not saying, for example, that grass grows to feed the sheep and that sheep exist in order that human beings should have food and clothing. It is of the unconscious co-operation of different kinds of material things in the production and maintenance of a relatively stable cosmic system that he is thinking, not of the benefits accruing to us from our use of certain objects. And his argument is that this co-operation on the part of heterogeneous material things clearly points to the existence of an extrinsic intelligent author of this co-operation, who operates with an end in view. If Aquinas had lived in the days of the evolutionary hypothesis, he would doubtless have argued that this hypothesis supports rather than invalidates the conclusion of the argument.

No one of these arguments was entirely new, as Aquinas himself was very well aware. But he developed them and arranged them to form a coherent whole. I do not mean that he regarded the validity of one particular argument as necessarily depending on the validity of the other four. He doubtless thought that each argument was valid in its own right. But, as I have already remarked, they conform to a certain pattern, and they are mutually complementary in the sense that in each argument things are considered from a different point of view or under a different aspect. They are so many different approaches to God.

D A V I D H U M E

Dialogues Concerning Natural Religion*

PART II

I must own, Cleanthes, said Demea, that nothing can more surprise me than the light in which you have all along put this argument. By the whole tenor of your discourse, one would imagine that you were maintaining the Being of a God against the cavils of atheists and infidels, and were necessitated to become a champion for that fundamental principle of all religion. But this, I hope, is not by any means a question among us. No man, no man at least of common sense, I am persuaded, ever entertained a serious doubt with regard to a truth so certain and self-evident. The question is not concerning the *being* but the *nature* of God. This I affirm, from the infirmities of human understanding, to be altogether incomprehensible and unknown to us. The essence of that supreme Mind, his attributes, the manner of his existence, the very nature of his duration—these and every particular which regards so divine a Being are mysterious to men. Finite, weak, and blind creatures, we ought to humble ourselves in his august presence, and, conscious of our frailties, adore in silence his infinite perfections which eye hath not seen, ear hath not heard, neither hath it entered into the heart of man to conceive. They are covered in a deep cloud from human curiosity; it is profaneness to attempt penetrating through these sacred obscurities, and, next to the impiety of denying his existence, is the temerity of prying into his nature and essence, decrees and attributes.

But lest you should think that my *piety* has here got the better of my *philosophy*, I shall support my opinion, if it needs any support, by a very great authority. I might cite all the divines, almost from the foundation of Christianity, who have ever treated of this or any other theological subject; but I shall confine myself, at present, to one equally celebrated for piety and philosophy. It is Father Malebranche who, I remember, thus expresses himself.[1] "One ought not so much," says he, "to call God a spirit in order to express positively what he is, as in order to signify that he

* David Hume, *Dialogues Concerning Natural Religion*, Parts II–XI. First published in 1779.

[1] *Recherche de la Vérité*, liv. 3, cap. 9.

is not matter. He is a Being infinitely perfect—of this we cannot doubt. But in the same manner as we ought not to imagine, even supposing him corporeal, that he is clothed with a human body, as the anthropomorphites asserted, under colour that that figure was the most perfect of any, so neither ought we to imagine that the spirit of God has human ideas or bears any resemblance to our spirit, under colour that we know nothing more perfect than a human mind. We ought rather to believe that as he comprehends the perfections of matter without being material . . . he comprehends also the perfections of created spirits without being spirit, in the manner we conceive spirit: that his true name is *He that is,* or, in other words, Being without restriction, All Being, the Being infinite and universal."

After so great an authority, Demea, replied Philo, as that which you have produced, and a thousand more which you might produce, it would appear ridiculous in me to add my sentiment or express my approbation of your doctrine. But surely, where reasonable men treat these subjects, the question can never be concerning the *being* but only the *nature* of the Deity. The former truth, as you well observe, is unquestionable and self-evident. Nothing exists without a cause; and the original cause of this universe (whatever it be) we call God, and piously ascribe to him every species of perfection. Whoever scruples this fundamental truth deserves every punishment which can be inflicted among philosophers, to wit, the greatest ridicule, contempt, and disapprobation. But as all perfection is entirely relative, we ought never to imagine that we comprehend the attributes of this divine Being, or to suppose that his perfections have any analogy or likeness to the perfections of a human creature. Wisdom, thought, design, knowledge—these we justly ascribe to him because these words are honourable among men, and we have no other language or other conceptions by which we can express our adoration of him. But let us beware lest we think that our ideas anywise correspond to his perfections, or that his attributes have any resemblance to these qualities among men. He is infinitely superior to our limited view and comprehension, and is more the object of worship in the temple than of disputation in the schools.

In reality, Cleanthes, continued he, there is no need of having recourse to that affected scepticism so displeasing to you in order to come at this determination. Our ideas reach no farther than our experience. We have no experience of divine attributes and operations. I need not conclude my syllogism, you can draw the inference yourself. And it is a pleasure to me (and I hope to you, too) that just reasoning and sound piety here concur in the same conclusion, and both of them establish the adorably mysterious and incomprehensible nature of the Supreme Being.

Not to lose any time in circumlocutions, said Cleanthes, addressing himself to Demea, much less in replying to the pious declamations of Philo, I shall briefly explain how I conceive this matter. Look round the world, contemplate the whole and every part of it: you will find it to be nothing but one great machine, subdivided into an infinite number of lesser machines, which again admit of subdivisions to a degree beyond what human senses and faculties can trace and explain. All these various machines, and even their most minute parts, are adjusted to each other with an accuracy which ravishes into admiration all men who have ever contemplated them. The curious adapting of means to ends, throughout all nature, resembles exactly, though it much exceeds, the productions of human contrivance—of human design, thought, wisdom, and intelligence. Since therefore the effects resemble each other, we are led to infer, by all the rules of analogy, that the causes also resemble, and that the Author of nature is somewhat similar to the mind of man, though possessed of much larger faculties, proportioned to the grandeur of the work which he has executed. By this argument *a posteriori,* and by this argument alone, do we prove at once the existence of a Deity and his similarity to human mind and intelligence.

I shall be so free, Cleanthes, said Demea, as to tell you that from the beginning I could not approve of your conclusion concerning the similarity of the Deity to men, still less can I approve of the mediums by which you endeavour to establish it. What! No demonstration of the Being of God! No abstract arguments! No proofs *a priori!* Are these which have hitherto been so much insisted on by philosophers all fallacy, all sophism? Can we reach no farther in this subject than experience and probability? I will not say that this is betraying the cause of a Deity; but surely, by this affected candour, you give advantages to atheists which they never could obtain by the mere dint of argument and reasoning.

What I chiefly scruple in this subject, said Philo, is not so much that all religious arguments are by Cleanthes reduced to experience, as that they appear not to be even the most certain and irrefragable of that inferior kind. That a stone will fall, that fire will burn, that the earth has solidity, we have observed a thousand and a thousand times; and when any new instance of this nature is presented, we draw without hesitation the accustomed inference. The exact similarity of the cases gives us a perfect assurance of a similar event, and a stronger evidence is never desired nor sought after. But wherever you depart, in the least, from the similarity of the cases, you diminish proportionably the evidence, and may at last bring it to a very weak *analogy,* which is confessedly liable to error and uncertainty. After having experienced the circulation of the blood in human creatures, we make no doubt that it takes place in Titius and Maevius; but from its circulation in frogs and fishes it is only a presumption, though a strong one, from analogy that it takes place in men and other animals. The analogical reasoning is much weaker when we infer the circulation of the sap in vegetables from our experience that the blood circulates in animals; and those who hastily followed that imperfect analogy are found, by more accurate experiments, to have been mistaken.

If we see a house, Cleanthes, we conclude, with the greatest certainty, that it had an architect or builder because this is precisely that species of effect which we have experienced to proceed from that species of cause. But surely you will not affirm that the universe bears such a resemblance to a house that we can with the same certainty infer a similar cause, or that the analogy is here entire and perfect. The dissimilitude is so striking that the utmost you can here pretend to is a guess, conjecture, a presumption concerning a similar cause; and how that pretension will be received in the world, I leave you to consider.

It would surely be very ill received, replied Cleanthes; and I should be deservedly blamed and detested did I allow that the proofs of Deity amounted to no more than a guess or conjecture. But is the whole adjustment of means to ends in a house and in the universe so slight a resemblance? the economy of final causes? the order, proportion, and arrangement of every part?

Steps of a stair are plainly contrived that human legs may use them in mounting; and this inference is certain and infallible. Human legs are also contrived for walking and mounting; and this inference, I allow, is not altogether so certain because of the dissimilarity which you remark; but does it, therefore, deserve the name only of presumption or conjecture?

Good God! cried Demea, interrupting him, where are we? Zealous defenders of religion allow that the proofs of a Deity fall short of perfect evidence! And you, Philo, on whose assistance I depended in proving the adorable mysteriousness of the Divine Nature, do you assent to all these extravagant opinions of Cleanthes? For what other name can I give them? or, why spare my censure when such principles are advanced, supported by such an authority, before so young a man as Pamphilus?

You seem not to apprehend, replied Philo, that I argue with Cleanthes in his own way, and, by showing him the dangerous consequences of his tenets, hope at last to reduce him to our opinion. But what sticks most with you, I observe, is the representation which Cleanthes has made of the argument *a posteriori;* and, finding that that argument is likely to escape your hold and vanish into air, you think it so disguised that you can scarcely believe it to be set in its true light. Now, however much I may dissent, in other respects, from the dangerous principle of Cleanthes, I must allow that he has fairly represented that argument, and I shall endeavour so to state the matter to you that you will entertain no further scruples with regard to it.

Were a man to abstract from everything which he knows or has seen, he would be altogether incapable, merely from his own ideas, to determine what kind of scene the universe must be, or to give the preference to one state or situation of things above another. For as nothing which he clearly conceives could be esteemed impossible or implying a contradiction, every chimera of his fancy would be upon an equal footing; nor could he assign any just reason why he adheres to one idea or system, and rejects the others which are equally possible.

Again, after he opens his eyes and contemplates the world as it really is, it would be impossible for him at first to assign the cause of any one event, much less of the whole of things, or of the universe. He might set his fancy a rambling, and she might bring him in an infinite variety of reports and representations. These would all be possible, but, being all equally possible, he would never of himself give a satisfactory account for his preferring one of them to the rest. Experience alone can point out to him the true cause of any phenomenon.

Now, according to this method of reasoning, Demea, it follows (and is, indeed, tacitly allowed by Cleanthes himself) that order, arrangement, or the adjustment of final causes, is not of itself any proof of design, but only so far as it has been experienced to proceed from that principle. Four aught we can know *a priori,* matter may contain the source or spring of order originally within itself, as well as mind does; and there is no more difficulty in conceiving that the several elements, from an internal unknown cause, may fall into the most exquisite arrangement, than to conceive that their ideas, in the great universal mind, from a like internal unknown cause, fall into that arrangement. The equal possibility of both these suppositions is allowed. But, by experience, we find (according to Cleanthes) that there is a difference between them. Throw several pieces of steel together, without shape or form, they will never arrange themselves so as to compose a watch. Stone and mortar and wood, without an architect, never erect a house. But the ideas in a human mind, we see, by an unknown, inexplicable economy, arrange themselves so as to form the plan of a watch or house. Experience, therefore, proves that there is an original principle of order in mind, not in matter. From similar effects we infer similar causes. The adjustment of means to ends is alike in the universe, as in a machine of human contrivance. The causes, therefore, must be resembling.

I was from the beginning scandalized, I must own, with this resemblance which is asserted between the Deity and human creatures, and must conceive it to imply such a degradation of the Supreme Being as no sound theist could endure. With your assistance, therefore, Demea, I shall endeavour to defend what you justly call the adorable mysteriousness of the Divine Nature, and shall refute this reasoning of Cleanthes, provided he allows that I have made a fair representation of it.

When Cleanthes had assented, Philo, after a short pause, proceeded in the following manner.

That all inferences, Cleanthes, concerning fact are founded on experience, and that all experimental reasonings are founded on the supposition that similar causes prove similar effects, and similar effects similar causes, I shall not at present much dispute with you. But observe, I entreat you, with what extreme caution all just reasoners proceed in the transferring of experiments to similar cases. Unless the cases be exactly similar, they repose no perfect confidence in applying their past observation to any particular phenomenon. Every alteration of circumstances occasions a doubt concerning the event; and it requires new experiments to prove certainly that the new circumstances are of no moment or importance. A change in bulk, situation, arrangement, age, disposition of the air, or surrounding bodies—any of these particulars may be attended with the most unexpected consequences. And unless the objects be quite familiar to us, it is the highest temerity to expect with assurance, after any of these changes, an event similar to that which before fell under our observation. The slow and deliberate steps of philosophers here, if anywhere, are distinguished from the precipitate march of the vulgar, who, hurried on by the smallest similitude, are incapable of all discernment or consideration.

But can you think, Cleanthes, that your usual phlegm and philosophy have been preserved in so wide a step as you have taken when you compared to the universe houses, ships, furniture, machines, and, from their similarity in some circumstances, inferred a similarity in their causes? Thought, design, intelligence, such as we discover in men and other animals, is no more than one of the springs and principles of the universe, as well as heat or cold, attraction or repulsion, and a hundred others which fall under daily observation. It is an active cause by which some particular parts of nature, we find, produce alterations on other parts. But can a conclusion, with any propriety, be transferred from parts to the whole? Does not the great disproportion bar all comparison and inference? From observing the growth of a hair, can we learn anything concerning the generation of a man? Would the manner of a leaf's blowing, even though perfectly known, afford us any instruction concerning the vegetation of a tree?

But allowing that we were to take the *opera-*

tions of one part of nature upon another for the foundation of our judgment concerning the *origin* of the whole (which never can be admitted), yet why select so minute, so weak, so bounded a principle as the reason and design of animals is found to be upon this planet? What peculiar privilege has this little agitation of the brain which we call *thought,* that we must thus make it the model of the whole universe? Our partiality in our own favour does indeed present it on all occasions, but sound philosophy ought carefully to guard against so natural an illusion.

So far from admitting, continued Philo, that the operations of a part can afford us any just conclusion concerning the origin of the whole, I will not allow any one part to form a rule for another part if the latter be very remote from the former. Is there any reasonable ground to conclude that the inhabitants of other planets possess thought, intelligence, reason, or anything similar to these faculties in men? When nature has so extremely diversified her manner of operation in this small globe, can we imagine that she incessantly copies herself throughout so immense a universe? And if thought, as we may well suppose, be confined merely to this narrow corner and has even there so limited a sphere of action, with what propriety can we assign it for the original cause of all things? The narrow views of a peasant who makes his domestic economy the rule for the government of kingdoms is in comparison a pardonable sophism.

But were we ever so much assured that a thought and reason resembling the human were to be found throughout the whole universe, and were its activity elsewhere vastly greater and more commanding than it appears in this globe, yet I cannot see why the operations of a world constituted, arranged, adjusted, can with any propriety be extended to a world which is in its embryo state, and is advancing towards that constitution and arrangement. By observation we know somewhat of the economy, action, and nourishment of a finished animal, but we must transfer with great caution that observation to the growth of a fœtus in the womb, and still more to the formation of an animalcule in the loins of its male parent. Nature, we find, even from our limited experience, possesses an infinite number of springs and principles which incessantly discover themselves on every change of her position and situation. And what new and unknown principles would actuate her in so new and unknown a situation as that of the formation of a universe, we cannot, without the utmost temerity, pretend to determine.

A very small part of this great system, during a very short time, is very imperfectly discovered to us; and do we thence pronounce decisively concerning the origin of the whole?

Admirable conclusion! Stone, wood, brick, iron, brass, have not, at this time, in this minute globe of earth, an order or arrangement without human art and contrivance; therefore, the universe could not originally attain its order and arrangement without something similar to human art. But is a part of nature a rule for another part very wide of the former? Is it a rule for the whole? Is a very small part a rule for the universe? Is nature in one situation a certain rule for nature in another situation vastly different from the former?

And can you blame me, Cleanthes, if I here imitate the prudent reserve of Simonides, who, according to the noted story, being asked by Hiero, *What God was?* desired a day to think of it, and then two days more; and after that manner continually prolonged the term, without ever bringing in his definition or description? Could you even blame me if I had answered, at first, *that I did not know,* and was sensible that this subject lay vastly beyond the reach of my faculties? You might cry out sceptic and rallier, as much as you pleased; but, having found in so many other subjects much more familiar the imperfections and even contradictions of human reason, I never should expect any success from its feeble conjectures in a subject so sublime and so remote from the sphere of our observation. When two *species* of objects have always been observed to be conjoined together, I can *infer,* by custom, the existence of one wherever I *see* the existence of the other; and this I call an argument from experience. But how this argument can have place where the objects, as in the present case, are single, individual, without parallel or specific resemblance, may be difficult to explain. And will any man tell me with a serious countenance that an orderly universe must arise from some thought and art like the human because we have experience of it? To ascertain this reasoning it were requisite that we had experience of the origin of worlds; and it is not sufficient, surely, that we have seen ships and cities arise from human art and contrivance.

Philo was proceeding in this vehement manner, somewhat between jest and earnest, as it appeared to me, when he observed some signs of impatience in Cleanthes, and then immediately stopped short. What I had to suggest, said Cleanthes, is only that you would not abuse terms, or make use of popular expressions to subvert philosophical reasonings. You know that the vulgar often distinguish reason from experience, even where the question relates only to matter of fact and existence, though it is found, where that *reason* is properly analyzed, that it is nothing but a species of experience. To prove by experience the origin of the universe from mind is not more contrary to common speech than to prove the motion of the earth from the same principle. And a caviller might raise all the same objections to the Copernican system which you have urged against my reasonings. Have you other earths, might he say, which you have seen to move? Have . . .

Yes! cried Philo, interrupting him, we have other earths. Is not the moon another earth, which we see to turn around its centre? Is not Venus another earth, where we observe the same phenomenon? Are not the revolutions of the sun also a confirmation, from analogy, of the same theory? All the planets, are they not earths which revolve about the sun? Are not the satellites moons which move round Jupiter and Saturn, and along with these primary planets round the sun? These analogies and resemblances, with others which I have not mentioned, are the sole proofs of the Copernican system; and to you it belongs to consider whether you have any analogies of the same kind to support your theory.

In reality, Cleanthes, continued he, the modern system of astronomy is now so much received by all inquirers, and has become so essential a part even of our earliest education, that we are not commonly very scrupulous in examining the reasons upon which it is founded. It is now become a matter of mere curiosity to study the first writers of that subject who had the full force of prejudice to encounter, and were obliged to turn their arguments on every side in order to render them popular and convincing. But if we peruse Galileo's famous *Dialogues* concerning the system of the world, we shall find that the great genius, one of the sublimest that ever existed, first bent all his endeavours to prove that there was no foundation for the distinction commonly made between elementary and celestial substances. The schools, proceeding from the illusions of sense, had carried this distinction very far; and had established the latter substances to be ingenerable, incorruptible, unalterable, impassible; and had assigned all the opposite qualities to the former. But Galileo, beginning with the moon, proved its similarity in every particular to the earth: its convex figure, its natural darkness when not illuminated, its density, its distinction into solid and liquid, the variations of its phases, the mutual illuminations of the earth and moon, their mutual eclipses, the inequalities of the lunar surface, etc. After many instances of this kind, with regard to all the planets, men plainly saw that these bodies became proper objects of experience, and that the similarity of their nature enabled us to extend the same arguments and phenomena from one to the other.

In this cautious proceeding of the astronomers you may read your own condemnation, Cleanthes, or rather may see that the subject in which you are engaged exceeds all human reason and inquiry. Can you pretend to show any such similarity between the fabric of a house and the generation of a universe? Have you ever seen nature in any such situation as resembles the first arrangement of the elements? Have worlds ever been formed under your eye, and have you had leisure to observe the whole progress of the phenomenon, from the first appearance of order to its final consummation? If you have, then cite your experience and deliver your theory.

PART III

How the most absurd argument, replied Cleanthes, in the hands of a man of ingenuity and invention, may acquire an air of probability! Are you not aware, Philo, that it became necessary for Copernicus and his first disciples to prove the similarity of the terrestrial and celestial matter because several philosophers, blinded by old systems and supported by some sensible appearances, had denied this similarity? But that it is by no means necessary that theists should prove the similarity of the works of *nature* to those of *art* because this similarity is self-evident and undeniable? The same matter, a like form; what more is requisite to show an analogy between their causes, and to ascertain the origin of all things from a divine purpose and intention? Your objections, I must freely tell you, are no better than the abstruse cavils of those philosophers who denied motion, and ought to be refuted in the same manner—by illustrations, examples, and instances rather than by serious argument and philosophy.

Suppose, therefore, that an articulate voice were heard in the clouds, much louder and more melodious than any which human art could ever reach; suppose that this voice were extended in the same instant over all nations and spoke to each nation in its own language and dialect; suppose that the words delivered not only contain a just sense and meaning, but convey some instruction altogether worthy of a benevolent Being superior to mankind—could you possibly hesitate a moment concerning the cause of this voice, and must you not instantly ascribe it to some design or purpose? Yet I cannot see but all the same objections (if they merit that appellation) which lie against the system of theism may also be produced against this inference.

Might you not say that all conclusions concerning fact were founded on experience; that, when we hear an articulate voice in the dark and thence infer a man, it is only the resemblance of the effects which leads us to conclude that there is a like resemblance in the cause; but that this extraordinary voice, by its loudness, extent, and flexibility to all languages, bears so little analogy to any human voice that we have no reason to suppose any analogy in their causes; and, consequently, that a rational, wise, coherent speech proceeded, you know not whence, from some accidental whistling of the winds, not from any divine reason or intelligence? You see clearly your own objections in these cavils, and I hope too you see clearly that they cannot possibly have more force in the one case than in the other.

But to bring the case still nearer the present one of the universe, I shall make two suppositions which imply not any absurdity or impossibility. Suppose that there is a natural, universal, invariable language, common to every individual of human race, and that books are natural productions which perpetuate themselves in the same manner with animals and vegetables, by descent and propagation. Several expressions of our passions contain a universal language: all brute animals have a natural speech, which, however limited, is very intelligible to their own species. And as there are infinitely fewer parts and less contrivance in the finest composition of eloquence than in the coarsest organized body, the propagation of an *Iliad* or *Æneid* is an easier supposition than that of any plant or animal.

Suppose, therefore, that you enter into your library thus peopled by natural volumes containing the most refined reason and most exquisite beauty; could you possibly open one of them and doubt that its original cause bore the strongest analogy to mind and intelligence? When it reasons and discourses; when it expostulates, argues, and enforces its views and topics; when it applies sometimes to the pure intellect, sometimes to the affections; when it collects, disposes, and adorns every consideration suited to the subject; could you persist in asserting that all this, at the bottom, had really no meaning, and that the first formation of this volume in the loins of its original parent proceeded not from thought and design? Your obstinacy, I know, reaches not that degree of firmness; even your sceptical play and wantonness would be abashed at so glaring an absurdity.

But if there be any difference, Philo, between this supposed case and the real one of the universe, it is all to the advantage of the latter. The anatomy of an animal affords many stronger instances of design than the perusal of Livy or Tacitus; and any objection which you start in the former case, by carrying me back to so unusual and extraordinary a scene as the first formation of worlds, the same objection has place on the supposition of our vegetating library. Choose, then, your party, Philo, without ambiguity or evasion; assert either that a rational volume is no proof of a rational cause or admit of a similar cause to all the works of nature.

Let me here observe, too, continued Cleanthes, that this religious argument, instead of being weakened by that scepticism so much affected by you, rather acquires force from it and becomes more firm and undisputed. To exclude all argument or reasoning of every kind is either affectation or madness. The declared profession of every reasonable sceptic is only to reject abtruse, remote, and refined arguments; to adhere to common sense and the plain instincts of nature; and to assent, wherever any reasons strike him with so full a force that he cannot, without the greatest violence, prevent it. Now the arguments for natural religion are plainly of this kind; and nothing but the most perverse, obstinate metaphysics can reject them. Consider, anatomize the eye, survey its structure and contrivance, and tell me, from your own feeling, if the idea of a contriver does not immediately flow in upon you with a force like that of sensation. The most obvious conclusion, surely, is in favour of design; and it requires time, reflection, and study, to summon up those frivolous though abstruse objections which can support infidelity. Who can behold the male and female of each species, the correspondence of their parts and instincts, their passions and whole course of life before and after generation, but must be sensible that the propagation of the species is intended by nature? Millions and millions of such instances present themselves through every part of the universe, and no language can convey a more intelligible irresistible meaning than the curious adjustment of final causes. To what degree, therefore, of blind dogmatism must one have attained to reject such natural and such convincing arguments?

Some beauties in writing we may meet with which seem contrary to rules, and which gain the affections and animate the imagination in opposition to all the precepts of criticism and to the authority of the established masters of art. And if the argument for theism be, as you pretend, contradictory to the principles of logic, its universal, its irresistible influence proves clearly that there may be arguments of a like irregular nature. Whatever cavils may be urged, an orderly world, as well as a coherent, articulate speech, will still be received as an incontestable proof of design and intention.

It sometimes happens, I own, that the religious arguments have not their due influence on an ignorant savage and barbarian, not because they are obscure and difficult, but because he never asks himself any question with regard to them. Whence arises the curious structure of an animal? From the copulation of its parents. And these whence? From *their* parents? A few removes set the objects at such a distance that to him they are lost in darkness and confusion; nor is he actuated by any curiosity to trace them farther. But this is neither dogmatism nor scepticism, but stupidity: a state of mind very different from your sifting, inquisitive disposition, my ingenious friend. You can trace causes from effects; you can compare the most distant and remote objects; and your greatest errors proceed not from barrenness of thought and invention, but from too luxuriant a fertility which suppresses your natural good sense by a profusion of unnecessary scruples and objections.

Here I could observe, Hermippus, that Philo was a little embarrassed and confounded; but, while he hesitated in delivering an answer, luckily for him, Demea broke in upon the discourse and saved his countenance.

Your instance, Cleanthes, said he, drawn from books and language, being familiar, has, I confess, so much more force on that account; but is there not some danger, too, in this very circumstance, and may it not render us presumptuous, by making us imagine we comprehend the Deity and have some adequate idea of his nature and attributes? When I read a volume, I enter into the mind and intention of the author; I become him, in a manner, for the instant, and have an immediate feeling and conception of those ideas which revolved in his imagination while employed in that composition. But so near an approach we never surely can make to the Deity. His ways are not our ways. His attributes are perfect but incomprehensible. And this volume of nature contains a great and inexplicable riddle, more than any intelligible discourse or reasoning.

The ancient Platonists, you know, were the most religious and devout of all the pagan philosophers, yet many of them, particularly Plotinus, expressly declare that intellect or understanding is not to be ascribed to the Deity, and that our most perfect worship of him consists, not in acts of veneration, reverence, gratitude, or love, but in a certain mysterious self-annihilation or total extinction of all our faculties. These ideas are, perhaps, too far stretched, but still it must be acknowledged that, by representing the Deity as so intelligible and comprehensible, and so similar to a human mind, we are guilty of the grossest and most narrow partiality, and make ourselves the model of the whole universe.

All the *sentiments* of the human mind, gratitude, resentment, love, friendship, approbation, blame, pity, emulation, envy, have a plain reference to the state and situation of man, and are calculated for preserving the existence and promoting the activity of such a being in such circumstances. It seems, therefore, unreasonable to transfer such sentiments to a supreme existence or to suppose him actuated by them; and the phenomena, besides, of the universe will not support us in such a theory. All our *ideas* derived from the senses are confessedly false and illusive, and cannot therefore be supposed to have place in a supreme intelligence. And as the ideas of internal sentiment, added to those of the external senses, composed the whole furniture of human understanding, we may conclude that none of the *materials* of thought are in any respect similar in the human and in the divine intelligence. Now, as to the *manner* of thinking, how can we make any comparison between them or suppose them anywise resembling? Our thought is fluctuating, uncertain, fleeting, successive, and compounded; and were we to remove these circumstances, we absolutely annihilate its essence, and it would in such a case be an abuse of terms to apply to it the name of thought or reason. At least, if it appear more pious and respectful (as it really is) still to retain these terms when we mention the Supreme Being, we ought to acknowledge that their meaning, in that case, is totally incomprehensible, and that the infirmities of our nature do not permit us to reach any ideas which in the least correspond to the ineffable sublimity of the Divine attributes.

PART IV

It seems strange to me, said Cleanthes, that you, Demea, who are so sincere in the cause of religion, should still maintain the mysterious, incomprehensible nature of the Deity, and should insist so strenuously that he has no manner of likeness or resemblance to human creatures. The Deity, I can readily allow, possesses many powers and attributes of which we can have no comprehension; but, if our ideas, so far as they go, be not just and adequate and correspondent to his real nature, I know not what there is in this subject worth insisting on. Is the name, without any meaning, of such mighty importance? Or how do you mystics, who maintain the absolute incomprehensibility of the Deity, differ from sceptics or atheists, who assert that the first cause of all is unknown and unintelligible? Their temerity must be very great if, after rejecting the production by a mind—I mean a mind resembling the human (for I know of no other)—they pretend to assign, with certainty, any other specific intelligible cause; and their conscience must be very scrupulous, indeed, if they refuse to call the universal unknown cause a God or Deity, and to bestow on him as many sublime eulogies and unmeaning epithets as you shall please to require of them.

Who could imagine, replied Demea, that Cleanthes, the calm philosophical Cleanthes, would attempt to refute his antagonists by affixing a nickname to them, and, like the common bigots and inquisitors of the age, have recourse to invective and declamation instead of reasoning? Or does he not perceive that these topics are easily retorted, and that *anthropomorphite* is an appellation as invidious, and implies as dangerous consequences, as the epithet of *mystic* with which he has honoured us? In reality, Cleanthes, consider what it is you assert when you represent the Deity as similar to a human mind and understanding. What is the soul of man? A composition of various faculties, passions, sentiments, ideas—united, indeed, into one self or person, but still distinct from each other. When it reasons, the ideas which are the parts of its discourse arrange themselves in a certain form or order which is not preserved entire for a moment, but immediately gives place to another arrangement. New opinions, new passions, new affections, new feelings arise which continually diversify the mental scene and produce in it the greatest variety and most rapid succession imaginable. How is this compatible with that perfect immutability and simplicity which all true theists ascribe to the Deity? By the same act, say they, he sees past, present, and future; his love and hatred, his mercy and justice, are one individual operation; he is entire in every point of space, and complete in every instant of duration. No succession, no change, no acquisition, no diminution. What he is implies not in it any shadow of distinction or diversity. And what he is this moment he ever has been and ever will be, without any new judgment, sentiment, or operation. He stands fixed in one simple, perfect state; nor can you ever say, with any propriety, that this act of his is different from that other, or that this judgment or idea has been lately formed and will give place, by succession, to any different judgment or idea.

I can readily allow, said Cleanthes, that those who maintain the perfect simplicity of the Supreme Being, to the extent in which you have explained it, are complete mystics, and chargeable with all the consequences which I have drawn from their opinion. They are, in a word, atheists, without knowing it. For though it be allowed that the Deity possesses attributes of which we have no comprehension, yet ought we never to ascribe to him any attributes which are absolutely incompatible with that intelligent nature essential to him. A mind whose acts and sentiments and ideas are not distinct and successive, one that is wholly simple and totally immutable, is a mind which has no thought, no reason, no will, no sentiment, no love, no hatred; or, in a word, is no mind at all. It is an abuse of terms to give it that appellation, and we may as well speak of limited extension without figure, or of number without composition.

Pray consider, said Philo, whom you are at present inveighing against. You are honouring with the appellation of *atheist* all the sound, orthodox divines, almost, who have treated of this subject; and you will at last be, yourself, found, according to your reckoning, the only sound theist in the world. But if idolaters be atheists, as, I think, may justly be asserted, and Christian theologians the same, what becomes of the argument, so much celebrated, derived from the universal consent of mankind?

But, because I know you are not much swayed by names and authorities, I shall endeavour to show you, a little more distinctly, the inconveniences of that anthropomorphism which you have embraced, and shall prove that there is no ground to suppose a plan of the world to be formed in the Divine mind, consisting of distinct ideas, differently arranged, in the same manner as an architect forms in his head the plan of a house which he intends to execute.

It is not easy, I own, to see what is gained by this supposition, whether we judge of the matter by *reason* or by *experience*. We are still obliged to mount higher in order to find the cause of this cause which you had assigned as satisfactory and conclusive.

If *reason* (I mean abstract reason derived from inquiries *a priori*) be not alike mute with regard to all questions concerning cause and effect, this sentence at least it will venture to pronounce: that a mental world or universe of ideas requires a cause as much as does a material world or universe of objects, and, if similar in its arrangement, must require a similar cause. For what is there in this subject which should occasion a different conclusion or inference? In an abstract view, they are entirely alike; and no difficulty attends the one supposition which is not common to both of them.

Again, when we will needs force *experience* to pronounce some sentence, even on these subjects which lie beyond her sphere, neither can she perceive any material difference in this particular between these two kinds of worlds, but finds them to be governed by similar principles, and to depend upon an equal variety of causes in their operations. We have specimens in miniature of both of them. Our own mind resembles the one; a vegetable or animal body the other. Let experience, therefore, judge from these samples. Nothing seems more delicate, with regard to its causes, than thought; and as these causes never operate in two persons after the same manner, so we never find two persons who think exactly alike. Nor indeed does the same person think exactly alike at any two different periods of time. A difference of age, of the disposition of his body, of weather, of food, of company, of books, of passions—any of these particulars, or others more minute, are sufficient to alter the curious machinery of thought and communicate to it very different movements and operations. As far as we can judge, vegetables and animal bodies are not more delicate in their motions, nor depend upon a greater variety or more curious adjustment of springs and principles.

How, therefore, shall we satisfy ourselves concerning the cause of that Being whom you suppose the Author of nature, or, according to your system of anthropomorphism, the ideal world into which you trace the material? Have we not the same reason to trace that ideal world into another ideal world or new intelligent principle? But if we stop and go no farther, why go so far? why not stop at the material world? How can we satisfy ourselves without going on *in infinitum?* And, after all, what satisfaction is there in that infinite progression? Let us remember the story of the Indian philosopher and his elephant. It was never more applicable than to the present subject. If the material world rests upon a similar ideal world, this ideal world must rest upon some other, and so on without end. It were better, therefore, never to look beyond the present material world. By supposing it to contain the principle of its order within itself, we really assert it to be God; and the sooner we arrive at that Divine Being, so much the better. When you go one step beyond the mundane system, you only excite an inquisitive humour which it is impossible ever to satisfy.

To say that the different ideas which compose the reason of the Supreme Being fall into order of themselves and by their own nature is really to talk without any precise meaning. If it has a meaning, I would fain know why it is not as good sense to say that the parts of the material world fall into order of themselves and by their own nature. Can the one opinion be intelligible, while the other is not so?

We have, indeed, experience of ideas which fall into order of themselves and without any *known* cause. But, I am sure, we have a much larger experience of matter which does the same, as in all instances of generation and vegetation where the accurate analysis of the cause exceeds all human comprehension. We have also experience of particular systems of thought and of matter which have no order; of the first in madness, of the second in corruption. Why, then, should we think that order is more essential to one than the other? And if it requires a cause in both, what do we gain by your system, in tracing the universe of objects into a similar universe of ideas? The first step which we make leads us on for ever. It were, therefore, wise in us to limit all our inquiries to the present world, without looking farther. No satisfaction can ever be attained by these speculations which so far exceed the narrow bounds of human understanding.

It was usual with the Peripatetics, you know, Cleanthes, when the cause of any phenomenon was demanded, to have recourse to their *faculties* or *occult qualities,* and to say, for instance, that bread nourished by its nutritive faculty, and senna purged by its purgative. But it has been discovered that this subterfuge was nothing but the disguise of ignorance, and that these philosophers, though less ingenuous, really said the same thing with the sceptics or the vulgar who fairly confessed that they knew not the cause of these phenomena. In like manner, when it is asked, what cause produced order in the ideas of the Supreme Being, can any other reason be assigned by you, anthropomorphites, than that it is a *rational* faculty, and that such is the nature of the Deity? But why a similar answer will not be equally satisfactory in accounting for the order of the world, without having recourse to any such intelligent creator as you insist on, may be difficult to determine. It is only to say that *such* is the nature of material objects, and that they are all originally possessed of a *faculty* of order and proportion. These are only more learned and elaborate ways of confessing our ignorance; nor has the one hypothesis any real advantage above the other, except in its greater conformity to vulgar prejudices.

You have displayed this argument with great emphasis, replied Cleanthes: You seem not sensible how easy it is to answer it. Even in common life, if I assign a cause for any event, is it any objection, Philo, that I cannot assign the cause of that cause, and answer every new question which may incessantly be started? And what philosophers could possibly submit to so rigid a rule?—philosophers who confess ultimate causes to be totally unknown, and are sensible that the most refined principles into which they trace the phenomena are still to them as inexplicable as these phenomena themselves are to the vulgar. The order and arrangement of nature, the curious adjustment of final causes, the plain use and intention of every part and organ—all these bespeak in the clearest language an intelligent cause or author. The heavens and the earth join in the same testimony: The whole chorus of nature raises one hymn to the praises of its Creator. You alone, or almost alone, disturb this general harmony. You start abstruse doubts, cavils, and objections; you ask me what is the cause of this cause? I know not; I care not; that concerns not me. I have found a Deity; and here I stop my inquiry. Let those go farther who are wiser or more enterprising.

I pretend to be neither, replied Philo; and for that very reason I should never, perhaps, have attempted to go so far, especially when I am sensible that I must at last be contented to sit down with the same answer which, without further trouble, might have satisfied me from the beginning. If I am still to remain in utter ignorance of causes and can absolutely give an explication of nothing, I shall never esteem it any advantage to shove off for a moment a difficulty which you acknowledge must immediately, in its full force, recur upon me. Naturalists indeed very justly explain particular effects by more general causes, though these general causes themselves should remain in the end totally inexplicable, but they never surely thought it satisfactory to explain a particular effect by a particular cause which was no more to be accounted for than the effect itself. An ideal system, arranged of itself, without a precedent design, is not a whit more explicable than a material one which attains its order in a like manner; nor is there any more difficulty in the latter supposition than in the former.

PART V

But to show you still more inconveniences, continued Philo, in your anthropomorphism, please to take a new survey of your principles. *Like effects prove like causes.* This is the experimental argument; and this, you say too, is the sole theological argument. Now it is certain that the liker the effects are which are seen and the liker the causes which are inferred, the stronger is the argument. Every departure on either side diminishes the probability and renders the experiment less conclusive. You cannot doubt of the principle; neither ought you to reject its consequences.

All the new discoveries in astronomy which prove the immense grandeur and magnificence of the works of nature are so many additional arguments for a Deity, according to the true system of theism; but, according to your hypothesis of experimental theism, they become so many objections, by removing the effect still farther from all resemblance to the effects of human art and contrivance. For if Lucretius, even following the old system of the world, could exclaim:

Quis regere immensi summam, quis habere profundi
Indu manu validas potis est moderanter habenas?
Quis pariter cœlos omnes convertere? et omnes
Ignibus ætheriis terras suffire feraces?
Omnibus inque locis esse omni tempore præsto?[2]

If Tully [Cicero] esteemed this reasoning so natural as to put it into the mouth of his Epicurean:

Quibus enim oculis animi intueri potuit vester Plato fabricam illam tanti operis, qua construi a Deo atque ædificari mundum facit? quæ molitio? quæ ferramenta? qui vectes? quæ machinæ? qui minstri tanti muneris fuerunt? quemadmodum autem obedire et parere voluntati architecti aer, ignis, aqua, terra potuerunt?[3]

If this argument, I say, had any force in former ages, how much greater must it have at present when the bounds of Nature are so infinitely enlarged and such a magnificent scene is opened to us? It is still more unreasonable to form our idea of so unlimited a cause from our experience of the narrow productions of human design and invention.

The discoveries by microscopes, as they open a new universe in miniature, are still objections, according to you, arguments, according to me. The further we push our researches of this kind, we are still led to infer the universal cause of all to be vastly different from mankind, or from any object of human experience and observation.

And what say you to the discoveries in anatomy, chemistry, botany? . . . These surely are no objections, replied Cleanthes; they only discover new instances of art and contrivance. It is still the image of mind reflected on us from innumerable objects. Add a mind *like the human,* said Philo. I know of no other, replied Cleanthes. And the liker, the better, insisted Philo. To be sure, said Cleanthes.

Now, Cleanthes, said Philo, with an air of alacrity and triumph, mark the consequences. *First,* by this method of reasoning you renounce all claim to infinity in any of the attributes of the Deity. For, as the cause ought only to be proportioned to the effect, and the effect, so far as it falls under our cognizance, is not infinite, what pretensions have we, upon your suppositions, to ascribe that attribute to the Divine Being? You will still insist that, by removing him so much from all similarity to human creatures, we give in to the most arbitrary hypothesis, and at the same time weaken all proofs of his existence.

Secondly, you have no reason, on your theory, for ascribing perfection to the Deity, even in his finite capacity, or for supposing him free from

[2] *De Rerum Natura,* lib. XI [II], 1094. (Who can rule the sum, who hold in his hand with controlling force the strong reins, of the immeasurable deep? Who can at once make all the different heavens to roll and warm with ethereal fires all the fruitful earths, or be present in all places at all times?—(Translation by H. A. J. Munro, G. Bell & Sons, 1920.)

[3] *De Natura Deorum,* lib. I [cap. VIII]. (For with what eyes could your Plato see the construction of so vast a work which, according to him, God was putting together and building? What materials, what tools, what bars, what machines, what servants were employed in such gigantic work? How could the air, fire, water, and earth pay obedience and submit to the will of the architect?)

every error, mistake, or incoherence, in his undertakings. There are many inexplicable difficulties in the works of nature which, if we allow a perfect author to be proved *a priori,* are easily solved, and become only seeming difficulties from the narrow capacity of man, who cannot trace infinite relations. But according to your method of reasoning, these difficulties become all real, and, perhaps, will be insisted on as new instances of likeness to human art and contrivance. At least, you must acknowledge that it is impossible for us to tell, from our limited views, whether this system contains any great faults or deserves any considerable praise if compared to other possible and even real systems. Could a peasant, if the *Æneid* were read to him, pronounce that poem to be absolutely faultless, or even assign to it its proper rank among the productions of human wit, he who had never seen any other production?

But were this world ever so perfect a production, it must still remain uncertain whether all the excellences of the work can justly be ascribed to the workman. If we survey a ship, what an exalted idea must we form of the ingenuity of the carpenter who framed so complicated, useful, and beautiful a machine? And what surprise must we feel when we find him a stupid mechanic who imitated others, and copied an art which, through a long succession of ages, after multiplied trials, mistakes, corrections, deliberations, and controversies, had been gradually improving? Many worlds might have been botched and bungled, throughout an eternity, ere this system was struck out; much labour lost, many fruitless trials made, and a slow but continued improvement carried on during infinite ages in the art of world-making. In such subjects, who can determine where the truth, nay, who can conjecture where the probability lies, amidst a great number of hypotheses which may be proposed, and a still greater which may be imagined?

And what shadow of an argument, continued Philo, can you produce from your hypothesis to prove the unity of the Deity? A great number of men join in building a house or ship, in rearing a city, in framing a commonwealth; why may not several deities combine in contriving and framing a world? This is only so much greater similarity to human affairs. By sharing the work among several, we may so much further limit the attributes of each, and get rid of that extensive power and knowledge which must be supposed in one deity, and which, according to you, can only serve to weaken the proof of his existence. And if such foolish, such vicious creatures as man can yet often unite in framing and executing one plan, how much more those deities or demons, whom we may suppose several degrees more perfect!

To multiply causes without necessity is indeed contrary to true philosophy, but this principle applies not to the present case. Were one deity antecedently proved by your theory who were possessed of every attribute requisite to the production of the universe, it would be needless, I own, (though not absurd) to suppose any other deity existent. But while it is still a question whether all these attributes are united in one subject or dispersed among several independent beings, by what phenomena in nature can we pretend to decide the controversy? Where we see a body raised in a scale, we are sure that there is in the opposite scale, however concealed from sight, some counterpoising weight equal to it; but it is still allowed to doubt whether that weight be an aggregate of several distinct bodies or one uniform united mass. And if the weight requisite very much exceeds anything which we have ever seen conjoined in any single body, the former supposition becomes still more probable and natural. An intelligent being of such vast power and capacity as is necessary to produce the universe, or, to speak in the language of ancient philosophy, so prodigious an animal exceeds all analogy and even comprehension.

But further, Cleanthes: Men are mortal, and renew their species by generation; and this is common to all living creatures. The two great sexes of male and female, says Milton, animate the world. Why must this circumstance, so universal, so essential, be excluded from those numerous and limited deities? Behold, then, the theogeny of ancient times brought back upon us.

And why not become a perfect anthropomorphite? Why not assert the deity or deities to be corporeal, and to have eyes, a nose, mouth, ears, etc.? Epicurus maintained that no man had ever seen reason but in a human figure; therefore, the gods must have a human figure. And this argument, which is deservedly so much ridiculed by Cicero, becomes, according to you, solid and philosophical.

In a word, Cleanthes, a man who follows your hypothesis is able, perhaps, to assert or conjecture that the universe sometime arose from something like design; but beyond that position he cannot ascertain one single circumstance, and is left afterwards to fix every point of his theology by the utmost license of fancy and hypothesis. This world, for aught he knows, is very faulty and imperfect, compared to a superior standard, and was only the first rude essay of some infant deity who afterwards abandoned it, ashamed of his lame performance; it is the work only of some dependent, inferior deity, and is the object of derision to his superiors; it is the production of old age and dotage in some superannuated deity, and ever since his death has run on at adventures, from the first impulse and active force which it received from him. You justly give signs of horror, Demea, at these strange suppositions; but these, and a thousand more of the same kind, are Cleanthes' suppositions, not mine. From the moment the attributes of the Deity are supposed finite, all these have place. And I cannot, for my part, think that so wild and unsettled a system of theology is, in any respect, preferable to none at all.

These suppositions I absolutely disown, cried Cleanthes: they strike me, however, with no horror, especially when proposed in that rambling way in which they drop from you. On the contrary, they give me pleasure when I see that, by the utmost indulgence of your imagination, you never get rid of the hypothesis of design in the universe, but are obliged at every turn to have recourse to it. To this concession I adhere steadily; and this I regard as a sufficient foundation for religion.

PART VI

It must be a slight fabric, indeed, said Demea, which can be erected on so tottering a foundation. While we are uncertain whether there is one deity or many, whether the deity or deities, to whom we owe our existence, be perfect or imperfect, subordinate or supreme, dead or alive, what trust or confidence can we repose in them? What devotion or worship address to them? What veneration or obedience pay them? To all the purposes of life the theory of religion becomes altogether useless; and even with regard to speculative consequences its uncertainty, according to you, must render it totally precarious and unsatisfactory.

To render it still more unsatisfactory, said Philo, there occurs to me another hypothesis which must acquire an air of probability from the method of reasoning so much insisted on by Cleanthes. That like effects arise from like causes—this principle he supposes the foundation of all religion. But there is another principle of the same kind, no less certain and derived from the same source of experience, that, where several known circumstances are observed to be similar, the unknown will also be found similar. Thus, if we see the limbs of a human body, we conclude that it is also attended with a human head, though hid from us. Thus, if we see, through a chink in a wall, a small part of the sun, we conclude that were the wall removed we should see the whole body. In short, this method of reasoning is so obvious and familiar that no scruple can ever be made with regard to its solidity.

Now, if we survey the universe, so far as it falls under our knowledge, it bears a great resemblance to an animal or organized body, and seems actuated with a like principle of life and motion. A continual circulation of matter in it produces no disorder; a continual waste in every part is incessantly repaired; the closest sympathy is perceived throughout the entire system; and each part or member, in performing its proper offices, operates both to its own preservation and to that of the whole. The world, therefore, I infer, is an animal; and the Deity is the *soul* of the world, actuating it, and actuated by it.

You have too much learning, Cleanthes, to be at all surprised at this opinion which, you know, was maintained by almost all the theists of antiquity, and chiefly prevails in their discourses and reasonings. For though, sometimes, the ancient philosophers reason from final causes, as if they thought the world the workmanship of God, yet it appears rather their favourite notion to consider it as his body whose organization renders it subservient to him. And it must be confessed that, as the universe resembles more a human body than it does the works of human art and contrivance, if our limited analogy could ever, with any propriety, be extended to the whole of nature, the inference seems juster in favour of the ancient than the modern theory.

There are many other advantages, too, in the former theory which recommended it to the ancient theologians. Nothing more repugnant to all their notions because nothing more repugnant to common experience than mind without body, a mere spiritual substance which fell not under their senses nor comprehension, and of which they had not observed one single instance throughout all nature. Mind and body they knew because they felt both; an order, arrangement, organization, or internal machinery, in both they likewise knew, after the same manner; and it could not but seem reasonable to transfer this experience to the universe, and to suppose the divine mind and body to be also coeval and to have, both of them, order and arrangement naturally inherent in them and inseparable from them.

Here, therefore, is a new species of *anthropomorphism,* Cleanthes, on which you may deliberate, and a theory which seems not liable to any considerable difficulties. You are too much superior, surely, to *systematical prejudices* to find any more difficulty in supposing an animal body to be, originally, of itself or from unknown causes, possessed of order and organization, than in supposing a similar order to belong to mind. But the *vulgar prejudice* that body and mind ought always to accompany each other ought not, one should think, to be entirely neglected; since it is founded on *vulgar experience,* the only guide which you profess to follow in all these theological inquiries. And if you assert that our limited experience is an unequal standard by which to judge of the unlimited extent of nature, you entirely abandon your own hypothesis, and must thenceforward adopt our mysticism, as you call it, and admit of the absolute incomprehensibility of the Divine Nature.

This theory, I own, replied Cleanthes, has never before occurred to me, though a pretty natural one; and I cannot readily, upon so short an examination and reflection, deliver any opinion with regard to it. You are very scrupulous, indeed, said Philo, were I to examine any system of yours, I should not have acted with half that caution and reserve, in starting objections and difficulties to it. However, if anything occur to you, you will oblige us by proposing it.

Why then, replied Cleanthes, it seems to me that, though the world does, in many circumstances, resemble an animal body, yet is the analogy also defective in many circumstances the most material: no organs of sense; no seat of thought or reason; no one precise origin of motion and action. In short, it seems to bear a stronger resemblance to a vegetable than to an animal, and your inference would be so far inconclusive in favour of the soul of the world.

But, in the next place, your theory seems to imply the eternity of the world; and that is a principle which, I think, can be refuted by the strongest reasons and probabilities. I shall suggest an argument to this purpose which, I believe, has not been insisted on by any writer. Those who reason from the late origin of arts and sciences, though their inference wants not force, may perhaps be refuted by considerations derived from the nature of human society, which is in continual revolution between ignorance and knowledge, liberty and slavery, riches and poverty; so that it is impossible for us, from our limited experience, to foretell with assurance what events may or may not be expected. Ancient learning and history seem to have been in great danger of entirely perishing after the inundation of the barbarous nations; and had these convulsions continued a little longer or been a little more violent, we should not probably have now known what passed in the world a few centuries before us. Nay, were it not for the superstition of the popes, who preserved a little jargon of Latin in order to support the appearance of an ancient and universal church, that tongue must have been utterly lost; in which case the Western world, being totally barbarous, would not have been in a fit disposition for receiving the Greek language and learning, which was conveyed to them after the sacking of Constantinople. When learning and books had been extinguished, even the mechanical arts would have fallen considerably to decay; and it is easily imagined that fable or tradition might ascribe to them a much later origin than the true one. This vulgar argument, therefore, against the eternity of the world seems a little precarious.

But here appears to be the foundation of a better argument. Lucullus was the first that brought cherry-trees from Asia to Europe, though that tree thrives so well in many European climates that it grows in the woods without any culture. Is it possible that, throughout a whole eternity, no European had ever passed into Asia and thought of transplanting so delicious a fruit into his own country? Or if the tree was once transplanted and propagated, how could it ever afterwards perish? Empires may rise and fall, liberty and slavery succeed alternately, ignorance and knowledge give place to each other; but the cherry-tree will still remain in the woods of Greece, Spain, and Italy, and will never be affected by the revolutions of human society.

It is not two thousand years since vines were transplanted into France, though there is no climate in the world more favourable to them. It is not three centuries since horses, cows, sheep, swine, dogs, corn, were known in America. Is it possible that during the revolutions of a whole eternity there never arose a Columbus who might open the communication between Europe and that continent? We may as well imagine that all men would wear stockings for ten thousand years, and never have the sense to think of garters to tie them. All these seem convincing proofs of the youth or rather infancy of the world, as being founded on the operation of principles more constant and steady than those by which human society is governed and directed. Nothing less than a total convulsion of the elements will ever destroy all the European animals and vegetables which are now to be found in the Western world.

And what argument have you against such convulsions? replied Philo. Strong and almost incontestable proofs may be traced over the whole earth that every part of this globe has continued for many ages entirely covered with water. And though order were supposed inseparable from matter, and inherent in it, yet may matter be susceptible of many and great revolutions, through the endless periods of eternal duration. The incessant changes to which every part of it is subject seem to intimate some such general transformations; though, at the same time, it is observable that all the changes and corruptions of which we have ever had experience are but passages from one state of order to another; nor can matter ever rest in total deformity and confusion. What we see in the parts, we may infer in the whole; at least, that is the method of reasoning on which you rest your whole theory. And were I obliged to defend any particular system of this nature, which I never willingly should do, I esteem none more plausible than that which ascribes an eternal inherent principle of order to the world, though attended with great and continual revolutions and alterations. This at once solves all difficulties; and if the solution, by being so general, is not entirely complete and satisfactory, it is at least a theory that we must sooner or later have recourse to, whatever system we embrace. How could things have been as they are, were there not an original inherent principle of order somewhere, in thought or in matter? And it is very indifferent to which of these we give the preference. Chance has no place, on any hypothesis, sceptical or religious. Everything is surely governed by steady, inviolable laws. And were the inmost essence of things laid open to us, we should then discover a scene of which, at present, we can have no idea. Instead of admiring the order of natural beings, we should clearly see that it was absolutely impossible for them, in the smallest article, ever to admit of any other disposition.

Were anyone inclined to revive the ancient pagan theology which maintained, as we learn from Hesiod, that this globe was governed by 30,000 deities, who arose from the unknown powers of nature, you would naturally object, Cleanthes, that nothing is gained by this hypothesis; and that it is as easy to suppose all men animals, beings more numerous but less perfect, to have sprung immediately from a like origin. Push the same inference a step further, and you will find a numerous society of deities as explicable as one universal deity who possesses within himself the powers and perfections of the whole society. All these systems, then, of Scepticism, Polytheism, and Theism, you must allow, on your principles, to be on a like footing, and that no one of them has any advantage over the others. You may thence learn the fallacy of your principles.

PART VII

But here, continued Philo, in examining the ancient system of the soul of the world there strikes me, all of a sudden, a new idea which, if just, must go near to subvert all your reasoning, and destroy even your first inferences on which you repose such confidence. If the universe bears a greater likeness to animal bodies and to vegetables than to the works of human art, it is more probable that its cause resembles the cause of the former than that of the latter, and its origin ought rather to be ascribed to generation or vegetation than to reason or design. Your conclusion, even according to your own principles, is therefore lame and defective.

Pray open up this argument a little further, said Demea, for I do not rightly apprehend it in that concise manner in which you have expressed it.

Our friend Cleanthes, replied Philo, as you have heard, asserts that, since no question of fact can be proved otherwise than by experience, the existence of a Deity admits not of proof from any other medium. The world, says he, resembles the works of human contrivance; therefore its cause must also resemble that of the other. Here we may remark that the operation of one very small part of nature, to wit, man, upon another very small part, to wit, that inanimate matter lying within his reach, is the rule by which Cleanthes judges of the origin of the whole; and he measures objects, so widely disproportioned, by the same individual standard. But to waive all objections drawn from this topic, I affirm that there are other parts of the universe (besides the machines of human invention) which bear still a greater resemblance to the fabric of the world, and which, therefore, afford a better conjecture concerning the universal origin of this system. These parts are animals and vegetables. The world plainly resembles more an animal or a vegetable than it does a watch or a knitting-loom. Its cause, therefore, it is more probable, resembles the cause of the former. The cause of the former is generation or vegetation. The cause, therefore, of the world we may infer to be something similar or analogous to generation or vegetation.

But how is it conceivable, said Demea, that the world can arise from anything similar to vegetation or generation?

Very easily, replied Philo. In like manner as a tree sheds its seed into the neighbouring fields and produces other trees, so the great vegetable, the world, or this planetary system, produces within itself certain seeds which, being scattered into the surrounding chaos, vegetate into new worlds. A comet, for instance, is the seed of a world; and after it has been fully ripened, by passing from sun to sun, and star to star, it is, at last, tossed into the unformed elements which everywhere surround this universe, and immediately sprouts up into a new system.

Or if, for the sake of variety (for I see no other advantage), we should suppose this world to be an animal: a comet is the egg of this animal; and in like manner as an ostrich lays its egg in the sand, which, without any further care, hatches the egg and produces a new animal, so . . . I understand you, says Demea. But what wild, arbitrary suppositions are these! What *data* have you for such extraordinary conclusions? And is the slight, imaginary resemblance of the world to a vegetable or an animal sufficient to establish the same inference with regard to both? Objects which are in general so widely different ought they to be a standard for each other?

Right, cries Philo: This is the topic on which I have all along insisted. I have still asserted that we have no *data* to establish any system of cosmogony. Our experience, so imperfect in itself and so limited both in extent and duration, can afford us no probable conjecture concerning the whole of things. But if we must needs fix on some hypothesis, by what rule, pray, ought we to determine our choice? Is there any other rule than the greater similarity of the objects compared? And does not a plant or an animal, which springs from vegetation or generation, bear a stronger resemblance to the world than does any artificial machine, which arises from reason and design?

But what is this vegetation and generation of which you talk? said Demea. Can you explain their operations, and anatomize that fine internal structure on which they depend?

As much, at least, replied Philo, as Cleanthes can explain the operations of reason, or anatomize that internal structure on which it depends. But without any such elaborate disquisitions, when I see an animal, I infer that it sprang from generation; and that with as great certainty as you conclude a house to have been reared by design. These words *generation, reason* mark only certain powers and energies in nature whose effects are known, but whose essence is incomprehensible; and one of these principles, more than the other, has no privilege for being made a standard to the whole of nature.

In reality, Demea, it may reasonably be expected that the larger the views are which we take of things, the better will they conduct us in our conclusions concerning such extraordinary and such magnificent subjects. In this little corner of the world alone, there are four principles, *reason, instinct, generation, vegetation,* which are similar to each other, and are the causes of similar effects. What a number of other principles may we naturally suppose in the immense extent and variety of the universe could we travel from planet to planet, and from system to system, in order to examine each part of this mighty fabric? Any one of these four principles above mentioned (and a hundred others which lie open to our conjecture) may afford us a theory by which to judge of the origin of the world; and it is a palpable and egregious partiality to confine our view entirely to that principle by which our own minds operate. Were this principle more intelligible on that account, such a partiality might be somewhat excusable; but reason, in its internal fabric and structure, is really as little known to us as instinct or vegetation; and, perhaps, even that vague, undeterminate word *nature* to which the vulgar refer everything is not at the bottom more inexplicable. The effects of these principles are all known to us from experience; but the principles themselves and their manner of operation are totally unknown; nor is it less intelligible or less conformable to experience to say that the world arose by vegetation, from a seed shed by another world, than to say that it arose from a divine reason or contrivance, according to the sense in which Cleanthes understands it.

But methinks, said Demea, if the world had a vegetative quality and could sow the seeds of new worlds into the infinite chaos, this power would be still an additional argument for design in its author. For whence could arise so wonderful a faculty but from design? Or how can order spring from anything which perceives not that order which it bestows?

You need only look around you, replied Philo, to satisfy yourself with regard to this question. A tree bestows order and organization on that tree which springs from it, without knowing the order; an animal in the same manner on its offspring; a bird on its nest; and instances of this kind are even more frequent in the world than those of order which arise from reason and contrivance. To say that all this order in animals and vegetables proceeds ultimately from design is begging the question; nor can that great point be ascertained otherwise than by proving, *a priori,* both that order is, from its nature, inseparably attached to thought and that it can never of itself or from original unknown principles belong to matter.

But further, Demea, this objection which you urge can never be made use of by Cleanthes, without renouncing a defence which he has already made against one of my objections. When I inquired concerning the cause of that supreme reason and intelligence into which he resolves everything, he told me that the impossibility of satisfying such inquiries could never be admitted as an objection in any species of philosophy. *We must stop somewhere,* says he; *nor is it ever within the reach of human capacity to explain ultimate causes or show the last connections of any objects. It is sufficient if any steps, so far as we go, are supported by experience and observation.* Now that vegetation and generation, as well as reason, are experienced to be principles of order in nature is undeniable. If I rest my system of cosmogony on the former, preferably to the latter, it is at my choice. The matter seems entirely arbitrary. And when Cleanthes asks me what is the cause of my great vegetative or generative faculty, I am equally entitled to ask him the cause of his great reasoning principle. These questions we have agreed to forbear on both sides; and it is chiefly his interest on the present occasion to stick to this agreement. Judging by our limited and imperfect experience, generation has some privileges above reason; for we see every day the latter arise from the former, never the former from the latter.

Compare, I beseech you, the consequences on both sides. The world, say I, resembles an animal; therefore it is an animal, therefore it arose from generation. The steps, I confess, are wide, yet there is some small appearance of analogy in each step. The world, says Cleanthes, resembles a machine; therefore it is a machine, therefore it arose from design. The steps are here equally wide, and the analogy less striking. And if he pretends to carry on *my* hypothesis a step further, and to infer design or reason from the great principle of generation on which I insist, I may, with better authority, use the same freedom to push further *his* hypothesis, and infer a divine generation or theogony from his principle of reason. I have at least some faint shadow of experience, which is the utmost that can ever be attained in the present subject. Reason, in innumerable instances, is observed to arise from the principle of generation, and never to arise from any other principle.

Hesiod and all the ancient mythologists were so struck with this analogy that they universally explained the origin of nature from an animal birth, and copulation. Plato, too, so far as he is intelligible, seems to have adopted some such notion in his *Timæus*.

The Brahmins assert that the world arose from an infinite spider, who spun this whole complicated mass from his bowels, and annihilates afterwards the whole or any part of it, by absorbing it again and resolving it into his own essence. Here is a species of cosmogony which appears to us ridiculous because a spider is a little contemptible animal whose operations we are never likely to take for a model of the whole universe. But still here is a new species of analogy, even in our globe. And were there a planet wholly inhabited by spiders (which is very possible), this inference would there appear as natural and irrefragable as that which in our planet ascribes the origin of all things to design and intelligence, as explained by Cleanthes. Why an orderly system may not be spun from the belly as well as from the brain, it will be difficult for him to give a satisfactory reason.

I must confess, Philo, replied Cleanthes, that, of all men living, the task which you have undertaken, of raising doubts and objections, suits you best and seems, in a manner, natural and unavoidable to you. So great is your fertility of invention that I am not ashamed to acknowledge myself unable, on a sudden, to solve regularly such out-of-the-way difficulties as you incessantly start upon me, though I clearly see, in general, their fallacy and error. And I question not, but you are yourself, at present, in the same case, and have not the solution so ready as the objection, while you must be sensible that common sense and reason are entirely against you, and that such whimsies as you have delivered may puzzle but never can convince us.

PART VIII

What you ascribe to the fertility of my invention, replied Philo, is entirely owing to the nature of the subject. In subjects adapted to the narrow compass of human reason there is commonly but one determination which carries probability or conviction with it; and to a man of sound judgment all other suppositions but that one appear entirely absurd and chimerical. But in such questions as the present, a hundred contradictory views may preserve a kind of imperfect analogy, and invention has here full scope to exert itself. Without any great effort of thought, I believe that I could, in an instant, propose other systems of cosmogony which would have some faint appearance of truth, though it is a thousand, a million to one if either yours or any one of mine be the true system.

For instance, what if I should revive the old Epicurean hypothesis? This is commonly, and I believe justly, esteemed the most absurd system that has yet been proposed; yet I know not whether, with a few alterations, it might not be brought to bear a faint appearance of probability. Instead of supposing matter infinite, as Epicurus did, let us suppose it finite. A finite number of particles is only susceptible of finite transpositions; and it must happen, in an eternal duration, that every possible order or position must be tried an infinite number of times. This world, therefore, with all its events, even the most minute, has before been produced and destroyed, and will again be produced and destroyed, without any bounds and limitations. No one who has a conception of the powers of infinite, in comparison of finite, will ever scruple this determination.

But this supposes, said Demea, that matter can acquire motion without any voluntary agent or first mover.

And where is the difficulty, replied Philo, of that supposition? Every event, before experience, is equally difficult and incomprehensible; and every event, after experience, is equally easy and intelligible. Motion, in many instances, from gravity, from elasticity, from electricity, begins in matter, without any known voluntary agent; and to suppose always, in these cases, an unknown voluntary agent is mere hypothesis and hypothesis attended with no advantages. The beginning of motion in matter itself is as conceivable *a priori* as its communication from mind and intelligence.

Besides, why may not motion have been propagated by impulse through all eternity, and the same stock of it, or nearly the same, be still upheld in the universe? As much is lost by the composition of motion, as much is gained by its resolution. And whatever the causes are, the fact is certain that matter is and always has been in continual agitation, as far as human experience or tradition reaches. There is not probably, at present, in the whole universe, one particle of matter at absolute rest.

And this very consideration, too, continued Philo, which we have stumbled on in the course of the argument, suggests a new hypothesis of cosmogony that is not absolutely absurd and improbable. Is there a system, an order, an economy of things, by which matter can preserve that perpetual agitation which seems essential to it, and yet maintain a constancy in the forms which it produces? There certainly is such an economy, for this is actually the case with the present world. The continual motion of matter, therefore, in less than infinite transpositions, must produce this economy or order, and, by its very nature, that order, when once established, supports itself for many ages if not to eternity. But wherever matter is so poised, arranged, and adjusted, as to continue in perpetual motion, and yet preserve a constancy in the forms, its situation must, of necessity, have all the same appearance of art and contrivance which we observe at present. All the parts of each form must have a relation to each other and to the whole; and the whole itself must have a relation to the other parts of the universe, to the element in which the form subsists, to the materials with which it repairs its waste and decay, and to every other form which is hostile or friendly. A defect in any of these particulars destroys the form, and the matter of which it is composed is again set loose, and is thrown into irregular motions and fermentations till it unite itself to some other regular form. If no such form be prepared to receive it, and if there be a great quantity of this corrupted matter in the universe, the universe itself is entirely disordered, whether it be the feeble embryo of a world in its first beginnings that is thus destroyed or the rotten carcase of one languishing in old age and infirmity. In either case, a chaos ensues till finite though innumerable revolutions produce, at last, some forms whose parts and organs are so adjusted as to support the forms amidst a continued succession of matter.

Suppose (for we shall endeavour to vary the expression) that matter were thrown into any position by a blind, unguided force; it is evident that this first position must, in all probability, be the most confused and most disorderly imaginable, without any resemblance to those works of human contrivance which, along with a symmetry of parts, discover an adjustment of means to ends and a tendency to self-preservation. If the actuating force cease after this operation, matter must remain for ever in disorder and continue an immense chaos, without any proportion or activity. But suppose that the actuating force, whatever it be, still continues in matter, this first position will immediately give place to a second which will likewise, in all probability, be as disorderly as the first, and so on through many successions of changes and revolutions. No particular order or position ever continues a moment unaltered. The original force, still remaining in activity, gives a perpetual restlessness to matter. Every possible situation is produced, and instantly destroyed. If a glimpse or dawn of order appears for a moment, it is instantly hurried away and confounded by that never-ceasing force which actuates every part of matter.

Thus the universe goes on for many ages in a continued succession of chaos and disorder. But is it not possible that it may settle at last, so as not to lose its motion and active force (for that we have supposed inherent in it), yet so as to preserve an uniformity of appearance, amidst the continual motion and fluctuation of its parts? This we find to be the case with the universe at present. Every individual is perpetually changing, and every part of every individual; and yet the whole remains, in appearance, the same. May we not hope for such a position or rather be assured of it from the eternal revolutions of unguided matter; and may not this account for all the appearing wisdom and contrivance which is in the universe? Let us contemplate the subject a little, and we shall find that this adjustment if attained by matter of a seeming stability in the forms, with a real and perpetual revolution or motion of parts, affords a plausible, if not a true, solution of the difficulty.

It is in vain, therefore, to insist upon the uses of the parts in animals or vegetables, and their curious adjustment to each other. I would fain know how an animal could subsist unless its parts were so adjusted? Do we not find that it immediately perishes whenever this adjustment ceases, and that its matter, corrupting, tries some new form? It happens indeed that the parts of the world are so well adjusted that some regular form immediately lays claim to this corrupted matter; and if it were not so, could the world subsist? Must it not dissolve, as well as the animal, and pass through new positions and situations till in great but finite succession it fall, at last, into the present or some such order?

It is well, replied Cleanthes, you told us that this hypothesis was suggested on a sudden, in the course of the argument. Had you had leisure to examine it, you would soon have perceived the insuperable objections to which it is exposed. No form, you say, can subsist unless it possess those powers and organs requisite for its subsistence; some new order or economy must be tried, and so on, without intermission, till at last some order which can support and maintain itself is fallen upon. But according to this hypothesis, whence arise the many conveniences and advantages which men and all animals possess? Two eyes, two ears are not absolutely necessary for the subsistence of the species. Human race might have been propagated and preserved without horses, dogs, cows, sheep, and those innumerable fruits and products which serve to our satisfaction and enjoyment. If no camels had been created for the use of man in the sandy deserts of Africa and Arabia, would the world have been dissolved? If no loadstone has been framed to give that wonderful and useful direction to the needle, would human society and the human kind have been immediately extinguished? Though the maxims of nature be in general very frugal, yet instances of this kind are far from being rare; and any one of them is a sufficient proof of design—and of a benevolent design—which gave rise to the order and arrangement of the universe.

At least, you may safely infer, said Philo, that the foregoing hypothesis is so far incomplete and imperfect, which I shall not scruple to allow. But can we ever reasonably expect greater success in any attempts of this nature? Or can we ever hope to erect a system of cosmogony that will be liable to no exceptions, and will contain no circumstance repugnant to our limited and imperfect experience of the analogy of nature? Your theory itself cannot surely pretend to any such advantage, even though you have run into *anthropomorphism,* the better to preserve a conformity to common experience. Let us once more put it to trial. In all instances which we have ever seen, ideas are copied from real objects, and are ectypal, not archetypal, to express myself in learned terms. You reverse this order and give thought the precedence. In all instances which we have ever seen, thought has no influence upon matter except where that matter is so conjoined with it as to have an equal reciprocal influence upon it. No animal can move immediately anything but the members of its own body; and, indeed, the equality of action and reaction seems to be an universal law of nature; but your theory implies a contradiction to this experience. These instances, with many more which it were easy to collect (particularly the supposition of a mind or system of thought that is eternal or, in other words, an animal ingenerable and immortal)—these instances, I say, may teach all of us sobriety in condemning each other, and let us see that as no system of this kind ought ever to be received from a slight analogy, so neither ought any to be rejected on account of a small incongruity. For that is an inconvenience from which we can justly pronounce no one to be exempted.

All religious systems, it is confessed, are subject to great and insuperable difficulties. Each disputant triumphs in his turn, while he carries on an offensive war, and exposes the absurdities, barbarities, and pernicious tenets of his antagonist. But all of them, on the whole, prepare a complete triumph for the *sceptic,* who tells them that no system ought ever to be embraced with regard to such subjects: for this plain reason that no absurdity ought ever to be assented to with regard to any subject. A total suspense of judgment is here our only reasonable resource. And if every attack, as is commonly observed, and no defence among theologians is successful, how complete must be *his* victory who remains always, with all mankind, on the offensive, and has himself no fixed station or abiding city which he is ever, on any occasion, obliged to defend?

PART IX

But if so many difficulties attend the argument *a posteriori,* said Demea, had we not better adhere to that simple and sublime argument *a priori* which, by offering to us infallible demonstration, cuts off at once all doubt and difficulty? By this argument, too, we may prove the *infinity* of the Divine attributes, which, I am afraid, can never be ascertained with certainty from any other topic. For how can an effect which either is finite or, for aught we know, may be so—how can such an effect, I say, prove an infinite cause? The unity, too, of the Divine Nature it is very difficult, if not absolutely impossible, to deduce merely from contemplating the works of nature; nor will the uniformity alone of the plan, even were it allowed, give us any assurance of that attribute. Whereas the argument *a priori* . . .

You seem to reason, Demea, interposed Cleanthes, as if those advantages and conveniences in the abstract argument were full proofs of its solidity. But it is first proper, in my opinion, to determine what argument of this nature you choose to insist on; and we shall afterwards, from itself, better than from its *useful* consequences, endeavour to determine what value we ought to put upon it.

The argument, replied Demea, which I would insist on is the common one. Whatever exists must have a cause or reason of its existence, it being absolutely impossible for anything to produce itself or be the cause of its own existence. In mounting up, therefore, from effect to causes, we must either go on in tracing an infinite succession, without any ultimate cause at all, or must at least have recourse to some ultimate cause that is *necessarily* existent. Now that the first supposition is absurd may be thus proved. In the infinite chain or succession of causes and effects, each single effect is determined to exist by the power and efficacy of that cause which immediately preceded; but the whole eternal chain or succession, taken together, is not determined or caused by anything, and yet it is evident that it requires a cause or reason, as much as any particular object which begins to exist in time. The question is still reasonable why this particular succession of causes existed from eternity, and not any other succession or no succession at all. If there be no necessarily existent being, any supposition which can be formed is equally possible; nor is there any more absurdity in *nothing's* having existed from eternity than there is in that succession of causes which constitutes the universe. What was it, then, which determined *something* to exist rather than *nothing*, and bestowed being on a particular possibility, exclusive of the rest? *External causes*, there are supposed to be none. *Chance* is a word without a meaning. Was it *nothing?* But that can never produce anything. We must, therefore, have recourse to a necessarily existent Being who carries the *reason* of his existence in himself, and who cannot be supposed not to exist, without an express contradiction. There is, consequently, such a Being—that is, there is a Deity.

I shall not leave it to Philo, said Cleanthes, though I know that the starting objections is his chief delight, to point out the weakness of this metaphysical reasoning. It seems to me so obviously ill-grounded, and at the same time of so little consequence to the cause of true piety and religion, that I shall myself venture to show the fallacy of it.

I shall begin with observing that there is an evident absurdity in pretending to demonstrate a matter of fact, or to prove it by any arguments *a priori*. Nothing is demonstrable unless the contrary implies a contradiction. Nothing that is distinctly conceivable implies a contradiction. Whatever we conceive as existent, we can also conceive as non-existent. There is no being, therefore, whose non-existence implies a contradiction. Consequently there is no being whose existence is demonstrable. I propose this argument as entirely decisive, and am willing to rest the whole controversy upon it.

It is pretended that the Deity is a necessarily existent being; and this necessity of his existence is attempted to be explained by asserting that, if we knew his whole essence or nature, we should perceive it to be as impossible for him not to exist, as for twice two not to be four. But it is evident that this can never happen, while our faculties remain the same as at present. It will still be possible for us, at any time, to conceive the non-existence of what we formerly conceived to exist; nor can the mind ever lie under a necessity of supposing any object to remain always in being; in the same manner as we lie under a necessity of always conceiving twice two to be four. The words, therefore, *necessary existence* have no meaning or, which is the same thing, none that is consistent.

But further, why may not the material universe be the necessarily existent Being, according to this pretended explication of necessity? We dare not affirm that we know all the qualities of matter; and, for aught we can determine, it may contain some qualities which, were they known, would make its non-existence appear as great a contradiction as that twice two is five. I find only one argument employed to prove that the material world is not the necessarily existent Being; and this argument is derived from the contingency both of the matter and the form of the world. "Any particle of matter," it is said, "may be *conceived* to be annihilated, and any form may be *conceived* to be altered. Such an annihilation or alteration, therefore, is not impossible."[4] But it seems a great partiality not to perceive that the same argument extends equally to the Deity, so far as we have any conception of him, and that the mind can at least imagine him to be non-existent or his attributes to be altered. It must be some unknown, inconceivable qualities which can make his non-existence appear impossible or his attributes unalterable; and no reason can be assigned why these qualities may not belong to matter. As they are altogether unknown and inconceivable, they can never be proved incompatible with it.

Add to this that in tracing an eternal succession of objects it seems absurd to inquire for a general cause or first author. How can anything that exists from eternity have a cause, since that relation implies a priority in time and a beginning of existence?

In such a chain, too, or succession of objects, each part is caused by that which preceded it, and causes that which succeeds it. Where then is the difficulty? But the *whole,* you say, wants a cause. I answer that the uniting of these parts into a whole, like the uniting of several distinct countries into one kingdom, or several distinct members into one body, is performed merely by an arbitrary act of the mind, and has no influence on the nature of things. Did I show you the particular causes of each individual in a collection of twenty particles of matter, I should think it very unreasonable should you afterwards ask me what was the cause of the whole twenty. This is sufficiently explained in explaining the cause of the parts.

Though the reasonings which you have urged, Cleanthes, may well excuse me, said Philo, from starting any further difficulties, yet I cannot forbear insisting still upon another topic. It is observed by arithmeticians that the products of 9 compose always either 9 or some lesser product of 9 if you add together all the characters of which any of the former products is composed. Thus, of 18, 27, 36, which are products of 9, you make 9 by adding 1 to 8, 2 to 7, 3 to 6. Thus 369 is a product also of 9; and if you add 3, 6, and 9, you make 18, a lesser product of 9.[5] To a superficial observer so wonderful a regularity may be admired as the effect either of chance or design; but a skilful algebraist immediately concludes it to be the work of necessity, and demonstrates that it must for ever result from the nature of these numbers. Is it not probable, I ask, that the whole economy of the universe is conducted by a like necessity, though no human algebra can furnish a key which solves the difficulty? And instead of admiring the order of natural beings, may it not happen that, could we penetrate into the intimate nature of bodies, we should clearly see why it was absolutely impossible they could ever admit of any other disposition? So dangerous is it to introduce this idea of necessity into the present question! and so naturally does it afford an inference directly opposite to the religious hypothesis!

But dropping all these abstractions, continued Philo, and confining ourselves to more familiar topics, I shall venture to add an observation that the argument *a priori* has seldom been found very convincing, except to people of a metaphysical head who have accustomed themselves to abstract reasoning, and who, finding from mathematics that the understanding frequently leads to truth through obscurity, and contrary to first appearances, have transferred the same habit of thinking to subjects where it ought not to have place. Other people, even of good sense and the best inclined to religion, feel always some deficiency in such arguments, though they are not perhaps able to explain distinctly where it lies—a certain proof that men ever did and ever will derive their religion from other sources than from this species of reasoning.

PART X

It is my opinion, I own, replied Demea, that each man feels, in a manner, the truth of religion within his own breast, and, from a consciousness of his imbecility and misery rather than from any reasoning, is led to seek protection from that Being on whom he and all nature is dependent. So anxious or so tedious are even the best scenes of life that futurity is still the object of all our hopes and fears. We incessantly look forward and endeavour, by prayers, adoration, and sacrifice, to appease those unknown powers whom we find, by experience, so able to afflict and oppress us. Wretched creatures that we are! What resource for us amidst the innumerable ills of life did not religion suggest some methods of

[4] Dr. Clarke [Samuel Clarke, the rationalist theologian (1675–1729).]

[5] *Republique des Lettres,* Aut 1685.

atonement, and appease those terrors with which we are incessantly agitated and tormented?

I am indeed persuaded, said Philo, that the best and indeed the only method of bringing everyone to a due sense of religion is by just representations of the misery and wickedness of men. And for that purpose a talent of eloquence and strong imagery is more requisite than that of reasoning and argument. For is it necessary to prove what everyone feels within himself? It is only necessary to make us feel it, if possible, more intimately and sensibly.

The people, indeed, replied Demea, are sufficiently convinced of this great and melancholy truth. The miseries of life, the unhappiness of man, the general corruptions of our nature, the unsatisfactory enjoyment of pleasures, riches, honours—these phrases have become almost proverbial in all languages. And who can doubt of what all men declare from their own immediate feeling and experience?

In this point, said Philo, the learned are perfectly agreed with the vulgar; and in all letters, *sacred* and *profane,* the topic of human misery has been insisted on with the most pathetic eloquence that sorrow and melancholy could inspire. The poets, who speak from sentiment, without a system, and whose testimony has therefore the more authority, abound in images of this nature. From Homer down to Dr. Young, the whole inspired tribe have ever been sensible that no other representation of things would suit the feeling and observation of each individual.

As to authorities, replied Demea, you need not seek them. Look round this library of Cleanthes. I shall venture to affirm that, except authors of particular sciences, such as chemistry or botany, who have no occasion to treat of human life, there is scarce one of those innumerable writers from whom the sense of human misery has not, in some passage or other, extorted a complaint and confession of it. At least, the chance is entirely on that side; and no one author has ever, so far as I can recollect, been so extravagant as to deny it.

There you must excuse me, said Philo: Leibniz has denied it, and is perhaps the first[6] who ventured upon so bold and paradoxical an opinion; at least, the first who made it essential to his philosophical system.

And by being the first, replied Demea, might he not have been sensible of his error? For is this a subject in which philosophers can propose to make discoveries especially in so late an age? And can any man hope by a simple denial (for the subject scarcely admits of reasoning) to bear down the united testimony of mankind, founded on sense and consciousness?

And why should man, added he, pretend to an exemption from the lot of all other animals? The whole earth, believe me, Philo, is cursed and polluted. A perpetual war is kindled amongst all living creatures. Necessity, hunger, want stimulate the strong and courageous; fear, anxiety, terror agitate the weak and infirm. The first entrance into life gives anguish to the new-born infant and to its wretched parent; weakness, impotence, distress attend each stage of that life, and it is, at least, finished in agony and horror.

Observe, too, says Philo, the curious artifices of nature in order to embitter the life of every living being. The stronger prey upon the weaker and keep them in perpetual terror and anxiety. The weaker, too, in their turn, often prey upon the stronger, and vex and molest them without relaxation. Consider that innumerable race of insects, which either are bred on the body of each animal or, flying about, infix their stings in him. These insects have others still less than themselves which torment them. And thus on each hand, before and behind, above and below, every animal is surrounded with enemies which incessantly seek his misery and destruction.

Man alone, said Demea, seems to be, in part, an exception to this rule. For by combination in society he can easily master lions, tigers, and bears, whose greater strength and agility naturally enable them to prey upon him.

On the contrary, it is here chiefly, cried Philo, that the uniform and equal maxims of nature are most apparent. Man, it is true, can, by combination, surmount all his *real* enemies and become master of the whole animal creation; but does he not immediately raise up to himself *imaginary* enemies, the demons of his fancy, who haunt him with superstitious terrors and blast every enjoyment of life? His pleasure, as he imagines, becomes in their eyes a crime; his food and repose give them umbrage and offence; his very sleep and dreams furnish new materials to anxious fear; and even death, his refuge from every other

[6] That sentiment had been maintained by Dr. King and some few others before Leibniz, though by none of so great fame as that German philosopher.

ill, presents only the dread of endless and innumerable woes. Nor does the wolf molest more the timid flock than superstition does the anxious breast of wretched mortals.

Besides, consider, Demea: This very society by which we surmount those wild beasts, our natural enemies, what new enemies does it not raise to us? What woe and misery does it not occasion? Man is the greatest enemy of man. Oppression, injustice, contempt, contumely, violence, sedition, war, calumny, treachery, fraud—by these they mutually torment each other, and they would soon dissolve that society which they had formed were it not for the dread of still greater ills which must attend their separation.

But though these external insults, said Demea, from animals, from men, from all the elements, which assault us from a frightful catalogue of woes, they are nothing in comparison of those which arise within ourselves, from the distempered condition of our mind and body. How many lie under the lingering torment of disease? Hear the pathetic enumeration of the great poet.

> Intestine stone and ulcer, colic-pangs,
> Demoniac frenzy, moping melancholy,
> And moon-struck madness, pining atrophy,
> Marasmus, and wide-wasting pestilence.
> Dire was the tossing, deep the groans: *Despair*
> Tended the sick, busiest from couch to couch.
> And over them triumphant *Death* his dart
> Shook: but delay'd to strike, though oft invok'd
> With vows, as their chief good and final hope.[7]

The disorders of the mind, continued Demea, though more secret, are not perhaps less dismal and vexatious. Remorse, shame, anguish, rage, disappointment, anxiety, fear, dejection, despair—who has ever passed through life without cruel inroads from these tormentors? How many have scarcely ever felt any better sensations? Labour and poverty, so abhorred by everyone, are the certain lot of the far greater number; and those few privileged persons who enjoy ease and opulence never reach contentment or true felicity. All the goods of life united would not make a very happy man, but all the ills united would make a wretch indeed; and any one of them almost (and who can be free from every one?), nay, often the absence of one good (and who can possess all?) is sufficient to render life ineligible.

Were a stranger to drop on a sudden into this world, I would show him, as a specimen of its ills, an hospital full of diseases, a prison crowded with malefactors and debtors, a field of battle strewed with carcases, a fleet foundering in the ocean, a nation languishing under tyranny, famine, or pestilence. To turn the gay side of life to him and give him a notion of its pleasures—whither should I conduct him? To a ball, to an opera, to court? He might justly think that I was only showing him a diversity of distress and sorrow.

There is no evading such striking instances, said Philo, but by apologies which still further aggravate the charge. Why have all men, I ask, in all ages, complained incessantly of the miseries of life? . . . They have no just reason, says one: these complaints proceed only from their discontented, repining, anxious disposition. . . . And can there possibly, I reply, be a more certain foundation of misery than such a wretched temper?

But if they were really as unhappy as they pretend, says my antagonist, why do they remain in life? . . .

> Not satisfied with life, afraid of death—

this is the secret chain, say I, that holds us. We are terrified, not bribed to the continuance of our existence.

It is only a false delicacy, he may insist, which a few refined spirits indulge, and which has spread these complaints among the whole race of mankind. . . . And what is this delicacy, I ask, which you blame? Is it anything but a greater sensibility to all the pleasures and pains of life? And if the man of a delicate, refined temper, by being so much more alive than the rest of the world, is only so much more unhappy, what judgment must we form in general of human life?

Let men remain at rest, says our adversary, and they will be easy. They are willing artificers of their own misery. . . . No! reply I: an anxious languor follows their repose; disappointment, vexation, trouble, their activity and ambition.

I can observe something like what you mention in some others, replied Cleanthes, but I confess I feel little or nothing of it in myself, and hope that it is not so common as you represent it.

[7] Milton: *Paradise Lost,* Bk. XI.

If you feel not human misery yourself, cried Demea, I congratulate you on so happy a singularity. Others, seemingly the most prosperous, have not been ashamed to vent their complaints in the most melancholy strains. Let us attend to the great, the fortunate emperor, Charles V, when tired with human grandeur, he resigned all his extensive dominions into the hands of his son. In the last harangue which he made on that memorable occasion, he publicly avowed *that the greatest prosperities which he had ever enjoyed had been mixed with so many adversities that he might truly say he had never enjoyed any satisfaction or contentment.* But did the retired life in which he sought for shelter afford him any greater happiness? If we may credit his son's account, his repentance commenced the very day of his resignation.

Cicero's fortune, from small beginnings, rose to the greatest lustre and renown; yet what pathetic complaints of the ills of life do his familiar letters, as well as philosophical discourses, contain? And suitably to his own experience, he introduces Cato, the great, the fortunate Cato protesting in his old age that had he a new life in his offer he would reject the present.

Ask yourself, ask any of your acquaintance, whether they would live over again the last ten or twenty years of their life. No! but the next twenty, they say, will be better:

> And from the dregs of life, hope to receive
> What the first sprightly running could not give.[8]

Thus, as last, they find (such is the greatness of human misery, it reconciles even contradictions) that they complain at once of the shortness of life and of its vanity and sorrow.

And is it possible, Cleanthes, said Philo, that after all these reflections, and infinitely more which might be suggested, you can still persevere in your anthropomorphism, and assert the moral attributes of the Deity, his justice, benevolence, mercy, and rectitude, to be of the same nature with these virtues in human creatures? His power, we allow, is infinite; whatever he wills is executed; but neither man nor any other animal is happy; therefore, he does not will their happiness. His wisdom is infinite; he is never mistaken in choosing the means to any end; but the course of nature tends not to human or animal felicity; therefore, it is not established for that purpose. Through the whole compass of human knowledge there are no inferences more certain and infallible than these. In what respect, then, do his benevolence and mercy resemble the benevolence and mercy of men?

Epicurus' old questions are yet unanswered.

Is he willing to prevent evil, but not able? then is he impotent. Is he able, but not willing? then is he malevolent. Is he both able and willing? whence then is evil?

You ascribe, Cleanthes, (and I believe justly) a purpose and intention to nature. But what, I beseech you, is the object of that curious artifice and machinery which she has displayed in all animals—the preservation alone of individuals, and propagation of the species? It seems enough for her purpose, if such a rank be barely upheld in the universe, without any care or concern for the happiness of the members that compose it. No resource for this purpose: no machinery in order merely to give pleasure or ease; no fund of pure joy and contentment; no indulgence without some want or necessity accompanying it. At least, the few phenomena of this nature are overbalanced by opposite phenomena of still greater importance.

Our sense of music, harmony, and indeed beauty of all kinds, gives satisfaction, without being absolutely necessary to the preservation and propagation of the species. But what racking pains, on the other hand, arise from gouts, gravels, megrims, toothaches, rheumatisms, where the injury to the animal machinery is either small or incurable? Mirth, laughter, play, frolic seem gratuitous satisfactions which have no further tendency; spleen, melancholy, discontent, superstition are pains of the same nature. How then does the Divine benevolence display itself, in the sense of you anthropomorphites? None but we mystics, as you were pleased to call us, can account for this strange mixture of phenomena, by deriving it from attributes infinitely perfect but incomprehensible.

And have you, at last, said Cleanthes smiling, betrayed your intentions, Philo? Your long agreement with Demea did indeed a little surprise me, but I find you were all the while erecting a concealed battery against me. And I must confess that you have now fallen upon a subject worthy of your noble spirit of opposition and contro-

[8] John Dryden, *Aureng-Zebe,* Act IV, sc. 1.

versy. If you can make out the present point, and prove mankind to be unhappy or corrupted, there is an end at once of all religion. For to what purpose establish the natural attributes of the Deity, while the moral are still doubtful and uncertain?

You take umbrage very easily, replied Demea, at opinions the most innocent and the most generally received, even amongst the religious and devout themselves; and nothing can be more surprising than to find a topic like this—concerning the wickedness and misery of man—charged with no less than atheism and profaneness. Have not all pious divines and preachers who have indulged their rhetoric on so fertile a subject, have they not easily, I say, given a solution of any difficulties which may attend it? This world is but a point in comparison of the universe; this life but a moment in comparison of eternity. The present evil phenomena, therefore, are rectified in other regions, and in some future period of existence. And the eyes of men, being then opened to larger views of things, see the whole connection of general laws, and trace, with adoration, and benevolence and rectitude of the Deity through all the mazes and intricacies of his providence.

No! replied Cleanthes, no! These arbitrary suppositions can never be admitted, contrary to matter of fact, visible and uncontroverted. Whence can any cause be known but from its known effects? Whence can any hypothesis be proved but from the apparent phenomena? To establish one hypothesis upon another is building entirely in the air; and the utmost we ever attain by these conjectures and fictions is to ascertain the bare possibility of our opinion, but never can we, upon such terms, establish its reality.

The only method of supporting Divine benevolence—and it is what I willingly embrace—is to deny absolutely the misery and wickedness of man. Your representations are exaggerated; your melancholy views mostly fictitious; your inferences contrary to fact and experience. Health is more common than sickness; pleasure than pain; happiness than misery. And for one vexation which we meet with, we attain, upon computation, a hundred enjoyments.

Admitting your position, replied Philo, which yet is extremely doubtful, you must at the same time allow that, if pain be less frequent than pleasure, it is infinitely more violent and durable. One hour of it is often able to outweigh a day, a week, a month of our common insipid enjoyments; and how many days, weeks, and months are passed by several in the most acute torments? Pleasure, scarcely in one instance, is ever able to reach ecstasy and rapture; and in no one instance can it continue for any time at its highest pitch and altitude. The spirits evaporate, the nerves relax, the fabric is disordered, and the enjoyment quickly degenerates into fatigue and uneasiness. But pain often, good God, how often! rises to torture and agony; and the longer it continues, it becomes still more genuine agony and torture. Patience is exhausted, courage languishes, melancholy seizes us, and nothing terminates our misery but the removal of its cause or another event which is the sole cure of all evil, but which, from our natural folly, we regard with still greater horror and consternation.

But not to insist upon these topics, continued Philo, though most obvious, certain, and important, I must use the freedom to admonish you, Cleanthes, that you have put the controversy upon a most dangerous issue, and are unawares introducing a total scepticism into the most essential articles of natural and revealed theology. What! no method of fixing a just foundation for religion unless we allow the happiness of human life, and maintain a continued existence even in this world, with all our present pains, infirmities, vexations, and follies, to be eligible and desirable! But this is contrary to everyone's feeling and experience; it is contrary to an authority so established as nothing can subvert. No decisive proofs can ever be produced against this authority; nor is it possible for you to compute, estimate, and compare all the pains and all the pleasures in the lives of all men and of all animals; and thus, by your resting the whole system of religion on a point which, from its very nature, must for ever be uncertain, you tacitly confess that that system is equally uncertain.

But allowing you what never will be believed, at least, what you never possibly can prove, that animal or, at least, human happiness in this life exceeds its misery, you have yet done nothing; for this is not, by any means, what we expect from infinite power, infinite wisdom, and infinite goodness. Why is there any misery at all in the world? Not by chance, surely. From some cause then. Is it from the intention of the Deity? But he is perfectly benevolent. Is it contrary to his intention? But he is almighty. Nothing can shake the solidity of this reasoning, so short, so clear, so decisive, except we assert that these subjects exceed all human capacity, and that our common measures of truth and falsehood are not applicable to them—a topic which I have all along insisted on, but which you have, from the beginning, rejected with scorn and indignation.

But I will be contented to retire still from this intrenchment, for I deny that you can ever force me in it. I will allow that pain or misery in man is *compatible* with infinite power and goodness in the Deity, even in your sense of these attributes: what are you advanced by all these concessions? A mere possible compatibility is not sufficient. You must *prove* these pure, unmixt, and uncontrollable attributes from the present mixed and confused phenomena, and from these alone. A hopeful undertaking! Were the phenomena ever so pure and unmixed, yet, being finite, they would be insufficient for that purpose. How much more, where they are also so jarring and discordant!

Here, Cleanthes, I find myself at ease in my argument. Here I triumph. Formerly, when we argued concerning the natural attributes of intelligence and design, I needed all my sceptical and metaphysical subtilty to elude your grasp. In many views of the universe and of its parts, particularly the matter, the beauty and fitness of final causes strike us with such irresistible force that all objections appear (what I believe they really are) mere cavils and sophisms; nor can we then imagine how it was ever possible for us to repose any weight on them. But there is no view of human life or of the condition of mankind from which, without the greatest violence, we can infer the moral attributes or learn that infinite benevolence, conjoined with infinite power and infinite wisdom, which we must discover by the eyes of faith alone. It is your turn now to tug the labouring oar, and to support your philosophical subtilties against the dictates of plain reason and experience.

PART XI

I scruple not to allow, said Cleanthes, that I have been apt to suspect the frequent repetition of the word *infinite,* which we meet with in all theological writers, to savour more of panegyric than of philosophy, and that any purposes of reasoning, and even of religion, would be better served were we to rest contented with more accurate and more moderate expressions. The terms *admirable, excellent, superlatively great, wise,* and *holy*—these sufficiently fill the imaginations of men, and anything beyond, besides that it leads into absurdities, has no influence on the affections or sentiments. Thus, in the present subject, if we abandon all human analogy, as seems your intention, Demea, I am afraid we abandon all religion and retain no conception of the great object of our adoration. If we preserve human analogy, we must forever find it impossible to reconcile any mixture of evil in the universe with infinite attributes; much less can we ever prove the latter from the former. But supposing the Author of nature to be finitely perfect, though far exceeding mankind, a satisfactory account may then be given of natural and moral evil, and every untoward phenomenon be explained and adjusted. A less evil may then be chosen in order to avoid a greater; inconveniences be submitted to in order to reach a desirable end; and, in a word, benevolence, regulated by wisdom and limited by necessity, may produce just such a world as the present. You, Philo, who are so prompt at starting views and reflections and analogies, I would gladly hear, at length, without interruption, your opinion of this new theory; and if it deserve our attention, we may afterwards, at more leisure, reduce it into form.

My sentiments, replied Philo, are not worth being made a mystery of; and, therefore, without any ceremony, I shall deliver what occurs to me with regard to the present subject. It must, I think, be allowed that, if a very limited intelligence whom we shall suppose utterly unacquainted with the universe were assured that it were the production of a very good, wise, and powerful Being, however finite, he would, from his conjectures, form *beforehand* a different notion of it from what we find it to be by experience; nor would he ever imagine, merely from these attributes of the cause of which he is informed, that the effect could be so full of vice and misery and disorder, as it appears in this life. Supposing now that this person were brought into the world, still assured that it was the workmanship of such a sublime and benevolent Being, he might, perhaps, be surprised at the disappointment, but would never retract his former belief if founded on any very solid argument, since such a limited intelligence must be sensible of his own blindness and ignorance, and must allow that there may be many solutions of those phenomena which will for ever escape his comprehension. But supposing, which is the real case with regard to man, that this creature is not antecedently convinced of a supreme intelligence, benevolent, and powerful, but is left to gather such a belief from the appearances of things—this entirely alters the case, nor will he ever find any reason for such a conclusion. He may be fully convinced of the narrow limits of his understanding, but this will not help him in forming an inference concerning the goodness of superior powers, since he must form that inference from what he knows, not from what he is ignorant of. The more you exaggerate his weakness and ignorance, the more diffident you render him, and give him the greater suspicion that such subjects are beyond the reach of his faculties. You are obliged, therefore, to reason with him merely from the known phenomena, and to drop every arbitrary supposition or conjecture.

Did I show you a house or palace where there was not one apartment convenient or agreeable, where the windows, doors, fires, passages, stairs, and the whole economy of the building were the source of noise, confusion, fatigue, darkness, and the extremes of heat and cold, you would certainly blame the contrivance, without any further examination. The architect would in vain display his subtilty, and prove to you that, if this door or that window were altered, greater ills would ensue. What he says may be strictly true: the alteration of one particular, while the other parts of the building remain, may only augment the inconveniences. But still you would assert in general that, if the architect had had skill and good intentions, he might have formed such a plan of the whole, and might have adjusted the parts in such a manner as would have remedied all or most of these inconveniences. His ignorance, or even your own ignorance of such a plan, will never convince you of the impossibility of it. If you find any inconveniences and deformities in the building, you will always, without entering into any detail, condemn the architect.

In short, I repeat the question: Is the world, considered in general and as it appears to us in this life, different from what a man or such a limited being would, *beforehand,* expect from a very powerful, wise, and benevolent Deity? It must be strange prejudice to assert the contrary. And from thence I conclude that, however consistent the world may be, allowing certain suppositions and conjectures with the idea of such a Deity, it can never afford us an inference concerning his existence. The consistency is not absolutely denied, only the inference. Conjectures, especially where infinity is excluded from the Divine attributes, may perhaps be sufficient to prove a consistency, but can never be foundations for any inference.

There seem to be *four* circumstances on which depend all or the greatest part of the ills that molest sensible creatures; and it is not impossible but all these circumstances may be necessary and unavoidable. We know so little beyond common life, or even of common life, that, with regard to the economy of a universe, there is no conjecture, however wild, which may not be just, nor any one, however plausible, which may not be erroneous. All that belongs to human understanding, in this deep ignorance and obscurity, is to be sceptical or at least cautious, and not to admit of any hypothesis whatever, much less of any which is supported by no appearance of probability. Now this I assert to be the case with regard to all the causes of evil and the circumstances on which it depends. None of them appear to human reason in the least degree necessary or unavoidable, nor can we suppose them such, without the utmost license of imagination.

The *first* circumstance which introduces evil is that contrivance or economy of the animal creation by which pains, as well as pleasures, are employed to excite all creatures to action, and make them vigilant in the great work of self-preservation. Now pleasure alone, in its various degrees, seems to human understanding sufficient for this purpose. All animals might be constantly in a state of enjoyment; but when urged by any of the necessities of nature, such as thirst, hunger, weariness, instead of pain, they might feel a diminution of pleasure by which they might be prompted to seek that object which is necessary to their subsistence. Men pursue pleasure as eagerly as they avoid pain; at least, they might have been so constituted. It seems, therefore, plainly possible to carry on the business of life without any pain. Why then is any animal ever rendered susceptible of such a sensation? If animals can be free from it an hour, they might enjoy a perpetual exemption from it, and it required as particular a contrivance of their organs to produce that feeling as to endow them with sight, hearing, or any of the senses. Shall we conjecture that such a contrivance was necessary, without any appearance of reason, and shall we build on that conjecture as on the most certain truth?

But a capacity of pain would not alone produce pain were it not for the *second* circumstance, viz., the conducting of the world by general laws; and this seems nowise necessary to a very perfect Being. It is true, if everything were conducted by particular volitions, the course of nature would be perpetually broken, and no man could employ his reason in the conduct of life. But might not other particular volitions remedy this inconvenience? In short, might not the Deity exterminate all ill, wherever it were to be found, and produce all good, without any preparation or long progress of causes and effects?

Besides, we must consider that, according to the present economy of the world, the course of nature, though supposed exactly regular, yet to us appears not so, and many events are uncertain, and many disappoint our expectations. Health and sickness, calm and tempest, with an infinite number of other accidents whose causes are unknown and variable, have a great influence both on the fortunes of particular persons and on the prosperity of public societies; and indeed all human life, in a manner, depends on such accidents. A being, therefore, who knows the secret springs of the universe might easily, by particular volitions, turn all these accidents to the good of mankind and render the whole world happy, without discovering himself in any operation. A fleet whose purposes were salutary to society might always meet with a fair wind. Good princes enjoy sound health and long life. Persons born to power and authority be framed with good tempers and virtuous dispositions. A few such events as these, regularly and wisely conducted, would change the face of the world, and yet would no more seem to disturb the course of nature or confound human conduct than the present economy of things where the causes are secret and variable and compounded. Some small touches given to Caligula's brain in his infancy might have converted him into a Trajan. One wave, a little higher than the rest, by burying Caesar and his fortune in the bottom of the ocean, might have restored liberty to a considerable part of mankind. There may, for aught we know, be good reasons why Providence interposes not in this manner, but they are unknown to us; and, though the mere supposition that such reasons exist may be sufficient to *save* the conclusion concerning the Divine attributes, yet surely it can never be sufficient to *establish* that conclusion.

If everything in the universe be conducted by general laws, and if animals be rendered susceptible of pain, it scarcely seems possible but some ill must arise in the various shocks of matter and the various concurrence and opposition of general laws; but this ill would be very rare were it not for the *third* circumstance which I proposed to mention, viz., the great frugality with which all powers and faculties are distributed to every particular being. So well adjusted are the organs and capacities of all animals, and so well fitted to their preservation, that, as far as history or tradition reaches, there appears not to be any single species which has yet been extinguished in the universe. Every animal has the requisite endowments, but these endowments are bestowed with so scrupulous an economy that any considerable diminution must entirely destroy the creature. Wherever one power is increased, there is a proportional abatement in the others. Animals which excel in swiftness are commonly defective in force. Those which possess both are either imperfect in some of their senses or are oppressed with the most craving wants. The human species, whose chief excellence is reason and sagacity, is of all others the most necessitous, and the most deficient in bodily advantages, without clothes, without arms, without food, without lodging, without any convenience of life, except what they owe to their own skill and industry. In short, nature seems to have formed an exact calculation of the necessities of her creatures, and, like a *rigid master,* has afforded them little more powers or endowments than what are strictly sufficient to supply those necessities. An *indulgent parent* would have bestowed a large stock in order to guard against accidents, and secure the happiness and welfare of the creature in the most unfortunate concurrence of circumstances. Every course of life would not have been so surrounded with precipices that the least departure from the true path, by mistake or necessity, must involve us in misery and ruin. Some reserve, some fund, would have been provided to ensure happiness, nor would the powers and the necessities have been adjusted with so rigid an economy. The Author of nature is inconceivably powerful; his force is supposed great, if not altogether inexhaustible, nor is there any reason, as far as we can judge, to make him observe this strict frugality in his dealings with his creatures. It would have been better, were his power extremely limited, to have created fewer animals, and to have endowed these with more faculties for their happiness and preservation. A builder is never esteemed prudent who undertakes a plan beyond what his stock will enable him to finish.

In order to cure most of the ills of human life, I require not that man should have the wings of the eagle, the swiftness of the stag, the force of the ox, the arms of the lion, the scales of the crocodile or rhinoceros; much less do I demand the sagacity of an angel or cherubim. I am contented to take an increase in one single power or faculty of his soul. Let him be endowed with a greater propensity to industry and labour, a more vigorous spring and activity of mind, a more constant bent to business and application. Let the whole species possess naturally an equal diligence with that which many individuals are able to attain by habit and reflection, and the most beneficial consequences, without any allay of ill, is the immediate and necessary result of this endowment. Almost all the moral as well as natural evils of human life arise from idleness; and were our species, by the original constitution of their frame, exempt from this vice or infirmity, the perfect cultivation of land, the improvement of arts and manufactures, the exact execution of every office and duty, immediately follow; and men at once may fully reach that state of society which is so imperfectly attained by the best regulated government. But as industry is a power, and the most valuable of any, nature seems determined, suitably to her usual maxims, to bestow it on men with a very sparing hand, and rather to punish him severely for his deficiency in it than to reward him for his attainments. She has so contrived his frame that nothing but the most violent necessity can oblige him to labour; and she employs all his other wants to overcome, at least in part, the want of diligence, and to endow him with some share of a faculty of which she has thought fit naturally to bereave him. Here our demands may be allowed very humble, and therefore the more reasonable. If we required the endowments of superior penetration and judgment, of a more delicate taste of beauty, of a nicer sensibility to benevolence and friendship, we might be told that we impiously pretend to break the order of nature, that we want to exalt ourselves into a higher rank of being, that the presents which we require, not being suitable to our state and condition, would only be pernicious to us. But it is hard, I dare to repeat it, it is hard that, being placed in a world so full of wants and necessities, where almost every being and element is either our foe or refuses its assistance . . . we should also have our own temper to struggle with, and should be deprived of that faculty which can alone fence against these multiplied evils.

The *fourth* circumstance whence arises the misery and ill of the universe is the inaccurate workmanship of all the springs and principles of the great machine of nature. It must be acknowledged that there are few parts of the universe which seem not to serve some purpose, and whose removal would not produce a visible defect and disorder in the whole. The parts hang all together, nor can one be touched without affecting the rest, in a greater or less degree. But at the same time, it must be observed that none of these parts or principles, however useful, are so accurately adjusted as to keep precisely within those bounds in which their utility consists; but they are, all of them, apt, on every occasion, to run into the one extreme or the other. One would imagine that this grand production had not received the last hand of the maker—so little finished is every part, and so coarse are the strokes with which it is executed. Thus the winds are requisite to convey the vapours along the surface of the globe, and to assist men in navigation; but how often, rising up to tempests and hurricanes, do they become pernicious? Rains are necessary to nourish all the plants and animals of the earth; but how often are they defective? how often excessive? Heat is requisite to all life and vegetation, but is not always found in the due proportion. On the mixture and secretion of the humours and juices of the body depend the health and prosperity of the animal; but the parts perform not regularly their proper function. What more useful than all the passions of the mind, ambition, vanity, love, anger? But how often do they break their bounds and cause the greatest convulsions in society? There is nothing so advantageous in the universe but what frequently becomes pernicious, by its excess or defect; nor has nature guarded, with the requisite accuracy, against all disorder or confusion. The irregularity is never perhaps so great as to destroy any species, but is often sufficient to involve the individuals in ruin and misery.

On the concurrence, then, of these *four* circumstances does all or the greatest part of natural evil depend. Were all living creatures incapable of pain, or were the world administered by particular volitions, evil never could have found access into the universe; and were animals endowed with a large stock of powers and faculties, beyond what strict necessity requires, or were the several springs and principles of the universe so accurately framed as to preserve always the just temperament and medium, there must have been very little ill in comparison of what we feel at present. What then shall we pronounce on this occasion? Shall we say that these circumstances are not necessary, and that they might easily have been altered in the contrivance of the universe? This decision seems too presumptuous for creatures so blind and ignorant. Let us be more modest in our conclusions. Let us allow that, if the goodness of the Deity (I mean a goodness like the human) could be established on any tolerable reasons *a priori,* these phenomena, however untoward, would not be sufficient to subvert that principle, but might easily, in some unknown manner, be reconcilable to it. But let us still assert that, as this goodness is not antecedently established but must be inferred from the phenomena, there can be no grounds for such an inference while there are so many ills in the universe, and while these ills might so easily have been remedied, as far as human understanding can be allowed to judge on such a subject. I am sceptic enough to allow that the bad appearances, notwithstanding all my reasonings, may be compatible with such attributes as you suppose, but surely they can never prove these attributes. Such a conclusion cannot result from scepticism, but must arise from the phenomena, and from our confidence in the reasonings which we deduce from these phenomena.

Look round this universe. What an immense profusion of beings, animated and organized, sensible and active! You admire this prodigious variety and fecundity. But inspect a little more narrowly these living existences, the only beings worth regarding. How hostile and destructive to each other! How insufficient all of them for their own happiness! How contemptible or odious to the spectator! The whole presents nothing but the idea of a blind nature, impregnated by a great vivifying principle, and pouring forth from her lap, without discernment or parental care, her maimed and abortive children!

Here the Manichaean system occurs as a proper hypothesis to solve the difficulty; and, no doubt, in some respects it is very specious and has more probability than the common hypothesis, by giving a plausible account of the strange mixture of good and ill which appears in life. But if we consider, on the other hand, the perfect uniformity and agreement of the parts of the universe, we shall not discover in it any marks of the combat of a malevolent with a benevolent being. There is indeed an opposition of pains and pleasures in the feelings of sensible creatures; but are not all the operations of nature carried on by an opposition of principles, of hot and cold, moist and dry, light and heavy? The true conclusion is that the original Source of all things is entirely indifferent to all these principles, and has no more regard to good above ill than to heat above cold, or to drought above moisture, or to light above heavy.

There may *four* hypotheses be framed concerning the first causes of the universe: that they are endowed with perfect goodness; that they have perfect malice; that they are opposite and have both goodness and malice; that they have neither goodness nor malice. Mixed phenomena can never prove the two former unmixed principles; and the uniformity and steadiness of general laws seem to oppose the third. The fourth, therefore, seems by far the most probable.

What I have said concerning natural evil will apply to moral with little or no variation; and we have no more reason to infer that the rectitude of the Supreme Being resembles human rectitude than that his benevolence resembles the human. Nay, it will be thought that we have still greater cause to exclude from him moral sentiments, such as we feel them, since moral evil, in the opinion of many, is much more predominant above moral good than natural evil above natural good.

But even though this should not be allowed, and though the virtue which is in mankind should be acknowledged much superior to the vice, yet, so long as there is any vice at all in the universe, it will very much puzzle you anthropomorphites how to account for it. You must assign a cause for it, without having recourse to the first cause. But as every effect must have a cause, and that cause another, you must either carry on the progression *in infinitum* or rest on that original principle, who is the ultimate cause of all things. . . .

Hold! hold! cried Demea: Whither does your imagination hurry you? I joined in alliance with you in order to prove the incomprehensible nature of the Divine Being, and refute the principles of Cleanthes, who would measure everything by human rule and standard. But I now find you running into all the topics of the greatest libertines and infidels, and betraying that holy cause which you seemingly espoused. Are you secretly, then, a more dangerous enemy than Cleanthes himself?

And are you so late in perceiving it? replied Cleanthes. Believe me, Demea, your friend Philo, from the beginning, has been amusing himself at both our expense; and it must be confessed that the injudicious reasoning of our vulgar theology has given him but too just a handle of ridicule. The total infirmity of human reason, the absolute incomprehensibility of the Divine Nature, the great and universal misery, and still greater wickedness of men—these are strange topics, surely, to be so fondly cherished by orthodox divines and doctors. In ages of stupidity and ignorance, indeed, these principles may safely be espoused; and perhaps no views of things are more proper to promote superstition than such as encourage the blind amazement, the diffidence, and melancholy of mankind. But at present . . .

Blame not so much, interposed Philo, the ignorance of these reverend gentlemen. They know how to change their style with the times. Formerly, it was a most popular theological topic to maintain that human life was vanity and misery, and to exaggerate all the ills and pains which are incident to men. But of late years, divines, we find, begin to retract this position and maintain, though still with some hesitation, that there are more goods than evils, more pleasures than pains, even in this life. When religion stood entirely upon temper and education, it was thought proper to encourage melancholy, as, indeed, mankind never have recourse to superior powers so readily as in that disposition. But as men have now learned to form principles and to draw consequences, it is necessary to change the batteries, and to make use of such arguments as will endure at least some scrutiny and examination. This variation is the same (and from the same causes) with that which I formerly remarked with regard to scepticism.

Thus Philo continued to the last his spirit of opposition, and his censure of established opinions. But I could observe that Demea did not at all relish the latter part of the discourse; and he took occasion soon after, on some pretence or other, to leave the company.

ANTONY FLEW, R. M. HARE, BASIL MITCHELL

Theology and Falsification*

ANTONY FLEW

Let us begin with a parable. It is a parable developed from a tale told by John Wisdom in his haunting and revelatory article 'Gods'.[1] Once upon a time two explorers came upon a clearing in the jungle. In the clearing were growing many flowers and many weeds. One explorer says, 'Some gardener must tend this plot'. The other disagrees, 'There is no gardener'. So they pitch their tents and set a watch. No gardener is ever seen. 'But perhaps he is an invisible gardener.' So they set up a barbed-wire fence. They electrify it. They patrol with bloodhounds. (For they remember how H. G. Wells's *The Invisible Man* could be both smelt and touched though he could not be seen.) But no shrieks ever suggest that some intruder has received a shock. No movements of the wire ever betray an invisible climber. The bloodhounds never give cry. Yet still the Believer is not convinced. 'But there is a gardener, invisible, intangible, insensible to electric shocks, a gardener who has no scent and makes no sound, a gardener who comes secretly to look after the garden which he loves.' At last the Sceptic despairs, 'But what remains of your original assertion? Just how does what you call an invisible, intangible, eternally elusive gardener differ from an imaginary gardener or even from no gardener at all?'

In this parable we can see how what starts as an assertion, that something exists or that there is some analogy between certain complexes of phenomena, may be reduced step by step to an altogether different status, to an expression perhaps of a 'picture preference'.[2] The Sceptic says there is no gardener. The Believer says there is a gardener (but invisible, etc.). One man talks about sexual behaviour. Another man prefers to talk of Aphrodite (but knows that there is not really a superhuman person additional to, and somehow responsible for, all sexual phenomena).[3] The process of qualification may be checked at any point before the original assertion is completely withdrawn and something of that first assertion will remain (Tautology). Mr. Wells's invisible man could not, admittedly, be seen, but in all other respects he was a man like the rest of us. But though the process of qualification may be, and of course usually is, checked in time, it is not always judiciously so halted. Someone may dissipate his assertion completely without noticing that he has done so. A fine brash hypothesis may thus be killed by inches, the death by a thousand qualifications.

And in this, it seems to me, lies the peculiar danger, the endemic evil, of theological utterance. Take such utterances as 'God has a plan', 'God created the world', 'God loves us as a father loves his children'. They look at first sight very much like assertions, vast cosmological assertions. Of course, this is no sure sign that they either are,

* Antony Flew, R. M. Hare, Basil Mitchell, "Theology and Falsification," *University*, 1950–51. Reprinted in A. Flew and A. MacIntyre, eds., *New Essays in Philosophical Theology* (New York: Macmillan, 1955), pp. 96–108. The discussion is reprinted here by permission of the Macmillan Company. First printed 1955 by SCM Press Ltd.

[1] *P.A.S.*, 1944–5, reprinted as Ch. X of *Logic and Language,* Vol. I (Blackwell, 1951), and in his *Philosophy and Psychoanalysis* (Blackwell, 1953).

[2] Cf. J. Wisdom, 'Other Minds', *Mind,* 1940; reprinted in his *Other Minds* (Blackwell, 1952).

[3] Cf. Lucretius, *De Rerum Natura,* II, 655–60.

or are intended to be, assertions. But let us confine ourselves to the cases where those who utter such sentences intend them to express assertions. (Merely remarking parenthetically that those who intend or interpret such utterances as crypto-commands, expressions of wishes, disguised ejaculations, concealed ethics, or as anything else but assertions, are unlikely to succeed in making them either properly orthodox or practically effective).

Now to assert that such and such is the case is necessarily equivalent to denying that such and such is not the case.[4] Suppose then that we are in doubt as to what someone who gives vent to an utterance is asserting, or suppose that, more radically, we are sceptical as to whether he is really asserting anything at all, one way of trying to understand (or perhaps it will be to expose) his utterance is to attempt to find what he would regard as counting against, or as being incompatible with, its truth. For if the utterance is indeed an assertion, it will necessarily be equivalent to a denial of the negation of that assertion. And anything which would count against the assertion, or which would induce the speaker to withdraw it and to admit that it had been mistaken, must be part of (or the whole of) the meaning of the negation of that assertion. And to know the meaning of the negation of an assertion, is as near as makes no matter, to know the meaning of that assertion.[5] And if there is nothing which a putative assertion denies then there is nothing which it asserts either: and so it is not really an assertion. When the Sceptic in the parable asked the Believer, 'Just how does what you call an invisible, intangible, eternally elusive gardener differ from an imaginary gardener or even from no gardener at all?' he was suggesting that the Believer's earlier statement had been so eroded by qualification that it was no longer an assertion at all.

Now it often seems to people who are not religious as if there was no conceivable event or series of events the occurrence of which would be admitted by sophisticated religious people to be a sufficient reason for conceding 'there wasn't a God after all' or 'God does not really love us then'. Someone tells us that God loves us as a father loves his children. We are reassured. But then we see a child dying of inoperable cancer of the throat. His earthly father is driven frantic in his efforts to help, but his Heavenly Father reveals no obvious sign of concern. Some qualification is made—God's love is 'not a merely human love' or it is 'an inscrutable love', perhaps—and we realize that such sufferings are quite compatible with the truth of the assertion that 'God loves us as a father (but, of course, . . .)'. We are reassured again. But then perhaps we ask: what is this assurance of God's (appropriately qualified) love worth, what is this apparent guarantee really a guarantee against? Just what would have to happen not merely (morally and wrongly) to tempt but also (logically and rightly) to entitle us to say 'God does not love us' or even 'God does not exist'? I therefore put to the succeeding symposiasts the simple central questions, 'What would have to occur or to have occurred to constitute for you a disproof of the love of, or of the existence of, God?'

[4] For those who prefer symbolism: $p \equiv \sim\sim p$.

[5] For by simply negating $\sim p$ we get $p : \sim\sim p \equiv p$.

R. M. HARE[6]

I wish to make it clear that I shall not try to defend Christianity in particular, but religion in general—not because I do not believe in Christianity, but because you cannot understand what Christianity is, until you have understood what religion is.

I must begin by confessing that, on the ground marked out by Flew, he seems to me to be completely victorious. I therefore shift my ground by relating another parable. A certain lunatic is convinced that all dons want to murder him. His friends introduce him to all the mildest and most respectable dons that they can find, and after each of them has retired, they say, 'You see, he doesn't really want to murder you; he spoke to you in a most cordial manner; surely you are convinced now?' But the lunatic replies 'Yes, but that was only his diabolical cunning; he's really plotting against me the whole time, like the rest of them; I know it I tell you'. However many kindly dons are produced, the reaction is still the same.

Now we say that such a person is deluded. But what is he deluded about? About the truth or falsity of an assertion? Let us apply Flew's test to him. There is no behaviour of dons that can be

[6] Some references to intervening discussion have been excised by the editors of *New Essays in Philosophical Theology*.

enacted which he will accept as counting against his theory; and therefore his theory, on this test, asserts nothing. But it does not follow that there is no difference between what he thinks about dons and what most of us think about them—otherwise we should not call him a lunatic and ourselves sane, and dons would have no reason to feel uneasy about his presence in Oxford.

Let us call that in which we differ from this lunatic, our respective *bliks*. He has an insane *blik* about dons; we have a sane one. It is important to realize that we have a sane one, not no *blik* at all; for there must be two sides to any argument—if he has a wrong *blik*, then those who are right about dons must have a right one. Flew has shown that a *blik* does not consist in an assertion or system of them; but nevertheless it is very important to have the right *blik*.

Let us try to imagine what it would be like to have different *bliks* about other things than dons. When I am driving my car, it sometimes occurs to me to wonder whether my movements of the steering-wheel will always continue to be followed by corresponding alterations in the direction of the car. I have never had a steering failure, though I have had skids, which must be similar. Moreover, I know enough about how the steering of my car is made, to know the sort of thing that would have to go wrong for the steering to fail—steel joints would have to part, or steel rods break, or something—but how do I know that this won't happen? The truth is, I don't know; I just have a *blik* about steel and its properties, so that normally I trust the steering of my car; but I find it not at all difficult to imagine what it would be like to lose this *blik* and acquire the opposite one. People would say I was silly about steel; but there would be no mistaking the reality of the difference between our respective *bliks*—for example, I should never go in a motor-car. Yet I should hesitate to say that the difference between us was the difference between contradictory assertions. No amount of safe arrivals or bench-tests will remove my *blik* and restore the normal one; for my *blik* is compatible with any finite number of such tests.

It was Hume who taught us that our whole commerce with the world depends upon our *blik* about the world; and that difference between *bliks* about the world cannot be settled by observation of what happens in the world. That was why, having performed the interesting experiment of doubting the ordinary man's *blik* about the world, and showing that no proof could be given to make us adopt one *blik* rather than another, he turned to backgammon to take his mind off the problem. It seems, indeed, to be impossible even to formulate as an assertion the normal *blik* about the world which makes me put my confidence in the future reliability of steel joints, in the continued ability of the road to support my car, and not gape beneath it revealing nothing below; in the general non-homicidal tendencies of dons; in my own continued well-being (in some sense of that word that I may not now fully understand) if I continue to do what is right according to my lights; in the general likelihood of people like Hitler coming to a bad end. But perhaps a formulation less inadequate than most is to be found in the Psalms: 'The earth is weak and all the inhabiters thereof: I bear up the pillars of it'.

The mistake of the position which Flew selects for attack is to regard this kind of talk as some sort of *explanation*, as scientists are accustomed to use the word. As such, it would obviously be ludicrous. We no longer believe in God as an Atlas—*nous n'avons pas besoin de cette hypothèse*. But it is nevertheless true to say that, as Hume saw, without a *blik* there can be no explanation; for it is by our *bliks* that we decide what is and what is not an explanation. Suppose we believed that everything that happened, happened by pure chance. This would not of course be an assertion; for it is compatible with anything happening or not happening, and so, incidentally, is its contradictory. But if we had this belief, we should not be able to explain or predict or plan anything. Thus, although we should not be *asserting* anything different from those of a more normal belief, there would be a great difference between us; and this is the sort of difference that there is between those who really believe in God and those who really disbelieve in him.

The word 'really' is important, and may excite suspicion. I put it in, because when people have had a good Christian upbringing, as have most of those who now profess not to believe in any sort of religion, it is very hard to discover what they really believe. The reason why they find it so easy to think that they are not religious, is that they have never got into the frame of mind of one who suffers from the doubts to which religion is the answer. Not for them the terrors of the primitive jungle. Having abandoned some of the more picturesque fringes of religion, they think that they have abandoned the whole thing—whereas in fact they still have got, and could not live without, a religion of a comfortably substantial, albeit highly sophisticated, kind, which differs from that of many 'religious people' in little more than this, that 'religious people' like to sing Psalms about theirs—a very natural and proper thing to do. But nevertheless there may be a big difference lying behind—the difference between two people who, though side by side, are walking in different directions. I do not know in what direction Flew is walking; perhaps he does not know either. But we have had some examples recently of various ways in which one can walk away from Christianity, and there are any number of possibilities. After all, man has not changed biologically since primitive times; it is his religion that has changed, and it can easily change again. And if you do not think that such changes make a difference, get acquainted with some Sikhs and some Mussulmans of the same Punjabi stock; you will find them quite different sorts of people.

There is an important difference between Flew's parable and my own which we have not yet noticed. The explorers do not *mind* about their garden; they discuss it with interest, but not with concern. But my lunatic, poor fellow, minds about dons; and I mind about the steering of my car; it often has people in it that I care for. It is because I mind very much about what goes on in the garden in which I find myself, that I am unable to share the explorers' detachment.

BASIL MITCHELL

Flew's article is searching and perceptive, but there is, I think, something odd about his conduct of the theologian's case. The theologian surely would not deny that the fact of pain counts against the assertion that God loves men. This very incompatibility generates the most intractable of theological problems—the problem of evil. So the theologian *does* recognize the fact of pain as counting against Christian doctrine. But it is true that he will not allow it—or anything—to count decisively against it; for he is committed by his faith to trust in God. His attitude is not that of the detached observer, but of the believer.

Perhaps this can be brought out by yet another parable. In time of war in an occupied country, a member of the resistance meets one night a

stranger who deeply impresses him. They spend that night together in conversation. The Stranger tells the partisan that he himself is on the side of the resistance—indeed that he is in command of it, and urges the partisan to have faith in him no matter what happens. The partisan is utterly convinced at that meeting of the Stranger's sincerity and constancy and undertakes to trust him.

They never meet in conditions of intimacy again. But sometimes the Stranger is seen helping members of the resistance, and the partisan is grateful and says to his friends, 'He is on our side'.

Sometimes he is seen in the uniform of the police handing over patriots to the occupying power. On these occasions his friends murmur against him: but the partisan still says, 'He is on our side'. He still believes that, in spite of appearances, the Stranger did not deceive him. Sometimes he asks the Stranger for help and receives it. He is then thankful. Sometimes he asks and does not receive it. Then he says, 'The Stranger knows best'. Sometimes his friends, in exasperation, say 'Well, what *would* he have to do for you to admit that you were wrong and that he is not on our side?' But the partisan refuses to answer. He will not consent to put the Stranger to the test. And sometimes his friends complain, 'Well, if *that's* what you mean by his being on our side, the sooner he goes over to the other side the better'.

The partisan of the parable does not allow anything to count decisively against the proposition 'The Stranger is on our side'. This is because he has committed himself to trust the Stranger. But he of course recognizes that the Stranger's ambiguous behaviour *does* count against what he believes about him. It is precisely this situation which constitutes the trial of his faith.

When the partisan asks for help and doesn't get it, what can he do? He can (*a*) conclude that the stranger is not on our side or; (*b*) maintain that he is on our side, but that he has reasons for withholding help.

The first he will refuse to do. How long can he uphold the second position without its becoming just silly?

I don't think one can say in advance. It will depend on the nature of the impression created by the Stranger in the first place. It will depend, too, on the manner in which he takes the Stranger's behavior. If he blandly dismisses it as of no consequence, as having no bearing upon his belief, it will be assumed that he is thoughtless or insane. And it quite obviously won't do for him to say easily, 'Oh, when used of the Stranger the phrase "is on our side" *means* ambiguous behavior of this sort'. In that case he would be like the religious man who says blandly of a terrible disaster 'It is God's will'. No, he will only be regarded as sane and reasonable in his belief, if he experiences in himself the full force of the conflict.

It is here that my parable differs from Hare's. The partisan admits that many things may and do count against his belief: whereas Hare's lunatic who has a *blik* about dons doesn't admit that anything counts against his *blik*. Nothing *can* count against *bliks*. Also the partisan has a reason for having in the first instance committed himself, viz. The character of the Stranger; whereas the lunatic has no reason for his *blik* about dons—because, of course, you can't have reasons for *bliks*.

This means that I agree with Flew that theological utterances must be assertions. The partisan is making an assertion when he says, 'The Stranger is on our side'.

Do I want to say that the partisan's belief about the Stranger is, in any sense, an explanation? I think I do. It explains and makes sense of the Stranger's behaviour: it helps to explain also the resistance movement in the context of which he appears. In each case it differs from the interpretation which the others put upon the same facts.

'God loves men' resembles 'the Stranger is on our side' (and many other significant statements, e.g. historical ones) in not being conclusively falsifiable. They can both be treated in at least three different ways: (1) As provisional hypotheses to be discarded if experience tells against them; (2) As significant articles of faith; (3) As vacuous formulae (expressing, perhaps, a desire for reassurance) to which experience makes no difference and which make no difference to life.

The Christian, once he has committed himself, is precluded by his faith from taking up the first attitude: 'Thou shalt not tempt the Lord thy God'. He is in constant danger, as Flew has observed, of slipping into the third. But he need not; and, if he does, it is a failure in faith as well as in logic.

ANTONY FLEW

It has been a good discussion: and I am glad to have helped to provoke it. But now—at least in *University*—it must come to an end: and the Editors of *University* have asked me to make some concluding remarks. Since it is impossible to deal with all the issues raised or to comment separately upon each contribution, I will concentrate on Mitchell and Hare, as representative of two very different kinds of response to the challenge made in 'Theology and Falsification'.

The challenge, it will be remembered, ran like this. Some theological utterances seem to, and are intended to, provide explanations or express assertions. Now an assertion, to be an assertion at all, must claim that things stand thus and thus; *and not otherwise*. Similarly an explanation, to be an explanation at all, must explain why this particular thing occurs; *and not something else*. Those last clauses are crucial. And yet sophisticated religious people—or so it seemed to me—are apt to overlook this, and tend to refuse to allow, not merely that anything actually does occur, but that anything conceivably could occur, which would count against their theological assertions and explanations. But in so far as they do this their supposed explanations are actually bogus, and their seeming assertions are really vacuous.

Mitchell's response to this challenge is admirably direct, straightforward, and understanding. He agrees 'that theological utterances must be assertions'. He agrees that if they are to be assertions, there must be something that would count against their truth. He agrees, too, that believers are in constant danger of transforming their would-be assertions into 'vacuous formulae'. But he takes me to task for an oddity in my 'conduct of the theologian's case. The theologian surely would not deny that the fact of pain counts against the assertion that God loves men. This very incompatibility generates the most intractable of theological problems, the problem of evil'. I think he is right. I should have made a distinction between two very different ways of dealing with what looks like evidence against the love of God: the way I stressed was the expedient of qualifying the original assertion; the way the theologian usually takes, at first, is to admit that it looks bad but to insist that there is—there must be—some explanation which will show that, in spite of appearances, there really is a God who loves us. His difficulty, it seems to me, is that he has given God attributes which rule out all possible saving explanations. In Mitchell's parable of the Stranger it is easy for the believer to find plausible excuses for ambiguous behavior: for the Stranger is a man. But suppose the Stranger is God. We cannot say that he would like to help but cannot: God is omnipotent. We cannot say that he would help if he only knew: God is omniscient. We cannot say that he is not responsible for the wickedness of others: God creates those others. Indeed an omnipotent, omniscient God must be an accessory before (and during) the fact to every human misdeed; as well as being responsible for every non-moral defect in the universe. So, though I entirely concede that Mitchell was absolutely right to insist against me that the theologian's first move is to look for an *explanation,* I still think that in the end, if relentlessly pursued, he will have to resort to the avoiding action of *qualification.* And there lies the danger of that death by a thousand qualifications, which would, I agree, constitute 'a failure in faith as well as in logic'.

Hare's approach is fresh and bold. He confesses that 'on the ground marked out by Flew, he seems to me to be completely victorious'. He therefore introduces the concept of *blik.* But while I think that there is room for some such concept in philosophy, and that philosophers should be grateful to Hare for his invention, I nevertheless want to insist that any attempt to analyse Christian religious utterances as expressions or affirmations of a *blik* rather than as (at least would-be) assertions about the cosmos is fundamentally misguided. *First,* because thus interpreted they would be entirely unorthodox. If Hare's religion really is a *blik,* involving no cosmological assertions about the nature and activities of a supposed personal creator, then surely he is not a Christian at all? *Second,* because thus interpreted, they could scarcely do the job they do. If they were not even intended as assertions then many religious activities would become fraudulent, or merely silly. If 'You ought *because* it is God's will' asserts no more than 'You ought', then the person who prefers the former phraseology is not really giving a reason, but a fraudulent substitute for one, a dialectical dud cheque. If 'My soul must be immortal *because* God loves his children, etc.' asserts no more than 'My soul must be immortal', then the man who reassures himself with theological arguments for immortality is being as silly as the man who tries to clear his overdraft by writing his bank a cheque on the same account. (Of course neither of these utterances would be distinctively Christian: but this discussion never pretended to be so confined.) Religious utterances may indeed express false or even bogus assertions: but I simply do not believe that they are not both intended and interpreted to be or at any rate to presuppose assertions, at least in the context of religious practice; whatever shifts may be demanded, in another context, by the exigencies of theological apologetic.

One final suggestion. The philosophers of religion might well draw upon George Orwell's last appalling nightmare *1984* for the concept of *doublethink.* '*Doublethink* means the power of holding two contradictory beliefs simultaneously, and accepting both of them. The party intellectual knows that he is playing tricks with reality, but by the exercise of *doublethink* he also satisfies himself that reality is not violated' (*1984,* p. 220). Perhaps religious intellectuals too are sometimes driven to doublethink in order to retain their faith in a loving God in face of the reality of a heartless and indifferent world. But of this more another time, perhaps.

WILLIAM JAMES

Mysticism*

Over and over again in these lectures I have raised points and left them open and unfinished until we should have come to the subject of Mysticism. Some of you, I fear, may have smiled as you noted my reiterated postponements. But now the hour has come when mysticism must be faced in good earnest, and those broken threads wound up together. One may say truly, I think, that personal religious experience has its root and centre in mystical states of consciousness; so for us, who in these lectures are treating personal experience as the exclusive subject of our study, such states of consciousness ought to form the vital chapter from which the other chapters get their light. Whether my treatment of mystical states will shed more light or darkness, I do not know, for my own constitution shuts me out from their enjoyment almost entirely, and I can speak of them only at second hand. But though forced to look upon the subject so externally, I will be as objective and receptive as I can; and I think I shall at least succeed in convincing you of the reality of the states in question, and of the paramount importance of their function.

First of all, then, I ask, What does the expression "mystical states of consciousness" mean? How do we part off mystical states from other states?

The words "mysticism" and "mystical" are often used as terms of mere reproach, to throw at any opinion which we regard as vague and vast and sentimental, and without a base in either facts or logic. For some writers a "mystic" is any person who believes in thought-transference, or spirit-return. Employed in this way the word has little value: there are too many less ambiguous synonyms. So, to keep it useful by restricting it, I will do what I did in the case of the word "religion," and simply propose to you four marks which, when an experience has them, may justify us in calling it mystical for the purpose of the present lectures. In this way we shall save verbal disputation, and the recriminations that generally go therewith.

1. *Ineffability*.—The handiest of the marks by which I classify a state of mind as mystical is negative. The subject of it immediately says that it defies expression, that no adequate report of its contents can be given in words. It follows from this that its quality must be directly experienced; it cannot be imparted or transferred to others. In this peculiarity mystical states are more like states of feeling than like states of intellect. No one can make clear to another who has never had a certain feeling, in what the quality or worth of it consists. One must have musical ears to know the value of a symphony; one must have been in love one's self to understand a lover's state of mind. Lacking the heart or ear, we cannot interpret the musician or the lover justly, and are even likely to consider him weak-minded or absurd. The mystic finds that most of us accord to his experiences an equally incompetent treatment.

2. *Noetic quality*.—Although so similar to states of feeling, mystical states seem to those who experience them to be also states of knowledge. They are states of insight into depths of truth unplumbed by the discursive intellect. They are illuminations, revelations, full of significance and importance, all inarticulate though they remain; and as a rule they carry with them a curious sense of authority for after-time.

These two characters will entitle any state to

* From William James, *The Varieties of Religious Experience* (1902). Extracts from Lectures XVI and XVII. Lengthy footnote discussions have been omitted.

be called mystical, in the sense in which I use the word. Two other qualities are less sharply marked, but are usually found. These are:—

3. *Transiency.*—Mystical states cannot be sustained for long. Except in rare instances, half an hour, or at most an hour or two, seems to be the limit beyond which they fade into the light of common day. Often, when faded, their quality can but imperfectly be reproduced in memory; but when they recur it is recognized; and from one recurrence to another it is susceptible of continuous development in what is felt as inner richness and importance.

4. *Passivity.*—Although the oncoming of mystical states may be facilitated by preliminary voluntary operations, as by fixing the attention, or going through certain bodily performances, or in other ways which manuals of mysticism prescribe; yet when the characteristic sort of consciousness once has set in, the mystic feels as if his own will were in abeyance, and indeed sometimes as if he were grasped and held by a superior power. This latter peculiarity connects mystical states with certain definite phenomena of secondary or alternative personality, such as prophetic speech, automatic writing, or the mediumistic trance. When these latter conditions are well pronounced, however, there may be no recollection whatever of the phenomenon, and it may have no significance for the subject's usual inner life, to which, as it were, it makes a mere interruption. Mystical states, strictly so-called, are never merely interruptive. Some memory of their content always remains, and a profound sense of their importance. They modify the inner life of the subject between the times of their recurrence. Sharp divisions in this region are, however, difficult to make, and we find all sorts of gradations and mixtures.

These four characteristics are sufficient to mark out a group of states of consciousness peculiar enough to deserve a special name and to call for careful study. Let it then be called the mystical group.

Our next step should be to gain acquaintance with some typical examples. Professional mystics at the height of their development have often elaborately organized experiences and a philosophy based thereupon. But you remember what I said in my first lecture: phenomena are best understood when placed within their series, studied in their germ and in their over-ripe decay, and compared with their exaggerated and degenerated kindred. The range of mystical experience is very wide, much too wide for us to cover in the time at our disposal. Yet the method of serial study is so essential for interpretation that if we really wish to reach conclusions we must use it. I will begin, therefore, with phenomena which claim no special religious significance, and end with those of which the religious pretensions are extreme.

The simplest rudiment of mystical experience would seem to be that deepened sense of the significance of a maxim or formula which occasionally sweeps over one. "I've heard that said all my life," we exclaim, "but I never realized its full meaning until now." "When a fellow-monk," said Luther, "one day repeated the words of the Creed: 'I believe in the forgiveness of sins,' I saw the Scripture in an entirely new light; and straightway I felt as if I were born anew. It was as if I had found the door of paradise thrown wide open." This sense of deeper significance is not confined to rational propositions. Single words, and conjunctions of words, effects of light on land and sea, odors and musical sounds, all bring it when the mind is tuned aright. Most of us can remember the strangely moving power of passages in certain poems read when we were young, irrational doorways as they were through which the mystery of fact, the wildness and the pang of life, stole into our hearts and thrilled them. The words have now perhaps become mere polished surfaces for us; but lyric poetry and music are alive and significant only in proportion as they fetch these vague vistas of a life continuous with our own, beckoning and inviting, yet ever eluding our pursuit. We are alive or dead to the eternal inner message of the arts according as we have kept or lost this mystical susceptibility.

A more pronounced step forward on the mystical ladder is found in an extremely frequent phenomenon, that sudden feeling, namely, which sometimes sweeps over us, of having "been here before," as if at some indefinite past time, in just this place, with just these people, we were already saying just these things. As Tennyson writes:

> Moreover, something is or seems
> That touches me with mystic gleams,
> Like glimpses of forgotten dreams—

> Of something felt, like something here;
> Of something done, I know not where;
> Such as no language may declare.[1]

Sir James Crichton-Browne has given the technical name of "dreamy states" to these sudden invasions of vaguely reminiscent consciousness. They bring a sense of mystery and of the metaphysical duality of things, and the feeling of an enlargement of perception which seems imminent but which never completes itself. . . .

The next step into mystical states carries us into a realm that public opinion and ethical philosophy have long since branded as pathological, though private practice and certain lyric strains of poetry seem still to bear witness to its ideality. I refer to the consciousness produced by intoxicants and anæsthetics, especially by alcohol. The sway of alcohol over mankind is unquestionably due to its power to stimulate the mystical faculties of human nature, usually crushed to earth by the cold facts and dry criticisms of the sober hour. Sobriety diminishes, discriminates, and says no; drunkenness expands, unites, and says yes. It is in fact the great exciter of the *Yes* function in man. It brings its votary from the chill periphery of things to the radiant core. It makes him for the moment one with truth. Not through mere perversity do men run after it. To the poor and the unlettered it stands in the place of symphony concerts and of literature; and it is part of the deeper mystery and tragedy of life that whiffs and gleams of something that we immediately recognize as excellent should be vouch-safed to so many of us only in the fleeting earlier phases of what in its totality is so degrading a poisoning. The drunken consciousness is one bit of the mystic consciousness, and our total opinion of it must find its place in our opinion of that larger whole.

Nitrous oxide and ether, especially nitrous oxide, when sufficiently diluted with air, stimulate the mystical consciousness in an extraordinary degree. Depth beyond depth of truth seems revealed to the inhaler. This truth fades out, however, or escapes, at the moment of coming to; and if any words remain over in which it seemed to clothe itself, they prove to be the veriest nonsense. Nevertheless, the sense of a profound meaning having been there persists; and I know more than one person who is persuaded that in the nitrous oxide trance we have a genuine metaphysical revelation.

Some years ago I myself made some observations on this aspect of nitrous oxide intoxication, and reported them in print. One conclusion was forced upon my mind at that time, and my impression of its truth has ever since remained unshaken. It is that our normal waking consciousness, rational consciousness as we call it, is but one special type of consciousness, whilst all about it, parted from it by the filmiest of screens, there lie potential forms of consciousness entirely different. We may go through life without suspecting their existence; but apply the requisite stimulus, and at a touch they are there in all their completeness, definite types of mentality which probably somewhere have their field of application and adaptation. No account of the universe in its totality can be final which leaves these other forms of consciousness quite disregarded. How to regard them is the question—for they are so discontinuous with ordinary consciousness. Yet they may determine attitudes though they cannot furnish formulas, and open a region though they fail to give a map. At any rate, they forbid a premature closing of our accounts with reality. Looking back on my own experiences, they all converge towards a kind of insight to which I cannot help ascribing some metaphysical significance. The keynote of it is invariably a reconciliation. It is as if the opposites of the world, whose contradictoriness and conflict make all our difficulties and troubles, were melted into unity. Not only do they, as contrasted species, belong to one and the same genus, but *one of the species,* the nobler and better one, *is itself the genus, and so soaks up and absorbs its opposite into itself.* This is a dark saying, I know, when thus expressed in terms of common logic, but I cannot wholly escape from its authority. I feel as if it must mean something, something like what the hegelian philosophy means, if one could only lay hold of it more clearly. Those who have ears to hear, let them hear; to me the living sense of its reality only comes in the artificial mystic state of mind.[2]

[1] "The Two Voices."

[2] What reader of Hegel can doubt that that sense of a perfected Being with all its otherness soaked up into itself, which dominates his whole philosophy, must have come from the prominence in his consciousness of mystical moods like this, in most persons kept

I just now spoke of friends who believe in the anæsthetic revelation. For them too it is a monistic insight, in which the *other* in its various forms appears absorbed into the One.

"Into this pervading genius," writes one of them, "we pass, forgetting and forgotten, and thenceforth each is all, in God. There is no higher, no deeper, no other, than the life in which we are founded. 'The One remains, the many change and pass;' and each and every one of us *is* the One that remains. . . . This is the ultimatum. . . . As sure as being—whence is all our care—so sure is content, beyond duplexity, antithesis, or trouble, where I have triumphed in a solitude that God is not above."

This has the genuine religious mystic ring! . . .

Certain aspects of nature seem to have a peculiar power of awakening such mystical moods. Most of the striking cases which I have collected have occurred out of doors. Literature has commemorated this fact in many passages of great beauty—this extract, for example, from Amiel's Journal Intime:—

> Shall I ever again have any of those prodigious reveries which sometimes came to me in former days? One day, in youth, at sunrise, sitting in the ruins of the castle of Faucigny; and again in the mountains, under the noonday sun, above Lavey, lying at the foot of a tree and visited by three butterflies; once more at night upon the shingly shore of the Northern Ocean, my back upon the sand and my vision ranging through the milky way;—such grand and spacious, immortal, cosmogonic reveries, when one reaches to the stars, when one owns the infinite! Moments divine, ecstatic hours; in which our thought flies from world to world, pierces the great enigma, breathes with a respiration broad, tranquil, and deep as the respiration of the ocean, serene and limitless as the blue firmament; . . . instants of irresistible intuition in which one feels one's self great as the universe, and calm as a god. . . . What hours, what memories! The vestiges they leave behind are enough to fill us with belief and enthusiasm, as if they were visits of the Holy Ghost. . . .

Even the least mystical of you must by this time be convinced of the existence of mystical moments as states of consciousness of an entirely specific quality, and of the deep impression which they make on those who have them. A Canadian psychiatrist, Dr. R. M. Bucke, gives to the more distinctly characterized of these phenomena the name of cosmic consciousness. "Cosmic consciousness in its more striking instances is not," Dr. Bucke says, "simply an expansion or extension of the self-conscious mind with which we are all familiar, but the superaddition of a function as distinct from any possessed by the average man as *self*-consciousness is distinct from any function possessed by one of the higher animals."

> The prime characteristic of cosmic consciousness is a consciousness of the cosmos, that is, of the life and order of the universe. Along with the consciousness of the cosmos there occurs an intellectual enlightenment which alone would place the individual on a new plane of existence—would make him almost a member of a new species. To this is added a state of moral exaltation, an indescribable feeling of elevation, elation, and joyousness, and a quickening of the moral sense, which is fully as striking, and more important than is the enhanced intellectual power. With these come what may be called a sense of immortality, a consciousness of eternal life, not a conviction that he shall have this, but the consciousness that he has it already.[3]

It was Dr. Bucke's own experience of a typical onset of cosmic consciousness in his own person which led him to investigate it in others. He has printed his conclusions in a highly interesting volume, from which I take the following account of what occurred to him:—

> I had spent the evening in a great city, with two friends, reading and discussing poetry and philosophy. We parted at midnight. I had a long drive in a hansom to my lodging. My mind, deeply under the influence of the ideas, images, and emotions called up by the reading and talk, was calm and peaceful. I was in a state of quiet, almost passive enjoyment, not actually thinking, but letting ideas, images, and emotions flow of themselves, as it were, through my mind. All at once, without warning of any kind, I found myself wrapped in a flame-colored cloud. For an instant I thought of fire, an immense conflagration somewhere close by in that great city; the next, I knew that the fire was within

---

subliminal? The notion is thoroughly characteristic of the mystical level, and the *Aufgabe* of making it articulate was surely set to Hegel's intellect by mystical feeling.

[3] *Cosmic Consciousness: a Study in the Evolution of the Human Mind* (Philadelphia, 1901) p. 2.

myself. Directly afterward there came upon me a sense of exultation, of immense joyousness accompanied or immediately followed by an intellectual illumination impossible to describe. Among other things, I did not merely come to believe, but I saw that the universe is not composed of dead matter, but is, on the contrary, a living Presence; I became conscious in myself of eternal life. It was not a conviction that I would have eternal life, but a consciousness that I possessed eternal life then; I saw that all men are immortal; that the cosmic order is such that without any peradventure all things work together for the good of each and all; that the foundation principle of the world, of all the worlds, is what we call love, and that the happiness of each and all is in the long run absolutely certain. The vision lasted a few seconds and was gone but the memory of it and the sense of the reality of what it taught has remained during the quarter of a century which has since elapsed. I knew that what the vision showed was true. I had attained to a point of view from which I saw that it must be true. That view, that conviction, I may say that consciousness, has never, even during periods of the deepest depression, been lost.[4]

We have now seen enough of this cosmic or mystic consciousness, as it comes sporadically. We must next pass to its methodical cultivation as an element of the religious life. Hindus, Buddhists, Mohammedans, and Christians all have cultivated it methodically.

In India, training in mystical insight has been known from time immemorial under the name of yoga. Yoga means the experimental union of the individual with the divine. It is based on persevering exercise; and the diet, posture, breathing, intellectual concentration, and moral discipline vary slightly in the different systems which teach it. The yogi, or disciple, who has by these means overcome the obscurations of his lower nature sufficiently, enters into the condition termed *samâdhi,* "and comes face to face with facts which no instinct or reason can ever know." He learns—

That the mind itself has a higher state of existence, beyond reason, a superconscious state, and that when the mind gets to that higher state, then this knowledge beyond reasoning comes. . . . All the different steps in yoga are intended to bring us scientifically to the superconscious state of Samâdhi. . . . Just as unconscious work is beneath consciousness, so there is another work which is above consciousness, and which, also, is not accompanied with the feeling of egoism. . . . There is no feeling of *I,* and yet the mind works, desireless, free from restlessness, objectless, bodiless. Then the Truth shines in its full effulgence, and we know ourselves—for Samâdhi lies potential in us all—for what we truly are, free, immortal, omnipotent, loosed from the finite, and its contrasts of good and evil altogether, and identical with the Atman or Universal Soul.[5]

The Vedantists say that one may stumble into superconsciousness sporadically, without the previous discipline, but it is then impure. Their test of its purity, like our test of religion's value, is empirical: its fruits must be good for life. When a man comes out of Samâdhi, they assure us that he remains "enlightened, a sage, a prophet, a saint, his whole character changed, his life changed, illumined.". . .

In the Christian church there have always been mystics. Although many of them have been viewed with suspicion, some have gained favor in the eyes of the authorities. The experiences of these have been treated as precedents, and a codified system of mystical theology has been based upon them, in which everything legitimate finds its place.[6] The basis of the system is "orison" or meditation, the methodical elevation of the soul towards God. Through the practice of orison the higher levels of mystical experience may be attained. It is odd that Protestantism, especially evangelical Protestantism, should seemingly have abandoned everything methodical in this line. Apart from what prayer may lead to, Protestant mystical experience appears to have been almost exclusively sporadic. It has been left to our mind-curers to reintroduce methodical meditation into our religious life.

The first thing to be aimed at in orison is the mind's detachment from outer sensations, for these interfere with its concentration upon ideal things. Such manuals as Saint Ignatius's Spirit-

[4] *Loc. cit.,* pp. 7, 8. My quotation follows the privately printed pamphlet which preceded Dr. Bucke's larger work, and differs verbally a little from the text of the latter.

[5] My quotations are from Vivekananda, *Raja Yoga* (London, 1896).

[6] Görres's *Christliche Mystik* gives a full account of the facts. So does Ribet's *Mystique Divine,* 2 vols. (Paris, 1890). A still more methodical modern work is the *Mystica Theologia* of Vallgornera, 2 vols. (Turin, 1890).

ual Exercises recommend the disciple to expel sensation by a graduated series of efforts to imagine holy scenes. The acme of this kind of discipline would be a semi-hallucinatory monoideism—an imaginary figure of Christ, for example, coming fully to occupy the mind. Sensorial images of this sort, whether literal or symbolic, play an enormous part in mysticism. But in certain cases imagery may fall away entirely, and in the very highest raptures it tends to do so. The state of consciousness becomes then insusceptible of any verbal description. Mystical teachers are unanimous as to this. Saint John of the Cross, for instance, one of the best of them, thus describes the condition called the "union of love," which, he says, is reached by "dark contemplation." In this the Deity compenetrates the soul, but in such a hidden way that the soul—

> finds no terms, no means, no comparison whereby to render the sublimity of the wisdom and the delicacy of the spiritual feeling with which she is filled. . . . We receive this mystical knowledge of God clothed in none of the kinds of images, in none of the sensible representations, which our mind makes use of in other circumstances. Accordingly in this knowledge, since the senses and the imagination are not employed, we get neither form nor impression, nor can we give any account or furnish any likeness, although the mysterious and sweet-tasting wisdom comes home so clearly to the inmost parts of our soul. Fancy a man seeing a certain kind of thing for the first time in his life. He can understand it, use and enjoy it, but he cannot apply a name to it, nor communicate any idea of it, even though all the while it be a mere thing of sense. How much greater will be his powerlessness when it goes beyond the senses! This is the peculiarity of the divine language. The more infused, intimate, spiritual, and supersensible it is, the more does it exceed the senses, both inner and outer, and impose silence upon them. . . . The soul then feels as if placed in a vast and profound solitude, to which no created thing has access, in an immense and boundless desert, desert the more delicious the more solitary it is. There, in this abyss of wisdom, the soul grows by what it drinks in from the well-springs of the comprehension of love, . . . and recognizes, however sublime and learned may be the terms we employ, how utterly vile, insignificant, and improper they are, when we seek to discourse of divine things by their means.[7]

[7] Saint John of the Cross: *The Dark Night of the Soul,* book ii. ch. xvii., in *Vie et œuvres,* 3me édition (Paris, 1893), iii. 428–432.

I cannot pretend to detail to you the sundry stages of the Christian mystical life. Our time would not suffice, for one thing; and moreover, I confess that the subdivisions and names which we find in the Catholic books seem to me to represent nothing objectively distinct. So many men, so many minds: I imagine that these experiences can be as infinitely varied as are the idiosyncrasies of individuals. . . .

To the medical mind these ecstasies signify nothing but suggested and imitated hypnoid states, on an intellectual basis of superstition, and a corporeal one of degeneration and hysteria. Undoubtedly these pathological conditions have existed in many and possibly in all the cases, but that fact tells us nothing about the value for knowledge of the consciousness which they induce. To pass a spiritual judgment upon these states, we must not content ourselves with superficial medical talk, but inquire into their fruits for life.

Their fruits appear to have been various. Stupefaction, for one thing, seems not to have been altogether absent as a result. You may remember the helplessness in the kitchen and schoolroom of poor Margaret Mary Alacoque. Many other ecstatics would have perished but for the care taken of them by admiring followers. The "other-worldliness" encouraged by the mystical consciousness makes this over-abstraction from practical life peculiarly liable to befall mystics in whom the character is naturally passive and the intellect feeble; but in natively strong minds and characters we find quite opposite results. The great Spanish mystics, who carried the habit of ecstasy as far as it has often been carried, appear for the most part to have shown indomitable spirit and energy, and all the more so for the trances in which they indulged.

Saint Ignatius was a mystic, but his mysticism made him assuredly one of the most powerfully practical human engines that ever lived. Saint John of the Cross, writing of the intuitions and "touches" by which God reaches the substance of the soul, tells us that—

> They enrich it marvelously. A single one of them may be sufficient to abolish at a stroke certain imperfections of which the soul during its whole life had vainly tried to rid itself, and to leave it adorned with virtues and loaded with supernatural gifts. A

single one of these intoxicating consolations may reward it for all the labors undergone in its life—even were they numberless. Invested with an invincible courage, filled with an impassioned desire to suffer for its God, the soul then is seized with a strange torment—that of not being allowed to suffer enough.

Saint Teresa is as emphatic, and much more detailed. . . .

Mystical conditions may, therefore, render the soul more energetic in the lines which their inspiration favors. But this could be reckoned an advantage only in case the inspiration were a true one. If the inspiration were erroneous, the energy would be all the more mistaken and misbegotten. So we stand once more before that problem of truth which confronted us at the end of the lectures on saintliness. You will remember that we turned to mysticism precisely to get some light on truth. Do mystical states establish the truth of those theological affections in which the saintly life has its root?

In spite of their repudiation of articulate self-description, mystical states in general assert a pretty distinct theoretic drift. It is possible to give the outcome of the majority of them in terms that point in definite philosophical directions. One of these directions is optimism, and the other is monism. We pass into mystical states from out of ordinary consciousness as from a less into a more, as from a smallness into a vastness, and at the same time as from an unrest to a rest. We feel them as reconciling, unifying states. They appeal to the yes-function more than to the no-function in us. In them the unlimited absorbs the limits and peacefully closes the account. Their very denial of every adjective you may propose as applicable to the ultimate truth—He, the Self, the Atman, is to be described by "No! no!" only, say the Upanishads—though it seems on the surface to be a no-function, is a denial made on behalf of a deeper yes. Whoso calls the Absolute anything in particular, or says that it is *this,* seems implicitly to shut it off from being *that*—it is as if he lessened it. So we deny the "this," negating the negation which it seems to us to imply, in the interests of the higher affirmative attitude by which we are possessed. . . .

In mystical literature such self-contradictory phrases as "dazzling obscurity," "whispering silence," "teeming desert," are continually met with. They prove that not conceptual speech, but music rather, is the element through which we are best spoken to by mystical truth. Many mystical scriptures are indeed little more than musical compositions.

He who would hear the voice of Nada, 'the Soundless Sound,' and comprehend it, he has to learn the nature of Dhâranâ. . . . When to himself his form appears unreal, as do on waking all the forms he sees in dreams; when he has ceased to hear the many, he may discern the ONE—the inner sound which kills the outer. . . . For then the soul will hear, and will remember. And then to the inner ear will speak THE VOICE OF THE SILENCE. . . . And now thy *Self* is lost in SELF, *thyself* unto THYSELF, merged in that SELF from which thou first didst radiate. . . . Behold! thou hast become the Light, thou has become the Sound, thou art thy Master and thy God. Thou art THYSELF the object of thy search: the VOICE unbroken, that resounds throughout eternities, exempt from change, from sin exempt, the seven sounds in one, the VOICE OF THE SILENCE. *Om tat Sat.*

These words, if they do not awaken laughter as you receive them, probably stir chords within you which music and language touch in common. Music gives us ontological messages which non-musical criticism is unable to contradict, though it may laugh at our foolishness in minding them. There is a verge of the mind which these things haunt; and whispers therefrom mingle with the operations of our understanding, even as the waters of the infinite ocean send their waves to break among the pebbles that lie upon our shores. . . .

That doctrine, for example, that eternity is timeless, that our "immortality," if we live in the eternal, is not so much future as already now and here, which we find so often expressed to-day in certain philosophic circles, finds its support in a "hear, hear!" or an "amen," which floats up from that mysteriously deeper level. We recognize the passwords to the mystical region as we hear them, but we cannot use them ourselves; it alone has the keeping of "the password primeval."

I have now sketched with extreme brevity and insufficiency, but as fairly as I am able in the time allowed, the general traits of the mystic range of consciousness. *It is on the whole pantheistic and optimistic, or at least the opposite of pessimistic. It is anti-naturalistic, and harmonizes best with twice-bornness and so-called other-worldly states of mind.*

My next task is to inquire whether we can invoke it as authoritative. Does it furnish any *warrant for the truth* of the twice-bornness and supernaturality and pantheism which it favors? I must give my answer to this question as concisely as I can.

In brief my answer is this—and I will divide it into three parts:—

(1) Mystical states, when well developed, usually are, and have the right to be, absolutely authoritative over the individuals to whom they come.

(2) No authority emanates from them which should make it a duty for those who stand outside of them to accept their revelations uncritically.

(3) They break down the authority of the non-mystical or rationalistic consciousness, based upon the understanding and the senses alone. They show it to be only one kind of consciousness. They open out the possibility of other orders of truth, in which, so far as anything in us vitally responds to them, we may freely continue to have faith.

I will take up these points one by one.

1

As a matter of psychological fact, mystical states of a well-pronounced and emphatic sort *are* usually authoritative over those who have them. They have been "there," and know. It is vain for rationalism to grumble about this. If the mystical truth that comes to a man proves to be a force that he can live by, what mandate have we of the majority to order him to live in another way? We can throw him into a prison or a madhouse, but we cannot change his mind—we commonly attach it only the more stubbornly to its beliefs. It mocks our utmost efforts, as a matter of fact, and in point of logic it absolutely escapes our jurisdiction. Our own more "rational" beliefs are based on evidence exactly similar in nature to that which mystics quote for theirs. Our senses, namely, have assured us of certain states of fact; but mystical experiences are as direct perceptions of fact for those who have them as any sensations ever were for us. The records show that even though the five senses be in abeyance in them, they are absolutely sensational in their epistemological quality, if I may be pardoned the barbarous expression—that is, they are face to face presentations of what seems immediately to exist.

The mystic is, in short, *invulnerable,* and must be left whether we relish it or not, in undisturbed enjoyment of his creed. Faith, says Tolstoy, is that by which men live. And faith-state and mystic state are practically convertible terms.

2

But I now proceed to add that mystics have no right to claim that we ought to accept the deliverance of their peculiar experiences, if we are ourselves outsiders and feel no private call thereto. The utmost they can ever ask of us in this life is to admit that they establish a presumption. They form a consensus and have an unequivocal outcome; and it would be odd, mystics might say, if such a unanimous type of experience should prove to be altogether wrong. At bottom, however, this would only be an appeal to numbers like the appeal of rationalism the other way; and the appeal to numbers has no logical force. If we acknowledge it, it is for "suggestive," not for logical reasons: we follow the majority because to do so suits our life.

But even this presumption from the unanimity of mystics is far from being strong. In characterizing mystic states as pantheistic, optimistic, etc., I am afraid I over-simplified the truth. I did so for expository reasons, and to keep the closer to the classic mystical tradition. The classic religious mysticism, it now must be confessed, is only a "privileged case." It is an *extract,* kept true to type by the selection of the fittest specimens and their preservation in "schools." It is carved out from a much larger mass; and if we take the larger mass as seriously as religious mysticism has historically taken itself, we find that the supposed unanimity largely disappears. To begin with, even religious mysticism itself, the kind that accumulates traditions and makes schools, is much less unanimous than I have allowed. It has been both ascetic and antinomianly self-indulgent within the Christian church. It is dualistic in Sankhya, and monistic in Vedanta philosophy. I called it pantheistic; but the great Spanish mystics are anything but pantheists. They are with few exceptions non-metaphysical minds, for whom "the category of personality" is absolute. The "union" of man with God is for them much more like an occasional miracle than like an original identity. How different again, apart from the happiness common to all, is the mysticism of Walt Whitman, Edward Carpenter, Richard Jefferies, and other naturalistic pantheists, from the more distinctively Christian sort. The fact is that the mystical feeling of enlargement, union, and emancipation has no specific intellectual content whatever of its own. It is capable of forming matrimonial alliances with material furnished by the most diverse philosophies and theologies, provided only they can find a place in their framework for its peculiar emotional mood. We have no right, therefore, to invoke its prestige as distinctively in favor of any special belief, such as that in absolute idealism, or in the absolute monistic identity, or in the absolute goodness, of the world. It is only relatively in favor of all these things—it passes out of common human consciousness in the direction in which they lie.

So much for religious mysticism proper. But more remains to be told, for religious mysticism is only one half of mysticism. The other half has no accumulated traditions except those which the text-books on insanity supply. Open any one of these, and you will find abundant cases in which "mystical ideas" are cited as characteristic symptoms of enfeebled or deluded states of mind. In delusional insanity, paranoia, as they sometimes call it, we may have a *diabolical* mysticism, a sort of religious mysicism turned upside down. The same sense of ineffable importance in the smallest events, the same texts and words coming with new meanings, the same voices and visions and leadings and missions, the same controlling by extraneous powers; only this time the emotion is pessimistic: instead of consolations we have desolations; the meanings are dreadful; and the powers are enemies to life. It is evident that from the point of view of their psychological mechanism, the classic mysticism and these lower mysticisms spring from the same mental level, from that great subliminal or transmarginal region of which science is beginning to admit the existence, but of which so little is really known. That region contains every kind of matter: "seraph and snake" abide there side by side. To come from thence is no infallible credential. What comes must be sifted and tested, and run the gauntlet of confrontation with the total context of experience, just like what comes from the outer world of sense. Its value must be ascertained by empirical methods, so long as we are not mystics ourselves.

Once more, then, I repeat that non-mystics are under no obligation to acknowledge in mystical states a superior authority conferred on them by their intrinsic nature.

3

Yet, I repeat once more, the existence of mystical states absolutely overthrows the pretension of non-mystical states to be the sole and ultimate dictators of what we may believe. As a rule, mystical states merely add a supersensuous meaning to the ordinary outward data of consciousness. They are excitements like the emotions of love or ambition, gifts to our spirit by means of which facts already objectively before us fall into a new expressiveness and make a new connection with our active life. They do not contradict these facts as such, or deny anything that our senses have immediately seized. It is the rationalistic critic rather who plays the part of denier in the controversy, and his denials have no strength, for there never can be a state of facts to which new meaning may not truthfully be added, provided the mind ascend to a more enveloping point of view. It must always remain an open question whether mystical states may not possibly be such superior points of view, windows through which the mind looks out upon a more extensive and inclusive world. The difference of the views seen from the different mystical windows need not prevent us from entertaining this supposition. The wider world would in that case prove to have a mixed constitution like that of this world, that is all. It would have its celestial and its infernal regions, its tempting and its saving moments, its valid experiences and its counterfeit ones, just as our world has them; but it would be a wider world all the same. We should have to use its experiences by selecting and subordinating and substituting just as is our custom in this ordinary naturalistic world; we should be liable to error just as we are now; yet the counting in of that wider world of meanings, and the serious dealing with it, might, in spite of all the perplexity, be indispensable stages in our approach to the final fullness of the truth.

In this shape, I think, we have to leave the subject. Mystical states indeed wield no authority due simply to their being mystical states. But the higher ones among them point in directions to which the religious sentiments even of non-mystical men incline. They tell of the supremacy of the ideal, of vastness, of union, of safety, and of rest. They offer us *hypotheses*, hypotheses which we may voluntarily ignore, but which as thinkers we cannot possibly upset. The supernaturalism and optimism to which they would persuade us may, interpreted in one way or another, be after all the truest of insights into the meaning of this life.

BERTRAND RUSSELL

Critique of Mysticism*

Ought we to admit that there is available, in support of religion, a source of knowledge which lies outside science and may properly be described as "revelation"? This is a difficult question to argue, because those who believe that truths have been revealed to them profess the same kind of certainty in regard to them that we have in regard to objects of sense. We believe the man who has seen things through the telescope that we have never seen; why, then, they ask, should we not believe them when they report things that are to them equally unquestionable?

It is, perhaps, useless to attempt an argument such as will appeal to the man who has himself enjoyed mystic illumination. But something can be said as to whether we others should accept this testimony. In the first place, it is not subject to the ordinary tests. When a man of science tells us the result of an experiment, he also tells us how the experiment was performed; others can repeat it, and if the result is not confirmed it is not accepted as true; but many men might put themselves into the situation in which the mystic's vision occurred without obtaining the same revelation. To this it may be answered that a man must use the appropriate sense: a telescope is useless to a man who keeps his eyes shut. The argument as to the credibility of the mystic's testimony may be prolonged almost indefinitely. Science should be neutral, since the argument is a scientific one, to be conducted exactly as an argument would be conducted about an uncertain experiment. Science depends upon perception and inference; its credibility is due to the fact that the perceptions are such as any observer can test. The mystic himself may be certain that he *knows*, and has no need of scientific tests; but those who are asked to accept his testimony will subject it to the same kind of scientific tests as those applied to men who say they have been to the North Pole. Science, as such, should have no expectation, positive or negative, as to the result.

The chief argument in favour of the mystics is their agreement with each other. "I know nothing more remarkable," says Dean Inge, "than the unanimity of the mystics, ancient, mediaeval, and modern, Protestant, Catholic, and even Buddhist or Mohammedan, though the Christian mystics are the most trustworthy." I do not wish to underrate the force of this argument, which I acknowledged long ago in a book called *Mysticism and Logic*. The mystics vary greatly in their capacity for giving verbal expression to their experiences, but I think we may take it that those who succeeded best all maintain: (1) that all division and separateness is unreal, and that the universe is a single indivisible unity; (2) that evil is illusory, and that the illusion arises through falsely regarding a part as self-subsistent; (3) that time is unreal, and that reality is eternal, not in the sense of being everlasting, but in the

* From Bertrand Russell, *Religion and Science*, Home University Library 178 (New York: Oxford University Press, 1961), pp. 177–189. First published in 1935. Reprinted by permission of the publisher.

sense of being wholly outside time. I do not pretend that this is a complete account of the matters on which all mystics concur, but the three propositions that I have mentioned may serve as representatives of the whole. Let us now imagine ourselves a jury in a law-court, whose business it is to decide on the credibility of the witnesses who make these three somewhat surprising assertions.

We shall find, in the first place, that, while the witnesses agree up to a point, they disagree totally when that point is passed, although they are just as certain as when they agree. Catholics, but not Protestants, may have visions in which the Virgin appears; Christians and Mohammedans, but not Buddhists, may have great truths revealed to them by the Archangel Gabriel; the Chinese mystics of the Tao tell us, as a direct result of their central doctrine, that all government is bad, whereas most European and Mohammedan mystics, with equal confidence, urged submission to constituted authority. As regards the points where they differ, each group will argue that the other groups are untrustworthy; we might, therefore, if we were content with a mere forensic triumph, point out that most mystics think most other mystics mistaken on most points. They might, however, make this only half a triumph by agreeing on the greater importance of the matters about which they are at one, as compared with those as to which their opinions differ. We will, in any case, assume that they have composed their differences, and concentrated the defence at these three points—namely, the unity of the world, the illusory nature of evil, and the unreality of time. What test can we, as impartial outsiders, apply to their unanimous evidence?

As men of scientific temper, we shall naturally first ask whether there is any way by which we can ourselves obtain the same evidence at first hand. To this we shall receive various answers. We may be told that we are obviously not in a receptive frame of mind, and that we lack the requisite humility; or that fasting and religious meditation are necessary; or (if our witness is Indian or Chinese) that the essential prerequisite is a course of breathing exercises. I think we shall find that the weight of experimental evidence is in favour of this last view, though fasting also has been frequently found effective. As a matter of fact, there is a definite physical discipline, called yoga, which is practised in order to produce the mystic's certainty, and which is recommended with much confidence by those who have tried it.[1] Breathing exercises are its most essential feature, and for our purposes we may ignore the rest.

In order to see how we could test the assertion that yoga gives insight, let us artificially simplify this assertion. Let us suppose that a number of people assure us that if, *for a certain time,* we breathe in a certain way, we shall become convinced that time is unreal. Let us go further, and suppose that, having tried their recipe, we have ourselves experienced a state of mind such as they describe. But now, having returned to our normal mode of respiration, we are not quite sure whether the vision was to be believed. How shall we investigate this question?

First of all, what can be meant by saying that time is unreal? If we really mean what we say, we must mean that such statements as "this is before that" are mere empty noise, like "twas brillig." If we suppose anything less than this—as, for example, that there is a relation between events which puts them in the same order as the relation of earlier and later, but that it is a different relation—we shall not have made any assertion that makes any real change in our outlook. It will be merely like supposing that the Iliad was not written by Homer, but by another man of the same name. We have to suppose that there are no "events" at all; there must be only the one vast whole of the universe, embracing whatever is real in the misleading appearance of a temporal procession. There must be nothing in reality corresponding to the apparent distinction between earlier and later events. To say that we are born, and then grow, and then die, must be just as false as to say that we die, then grow small, and finally are born. The truth of what seems an individual life is merely the illusory isolation of one element in the timeless and indivisible being of the universe. There is no distinction between improvement and deterioration, no difference between sorrows that end in happiness and happiness that ends in sorrow. If you find a corpse with a dagger in it, it makes no difference whether the man died of the wound or the dagger was plunged in after death. Such a view,

[1] As regards yoga in China, see Waley, *The Way and Its Power,* pp. 117–18.

if true, puts an end, not only to science, but to prudence, hope, and effort; it is incompatible with worldly wisdom, and—what is more important to religion—with morality.

Most mystics, of course, do not accept these conclusions in their entirety, but they urge doctrines from which these conclusions inevitably follow. Thus Dean Inge rejects the kind of religion that appeals to evolution, because it lays too much stress upon a temporal process. "There is no law of progress, and there is no universal progress," he says. And again: "The doctrine of automatic and universal progress, the lay religion of many Victorians, labours under the disadvantage of being almost the only philosophical theory which can be definitely disproved." On this matter, which I shall discuss at a later stage, I find myself in agreement with the Dean, for whom, on many grounds, I have a very high respect. But he naturally does not draw from his premisses all the inferences which seem to me to be warranted.

It is important not to caricature the doctrine of mysticism, in which there is, I think, a core of wisdom. Let us see how it seeks to avoid the extreme consequences which seem to follow from the denial of time.

The philosophy based upon mysticism has a great tradition, from Parmenides to Hegel. Parmenides says: "What is, is uncreated and indestructible; for it is complete, immovable, and without end. Nor was it ever, nor will it be; for now *it is,* all at once, a continuous one."[2] He introduced into metaphysics the distinction between reality and appearance, or the way of truth and the way of opinion, as he calls them. It is clear that whoever denies the reality of time must introduce some such distinction, since obviously the world *appears* to be in time. It is also clear that, if everyday experience is not to be *wholly* illusory, there must be some relation between appearance and the reality behind it. It is at this point, however, that the greatest difficulties arise: if the relation between appearance and reality is made too intimate, all the unpleasant features of appearance will have their unpleasant counterparts in reality, while if the relation is made too remote, we shall be unable to make inferences from the character of appearance to that of reality, and reality will be left a vague Unknowable, as with Herbert Spencer. For Christians, there is the related difficulty of avoiding pantheism: if the world is *only* apparent, God created nothing, and the reality corresponding to the world is a part of God; but if the world is in any degree real and distinct from God, we abandon the wholeness of everything, which is an essential doctrine of mysticism, and we are compelled to suppose that, in so far as the world is real, the evil which it contains is also real. Such difficulties make thorough-going mysticism very difficult for an orthodox Christian. As the Bishop of Birmingham says: "All forms of pantheism . . . as it seems to me, must be rejected because, if man is actually a part of God, the evil in man is also in God."

All this time I have been supposing that we are a jury, listening to the testimony of the mystics, and trying to decide whether to accept or reject it. If, when they deny the reality of the world of sense, we took them to mean "reality" in the ordinary sense of the law-courts, we should have no hesitation in rejecting what they say, since we should find that it runs counter to all other testimony, and even to their own in their mundane moments. We must therefore look for some other sense. I believe that, when the mystics contrast "reality" with "appearance," the word "reality" has not a logical, but an emotional, significance: it means what is, in some sense, important. When it is said that time is "unreal," what should be said is that, in some sense and on some occasions, it is important to conceive the universe as a whole, as the Creator, if He existed, must have conceived it in deciding to create it. When so conceived, all process is within one completed whole; past, present, and future, all exist, in some sense, together, and the present does not have that pre-eminent reality which it has to our usual ways of apprehending the world. If this interpretation is accepted, mysticism expresses an emotion, not a fact; it does not assert anything, and therefore can be neither confirmed nor contradicted by science. The fact that mystics do make assertions is owing to their inability to separate emotional importance from scientific validity. It is, of course, not to be expected that they will accept this view, but it is the only one, so far as I can see, which, while admitting something of their claim, is not repugnant to the scientific intelligence.

[2] Quoted from Burnet's *Early Greek Philosophy,* p. 199.

The certainty and partial unanimity of mystics is no conclusive reason for accepting their testimony on a matter of fact. The man of science, when he wishes others to see what he has seen, arranges his microscope or telescope; that is to say, he makes changes in the external world, but demands of the observer only normal eyesight. The mystic, on the other hand, demands changes in the observer, by fasting, by breathing exercises, and by a careful abstention from external observation. (Some object to such discipline, and think that the mystic illumination cannot be artificially achieved; from a scientific point of view, this makes their case more difficult to test than that of those who rely on yoga. But nearly all agree that fasting and an ascetic life are helpful.) We all know that opium, hashish, and alcohol produce certain effects on the observer, but as we do not think these effects admirable we take no accournt of them in our theory of the universe. They may even, sometimes, reveal fragments of truth; but we do not regard them as sources of general wisdom. The drunkard who sees snakes does not imagine, afterwards, that he has had a revelation of a reality hidden from others, though some not wholly dissimilar belief must have given rise to the worship of Bacchus. In our own day, as William James related,[3] there have been people who considered that the intoxication produced by laughing-gas revealed truths which are hidden at normal times. From a scientific point of view, we can make no distinction between the man who eats little and sees heaven and the man who drinks much and sees snakes. Each is in an abnormal physical condition, and therefore has abnormal perceptions. Normal perceptions, since they have to be useful in the struggle for life, must have some correspondence with fact; but in abnormal perceptions there is no reason to expect such correspondence, and their testimony, therefore, cannot outweigh that of normal perception.

The mystic emotion, if it is freed from unwarranted beliefs, and not so overwhelming as to remove a man wholly from the ordinary business of life, may give something of very great value—the same kind of thing, though in a heightened form, that is given by contemplation. Breadth and calm and profundity may all have their source in this emotion, in which, for the moment, all self-centred desire is dead, and the mind becomes a mirror for the vastness of the universe. Those who have had this experience, and believe it to be bound up unavoidably with assertions about the nature of the universe, naturally cling to these assertions. I believe myself that the assertions are inessential, and that there is no reason to believe them true. I cannot admit any method of arriving at truth except that of science, but in the realm of the emotions I do not deny the value of the experiences which have given rise to religion. Through association with false beliefs, they have led to much evil as well as good; freed from this association, it may be hoped that the good alone will remain.

[3] See his *Varieties of Religious Experience.*

SIGMUND FREUD

Analysis of "the Oceanic Feeling"*

It is impossible to escape the impression that people commonly use false standards of measurement—that they seek power, success and wealth for themselves and admire them in others, and that they underestimate what is of true value in life. And yet, in making any general judgement of this sort, we are in danger of forgetting how variegated the human world and its mental

* Reprinted from *Civilization and Its Discontents* (pp. 11–16) by Sigmund Freud, translated from the German and edited by James Strachey.

life are. There are a few men from whom their contemporaries do not withhold admiration, although their greatness rests on attributes and achievements which are completely foreign to the aims and ideals of the multitude. One might easily be inclined to suppose that it is after all only a minority which appreciates these great men, while the large majority cares nothing for them. But things are probably not as simple as that, thanks to the discrepancies between people's thoughts and their actions, and to the diversity of their wishful impulses.

One of these exceptional few calls himself my friend in his letters to me. I had sent him my small book that treats religion as an illusion,[1] and he answered that he entirely agreed with my judgement upon religion, but that he was sorry I had not properly appreciated the true source of religious sentiments. This, he says, consists in a peculiar feeling, which he himself is never without, which he finds confirmed by many others, and which he may suppose is present in millions of people. It is a feeling which he would like to call a sensation of "eternity", a feeling as of something limitless, unbounded—as it were, "oceanic". This feeling, he adds, is a purely subjective fact, not an article of faith; it brings with it no assurance of personal immortality, but it is the source of the religious energy which is seized upon by the various Churches and religious systems, directed by them into particular channels, and doubtless also exhausted by them. One may, he thinks, rightly call oneself religious on the ground of this oceanic feeling alone, even if one rejects every belief and every illusion.

The views expressed by the friend whom I so much honour, and who himself once praised the magic of illusion in a poem,[2] caused me no small difficulty. I cannot discover this "oceanic" feeling in myself. It is not easy to deal scientifically with feelings. One can attempt to describe their physiological signs. Where this is not possible—and I am afraid that the oceanic feeling too will defy this kind of characterization—nothing remains but to fall back on the ideational content which is most readily associated with the feeling. If I have understood my friend rightly, he means the same thing by it as the consolation offered by an original and somewhat eccentric dramatist to his hero who is facing a self-inflicted death. "We cannot fall out of this world."[3] That is to say, it is a feeling of an indissoluble bond, of being one with the external world as a whole. I may remark that to me this seems something rather in the nature of an intellectual perception, which is not, it is true, without an accompanying feeling-tone, but only such as would be present with any other act of thought of equal range. From my own experience I could not convince myself of the primary nature of such a feeling. But this gives me no right to deny that it does in fact occur in other people. The only question is whether it is being correctly interpreted and whether it ought to be regarded as the *fons et origo* of the whole need for religion.

I have nothing to suggest which could have a decisive influence on the solution of this problem. The idea of men's receiving an intimation of their connection with the world around them through an immediate feeling which is from the outset directed to that purpose sounds so strange and fits in so badly with the fabric of our psychology that one is justified in attempting to discover a psycho-analytic—that is, a genetic—explanation of such a feeling. The following line of thought suggests itself. Normally, there is nothing of which we are more certain than the feeling of our self, of our own ego.[4] This ego appears to us as something autonomous and unitary, marked off distinctly from everything else. That such an appearance is deceptive, and that on the contrary the ego is continued inwards, without any sharp delimitation, into an unconscious mental entity which we designate as the id and for which it serves as a kind of façade—this was a discovery first made by psycho-analytic research, which should still have much more to tell us about the relation of the ego to the id. But towards the outside, at any rate, the ego seems to maintain clear and sharp lines of demarcation. There is

[1] *The Future of an Illusion* (1927).

[2] [*Footnote added* 1931:] *Liluli* [1919].—Since the publication of his two books *La vie de Ramakrishna* [1929] and *La vie de Vivekananda* [1930], I need no longer hide the fact that the friend spoken of in the text is Romain Rolland. [Romain Rolland had written to Freud about the "oceanic feeling" in a letter of December 5, 1927, very soon after the publication of *The Future of an Illusion*.]

[3] Christian Dietrich Grabbe [1801–36], *Hannibal*: "Ja, aus der Welt werden wir nicht fallen. Wir sind einmal darin." ["Indeed, we shall not fall out of this world. We are in it once and for all."]

[4] [Some remarks on Freud's use of the terms "ego" and "self" will be found in the Editor's Introduction to *The Ego and the Id* (1923), *Standard Ed.*, 19, 7.]

only one state—admittedly an unusual state, but not one that can be stigmatized as pathological—in which it does not do this. At the height of being in love the boundary between ego and object threatens to melt away. Against all the evidence of his senses, a man who is in love declares that "I" and "you" are one, and is prepared to behave as if it were a fact.[5] What can be temporarily done away with by a physiological [i.e. normal] function must also, of course, be liable to be disturbed by pathological processes. Pathology has made us acquainted with a great number of states in which the boundary lines between the ego and the external world become uncertain or in which they are actually drawn incorrectly. There are cases in which parts of a person's own body, even portions of his own mental life—his perceptions, thoughts and feelings—, appear alien to him and as not belonging to his ego; there are other cases in which he ascribes to the external world things that clearly originate in his own ego and that ought to be acknowledged by it. Thus even the feeling of our own ego is subject to disturbances and the boundaries of the ego are not constant.

Further reflection tells us that the adult's ego-feeling cannot have been the same from the beginning. It must have gone through a process of development, which cannot, of course, be demonstrated but which admits of being constructed with a fair degree of probability.[6] An infant at the breast does not as yet distinguish his ego from the external world as the source of the sensations flowing in upon him. He gradually learns to do so, in response to various promptings.[7] He must be very strongly impressed by the fact that some sources of excitation, which he will later recognize as his own bodily organs, can provide him with sensations at any moment, whereas other sources evade him from time to time—among them what he desires most of all, his mother's breast—and only reappear as a result of his screaming for help. In this way there is for the first time set over against the ego an 'object', in the form of something which exists "outside" and which is only forced to appear by a special action.[8] A further incentive to a disengagement of the ego from the general mass of sensations—that is, to the recognition of an "outside", an external world—is provided by the frequent, manifold and unavoidable sensations of pain and unpleasure the removal and avoidance of which is enjoined by the pleasure principle, in the exercise of its unrestricted domination. A tendency arises to separate from the ego everything that can become a source of such unpleasure, to throw it outside and to create a pure pleasure-ego which is confronted by a strange and threatening "outside". The boundaries of this primitive pleasure-ego cannot escape rectification through experience. Some of the things that one is unwilling to give up, because they give pleasure, are nevertheless not ego but object; and some sufferings that one seeks to expel turn out to be inseparable from the ego in virtue of their internal origin. One comes to learn a procedure by which, through a deliberate direction of one's sensory activities and through suitable muscular action, one can differentiate between what is internal—what belongs to the ego—and what is external—what emanates from the outer world. In this way one makes the first step towards the introduction of the reality principle which is to dominate future development.[9] This differentiation, of course, serves the practical purpose of enabling one to defend oneself against sensations of unpleasure which one actually feels or with which one is threatened. In order to fend off certain unpleasurable excitations arising from within, the ego can use no other methods than those which it uses against unpleasure coming from without, and this is the starting-point of important pathological disturbances.

In this way, then, the ego detaches itself from the external world. Or, to put it more correctly, originally the ego includes everything, later it separates off an external world from itself. Our

[5] [Cf. a footnote to Section III of the Schreber case history (1911), *Standard Ed.*, 12, 69.]

[6] Cf. the many writings on the topic of ego-development and ego-feeling, dating from Ferenczi's paper on "Stages in the Development of the Sense of Reality" (1913) to Federn's contributions of 1926, 1927 and later.

[7] [In this paragraph Freud was going over familiar ground. He had discussed the matter not long before, in his paper on "Negation" (1925*h*), *Standard Ed.*, 19, 236–8. But he had dealt with it on several earlier occasions. See, for instance, "Instincts and their Vicissitudes" (1915), ibid., 14, 119 and 134–6, and *The Interpretation of Dreams* (1900), ibid., 5, 565–6. Its essence, indeed, is already to be found in the "Project" of 1895, Sections 1, 2, 11 and 16 of Part I (Freud, 1950).

[8] [The "specific action" of the "Project".]

[9] [Cf. "Formulations on the Two Principles of Mental Functioning" (1911), *Standard Ed.*, 12, 222–3.]

present ego-feeling is, therefore, only a shrunken residue of a much more inclusive—indeed, an all-embracing—feeling which corresponded to a more intimate bond between the ego and the world about it. If we may assume that there are many people in whose mental life this primary ego-feeling has persisted to a greater or less degree, it would exist in them side by side with the narrower and more sharply demarcated ego-feeling of maturity, like a kind of counterpart to it. In that case, the ideational contents appropriate to it would be precisely those of limitlessness and of a bond with the universe—the same ideas with which my friend elucidated the "oceanic" feeling.

But have we a right to assume the survival of something that was originally there, alongside of what was later derived from it? Undoubtedly. There is nothing strange in such a phenomenon, whether in the mental field or elsewhere. In the animal kingdom we hold to the view that the most highly developed species have proceeded from the lowest; and yet we find all the simple forms still in existence to-day. The race of the great saurians is extinct and has made way for the mammals; but a true representative of it, the crocodile, still lives among us. This analogy may be too remote, and it is also weakened by the circumstance that the lower species which survive are for the most part not the true ancestors of the present-day more highly developed species. As a rule the intermediate links have died out and are known to us only through reconstruction. In the realm of the mind, on the other hand, what is primitive is so commonly preserved alongside of the transformed version which has arisen from it that it is unnecessary to give instances as evidence. When this happens it is usually in consequence of a divergence in development: one portion (in the quantitative sense) of an attitude or instinctual impulse has remained unaltered, while another portion has undergone further development.

HUSTON SMITH

Do Drugs Have Religious Import?*

Until six months ago, if I picked up my phone in the Cambridge area and dialed KISS-BIG, a voice would answer, "If-if." These were coincidences: KISS-BIG happened to be the letter equivalents of an arbitrarily assigned telephone number, and I.F.I.F. represented the initials of an organization with the improbable name of the International Federation for Internal Freedom. But the coincidences were apposite to the point of being poetic. "Kiss big" caught the euphoric, manic, life-embracing attitude that characterized this most publicized of the organizations formed to explore the newly synthesized consciousness-changing substances; the organization itself was surely one of the "iffyest" phenomena to appear on our social and intellectual scene in some time. It produced the first firings in Harvard's history, an ultimatum to get out of Mexico in five days, and "the miracle of Marsh Chapel," in which, during a two-and-one-half-hour Good Friday service, ten theological students and professors ingested psilocybin and were visited by what they generally reported to be the deepest religious experiences of their lives.

Despite the last of these phenomena and its numerous if less dramatic parallels, students of religion appear by and large to be dismissing the psychedelic drugs that have sprung to our atten-

* Huston Smith, "Do Drugs Have Religious Import?" *Journal of Philosophy,* LXI (1964), 517–530, reprinted by permission of the author and the editor of the *Journal of Philosophy*. This is the emended version of a paper presented to The Woodrow Wilson Society, Princeton University, on May 16, 1964.

tion in the '60s as having little religious relevance. The position taken in one of the most forward-looking volumes of theological essays to have appeared in recent years—*Soundings,* edited by A. R. Vidler[1]—accepts R. C. Zaehner's *Mysticism Sacred and Profane* as having "fully examined and refuted" the religious claims for mescalin which Aldous Huxley sketched in *The Doors of Perception.* This closing of the case strikes me as premature, for it looks as if the drugs have light to throw on the history of religion, the phenomenology of religion, the philosophy of religion, and the practice of the religious life itself.

1. DRUGS AND RELIGION VIEWED HISTORICALLY

In his trial-and-error life explorations man almost everywhere has stumbled upon connections between vegetables (eaten or brewed) and actions (yogi breathing exercises, whirling-dervish dances, flagellations) that alter states of consciousness. From the psychopharmacological standpoint we now understand these states to be the products of changes in brain chemistry. From the sociological perspective we see that they tend to be connected in some way with religion. If we discount the wine used in Christian communion services, the instances closest to us in time and space are the peyote of The Native American [Indian] Church and Mexico's 2000-year-old "sacred mushrooms," the latter rendered in Aztec as "God's Flesh"—striking parallel to "the body of our Lord" in the Christian eucharist. Beyond these neighboring instances lie the *soma* of the Hindus, the *haoma* and hemp of the Zoroastrians, the Dionysus of the Greeks who "everywhere . . . taught men the culture of the vine and the mysteries of his worship and everywhere [was] accepted as a god,"[2] the *benzoin* of Southeast Asia, Zen's tea whose fifth cup purifies and whose sixth "calls to the realm of the immortals,"[3] the *pituri* of the Australian aborigines, and probably the mystic *kykeon* that was eaten and drunk at the climactic close of the sixth day of the Eleusinian mysteries.[4] There is no need to extend the list, as a reasonably complete account is available in Philippe de Félice's comprehensive study of the subject, *Poisons sacrés, ivresses divines.*

More interesting than the fact that consciousness-changing devices have been linked with religion is the possibility that they actually initiated many of the religious perspectives which, taking root in history, continued after their psychedelic origins were forgotten. Bergson saw the first movement of Hindus and Greeks toward "dynamic religion" as associated with the "divine rapture" found in intoxicating beverages;[5] more recently Robert Graves, Gordon Wasson, and Alan Watts have suggested that most religions arose from such chemically induced theophanies. Mary Barnard is the most explicit proponent of this thesis. "Which . . . was more likely to happen first," she asks,[6] "the spontaneously generated idea of an afterlife in which the disembodied soul, liberated from the restrictions of time and space, experiences eternal bliss, or the accidental discovery of hallucinogenic plants that give a sense of euphoria, dislocate the center of consciousness, and distort time and space, making them balloon outward in greatly expanded vistas?" Her own answer is that "the [latter] experience might have had . . . an almost explosive effect on the largely dormant minds of men, causing them to think of things they had never thought of before. This, if you like, is direct revelation." Her use of the subjunctive "might" renders this formulation of her answer equivocal, but she concludes her essay on a note that is completely unequivocal: "Looking at the matter coldly, unintoxicated and unentranced, I am willing to prophesy that fifty theobotanists working for fifty years would make the current theories concerning the origins of much mythology and theology as out-of-date as pre-Copernican astronomy."

This is an important hypothesis—one which must surely engage the attention of historians of religion for some time to come. But as I am

[1] *Soundings: Essays concerning Christian Understandings,* A. R. Vidler, ed. (Cambridge: University Press, 1962). The statement cited appears on page 72, in H. A. Williams's essay on "Theology and Self-awareness."

[2] Edith Hamilton, *Mythology* (New York: Mentor, 1953), p. 55.

[3] Quoted in Alan Watts, *The Spirit of Zen* (New York: Grove Press, 1958), p. 110.

[4] George Mylonas, *Eleusis and the Eleusinian Mysteries* (Princeton, N.J.: Princeton Univ. Press, 1961), p. 284.

[5] *Two Sources of Morality and Religion* (New York: Holt, 1935), pp. 206–212.

[6] "The God in the Flowerpot," *The American Scholar* 32, No. 4 (Autumn 1963), 584, 586.

concerned here only to spot the points at which the drugs erupt onto the field of serious religious study, not to ride the geysers to whatever heights, I shall not pursue Miss Barnard's thesis. Having located what appears to be the crux of the historical question, namely the extent to which drugs not merely duplicate or simulate theologically sponsored experiences but generate or shape theologies themselves, I turn to phenomenology.

2. DRUGS AND RELIGION VIEWED PHENOMENOLOGICALLY

Phenomenology attempts a careful description of human experience. The question the drugs pose for the phenomenology of religion, therefore, is whether the experiences they induce differ from religious experiences reached naturally, and if so how.

Even the Bible notes that chemically induced psychic states bear *some* resemblance to religious ones. Peter had to appeal to a circumstantial criterion—the early hour of the day—to defend those who were caught up in the Pentecostal experience against the charge that they were merely drunk: "These men are not drunk, as you suppose, since it is only the third hour of the day" (Acts 2:15); and Paul initiates the comparison when he admonishes the Ephesians not to "get drunk with wine . . . but [to] be filled with the spirit" (Ephesians 5:18). Are such comparisons, paralleled in the accounts of virtually every religion, superficial? How far can they be pushed?

Not all the way, students of religion have thus far insisted. With respect to the new drugs, Prof. R. C. Zaehner has drawn the line emphatically. "The importance of Huxley's *Doors of Perception,*" he writes, "is that in it the author clearly makes the claim that what he experienced under the influence of mescalin is closely comparable to a genuine mystical experience. If he is right, . . . the conclusions . . . are alarming."[7] Zaehner thinks that Huxley is not right, but I fear that it is Zaehner who is mistaken.

There are, of course, innumerable drug experiences that have no religious feature; they can be sensual as readily as spiritual, trivial as readily as transforming, capricious as readily as sacramental. If there is one point about which every student of the drugs agrees, it is that there is no such thing as the drug experience *per se*—no experience that the drugs, as it were, merely secrete. Every experience is a mix of three ingredients: drug, set (the psychological make-up of the individual), and setting (the social and physical environment in which it is taken). But given the right set and setting, the drugs can induce religious experiences indistinguishable from experiences that occur spontaneously. Nor need set and setting be exceptional. The way the statistics are currently running, it looks as if from one-fourth to one-third of the general population will have religious experiences if they take the drugs under naturalistic conditions, meaning by this conditions in which the researcher supports the subject but does not try to influence the direction his experience will take. Among subjects who have strong religious inclinations to begin with, the proportion of those having religious experiences jumps to three-fourths. If they take the drugs in settings that are religious too, the ratio soars to nine in ten.

How do we know that the experiences these people have really are religious? We can begin with the fact that they say they are. The "one-fourth to one-third of the general population" figure is drawn from two sources. Ten months after they had had their experiences, 24 per cent of the 194 subjects in a study by the California psychiatrist Oscar Janiger characterized their experiences as having been religious.[8] Thirty-two per cent of the 74 subjects in Ditman and Hayman's study reported, looking back on their LSD experience, that it looked as if it had been "very much" or "quite a bit" a religious experience; 42 per cent checked as true the statement that they "were left with a greater awareness of God, or a higher power, or ultimate reality."[9] The statement that three-fourths of subjects having religious "sets" will have religious experiences comes from the reports of sixty-nine religious professionals who took the drugs while the Harvard project was in progress.[10]

In the absence of (a) a single definition of religious experience acceptable to psychologists

[7] *Mysticism, Sacred and Profane* (New York: Oxford, 1961), p. 12.

[8] Quoted in William H. McGlothlin, "Long-lasting Effects of LSD on Certain Attitudes in Normals," printed for private distribution by the RAND Corporation, May 1962, p. 16.

[9] *Ibid.*, pp. 45, 46.

[10] Timothy Leary, "The Religious Experience: Its Production and Interpretation," *The Psychedelic Review*, 1, No. 3 (1964), 325.

of religion generally and (b) foolproof ways of ascertaining whether actual experiences exemplify any definition, I am not sure there is any better way of telling whether the experiences of the 333 men and women involved in the above studies were religious than by noting whether they seemed so to them. But if more rigorous methods are preferred, they exist; they have been utilized, and they confirm the conviction of the man in the street that drug experiences can indeed be religious. In his doctoral study at Harvard University, Walter Pahnke worked out a typology of religious experience (in this instance of the mystical variety) based on the classic cases of mystical experiences as summarized in Walter Stace's *Mysticism and Philosophy*. He then administered psilocybin to ten theology students and professors in the setting of a Good Friday service. The drug was given "double-blind," meaning that neither Dr. Pahnke nor his subjects knew which ten were getting psilocybin and which ten placebos to constitute a control group. Subsequently the reports the subjects wrote of their experiences were laid successively before three college-graduate housewives who, without being informed about the nature of the study, were asked to rate each statement as to the degree (strong, moderate, slight, or none) to which it exemplified each of the nine traits of mystical experience enumerated in the typology of mysticism worked out in advance. When the test of significance was applied to their statistics, it showed that "those subjects who received psilocybin experienced phenomena which were indistinguishable from, if not identical with . . . the categories defined by our typology of mysticism."[11]

With the thought that the reader might like to test his own powers of discernment on the question being considered, I insert here a simple test I gave to a group of Princeton students following a recent discussion sponsored by the Woodrow Wilson Society:

Below are accounts of two religious experiences. One occurred under the influence of drugs, one without their influence. Check the one you think *was* drug-induced.

I

Suddenly I burst into a vast, new, indescribably wonderful universe. Although I am writing this over a year later, the thrill of the surprise and amazement, the awesomeness of the revelation, the engulfment in an overwhelming feeling-wave of gratitude and blessed wonderment, are as fresh, and the memory of the experience is as vivid, as if it had happened five minutes ago. And yet to concoct anything by way of description that would even hint at the magnitude, the sense of ultimate reality . . . this seems such an impossible task. The knowledge which has infused and affected every aspect of my life came instantaneously and with such complete force of certainty that it was impossible, then or since, to doubt its validity.

II

All at once, without warning of any kind, I found myself wrapped in a flame-colored cloud. For an instant I thought of fire . . . the next, I knew that the fire was within myself. Directly afterward there came upon me a sense of exultation, of immense joyousness accompanied or immediately followed by an intellectual illumination impossible to describe. Among other things, I did not merely come to believe, but I saw that the universe is not composed of dead matter, but is, on the contrary, a living Presence; I became conscious in myself of eternal life. . . . I saw that all men are immortal: that the cosmic order is such that without any preadventure all things work together for the good of each and all; that the foundation principle of the world . . . is what we call love, and that the happiness of each and all is in the long run absolutely certain.

On the occasion referred to, twice as many students (46) answered incorrectly as answered correctly (23). I bury the correct answer in a footnote to preserve the reader's opportunity to test himself.[12]

Why, in the face of this considerable evidence, does Zaehner hold that drug experiences cannot

[11] "Drugs and Mysticism: An Analysis of the Relationship between Psychedelic Drugs and the Mystical Consciousness," a thesis presented to the Committee on Higher Degrees in History and Philosophy of Religion, Harvard University, June 1963.

[12] The first account is quoted anonymously in "The Issue of the Consciousness-expanding Drugs," *Main Currents in Modern Thought,* 20, No. 1 (September-October 1963), 10–11. The second experience was that of Dr. R. M. Bucke, the author of *Cosmic Consciousness,* as quoted in William James, *The Varieties of Religious Experience* (New York: Modern Library, 1902), pp. 390–391. The former experience occurred under the influence of drugs; the latter did not.

be authentically religious? There appear to be three reasons:

1. His own experience was "utterly trivial." This of course proves that not all drug experiences are religious; it does not prove that no drug experiences are religious.

2. He thinks the experiences of others that appear religious to them are not truly so. Zaehner distinguishes three kinds of mysticism: nature mysticism, in which the soul is united with the natural world; monistic mysticism, in which the soul merges with an impersonal absolute; and theism, in which the soul confronts the living, personal God. He concedes that drugs can induce the first two species of mysticism, but not its supreme instance, the theistic. As proof, he analyzes Huxley's experience as recounted in *The Doors of Perception* to show that it produced at best a blend of nature and monistic mysticism. Even if we were to accept Zaehner's evaluation of the three forms of mysticism, Huxley's case, and indeed Zaehner's entire book, would prove only that not every mystical experience induced by the drugs is theistic. Insofar as Zaehner goes beyond this to imply that drugs do not and cannot induce theistic mysticism, he not only goes beyond the evidence but proceeds in the face of it. James Slotkin reports that the peyote Indians "see visions, which may be of Christ Himself. Sometimes they hear the voice of the Great Spirit. Sometimes they become aware of the presence of God and of those personal shortcomings which must be corrected if they are to do His will."[13] And G. M. Carstairs, reporting on the use of psychedelic *bhang* in India, quotes a Brahmin as saying, "It gives good bhakti. . . . You get a very good bhakti with bhang," *bhakti* being precisely Hinduism's theistic variant.[14]

3. There is a third reason why Zaehner might doubt that drugs can induce genuinely mystical experiences. Zaehner is a Roman Catholic, and Roman Catholic doctrine teaches that mystical rapture is a gift of grace and as such can never be reduced to man's control. This may be true; certainly the empirical evidence cited does not preclude the possibility of a genuine ontological or theological difference between natural and drug-induced religious experiences. At this point, however, we are considering phenomenology rather than ontology, description rather than interpretation, and on this level there is no difference. Descriptively, drug experiences cannot be distinguished from their natural religious counterpart. When the current philosophical authority on mysticism, W. T. Stace, was asked whether the drug experience is similar to the mystical experience, he answered, "It's not a matter of its being *similar* to mystical experience; it *is* mystical experience."

What we seem to be witnessing in Zaehner's *Mysticism Sacred and Profane* is a reenactment of the age-old pattern in the conflict between science and religion. Whenever a new controversy arises, religion's first impulse is to deny the disturbing evidence science has produced. Seen in perspective, Zaehner's refusal to admit that drugs can induce experiences descriptively indistinguishable from those which are spontaneously religious is the current counterpart of the seventeenth-century theologians' refusal to look through Galileo's telescope or, when they did, their persistence on dismissing what they saw as machinations of the devil. When the fact that drugs can trigger religious experiences becomes incontrovertible, discussion will move to the more difficult question of how this new fact is to be interpreted. The latter question leads beyond phenomenology into philosophy.

3. DRUGS AND RELIGION VIEWED PHILOSOPHICALLY

Why do people reject evidence? Because they find it threatening, we may suppose. Theologians are not the only professionals to utilize this mode of defense. In his *Personal Knowledge*,[15] Michael Polanyi recounts the way the medical profession ignored such palpable facts as the painless amputation of human limbs, performed before their own eyes in hundreds of successive cases, concluding that the subjects were impostors who were either deluding their physicians or colluding with them. One physician, Esdaile, carried out about 300 major operations painlessly under mesmeric trance in India, but neither in India nor in Great Britain could he get medical journals to print accounts of his work. Polanyi attributes this closed-mindedness to "lack of a conceptual framework in which their

[13] James S. Slotkin, *Peyote Religion* (New York: Free Press of Glencoe, 1956).

[14] "Daru and Bhang," *Quarterly Journal of the Study of Alcohol*, 15 (1954), 229.

[15] Chicago: Univ. of Chicago Press, 1958.

discoveries could be separated from specious and untenable admixtures."

The "untenable admixture" in the fact that psychotomimetic drugs can induce religious experience is its apparent implicate: that religious disclosures are no more veridical than psychotic ones. For religious skeptics, this conclusion is obviously not untenable at all; it fits in beautifully with their thesis that *all* religion is at heart an escape from reality. Psychotics avoid reality by retiring into dream worlds of make-believe; what better evidence that religious visionaries do the same than the fact that identical changes in brain chemistry produce both states of mind? Had not Marx already warned us that religion is the "opiate" of the people?—apparently he was more literally accurate than he supposed. Freud was likewise too mild. He "never doubted that religious phenomena are to be understood only on the model of the neurotic symptoms of the individual."[16] He should have said "psychotic symptoms."

So the religious skeptic is likely to reason. What about the religious believer? Convinced that religious experiences are not fundamentally delusory, can he admit that psychotomimetic drugs can occasion them? To do so he needs (to return to Polanyi's words) "a conceptual framework in which [the discoveries can] be separated from specious and untenable admixtures," the "untenable admixture" being in this case the conclusion that religious experiences are in general delusory.

One way to effect the separation would be to argue that, despite phenomenological similarities between natural and drug-induced religious experiences, they are separated by a crucial *ontological* difference. Such an argument would follow the pattern of theologians who argue for the "real presence" of Christ's body and blood in the bread and wine of the Eucharist despite their admission that chemical analysis, confined as it is to the level of "accidents" rather than "essences," would not disclose this presence. But this distinction will not appeal to many today, for it turns on an essence-accident metaphysics which is not widely accepted. Instead of fighting a rear-guard action by insisting that if drug and non-drug religious experiences cannot be distinguished empirically there must be some transempirical factor that distinguishes them and renders the drug experience profane, I wish to explore the possibility of accepting drug-induced experiences as religious without relinquishing confidence in the truth-claims of religious experience generally.

To begin with the weakest of all arguments, the argument from authority: William James did not discount *his* insights that occurred while his brain chemistry was altered. The paragraph in which he retrospectively evaluates his nitrous oxide experiences has become classic, but it is so pertinent to the present discussion that it merits quoting once again.

> One conclusion was forced upon my mind at that time, and my impression of its truth has ever since remained unshaken. It is that our normal waking consciousness, rational consciousness as we call it, is but one special type of consciousness, whilst all about it, parted from it by the filmiest of screens, there lie potential forms of consciousness entirely different. We may go through life without suspecting their existence; but apply the requisite stimulus, and at a touch they are there in all their completeness, definite types of mentality which probably somewhere have their field of application and adaptation. No account of the universe in its totality can be final which leaves these other forms of consciousness quite disregarded. How to regard them is the question—for they are so discontinuous with ordinary consciousness. Yet they may determine attitudes though they cannot furnish formulas, and open a region though they fail to give a map. At any rate, they forbid a premature closing of our accounts with reality. Looking back on my own experiences, they all converge toward a kind of insight to which I cannot help ascribing some metaphysical significance (*op. cit.*, 378–379).

To this argument from authority, I add two arguments that try to provide something by way of reasons. Drug experiences that assume a religious cast tend to have fearful and/or beatific features, and each of my hypotheses relates to one of these aspects of the experience.

Beginning with the ominous, "fear of the Lord," awe-ful features, Gordon Wasson, the New York banker-turned-mycologist, describes these as he encountered them in his psilocybin experience as follows: "Ecstasy! In common parlance . . . ecstasy is fun. . . . But ecstasy is not fun. Your very soul is seized and shaken until it tingles. After all, who will choose to feel undi-

[16] *Totem and Taboo* (New York: Modern Library, 1938).

luted awe? . . . The unknowing vulgar abuse the word; we must recapture its full and terrifying sense."[17] Emotionally the drug experience can be like having forty-foot waves crash over you for several hours while you cling desperately to a life-raft which may be swept from under you at any minute. It seems quite possible that such an ordeal, like any experience of a close call, could awaken rather fundamental sentiments respecting life and death and destiny and trigger the "no atheists in foxholes" effect. Similarly, as the subject emerges from the trauma and realizes that he is not going to be insane as he had feared, there may come over him an intensified appreciation like that frequently reported by patients recovering from critical illness. "It happened on the day when my bed was pushed out of doors to the open gallery of the hospital," reads one such report:

> I cannot now recall whether the revelation came suddenly or gradually; I only remember finding myself in the very midst of those wonderful moments, beholding life for the first time in all its young intoxication of loveliness, in its unspeakable joy, beauty, and importance. I cannot say exactly what the mysterious change was. I saw no new thing, but I saw all the usual things in a miraculous new light—in what I believe is their true light. I saw for the first time how wildly beautiful and joyous, beyond any words of mine to describe, is the whole of life. Every human being moving across that porch, every sparrow that flew, every branch tossing in the wind, was caught in and was a part of the whole mad ecstasy of loveliness, of joy, of importance, of intoxication of life.[18]

If we do not discount religious intuitions because they are prompted by battlefields and *physical* crises; if we regard the latter as "calling us to our senses" more often than they seduce us into delusions, need comparable intuitions be discounted simply because the crises that trigger them are of an inner, *psychic* variety?

Turning from the hellish to the heavenly aspects of the drug experience, *some* of the latter may be explainable by the hypothesis just stated; that is, they may be occasioned by the relief that attends the sense of escape from high danger. But this hypothesis cannot possibly account for *all* the beatific episodes, for the simple reason that the positive episodes often come first, or to persons who experience no negative episodes whatever. Dr. Sanford Unger of the National Institute of Mental Health reports that among his subjects "50 to 60% will not manifest any real disturbance worthy of discussion," yet "around 75% will have at least one episode in which exaltation, rapture, and joy are the key descriptions."[19] How are we to account for the drug's capacity to induce peak experiences, such as the following, which are *not* preceded by fear?

> A feeling of great peace and contentment seemed to flow through my entire body. All sound ceased and I seemed to be floating in a great, very very still void or hemisphere. It is impossible to describe the overpowering feeling of peace, contentment, and being a part of goodness itself that I felt. I could feel my body dissolving and actually becoming a part of the goodness and peace that was all around me. Words can't describe this. I feel an awe and wonder that such a feeling could have occurred to me.[20]

Consider the following line of argument. Like every other form of life, man's nature has become distinctive through specialization. Man has specialized in developing a cerebral cortex. The analytic powers of this instrument are a standing wonder, but the instrument seems less able to provide man with the sense that he is meaningfully related to his environment: to life, the world, and history in their wholeness. As Albert Camus describes the situation, "If I were . . . a cat among animals, this life would have a meaning, or rather this problem would not arise, for I should belong to this world. I would *be* this world to which I am now opposed by my whole consciousness."[21] Note that it is Camus' consciousness that opposes him to his world. The

[17] "The Hallucinogenic Fungi of Mexico: An Inquiry into the Origins of the Religious Idea among Primitive Peoples," *Harvard Botanical Museum Leaflets*, 19, 7 (1961).

[18] Margaret Prescott Montague, *Twenty Minutes of Reality* (St. Paul, Minn.: Macalester Park, 1947), pp. 15, 17.

[19] "The Current Scientific Status of Psychedelic Drug Research," read at the Conference on Methods in Philosophy and the Sciences, New School for Social Research, May 3, 1964, and scheduled for publication in David Solomon, ed., *The Conscious Expanders* (New York: Putnam, fall of 1964).

[20] Quoted by Dr. Unger in the paper just mentioned.

[21] *The Myth of Sisyphus* (New York: Vintage, 1955), p. 38.

drugs do not knock this consciousness out, but while they leave it operative they also activate areas of the brain that normally lie below its threshold of awareness. One of the clearest objective signs that the drugs are taking effect is the dilation they produce in the pupils of the eyes, and one of the most predictable subjective signs is the intensification of visual perception. Both of these responses are controlled by portions of the brain that lie deep, further to the rear than the mechanisms that govern consciousness. Meanwhile we know that the human organism is interlaced with its world in innumerable ways it normally cannot sense—through gravitational fields, body respiration, and the like: the list could be multiplied until man's skin began to seem more like a thoroughfare than a boundary. Perhaps the deeper regions of the brain which evolved earlier and are more like those of the lower animals—"If I were . . . a cat . . . I should belong to this world"—can sense this relatedness better than can the cerebral cortex which now dominates our awareness. If so, when the drugs rearrange the neurohumors that chemically transmit impulses across synapses between neurons, man's consciousness and his submerged, intuitive, ecological awareness might for a spell become interlaced. This is, of course, no more than a hypothesis, but how else are we to account for the extraordinary incidence under the drugs of that kind of insight the keynote of which James described "invariably a reconciliation"? "It is as if the opposites of the world, whose contradictoriness and conflict make all our difficulties and troubles, were melted into one and the same genus, but *one of the species,* the nobler and better one, *is itself the genus, and so soaks up and absorbs its opposites into itself*" (*op. cit.,* 379).

4. THE DRUGS AND RELIGION VIEWED "RELIGIOUSLY"

Suppose that drugs can induce experiences indistinguishable from religious experiences and that we can respect their reports. Do they shed any light, not (we now ask) on life, but on the nature of the religious life?

One thing they may do is throw religious experience itself into perspective by clarifying its relation to the religious life as a whole. Drugs appear able to induce religious experiences; it is less evident that they can produce religious lives. It follows that religion is more than religious experiences. This is hardly news, but it may be a useful reminder, especially to those who incline toward "the religion of religion experience"; which is to say toward lives bent on the acquisition of desired states of experience irrespective of their relation to life's other demands and components.

Despite the dangers of faculty psychology, it remains useful to regard man as having a mind, a will, and feelings. One of the lessons of religious history is that, to be adequate, a faith must rouse and involve all three components of man's nature. Religions of reason grow arid; religions of duty, leaden. Religions of experience have their comparable pitfalls, as evidenced by Taoism's struggle (not always successful) to keep from degenerating into quietism, and the vehemence with which Zen Buddhism has insisted that once students have attained *satori,* they must be driven out of it, back into the world. The case of Zen is especially pertinent here, for it pivots on an enlightenment experience—*satori,* or *kensho* —which some (but not all) Zennists say resembles LSD. Alike or different, the point is that Zen recognizes that unless the experience is joined to discipline, it will come to naught:

> Even the Buddha . . . had to sit. . . . Without *joriki,* the particular power developed through *zazen* [seated meditation], the vision of oneness attained in enlightenment . . . in time becomes clouded and eventually fades into a pleasant memory instead of remaining an omnipresent reality shaping our daily life. . . . To be able to live in accordance with what the Mind's eye has revealed through *satori* requires, like the purification of character and the development of personality, a ripening period of *zazen.*[22]

If the religion of religious experience is a snare and a delusion, it follows that no religion that fixes its faith primarily in substances that induce religious experiences can be expected to come to a good end. What promised to be a short cut will prove to be a short circuit; what began as a religion will end as a religion surrogate. Whether chemical substances can be helpful *adjuncts* to faith is another question. The peyote-using Native American Church seems to indicate that they can be; anthropologists give this church a

[22] Philip Kapleau, *Zen Practice and Attainment,* a manuscript in process of publication.

good report, noting among other things that members resist alcohol and alcoholism better than do nonmembers.[23] The conclusion to which evidence currently points would seem to be that chemicals *can* aid the religious life, but only where set within a context of faith (meaning by this the conviction that what they disclose is true) and discipline (meaning diligent exercise of the will in the attempt to work out the implications of the disclosures for the living of life in the everyday, common-sense world).

Nowhere today in Western civilization are these two conditions jointly fulfilled. Churches lack faith in the sense just mentioned; hipsters lack discipline. This might lead us to forget about the drugs, were it not for one fact: the distinctive religious emotion and the emotion that drugs unquestionably can occasion—Otto's *mysterium tremendum, majestas, mysterium fascinans;* in a phrase, the phenomenon of religious awe—seems to be declining sharply. As Paul Tillich said in an address to the Hillel Society at Harvard several years ago:

> The question our century puts before us [is]: Is it possible to regain the lost dimension, the encounter with the Holy, the dimension which cuts through the world of subjectivity and objectivity and goes down to that which is not world but is the mystery of the Ground of Being?

Tillich may be right; this may be the religious question of our century. For if (as we have insisted) religion cannot be equated with religious experiences, neither can it long survive their absence.

[23] Slotkin, *op. cit.*

B L A I S E P A S C A L

The Wager*

Infinite—nothing.—Our soul is cast into a body, where it finds number, time, dimension. Thereupon it reasons, and calls this nature, necessity, and can believe nothing else.

Unity joined to infinity adds nothing to it, no more than one foot to an infinite measure. The finite is annihilated in the presence of the infinite, and becomes a pure nothing. So our spirit before God, so our justice before divine justice. There is not so great a disproportion between our justice and that of God, as between unity and infinity.

The justice of God must be vast like His compassion. Now justice to the outcast is less vast, and ought less to offend our feelings than mercy towards the elect.

We know that there is an infinite, and are ignorant of its nature. As we know it to be false that numbers are finite, it is therefore true that there is an infinity in number. But we do not know what it is. It is false that it is even, it is false that it is odd; for the addition of a unit can make no change in its nature. Yet it is a number, and every number is odd or even (this is certainly true of every finite number). So we may well know that there is a God without knowing what He is. Is there not one substantial truth, seeing there are so many things which are not the truth itself?

We know then the existence and nature of the finite, because we also are finite and have extension. We know the existence of the infinite, and are ignorant of its nature, because it has extension like us, but not limits like us. But we know neither the existence nor the nature of God, because He has neither extension nor limits.

But by faith we know His existence; in glory

* From Blaise Pascal, *Thoughts,* trans. W. F. Trotter (New York: P. F. Collier & Son, 1910), 233. This material reprinted with the kind permission of Crowell Collier and Macmillan, Inc.

we shall know His nature. Now, I have already shown that we may well know the existence of a thing, without knowing its nature.

Let us now speak according to natural lights.

If there is a God, He is infinitely incomprehensible, since, having neither parts nor limits, He has no affinity to us. We are then incapable of knowing either what He is or if He is. This being so, who will dare to undertake the decision of the question? Not we, who have no affinity to Him.

Who then will blame Christians for not being able to give a reason for their belief, since they profess a religion for which they cannot give a reason? They declare, in expounding it to the world, that it is a foolishness, *stultitiam;* and then you complain that they do not prove it! If they proved it, they would not keep their word; it is in lacking proofs, that they are not lacking in sense. "Yes, but although this excuses those who offer it as such, and take away from them the blame of putting it forward without reason, it does not excuse those who receive it." Let us then examine this point, and say, "God is, or He is not." But to which side shall we incline? Reason can decide nothing here. There is an infinite chaos which separates us. A game is being played at the extremity of this infinite distance where heads or tails will turn up. What will you wager? According to reason, you can do neither the one thing nor the other; according to reason, you can defend neither of the propositions.

Do not then reprove for error those who have made a choice; for you know nothing about it. "No, but I blame them for having made, not this choice, but a choice; for again both he who chooses heads and he who chooses tails are equally at fault, they are both in the wrong. The true course is not to wager at all."

—Yes; but you must wager. It is not optional. You are embarked. Which will you choose then? Let us see. Since you must choose, let us see which interests you least. You have two things to lose, the true and the good; and two things to stake, your reason and your will, your knowledge and your happiness; and your nature has two things to shun, error and misery. Your reason is no more shocked in choosing one rather than the other, since you must of necessity choose. This is one point settled. But your happiness? Let us weigh the gain and the loss in wagering that God is. Let us estimate these two chances. If you gain, you gain all; if you lose, you lose nothing. Wager then without hesitation that He is.—"That is very fine. Yes, I must wager; but I may perhaps wager too much."—Let us see. Since there is an equal risk of gain and of loss, if you had only to gain two lives, instead of one, you might still wager. But if there were three lives to gain, you would have to play (since you are under the necessity of playing), and you would be imprudent, when you are forced to play, not to chance your life to gain three at a game where there is an equal risk of loss and gain. But there is an eternity of life and happiness. And this being so, if there were an infinity of chances, of which one only would be for you, you would still be right in wagering one to win two, and you would act stupidly, being obliged to play, by refusing to stake one life against three at a game in which out of an infinity of chances there is one for you, if there were an infinity of an infinitely happy life to gain. But there is here an infinity of an infinitely happy life to gain, a chance of gain against a finite number of chances of loss, and what you stake is finite. It is all divided; wherever the infinite is and there is not an infinity of chances of loss against that of gain, there is no time to hesitate, you must give all. And thus, when one is forced to play, he must renounce reason to preserve his life, rather than risk it for infinite gain, as likely to happen as the loss of nothingness.

For it is no use to say it is uncertain if we will gain, and it is certain that we risk, and that the infinite distance between the *certainty* of what is staked and the *uncertainty* of what will be gained, equals the finite good which is certainly staked against the uncertain infinite. It is not so, as every player stakes a certainty to gain an uncertainty, and yet he stakes a finite certainty to gain a finite uncertainty, without transgressing against reason. There is not an infinite distance between the certainty staked and the uncertainty of the gain; that is untrue. In truth, there is an infinity between the certainty of gain and the certainty of loss. But the uncertainty of the gain is proportioned to the certainty of the stake according to the proportion of the chances of gain and loss. Hence it comes that, if there are as many risks on one side as on the other, the course is to play even; and then the certainty of the stake is equal to the uncertainty of the gain, so far is it from fact that there is an infinite distance between them. And so our proposition is of infinite force, when there is the finite to stake in a game where there are equal risks of gain and of loss, and the infinite to gain. This is demonstrable; and if men are capable of any truths, this is one.

"I confess it, I admit it. But still is there no means of seeing the faces of the cards?"—Yes, Scripture and the rest, &c.—"Yes, but I have my hands tied and my mouth closed; I am forced to wager, and am not free. I am not released, and am so made that I cannot believe. What then would you have me do?"

True. But at least learn your inability to believe, since reason brings you to this, and yet you cannot believe. Endeavour then to convince yourself, not by increase of proofs of God, but by the abatement of your passions. You would like to attain faith, and do not know the way; you would like to cure yourself of unbelief, and ask the remedy for it. Learn of those who have been bound like you, and who now stake all their possessions. These are people who know the way which you would follow, and who are cured of an ill of which you would be cured. Follow the way by which they began; by acting as if they believe, taking the holy water, having masses said, &c. Even this will naturally make you believe, and deaden your acuteness.—"But this is what I am afraid of."—And why? What have you to lose?

But to show you that this leads you there, it is this which will lessen the passions, which are your stumbling-blocks.

The end of this discourse.—Now what harm will befall you in taking this side? You will be faithful, honest, humble, grateful, generous, a sincere friend, truthful. Certainly you will not have those poisonous pleasures, glory and luxury; but will you not have others? I will tell you that you will thereby gain in this life, and that, at each step you take on this road, you will see so great certainty of gain, so much nothingness in what you risk, that you will at last recognize that you have wagered for something certain and infinite, for which you have given nothing.

"Ah! This discourse transports me, charms me," &c.

If this discourse pleases you and seems impressive, know that it is made by a man who has knelt, both before and after it, in prayer to that Being, infinite and without parts, before whom he lays all he has, for you also to lay before Him all you have for your own good and for His glory, that so strength may be given to lowliness.

WILLIAM JAMES

The Will to Believe*

I

Let us give the name of hypothesis to anything that may be proposed to our belief; and just as the electricians speak of live and dead wires, let us speak of any hypothesis as either *live* or *dead*. A live hypothesis is one which appeals as a real possibility to him to whom it is proposed. If I ask you to believe in the Mahdi, the notion makes no electric connection with your nature—it refuses to scintillate with any credibility at all. As an hypothesis it is completely dead. To an Arab, however (even if he be not one of the Mahdi's followers), the hypothesis is among the mind's possibilities: it is alive. This shows that deadness and liveness in an hypothesis are not intrinsic properties, but relations to the individual thinker. They are measured by his willingness to

* Extracts from William James, "The Will to Believe," an Address to the Philosophical Clubs of Yale and Brown Universities. First published in the *New World*, 1896.

act. The maximum of liveness in an hypothesis means willingness to act irrevocably. Practically, that means belief; but there is some believing tendency wherever there is willingness to act at all.

Next, let us call the decision between two hypotheses an *option*. Options may be of several kinds. They may be—first, *living* or *dead;* secondly, *forced* or *avoidable;* thirdly, *momentous* or *trivial;* and for our purposes we may call an option a *genuine* option when it is of the forced, living, and momentous kind.

1. A living option is one in which both hypotheses are live ones. If I say to you: "Be a theosophist or be a Mohammedan," it is probably a dead option, because for you neither hypothesis is likely to be alive. But if I say: "Be an agnostic or be a Christian," it is otherwise: trained as you are, each hypothesis makes some appeal, however small, to your belief.

2. Next, if I say to you: "Choose between going out with your umbrella or without it," I do not offer you a genuine option, for it is not forced. You can easily avoid it by not going out at all. Similarly, if I say, "Either love me or hate me," "Either call my theory true or call it false," your option is avoidable. You may remain indifferent to me, neither loving nor hating, and you may decline to offer any judgment as to my theory. But if I say, "Either accept this truth or go without it," I put on you a forced option, for there is no standing place outside of the alternative. Every dilemma based on a complete logical disjunction, with no possibility of not choosing, is an option of this forced kind.

3. Finally, if I were Dr. Nansen and proposed to you to join my North Pole expedition, your option would be momentous; for this would probably be your only similar opportunity, and your choice now would either exclude you from the North Pole sort of immortality altogether or put at least the chance of it into your hands. He who refuses to embrace a unique opportunity loses the prize as surely as if he tried and failed. *Per contra,* the option is trivial when the opportunity is not unique, when the stake is insignificant, or when the decision is reversible if it later prove unwise. Such trivial options abound in the scientific life. A chemist finds an hypothesis live enough to spend a year in its verification: he believes in it to that extent. But if his experiments prove inconclusive either way, he is quit for his loss of time, no vital harm being done.

It will facilitate our discussion if we keep all these distinctions well in mind.

II

The next matter to consider is the actual psychology of human opinion. When we look at certain facts, it seems as if our passional and volitional nature lay at the root of all our convictions. When we look at others, it seems as if they could do nothing when the intellect had once said its say. Let us take the latter facts up first.

Does it not seem preposterous on the very face of it to talk of our opinions being modifiable at will? Can our will either help or hinder our intellect in its perceptions of truth? Can we, by just willing it, believe that Abraham Lincoln's existence is a myth, and that the portraits of him in *McClure's Magazine* are all of some one else? Can we, by any effort of our will, or by any strength of wish that it were true, believe ourselves well and about when we are roaring with rheumatism in bed, or feel certain that the sum of the two one-dollar bills in our pocket must be a hundred dollars? We can *say* any of these things, but we are absolutely impotent to believe them; and of just such things is the whole fabric of the truths that we do believe in made up—matters of fact, immediate or remote, as Hume said, and relations between ideas, which are either there or not there for us if we see them so, and which if not there cannot be put there by any action of our own.

In Pascal's *Thoughts* there is a celebrated passage known in literature as Pascal's wager. In it he tries to force us into Christianity by reasoning as if our concern with truth resembled our concern with the stakes in a game of chance. Translated freely his words are these: You must either believe or not believe that God is—which will you do? Your human reason cannot say. A game is going on between you and the nature of things which at the day of judgment will bring out either heads or tails. Weigh what your gains and your losses would be if you should stake all you have on heads, or God's existence: if you win in such case, you gain eternal beatitude; if you lose, you lose nothing at all. If there were an infinity of chances, and only one for God in this wager, still you ought to stake your all on God; for though you surely risk a finite loss by this procedure, any finite loss is reasonable, even a certain one is reasonable, if there is but the possibility of infinite gain. Go, then, and take holy water, and have masses said; belief will come and stupefy your scruples—*Cela vous fera croire et vous abêtira.* Why should you not? At bottom, what have you to lose?

You probably feel that when religious faith expresses itself thus, in the language of the gaming-table, it is put to its last trumps. Surely Pascal's own personal belief in masses and holy water had far other springs; and this celebrated page of his is but an argument for others, a last desperate snatch at a weapon against the hardness of the unbelieving heart. We feel that a faith in masses and holy water adopted wilfully after such a mechanical calculation would lack the inner soul of faith's reality; and if we were ourselves in the place of the Deity, we should probably take particular pleasure in cutting off believers of this pattern from their infinite reward. It is evident that unless there be some pre-existing tendency to believe in masses and holy water, the option offered to the will by Pascal is not a living option. Certainly no Turk ever took to masses and holy water on its account; and even to us Protestants these means of salvation seem such foregone impossibilities that Pascal's logic, invoked for them specifically, leaves us unmoved. As well might the Mahdi write to us, saying, "I am the Expected One whom God has created in his effulgence. You shall be infinitely happy if you confess me; otherwise you shall be cut off from the light of the sun. Weigh, then, your infinite gain if I am genuine against your finite sacrifice if I am not!" His logic would be that of Pascal; but he would vainly use it on us, for the hypothesis he offers us is dead. No tendency to act on it exists in us to any degree.

The talk of believing by our volition seems, then, from one point of view, simply silly. From another point of view it is worse than silly, it is vile. When one turns to the magnificent edifice of the physical sciences, and sees how it was reared; what thousands of disinterested moral lives of men lie buried in its mere foundations; what patience and postponement, what choking down of preference, what submission to the icy laws of outer fact are wrought into its very stones and mortar; how absolutely impersonal it stands in its vast augustness—then how besotted and contemptible seems every little sentimentalist who comes blowing his voluntary smoke-wreaths, and pretending to decide things from out of his private dream! Can we wonder if those bred in the rugged and manly school of science should feel like spewing such subjectivism out of their mouths? The whole system of loyalties which grow up in the schools of science go dead against its toleration; so that it is only natural that those who have caught the scientific fever should pass over to the opposite extreme, and write sometimes as if the incorruptibly truthful intellect ought positively to prefer bitterness and unacceptableness to the heart in its cup.

> It fortifies my soul to know
> That though I perish, Truth is so—

sings Clough, while Huxley exclaims: "My only consolation lies in the reflection that, however bad our posterity may become, so far as they hold by the plain rule of not pretending to believe what they have no reason to believe, because it may be to their advantage so to pretend [the word 'pretend' is surely here redundant], they will not have reached the lowest depth of immorality." And that delicious *enfant terrible* Clifford writes: "Belief is desecrated when given to unproved and unquestioned statements for the solace and private pleasure of the believer. . . . Whoso would deserve well of his fellows in this matter will guard the purity of his belief with a very fanaticism of jealous care, lest at any time it should rest on an unworthy object, and catch a stain which can never be wiped away. . . . If [a] belief has been accepted on insufficient evidence [even though the belief be true, as Clifford on the same page explains] the pleasure is a stolen one. . . . It is sinful because it is stolen in defiance of our duty to mankind. That duty is to guard ourselves from such beliefs as from a pestilence which may shortly master our own body and then spread to the rest of the town. . . . It is wrong always, everywhere, and for every one, to believe anything upon insufficient evidence."

III

All this strikes one as healthy, even when expressed, as by Clifford, with somewhat too much of robustious pathos in the voice. Free will and simple wishing do seem, in the matter of our credences, to be only fifth wheels to the coach. Yet if any one should thereupon assume that intellectual insight is what remains after wish and will and sentimental preference have taken wing, or that pure reason is what then settles our opinions, he would fly quite as directly in the teeth of the facts.

It is only our already dead hypotheses that our willing nature is unable to bring to life again. But what has made them dead for us is for the most part a previous action of our willing nature of an antagonistic kind. When I say "willing nature," I do not mean only such deliberate volitions as may have set up habits of belief that we cannot now escape from—I mean all such factors of belief as fear and hope, prejudice and passion, imitation and partisanship, the circumpressure of our caste and set. As a matter of fact we find ourselves believing, we hardly know how or why. Mr. Balfour gives the name of "authority" to all those influences, born of the intellectual climate, that make hypotheses possible or impossible for us, alive or dead. Here in this room, we all of us believe in molecules and the conservation of energy, in democracy and necessary progress, in Protestant Christianity and the duty of fighting for "the doctrine of the immortal Monroe," all for no reasons worthy of the name. We see into these matters with no more inner clearness, and probably with much less, than any disbeliever in them might possess. His unconventionality would probably have some grounds to show for its conclusions; but for us, not insight, but the *prestige* of the opinions, is what makes the spark shoot from them and light up our sleeping magazines of faith. Our reason is quite satisfied, in nine hundred and ninety-nine cases out of every thousand of us, if it can find a few arguments that will do to recite in case our credulity is criticized by some one else. Our faith is faith in some one else's faith, and in the greatest matters this is most the case. . . .

Evidently, then, our non-intellectual nature does influence our convictions. There are passional tendencies and volitions which run before and others which come after belief, and it is only the latter that are too late for the fair; and they are not too late when the previous passional work has been already in their own direction. Pascal's argument, instead of being powerless, then seems a regular clincher, and is the last stroke needed to make our faith in masses and holy water complete. The state of things is evidently far from simple; and pure insight and logic, whatever they might do ideally, are not the only things that really do produce our creeds.

IV

Our next duty, having recognized this mixed-up state of affairs, is to ask whether it be simply reprehensible and pathological, or whether, on the contrary, we must treat it as a normal element in making up our minds. The thesis I defend is, briefly stated, this: *Our passional nature not only lawfully may, but must, decide an option between propositions, whenever it is a genuine option that cannot by its nature be decided on intellectual grounds; for to say, under such circumstances, "Do not decide, but leave the question open," is itself a passional decision—just like deciding yes or no—and is attended with the same risk of losing the truth. . . .*

VII

One more point, small but important, and our preliminaries are done. There are two ways of looking at our duty in the matter of opinion—ways entirely different, and yet ways about whose difference the theory of knowledge seems hitherto to have shown very little concern. *We must know the truth;* and *we must avoid error*—these are our first and great commandments as would-be knowers; but they are not two ways of stating an identical commandment, they are two separable laws. Although it may indeed happen that when we believe the truth *A,* we escape as an incidental consequence from believing the falsehood *B,* it hardly ever happens that by merely disbelieving *B* we necessarily believe *A.* We may in escaping *B* fall into believing other falsehoods, *C* or *D,* just as bad as *B;* or we may escape *B* by not believing anything at all, not even *A.*

Believe truth! Shun error!—these, we see, are two materially different laws; and by choosing between them we may end by coloring differently our whole intellectual life. We may regard the chase for truth as paramount, and the avoidance of error as secondary; or we may, on the other hand, treat the avoidance of error as more imperative, and let truth take its chance. Clifford, in the instructive passage which I have quoted, exhorts us to the latter course. Believe nothing, he tells us, keep your mind in suspense forever, rather than by closing it on insufficient evidence incur the awful risk of believing lies. You, on the other hand, may think that the risk of being in error is a very small matter when compared with the blessings of real knowledge, and be ready to be duped many times in your investigation rather than postpone indefinitely the chance of guessing true. I myself find it impossible to go with Clifford. We must remember that these feelings of our duty about either truth or error are in any case only expressions of our passional life. Biologically considered, our minds are as ready to grind out falsehood as veracity, and he who says, "Better go without belief forever than believe a lie!" merely shows his own preponderant private horror of becoming a dupe. He may be critical of many of his desires and fears, but this fear he slavishly obeys. He cannot imagine any one questioning its binding force. For my own part, I have also a horror of being duped; but I can believe that worse things than being duped may happen to a man in this world: so Clifford's exhortation has to my ears a thoroughly fantastic sound. It is like a general informing his soldiers that it is better to keep out of battle forever than to risk a single wound. Not so are victories either over enemies or over nature gained. Our errors are surely not such awfully solemn things. In a world where we are so certain to incur them in spite of all our caution, a certain lightness of heart seems healthier than this excessive nervousness on their behalf. At any rate, it seems the fittest thing for the empiricist philosopher.

VIII

And now, after all this introduction, let us go straight at our question. I have said, and now repeat it, that not only as a matter of fact do we find our passional nature influencing us in our opinions, but that there are some options between opinions in which this influence must be regarded both as an inevitable and as a lawful determinant of our choice.

I fear here that some of you my hearers will begin to scent danger, and lend an inhospitable ear. Two first steps of passion you have indeed had to admit as necessary—we must think so as to avoid dupery, and we must think so as to gain truth; but the surest path to those ideal consummations, you will probably consider, is from now onwards to take no further passional step.

Well, of course, I agree as far as the facts will allow. Wherever the option between losing truth

and gaining it is not momentous, we can throw the chance of *gaining truth* away, and at any rate save ourselves from any chance of *believing falsehood,* by not making up our minds at all till objective evidence has come. In scientific questions, this is almost always the case; and even in human affairs in general, the need of acting is seldom so urgent that a false belief to act on is better than no belief at all. Law courts, indeed, have to decide on the best evidence attainable for the moment, because a judge's duty is to make law as well as to ascertain it, and (as a learned judge once said to me) few cases are worth spending much time over: the great thing is to have them decided on *any* acceptable principle, and got out of the way. But in our dealings with objective nature we obviously are recorders, not makers, of the truth; and decisions for the mere sake of deciding promptly and getting on to the next business would be wholly out of place. Throughout the breadth of physical nature facts are what they are quite independently of us, and seldom is there any such hurry about them that the risks of being duped by believing a premature theory need be faced. The questions here are always trivial options, the hypotheses are hardly living (at any rate not living for us spectators), the choice between believing truth or falsehood is seldom forced. The attitude of sceptical balance is therefore the absolutely wise one if we would escape mistakes. What difference, indeed, does it make to most of us whether we have or have not a theory of the Röntgen rays, whether we believe or not in mind-stuff, or have a conviction about the causality of conscious states? It makes no difference. Such options are not forced on us. On every account it is better not to make them, but still keep weighing reasons *pro et contra* with an indifferent hand.

I speak, of course, here of the purely judging mind. For purposes of discovery such indifference is to be less highly recommended, and science would be far less advanced than she is if the passionate desires of individuals to get their own faiths confirmed had been kept out of the game. See for example the sagacity which Spencer and Weismann now display. On the other hand, if you want an absolute duffer in an investigation, you must, after all, take the man who has no interest whatever in its results: he is the warranted incapable, the positive fool. The most useful investigator, because the most sensitive observer, is always he whose eager interest in one side of the question is balanced by an equally keen nervousness lest he become deceived.[1] Science has organized this nervousness into a regular *technique,* her so-called method of verification; and she has fallen so deeply in love with the method that one may even say she has ceased to care for truth by itself at all. It is only truth as technically verified that interests her. The truth of truths might come in merely affirmative form, and she would decline to touch it. Such truth as that, she might repeat with Clifford, would be stolen in defiance of her duty to mankind. Human passions, however, are stronger than technical rules. "*Le cœur a ses raisons,*" as Pascal says, "*que la raison ne connaît pas*"; and however indifferent to all but the bare rules of the game the umpire, the abstract intellect, may be, the concrete players who furnish him the materials to judge of are usually, each one of them, in love with some pet "live hypothesis" of his own. Let us agree, however, that wherever there is no forced option, the dispassionately judicial intellect with no pet hypothesis, saving us, as it does, from dupery at any rate, ought to be our ideal.

The question next arises: Are there not somewhere forced options in our speculative questions, and can we (as men who may be interested at least as much in positively gaining truth as in merely escaping dupery) always wait with impunity till the coercive evidence shall have arrived? It seems *a priori* improbable that the truth should be so nicely adjusted to our needs and powers as that. In the great boarding-house of nature, the cakes and the butter and the syrup seldom come out so even and leave the plates so clean. Indeed, we should view them with scientific suspicion if they did.

IX

Moral questions immediately present themselves as questions whose solution cannot wait for sensible proof. A moral question is a question not of what sensibly exists, but of what is good, or would be good if it did exist. Science can tell us what exists; but to compare the *worths,* both of what exists and of what does not exist, we must consult not science, but what Pascal calls our heart. . . .

Turn now from these wide questions of good to a certain class of questions of fact, questions concerning personal relations, states of mind between one man and another. *Do you like me or not?*—for example. Whether you do or not depends, in countless instances, on whether I meet you half-way, am willing to assume that you must like me, and show you trust and expectation. The previous faith on my part in your liking's existence is in such cases what makes your liking come. But if I stand aloof, and refuse to budge an inch until I have objective evidence, until you shall have done something apt, as the absolutists say, *ad extorquendum assensum meum,* ten to one your liking never comes. How many women's hearts are vanquished by the mere sanguine insistence of some man that they *must* love him! he will not consent to the hypothesis that they cannot. The desire for a certain kind of truth here brings about that special truth's existence; and so it is in innumerable cases of other sorts. . . . *And where faith in a fact can help create the fact,* that would be an insane logic which should say that faith running ahead of scientific evidence is the "lowest kind of immorality" into which a thinking being can fall. Yet such is the logic by which our scientific absolutists pretend to regulate our lives!

X

In truths dependent on our personal action, then, faith based on desire is certainly a lawful and possibly an indispensable thing.

But now, it will be said, these are all childish human cases, and have nothing to do with great cosmical matters, like the question of religious faith. Let us then pass on to that. Religions differ so much in their accidents that in discussing the religious question we must make it very generic and broad. What then do we now mean by the religious hypothesis? Science says things are; morality says some things are better than other things; and religion says essentially two things.

First, she says that the best things are the more eternal things, the overlapping things, the things in the universe that throw the last stone, so to speak, and say the final word. "Perfection is

[1] Compare Wilfrid Ward's Essay "The Wish to Believe," in his *Witnesses to the Unseen* (Macmillan & Co., 1893).

eternal"—this phrase of Charles Secrétan seems a good way of putting this first affirmation of religion, an affirmation which obviously cannot yet be verified scientifically at all.

The second affirmation of religion is that we are better off even now if we believe her first affirmation to be true.

Now, let us consider what the logical elements of this situation are *in case the religious hypothesis in both its branches be really true.* (Of course, we must admit that possibility at the outset. If we are to discuss the question at all, it must involve a living option. If for any of you religion be a hypothesis that cannot, by any living possibility, be true, then you need go no farther. I speak to the "saving remnant" alone.) So proceeding, we see, first, that religion offers itself as a *momentous* option. We are supposed to gain, even now, by our belief, and to lose by our non-belief, a certain vital good. Secondly, religion is a *forced* option, so far as that good goes. We cannot escape the issue by remaining sceptical and waiting for more light, because, although we do avoid error in that way *if religion be untrue,* we lose the good, *if it be true,* just as certainly as if we positively chose to disbelieve. It is as if a man should hesitate indefinitely to ask a certain woman to marry him because he was not perfectly sure that she would prove an angel after he brought her home. Would he not cut himself off from that particular angel-possibility as decisively as if he went and married some one else? Scepticism, then, is not avoidance of option; it is option of a certain particular kind of risk. *Better risk loss of truth than chance of error*—that is your faith-vetoer's exact position. He is actively playing his stake as much as the believer is; he is backing the field against the religious hypothesis, just as the believer is backing the religious hypothesis against the field. To preach scepticism to us as a duty until "sufficient evidence" for religion be found, is tantamount therefore to telling us, when in presence of the religious hypothesis, that to yield to our fear of its being error is wiser and better than to yield to our hope that it may be true. It is not intellect against all passions, then; it is only intellect with one passion laying down its law. And by what, forsooth, is the supreme wisdom of this passion warranted? Dupery for dupery, what proof is there that dupery through hope is so much worse than dupery through fear? I, for one, can see no proof; and I simply refuse obedience to the scientist's command to imitate his kind of option, in a case where my own stake is important enough to give me the right to choose my own form of risk. If religion be true and the evidence for it be still insufficient, I do not wish, by putting your extinguisher upon my nature (which feels to me as if it had after all some business in this matter), to forfeit my sole chance in life of getting upon the winning side—that chance depending, of course, on my willingness to run the risk of acting as if my passional need of taking the world religiously might be prophetic and right.

All this is on the supposition that it really may be prophetic and right, and that, even to us who are discussing the matter, religion is a live hypothesis which may be true. Now, to most of us religion comes in a still further way that makes a veto on our active faith even more illogical. The more perfect and more eternal aspect of the universe is represented in our religions as having personal form. The universe is no longer a mere *It* to us, but a *Thou,* if we are religious; and any relation that may be possible from person to person might be possible here. For instance, although in one sense we are passive portions of the universe, in another we show a curious autonomy, as if we were small active centres on our own account. We feel, too, as if the appeal of religion to us were made to our own active goodwill, as if evidence might be forever withheld from us unless we met the hypothesis half-way. To take a trivial illustration: just as a man who in a company of gentlemen made no advances, asked a warrant for every concession, and believed no one's word without proof, would cut himself off by such churlishness from all the social rewards that a more trusting spirit would earn—so here, one who should shut himself up in snarling logicality and try to make the gods extort his recognition willy-nilly, or not get it at all, might cut himself off forever from his only opportunity of making the gods' acquaintance. This feeling, forced on us we know not whence, that by obstinately believing that there are gods (although not to do so would be so easy both for our logic and our life) we are doing the universe the deepest service we can, seems part of the living essence of the religious hypothesis. If the hypothesis *were* true in all its parts, including this one, then pure intellectualism, with its veto on our making willing advances, would be an absurdity; and some participation of our sympathetic nature would be logically required. I, therefore, for one, cannot see my way to accepting the agnostic rules for truth-seeking, or wilfully agree to keep my willing nature out of the game. I cannot do so for this plain reason, that *a rule of thinking which would absolutely prevent me from acknowledging certain kinds of truth if those kinds of truth were really there, would be an irrational rule.* That for me is the long and short of the formal logic of the situation, no matter what the kinds of truth might materially be.

I confess I do not see how this logic can be escaped. But sad experience makes me fear that some of you may still shrink from radically saying with me, *in abstracto,* that we have the right to believe at our own risk any hypothesis that is live enough to tempt our will. I suspect, however, that if this is so, it is because you have got away from the abstract logical point of view altogether, and are thinking (perhaps without realizing it) of some particular religious hypothesis which for you is dead. The freedom to "believe what we will" you apply to the case of some patent superstition; and the faith you think of is the faith defined by the schoolboy when he said, "Faith is when you believe something that you know ain't true." I can only repeat that this is misapprehension. *In concreto,* the freedom to believe can only cover living options which the intellect of the individual cannot by itself resolve; and living options never seem absurdities to him who has them to consider. When I look at the religious question as it really puts itself to concrete men, and when I think of all the possibilities which both practically and theoretically it involves, then this command that we shall put a stopper on our heart, instincts, and courage, and *wait*—acting of course meanwhile more or less as if religion were *not* true[2]—till doomsday, or till such time as our intellect and senses working together may have raked in evidence enough—this command, I say, seems to me the queerest idol ever manufactured in the philosophic cave. Were we scholastic absolutists, there might be more excuse. If we had an infallible intellect with its objective certitudes, we might feel ourselves disloyal to such a perfect organ of knowledge in not trusting to it exclusively, in not waiting for its releasing word. But if we are empiricists, if we believe that no bell in us tolls to let us know for certain when truth is in our grasp, then it seems a piece of idle fantasticality to preach so solemnly our duty of waiting for the bell. Indeed we *may* wait if we will—I hope you do not think that I am denying that—but if we do so, we do so at our peril as much as if we believed. In either case we *act,* taking our life in our hands. No one of us ought to issue vetoes to the other, nor should we bandy words of abuse. We ought, on the contrary, delicately and profoundly to respect one another's mental freedom: then only shall we bring about the intellectual republic; then only shall we have that spirit of inner tolerance without which all our outer tolerance is soulless, and which is empiricism's glory; then only shall we live and let live, in speculative as well as in practical things.

I began by a reference to Fitz-James Stephen; let me end by a quotation from him. "What do you think of yourself? What do you think of the world? . . . These are questions with which all must deal as it seems good to them. They are riddles of the Sphinx, and in some way or other we must deal with them. . . . In all important transactions of life we have to take a leap in the dark. . . . If we decide to leave the riddles unanswered, that is a choice; if we waver in our answer, that, too, is a choice: but whatever choice we make, we make it at our peril. If a man chooses to turn his back altogether on God and the future, no one can prevent him; no one can show beyond reasonable doubt that he is mistaken. If a man thinks otherwise and acts as he thinks, I do not see that any one can prove that he is mistaken. Each must act as he thinks best; and if he is wrong, so much the worse for him.

[2] Since belief is measured by action, he who forbids us to believe religion to be true, necessarily also forbids us to act as we should if we did believe it to be true. The whole defence of religious faith hinges upon action. If the action required or inspired by the religious hypothesis is in no way different from that dictated by the naturalistic hypothesis, then religious faith is a pure superfluity, better pruned away, and controversy about its legitimacy is a piece of idle trifling, unworthy of serious minds. I myself believe, of course, that the religious hypothesis gives to the world an expression which specifically determines our reactions, and makes them in a large part unlike what they might be on a purely naturalistic scheme of belief.

We stand on a mountain pass in the midst of whirling snow and blinding mist, through which we get glimpses now and then of paths which may be deceptive. If we stand still we shall be frozen to death. If we take the wrong road we shall be dashed to pieces. We do not certainly know whether there is any right one. What must we do? 'Be strong and of a good courage.' Act for the best, hope for the best, and take what comes. . . . If death ends all, we cannot meet death better."[3]

[3] *Liberty, Equality, Fraternity,* p. 353, 2d edition (London, 1874).

PART 2 HUMAN KNOWLEDGE:

During the great golden age of philosophy, in the seventeenth and eighteenth centuries, problems about the nature of human knowledge divided philosophers into two schools; and despite changing idioms and increased understanding of the methods of science, the division to a large degree persists. On the one hand, the *Empiricists,* whose leading thinkers were John Locke (1632–1704), George Berkeley (1685–1753), and David Hume (1711–1776), held that all our ideas come from experience and that no proposition about any matter of fact can be known to be true independently of experience. On the other hand, the *Rationalists,* whose most important representatives were René Descartes (1596–1650), Baruch Spinoza (1632–1677), and Gottfried Leibniz (1646–1716), maintained that there are "innate ideas," and that there are some general propositions (usually called "necessary" or "a priori" propositions) that we can know to be true in advance of, or in the absence of, empirical verification. It should be noted that both the rationalist and the empiricist are "rationalists" in the wider sense of the term that is opposed to fideism, romanticism, or irrationalism. Both can support rational inquiry as the sole road to truth, but they differ in their conceptions of what rational inquiry is, particularly regarding the role that sense experience plays in it.

Advocates of the theory of innate ideas did not, of course, hold that we are born literally thinking certain thoughts, but rather that we are born with inherited dispositions to have thoughts of a certain form and structure. Just as dehydrated milk has the disposition to become milk when water is added to it, so the mind, on this theory, has from birth the disposition to acquire the concepts of being, substance, duration—even infinitude and God—once a certain amount of experience is "added to it." Thus, rationalism holds that there can be in the mind ideas and truths that were not first present in experience but only later activated by experience. For the empiricist, on the other hand, the mind is (as Locke put it) like the tablet on which nothing has been written (a *tabula rasa*) until experience writes its message on it.

The writings of René Descartes, a leading mathematician and man of science as well as a philosopher, are a clear example not only of the rationalistic doctrine and method

ITS GROUNDS AND LIMITS

but also of the rationalistic temper of mind. In the autobiographical *Discourse on Method,* he compares the state of the sciences and philosophy to an ancient European town, grown helter-skelter from an older village, with crooked streets, random walls, and poor sanitation. Of course, we are not accustomed to rip down whole cities in order to start from scratch the task of rational redesign; but individuals can without arrogance or absurdity think of ripping down and rebuilding their own homes:

> . . . and the same I thought was true of any similar project for reforming the body of the Sciences, or the order of teaching them established in the Schools: but as for the opinions which up to that time I had embraced, I thought that I could not do better than resolve at once to sweep them wholly away, that I might afterwards be in a position to admit either others more correct, or even perhaps the same ones when they had undergone the scrutiny of reason. I firmly believed that in this way I should much better succeed in the conduct of my life, than if I built only upon old foundations, and leaned upon principles which, in my youth, I had taken upon trust.

Thus Descartes begins his dramatic quest for new "foundations," doubting everything that can be doubted until he finds a solid basis for reconstruction in the indubitable fact of his own existence as a "thinking substance." What makes the argument for his own existence so convincing, Descartes decides, is its "clearness and distinctness"; hence he has a working criterion of truth to use in the voyage away from his skeptical starting point: whatever he conceives clearly and distinctly is true. In the third Meditation (here omitted because of its difficult technicalities) Descartes finds in himself the idea of an infinite God. The idea, he argues, could not be his own invention, nor could it be derived from merely finite experience. Its only possible cause must be the actually existing deity. Then it is proved that God is no deceiver and (in the beginning of Meditation IV) that intellectual error springs from a kind of hasty willfulness in ourselves and not from God. Since God has given us such a powerful disposition to believe in the existence of material objects (e.g., human bodies), He would be a deceiver were there no such bodies in existence. And so, at last, almost everything doubted in the beginning, including a world of extended bodies in motion, has been demonstrated back into existence, every step of the way evident to the "natural light of reason," and the conclusion guaranteed by an eternally reliable God, who indeed is the foundation of it all.

Few philosophers today find Descartes's system of arguments convincing, but his method has left its mark on most of his successors. For three centuries philosophers have tried to give a rational reconstruction of our knowledge, beginning with the relatively indubitable and building on it, and taking very seriously as they work the nagging claims of imaginary skeptics that what we think we know with certainty we may not really know at all.

The empiricist George Berkeley also was concerned with skepticism. As an empiricist, he was concerned to show that all of our ideas, insofar as they are genuine (not merely confused), are derived from experience. What, then, of our idea of corporeal objects such as trees, tables, bodies? Berkeley is driven by his logic and his empiricist startings to conclude that physical objects, insofar as we have any clear idea of them at all, are simply collections of "ideas"—or, in more modern terminology, sense impressions. Those corporeal substances, of which Descartes had "a clear and distinct idea," turn out on analysis to be the figments of muddled thought.

Has empiricism then truly reconstructed our knowledge of the world, if this is its conclusion? Doesn't Berkeley's conception of a world "through and through mental" give a violent jolt to common sense? Not so, replies Berkeley's spokesman Philonous. Berkeley's idealism (idea-ism) implies that tables and trees and bodies are just exactly what they seem—colored, shaped, hard, and so on. There is indeed nothing to these things except the qualities they seem to have. Moreover, it is not true that tables "vanish" or "pop out of existence" the moment we turn our backs on them (that *would* be repugnant to common sense); for God is always perceiving them, and therefore they continue to exist as ideas in His mind. To many later empiricists this use of God seemed a desperate expedient to save Berkeley's theory from embarrassment. John Stuart Mill (1806–1873) was typical of later empiricists (often called Phenomenalists) who found ways to make the rejection of "corporeal substance" more palatable to common sense without invoking a *deus ex machina.* We can say that the table continues to exist when unperceived, if we wish; but all we can mean by this is that *if* someone were to look in a certain place, then he would have sense impressions of a certain (table-like) kind; for material objects, according to Mill, are not simply bundles of actual sense impressions; they are rather to be understood as "permanent possibilities of sensation," and this conception exhausts whatever clear idea we have of them.

David Hume applies the empiricist philosophy to other basic concepts, with results that even he was not reluctant to call skeptical. In the selections included here, he examines the concept of causation and finds no more sense in the idea of a "necessary connection" between cause and effect (when we drop a stone, it *must* fall—so we think) than Berkeley did in the idea of "corporeal substance." We may continue to talk, as Hume himself does, of one thing's causing another, but all we can *mean* is that events of the first kind are in fact constantly conjoined with events of the second kind; and the so-called necessity that the second follow the first is simply the reflection of our habitual expectation. If the reader can find no error in Hume's arguments, he must then either reject Hume's empiricist presuppositions or else revise his own commonsense view of the world. Hume would not have us deny the plain reports of our senses or the fruits of our mathematical deductions; but he is a skeptic in the sense that he denies that there can be any logically infallible method of achieving truth about matters of fact, or indeed any method at all for reasoning about matters that lie beyond all experience. But this kind of skepticism need not force us into a permanent suspension of judgment about all things, even in the practical affairs of life; for we will (as Hume elsewhere puts it) continue to leave buildings by the first-floor door rather than the upstairs window, and "Nature will always maintain her rights and prevail in the end over any abstract reasoning whatever."

The issue between rationalism and empiricism can be put very precisely, indeed even pithily, in a single short question: Are there any synthetic a priori propositions? Are there any general statements we can know with perfect certainty to be true prior to an examination of all (or even many) of the cases to which they apply? We cannot know for certain that *all kittens are playful* without checking each and every kitten, because, for all we know, we may one day discover a non-playful kitten. There is surely no logical absurdity in the supposition. Without making any investigation, on the other hand, we can know that *all kittens are young cats;* for this is a necessary truth—one we can know, so to speak, without leaving our armchairs. But then, necessary though it be, it is perfectly trivial; it tells us nothing at all about kittens, since it is true not by virtue of some *fact* about kittens, but rather by virtue of what we *mean* by the word "kitten." Are there, then, any general propositions that are necessary (a priori) yet genuinely informative (synthetic)? That is the question that divided Hume and Kant in their day, and the selections from Ayer and Ewing carry on the debate in twentieth-century idiom.

It is often said that *Pragmatism,* the distinctively American contribution to the history of philosophy, is a third major theory of knowledge. There is some truth in this, without question; but Charles Saunders Peirce and William James both regarded the pragmatic maxim as an explication of a methodological principle implicit in the writings of the great British empiricists. The concluding selection, by John Hospers, is a remarkably clear and penetrating discussion of questions that have been in the background in most of the articles preceding it: What is it *to explain,* and (correlatively) what is it *to understand?*

RENÉ DESCARTES

*Meditations on First Philosophy**

MEDITATION I

Of the things which may be brought within the sphere of the doubtful.

It is now some years since I detected how many were the false beliefs that I had from my earliest youth admitted as true, and how doubtful was everything I had since constructed on this basis; and from that time I was convinced that I must once for all seriously undertake to rid myself of all the opinions which I had formerly accepted, and commence to build anew from the foundation, if I wanted to establish any firm and permanent structure in the sciences. But as this enterprise appeared to be a very great one, I waited until I had attained an age so mature that I could not hope that at any later date I should be better fitted to execute my design. This reason caused me to delay so long that I should feel that I was doing wrong were I to occupy in deliberation the time that yet remains to me for action. To-day, then, since very opportunely for the plan I have in view I have delivered my mind from every care [and am happily agitated by no passions] and since I have procured for myself an assured leisure in a peaceable retirement, I shall at last seriously and freely address myself to the general upheaval of all my former opinions.

Now for this object it is not necessary that I should show that all of these are false—I shall perhaps never arrive at this end. But inasmuch as reason already persuades me that I ought no less carefully to withhold my assent from matters which are not entirely certain and indubitable than from those which appear to me manifestly to be false, if I am able to find in each one some reason to doubt, this will suffice to justify my rejecting the whole. And for that end it will not be requisite that I should examine each in particular, which would be an endless undertaking; for owing to the fact that the destruction of the foundations of necessity brings with it the downfall of the rest of the edifice, I shall only in the first place attack those principles upon which all my former opinions rested.

All that up to the present time I have accepted as most true and certain I have learned either from the senses or through the senses; but it is sometimes proved to me that these senses are deceptive, and it is wiser not to trust entirely to any thing by which we have once been deceived.

But it may be that although the senses sometimes deceive us concerning things which are hardly perceptible, or very far away, there are yet many others to be met with as to which we cannot reasonably have any doubt, although we recognise them by their means. For example, there is the fact that I am here, seated by the fire, attired in a dressing gown, having this paper in my hands and other similar matters. And how could I deny that these hands and this body are mine, were it not perhaps that I compare myself to certain persons, devoid of sense, whose cerebella are so troubled and clouded by the violent vapours of black bile, that they constantly assure us that they think they are kings when they are really quite poor, or that they are clothed in purple when they are really without covering, or who imagine that they have an earthenware head or are nothing but pumpkins or are made of glass. But they are mad, and I should not be any the less insane were I to follow examples so extravagant.

At the same time I must remember that I am a

* From René Descartes, *Meditations on First Philosophy,* trans. Elizabeth Haldane and G. R. T. Ross (London: Cambridge University Press, 1931), Meditations I, II, IV, V. Reprinted by permission of the publisher. First published in Latin in 1641.

man, and that consequently I am in the habit of sleeping, and in my dreams representing to myself the same things or sometimes even less probable things, than do those who are insane in their waking moments. How often has it happened to me that in the night I dreamt that I found myself in this particular place, that I was dressed and seated near the fire, whilst in reality I was lying undressed in bed! At this moment it does indeed seem to me that it is with eyes awake that I am looking at this paper; that this head which I move is not asleep, that it is deliberately and of set purpose that I extend my hand and perceive it; what happens in sleep does not appear so clear nor so distinct as does all this. But in thinking over this I remind myself that on many occasions I have in sleep been deceived by similar illusions, and in dwelling carefully on this reflection I see so manifestly that there are no certain indications by which we may clearly distinguish wakefulness from sleep that I am lost in astonishment. And my astonishment is such that it is almost capable of persuading me that I now dream.

Now let us assume that we are asleep and that all these particulars, e.g. that we open our eyes, shake our head, extend our hands, and so on, are but false delusions; and let us reflect that possibly neither our hands nor our whole body are such as they appear to us to be. At the same time we must at least confess that the things which are represented to us in sleep are like painted representations which can only have been formed as the counterparts of something real and true, and that in this way those general things at least, i.e. eyes, a head, hands, and a whole body, are not imaginary things, but things really existent. For, as a matter of fact, painters, even when they study with the greatest skill to represent sirens and satyrs by forms the most strange and extraordinary, cannot give them natures which are entirely new, but merely make a certain medley of the members of different animals; or if their imagination is extravagant enough to invent something so novel that nothing similar has ever before been seen, and that then their work represents a thing purely fictitious and absolutely false, it is certain all the same that the colours of which this is composed are necessarily real. And for the same reason, although these general things, to wit, [a body,] eyes, a head, hands, and such like, may be imaginary, we are bound at the same time to confess that there are at least some other objects yet more simple and more universal, which are real and true; and of these just in the same way as with certain real colours, all these images of things which dwell in our thoughts, whether true and real or false and fantastic, are formed.

To such a class of things pertains corporeal nature in general, and its extension, the figure of extended things, their quantity or magnitude and number, as also the place in which they are, the time which measures their duration, and so on.

That is possibly why our reasoning is not unjust when we conclude from this that Physics, Astronomy, Medicine and all other sciences which have as their end the consideration of composite things, are very dubious and uncertain; but that Arithmetic, Geometry and other sciences of that kind which only treat of things that are very simple and very general, without taking great trouble to ascertain whether they are actually existent or not, contain some measure of certainty and an element of the indubitable. For whether I am awake or asleep, two and three together always form five, and the square can never have more than four sides, and it does not seem possible that truths so clear and apparent can be suspected of any falsity [or uncertainty].

Nevertheless I have long had fixed in my mind the belief that an all-powerful God existed by whom I have been created such as I am. But how do I know that He has not brought it to pass that there is no earth, no heaven, no extended body, no magnitude, no place, and that nevertheless [I possess the perceptions of all these things and that] they seem to me to exist just exactly as I now see them? And, besides, as I sometimes imagine that others deceive themselves in the things which they think they know best, how do I know that I am not deceived every time that I add two and three, or count the sides of a square, or judge of things yet simpler, if anything simpler can be imagined? But possibly God has not desired that I should be thus deceived, for He is said to be supremely good. If, however, it is contrary to His goodness to have made me such that I constantly deceive myself, it would also appear to be contrary to His goodness to permit me to be sometimes deceived, and nevertheless I cannot doubt that He does permit this.

There may indeed be those who would prefer to deny the existence of a God so powerful, rather than believe that all other things are uncertain. But let us not oppose them for the present, and grant that all that is here said of a God is a fable; nevertheless in whatever way they suppose that I have arrived at the state of being that I have reached—whether they attribute it to fate or to accident, or make out that it is by a continual succession of antecedents, or by some other method—since to err and deceive oneself is a defect, it is clear that the greater will be the probability of my being so imperfect as to deceive myself ever, as is the Author to whom they assign my origin the less powerful. To these reasons I have certainly nothing to reply, but at the end I feel constrained to confess that there is nothing in all that I formerly believed to be true, of which I cannot in some measure doubt, and that not merely through want of thought or through levity, but for reasons which are very powerful and maturely considered; so that henceforth I ought not the less carefully to refrain from giving credence to these opinions than to that which is manifestly false, if I desire to arrive at any certainty [in the sciences].

But it is not sufficient to have made these remarks, we must also be careful to keep them in mind. For these ancient and commonly held opinions still revert frequently to my mind, long and familiar custom having given them the right to occupy my mind against my inclination and rendered them almost masters of my belief; nor will I ever lose the habit of deferring to them or of placing my confidence in them, so long as I consider them as they really are, i.e. opinions in some measure doubtful, as I have just shown, and at the same time highly probable, so that there is much more reason to believe in than to deny them. That is why I consider that I shall not be acting amiss, if, taking of set purpose a contrary belief, I allow myself to be deceived, and for a certain time pretend that all these opinions are entirely false and imaginary, until at last, having thus balanced my former prejudices with my latter [so that they cannot divert my opinions more to one side than to the other], my judgment will no longer be dominated by bad usage or turned away from the right knowledge of the truth. For I am assured that there can be neither peril nor error in this course, and that I cannot at present yield too much to distrust, since I am not considering the question of action, but only of knowledge.

I shall then suppose, not that God who is supremely good and the fountain of truth, but some evil genius not less powerful than deceitful, has employed his whole energies in deceiving me; I shall consider that the heavens, the earth, colours, figures, sound, and all other external things are nought but the illusions and dreams of which this genius has availed himself in order to lay traps for my credulity; I shall consider myself as having no hands, no eyes, no flesh, no blood, nor any senses, yet falsely believing myself to possess all these things; I shall remain obstinately attached to this idea, and if by this means it is not in my power to arrive at the knowledge of any truth, I may at least do what is in my power [i.e. suspend my judgment], and with firm purpose avoid giving credence to any false thing, or being imposed upon by this arch deceiver, however powerful and deceptive he may be. But this task is a laborious one, and insensibly a certain lassitude leads me into the course of my ordinary life. And just as a captive who in sleep enjoys an imaginary liberty, when he begins to suspect that his liberty is but a dream, fears to awaken, and conspires with these agreeable illusions that the deception may be prolonged, so insensibly of my own accord I fall back into my former opinions, and I dread awakening from this slumber, lest the laborious wakefulness which would follow the tranquillity of this repose should have to be spent not in daylight, but in the excessive darkness of the difficulties which have just been discussed.

MEDITATION II

Of the Nature of the Human Mind; and that it is more easily known than the Body.

The Meditation of yesterday filled my mind with so many doubts that it is no longer in my power to forget them. And yet I do not see in what manner I can resolve them; and, just as if I had all of a sudden fallen into very deep water, I am so disconcerted that I can neither make certain of setting my feet on the bottom, nor can I swim and so support myself on the surface. I shall nevertheless make an effort and follow anew the same path as that on which I yesterday entered, i.e. I shall proceed by setting aside all that in which the least doubt could be supposed to exist, just as if I had discovered that it was absolutely false; and I shall ever follow in this road until I have met with something which is certain, or at least, if I can do nothing else, until I have learned for certain that there is nothing in the world that is certain. Archimedes, in order that he might draw the terrestrial globe out of its place, and transport it elsewhere, demanded only that one point should be fixed and immoveable; in the same way I shall have the right to conceive high hopes if I am happy enough to discover one thing only which is certain and indubitable.

I suppose, then, that all the things that I see are false; I persuade myself that nothing has ever existed of all that my fallacious memory represents to me. I consider that I possess no senses; I imagine that body, figure, extension, movement and place are but the fictions of my mind. What, then can be esteemed as true? Perhaps nothing at all, unless that there is nothing in the world that is certain.

But how can I know there is not something different from those things that I have just considered, of which one cannot have the slightest doubt? Is there not some God, or some other being by whatever name we call it, who puts these reflections into my mind? That is not necessary, for is it not possible that I am capable of producing them myself? I myself, am I not at least something? But I have already denied that I had senses and body. Yet I hesitate, for what follows from that? Am I so dependent on body and senses that I cannot exist without these? But I was persuaded that there was nothing in all the world, that there was no heaven, no earth, that there were no minds, nor any bodies: was I not then likewise persuaded that I did not exist? Not at all; of a surety I myself did exist since I persuaded myself of something [or merely because I thought of something]. But there is some deceiver or other, very powerful and very cunning, who ever employs his ingenuity in deceiving me. Then without doubt I exist also if he deceives me, and let him deceive me as much as he will, he can never cause me to be nothing so long as I think that I am something. So that after having reflected well and carefully examined all things, we must come to the definite conclusion that this proposition: I am, I exist, is necessarily true each time that I pronounce it, or that I mentally conceive it.

But I do not yet know clearly enough what I am, I who am certain that I am; and hence I must be careful to see that I do not imprudently take some other object in place of myself, and thus that I do not go astray in respect of this knowledge that I hold to be the most certain and most evident of all that I have formerly learned. That is why I shall now consider anew what I believed myself to be before I embarked upon these last reflections; and of my former opinions I shall withdraw all that might even in a small degree be invalidated by the reasons which I have just brought forward, in order that there may be nothing at all left beyond what is absolutely certain and indubitable.

What then did I formerly believe myself to be? Undoubtedly I believed myself to be a man. But what is a man? Shall I say a reasonable animal? Certainly not; for then I should have to inquire what an animal is, and what is reasonable; and thus from a single question I should insensibly fall into an infinitude of others more difficult; and I should not wish to waste the little time and leisure remaining to me in trying to unravel subtleties like these. But I shall rather stop here to consider the thoughts which of themselves spring up in my mind, and which were not inspired by anything beyond my own nature alone when I applied myself to the consideration of my being. In the first place, then, I considered myself as having a face, hands, arms, and all that system of members composed of bones and flesh as seen in a corpse which I designated by the name of body. In addition to this I considered that I was nourished, that I walked, that I felt, and that I thought, and I referred all these actions to the soul: but I did not stop to consider what the soul was, or if I did stop, I imagined that it was something extremely rare and subtle like a wind, a flame, or an ether, which was spread throughout my grosser parts. As to body I had no manner of doubt about its nature, but thought I had a very clear knowledge of it; and if I had desired to explain it according to the notions that I had then formed of it, I should have described it thus: By the body I understand all that which can be defined by a certain figure: something which can be confined in a certain place, and which can fill a given space in such a way that every other body will be excluded from it; which can be perceived either by touch, or by sight, or by hearing, or by taste, or by smell: which can be moved in many ways not, in truth, by itself, but by something which is foreign to it, by which it is touched [and from which it receives impressions]: for to have the power of self-movement, as also of feeling or of thinking, I did not consider to appertain to the nature of body: on the contrary, I was rather astonished to find that faculties similar to them existed in some bodies.

But what am I, now that I suppose that there is a certain genius which is extremely powerful, and, if I may say so, malicious, who employs all his powers in deceiving me? Can I affirm that I possess the least of all those things which I have just said pertain to the nature of body? I pause to consider, I revolve all these things in my mind, and I find none of which I can say that it pertains to me. It would be tedious to stop to enumerate them. Let us pass to the attributes of soul and see if there is any one which is in me? What of nutrition or walking [the first mentioned]? But if it is so that I have no body it is also true that I can neither walk nor take nourishment. Another attribute is sensation. But one cannot feel without body, and besides I have thought I perceived many things during sleep that I recognised in my waking moments as not having been experienced at all. What of thinking? I find here that thought is an attribute that belongs to me; it alone cannot be separated from me. I am, I exist, that is certain. But how often? Just when I think; for it might possibly be the case if I ceased entirely to think, that I should likewise cease altogether to exist. I do not now admit anything which is not necessarily true: to speak accurately I am not more than a thing which thinks, that is to say a mind or a soul, or an understanding, or a reason, which are terms whose significance was formerly unknown to me. I am, however, a real thing and really exist; but what thing? I have answered: a thing which thinks.

And what more? I shall exercise my imagination [in order to see if I am not something more]. I am not a collection of members which we call the human body: I am not a subtle air distributed through these members, I am not a wind, a fire, a vapour, a breath, nor anything at all which I can imagine or conceive; because I have assumed that all these were nothing. Without changing that supposition I find that I only leave myself certain of the fact that I am somewhat. But perhaps it is true that these same things which I supposed were non-existent because they are unknown to me, are really not different from the self which I know. I am not sure about this, I shall not dispute about it now; I can only give judgment on things that are known to me. I know that I exist, and I inquire what I am, I whom I know to exist. But it is very certain that the knowledge of my existence taken in its precise significance does not depend on things whose existence is not yet known to me; consequently it does not depend on those which I can feign in imagination. And indeed the very term *feign* in imagination proves to me my error, for I really do this if I image myself a something, since to imagine is nothing else than to contemplate the figure or image of a corporeal thing. But I already know for certain that I am, and that it may be that all these images, and, speaking generally, all things that relate to the nature of body are nothing but dreams [and chimeras]. For this reason I see clearly that I have as little reason to say, 'I shall stimulate my imagination in order to know more distinctly what I am,' than if I were to say, 'I am now awake, and I perceive somewhat that is real and true: but because I do not yet perceive it distinctly enough, I shall go to sleep of express purpose, so that my dreams may represent the perception with greatest truth and evidence,' And, thus, I know for certain that nothing of all that I can understand by means of my imagination belongs to this knowledge which I have of myself, and that it is necessary to recall the mind from this mode of thought with the utmost diligence in order that it may be able to know its own nature with perfect distinctness.

But what then am I? A thing which thinks. What is a thing which thinks? It is a thing which doubts, understands, [conceives,] affirms, denies, wills, refuses, which also imagines and feels.

Certainly it is no small matter if all these things pertain to my nature. But why should they not so pertain? Am I not that being who now doubts nearly everything, who nevertheless understands certain things, who affirms that one only is true, who denies all the others, who desires to know more, is averse from being deceived, who imagines many things, sometimes indeed despite his will, and who perceives many likewise, as by the intervention of the bodily organs? Is there nothing in all this which is as true as it is certain that I exist, even though I should always sleep and though he who has given me being employed all his ingenuity in deceiving me? Is there likewise any one of these attributes which can be distinguished from my thought, or which might be said to be separated from myself? For it is so evident of itself that it is I who doubts, who understands, and who desires, that there is no reason here to add anything to explain it. And I have certainly the power of imagining likewise; for although it may happen (as I formerly supposed) that none of the things which I imagine are true, nevertheless this power of imagining does not cease to be really in use, and it forms part of my thought. Finally, I am the same who feels, that is to say, who perceives certain things, as by the organs of sense, since in truth I see light, I hear noise, I feel heat. But it will be said that these phenomena are false and that I am dreaming. Let it be so; still it is at least quite certain that it seems to me that I see light, that I hear noise and that I feel heat. That cannot be false; properly speaking it is what is in me called feeling; and used in this precise sense that is no other thing than thinking.

From this time I begin to know what I am with a little more clearness and distinction than before; but nevertheless it still seems to me, and I cannot prevent myself from thinking, that corporeal things, whose images are framed by thought, which are tested by the senses, are much more distinctly known than that obscure part of me which does not come under the imagination. Although really it is very strange to say that I know and understand more distinctly these things whose existence seems to me dubious, which are unknown to me, and which do not belong to me, than others of the truth of which I am convinced, which are known to me and which pertain to my real nature, in a word, than myself. But I see clearly how the case stands: my mind loves to wander, and cannot yet suffer itself to be retained within the just limits of truth. Very good, let us once more give it the freest rein, so that, when afterwards we seize the proper occasion for pulling up, it may the more easily be regulated and controlled.

Let us begin by considering the commonest matters, those which we believe to be the most distinctly comprehended, to wit, the bodies which we touch and see; not indeed bodies in general, for these general ideas are usually a little more confused, but let us consider one body in particular. Let us take, for example, this piece of wax: it has been taken quite freshly from the hive, and it has not yet lost the sweetness of the honey which it contains; it still retains somewhat of the odour of the flowers from which it has been culled; its colour, its figure, its size are apparent; it is hard, cold, easily handled, and if you strike it with the finger, it will emit a sound. Finally all the things which are requisite to cause us distinctly to recognise a body, are met with in it. But notice that while I speak and approach the fire what remained of the taste is exhaled, the smell evaporates, the colour alters, the figure is destroyed, the size increases, it becomes liquid, it heats, scarcely can one handle it, and when one strikes it, no sound is emitted. Does the same wax remain after this change? We must confess that it remains; none would judge otherwise. What then did I know so distinctly in this piece of wax? It could certainly be nothing of all that the senses brought to my notice, since all these things which fall under taste, smell, sight, touch, and hearing, are found to be changed, and yet the same wax remains.

Perhaps it was what I now think, viz. that this wax was not that sweetness of honey, nor that agreeable scent of flowers, nor that particular whiteness, nor that figure, nor that sound, but simply a body which a little while before appeared to me as perceptible under these forms, and which is now perceptible under others. But what, precisely, is it that I imagine when I form such conceptions? Let us attentively consider this, and, abstracting from all that does not belong to the wax, let us see what remains. Certainly nothing remains excepting a certain extended thing which is flexible and movable. But what is the meaning of flexible and movable? Is it not that I imagine that this piece of wax being round is capable of becoming square and of passing from a square to a triangular figure? No, certainly it is not that, since I imagine it admits of an infinitude of similar changes, and I nevertheless do not know how to compass the infinitude by my imagination, and consequently this conception which I have of the wax is not brought about by the faculty of imagination. What now is this extension? Is it not also unknown? For it becomes greater when the wax is melted, greater when it is boiled, and greater still when the heat increases; and I should not conceive [clearly] according to truth what wax is, if I did not think that even this piece that we are considering is capable of receiving more variations in extension that I have ever imagined. We must then grant that I could not even understand through the imagination what this piece of wax is, and that it is my mind alone which perceives it. I say this piece of wax in particular, for as to wax in general it is yet clearer. But what is this piece of wax which cannot be understood excepting by the [understanding or] mind? It is certainly the same that I see, touch, imagine, and finally it is the same which I have always believed it to be from the beginning. But what must particularly be observed is that its perception is neither an act of vision, nor of touch, nor of imagination, and has never been such although it may have appeared formerly to be so, but only an intuition of the mind, which may be imperfect and confused as it was formerly, or clear and distinct as it is at present, according as my attention is more or less directed to the elements which are found in it, and of which it is composed.

Yet in the meantime I am greatly astonished when I consider [the great feebleness of mind] and its proneness to fall [insensibly] into error; for although without giving expression to my thoughts I consider all this in my own mind, words often impede me and I am almost deceived by the terms of ordinary language. For we say that we see the same wax, if it is present, and not that we simply judge that it is the same from its having the same colour and figure. From this I should conclude that I knew the wax by means of vision and not simply by the intuition of the mind; unless by chance I remember that, when looking from a window and saying I see men who pass in the street, I really do not see them, but infer that what I see is men, just as I say that I see wax. And yet what do I see from the window but hats and coats which may cover automatic machines? Yet I judge these to be men. And similarly solely by the faculty of judgment which rests in my mind, I comprehend that which I believed I saw with my eyes.

A man who makes it his aim to raise his knowledge above the common should be ashamed to derive the occasion for doubting from the forms of speech invented by the vulgar; I prefer to pass on and consider whether I had a more evident and perfect conception of what the wax was when I first perceived it, and when I believed I knew it by means of the external senses or at least by the common sense as it is called, that is to say by the imaginative faculty, or whether my present conception is clearer now that I have most carefully examined what it is, and in what way it can be known. It would certainly be absurd to doubt as to this. For what was there in this first perception which was distinct? What was there which might not as well have been perceived by any of the animals? But when I distinguish the wax from its external forms, and when, just as if I had taken from it its vestments, I consider it quite naked, it is certain that although some error may still be found in my judgment, I can nevertheless not perceive it thus without a human mind.

But finally what shall I say of this mind, that is, of myself, for up to this point I do not admit in myself anything but mind? What then, I who seem to perceive this piece of wax so distinctly, do I not know myself, not only with much more truth and certainty, but also with much more distinctness and clearness? For if I judge that the wax is or exists from the fact that I see it, it certainly follows much more clearly that I am or that I exist myself from the fact that I see it. For it may be that what I see is not really wax, it may also be that I do not possess eyes with which to see anything; but it cannot be that when I see, or (for I no longer take account of the distinction) when I think I see, that I myself who think am nought. So if I judge that the wax exists from the fact that I touch it, the same thing will follow, to wit, that I am; and if I judge that my imagination, or some other cause, whatever it is, persuades me that the wax exists, I shall still conclude the same. And what I have here remarked of wax may be applied to all other things which are external to me [and which are met with outside of me]. And further, if the [notion or] perception of wax has seemed to me clearer and more distinct, not only after the sight or the touch, but also after many other causes have rendered it quite manifest to me, with how much more [evidence] and distinctness must it be said that I now know myself, since all the reasons which contribute to the knowledge of wax, or any other body whatever, are yet better proofs of the nature of my mind! And there are so many other things in the mind itself which may contribute to the elucidation of its nature, that those which depend on body such as these just mentioned, hardly merit being taken into account.

But finally here I am, having insensibly reverted to the point I desired, for, since it is now manifest to me that even bodies are not properly speaking known by the senses or by the faculty of imagination, but by the understanding only, and since they are not known from the fact that they are seen or touched, but only because they are understood, I see clearly that there is nothing which is easier for me to know than my mind. But because it is difficult to rid oneself so promptly of an opinion to which one was accustomed for so long, it will be well that I should halt a little at this point, so that by the length of my meditation I may more deeply imprint on my memory this new knowledge. . . .

MEDITATION IV

Of the True and the False

I have been well accustomed these past days to detach my mind from my senses, and I have accurately observed that there are very few things that one knows with certainty respecting corporeal objects, that there are many more which are known to us respecting the human mind, and yet more still regarding God Himself; so that I shall now without any difficulty abstract my thoughts from the consideration of [sensible or] imaginable objects, and carry them to those which, being withdrawn from all contact with matter, are purely intelligible. And certainly the idea which I possess of the human mind inasmuch as it is a thinking thing, and not extended in length, width and depth, nor participating in anything pertaining to body, is incomparably more distinct than is the idea of any corporeal thing. And when I consider that I doubt, that is to say, that I am an incomplete and dependent being, the idea of a being that is complete and independent, that is of God, presents itself to my mind with so much distinctness and clearness—and from the fact alone that this idea is found in me, or that I who possess this idea exist, I conclude so certainly that God exists, and that my existence depends entirely on Him in every moment of my life—that I do not think that the human mind is capable of knowing anything with more evidence and certitude. And it seems to me that I now have before me a road which will lead us from the contemplation of the true God (in whom all the treasures of science and wisdom are contained) to the knowledge of the other objects of the universe.

For, first of all, I recognise it to be impossible that He should ever deceive me; for in all fraud and deception some imperfection is to be found, and although it may appear that the power of deception is a mark of subtilty or power, yet the desire to deceive without doubt testifies to malice or feebleness, and accordingly cannot be found in God.

In the next place I experienced in myself a certain capacity for judging which I have doubtless received from God, like all the other things that I possess; and as He could not desire to deceive me, it is clear that He has not given me a faculty that will lead me to err if I use it aright.

And no doubt respecting this matter could remain, if it were not that the consequence would seem to follow that I can thus never be deceived; for if I hold all that I possess from God, and if He has not placed in me the capacity for error, it seems as though I could never fall into error. And it is true that when I think only of God [and direct my mind wholly to Him], I discover [in myself] no cause of error, or falsity; yet directly afterwards, when recurring to myself, experience shows me that I am nevertheless subject to an infinitude of errors, as to which, when we come to investigate them more closely, I notice that not only is there a real and positive idea of God or of a Being of supreme perfection present to my mind, but also, so to speak, a certain negative idea of nothing, that is, of that which is infinitely removed from any kind of perfection; and that I am in a sense something intermediate between God and nought, i.e. placed in such a manner between the supreme Being and non-being, that there is in truth nothing in me that can lead to error in so far as a sovereign Being has formed me; but that, as I in some degree participate likewise in nought or in non-being, i.e. in so far as I am not myself the supreme Being, and as I find myself subject to an infinitude of imperfections, I ought not to be astonished if I should fall into error. Thus do I recognise that error, in so far as it is such, is not a real thing depending on God, but simply a defect; and therefore, in order to fall into it, that I have no need to possess a special faculty given me by God for this very purpose, but that I fall into error from the fact that the power given me by God for the purpose of distinguishing truth from error is not infinite.

Nevertheless this does not quite satisfy me; for error is not a pure negation [i.e. is not the simple defect or want of some perfection which ought not to be mine], but it is a lack of some knowledge which it seems that I ought to possess. And on considering the nature of God it does not appear to me possible that He should have given me a faculty which is not perfect of its kind, that is, which is wanting in some perfection due to it. For if it is true that the more skilful the artizan, the more perfect is the work of his hands, what can have been produced by this supreme Creator of all things that is not in all its parts perfect? And certainly there is no doubt that God could have created me so that I could never have been subject to error; it is also certain that He ever wills what is best; is it then better that I should be subject to err than that I should not?

In considering this more attentively, it occurs to me in the first place that I should not be astonished if my intelligence is not capable of comprehending why God acts as He does; and that there is thus no reason to doubt of His existence from the fact that I may perhaps find many other things besides this as to which I am able to understand neither for what reason nor how God has produced them. For, in the first place, knowing that my nature is extremely feeble and limited, and that the nature of God is on the contrary immense, incomprehensible, and infinite, I have no further difficulty in recognising that there is an infinitude of matters in His power, the causes of which transcend my knowledge; and this reason suffices to convince me that the species of cause termed final, finds no useful employment in physical [or natural] things; for it does not appear to me that I can without temerity seek to investigate the [inscrutable] ends of God.

It further occurs to me that we should not consider one single creature separately, when we inquire as to whether the works of God are perfect, but should regard all his creations together. For the same thing which might possibly seem very imperfect with some semblance of reason if regarded by itself, is found to be very perfect if regarded as part of the whole universe; and although, since I resolved to doubt all things, I as yet have only known certainly my own existence and that of God, nevertheless since I have recognised the infinite power of God, I cannot deny that He may have produced many other things, or at least that He has the power of producing them, so that I may obtain a place as a part of a great universe.

Whereupon, regarding myself more closely, and considering what are my errors (for they alone testify to there being any imperfection in me), I answer that they depend on a combination of two causes, to wit, on the faculty of knowledge that rests in me, and on the power of choice or of free will—that is to say, of the understanding and at the same time of the will. For by the understanding alone I [neither assert nor deny anything, but] apprehend the ideas of things as to which I can form a judgment. But no error is properly speaking found in it, provided the word error is taken in its proper signification; and though there is possibly an infinitude of things in the world of which I have no idea in my understanding, we cannot for all that say that it is deprived of these ideas [as we might say of something which is required by its nature], but simply it does not possess these; because in truth there is no reason to prove that God should have given me a greater faculty of knowledge than He has given me; and however skilful a workman I represent Him to be, I should not for all that consider that He was bound to have placed in each of His works all the perfections which He may have been able to place in some. I likewise cannot complain that God has not given me a free choice or a will which is sufficient, ample and perfect, since as a matter of fact I am conscious of a will so extended as to be subject to no limits. And what seems to me very remarkable in this regard is that of all the qualities which I possess there is no one so perfect and so comprehensive that I do not very clearly recognise that it might be yet greater and more perfect. For, to take an example, if I consider the faculty of comprehension which I possess, I find that it is of very small extent and extremely limited, and at the same time I find the idea of another faculty much more ample and even infinite, and seeing that I can form the idea of it, I recognise from this very fact that it pertains to the nature of God. If in the same way I examine the memory, the imagination, or some other faculty, I do not find any which is not small and circumscribed, while in God it is immense [or infinite]. It is free will alone or liberty of choice which I find to be so great in me that I can conceive no other idea to be more great; it is indeed the case that it is for the most part this will that causes me to know that in some manner I bear the image and similitude of God. For although the power of will is incomparably greater in God than in me, both by reason of the knowledge and the power which, conjoined with it, render it stronger and more efficacious, and by reason of its object, inasmuch as in God it extends to a great many things; it nevertheless does not seem to me greater if I consider it formally and precisely in itself: for the faculty of will consists alone in our having the power of choosing to do a thing or choosing not to do it (that is, to affirm or deny, to pursue or to shun it), or rather it consists alone in the fact that in order to affirm or deny, pursue or shun those things placed before us by the understanding, we act so that we are unconscious that any outside force constrains us in doing so. For in order that I should be free it is not necessary that I should be indifferent as to the choice of one or the other of two contraries; but contrariwise the more I lean to the one—whether I recognise clearly that the reasons of the good and true are to be found in it, or whether God so disposes my inward thought—the more freely do I choose and embrace it. And undoubtedly both divine grace and natural knowledge, far from diminishing my liberty, rather increase it and strengthen it. Hence this indifference which I feel, when I am not swayed to one side rather than to the other by lack of reason, is the lowest grade of liberty, and rather evinces a lack or negation in knowledge than a perfection of will: for if I always recognised clearly what was true and good, I should never have trouble in deliberating as to what judgment or choice I should make, and then I should be entirely free without ever being indifferent.

From all this I recognise that the power of will which I have received from God is not of itself the source of my errors—for it is very ample and very perfect of its kind—any more than is the power of understanding; for since I understand nothing but by the power which God has given me for understanding, there is no doubt that all that I understand, I understand as I ought, and it is not possible that I err in this. Whence then come my errors? They come from the sole fact that since the will is much wider in its range and compass than the understanding, I do not restrain it within the same bounds, but extend it also to things which I do not understand: and as the will is of itself indifferent to these, it easily falls into error and sin, and chooses the evil for the good, or the false for the true.

For example, when I lately examined whether anything existed in the world, and found that from the very fact that I considered this question it followed very clearly that I myself existed, I could not prevent myself from believing that a thing I so clearly conceived was true: not that I found myself compelled to do so by some external cause, but simply because from great clearness in my mind there followed a great inclination of my will; and I believed this with so much the greater freedom or spontaneity as I possessed the less indifference towards it. Now, on the contrary, I not only know that I exist, inasmuch as I am a thinking thing, but a certain representation of corporeal nature is also presented to my mind; and it comes to pass that I doubt whether this thinking nature which is in me, or rather by which I am what I am, differs from this corporeal nature, or whether both are not simply the same thing; and I here suppose that I do not yet know any reason to persuade me to adopt the one belief rather than the other. From this it follows that I am entirely indifferent as to which of the two I affirm or deny, or even whether I abstain from forming any judgment in the matter.

And this indifference does not only extend to matters as to which the understanding has no knowledge, but also in general to all those which are not apprehended with perfect clearness at the moment when the will is deliberating upon them: for, however probable are the conjectures which render me disposed to form a judgment respecting anything, the simple knowledge that I have that those are conjectures alone and not certain and indubitable reasons, suffices to occasion me to judge the contrary. Of this I have had great experience of late when I set aside as false all that I had formerly held to be absolutely true, for the sole reason that I remarked that it might in some measure be doubted.

But if I abstain from giving my judgment on any thing when I do not perceive it with sufficient clearness and distinctness, it is plain that I act rightly and am not deceived. But if I determine to deny or affirm, I no longer make use as I should of my free will, and if I affirm what is not true, it is evident that I deceive myself; even though I judge according to truth, this comes about only by chance, and I do not escape the blame of misusing my freedom; for the light of nature teaches us that the knowledge of the understanding should always precede the determination of the will. And it is in the misuse of the free will that the privation which constitutes the characteristic nature of error is met with. Privation, I say, is found in the act, in so far as it proceeds from me, but it is not found in the faculty which I have received from God, nor even in the act in so far as it depends on Him.

For I have certainly no cause to complain that God has not given me an intelligence which is more powerful, or a natural light which is stronger than that which I have received from Him, since it is proper to the finite understanding not to comprehend a multitude of things, and it is proper to a created understanding to be finite; on the contrary, I have every reason to render thanks to God who owes me nothing and who has given me all the perfections I possess, and I should be far from charging Him with injustice, and with having deprived me of, or wrongfully withheld from me, these perfections which He has not bestowed upon me.

I have further no reason to complain that He has given me a will more ample than my understanding, for since the will consists only of one single element, and is so to speak indivisible, it appears that its nature is such that nothing can be abstracted from it [without destroying it]; and certainly the more comprehensive it is found to be, the more reason I have to render gratitude to the giver.

And, finally, I must also not complain that God concurs with me in forming the acts of the will, that is the judgment in which I go astray, because these acts are entirely true and good, inasmuch as they depend on God; and in a certain sense more perfection accrues to my nature from the fact that I can form them, than if I could not do so. As to the privation in which alone the formal reason of error or sin consists, it has no need of any concurrence from God, since it is not a thing [or an existence], and since it is not related to God as to a cause, but should be termed merely a negation [according to the significance given to these words in the Schools]. For in fact it is not an imperfection in God that He has given me the liberty to give or withhold my assent from certain things as to which He has not placed a clear and dintinct knowledge in my understanding; but it is without doubt an imperfection in me not to make a good use of my freedom, and to give my judgment readily on matters which I only understand obscurely. I nevertheless perceive that God could easily have created me so that I never should err, although I still remained free, and endowed with a limited knowledge, viz. by giving to my understanding a clear and distinct intelligence of all things as to which I should ever have to deliberate; or simply by His engraving deeply in my memory the resolution never to form a judgment on anything without having a clear and distinct understanding of it, so that I could never forget it. And it is easy for me to understand that, in so far as I consider myself alone, and as if there were only myself in the world, I should have been much more perfect than I am, if God had created me so that I could never err. Nevertheless I cannot deny that in some sense it is a greater perfection in the whole universe that certain parts should not be exempt from error as others are than that all parts should be exactly similar. And I have no right to complain if God, having placed me in the world, has not called upon me to play a part that excels all others in distinction and perfection.

And further I have reason to be glad on the ground that if He has not given me the power of never going astray by the first means pointed out above, which depends on a clear and evident knowledge of all the things regarding which I can deliberate, He has at least left within my power the other means, which is firmly to adhere to the resolution never to give judgment on matters whose truth is not clearly known to me; for although I notice a certain weakness in my nature in that I cannot continually concentrate my mind on one single thought, I can yet, by attentive and frequently repeated meditation, impress it so forcibly on my memory that I shall never fail to recollect it whenever I have need of it, and thus acquire the habit of never going astray.

And inasmuch as it is in this that the greatest and principal perfection of man consists, it seems to me that I have not gained little by this day's Meditation, since I have discovered the source of falsity and error. And certainly there can be no other source than that which I have explained; for as often as I so restrain my will within the limits of my knowledge that it forms no judgment except on matters which are clearly and distinctly represented to it by the understanding, I can never be deceived; for every clear and distinct conception is without doubt something, and hence cannot derive its origin from what is nought, but must of necessity have God as its author—God, I say, who being supremely perfect, cannot be the cause of any error; and consequently we must conclude that such a conception [or such a judgment] is true. Nor have I only learned to-day what I should avoid in order that I may not err, but also how I should act in order to arrive at a knowledge of the truth; for without doubt I shall arrive at this end if I devote my attention sufficiently to those things which I perfectly understand; and if I separate from these that which I only understand confusedly and with obscurity. To these I shall henceforth diligently give heed.

MEDITATION V

Of the essence of material things, and, again, of God that He exists.

Many other matters respecting the attributes of God and my own nature or mind remain for consideration; but I shall possibly on another occasion resume the investigation of these. Now (after first noting what must be done or avoided, in order to arrive at a knowledge of the truth) my principal task is to endeavour to emerge from the state of doubt into which I have these last days fallen, and to see whether nothing certain can be known regarding material things.

But before examining whether any such objects as I conceive exist outside of me, I must consider the ideas of them in so far as they are in my thought, and see which of them are distinct and which confused.

In the first place, I am able distinctly to imagine that quantity which philosophers commonly call continuous, or the extension in length, breadth, or depth, that is in this quantity, or rather in the object to which it is attributed. Further, I can number in it many different parts, and attribute to each of its parts many sorts of size, figure, situation and local movements, and, finally, I can assign to each of these movements all degrees of duration.

And not only do I know these things with distinctness when I consider them in general, but, likewise [however little I apply my attention to the matter], I discover an infinitude of particulars respecting numbers, figures, movements, and other such things, whose truth is so manifest, and so well accords with my nature, that when I begin to discover them, it seems to me that I learn nothing new, or recollect what I formerly knew—that is to say, that I for the first time perceive things which were already present to my mind, although I had not as yet applied my mind to them.

And what I here find to be most important is that I discover in myself an infinitude of ideas of certain things which cannot be esteemed as pure negations, although they may possibly have no existence outside of my thought, and which are not framed by me, although it is within my power either to think or not to think them, but which possess natures which are true and immutable. For example, when I imagine a triangle, although there may nowhere in the world be such a figure outside my thought, or ever have been, there is nevertheless in this figure a certain determinate nature, form, or essence, which is immutable and eternal, which I have not invented, and which in no wise depends on my mind, as appears from the fact that diverse properties of that triangle can be demonstrated, viz. that its three angles are equal to two right angles, that the greatest side is subtended by the greatest angle, and the like, which now, whether I wish it or do not wish it, I recognise very clearly as pertaining to it, although I never thought of the matter at all when I imagined a triangle for the first time, and which therefore cannot be said to have been invented by me.

Nor does the objection hold good that possibly this idea of a triangle has reached my mind through the medium of my senses, since I have sometimes seen bodies triangular in shape; because I can form in my mind an infinitude of other figures regarding which we cannot have the least conception of their ever having been objects of sense, and I can nevertheless demonstrate various properties pertaining to their nature as well as to that of the triangle, and these must certainly all be true since I conceive them clearly. Hence they are something, and not pure negation; for it is perfectly clear that all that is true is something, and I have already fully demonstrated that all that I know clearly is true. And even although I had not demonstrated this, the nature of my mind is such that I could not prevent myself from holding them to be true so long as I conceive them clearly; and I recollect that even when I was still strongly attached to the objects of sense, I counted as the most certain those truths which I conceived clearly as regards figures, numbers, and the other matters which pertain to arithmetic and geometry, and, in general, to pure and abstract mathematics.

But now, if just because I can draw the idea of something from my thought, it follows that all which I know clearly and distinctly as pertaining to this object does really belong to it, may I not derive from this an argument demonstrating the existence of God? It is certain that I no less find the idea of God, that is to say, the idea of a supremely perfect Being, in me, than that of any figure or number whatever it is; and I do not know any less clearly and distinctly that an [actual and] eternal existence pertains to this nature than I know that all that which I am able to demonstrate of some figure or number truly pertains to the nature of this figure or number, and therefore, although all that I concluded in the preceding Meditations were found to be false, the existence of God would pass with me as at least as certain as I have ever held the truths of mathematics (which concern only numbers and figures) to be.

This indeed is not at first manifest, since it would seem to present some appearance of being a sophism. For being accustomed in all other things to make a distinction between existence and essence, I easily persuade myself that the existence can be separated from the essence of God, and that we can thus conceive God as not actually existing. But, nevertheless, when I think of it with more attention, I clearly see that existence can no more be separated from the essence of God than can its having its three angles equal to two right angles be separated from the essence of a [rectilinear] triangle, or the idea of a mountain from the idea of a valley; and so there is not any less repugnance to our conceiving a God (that is, a Being supremely perfect) to whom existence is lacking (that is to say, to whom a certain perfection is lacking), than to conceive of a mountain which has no valley.

But although I cannot really conceive of a God without existence any more than a mountain without a valley, still from the fact that I conceive of a mountain with a valley, it does not follow that there is such a mountain in the world; similarly although I conceive of God as possessing existence, it would seem that it does not follow that there is a God which exists; for my thought does not impose any necessity upon things, and just as I may imagine a winged horse, although no horse with wings exists, so I could perhaps attribute existence to God, although no God existed.

But a sophism is concealed in this objection; for from the fact that I cannot conceive a mountain without a valley, it does not follow that there is any mountain or any valley in existence, but only that the mountain and the valley, whether they exist or do not exist, cannot in any way be separated one from the other. While from the fact that I cannot conceive God without existence, it follows that existence is inseparable from Him, and hence that He really exists; not that my thought can bring this to pass, or impose any necessity on things, but, on the contrary, because the necessity which lies in the thing itself, i.e. the necessity of the existence of God determines me to think in this way. For it is not within my power to think of God without existence (that is of a supremely perfect Being devoid of a supreme perfection) though it is in my power to imagine a horse either with wings or without wings.

And we must not here object that it is in truth necessary for me to assert that God exists after having presupposed that He possesses every sort of perfection, since existence is one of these, but that as a matter of fact my original supposition was not necessary, just as it is not necessary to consider that all quadrilateral figures can be inscribed in the circle; for supposing I thought this, I should be constrained to admit that the rhombus might be inscribed in the circle since it is a quadrilateral figure, which, however, is manifestly false. [We must not, I say, make any such allegations because] although it is not necessary that I should at any time entertain the notion of God, nevertheless whenever it happens that I think of a first and a sovereign Being, and, so to speak, derive the idea of Him from the storehouse of my mind, it is necessary that I should attribute to Him every sort of perfection, although I do not get so far as to enumerate them all, or to apply my mind to each one in particular.

And this necessity suffices to make me conclude (after having recognised that existence is a perfection) that this first and sovereign Being really exists; just as though it is not necessary for me ever to imagine any triangle, yet, whenever I wish to consider a rectilinear figure composed only of three angles, it is absolutely essential that I should attribute to it all those properties which serve to bring about the conclusion that its three angles are not greater than two right angles, even although I may not then be considering this point in particular. But when I consider which figures are capable of being inscribed in the circle, it is in no wise necessary that I should think that all quadrilateral figures are of this number; on the contrary, I cannot even pretend that this is the case, so long as I do not desire to accept anything which I cannot conceive clearly and distinctly. And in consequence there is a great difference between the false suppositions such as this, and the true ideas born within me, the first and principal of which is that of God. For really I discern in many ways that this idea is not something factitious, and depending solely on my thought, but that it is the image of a true and immutable nature; first of all, because I cannot conceive anything but God himself to whose essence existence [necessarily] pertains; in the second place because it is not possible for me to conceive two or more Gods in this same position; and, granted that there is one such God who now exists, I see clearly that it is necessary that He should have existed from all eternity, and that He must exist eternally; and finally, because I know an infinitude of other properties in God, none of which I can either diminish or change.

For the rest, whatever proof or argument I avail myself of, we must always return to the point that it is only those things which we conceive clearly and distinctly that have the power of persuading me entirely. And although amongst the matters which I conceive of in this way, some indeed are manifestly obvious to all, while others only manifest themselves to those who consider them closely and examine them attentively; still, after they have once been discovered, the latter are not esteemed as any less certain that the former. For example, in the case of every right-angled triangle, although it does not so manifestly appear that the square of the base is equal to the squares of the two other sides as that this base is opposite to the greatest angle; still, when this has once been apprehended, we are just as certain of its truth as of the truth of the other. And as regards God, if my mind were not pre-occupied with prejudices, and if my thought did not find itself on all hands diverted by the continual pressure of sensible things, there would be nothing which I could know more immediately and more easily than Him. For is there anything more manifest than that there is a God, that is to say, a Supreme Being, to whose essence alone existence pertains?

And although for a firm grasp of this truth I have need of a strenuous application of mind, at present I not only feel myself to be as assured of it as of all that I hold as most certain, but I also remark that the certainty of all other things depends on it so absolutely, that without this knowledge it is impossible ever to know anything perfectly.

For although I am of such a nature that as long as I understand anything very clearly and distinctly, I am naturally impelled to believe it to be true, yet because I am also of such a nature that I cannot have my mind constantly fixed on the same object in order to perceive it clearly, and as I often recollect having formed a past judgment without at the same time properly recollecting the reasons that led me to make it, it may happen meanwhile that other reasons present themselves to me, which would easily cause me to change my opinion, if I were ignorant of the facts of the existence of God, and thus I should have no true and certain knowledge, but only vague and vacillating opinions. Thus, for example, when I consider the nature of a [rectilinear] triangle, I who have some little knowledge of the principles of geometry recognise quite clearly that the three angles are equal to two right angles, and it is not possible for me not to believe this so long as I apply my mind to its demonstration; but so soon as I abstain from attending to the proof, although I still recollect having clearly comprehended it, it may easily occur that I come to doubt its truth, if I am ignorant of there being a God. For I can persuade myself of having been so constituted by nature that I can easily deceive myself even in those matters which I believe myself to apprehend with the greatest evidence and certainty, especially when I recollect that I have frequently judged matters to be true and certain which other reasons have afterwards impelled me to judge to be altogether false.

But after I have recognised that there is a God—because at the same time I have also recognised that all things depend upon Him, and that He is not a deceiver, and from that have inferred that what I perceive clearly and distinctly cannot fail to be true—although I no longer pay attention to the reasons for which I have judged this to be true, provided that I recollect having clearly and distinctly perceived it, no contrary reason can be brought forward which could ever cause me to doubt of its truth; and thus I have a true and certain knowledge of it. And this same knowledge extends likewise to all other things which I recollect having formerly demonstrated, such as the truths of geometry and the like; for what can be alleged against them to cause me to place them in doubt? Will it be said that my nature is such as to cause me to be frequently deceived? But I already know that I cannot be deceived in the judgment whose grounds I know clearly. Will it be said that I formerly held many things to be true and certain which I have afterwards recognised to be false? But I had not had any clear and distinct knowledge of these things, and not as yet knowing the rule whereby I assure myself of the truth, I had been impelled to give my assent from reasons which I have since recognised to be less strong than I had at the time imagined them to be. What further objection can then be raised? That possibly I am dreaming (an objection I myself made a little while ago), or that all the thoughts which I now have are no more true than the phantasies of my dreams? But even though I slept the case would be the same, for all that is clearly present to my mind is absolutely true.

And so I very clearly recognise that the certainty and truth of all knowledge depends alone on the knowledge of the true God, in so much that, before I knew Him, I could not have a perfect knowledge of any other thing. And now that I know Him I have the means of acquiring a perfect knowledge of an infinitude of things, not only of those which relate to God Himself and other intellectual matters, but also of those which pertain to corporeal nature in so far as it is the object of pure mathematics [which have no concern with whether it exists or not].

GEORGE BERKELEY

Three Dialogues between Hylas and Philonous*

THE FIRST DIALOGUE

Philonous. Good morrow, Hylas. I did not expect to find you abroad so early.

Hylas. It is indeed something unusual; but my thoughts were so taken up with a subject I was discoursing of last night that, finding I could not sleep, I resolved to rise and take a turn in the garden.

Phil. It happened well, to let you see what innocent and agreeable pleasures you lose every morning. Can there be a pleasanter time of the day or a more delightful season of the year? That purple sky, these wild but sweet notes of birds, the fragrant bloom upon the trees and flowers, the gentle influence of the rising sun—these and a thousand nameless beauties of nature inspire the soul with secret transports; its faculties, too, being at this time fresh and lively, are fit for those meditations which the solitude of a garden and tranquility of the morning naturally dispose us to. But I am afraid I interrupt your thoughts, for you seemed very intent on something.

* From George Berkeley, *Three Dialogues between Hylas and Philonous, in Opposition to Skeptics and Atheists.* The First Dialogue and some objections and replies from the Third Dialogue. First published in 1713.

Hyl. It is true, I was, and shall be obliged to you if you will permit me to go on in the same vein; not that I would by any means deprive myself of your company, for my thoughts always flow more easily in conversation with a friend than when I am alone; but my request is that you would suffer me to impart my reflections to you.

Phil. With all my heart, it is what I should have requested myself if you had not prevented me.

Hyl. I was considering the odd fate of those men who have in all ages, through an affectation of being distinguished from the vulgar, or some unaccountable turn of thought, pretended either to believe nothing at all or to believe the most extravagant things in the world. This, however, might be borne if their paradoxes and skepticism did not draw after them some consequences of general disadvantage to mankind. But the mischief lies here: that when men of less leisure see them who are supposed to have spent their whole time in the pursuits of knowledge professing an entire ignorance of all things or advancing such notions as are repugnant to plain and commonly received principles, they will be tempted to entertain suspicions concerning the most important truths, which they had hitherto held sacred and unquestionable.

Phil. I entirely agree with you as to the ill tendency of the affected doubts of some philosophers and fantastical conceits of others. I am even so far gone of late in this way of thinking that I have quitted several of the sublime notions I had got in their schools for vulgar opinions. And I give it you on my word, since this revolt from metaphysical notions to the plain dictates of nature and common sense, I find my understanding strangely enlightened, so that I can now easily comprehend a great many things which before were all mystery and riddle.

Hyl. I am glad to find there was nothing in the accounts I heard of you.

Phil. Pray, what were those?

Hyl. You were represented in last night's conversation as one who maintained the most extravagant opinion that ever entered into the mind of man, to wit, that there is no such thing as "material substance" in the world.

Phil. That there is no such thing as what philosophers call "material substance," I am seriously persuaded; but if I were made to see anything absurd or skeptical in this, I should then have the same reason to renounce this that I imagine I have now to reject the contrary opinion.

Hyl. What! Can anything be more fantastical, more repugnant to common sense or a more manifest piece of skepticism than to believe there is no such thing as matter?

Phil. Softly, good Hylas. What if it should prove that you, who hold there is, are, by virtue of that opinion, a greater skeptic and maintain more paradoxes and repugnances to common sense than I who believe no such thing?

Hyl. You may as soon persuade me the part is greater than the whole, as that, in order to avoid absurdity and skepticism, I should ever be obliged to give up my opinion in this point.

Phil. Well then, are you content to admit that opinion for true which, upon examination, shall appear most agreeable to common sense and remote from skepticism?

Hyl. With all my heart. Since you are for raising disputes about the plainest things in nature, I am content for once to hear what you have to say.

Phil. Pray, Hylas, what do you mean by a "skeptic?"

Hyl. I mean what all men mean, one that doubts of everything.

Phil. He then who entertains no doubt concerning some particular point, with regard to that point cannot be thought a skeptic.

Hyl. I agree with you.

Phil. Whether does doubting consist in embracing the affirmative or negative side of a question?

Hyl. In neither; for whoever understands English cannot but know that *doubting* signifies a suspense between both.

Phil. He then that denies any point can no more be said to doubt of it than he who affirms it with the same degree of assurance.

Hyl. True.

Phil. And, consequently, for such his denial is no more to be esteemed a skeptic than the other.

Hyl. I acknowledge it.

Phil. How comes it to pass then, Hylas, that you pronounce me a skeptic because I deny what you affirm, to wit, the existence of matter? Since, for aught you can tell, I am as peremptory in my denial as you in your affirmation.

Hyl. Hold, Philonous, I have been a little out in my definition; but every false step a man makes in discourse is not to be insisted on. I said indeed that a "skeptic" was one who doubted of everything; but I should have added: or who denies the reality and truth of things.

Phil. What things? Do you mean the principles and theorems of sciences? But these you know are universal intellectual notions, and consequently independent of matter; the denial therefore of this does not imply the denying them.

Hyl. I grant it. But are there no other things? What think you of distrusting the senses, of denying the real existence of sensible things, or pretending to know nothing of them. Is not this sufficient to denominate a man a skeptic?

Phil. Shall we therefore examine which of us it is that denies the reality of sensible things or professes the greatest ignorance of them, since, if I take you rightly, he is to be esteemed the greatest skeptic?

Hyl. That is what I desire.

Phil. What mean you by "sensible things?"

Hyl. Those things which are perceived by the senses. Can you imagine that I mean anything else?

Phil. Pardon me, Hylas, if I am desirous clearly to apprehend your notions, since this may much shorten our inquiry. Suffer me then to ask you this further question. Are those things only perceived by the senses which are perceived immediately? Or may those things properly be said to be "sensible" which are perceived mediately, or not without the intervention of others?

Hyl. I do not sufficiently understand you.

Phil. In reading a book, what I immediately perceive are the letters, but mediately, or by means of these, are suggested to my mind the notions of God, virtue, truth, etc. Now, that the letters are truly sensible things, or perceived by sense, there is no doubt; but I would know whether you take the things suggested by them to be so too.

Hyl. No, certainly; it were absurd to think God or virtue sensible things, though they may be signified and suggested to the mind by sensible marks with which they have an arbitrary connection.

Phil. It seems, then, that by "sensible things" you mean those only which can be perceived immediately by sense.

Hyl. Right.

Phil. Does it not follow from this that, though I see one part of the sky red, and another blue, and that my reason does thence evidently conclude there must be some cause of that diversity of colors, yet that cause cannot be said to be a sensible thing or perceived by the sense of seeing?

Hyl. It does.

Phil. In like manner, though I hear variety of sounds, yet I cannot be said to hear the causes of those sounds.

Hyl. You cannot.

Phil. And when by my touch I perceive a thing to be hot and heavy, I cannot say, with any truth or propriety, that I feel the cause of its heat or weight.

Hyl. To prevent any more questions of this kind, I tell you once for all that by "sensible things" I mean those only which are perceived by sense, and that in truth the senses perceive nothing which they do not perceive immediately, for they make no inferences. The deducing therefore of causes or occasions from effects and appearances, which alone are perceived by sense, entirely relates to reason.

Phil. This point then is agreed between us—that *sensible things are those only which are immediately perceived by sense.* You will further inform me whether we immediately perceive by sight anything besides light and colors and figures; or by hearing, anything but sounds; by the palate, anything beside tastes; by the smell, besides odors; or by the touch, more than tangible qualities.

Hyl. We do not.

Phil. It seems, therefore, that if you take away all sensible qualities, there remains nothing sensible?

Hyl. I grant it.

Phil. Sensible things therefore are nothing else but so many sensible qualities or combinations of sensible qualities?

Hyl. Nothing else.

Phil. Heat is then a sensible thing?

Hyl. Certainly.

Phil. Does the reality of sensible things consist in being perceived, or is it something distinct from their being perceived, and that bears no relation to the mind?

Hyl. To *exist* is one thing, and to be *perceived* is another.

Phil. I speak with regard to sensible things only; and of these I ask, whether by their real existence you mean a subsistence exterior to the mind and distinct from their being perceived?

Hyl. I mean a real absolute being, distinct from and without any relation to their being perceived.

Phil. Heat therefore, if it be allowed a real being, must exist without the mind?

Hyl. It must.

Phil. Tell me, Hylas, is this real existence equally compatible to all degrees of heat, which we perceive, or is there any reason why we should attribute it to some and deny it to others? And if there be, pray let me know that reason.

Hyl. Whatever degree of heat we perceive by sense, we may be sure the same exists in the object that occasions it.

Phil. What! the greatest as well as the least?

Hyl. I tell you, the reason is plainly the same in respect of both: they are both perceived by sense; nay, the greater degree of heat is more sensibly perceived; and consequently, if there is any difference, we are more certain of its real existence than we can be of the reality of a lesser degree.

Phil. But is not the most vehement and intense degree of heat a very great pain?

Hyl. No one can deny it.

Phil. And is any unperceiving thing capable of pain or pleasure?

Hyl. No, certainly.

Phil. Is your material substance a senseless being or a being endowed with sense and perception?

Hyl. It is senseless, without doubt.

Phil. It cannot, therefore, be the subject of pain?

Hyl. By no means.

Phil. Nor, consequently, of the greatest heat perceived by sense, since you acknowledge this to be no small pain?

Hyl. I grant it.

Phil. What shall we say then of your external object: is it a material substance, or no?

Hyl. It is a material substance with the sensible qualities inhering in it.

Phil. How then can a great heat exist in it, since you own it cannot in a material substance? I desire you would clear this point.

Hyl. Hold, Philonous, I fear I was out in yielding intense heat to be a pain. It should seem rather that pain is something distinct from heat, and the consequence or effect of it.

Phil. Upon putting your hand near the fire, do you perceive one simple uniform sensation or two distinct sensations?

Hyl. But one simple sensation.

Phil. Is not the heat immediately perceived?

Hyl. It is.

Phil. And the pain?

Hyl. True.

Phil. Seeing therefore they are both immediately perceived at the same time, and the fire affects you only with one simple or uncompounded idea, it follows that this same simple idea is both the intense heat immediately perceived and the pain; and, consequently, that the intense heat immediately perceived is nothing distinct from a particular sort of pain.

Hyl. It seems so.

Phil. Again, try in your thoughts, Hylas, if you can conceive a vehement sensation to be without pain or pleasure.

Hyl. I cannot.

Phil. Or can you frame to yourself an idea of sensible pain or pleasure, in general, abstracted from every particular idea of heat, cold, tastes, smells, etc.?

Hyl. I do not find that I can.

Phil. Does it not therefore follow that sensible pain is nothing distinct from those sensations or ideas—in an intense degree?

Hyl. It is undeniable; and, to speak the truth, I begin to suspect a very great heat cannot exist but in a mind perceiving it.

Phil. What! are you then in that *skeptical* state of suspense, between affirming and denying?

Hyl. I think I may be positive in the point. A very violent and painful heat cannot exist without the mind.

Phil. It has not therefore, according to you, any real being?

Hyl. I own it.

Phil. Is it therefore certain that there is no body in nature really hot?

Hyl. I have not denied there is any real heat in bodies. I only say there is no such thing as an intense real heat.

Phil. But did you not say before that all degrees of heat were equally real, or, if there was any difference, that the greater were more undoubtedly real than the lesser?

Hyl. True; but it was because I did not then consider the ground there is for distinguishing between them, which I now plainly see. And it is this: because intense heat is nothing else but a particular kind of painful sensation, and pain cannot exist but in a perceiving being, it follows that no intense heat can really exist in an unperceiving corporeal substance. But this is no reason why we should deny heat in an inferior degree to exist in such a substance.

Phil. But how shall we be able to discern those degrees of heat which exist only in the mind from those which exist without it?

Hyl. That is no difficult matter. You know the least pain cannot exist unperceived; whatever, therefore, degree of heat is a pain exists only in the mind. But as for all other degrees of heat nothing obliges us to think the same of them.

Phil. I think you granted before that no unperceiving being was capable of pleasure any more than of pain.

Hyl. I did.

Phil. And is not warmth, or a more gentle degree of heat than what causes uneasiness, a pleasure?

Hyl. What then?

Phil. Consequently, it cannot exist without the mind in an unperceiving substance, or body.

Hyl. So it seems.

Phil. Since, therefore, as well those degrees of heat that are not painful, as those that are, can exist only in a thinking substance, may we not conclude that external bodies are absolutely incapable of any degree of heat whatsoever?

Hyl. On second thoughts, I do not think it is so evident that warmth is a pleasure as that a great degree of heat is a pain.

Phil. I do not pretend that warmth is as great a pleasure as heat is a pain. But if you grant it to be even a small pleasure, it serves to make good my conclusion.

Hyl. I could rather call it an "indolence." It seems to be nothing more than a privation of both pain and pleasure. And that such a quality or state as this may agree to an unthinking substance, I hope you will not deny.

Phil. If you are resolved to maintain that warmth, or a gentle degree of heat, is no pleasure, I know not how to convince you otherwise than by appealing to your own sense. But what think you of cold?

Hyl. The same that I do of heat. An intense degree of cold is a pain; for to feel a very great cold is to perceive a great uneasiness; it cannot therefore exist without the mind; but a lesser degree of cold may, as well as a lesser degree of heat.

Phil. Those bodies, therefore, upon whose application to our own we perceive a moderate degree of heat must be concluded to have a moderate degree of heat or warmth in them; and those upon whose application we feel a like degree of cold must be thought to have cold in them.

Hyl. They must.

Phil. Can any doctrine be true that necessarily leads a man into an absurdity?

Hyl. Without doubt it cannot.

Phil. Is it not an absurdity to think that the same thing should be at the same time both cold and warm?

Hyl. It is.

Phil. Suppose now one of your hands hot, and the other cold, and that they are both at once put into the same vessel of water, in an intermediate state, will not the water seem cold to one hand, and warm to the other?

Hyl. It will.

Phil. Ought we not therefore, by your principles, to conclude it is really both cold and warm at the same time, that is, according to your own concession, to believe an absurdity?

Hyl. I confess it seems so.

Phil. Consequently, the principles themselves are false, since you have granted that no true principle leads to an absurdity.

Hyl. But, after all, can anything be more absurd than to say, *there is no heat in the fire?*

Phil. To make the point still clearer; tell me whether, in two cases exactly alike, we ought not to make the same judgment?

Hyl. We ought.

Phil. When a pin pricks your finger, does it not rend and divide the fibres of your flesh?

Hyl. It does.

Phil. And when a coal burns your finger, does it any more?

Hyl. It does not.

Phil. Since, therefore, you neither judge the sensation itself occasioned by the pin, nor anything like it to be in the pin, you should not, conformably to what you have now granted, judge the sensation occasioned by the fire, or anything like it, to be in the fire.

Hyl. Well, since it must be so, I am content to yield this point and acknowledge that heat and cold are only sensations existing in our minds. But there still remain qualities enough to secure the reality of external things.

Phil. But what will you say, Hylas, if it shall appear that the case is the same with regard to all other sensible qualities, and that they can no more be supposed to exist without the mind than heat and cold?

Hyl. Then, indeed, you will have done something to the purpose; but that is what I despair of seeing proved.

Phil. Let us examine them in order. What think you of tastes—do they exist without the mind, or no?

Hyl. Can any man in his senses doubt whether sugar is sweet, or wormwood bitter?

Phil. Inform me, Hylas. Is a sweet taste a particular kind of pleasure or pleasant sensation, or is it not?

Hyl. It is.

Phil. And is not bitterness some kind of uneasiness or pain?

Hyl. I grant it.

Phil. If, therefore, sugar and wormwood are unthinking corporeal substances existing without the mind, how can sweetness and bitterness, that is, pleasure and pain, agree to them?

Hyl. Hold, Philonous. I now see what it was [that] deluded me all this time. You asked whether heat and cold, sweetness and bitterness, were not particular sorts of pleasure and pain; to which I answered simply that they were. Whereas I should have thus distinguished: those qualities as perceived by us are pleasures or pains, but not as existing in the external objects. We must not therefore conclude absolutely that there is no heat in the fire or sweetness in the sugar, but only that heat or sweetness, as perceived by us, are not in the fire or sugar. What say you to this?

Phil. I say it is nothing to the purpose. Our discourse proceeded altogether concerning sensible things, which you defined to be "the things we immediately perceive by our senses." Whatever other qualities, therefore, you speak of, as distinct from these, I know nothing of them, neither do they at all belong to the point in dispute. You may, indeed, pretend to have discovered certain qualities which you do not perceive and assert those insensible qualities exist in fire and sugar. But what use can be made of this to your present purpose, I am at a loss to conceive. Tell me then once more, do you acknowledge that heat and cold, sweetness and bitterness (meaning those qualities which are perceived by the senses), do not exist without the mind?

Hyl. I see it is to no purpose to hold out, so I give up the cause as to those mentioned qualities, though I profess it sounds oddly to say that sugar is not sweet.

Phil. But, for your further satisfaction, take this along with you: that which at other times seems sweet shall, to a distempered palate, appear bitter. And nothing can be plainer than that divers persons perceive different tastes in the same food, since that which one man delights in, another abhors. And how could this be if the taste was something really inherent in the food?

Hyl. I acknowledge I know not how.

Phil. In the next place, odors are to be considered. And with regard to these I would fain know whether what has been said of tastes does not exactly agree to them? Are they not so many pleasing or displeasing sensations?

Hyl. They are.

Phil. Can you then conceive it possible that they should exist in an unperceiving thing?

Hyl. I cannot.

Phil. Or can you imagine that filth and ordure affect those brute animals that feed on them out of choice with the same smells which we perceive in them?

Hyl. By no means.

Phil. May we not therefore conclude of smells, as of the other forementioned qualities, that they cannot exist in any but a perceiving substance or mind?

Hyl. I think so.

Phil. Then as to sounds, what must we think of them, are they accidents really inherent in external bodies or not?

Hyl. That they inhere not in the sonorous bodies is plain from hence; because a bell struck in the exhausted receiver of an air-pump sends forth no sound. The air, therefore, must be thought the subject of sound.

Phil. What reason is there for that, Hylas?

Hyl. Because, when any motion is raised in the air, we perceive a sound greater or less, in proportion to the air's motion; but without some motion in the air we never hear any sound at all.

Phil. And granting that we never hear a sound but when some motion is produced in the air, yet I do not see how you can infer from thence that the sound itself is in the air.

Hyl. It is this very motion in the external air that produces in the mind the sensation of sound. For, striking on the drum of the ear, it causes a vibration which by the auditory nerves being communicated to the brain, the soul is thereupon affected with the sensation called "sound."

Phil. What! is sound then a sensation?

Hyl. I tell you, as perceived by us it is a particular sensation in the mind.

Phil. And can any sensation exist without the mind?

Hyl. No, certainly.

Phil. How then can sound, being a sensation, exist in the air if by the "air" you mean a senseless substance existing without the mind?

Hyl. You must distinguish, Philonous, between sound as it is perceived by us, and as it is in itself; or (which is the same thing) between the sound we immediately perceive and that which exists without us. The former, indeed, is a particular kind of sensation, but the latter is merely a vibrative or undulatory motion in the air.

Phil. I thought I had already obviated that distinction by the answer I gave when you were applying it in a like case before. But, to say no more of that, are you sure then that sound is really nothing but motion?

Hyl. I am.

Phil. Whatever, therefore, agrees to real sound may with truth be attributed to motion?

Hyl. It may.

Phil. It is then good sense to speak of "motion" as of a thing that is *loud, sweet, acute,* or *grave.*

Hyl. I see you are resolved not to understand me. Is it not evident those accidents or modes belong only to sensible sound, or sound in the common acceptation of the word, but not to sound in the real and philosophic sense, which, as I just now told you, is nothing but a certain motion of the air?

Phil. It seems then there are two sorts of sound—the one vulgar, or that which is heard, the other philosophical and real?

Hyl. Even so.

Phil. And the latter consists in motion?

Hyl. I told you so before.

Phil. Tell me, Hylas, to which of the senses, think you, the idea of motion belongs? To the hearing?

Hyl. No, certainly; but to the sight and touch.

Phil. It should follow then that, according to you, real sounds may possibly be *seen* or *felt,* but never *heard.*

Hyl. Look you, Philonous, you may, if you please, make a jest of my opinion, but that will not alter the truth of things. I own, indeed, the inferences you draw me into sound something oddly, but common language, you know, is framed by, and for the use of, the vulgar. We must not therefore wonder if expressions adapted to exact philosophic notions seem uncouth and out of the way.

Phil. Is it come to that? I assure you I imagine myself to have gained no small point since you make so light of departing from common phrases and opinions, it being a main part of our inquiry to examine whose notions are widest of the common road and most repugnant to the general sense of the world. But can you think it no more than a philosophical paradox to say that "real sounds are never heard," and that the idea of them is obtained by some other sense? And is there nothing in this contrary to nature and the truth of things?

Hyl. To deal ingenuously, I do not like it. And, after the concessions already made, I had as well grant that sounds, too, have no real being without the mind.

Phil. And I hope you will make no difficulty to acknowledge the same of colors.

Hyl. Pardon me; the case of colors is very different. Can anything be plainer than that we see them on the objects?

Phil. The objects you speak of are, I suppose, corporeal substances existing without the mind?

Hyl. They are.

Phil. And have true and real colors inhering in them?

Hyl. Each visible object has that color which we see in it.

Phil. How! is there anything visible but what we perceive by sight?

Hyl. There is not.

Phil. And do we perceive anything by sense which we do not perceive immediately?

Hyl. How often must I be obliged to repeat the same thing? I tell you, we do not.

Phil. Have patience, good Hylas, and tell me once more whether there is anything immediately perceived by the senses except sensible qualities. I know you asserted there was not; but I would now be informed whether you still persist in the same opinion.

Hyl. I do.

Phil. Pray, is your corporeal substance either a sensible quality or made up of sensible qualities?

Hyl. What a question that is! Who ever thought it was?

Phil. My reason for asking was, because in saying "each visible object has that color which we see in it," you make visible objects to be corporeal substances, which implies either that corporeal substances are sensible qualities or else that there is something besides sensible qualities perceived by sight; but as this point was formerly agreed between us, and is still maintained by you, it is a clear consequence that your corporeal substance is nothing distinct from sensible qualities.

Hyl. You may draw as many absurd consequences as you please and endeavor to perplex the plainest things, but you shall never persuade me out of my senses. I clearly understand my own meaning.

Phil. I wish you would make me understand it, too. But, since you are unwilling to have your notion of corporeal substance examined, I shall urge that point no further. Only be pleased to let me know whether the same colors which we see exist in external bodies or some other.

Hyl. The very same.

Phil. What! are then the beautiful red and purple we see on yonder clouds really in them? Or do you imagine they have in themselves any other form than that of a dark mist or vapor?

Hyl. I must own, Philonous, those colors are not really in the clouds as they seem to be at this distance. They are only apparent colors.

Phil. "Apparent" call you them? How shall we distinguish these apparent colors from real?

Hyl. Very easily. Those are to be thought apparent which, appearing only at a distance, vanish upon a nearer approach.

Phil. And those, I suppose, are to be thought real which are discovered by the most near and exact survey.

Hyl. Right.

Phil. Is the nearest and exactest survey made by the help of a microscope or by the naked eye?

Hyl. By a microscope, doubtless.

Phil. But a microscope often discovers colors in an object different from those perceived by the unassisted sight. And, in case we had microscopes magnifying to any assigned degree, it is certain that no object whatsoever, viewed through them, would appear in the same color which it exhibits to the naked eye.

Hyl. And what will you conclude from all this? You cannot argue that there are really and naturally no colors on objects because by artificial managements they may be altered or made to vanish.

Phil. I think it may evidently be concluded from your own concessions that all the colors we see with our naked eyes are only apparent as those on the clouds, since they vanish upon a more close and accurate inspection which is afforded us by a microscope. Then, as to what you say by way of prevention: I ask you whether the real and natural state of an object is better discovered by a very sharp and piercing sight or by one which is less sharp?

Hyl. By the former without doubt.

Phil. Is it not plain from dioptrics that microscopes make the sight more penetrating and represent objects as they would appear to the eye in case it were naturally endowed with a most exquisite sharpness?

Hyl. It is.

Phil. Consequently, the microscopical representation is to be thought that which best sets forth the real nature of the thing, or what it is in itself. The colors, therefore, by it perceived are more genuine and real than those perceived otherwise.

Hyl. I confess there is something in what you say.

Phil. Besides, it is not only possible but manifest that there actually are animals whose eyes are by nature framed to perceive those things which by reason of their minuteness escape our sight. What think you of those inconceivably small animals perceived by glasses? Must we suppose they are all stark blind? Or, in case they see, can it be imagined their sight has not the same use in preserving their bodies from injuries which appears in that of all other animals? And if it has, is it not evident they must see particles less than their own bodies, which will present them with a far different view in each object from that which strikes our senses? Even our own eyes do not always represent objects to us after the same manner. In the jaundice everyone knows that all things seem yellow. Is it not therefore highly probable those animals in whose eyes we discern a very different texture from that of ours, and whose bodies abound with different humors, do not see the same colors in every object that we do? From all which should it not seem to follow that all colors are equally apparent, and that none of those which we perceive are really inherent in any outward object?

Hyl. It should.

Phil. The point will be past all doubt if you consider that, in case colors were real properties or affections inherent in external bodies, they could admit of no alteration without some change wrought in the very bodies themselves; but is it not evident from what has been said that, upon the use of microscopes, upon a change happening in the humors of the eye, or a variation of distance, without any manner of real alteration in the thing itself, the colors of any object are either changed or totally disappear? Nay, all other circumstances remaining the same, change but the situation of some objects and they shall present different colors to the eye. The same thing happens upon viewing an object in various degrees of light. And what is more known than that the same bodies appear differently colored by candlelight from what they do in the open day? Add to these the experiment of a prism which, separating the heterogeneous rays of light, alters the color of any object and will cause the whitest to appear of a deep blue or red to the naked eye. And now tell me whether you are still of opinion that every body has its true real color inhering in it; and if you think it has, I would fain know further from you what certain distance and position of the object, what peculiar texture and formation of the eye, what degree or kind of light is necessary for ascertaining that true color and distinguishing it from apparent ones.

Hyl. I own myself entirely satisfied that they are all equally apparent and that there is no such thing as color really inhering in external bodies, but that it is altogether in the light. And what confirms me in this opinion is that in proportion to the light colors are still more or less vivid; and if there be no light, then are there no colors perceived. Besides, allowing there are colors on external objects, yet, how is it possible for us to perceive them? For no external body affects the mind unless it acts first on our organs of sense. But the only action of bodies is motion, and motion cannot be communicated otherwise than by impulse. A distant object, therefore, cannot act on the eye, nor consequently make itself or its properties perceivable to the soul. Whence it plainly follows that it is immediately some contiguous substance which, operating on the eye, occasions a perception of colors; and such is light.

Phil. How! is light then a substance?

Hyl. I tell you, Philonous, external light is nothing but a thin fluid substance whose minute particles, being agitated with a brisk motion and in various manners reflected from the different surfaces of outward objects to the eyes, communicate different motions to the optic nerves; which, being propagated to the brain, cause therein various impressions, and these are attended with the sensations of red, blue, yellow, etc.

Phil. It seems, then, the light does no more than shake the optic nerves.

Hyl. Nothing else.

Phil. And, consequent to each particular motion of the nerves, the mind is affected with a sensation which is some particular color.

Hyl. Right.

Phil. And these sensations have no existence without the mind.

Hyl. They have not.

Phil. How then do you affirm that colors are in the light, since by "light" you understand a corporeal substance external to the mind?

Hyl. Light and colors, as immediately perceived by us, I grant cannot exist without the mind. But in themselves they are only the motions and configurations of certain insensible particles of matter.

Phil. Colors, then, in the vulgar sense, or taken for the immediate objects of sight, cannot agree to any but a perceiving substance.

Hyl. That is what I say.

Phil. Well then, since you give up the point as to those sensible qualities which are alone thought colors by all mankind besides, you may hold what you please with regard to those invisible ones of the philosophers. It is not my business to dispute about them; only I would advise you to bethink yourself whether, considering the inquiry we are upon, it be prudent for you to affirm—*the red and blue which we see are not real colors, but certain unknown motions and figures which no man ever did or can see are truly so.* Are not these shocking notions, and are not they subject to as many ridiculous inferences as those you were obliged to renounce before in the case of sounds?

Hyl. I frankly own, Philonous, that it is in vain to stand out any longer. Colors, sounds, tastes, in a word, all those termed "secondary qualities," have certainly no existence without the mind. But by this acknowledgment I must not be supposed to derogate anything from the reality of matter or external objects; seeing it is no more than several philosophers maintain, who nevertheless are the farthest imaginable from denying matter. For the clearer understanding of this you must know sensible qualities are by philosophers divided into "primary" and "secondary." The former are extension, figure, solidity, gravity, motion, and rest. And these they hold exist really in bodies. The latter are those above enumerated, or, briefly, all sensible qualities besides the primary, which they assert are only so many sensations or ideas existing nowhere but in the mind. But all this, I doubt not, you are already apprised of. For my part I have been a long time sensible there was such an opinion current among philosophers, but was never thoroughly convinced of its truth till now.

Phil. You are still then of opinion that *extension* and *figures* are inherent in external unthinking substances?

Hyl. I am.

Phil. But what if the same arguments which are brought against secondary qualities will hold good against these also?

Hyl. Why then I shall be obliged to think they too exist only in the mind.

Phil. Is it your opinion the very figure and extension which you perceive by sense exist in the outward object or material substance?

Hyl. It is.

Phil. Have all other animals as good grounds to think the same of the figure and extension which they see and feel?

Hyl. Without doubt, if they have any thought at all.

Phil. Answer me, Hylas. Think you the senses were bestowed upon all animals for their preservation and well-being in life? Or were they given to men alone for this end?

Hyl. I make no question but they have the same use in all other animals.

Phil. If so, is it not necessary they should be enabled by them to perceive their own limbs and those bodies which are capable of harming them?

Hyl. Certainly.

Phil. A mite therefore must be supposed to see his own foot, and things equal or even less than it, as bodies of some considerable dimension, though at the same time they appear to you scarce discernible or at best as so many visible points?

Hyl. I cannot deny it.

Phil. And to creatures less than the mite they will seem yet larger?

Hyl. They will.

Phil. Insomuch that what you can hardly discern will to another extremely minute animal appear as some huge mountain?

Hyl. All this I grant.

Phil. Can one and the same thing be at the same time in itself of different dimensions?

Hyl. That were absurd to imagine.

Phil. But from what you have laid down it follows that both the extension by you perceived and that perceived by the mite itself, as likewise all those perceived by lesser animals, are each of them the true extension of the mite's foot; that is to say, by your own principles you are led into an absurdity.

Hyl. There seems to be some difficulty in the point.

Phil. Again, have you not acknowledged that no real inherent property of any object can be changed without some change in the thing itself?

Hyl. I have.

Phil. But, as we approach to or recede from an object, the visible extension varies, being at one distance ten or a hundred times greater than at another. Does it not therefore follow from hence likewise that it is not really inherent in the object?

Hyl. I own I am at a loss what to think.

Phil. Your judgment will soon be determined if you will venture to think as freely concerning this quality as you have done concerning the rest.

Was it not admitted as a good argument that neither heat nor cold was in the water because it seemed warm to one hand and cold to the other?

Hyl. It was.

Phil. Is it not the very same reasoning to conclude there is no extension or figure in an object because to one eye it shall seem little, smooth, and round, when at the same time it appears to the other great, uneven, and angular?

Hyl. The very same. But does this latter fact ever happen?

Phil. You may at any time make the experiment by looking with one eye bare and with the other through a microscope.

Hyl. I know not how to maintain it, and yet I am loath to give up *extension;* I see so many odd consequences following upon such a concession.

Phil. Odd, say you? After the concessions already made, I hope you will stick at nothing for its oddness. [But,[1] on the other hand, should it not seem very odd if the general reasoning which includes all other sensible qualities did not also include extension? If it be allowed that no idea nor anything like an idea can exist in an unperceiving substance, then surely it follows that no figure or mode of extension, which we can either perceive or imagine, or have any idea of, can be really inherent in matter, not to mention the peculiar difficulty there must be in conceiving a material substance, prior to and distinct from extension, to be the *substratum* of extension. Be the sensible quality what it will—figure or sound or color—it seems alike impossible it should subsist in that which does not perceive it.]

Hyl. I give up the point for the present, reserving still a right to retract my opinion in case I shall hereafter discover any false step in my progress to it.

Phil. That is a right you cannot be denied. Figures and extension being dispatched, we proceed next to *motion*. Can a real motion in any external body be at the same time both very swift and very slow?

Hyl. It cannot.

Phil. Is not the motion of a body swift in a reciprocal proportion to the time it takes up in describing any given space? Thus a body that describes a mile in an hour moves three times faster than it would in case it described only a mile in three hours.

Hyl. I agree with you.

Phil. And is not time measured by the succession of ideas in our minds?

Hyl. It is.

Phil. And is it not possible ideas should succeed one another twice as fast in your mind as they do in mine, or in that of some spirit of another kind?

Hyl. I own it.

Phil. Consequently, the same body may to another seem to perform its motion over any space in half the time that it does to you. And the same reasoning will hold as to any other proportion; that is to say, according to your principles (since the motions perceived are both really in the object) it is possible one and the same body shall be really moved the same way at once, both very swift and very slow. How is this consistent either with common sense or with what you just now granted?

Hyl. I have nothing to say to it.

Phil. Then as for *solidity;* either you do not mean any sensible quality by that word, and so it is beside our inquiry; or if you do, it must be either hardness or resistance. But both the one and the other are plainly relative to our senses: it being evident that what seems hard to one animal may appear soft to another who has greater force and firmness of limbs. Nor is it less plain that the resistance I feel is not in the body.

Hyl. I own the very sensation of resistance, which is all you immediately perceive, is not in the *body,* but the cause of that sensation is.

Phil. But the causes of our sensations are not things immediately perceived, and therefore not sensible. This point I thought had been already determined.

Hyl. I own it was; but you will pardon me if I seem a little embarrassed; I know not how to quit my old notions.

Phil. To help you out, do but consider that if *extension* be once acknowledged to have no existence without the mind, the same must necessarily be granted of motion, solidity, and gravity, since they all evidently suppose extension. It is therefore superfluous to inquire particularly concerning each of them. In denying extension, you have denied them all to have any real existence.

[1] The remainder of the present paragraph did not appear in the first and second editions.

Hyl. I wonder, Philonous, if what you say be true, why those philosophers who deny the secondary qualities any real existence should yet attribute it to the primary. If there is no difference between them, how can this be accounted for?

Phil. It is not my business to account for every opinion of the philosophers. But, among other reasons which may be assigned for this, it seems probable that pleasure and pain being rather annexed to the former than the latter may be one. Heat and cold, tastes and smells have something more vividly pleasing or disagreeable than the ideas of extension, figure, and motion affect us with. And, it being too visibly absurd to hold that pain or pleasure can be in an unperceiving substance, men are more easily weaned from believing the external existence of the secondary than the primary qualities. You will be satisfied there is something in this if you recollect the difference you made between an intense and more moderate degree of heat, allowing the one a real existence while you denied it to the other. But, after all, there is no rational ground for that distinction, for surely an indifferent sensation is as truly a *sensation* as one more pleasing or painful, and consequently should not any more than they be supposed to exist in an unthinking subject.

Hyl. It is just come into my head, Philonous, that I have somewhere heard of a distinction between *absolute* and *sensible* extension. Now though it be acknowledged that *great* and *small,* consisting merely in the relation which other extended beings have to the parts of our own bodies, do not really inhere in the substances themselves, yet nothing obliges us to hold the same with regard to *absolute* extension, which is something abstracted from *great* and *small,* from this or that particular magnitude or figure. So likewise as to motion: *swift* and *slow* are altogether relative to the succession of ideas in our own minds. But it does not follow, because those modifications of motion exist not without the mind, that therefore absolute motion abstracted from them does not.

Phil. Pray what is it that distinguishes one motion, or one part of extension, from another? Is it not something sensible, as some degree of swiftness or slowness, some certain magnitude or figure peculiar to each?

Hyl. I think so.

Phil. These qualities, therefore, stripped of all sensible properties, are without all specific and numerical differences, as the schools call them.

Hyl. They are.

Phil. That is to say, they are extension in general, and motion in general.

Hyl. Let it be so.

Phil. But it is a universally received maxim that *everything which exists is particular.* How then can motion in general, or extension in general, exist in any corporeal substance?

Hyl. I will take time to solve your difficulty.

Phil. But I think the point may be speedily decided. Without doubt you can tell whether you are able to frame this or that idea. Now I am content to put our dispute on this issue. If you can frame in your thoughts a distinct abstract idea of motion or extension divested of all those sensible modes as swift and slow, great and small, round and square, and the like, which are acknowledged to exist only in the mind, I will then yield the point you contend for. But if you cannot, it will be unreasonable on your side to insist any longer upon what you have no notion of.

Hyl. To confess ingenuously, I cannot.

Phil. Can you even separate the ideas of extension and motion from the ideas of all those qualities which they who make the distinction term "secondary?"

Hyl. What! is it not an easy matter to consider extension and motion by themselves, abstracted from all other sensible qualities? Pray how do the mathematicians treat of them?

Phil. I acknowledge, Hylas, it is not difficult to form general propositions and reasonings about those qualities without mentioning any other, and, in this sense, to consider or treat of them abstractedly. But how does it follow that, because I can pronounce the word "motion" by itself, I can form the idea of it in my mind exclusive of body? Or because theorems may be made of extension and figures, without any mention of *great* or *small,* or any other sensible mode or quality, that therefore it is possible such an abstract idea of extension, without any particular size or figure or sensible quality, should be distinctly formed and apprehended by the mind? Mathematicians treat of quantity without regarding what other sensible qualities it is attended with, as being altogether indifferent to their demonstrations. But when, laying aside the words, they contemplate the bare ideas, I believe you will find they are not the pure abstracted ideas of extension.

Hyl. But what say you to *pure intellect?* May not abstracted ideas be framed by that faculty?

Phil. Since I cannot frame abstract ideas at all, it is plain I cannot frame them by the help of pure intellect, whatsoever faculty you understand by those words. Besides, not to inquire into the nature of pure intellect and its spiritual objects, as *virtue, reason, God,* or the like, thus much seems manifest that sensible things are only to be perceived by sense or represented by the imagination. Figures, therefore, and extension, being originally perceived by sense, do not belong to pure intellect; but, for your further satisfaction, try if you can frame the idea of any figure abstracted from all particularities of size or even from other sensible qualities.

Hyl. Let me think a little—I do not find that I can.

Phil. And can you think it possible that should really exist in nature which implies a repugnancy in its conception?

Hyl. By no means.

Phil. Since therefore it is impossible even for the mind to disunite the ideas of extension and motion from all other sensible qualities, does it not follow that where the one exist there necessarily the other exist likewise?

Hyl. It should seem so.

Phil. Consequently, the very same arguments which you admitted as conclusive against the secondary qualities are, without any further application of force, against the primary, too. Besides, if you will trust your senses, is it not plain all sensible qualities coexist, or to them appear as being in the same place? Do they ever represent a motion or figure as being divested of all other visible and tangible qualities?

Hyl. You need say no more on this head. I am free to own, if there be no secret error or oversight in our proceedings hitherto, that all sensible qualities are alike to be denied existence without the mind. But my fear is that I have been too liberal in my former concessions, or overlooked some fallacy or other. In short, I did not take time to think.

Phil. For that matter, Hylas, you may take what time you please in reviewing the progress of our inquiry. You are at liberty to recover any slips you might have made, or offer whatever you have omitted which makes for your first opinion.

Hyl. One great oversight I take to be this—that I did not sufficiently distinguish the *object* from the *sensation.* Now, though this latter may not exist without the mind, yet it will not thence follow that the former cannot.

Phil. What object do you mean? The object of the senses?

Hyl. The same.

Phil. It is then immediately perceived?

Hyl. Right.

Phil. Make me to understand the difference between what is immediately perceived and a sensation.

Hyl. The sensation I take to be an act of the mind perceiving; besides which there is something perceived, and this I call the "object." For example, there is red and yellow on that tulip. But then the act of perceiving those colors is in me only, and not in the tulip.

Phil. What tulip do you speak of? Is it that which you see?

Hyl. The same.

Phil. And what do you see besides color, figure, and extension?

Hyl. Nothing.

Phil. What you would say then is that the red and yellow are coexistent with the extension; is it not?

Hyl. That is not all; I would say they have a real existence without the mind, in some unthinking substance.

Phil. That the colors are really in the tulip which I see is manifest. Neither can it be denied that this tulip may exist independent of your mind or mine; but that any immediate object of the senses—that is, any idea, or combination of ideas—should exist in an unthinking substance, or exterior to all minds, is in itself an evident contradiction. Nor can I imagine how this follows from what you said just now, to wit, that the red and yellow were on the tulip *you saw,* since you do not pretend to *see* that unthinking substance.

Hyl. You have an artful way, Philonous, of diverting our inquiry from the subject.

Phil. I see you have no mind to be pressed that way. To return then to your distinction between *sensation* and *object;* if I take you right, you distinguish in every perception two things, the one an action of the mind, the other not.

Hyl. True.

Phil. And this action cannot exist in, or belong to, any unthinking thing, but whatever besides is implied in a perception may?

Hyl. That is my meaning.

Phil. So that if there was a perception without any act of the mind, it were possible such a perception should exist in an unthinking substance?

Hyl. I grant it. But it is impossible there should be such a perception.

Phil. When is the mind said to be active?

Hyl. When it produces, puts an end to, or changes anything.

Phil. Can the mind produce, discontinue, or change anything but by an act of the will?

Hyl. It cannot.

Phil. The mind therefore is to be accounted *active* in its perceptions so far forth as *volition* is included in them?

Hyl. It is.

Phil. In plucking this flower I am active, because I do it by the motion of my hand, which was consequent upon my volition; so likewise in applying it to my nose. But is either of these smelling?

Hyl. No.

Phil. I act, too, in drawing the air through my nose, because my breathing so rather than otherwise is the effect of my volition. But neither can this be called "smelling," for if it were I should smell every time I breathed in that manner?

Hyl. True.

Phil. Smelling then is somewhat consequent to all this?

Hyl. It is.

Phil. But I do not find my will concerned any further. Whatever more there is—as that I perceive such a particular smell, or any smell at all—this is independent of my will, and therein I am altogether passive. Do you find it otherwise with you, Hylas?

Hyl. No, the very same.

Phil. Then, as to seeing, it is not in your power to open your eyes or keep them shut, to turn them this or that way?

Hyl. Without doubt.

Phil. But does it in like manner depend on your will that in looking on this flower you perceive *white* rather than any other color? Or, directing your open eyes toward yonder part of the heaven, can you avoid seeing the sun? Or is light or darkness the effect of your volition?

Hyl. No, certainly.

Phil. You are then in these respects altogether passive?

Hyl. I am.

Phil. Tell me now whether *seeing* consists in perceiving light and colors or in opening and turning the eyes?

Hyl. Without doubt, in the former.

Phil. Since, therefore, you are in the very perception of light and colors altogether passive, what is become of that action you were speaking of as an ingredient in every sensation? And does it not follow from your own concessions that the perception of light and colors, including no action in it, may exist in an unperceiving substance? And is not this a plain contradiction?

Hyl. I know not what to think of it.

Phil. Besides, since you distinguish the *active* and *passive* in every perception, you must do it in that of pain. But how is it possible that pain, be it as little active as you please, should exist in an unperceiving substance? In short, do but consider the point and then confess ingenuously whether light and colors, tastes, sounds, etc. are not all equally passions or sensations in the soul. You may indeed call them "external objects" and give them in words what subsistence you please. But examine your own thoughts and then tell me whether it be not as I say?

Hyl. I acknowledge, Philonous, that, upon a fair observation of what passes in my mind, I can discover nothing else but that I am a thinking being affected with variety of sensations, neither is it possible to conceive how a sensation should exist in an unperceiving substance. But then, on the other hand, when I look on sensible things in a different view, considering them as so many modes and qualities, I find it necessary to suppose a material *substratum,* without which they cannot be conceived to exist.

Phil. "Material substratum" call you it? Pray, by which of your senses came you acquainted with that being?

Hyl. It is not itself sensible; its modes and qualities only being perceived by the senses.

Phil. I presume then it was by reflection and reason you obtained the idea of it?

Hyl. I do not pretend to any proper positive idea of it. However, I conclude it exists because qualities cannot be conceived to exist without a support.

Phil. It seems then you have only a relative

notion of it, or that you conceive it not otherwise than by conceiving the relation it bears to sensible qualities?

Hyl. Right.

Phil. Be pleased, therefore, to let me know wherein that relation consists.

Hyl. Is it not sufficiently expressed in the term "substratum" or "substance?"

Phil. If so, the word "substratum" should import that it is spread under the sensible qualities or accidents?

Hyl. True.

Phil. And consequently under extension?

Hyl. I own it.

Phil. It is therefore somewhat in its own nature entirely distinct from extension?

Hyl. I tell you extension is only a mode, and matter is something that supports modes. And is it not evident the thing supported is different from the thing supporting?

Phil. So that something distinct from, and exclusive of, extension is supposed to be the *substratum* of extension?

Hyl. Just so.

Phil. Answer me, Hylas, can a thing be spread without extension, or is not the idea of extension necessarily included in *spreading?*

Hyl. It is.

Phil. Whatsoever therefore you suppose spread under anything must have in itself an extension distinct from the extension of that thing under which it is spread?

Hyl. It must.

Phil. Consequently, every corporeal substance being the *substratum* of extension must have in itself another extension by which it is qualified to be a *substratum,* and so on to infinity? And I ask whether this be not absurd in itself and repugnant to what you granted just now, to wit, that the *substratum* was something distinct from and exclusive of extension?

Hyl. Aye, but, Philonous, you take me wrong. I do not mean that matter is *spread* in a gross literal sense under extension. The word "substratum" is used only to express in general the same thing with "substance."

Phil. Well then, let us examine the relation implied in the term "substance." Is it not that it stands under accidents?

Hyl. The very same.

Phil. But that one thing may stand under or support another, must it not be extended?

Hyl. It must.

Phil. Is not therefore this supposition liable to the same absurdity with the former?

Hyl. You still take things in a strict literal sense; that is not fair, Philonous.

Phil. I am not for imposing any sense on your words; you are at liberty to explain them as you please. Only, I beseech you, make me understand something by them. You tell me matter supports or stands under accidents. How! is it as your legs support your body?

Hyl. No; that is the literal sense.

Phil. Pray let me know any sense, literal or not literal, that you understand it in.—How long must I wait for an answer, Hylas?

Hyl. I declare I know not what to say. I once thought I understood well enough what was meant by matter's supporting accidents. But now, the more I think on it, the less can I comprehend it; in short, I find that I know nothing of it.

Phil. It seems then you have no idea at all, neither relative nor positive, of matter; you know neither what it is in itself nor what relation it bears to accidents?

Hyl. I acknowledge it.

Phil. And yet you asserted that you could not conceive how qualities or accidents should really exist without conceiving at the same time a material support of them?

Hyl. I did.

Phil. That is to say, when you conceive the real existence of qualities, you do withal conceive something which you cannot conceive?

Hyl. It was wrong I own. But still I fear there is some fallacy or other. Pray, what think you of this? It is just come into my head that the ground of all our mistake lies in your treating of each quality by itself. Now I grant that each quality cannot singly subsist without the mind. Color cannot without extension, neither can figure without some other sensible quality. But, as the several qualities united or blended together form entire sensible things, nothing hinders why such things may not be supposed to exist without the mind.

Phil. Either, Hylas, you are jesting or have a very bad memory. Though, indeed, we went through all the qualities by name one after another, yet my arguments, or rather your concessions, nowhere tended to prove that the secondary qualities did not subsist each alone by itself, but that they were not *at all* without the mind. Indeed, in treating of figure and motion we concluded they could not exist without the mind, because it was impossible even in thought to separate them from all secondary qualities, so as to conceive them existing by themselves. But then this was not the only argument made use of upon that occasion. But (to pass by all that has been hitherto said and reckon it for nothing, if you will have it so) I am content to put the whole upon this issue. If you can conceive it possible for any mixture or combination of qualities, or any sensible object whatever, to exist without the mind, then I will grant it actually to be so.

Hyl. If it comes to that the point will soon be decided. What more easy than to conceive a tree or house existing by itself, independent of, and unperceived by, any mind whatsoever? I do at this present time conceive them existing after that manner.

Phil. How say you, Hylas, can you see a thing which is at the same time unseen?

Hyl. No, that were a contradiction.

Phil. Is it not as great a contradiction to talk of *conceiving* a thing which is *unconceived?*

Hyl. It is.

Phil. The tree or house, therefore, which you think of is conceived by you?

Hyl. How should it be otherwise?

Phil. And what is conceived is surely in the mind?

Hyl. Without question, that which is conceived is in the mind.

Phil. How then came you to say you conceived a house or tree existing independent and out of all minds whatsoever?

Hyl. That was I own an oversight, but stay, let me consider what led me into it.—It is a pleasant mistake enough. As I was thinking of a tree in a solitary place where no one was present to see it, methought that was to conceive a tree as existing unperceived or unthought of, not considering that I myself conceived it all the while. But now I plainly see that all I can do is to frame ideas in my own mind. I may indeed conceive in my own thoughts the idea of a tree, or a house, or a mountain, but that is all. And this is far from proving that I can conceive them *existing out of the minds of all spirits.*

Phil. You acknowledge then that you cannot possibly conceive how any one corporeal sensible thing should exist otherwise than in a mind?

Hyl. I do.

Phil. And yet you will earnestly contend for the truth of that which you cannot so much as conceive?

Hyl. I profess I know not what to think; but still there are some scruples remain with me. Is it not certain I see things at a distance? Do we not perceive the stars and moon, for example, to be a great way off? Is not this, I say, manifest to the senses?

Phil. Do you not in a dream, too, perceive those or the like objects?

Hyl. I do.

Phil. And have they not then the same appearance of being distant?

Hyl. They have.

Phil. But you do not thence conclude the apparitions in a dream to be without the mind?

Hyl. By no means.

Phil. You ought not therefore to conclude that sensible objects are without the mind, from their appearance or manner wherein they are perceived.

Hyl. I acknowledge it. But does not my sense deceive me in those cases?

Phil. By no means. The idea or thing which you immediately perceive, neither sense nor reason informs you that it actually exists without the mind. By sense you only know that you are affected with such certain sensations of light and colors, etc. And these you will not say are without the mind.

Hyl. True, but, besides all that, do you not think the sight suggests something of *outness* or *distance?*

Phil. Upon approaching a distant object, do the visible size and figure change perpetually or do they appear the same at all distances?

Hyl. They are in a continual change.

Phil. Sight, therefore, does not suggest or any way inform you that the visible object you immediately perceive exists at a distance,[2] or will be perceived when you advance farther onward, there being a continued series of visible objects

[2] See the author's *An Essay towards a New Theory of Vision* (1709) and *The Theory of Vision Vindicated and Explained* (1733).

succeeding each other during the whole time of your approach.

Hyl. It does not; but still I know, upon seeing an object, what object I shall perceive after having passed over a certain distance; no matter whether it be exactly the same or no, there is still something of distance suggested in the case.

Phil. Good Hylas, do but reflect a little on the point, and then tell me whether there be any more in it than this. From the ideas you actually perceive by sight, you have by experience learned to collect what other ideas you will (according to the standing order of nature) be affected with, after such a certain succession of time and motion.

Hyl. Upon the whole, I take it to be nothing else.

Phil. Now is it not plain that if we suppose a man born blind was on a sudden made to see, he could at first have no experience of what may be suggested by sight?

Hyl. It is.

Phil. He would not then, according to you, have any notion of distance annexed to the things he saw, but would take them for a new set of sensations existing only in his mind?

Hyl. It is undeniable.

Phil. But to make it still more plain: is not *distance* a line turned endwise to the eye?

Hyl. It is.

Phil. And can a line so situated be perceived by sight?

Hyl. It cannot.

Phil. Does it not therefore follow that distance is not properly and immediately perceived by sight?

Hyl. It should seem so.

Phil. Again, it is your opinion that colors are at a distance?

Hyl. It must be acknowledged they are only in the mind.

Phil. But do not colors appear to the eye as coexisting in the same place with extension and figures?

Hyl. They do.

Phil. How can you then conclude from sight that figures exist without, when you acknowledge colors do not; the sensible appearance being the very same with regard to both?

Hyl. I know not what to answer.

Phil. But allowing that distance was truly and immediately perceived by the mind, yet it would not thence follow it existed out of the mind. For whatever is immediately perceived is an idea; and can any *idea* exist out of the mind?

Hyl. To suppose that were absurd; but, inform me, Philonous, can we perceive or know nothing besides our ideas?

Phil. As for the rational deducing of causes from effects, that is beside our inquiry. And by the senses you can best tell whether you perceive anything which is not immediately perceived. And I ask you whether the things immediately perceived are other than your own sensations or ideas? You have indeed more than once, in the course of this conversation, declared yourself on those points, but you seem, by this last question, to have departed from what you then thought.

Hyl. To speak the truth, Philonous, I think there are two kinds of objects: the one perceived immediately, which are likewise called "ideas"; the other are real things or external objects, perceived by the mediation of ideas which are their images and representations. Now I own ideas do not exist without the mind, but the latter sort of objects do. I am sorry I did not think of this distinction sooner; it would probably have cut short your discourse.

Phil. Are those external objects perceived by sense or by some other faculty?

Hyl. They are perceived by sense.

Phil. How! is there anything perceived by sense which is not immediately perceived?

Hyl. Yes, Philonous, in some sort there is. For example, when I look on a picture or statue of Julius Caesar, I may be said, after a manner, to perceive him (though not immediately) by my senses.

Phil. It seems then you will have our ideas, which alone are immediately perceived, to be pictures of external things: and that these also are perceived by sense inasmuch as they have a conformity or resemblance to our ideas?

Hyl. That is my meaning.

Phil. And in the same way that Julius Caesar, in himself invisible, is nevertheless perceived by sight, real things, in themselves imperceptible, are perceived by sense.

Hyl. In the very same.

Phil. Tell me, Hylas, when you behold the picture of Julius Caesar, do you see with your eyes any more than some colors and figures, with a certain symmetry and composition of the whole?

Hyl. Nothing else.

Phil. And would not a man who had never known anything of Julius Caesar see as much?

Hyl. He would.

Phil. Consequently, he has his sight and the use of it in as perfect a degree as you?

Hyl. I agree with you.

Phil. Whence comes it then that your thoughts are directed to the Roman emperor, and his are not? This cannot proceed from the sensations or ideas of sense by you then perceived, since you acknowledge you have no advantage over him in that respect. It should seem therefore to proceed from reason and memory, should it not?

Hyl. It should.

Phil. Consequently, it will not follow from that instance that anything is perceived by sense which is not immediately perceived. Though I grant we may, in one acceptation, be said to perceive sensible things mediately by sense—that is, when, from a frequently perceived connection, the immediate perception of ideas by one sense suggest to the mind others, perhaps belonging to another sense, which are wont to be connected with them. For instance, when I hear a coach drive along the streets, immediately I perceive only the sound; but from the experience I have had that such a sound is connected with a coach, I am said to hear the coach. It is nevertheless evident that, in truth and strictness, nothing can be *heard* but *sound;* and the coach is not then properly perceived by sense, but suggested from experience. So likewise when we are said to see a red-hot bar of iron; the solidity and heat of the iron are not the objects of sight, but suggested to the imagination by the color and figure which are properly perceived by that sense. In short, those things alone are actually and strictly perceived by any sense which would have been perceived in case that same sense had then been first conferred on us. As for other things, it is plain they are only suggested to the mind by experience grounded on former perceptions. But, to return to your comparison of Caesar's picture, it is plain, if you keep to that, you must hold the real things or archetypes of our ideas are not perceived by sense, but by some internal faculty of the soul, as reason or memory. I would, therefore, fain know what arguments you can draw from reason for the existence of what you call "real things" or "material objects," or whether you remember to have seen them formerly as they are in themselves, or if you have heard or read of anyone that did.

Hyl. I see, Philonous, you are disposed to raillery; but that will never convince me.

Phil. My aim is only to learn from you the way to come at the knowledge of "material beings." Whatever we perceive is perceived either immediately or mediately—by sense, or by reason and reflection. But, as you have excluded sense, pray show me what reason you have to believe their existence, or what *medium* you can possibly make use of to prove it, either to mine or your own understanding.

Hyl. To deal ingenuously, Philonous, now [that] I consider the point, I do not find I can give you any good reason for it. But this much seems pretty plain, that it is at least possible such things may really exist. And as long as there is no absurdity in supposing them, I am resolved to believe as I did, till you bring good reasons to the contrary.

Phil. What! is it come to this, that you only believe the existence of material objects, and that your belief is founded barely on the possibility of its being true? Then you will have me bring reasons against it, though another would think it reasonable the proof should lie on him who holds the affirmative. And, after all, this very point which you are now resolved to maintain, without any reason, is in effect what you have more than once during this discourse seen good reason to give up. But to pass over all this—if I understand you rightly, you say our ideas do not exist without the mind, but that they are copies, images, or representations of certain originals that do?

Hyl. You take me right.

Phil. They are then like external things?

Hyl. They are.

Phil. Have those things a stable and permanent nature, independent of our senses, or are they in a perpetual change, upon our producing any motions in our bodies, suspending, exerting, or altering our faculties or organs of sense?

Hyl. Real things, it is plain, have a fixed and real nature, which remains the same notwithstanding any change in our senses or in the posture and motion of our bodies; which indeed may affect the ideas in our minds, but it were absurd to think they had the same effect on things existing without the mind.

Phil. How then is it possible that things perpetually fleeting and variable as our ideas should be copies or images of anything fixed and constant? Or, in other words, since all sensible qualities, as size, figure, color, etc., that is, our ideas, are continually changing upon every alteration in the distance, medium, or instruments of sensation—how can any determinate material objects be properly represented or painted forth by several distinct things each of which is so different from and unlike the rest? Or, if you say it resembles some one only of our ideas, how shall we be able to distinguish the true copy from all the false ones?

Hyl. I profess, Philonous, I am at a loss. I know not what to say to this.

Phil. But neither is this all. Which are material objects in themselves—perceptible or imperceptible?

Hyl. Properly and immediately nothing can be perceived but ideas. All material things, therefore, are in themselves insensible and to be perceived only by their ideas.

Phil. Ideas then are sensible, and their archetypes or originals insensible?

Hyl. Right.

Phil. But how can that which is sensible be like that which is insensible? Can a real thing, in itself *invisible,* be like a *color,* or a real thing which is not *audible* be like a *sound?* In a word, can anything be like a sensation or idea, but another sensation or idea?

Hyl. I must own, I think not.

Phil. Is it possible there should be any doubt on the point? Do you not perfectly know your own ideas?

Hyl. I know them perfectly, since what I do not perceive or know can be no part of my idea.

Phil. Consider, therefore, and examine them, and then tell me if there be anything in them which can exist without the mind, or if you can conceive anything like them existing without the mind?

Hyl. Upon inquiry I find it is impossible for me to conceive or understand how anything but an idea can be like an idea. And it is most evident that *no idea can exist without the mind.*

Phil. You are, therefore, by your principles forced to deny the reality of sensible things, since you made it to consist in an absolute existence exterior to the mind. That is to say, you are a downright skeptic. So I have gained my point, which was to show your principles led to skepticism.

Hyl. For the present I am, if not entirely convinced, at least silenced.

Phil. I would fain know what more you would require in order to a perfect conviction. Have you not had the liberty of explaining yourself all manner of ways? Were any little slips in discourse laid hold and insisted on? Or were you not allowed to retract or reinforce anything you had offered, as best served your purpose? Has not everything you could say been heard and examined with all the fairness imaginable? In a word, have you not in every point been convinced out of your own mouth? And, if you can at present discover any flaw in any of your former concessions, or think of any remaining subterfuge, any new distinction, color, or comment whatsoever, why do you not produce it?

Hyl. A little patience, Philonous. I am at present so amazed to see myself ensnared, and as it were imprisoned in the labyrinths you have drawn me into, that on the sudden it cannot be expected I should find my way out. You must give me time to look about me and recollect myself.

Phil. Hark; is not this the college bell?

Hyl. It rings for prayers.

Phil. We will go in then, if you please, and meet here again tomorrow morning. In the meantime, you may employ your thoughts on this morning's discourse and try if you can find any fallacy in it, or invent any new means to extricate yourself.

Hyl. Agreed.

THE THIRD DIALOGUE

. . .

[*Hyl.*[3] You say your own soul supplies you with some sort of an idea or image of God. But, at the same time, you acknowledge you have, properly speaking, no idea of your own soul. You even affirm that spirits are a sort of beings altogether different from ideas. Consequently, that no idea can be like a spirit. We have, therefore, no idea of any spirit. You admit nevertheless that there is spiritual substance, although you have no idea of it, while you deny there can be such a thing as material substance, because you have no

[3] The four paragraphs following do not appear in the first and second editions.

notion or idea of it. Is this fair dealing? To act consistently, you must either admit matter or reject spirit. What say you to this?

Phil. I say, in the first place, that I do not deny the existence of material substance merely because I have no notion of it, but because the notion of it is inconsistent, or, in other words, because it is repugnant that there should be a notion of it. Many things, for aught I know, may exist whereof neither I nor any other man has or can have any idea or notion whatsoever. But then those things must be possible, that is, nothing inconsistent must be included in their definition. I say, secondly, that, although we believe things to exist which we do not perceive, yet we may not believe that any particular thing exists without some reason for such belief; but I have no reason for believing the existence of matter. I have no immediate intuition thereof, neither can I immediately from my sensations, ideas, notions, actions, or passions infer an unthinking, unperceiving, inactive substance, either by probable deduction or necessary consequence. Whereas the being of my self, that is, my own soul, mind, or thinking principle, I evidently know by reflection. You will forgive me if I repeat the same things in answer to the same objections. In the very notion or definition of "material substance" there is included a manifest repugnance and inconsistency. But this cannot be said of the notion of spirit. That ideas should exist in what does not perceive, or be produced by what does not act, is repugnant. But it is no repugnancy to say that a perceiving thing should be the subject of ideas, or an active thing the cause of them. It is granted we have neither an immediate evidence nor a demonstrative knowledge of the existence of other finite spirits, but it will not thence follow that such spirits are on a foot with material substances, if to suppose the one be inconsistent, and it be not inconsistent to suppose the other; if the one can be inferred by no argument, and there is a probability for the other; if we see signs and effects indicating distinct finite agents like ourselves, and see no sign or symptom whatever that leads to a rational belief of matter. I say, lastly, that I have a notion of spirit, though I have not, strictly speaking, an idea of it. I do not perceive it as an idea, or by means of an idea, but know it by reflection.

Hyl. Notwithstanding all you have said, to me it seems that, according to your own way of thinking, and in consequence of your own principles, it should follow that you are only a system of floating ideas without any substance to support them. Words are not to be used without a meaning. And, as there is no more meaning in *spiritual* substance than in *material* substance, the one is to be exploded as well as the other.

Phil. How often must I repeat that I know or am conscious of my own being, and that *I myself* am not my ideas, but somewhat else, a thinking, active principle that perceives, knows, wills, and operates about ideas. I know that I, one and the same self, perceive both colors and sounds, that a color cannot perceive a sound, nor a sound a color, that I am therefore one individual principle distinct from color and sound, and, for the same reason, from all other sensible things and inert ideas. But I am not in like manner conscious either of the existence or essence of matter. On the contrary, I know that nothing inconsistent can exist, and that the existence of matter implies an inconsistency. Further, I know what I mean when I affirm that there is a spiritual substance or support of ideas, that is, that a spirit knows and perceives ideas. But I do not know what is meant when it is said that an unperceiving substance has inherent in it and supports either ideas or the archetypes of ideas. There is, therefore, upon the whole no parity of case between spirit and matter.]

Hyl. I own myself satisfied in this point. But do you in earnest think the real existence of sensible things consists in their being actually perceived? If so, how comes it that all mankind distinguish between them? Ask the first man you meet, and he shall tell you, "to be perceived" is one thing, and "to exist" is another.

Phil. I am content, Hylas, to appeal to the common sense of the world for the truth of my notion. Ask the gardener why he thinks yonder cherry tree exists in the garden, and he shall tell you, because he sees and feels it; in a word, because he perceives it by his senses. Ask him why he thinks an orange tree not to be there, and he shall tell you, because he does not perceive it. What he perceives by sense, that he terms a real being and says it "is" or "exists"; but that which is not perceivable, the same, he says, has no being.

Hyl. Yes, Philonous, I grant the existence of a sensible thing consists in being perceivable, but not in being actually perceived.

Phil. And what is perceivable but an idea? And can an idea exist without being actually perceived? These are points long since agreed between us.

Hyl. But be your opinion never so true, yet surely you will not deny it is shocking and contrary to the common sense of men. Ask the fellow whether yonder tree has an existence out of his mind; what answer think you he would make?

Phil. The same that I should myself, to wit, that it does exist out of his mind. But then to a Christian it cannot surely be shocking to say, the real tree, existing without his mind, is truly known and comprehended by (that is, *exists in*) the infinite mind of God. Probably he may not at first glance be aware of the direct and immediate proof there is of this, inasmuch as the very being of a tree, or any other sensible thing, implies a mind wherein it is. But the point itself he cannot deny. The question between the materialists and me is not whether things have a *real* existence out of the mind of this or that person, but, whether they have an *absolute* existence, distinct from being perceived by God, and exterior to all minds. This, indeed, some heathens and philosophers have affirmed, but whoever entertains notions of the Deity suitable to the Holy Scriptures will be of another opinion.

Hyl. But, according to your notions, what difference is there between real things and chimeras formed by the imagination or the visions of a dream, since they are all equally in the mind?

Phil. The ideas formed by the imagination are faint and indistinct; they have, besides, an entire dependence on the will. But the ideas perceived by sense, that is, real things, are more vivid and clear, and, being imprinted on the mind by a spirit distinct from us, have not the like dependence on our will. There is, therefore, no danger of confounding these with the foregoing, and there is as little of confounding them with the visions of a dream, which are dim, irregular, and confused. And though they should happen to be never so lively and natural, yet, by their not being connected and of a piece with the preceding and subsequent transaction of our lives, they might easily be distinguished from realities. In short, by whatever method you distinguish *things* from *chimeras* on your own scheme, the same, it is evident, will hold also upon mine. For it must be, I presume, by some perceived difference, and I am not for depriving you of any one thing that you perceive.

Hyl. But still, Philonous, you hold there is nothing in the world but spirits and ideas. And this you must needs acknowledge sounds very oddly.

Phil. I own the word "idea," not being commonly used for "thing," sounds something out of the way. My reason for using it was because a necessary relation to the mind is understood to be implied by the term; and it is now commonly used by philosophers to denote the immediate objects of the understanding. But however oddly the proposition may sound in words, yet it includes nothing so very strange or shocking in its sense, which in effect amounts to no more than this, to wit, that there are only things perceiving and things perceived, or that every unthinking being is necessarily, and from the very nature of its existence, perceived by some mind, if not by any finite created mind, yet certainly by the infinite mind of God, in whom "we live, and move, and have our being." Is this as strange as to say the sensible qualities are not on the object or that we cannot be sure of the existence of things, or know anything of their real natures, though we both see and feel them and perceive them by all our senses?

Hyl. And, in consequence of this, must we not think there are no such things as physical or corporeal causes, but that a spirit is the immediate cause of all the *phenomena* in nature? Can there be anything more extravagant than this?

Phil. Yes, it is infinitely more extravagant to say a thing which is inert operates on the mind, and which is unperceiving is the cause of our perceptions. Besides, that which to you I know not for what reason seems so extravagant is no more than the Holy Scriptures assert in a hundred places. In them God is represented as the sole and immediate Author of all those effects which some heathens and philosophers are wont to ascribe to Nature, Matter, Fate, or the like unthinking principle. This is so much the constant language of Scripture that it were needless to confirm it by citations.

Hyl. You are not aware, Philonous, that, in making God the immediate Author of all the motions in nature, you make Him the Author of murder, sacrilege, adultery, and the like heinous sins.

Phil. In answer to that I observe, first, that the imputation of guilt is the same whether a person commits an action with or without an instrument. In case, therefore, you suppose God to act by the mediation of an instrument or occasion called "matter," you as truly make Him the author of sin as I, who think Him the immediate agent in all those operations vulgarly ascribed to Nature. I further observe that sin or moral turpitude does not consist in the outward physical action or motion, but in the internal deviation of the will from the laws of reason and religion. This is plain, in that the killing an enemy in a battle or putting a criminal legally to death is not thought sinful, though the outward act be the very same with that in the case of murder. Since, therefore, sin does not consist in the physical action, the making God an immediate cause of all such actions is not making Him the Author of sin. Lastly, I have nowhere said that God is the only agent who produces all the motions in bodies. It is true I have denied there are any other agents besides spirits, but this is very consistent with allowing to thinking rational beings, in the production of motions, the use of limited powers, ultimately, indeed, derived from God but immediately under the direction of their own wills, which is sufficient to entitle them to all the guilt of their actions.

Hyl. But the denying matter, Philonous, or corporeal substance, there is the point. You can never persuade me that this is not repugnant to the universal sense of mankind. Were our dispute to be determined by most voices, I am confident you would give up the point without gathering the votes.

Phil. I wish both our opinions were fairly stated and submitted to the judgment of men who had plain common sense, without the prejudices of a learned education. Let me be represented as one who trusts his senses, who thinks he knows the things he sees and feels, and entertains no doubts of their existence; and you fairly set forth with all your doubts, your paradoxes, and your skepticism about you, and I shall willingly acquiesce in the determination of any indifferent person. That there is no substance wherein ideas can exist besides spirit is to me evident. And that the objects immediately perceived are ideas is on all hands agreed. And that sensible qualities are objects immediately perceived no one can deny. It is therefore evident there can be no *substratum* of those qualities but spirit, in which they exist, not by way of mode or property, but as a thing perceived in that which perceives it. I deny, therefore, that there is any unthinking *substratum* of the objects of sense, and in that acceptation that there is any material substance. But if by "material substance" is meant only sensible body, that which is seen and felt (and the unphilosophical part of the world, I dare say, mean no more), then I am more certain of matter's existence than you or any other philosopher pretend to be. If there be anything which makes the generality of mankind averse from the notions I espouse, it is a misapprehension that I deny the reality of sensible things; but as it is you who are guilty of that and not I, it follows that in truth their aversion is against your notions and not mine. I do therefore assert that I am as certain as of my own being that there are bodies or corporeal substances (meaning the things I perceive by my senses), and that, granting this, the bulk of mankind will take no thought about, nor think themselves at all concerned in the fate of, those unknown natures and philosophical quiddities which some men are so fond of.

Hyl. What say you to this? Since, according to you, men judge of the reality of things by their senses, how can a man be mistaken in thinking the moon a plain lucid surface, about a foot in diameter, or a square tower, seen at a distance, round, or an oar, with one end in the water, crooked?

Phil. He is not mistaken with regard to the ideas he actually perceives, but in the inferences he makes from his present perceptions. Thus, in the case of the oar, what he immediately perceives by sight is certainly crooked, and so far he is in the right. But if he thence conclude that upon taking the oar out of the water he shall perceive the same crookedness, or that it would affect his touch as crooked things are wont to do, in that he is mistaken. In like manner, if he shall conclude, from what he perceives in one station, that, in case he advances toward the moon or tower, he should still be affected with the like ideas, he is mistaken. But his mistake lies not in what he perceives immediately and at present (it being a manifest contradiction to suppose he should err in respect of that), but in the wrong judgment he makes concerning the ideas he apprehends to be connected with those immediately perceived, or, concerning the ideas, that from what he perceives at present he imagines would be perceived in other circumstances. The case is the same with regard to the Copernican system. We do not here perceive any motion of the earth, but it were erroneous thence to conclude that, in case we were placed at as great a distance from that as we are now from the other planets, we should not then perceive its motion.

Hyl. I understand you and must needs own you say things plausible enough, but give me leave to put you in mind of one thing. Pray, Philonous, were you not formerly as positive that matter existed as you are now that it does not?

Phil. I was. But here lies the difference. Before, my positiveness was founded, without examination, upon prejudice, but now, after inquiry, upon evidence.

Hyl. After all, it seems our dispute is rather about words than things. We agree in the thing, but differ in the name. That we are affected with ideas from without is evident; and it is no less evident that there must be (I will not say archetypes, but) powers without the mind corresponding to those ideas. And as these powers cannot subsist by themselves, there is some subject of them necessarily to be admitted, which I call "matter," and you call "spirit." This is all the difference.

Phil. Pray, Hylas, is that powerful being, or subject of powers, extended?

Hyl. It has not extension, but it has the power to raise in you the idea of extension.

Phil. It is therefore itself unextended?

Hyl. I grant it.

Phil. Is it not also active?

Hyl. Without doubt; otherwise, how could we attribute powers to it?

Phil. Now let me ask you two questions: *First,* whether it be agreeable to the usage either of philosophers or others to give the name "matter" to an unextended active being? And, secondly, whether it be not ridiculously absurd to misapply names contrary to the common use of language?

Hyl. Well then, let it not be called "matter," since you will have it so, but some "third nature," distinct from matter and spirit. For what reason is there why you should call it spirit? Does not the notion of spirit imply that it is thinking as well as active and unextended?

Phil. My reason is this: because I have a mind to have some notion or meaning in what I say, but I have no notion of any action distinct from volition, neither can I conceive volition to be anywhere but in a spirit; therefore, when I speak of an active being I am obliged to mean a spirit. Besides, what can be plainer than that a thing which has no ideas in itself cannot impart them to me; and, if it has ideas, surely it must be a spirit. To make you comprehend the point still more clearly, if it be possible: I assert as well as you that, since we are affected from without, we must allow powers to be without, in a being distinct from ourselves. So far we are agreed. But then we differ as to the kind of this powerful being. I will have it to be spirit, you matter or I know not what (I may add, too, you know not what) third nature. Thus I prove it to be spirit. From the effects I see produced I conclude there are actions; and because actions, volitions; and because there are volitions, there must be a will. Again, the things I perceive must have an existence, they or their archetypes, out of my mind; but, being ideas, neither they nor their achetypes can exist otherwise than in an understanding, there is therefore an understanding. But will and understanding constitute in the strictest sense a mind or spirit. The powerful cause, therefore, of my ideas is in strict propriety of speech a *spirit.*

Hyl. And now I warrant you think you have made the point very clear, little suspecting that what you advance leads directly to a contradiction. Is it not an absurdity to imagine any imperfection in God?

Phil. Without a doubt.

Hyl. To suffer pain is an imperfection?

Phil. Are we not sometimes affected with pain and uneasiness by some other being?

Phil. We are.

Hyl. And have you not said that being is a spirit, and is not that spirit God?

Phil. I grant it.

Hyl. But you have asserted that whatever ideas we perceive from without are in the mind which affects us. The ideas, therefore, of pain and uneasiness are in God, or, in other words, God suffers pain; that is to say, there is an imperfection in the divine nature, which, you acknowledge, was absurd. So you are caught in a plain contradiction.

Phil. That God knows or understands all things, and that He knows, among other things, what pain is, even every sort of painful sensation, and what it is for His creatures to suffer pain, I make no question. But that God, though He knows and sometimes causes painful sensations in us, can Himself suffer pain I positively deny. We, who are limited and dependent spirits, are liable to impressions of sense, the effects of an external agent, which, being produced against our wills, are sometimes painful and uneasy. But God, whom no external being can affect, who perceives nothing by sense as we do, whose will is absolute and independent, causing all things, and liable to be thwarted or resisted by nothing, it is evident such a Being as this can suffer nothing, nor be affected with any painful sensation or, indeed, any sensation at all. We are chained to a body; that is to say, our perceptions are connected with corporeal motions. By the law of our nature we are affected upon every alteration in the nervous parts of our sensible body; which sensible body, rightly considered, is nothing but a complexion of such qualities or ideas as have no existence distinct from being perceived by a mind; so that this connection of sensations with corporeal motions means no more than a correspondence in the order of nature between two sets of ideas, or things immediately perceivable. But God is a pure spirit, disengaged from all such sympathy or natural ties. No corporeal motions are attended with the sensations of pain or pleasure in His mind. To know everything knowable is certainly a perfection, but to endure or suffer or feel anything by sense is an imperfection. The former, I say, agrees to God, but not the latter. God knows or has ideas, but His ideas are not conveyed to Him by sense, as ours are. Your not distinguishing where there is so manifest a difference makes you fancy you see an absurdity where there is none.

Hyl. But all this while you have not considered that the quantity of matter has been demonstrated to be proportional to the gravity of bodies. And what can withstand demonstration?

Phil. Let me see how you demonstrate that point.

Hyl. I lay it down for a principle that the moments or quantities of motion in bodies are in a direct compounded reason of the velocities and quantities of matter contained in them. Hence, where the velocities are equal, it follows the moments are directly as the quantity of matter in each. But it is found by experience that all bodies (bating the small inequalities arising from the resistance of the air) descend with an equal velocity; the motion therefore of descending bodies, and consequently their gravity, which is the cause or principle of that motion, is proportional to the quantity of matter, which was to be demonstrated.

Phil. You lay it down as a self-evident principle that the quantity of motion in any body is proportional to the velocity and matter taken together; and this is made use of to prove a proposition from whence the existence of matter is inferred. Pray is not this arguing in a circle?

Hyl. In the premise I only mean that the motion is proportional to the velocity, jointly with the extension and solidity.

Phil. But allowing this to be true, yet it will not thence follow that gravity is proportional to matter in your philosophic sense of the word, except you take it for granted that unknown *substratum,* or whatever else you call it, is proportional to those sensible qualities which to suppose is plainly begging the question. That there is magnitude and solidity or resistance perceived by sense I readily grant, as likewise, that gravity may be proportional to those qualities I will not dispute. But that either these qualities as perceived by us, or the powers producing them, do exist in a *material substratum*—this is what I deny, and you, indeed, affirm but, notwithstanding your demonstration, have not yet proved.

Hyl. I shall insist no longer on that point. Do you think, however, you shall persuade me the natural philosophers have been dreaming all this while? Pray what becomes of all their hypotheses and explications of the phenomena which suppose the existence of matter?

Phil. What mean you, Hylas, by the "phenomena"?

Hyl. I mean the appearances which I perceive by my senses.

Phil. And the appearances perceived by sense, are they not ideas?

Hyl. I have told you so a hundred times.

Phil. Therefore, to explain the phenomena is to show how we come to be affected with ideas in that manner and order wherein they are imprinted on our senses. Is it not?

Hyl. It is.

Phil. Now, if you can prove that any philosopher has explained the production of any one idea in our minds by the help of *matter,* I shall forever acquiesce and look on all that has been said against it as nothing; but if you cannot, it is vain to urge the explication of phenomena. That a being endowed with knowledge and will should produce or exhibit ideas is easily understood. But that a being which is utterly destitute of these faculties should be able to produce ideas, or in any sort to affect an intelligence, this I can never understand. This I say, though we had some positive conception of matter, though we knew its qualities and could comprehend its existence, would yet be so far from explaining things that it is itself the most inexplicable thing in the world. And yet, for all this, it will not follow that philosophers have been doing nothing; for by observing and reasoning upon the connection of ideas, they discover the laws and methods of nature, which is a part of knowledge both useful and entertaining.

Hyl. After all, can it be supposed God would deceive all mankind? Do you imagine He would have induced the whole world to believe the being of matter if there was no such thing?

Phil. That every epidemical opinion arising from prejudice, or passion, or thoughtlessness may be imputed to God, as the Author of it, I believe you will not affirm. Whatsoever opinion we father on Him, it must be either because He has discovered it to us by supernatural revelation or because it is so evident to our natural faculties, which were framed and given us by God, that it is impossible we should withhold our assent from it. But where is the revelation? Or where is the evidence that extorts the belief of matter? Nay, how does it appear that matter, taken for something distinct from what we perceive by our senses, is thought to exist by all mankind, or, indeed, by any except a few philosophers who do not know what they would be at? Your question supposes these points are clear; and, when you have cleared them, I shall think myself obliged to give you another answer. In the meantime let it suffice that I tell you I do not suppose God has deceived mankind at all.

Hyl. But the novelty, Philonous, the novelty! There lies the danger. New notions should always be discountenanced; they unsettle men's minds, and nobody knows where they will end.

Phil. Why the rejecting a notion that has no foundation, either in sense or in reason or in Divine authority, should be thought to unsettle the belief of such opinions as are grounded on all or any of these, I cannot imagine. That innovations in government and religion are dangerous and ought to be discountenanced, I freely own. But is there the like reason why they should be discouraged in philosophy? The making anything known which was unknown before is an innovation in knowledge; and if all such innovations had been forbidden, men would [not] have made a notable progress in the arts and sciences. But it is none of my business to plead for novelties and paradoxes. That the qualities we perceive are not on the objects, that we must not believe our senses, that we know nothing of the real nature of things and can never be assured even of their existence, that real colors and sounds are nothing but certain unknown figures and motions, that motions are in themselves neither swift nor slow, that there are in bodies absolute extensions without any particular magnitude or figure, that a thing stupid, thoughtless, and inactive operates on a spirit, that the least particle of a body contains innumerable extended parts—these are the novelties, these are the strange notions which shock the genuine uncorrupted judgment of all mankind, and, being once admitted, embarrass the mind with endless doubts and difficulties. And it is against these and the like innovations I endeavor to vindicate Common Sense. It is true, in doing this I may, perhaps, be obliged to use some ambages and ways of speech not common. But if my notions are once thoroughly understood, that which is most singular in them will, in effect, be found to amount to no more than this—that it is absolutely impossible and a plain contradiction to suppose any unthinking being should exist without being perceived by a mind. And if this notion be singular, it is a shame it should be so at this time of day and in a Christian country.

Hyl. As for the difficulties other opinions may be liable to, those are out of the question. It is your business to defend your own opinion. Can anything be plainer than that you are for changing all things into ideas? You, I say, who are not ashamed to charge me with skepticism. This is so plain, there is no denying it.

Phil. You mistake me. I am not for changing things into ideas but rather ideas into things, since those immediate objects of perception, which, according to you, are only appearances of things, I take to be the real things themselves.

Hyl. Things! you may pretend what you please; but it is certain you leave us nothing but the empty forms of things, the outside only which strikes the senses.

Phil. What you call the empty forms and outside of things seem to me the very things themselves. Nor are they empty or incomplete otherwise than upon your supposition that matter is an essential part of all corporeal things. We both, therefore, agree in this, that we perceive only sensible forms; but herein we differ: you will have them to be empty appearances, I real beings. In short, you do not trust your senses, I do.

Hyl. You say you believe your senses, and seem to applaud yourself that in this you agree with the vulgar. According to you, therefore, the true nature of a thing is discovered by the senses. If so, whence comes that disagreement? Why, is not the same figure, and other sensible qualities, perceived all manner of ways? And why should we use a microscope the better to discover the true nature of a body, if it were discoverable to the naked eye?

Phil. Strictly speaking, Hylas, we do not see the same object that we feel; neither is the same object perceived by the microscope which was by the naked eye. But in case every variation was thought sufficient to constitute a new kind or individual, the endless number or confusion of names would render language impracticable. Therefore, to avoid this as well as other inconveniences which are obvious upon a little thought, men combine together several ideas, apprehended by divers senses, or by the same sense at different times or in different circumstances, but observed, however, to have some connection in nature, either with respect to coexistence or succession; all which they refer to one name and consider as one thing. Hence it follows that when I examine by my other senses a thing I have seen, it is not in order to understand better the same object which I had perceived by sight, the object of one sense not being perceived by the other senses. And when I look through a microscope, it is not that I may perceive more clearly what I perceived already with my bare eyes, the object perceived by the glass being quite different from the former. But in both cases my aim is only to know what ideas are connected together; and the more a man knows of the connection of ideas, the more he is said to know of the nature of things. What, therefore, if our ideas are variable, what if our senses are not in all circumstances affected with the same appearances? It will not thence follow they are not to be trusted or that they are inconsistent either with themselves or anything else, except it be with your preconceived notion of (I know not what) one single, unchanged, unperceivable, real nature, marked by each name; which prejudice seems to have taken its rise from not rightly understanding the common language of men speaking of several distinct ideas as united into one thing by the mind. And, indeed, there is cause to suspect several erroneous conceits of the philosophers are owing to the same original: while they began to build their schemes not so much on notions as words which were framed by the vulgar merely for convenience and dispatch in the common actions of life, without any regard to speculation.

Hyl. Methinks I apprehend your meaning.

Phil. It is your opinion the ideas we perceive by our senses are not real things, but images or copies of them. Our knowledge, therefore, is no further real than as our ideas are the true representations of those originals. But as these supposed originals are in themselves unknown, it is impossible to know how far our ideas resemble them, or whether they resemble them at all. We cannot, therefore, be sure we have any real knowledge. Further, as our ideas are perpetually varied, without any change in the supposed real things, it necessarily follows they cannot all be true copies of them, or, if some are and others are not, it is impossible to distinguish the former from the latter. And this plunges us yet deeper in uncertainty. Again, when we consider the point, we cannot conceive how any idea, or anything like an idea, should have an absolute existence out of a mind, nor consequently, according to you, how there should be any real thing in nature. The result of all which is that we are thrown into the most hopeless and abandoned skepticism. Now give me leave to ask you, *first,* whether your referring ideas to certain absolutely existing unperceived substances, as their originals, be not the source of all this skepticism? *Secondly,* whether you are informed, either by sense or reason, of the existence of those unknown originals? And in case you are not, whether it be not absurd to suppose them? *Thirdly,* whether, upon inquiry, you find there is anything distinctly conceived or meant by the "absolute or external existence of unperceiving substances?" *Lastly,* whether, the premises considered, it be not the wisest way to follow nature, trust your senses, and, laying aside all anxious thought about unknown natures or substances, admit with the vulgar those for real things which are perceived by the senses?

Hyl. For the present I have no inclination to the answering part. I would much rather see how you can get over what follows. Pray, are not the objects perceived by the senses of one likewise perceivable to others present? If there were a hundred more here, they would all see the garden, the trees and flowers, as I see them. But they are not in the same manner affected with the ideas I frame in my imagination. Does not this make a difference between the former sort of objects and the latter?

Phil. I grant it does. Nor have I ever denied a difference between the objects of sense and those of imagination. But what would you infer from thence? You cannot say that sensible objects exist unperceived because they are perceived by many.

Hyl. I own I can make nothing of that objection, but it has led me into another. Is it not your opinion that by our senses we perceive only the ideas existing in our minds?

Phil. It is.

Hyl. But the same idea which is in my mind cannot be in yours or in any other mind. Does it not, therefore, follow from your principles that no two can see the same thing? And is not this highly absurd?

Phil. If the term "same" be taken in the vulgar acceptation, it is certain (and not at all repugnant to the principles I maintain) that different persons may perceive the same thing, or the same thing or idea exist in different minds. Words are of arbitrary imposition; and since men are used to apply the word "same" where no distinction or variety is perceived, and I do not pretend to alter their perceptions, it follows that, as men have said before, *several saw the same thing,* so they may, upon like occasions, still continue to use the same phrase without any deviation either from propriety of language or the truth of things. But if the term "same" be used in the acceptation of philosophers who pretend to an abstracted notion of identity, then, according to their sundry definitions of this notion (for it is not yet agreed wherein that philosophic identity consists), it may or may not be possible for divers persons to perceive the same thing. But whether philosophers shall think fit to call a thing the "same" or no is, I conceive, of small importance. Let us suppose several men together, all endued with the same faculties, and consequently affected in like sort by their senses, and who had yet never known the use of language; they would without question agree in their perceptions. Though perhaps, when they came to the use of speech, some regarding the uniformness of what was perceived might call it the "same" thing; others, especially regarding the diversity of persons who perceived, might choose the denomination of "different" things. But who sees not that all the dispute is about a word, to wit, whether what is perceived by different persons may yet have the term "same" applied to it? Or suppose a house whose walls or outward shell remaining unaltered, the chambers are all pulled down, and new ones built in their place, and that you should call this the "same," and I should say it was not the "same," house—would we not, for all this, perfectly agree in our thoughts of the house considered in itself? And would not all the difference consist in a sound? If you should say we differed in our notions, for that you superadded to your idea of the house the simple abstracted idea of identity, whereas I did not, I would tell you I know not what you mean by that "abstracted idea of identity," and should desire you to look into your own thoughts and be sure you understood yourself.—Why so silent, Hylas? Are you not yet satisfied men may dispute about identity and diversity without any real difference in their thoughts and opinions abstracted from names? Take this further reflection with you—that, whether matter be allowed to exist or no, the case is exactly the same as to the point in hand. For the materialists themselves acknowledge what we immediately perceive by our senses to be our own ideas. Your difficulty, therefore, that no two see the same thing makes equally against the materialists and me. . . .

DAVID HUME

An Inquiry concerning Human Understanding*

SECTION IV. SKEPTICAL DOUBTS CONCERNING THE OPERATIONS OF THE UNDERSTANDING

PART I

All the objects of human reason or inquiry may naturally be divided into two kinds, to wit, "Relations of Ideas," and "Matters of Fact." Of the first kind are the sciences of Geometry, Algebra, and Arithmetic, and, in short, every affirmation which is either intuitively or demonstratively certain. *That the square of the hypotenuse is equal to the square of the two sides* is a proposition which expresses a relation between these figures. *That three times five is equal to the half of thirty* expresses a relation between these numbers. Propositions of this kind are discoverable by the mere operation of thought, without dependence on what is anywhere existent in the universe. Though there never were a circle or triangle in nature, the truths demonstrated by Euclid would forever retain their certainty and evidence.

Matters of fact, which are the second objects of human reason, are not ascertained in the same manner, nor is our evidence of their truth, however great, of a like nature with the foregoing. The contrary of every matter of fact is still possible, because it can never imply a contradiction and is conceived by the mind with the same facility and distinctness as if ever so conformable to reality. *That the sun will not rise tomorrow* is no less intelligible a proposition and implies no more contradiction than the affirmation *that it will rise*. We should in vain, therefore, attempt to demonstrate its falsehood. Were it demonstratively false, it would imply a contradiction and could never be distinctly conceived by the mind.

It may, therefore, be a subject worthy of curiosity to inquire what is the nature of that evidence which assures us of any real existence and matter of fact beyond the present testimony of our senses or the records of our memory. This part of philosophy, it is observable, had been little cultivated either by the ancients or moderns; and, therefore, our doubts and errors in the prosecution of so important an inquiry may be the more excusable while we march through such difficult paths without any guide or direction. They may even prove useful by exciting curiosity and destroying that implicit faith and security which is the bane of all reasoning and free inquiry. The discovery of defects in the common philosophy, if any such there be, will not, I presume, be a discouragement, but rather an incitement, as is usual, to attempt something more full and satisfactory than has yet been proposed to the public.

All reasonings concerning matter of fact seem to be founded on the relation of *cause* and *effect*. By means of that relation alone we can go beyond the evidence of our memory and senses. If you were to ask a man why he believes any matter of fact which is absent, for instance, that his friend is in the country or in France, he would give you a reason, and this reason would be some other fact: as a letter received from him or the knowledge of his former resolutions and promises. A man finding a watch or any other machine in a desert island would conclude that there had once been men in that island. All our reasonings concerning fact are of the same nature. And here it is constantly supposed that

* David Hume, *An Inquiry concerning Human Understanding*, Sections 4–7. First published in 1748.

there is a connection between the present fact and that which is inferred from it. Were there nothing to bind them together, the inference would be entirely precarious. The hearing of an articulate voice and rational discourse in the dark assures us of the presence of some person. Why? Because these are the effects of the human make and fabric, and closely connected with it. If we anatomize all the other reasonings of this nature, we shall find that they are founded on the relation of cause and effect, and that this relation is either near or remote, direct or collateral. Heat and light are collateral effects of fire, and the one effect may justly be inferred from the other.

If we would satisfy ourselves, therefore, concerning the nature of that evidence which assures us of matters of fact, we must inquire how we arrive at the knowledge of cause and effect.

I shall venture to affirm, as a general proposition which admits of no exception, that the knowledge of this relation is not, in any instance, attained by reasonings *a priori,* but arises entirely from experience, when we find that any particular objects are constantly conjoined with each other. Let an object be presented to a man of ever so strong natural reason and abilities—if that object be entirely new to him, he will not be able, by the most accurate examination of its sensible qualities, to discover any of its causes or effects. Adam, though his rational faculties be supposed, at the very first, entirely perfect, could not have inferred from the fluidity and transparency of water that it would suffocate him, or from the light and warmth of fire that it would consume him. No object ever discovers, by the qualities which appear to the senses, either the causes which produced it or the effects which will arise from it; nor can our reason, unassisted by experience, ever draw any inference concerning real existence and matter of fact.

This proposition, *that causes and effects are discoverable, not by reason, but by experience,* will readily be admitted with regard to such objects as we remember to have once been altogether unknown to us, since we must be conscious of the utter inability which we then lay under of foretelling what would arise from them. Present two smooth pieces of marble to a man who has no tincture of natural philosophy; he will never discover that they will adhere together in such a manner as to require great force to separate them in a direct line, while they make so small a resistance to a lateral pressure. Such events as bear little analogy to the common course of nature are also readily confessed to be known only by experience, nor does any man imagine that the explosion of gunpowder or the attraction of a loadstone could ever be discovered by arguments *a priori.* In like manner, when an effect is supposed to depend upon an intricate machinery or secret structure of parts, we make no difficulty in attributing all our knowledge of it to experience. Who will assert that he can give the ultimate reason why milk or bread is proper nourishment for a man, not for a lion or tiger?

But the same truth may not appear at first sight to have the same evidence with regard to events which have become familiar to us from our first appearance in the world, which bear a close analogy to the whole course of nature, and which are supposed to depend on the simple qualities of objects without any secret structure of parts. We are apt to imagine that we could discover these effects by the mere operation of our reason without experience. We fancy that, were we brought on a sudden into this world, we could at first have inferred that one billiard ball would communicate motion to another upon impulse, and that we needed not to have waited for the event in order to pronounce with certainty concerning it. Such is the influence of custom that where it is strongest it not only covers our natural ignorance but even conceals itself, and seems not to take place, merely because it is found in the highest degree.

But to convince us that all the laws of nature and all the operations of bodies without exception are known only by experience, the following reflections may perhaps suffice. Were any object presented to us, and were we required to pronounce concerning the effect which will result from it without consulting past observation, after what manner, I beseech you, must the mind proceed in this operation? It must invent or imagine some event which it ascribes to the object as its effect; and it is plain that this invention must be entirely arbitrary. The mind can never possibly find the effect in the supposed cause by the most accurate scrutiny and examination. For the effect is totally different from the cause, and consequently can never be discovered in it. Motion in the second billiard ball is a quite distinct event from motion in the first, nor is there anything in the one to suggest the smallest hint of the other. A stone or piece of metal raised into the air and left without any support immediately falls. But to consider the matter *a priori,* is there anything we discover in this situation which can beget the idea of a downward rather than an upward or any other motion in the stone or metal?

And as the first imagination or invention of a particular effect in all natural operations is arbitrary where we consult not experience, so must we also esteem the supposed tie or connection between the cause and effect which binds them together and renders it impossible that any other effect could result from the operation of that cause. When I see, for instance, a billiard ball moving in a straight line toward another, even suppose motion in the second ball should by accident be suggested to me as the result of their contact or impulse, may I not conceive that a hundred different events might as well follow from that cause? May not both these balls remain at absolute rest? May not the first ball return in a straight line or leap off from the second in any line or direction? All these suppositions are consistent and conceivable. Why, then, should we give the preference to one which is no more consistent or conceivable than the rest? All our reasonings *a priori* will never be able to show us any foundation for this preference.

In a word, then, every effect is a distinct event from its cause. It could not, therefore, be discovered in the cause, and the first invention or conception of it, *a priori,* must be entirely arbitrary. And even after it is suggested, the conjunction of it with the cause must appear equally arbitrary, since there are always many other effects which, to reason, must seem fully as consistent and natural. In vain, therefore, should we pretend to determine any single event or infer any cause or effect without the assistance of observation and experience.

Hence we may discover the reason why no philosopher who is rational and modest has ever pretended to assign the ultimate cause of any natural operation, or to show distinctly the action of that power which produces any single effect in the universe. It is confessed that the utmost effort of human reason is to reduce the principles productive of natural phenomena to a greater simplicity, and to resolve the many particular effects into a few general causes, by means of reasonings from analogy, experience, and observation. But as to the causes of these general causes, we should in vain attempt their discovery, nor shall we ever be able to satisfy ourselves by any particular explication of them. These ultimate springs and principles are totally shut up from human curiosity and inquiry. Elasticity, gravity, cohesion of parts, communication of motion by impulse—these are probably the ultimate causes and principles which we shall ever discover in nature; and we may esteem ourselves sufficiently happy if, by accurate inquiry and reasoning, we can trace up the particular phenomena to, or near to, these general principles. The most perfect philosophy of the natural kind only staves off our ignorance a little longer, as perhaps the most perfect philosophy of the moral or metaphysical kind serves only to discover larger portions of it. Thus the observation of human blindness and weakness is the result of all philosophy, and meets us, at every turn, in spite of our endeavors to elude or avoid it.

Nor is geometry, when taken into the assistance of natural philosophy, ever able to remedy this defect or lead us into the knowledge of ultimate causes by all that accuracy of reasoning for which it is so justly celebrated. Every part of mixed mathematics proceeds upon the supposition that certain laws are established by nature in her operations, and abstract reasonings are employed either to assist experience in the discovery of these laws or to determine their influence in particular instances where it depends upon any precise degree of distance and quantity. Thus it is a law of motion, discovered by experience, that the moment or force of any body in motion is in the compound ratio or proportion of its solid contents and its velocity, and, consequently, that a small force may remove the greatest obstacle or raise the greatest weight if by any contrivance or machinery we can increase the velocity of that force so as to make it an overmatch for its antagonist. Geometry assists us in the application of this law by giving us the just dimensions of all the parts and figures which can enter into any species of machine, but still the discovery of the law itself is owing merely to experience; and all the abstract reasonings in the world could never lead us one step toward the knowledge of it. When we reason *a priori* and consider merely any object or cause as it appears to the mind, independent of all observation, it never could suggest to us the notion of any distinct object, such as its effect, much less show us the inseparable and inviolable connection between them. A man must be very sagacious who could discover by reasoning that crystal is the effect of heat, and ice of cold, without being previously acquainted with the operation of these qualities.

PART II

But we have not yet attained any tolerable satisfaction with regard to the question first proposed. Each solution still gives rise to a new question as difficult as the foregoing and leads us on to further inquiries. When it is asked, *What is the nature of all our reasonings concerning matter of fact?* the proper answer seems to be, That they are founded on the relation of cause and effect. When again it is asked, *What is the foundation of all our reasonings and conclusions concerning that relation?* it may be replied in one word, *experience.* But if we still carry on our sifting humor and ask, *What is the foundation of all conclusions from experience?* this implies a new question which may be of more difficult solution and explication. Philosophers that give themselves airs of superior wisdom and sufficiency have a hard task when they encounter persons of inquisitive dispositions, who push them from every corner to which they retreat, and who are sure at last to bring them to some dangerous dilemma. The best expedient to prevent this confusion is to be modest in our pretensions and even to discover the difficulty ourselves before it is objected to us. By this means we may make a kind of merit of our very ignorance.

I shall content myself in this section with an easy task and shall pretend only to give a negative answer to the question here proposed. I say, then, that even after we have experience of the operations of cause and effect, our conclusions from that experience are *not* founded on reasoning or any process of the understanding. This answer we must endeavor both to explain and to defend.

It must certainly be allowed that nature has kept us at a great distance from all her secrets and has afforded us only the knowledge of a few superficial qualities of objects, while she conceals from us those powers and principles on which the influence of these objects entirely depends. Our senses inform us of the color, weight, and consistency of bread, but neither sense nor reason can ever inform us of those qualities which fit it for the nourishment and support of the human body. Sight or feeling conveys an idea of the actual motion of bodies, but as to that wonderful force or power which would carry on a moving body forever in a continued change of place, and which bodies never lose but by communicating it to others, of this we cannot form the most distant conception. But notwithstanding this ignorance of natural powers[1] and principles, we always presume when we see like sensible qualities that they have like secret powers, and expect that effects similar to those which we have experienced will follow from them. If a body of like color and consistency with that bread which we have formerly eaten be presented to us, we make no scruple of repeating the experiment and foresee with certainty like nourishment and support. Now this is a process of the mind or thought of which I would willingly know the foundation. It is allowed on all hands that there is no known connection between the sensible qualities and the secret powers, and, consequently, that the mind is not led to form such a conclusion concerning their constant and regular conjunction by anything which it knows of their nature. As to past *experience,* it can be allowed to give *direct* and *certain* information of those precise objects only, and that precise period of time which fell under its cognizance: But why this experience should be extended to future times and to other objects which, for aught we know, may be only in appearance similar, this is the main question on which I would insist. The bread which I formerly ate nourished me; that is, a body of such sensible qualities was, at that time, endued with such secret powers. But does it follow that other bread must also nourish me at another time, and that like sensible qualities must always be attended with like secret powers? The consequence seems nowise necessary. At least, it must be acknowledged that there is here a consequence drawn by the mind that there is a certain step taken, a process of thought, and an inference which wants to be explained. These two propositions are far from being the same: *I have found that such an object has always been attended with such an effect,* and *I foresee that other*

[1] The word "power" is here used in a loose and popular sense. The more accurate explication of it would give additional evidence to this argument. See Section VII.

objects which are in appearance similar will be attended with similar effects. I shall allow, if you please, that the one proposition may justly be inferred from the other: I know, in fact, that it always is inferred. But if you insist that the inference is made by a chain of reasoning, I desire you to produce that reasoning. The connection between these propositions is not intuitive. There is required a medium which may enable the mind to draw such an inference, if indeed it be drawn by reasoning and argument. What that medium is I must confess passes my comprehension; and it is incumbent on those to produce it who assert that it really exists and is the original of all our conclusions concerning matter of fact.

This negative argument must certainly, in process of time, become altogether convincing if many penetrating and able philosophers shall turn their inquiries this way, and no one be ever able to discover any connecting proposition or intermediate step which supports the understanding in this conclusion. But as the question is yet new, every reader may not trust so far to his own penetration as to conclude, because an argument escapes his inquiry, that therefore it does not really exist. For this reason it may be requisite to venture upon a more difficult task, and, enumerating all the branches of human knowledge, endeavor to show that none of them can afford such an argument.

All reasonings may be divided into two kinds, namely, demonstrative reasoning, or that concerning relations of ideas, and moral reasoning, or that concerning matter of fact and existence. That there are no demonstrative arguments in the case seems evident, since it implies no contradiction that the course of nature may change and that an object, seemingly like those which we have experienced, may be attended with different or contrary effects. May I not clearly and distinctly conceive that a body, falling from the clouds and which in all other respects resembles snow, has yet the taste of salt or feeling of fire? Is there any more intelligible proposition than to affirm that all the trees will flourish in December and January, and will decay in May and June? Now, whatever is intelligible and can be distinctly conceived implies no contradiction and can never be proved false by any demonstrative argument or abstract reasoning *a priori*.

If we be, therefore, engaged by arguments to put trust in past experience and make it the standard of our future judgment, these arguments must be probable only, or such as regard matter of fact and real existence, according to the division above mentioned. But that there is no argument of this kind must appear if our explication of that species of reasoning be admitted as solid and satisfactory. We have said that all arguments concerning existence are founded on the relation of cause and effect, that our knowledge of that relation is derived entirely from experience, and that all our experimental conclusions proceed upon the supposition that the future will be conformable to the past. To endeavor, therefore, the proof of this last supposition by probable arguments, or arguments regarding existence, must be evidently going in a circle and taking that for granted which is the very point in question.

In reality, all arguments from experience are founded on the similarity which we discover among natural objects, and by which we are induced to expect effects similar to those which we have found to follow from such objects. And though none but a fool or madman will ever pretend to dispute the authority of experience or to reject that great guide of human life, it may surely be allowed a philosopher to have so much curiosity at least as to examine the principle of human nature which gives this mighty authority to experience and makes us draw advantage from that similarity which nature has placed among different objects. From causes which appear similar, we expect similar effects. This is the sum of all our experimental conclusions. Now it seems evident that, if this conclusion were formed by reason, it would be as perfect at first, and upon one instance, as after ever so long a course of experience; but the case is far otherwise. Nothing so like as eggs, yet no one, on account of this appearing similarity, expects the same taste and relish in all of them. It is only after a long course of uniform experiments in any kind that we attain a firm reliance and security with regard to a particular event. Now, where is that process of reasoning which, from one instance, draws a conclusion so different from that which it infers from a hundred instances that are nowise different from that single one? This question I propose as much for the sake of information as with an intention of raising difficulties. I cannot find, I cannot imagine any such reasoning. But I keep my mind still open to instruction if anyone will vouchsafe to bestow it on me.

Should it be said that, from a number of uniform experiments, we *infer* a connection between the sensible qualities and the secret powers, this, I must confess, seems the same difficulty, couched in different terms. The question still occurs, On what process of argument is this *inference* founded? Where is the medium, the interposing ideas which join propositions so very wide of each other? It is confessed that the color, consistency, and other sensible qualities of bread appear not of themselves to have any connection with the secret powers of nourishment and support; for otherwise we could infer these secret powers from the first appearance of these sensible qualities without the aid of experience, contrary to the sentiment of all philosophers, and contrary to plain matter of fact. Here, then, is our natural state of ignorance with regard to the powers and influence of all objects. How is this remedied by experience? It only shows us a number of uniform effects resulting from certain objects, and teaches us that those particular objects, at that particular time, were endowed with such powers and forces. When a new object endowed with similar sensible qualities is produced, we expect similar powers and forces, and look for a like effect. From a body of like color and consistency with bread, we expect like nourishment and support. But this surely is a step or progress of the mind which wants to be explained. When a man says, *I have found, in all past instances, such sensible qualities, conjoined with such secret powers,* and when he says, *similar sensible qualities will always be conjoined with similar secret powers,* he is not guilty of a tautology, nor are these propositions in any respect the same. You say that the one proposition is an inference from the other; but you must confess that the inference is not intuitive, neither is it demonstrative. Of what nature is it then? To say it is experimental is begging the question. For all inferences from experience suppose, as their foundation, that the future will resemble the past and that similar powers will be conjoined with similar sensible qualities. If there by any suspicion that the course of nature may change, and that the past may be no rule for the future, all experience becomes useless and can give rise to no inference or conclusion. It is impossible, therefore, that any arguments from experience can prove this resemblance of the past to the future, since all these arguments are founded on the supposition of that resemblance. Let the course of things be allowed hitherto ever so regular, that alone, without some new argument or inference, proves not that for the future it will continue so. In vain do you pretend to have learned the nature of bodies from your past experience. Their secret nature, and consequently all their efforts and influence, may change without any change in their sensible qualities. This happens sometimes, and with regard to some objects. Why may it not happen always, and with regard to all objects? What logic, what process of argument secures you against this supposition? My practice, you say, refutes my doubts. But you mistake the purport of my question. As an agent, I am quite satisfied in the point; but as a philosopher who has some share of curiosity, I will not say skepticism, I want to learn the foundation of this inference. No reading, no inquiry has yet been able to remove my difficulty or give me satisfaction in a matter of such importance. Can I do better than propose the difficulty to the public, even though, perhaps, I have small hopes of obtaining a solution? We shall at least, by this means, be sensible of our ignorance, if we do not augment our knowledge.

I must confess that a man is guilty of unpardonable arrogance who concludes, because an argument has escaped his own investigation, that therefore it does not really exist. I must also confess that, though all the learned, for several ages, should have employed themselves in fruitless search upon any subject, it may still, perhaps, be rash to conclude positively that the subject must therefore pass all human comprehension. Even though we examine all the sources of our knowledge and conclude them unfit for such a subject, there may still remain a suspicion that the enumeration is not complete or the examination not accurate. But with regard to the present subject, there are some considerations which seem to remove all this accusation of arrogance or suspicion of mistake.

It is certain that the most ignorant and stupid peasants, nay infants, nay even brute beasts, improve by experience and learn the qualities of natural objects by observing the effects which result from them. When a child has felt the sensation of pain from touching the flame of a candle, he will be careful not to put his hand near any candle, but will expect a similar effect from a cause which is similar in its sensible qualities and appearance. If you assert, therefore, that the understanding of the child is led into this conclusion by any process of argument or ratiocination, I may justly require you to produce that argument, nor have you any pretense to refuse so equitable a demand. You cannot say that the argument is abstruse and may possibly escape your inquiry, since you confess that it is obvious to the capacity of a mere infant. If you hesitate, therefore, a moment or if, after reflection, you produce an intricate or profound argument, you, in a manner, give up the question and confess that it is not reasoning which engages us to suppose the past resembling the future, and to expect similar effects from causes which are to appearance similar. This is the proposition which I intended to enforce in the present section. If I be right, I pretend not to have made any mighty discovery. And if I be wrong, I must acknowledge myself to be indeed a very backward scholar, since I cannot now discover an argument which, it seems, was perfectly familiar to me long before I was out of my cradle.

SECTION V. SKEPTICAL SOLUTION OF THESE DOUBTS

PART I

The passion for philosophy, like that for religion, seems liable to this inconvenience, that though it aims at the correction of our manners and extirpation of our vices, it may only serve, by imprudent management, to foster a predominant inclination and push the mind with more determined resolution toward that side which already *draws* too much by the bias and propensity of the natural temper. It is certain that, while we aspire to the magnanimous firmness of the philosophic sage and endeavor to confine our pleasures altogether within our own minds, we may, at last, render our philosophy, like that of Epictetus and other Stoics, only a more refined system of selfishness, and reason ourselves out of all virtue as well as social enjoyment. While we study with attention the vanity of human life and turn all our thoughts toward the empty and transitory nature of riches and honors, we are, perhaps, all the while flattering our natural indolence which, hating the bustle of the world and drudgery of business, seeks a pretense of reason to give itself a full and uncontrolled indulgence. There is, however, one species of philosophy which seems little liable to this inconvenience, and that because it strikes in with no disorderly passion of the human mind, nor can mingle itself with any natural affection or propensity; and that is the Academic or Skeptical philosophy. The Academics always talk of doubt and suspense of judgment, of danger in hasty determinations, of confining to very narrow bounds the inquiries of the understanding, and of renouncing all speculations which lie not within the limits of common life and practice. Nothing, therefore, can be more contrary than such a philosophy to the supine indolence of the mind, its rash arrogance, its lofty pretensions, and its superstitious credulity. Every passion is mortified by it, except the love of truth; and that passion never is nor can be carried to too high a degree. It is surprising, therefore, that this philosophy, which in almost every instance must be harmless and innocent, should be the subject of so much groundless reproach and obloquy. But, perhaps, the very circumstance which renders it so innocent is what chiefly exposes it to the public hatred and resentment. By flattering no irregular passion, it gains few partisans. By opposing so many vices and follies, it raises to itself abundance of enemies who stigmatize it as libertine, profane, and irreligious.

Nor need we fear that this philosophy, while it endeavors to limit our inquiries to common life, should ever undermine the reasonings of common life and carry its doubts so far as to destroy all action as well as speculation. Nature will always maintain her rights and prevail in the end over any abstract reasoning whatsoever. Though we should conclude, for instance, as in the foregoing section, that in all reasonings from experience there is a step taken by the mind which is not supported by any argument or process of the understanding, there is no danger that these reasonings, on which almost all knowledge depends, will ever be affected by such a discovery. If the mind be not engaged by argument to make this step, it must be induced by some other principle of equal weight and authority; and that principle will preserve its influence as long as human nature remains the same. What that principle is may well be worth the pains of inquiry.

Suppose a person, though endowed with the strongest faculties of reason and reflection, to be brought on a sudden into this world; he would, indeed, immediately observe a continual succession of objects and one event following another, but he would not be able to discover anything further. He would not at first, by any reasoning, be able to reach the idea of cause and effect, since the particular powers by which all natural operations are performed never appear to the senses; nor is it reasonable to conclude, merely because one event in one instance precedes another, that therefore the one is the cause, the other the effect. The conjunction may be arbitrary and casual. There may be no reason to infer the existence of one from the appearance of the other: and, in a word, such a person without more experience could never employ his conjecture or reasoning concerning any matter of fact or be assured of anything beyond what was immediately present to his memory or senses.

Suppose again that he has acquired more experience and has lived so long in the world as to have observed similar objects or events to be constantly conjoined together—what is the consequence of this experience? He immediately infers the existence of one object from the appearance of the other, yet he has not, by all his experience, acquired any idea or knowledge of the secret power by which the one object produces the other, nor is it by any process of reasoning he is engaged to draw this inference; but still he finds himself determined to draw it, and though he should be convinced that his understanding has no part in the operation, he would nevertheless continue in the same course of thinking. There is some other principle which determines him to form such a conclusion.

This principle is *custom* or *habit*. For wherever the repetition of any particular act or operation produces a propensity to renew the same act or operation without being impelled by any reasoning or process of the understanding, we always say that this propensity is the effect of *custom*. By employing that word we pretend not to have given the ultimate reason of such a propensity. We only point out a principle of human nature which is universally acknowledged, and which is well known by its effects. Perhaps we can push our inquiries no further or pretend to give the cause of this cause, but must rest contented with it as the ultimate principle which we can assign of all our conclusions from experience. It is sufficient satisfaction that we can go so far without repining at the narrowness of our faculties, because they will carry us no further. And it is certain we here advance a very intelligible proposition at least, if not a true one, when we assert that after the constant conjunction of two objects, heat and flame, for instance, weight and solidity, we are determined by custom alone to expect the one from the appearance of the other. This hypothesis seems even the only one which explains the difficulty why we draw from a thousand instances an inference which we are not able to draw from one instance that is in no respect different from them. Reason is incapable of any such variation. The conclusions which it draws from considering one circle are the same which it would form upon surveying all the circles in the universe. But no man, having seen only one body move after being impelled by another, could infer that every other body will move after a like impulse. All inferences from experience, therefore, are effects of custom, not of reasoning.[2]

[2] Nothing is more usual than for writers, even on *moral, political,* or *physical* subjects, to distinguish between *reason* and *experience,* and to suppose that these species of argumentation are entirely different from each other. The former are taken for the mere result of our intellectual faculties, which, by considering *a priori* the nature of things, and examining the effects that must follow from their operation, establish particular principles of science and philosophy. The latter are supposed to be derived entirely from sense and observation, by which we learn what has actually resulted from the operation of particular objects, and are thence able to infer what will for the future result from them. Thus, for instance, the limitations and restraints of civil government and a legal constitution may be defended, either from *reason,* which, reflecting on the great frailty and corruption of human nature, teaches that no man can safely be trusted with unlimited authority; or from *experience* and history, which inform us of the enormous abuses that ambition in every age and country has been found to make of so imprudent a confidence.

The same distinction between reason and experience is maintained in all our deliberations concerning the conduct of life, while the experienced statesman, general physician, or merchant, is trusted and followed, and the unpracticed novice, with whatever natural talents endowed, neglected and despised. Though it be allowed that reason may form very plausible conjectures with regard to the consequences of such a particular conduct in such particular circumstances, it is still supposed imperfect without the assistance of experience, which is alone able to give stability and certainty to the maxim derived from study and reflection.

But notwithstanding that this distinction be thus universally received, both in the active and speculative scenes of life, I shall not scruple to pronounce that it is, at bottom, erroneous, or at least superficial.

If we examine those arguments which, in any of

Custom, then, is the great guide of human life. It is that principle alone which renders our experience useful to us and makes us expect, for the future, a similar train of events with those which have appeared in the past. Without the influence of custom we should be entirely ignorant of every matter of fact beyond what is immediately present to the memory and senses. We should never know how to adjust means to ends or to employ our natural powers in the production of any effect. There would be an end at once of all action as well as of the chief part of speculation.

But here it may be proper to remark that though our conclusions from experience carry us beyond our memory and senses and assure us of matters of fact which happened in the most distant places and most remote ages, yet some fact must always be present to the senses or memory from which we may first proceed in drawing these conclusions. A man who should find in a desert country the remains of pompous buildings would conclude that the country had, in ancient times, been cultivated by civilized inhabitants; but did nothing of this nature occur to him, he could never form such an inference. We learn the events of former ages from history, but then we must peruse the volume in which this instruction is contained, and thence carry up our inferences from one testimony to another, till we arrive at the eyewitnesses and spectators of these distant events. In a word, if we proceed not upon some fact present to the memory or senses, our reasonings would be merely hypothetical; and however the particular links might be connected with each other, the whole chain of inferences would have nothing to support it, nor could we ever, by its means, arrive at the knowledge of any real existence. If I ask why you believe any particular matter of fact which you relate, you must tell me some reason; and this reason will be some other fact connected with it. But as you cannot proceed after this manner *in infinitum,* you must at last terminate in some fact which is present to your memory or senses or must allow that your belief is entirely without foundation.

What, then, is the conclusion of the whole matter? A simple one, though, it must be confessed, pretty remote from the common theories of philosophy. All belief of matter of fact or real existence is derived merely from some object present to the memory or senses and a customary conjunction between that and some other object; or, in other words, having found, in many instances, that any two kinds of objects, flame and heat, snow and cold, have always been conjoined together: if flame or snow be presented anew to the senses, the mind is carried by custom to expect heat or cold, and to *believe* that such a quality does exist and will discover itself upon a nearer approach. This belief is the necessary result of placing the mind in such circumstances. It is an operation of the soul, when we are so situated, as unavoidable as to feel the passion of love, when we receive benefits; or hatred, when we meet with injuries. All these operations are a species of natural instincts, which no reasoning or process of the thought and understanding is able either to produce or to prevent. At this point

---

the sciences above mentioned, are supposed to be the mere effects of reasoning and reflection, they will be found to terminate at last in some general principle or conclusion for which we can assign no reason but observation and experience. The only difference between them and those maxims which are vulgarly esteemed the result of pure experience is that the former cannot be established without some process of thought, and some reflection on what we have observed, in order to distinguish its circumstances and trace its consequences—whereas, in the latter, the experienced event is exactly and fully similar to that which we infer as the result of any particular situation. The history of a Tiberius or a Nero makes us dread a like tyranny, were our monarchs freed from the restraints of laws and senates: but the observation of any fraud or cruelty in private life is sufficient, with the aid of a little thought, to give us the same apprehension, while it serves as an instance of the general corruption of human nature, and shows us the danger which we must incur by reposing an entire confidence in mankind. In both cases, it is experience which is ultimately the foundation of our inference and conclusion.

There is no man so young and inexperienced as not to have formed from observation many general and just maxims concerning human affairs and the conduct of life; but it must be confessed that when a man comes to put these in practice he will be extremely liable to error, till time and further experience both enlarge these maxims, and teach him their proper use and application. In every situation or incident there are many particular and seemingly minute circumstances which the man of greatest talents is at first apt to overlook, though on them the justness of his conclusions, and consequently the prudence of his conduct, entirely depend. Not to mention that, to a young beginner, the general observations and maxims occur not always on the proper occasions, nor can be immediately applied with due calmness and distinction. The truth is, an inexperienced reasoner could be no reasoner at all were he absolutely inexperienced; and when we assign that character to anyone, we mean it only in a comparative sense, and suppose him possessed of experience in a smaller and more imperfect degree.

it would be very allowable for us to stop our philosophical researches. In most questions we can never make a single step further; and in all questions we must terminate here at last, after our most restless and curious inquiries. But still our curiosity will be pardonable, perhaps commendable, if it carry us on to still further researches and make us examine more accurately the nature of this *belief* and of the *customary conjunction* whence it is derived. By this means we may meet with some explications and analogies that will give satisfaction, at least to such as love the abstract sciences, and can be entertained with speculations which, however accurate, may still retain a degree of doubt and uncertainty. As to readers of a different taste, the remaining part of this Section is not calculated for them; and the following inquiries may well be understood, though it be neglected.

PART II

Nothing is more free than the imagination of man, and though it cannot exceed that original stock of ideas furnished by the internal and external senses, it has unlimited power of mixing, compounding, separating, and dividing these ideas in all the varieties of fiction and vision. It can feign a train of events with all the appearance of reality, ascribe to them a particular time and place, conceive them as existent, and paint them out to itself with every circumstance that belongs to any historical fact which it believes with the greatest certainty. Wherein, therefore, consists the difference between such a fiction and belief? It lies not merely in any peculiar idea which is annexed to such a conception as commands our assent, and which is wanting to every known fiction. For as the mind has authority over all its ideas, it could voluntarily annex this particular idea to any fiction, and consequently be able to believe whatever it pleases, contrary to what we find by daily experience. We can, in our conception, join the head of a man to the body of a horse, but it is not in our power to believe that such an animal has ever really existed.

It follows, therefore, that the difference between *fiction* and *belief* lies in some sentiment or feeling which is annexed to the latter, not to the former, and which depends not on the will, nor can be demanded at pleasure. It must be excited by nature like all other sentiments and must rise from the particular situation in which the mind is placed at any particular juncture. Whenever any object is presented to the memory or senses, it immediately, by the force of custom, carries the imagination to conceive that object which is usually conjoined to it; and this conception is attended with a feeling or sentiment different from the loose reveries of the fancy. In this consists the whole nature of belief. For as there is no matter of fact which we believe so firmly that we cannot conceive the contrary, there would be no difference between the conception assented to and that which is rejected were it not for some sentiment which distinguishes the one from the other. If I see a billiard ball moving toward another on a smooth table, I can easily conceive it to stop upon contact. This conception implies no contradiction, but still it feels very differently from that conception by which I represent to myself the impulse and the communication of motion from one ball to another.

Were we to attempt a *definition* of this sentiment, we should, perhaps, find it a very difficult, if not an impossible, task; in the same manner as if we should endeavor to define the feeling of cold, or passion of anger, to a creature who never had any experience of these sentiments. Belief is the true and proper name of this feeling, and no one is ever at a loss to know the meaning of that term, because every man is every moment conscious of the sentiment represented by it. It may not, however, be improper to attempt a *description* of this sentiment, in hopes we may by that means arrive at some analogies which may afford a more perfect explication of it. I say that belief is nothing but a more vivid, lively, forcible, firm, steady conception of an object than what the imagination alone is ever able to attain. This variety of terms, which may seem so unphilosophical, is intended only to express that act of the mind which renders realities, or what is taken for such, more present to us than fictions, causes them to weigh more in the thought, and gives them a superior influence on the passions and imagination. Provided we agree about the thing, it is needless to dispute about the terms. The imagination has the command over all its ideas and can join and mix and vary them in all the ways possible. It may conceive fictitious objects with all the circumstances of place and time. It may set them in a manner before our eyes, in their true colors, just as they might have existed. But as it is impossible that this faculty of imagination can ever, of itself, reach belief, it is evident that belief consists not in the peculiar nature or order of ideas, but in the *manner* of their conception and in their *feeling* to the mind. I confess that it is impossible perfectly to explain this feeling or manner of conception. We may make use of words which express something near it. But its true and proper name, as we observed before, is "belief," which is a term that everyone sufficiently understands in common life. And in philosophy we can go no further than assert that *belief* is something felt by the mind, which distinguishes the ideas of the judgment from the fictions of the imagination. It gives them more weight and influence, makes them appear of greater importance, enforces them in the mind, and renders them the governing principle of our actions. I hear at present, for instance, a person's voice with whom I am acquainted, and the sound comes as from the next room. This impression of my senses immediately conveys my thought to the person, together with all the surrounding objects. I paint them out to myself as existing at present, with the same qualities and relations of which I formerly knew them possessed. These ideas take faster hold of my mind than ideas of an enchanted castle. They are very different from the feeling and have a much greater influence of every kind, either to give pleasure or pain, joy or sorrow.

Let us, then, take in the whole compass of this doctrine and allow that the sentiment of belief is nothing but a conception more intense and steady than what attends the mere fictions of the imagination, and that this *manner* of conception arises from a customary conjunction of the object with something present to the memory or senses. I believe that it will not be difficult, upon these suppositions, to find other operations of the mind analogous to it and to trace up these phenomena to principles still more general.

We have already observed that nature has established connections among particular ideas, and that no sooner one idea occurs to our thoughts than it introduces its correlative and carries our attention toward it by a gentle and insensible movement. These principles of connection or association we have reduced to three, namely, "resemblance," "contiguity," and "causation," which are the only bonds that unite our thoughts together and beget that regular train of reflection or discourse which, in a greater or less degree, takes place among all mankind. Now here arises a question on which the solution of the present difficulty will depend. Does it happen in all these relations that when one of the objects is presented to the senses or memory, the mind is not only carried to the conception of the correlative, but reaches a steadier and stronger conception of it than what otherwise it would have been able to attain? This seems to be the case with that belief which arises from the relation of cause and effect. And if the case be the same with the other relations or principles of association, this may be established as a general law which takes place in all the operations of the mind.

We may, therefore, observe, as the first experiment to our present purpose, that upon the appearance of the picture of an absent friend our idea of him is evidently enlivened by the *resemblance,* and that every passion which that idea occasions, whether of joy or sorrow, acquires new force and vigor. In producing this effect there concur both a relation and a present impression. Where the picture bears him no resemblance, at least was not intended for him, it never so much as conveys our thought to him. And where it is absent, as well as the person, though the mind may pass from the thought of one to that of the other, it feels its idea to be rather weakened than enlivened by that transition. We take a pleasure in viewing the picture of a friend when it is set before us; but when it is removed, rather choose to consider him directly than by reflection on an image which is equally distant and obscure.

The ceremonies of the Roman Catholic religion may be considered as instances of the same nature. The devotees of that superstition usually plead, in excuse for the mummeries with which they are upbraided, that they feel the good effect of those external motions, and postures, and actions in enlivening their devotion and quickening their fervor, which otherwise would decay if directed entirely to distant and immaterial objects. We shadow out the objects of our faith, say they, in sensible types and images, and render them more present to us by the immediate presence of these types than it is possible for us to do merely by an intellectual view and contemplation. Sensible objects have always a greater influence on the fancy than any other, and this influence they readily convey to those ideas to which they are related and which they resemble.

I shall only infer from these practices and this reasoning that the effect of resemblance in enlivening the ideas is very common; and as in every case a resemblance and a present impression must concur, we are abundantly supplied with experiments to prove the reality of the foregoing principle.

We may add force to these experiments by others of a different kind, in considering the effects of *contiguity* as well as of *resemblance.* It is certain that distance diminishes the force of every idea and that, upon our approach to any object, though it does not discover itself to our senses, it operates upon the mind with an influence which imitates an immediate impression. The thinking on any object readily transports the mind to what is contiguous; but it is only the actual presence of an object that transports it with a superior vivacity. When I am a few miles from home, whatever relates to it touches me more nearly than when I am two hundred leagues distant, though even at that distance the reflecting on anything in the neighborhood of my friends or family naturally produces an idea of them. But, as in this latter case, both the objects of the mind are ideas, notwithstanding there is an easy transition between them; that transition alone is not able to give a superior vivacity to any of the ideas, for want of some immediate impression.[3]

No one can doubt but *causation* has the same influence as the other two relations of resemblance and contiguity. Superstitious people are fond of the relics of saints and holy men, for the same reason that they seek after types or images in order to enliven their devotion and give them a more intimate and strong conception of those exemplary lives which they desire to imitate. Now it is evident that one of the best relics which a devotee could procure would be the handiwork of a saint; and if his clothes and furniture are ever to be considered in this light, it is because they were once at his disposal and were moved and affected by him; in which respect they are to be considered as imperfect effects, and as connected with him by a shorter chain of consequences than any of those by which we learn the reality of his existence.

Suppose that the son of a friend who had been long dead or absent were presented to us; it is evident that this object would instantly revive its correlative idea and recall to our thoughts all past intimacies and familiarities in more lively color than they would otherwise have appeared to us. This is another phenomenon which seems to prove the principle above mentioned.

We may observe that in these phenomena the belief of the correlative object is always presupposed, without which the relation could have no effect. The influence of the picture supposes that we *believe* our friend to have once existed. Contiguity to home can never excite our ideas of home unless we *believe* that it really exists. Now I assert that this belief, where it reaches beyond the memory or senses, is of a similar nature and arises from similar causes with the transition of thought and vivacity of conception here explained. When I throw a piece of dry wood into a fire, my mind is immediately carried to conceive that it augments, not extinguishes, the flame. This transition of thought from the cause to the effect proceeds not from reason. It derives its origin altogether from custom and experience. And, as it first begins from an object present to the senses, it renders the idea or conception of flame more strong or lively than any loose floating reverie of the imagination. That idea arises immediately. The thought moves instantly toward it and conveys to it all that force of conception which is derived from the impression present to the senses. When a sword is leveled at my breast, does not the idea of wound and pain strike me more strongly than when a glass of wine is presented to me, even though by accident this idea should occur after the appearance of the latter object? But what is there in this whole matter to cause such a strong conception except only a present object and a customary transition to the idea of another object which we have been accustomed to conjoin with the former? This is the whole operation of the mind in all our conclusions concerning matter of fact and existence; and it is a satisfaction to find some analogies by which it may be explained. The transition from a present object does in all cases give strength and solidity to the related idea.

Here, then, is a kind of pre-established harmony between the course of nature and the succession of our ideas; and though the powers and forces by which the former is governed be wholly unknown to us, yet our thoughts and conceptions have still, we find, gone on in the same train with

[3] [A footnote containing a long quotation from Cicero deleted.]

the other works of nature. Custom is that principle by which this correspondence has been effected, so necessary to the subsistence of our species and the regulation of our conduct in every circumstance and occurrence of human life. Had not the presence of an object instantly excited the idea of those objects commonly conjoined with it, all our knowledge must have been limited to the narrow sphere of our memory and senses, and we should never have been able to adjust means to ends or employ our natural powers either to the producing of good or avoiding of evil. Those who delight in the discovery and contemplation of *final causes* have here ample subject to employ their wonder and admiration.

I shall add, for a further confirmation of the foregoing theory, that as this operation of the mind, by which we infer like effects from like causes, and *vice versa,* is so essential to the subsistence of all human creatures, it is not probable that it could be trusted to the fallacious deductions of our reason, which is slow in its operations, appears not, in any degree, during the first years of infancy, and, at best, is in every age and period of human life extremely liable to error and mistake. It is more conformable to the ordinary wisdom of nature to secure so necessary an act of the mind by some instinct or mechanical tendency which may be infallible in its operations, may discover itself at the first appearance of life and thought, and may be independent of all the labored deductions of the understanding. As nature has taught us the use of our limbs without giving us the knowledge of the muscles and nerves by which they are actuated, so has she implanted in us an instinct which carries forward the thought in a correspondent course to that which she has established among external objects, though we are ignorant of those powers and forces on which this regular course and succession of objects totally depends.

SECTION VI. OF PROBABILITY[4]

Though there be no such thing as *chance* in the world, our ignorance of the real cause of any event has the same influence on the understanding and begets a like species of belief or opinion.

There is certainly a probability which arises from a superiority of chances on any side; and, according as this superiority increases and surpasses the opposite chances, the probability receives a proportionable increase and begets still a higher degree of belief or assent to that side in which we discover the superiority. If a die were marked with one figure or number of spots on four sides, and with another figure or number of spots on the two remaining sides, it would be more probable that the former would turn up than the latter, though, if it had a thousand sides marked in the same manner, and only one side different, the probability would be much higher and our belief or expectation of the event more steady and secure. This process of the thought or reasoning may seem trivial and obvious; but to those who consider it more narrowly it may, perhaps, afford matter for curious speculation.

It seems evident that when the mind looks forward to discover the event which may result from the throw of such a die, it considers the turning up of each particular side as alike probable; and this is the very nature of chance, to render all the particular events comprehended in it entirely equal. But finding a greater number of sides concur in the one event than in the other, the mind is carried more frequently to that event and meets it oftener in revolving the various possibilities or chances on which the ultimate result depends. This concurrence of several views in one particular event begets immediately, by an explicable contrivance of nature, the sentiment of belief and gives that event the advantage over its antagonist which is supported by a smaller number of views and recurs less frequently to the mind. If we allow that belief is nothing but a firmer and stronger conception of an object than what attends the mere fictions of the imagination, this operation may, perhaps, in some measure be accounted for. The concurrence of these several views or glimpses imprints the idea more strongly on the imagination, gives it superior force and vigor, renders its influence on the passions and affections more sensible, and, in a word, begets that reliance or security which constitutes the nature of belief and opinion.

[4] Mr. Locke divides all arguments into "demonstrative" and "probable." In this view, we must say that it is only probable all men must die, or that the sun will rise tomorrow. But to conform our language more to common use, we ought to divide arguments into *demonstrations, proofs,* and *probabilities;* by proofs, meaning such arguments from experience as leave no room for doubt or opposition.

The case is the same with the probability of causes as with that of chance. There are some cases which are entirely uniform and constant in producing a particular effect, and no instance has ever yet been found of any failure or irregularity in their operation. Fire has always burned, and water suffocated, every human creature. The production of motion by impulse and gravity is a universal law which has hitherto admitted of no exception. But there are other causes which have been found more irregular and uncertain, nor has rhubarb always proved a purge, or opium a soporific, to everyone who has taken these medicines. It is true, when any cause fails of producing its usual effect, philosophers ascribe not this to any irregularity in nature, but suppose that some secret causes in the particular structure of parts have prevented the operation. Our reasonings, however, and conclusions concerning the event are the same as if this principle had no place. Being determined by custom to transfer the past to the future in all our inferences, where the past has been entirely regular and uniform we expect the event with the greatest assurance and leave no room for any contrary supposition. But where different effects have been found to follow from causes which are to *appearance* exactly similar, all these various effects must occur to the mind in transferring the past to the future, and enter into our consideration when we determine the probability of the event. Though we give the preference to that which has been found most usual, and believe that this effect will exist, we must not overlook the other effects, but must assign to each of them a particular weight and authority in proportion as we have found it to be more or less frequent. It is more probable, in almost every country of Europe, that there will be frost sometime in January than that the weather will continue open throughout that whole month, though this probability varies according to the different climates, and approaches to a certainty in the more northern kingdoms. Here, then, it seems evident that when we transfer the past to the future in order to determine the effect which will result from any cause, we transfer all the different events in the same proportion as they have appeared in the past, and conceive one to have existed a hundred times, for instance, another ten times, and another once. As a great number of views do here concur in one event, they fortify and confirm it to the imagination, beget that sentiment which we call "belief," and give its object the preference above the contrary event which is not supported by an equal number of experiments and recurs not so frequently to the thought in transferring the past to the future. Let anyone try to account for this operation of the mind upon any of the received systems of philosophy, and he will be sensible of the difficulty. For my part, I shall think it sufficient if the present hints excite the curiosity of philosophers and make them sensible how defective all common theories are in treating of such curious and such sublime subjects.

SECTION VII. OF THE IDEA OF NECESSARY CONNECTION

PART I

The great advantage of the mathematical sciences above the moral consists in this, that the ideas of the former, being sensible, are always clear and determinate, the smallest distinction between them is immediately perceptible, and the same terms are still expressive of the same ideas without ambiguity or variation. An oval is never mistaken for a circle, nor a hyperbola for an ellipsis. The isosceles and scalenum are distinguished by boundaries more exact than vice and virtue, right and wrong. If any term be defined in geometry, the mind readily, of itself, substitutes on all occasions the definition for the term defined, or, even when no definition is employed, the object itself may be presented to the senses and by that means be steadily and clearly apprehended. But the finer sentiments of the mind, the operations of the understanding, the various agitations of the passions, though really in themselves distinct, easily escape us when surveyed by reflection, nor is it in our power to recall the original object as often as we have occasion to contemplate it. Ambiguity, by this means, is gradually introduced into our reasonings: similar objects are readily taken to be the same, and the conclusion becomes at last very wide of the premises.

One may safely, however, affirm that if we consider these sciences in a proper light, their advantages and disadvantages nearly compensate each other and reduce both of them to a state of equality. If the mind, with greater facility, retains the ideas of geometry clear and determinate, it must carry on a much longer and more intricate chain of reasoning and compare ideas much wider of each other in order to reach the abstruser truths of that science. And if moral ideas are apt, without extreme care, to fall into obscurity and confusion, the inferences are always much shorter in these disquisitions, and the intermediate steps which lead to the conclusion much fewer than in the sciences which treat of quantity and number. In reality, there is scarcely a proposition in Euclid so simple as not to consist of more parts than are to be found in any moral reasoning which runs not into chimera and conceit. Where we trace the principles of the human mind through a few steps, we may be very well satisfied with our progress, considering how soon nature throws a bar to all our inquiries concerning causes and reduces us to an acknowledgment of our ignorance. The chief obstacle, therefore, to our improvement in the moral or metaphysical sciences is the obscurity of the ideas and ambiguity of the terms. The principal difficulty in the mathematics is the length of inferences and compass of thought requisite to the forming of any conclusion. And, perhaps, our progress in natural philosophy is chiefly retarded by the want of proper experiments and phenomena, which are often discovered by chance and cannot always be found when requisite, even by the most diligent and prudent inquiry. As moral philosophy seems hitherto to have received less improvement than either geometry or physics, we may conclude that if there be any difference in this respect among these sciences, the difficulties which obstruct the progress of the former require superior care and capacity to be surmounted.

There are no ideas which occur in metaphysics more obscure and uncertain than those of "power," "force," "energy," or "necessary connection," of which it is every moment necessary for us to treat in all our disquisitions. We shall, therefore, endeavor in this Section to fix, if possible, the precise meaning of these terms and thereby remove some part of that obscurity which is so much complained of in this species of philosophy.

It seems a proposition which will not admit of much dispute that all our ideas are nothing but copies of our impressions, or, in other words, that it is impossible for us to *think* of anything which we have not antecedently *felt,* either by our external or internal senses. I have endeavored[5] to explain and prove this proposition, and have expressed my hopes that by a proper application of it men may reach a greater clearness and precision in philosophical reasonings than what they have hitherto been able to attain. Complex ideas may, perhaps, be well known by definition, which is nothing but an enumeration of those parts or simple ideas that compose them. But when we have pushed up definitions to the most simple ideas and find still some ambiguity and obscurity, what resources are we then possessed of? By what invention can we throw light upon these ideas and render them altogether precise and determinate to our intellectual view? Produce the impressions or original sentiments from which the ideas are copied. These impressions are all strong and sensible. They admit not of ambiguity. They are not only placed in a full light themselves, but may throw light on their correspondent ideas, which lie in obscurity. And by this means we may perhaps obtain a new microscope or species of optics by which, in the moral sciences, the most minute and most simple ideas may be so enlarged as to fall readily under our apprehension and be equally known with the grossest and most sensible ideas that can be the object of our inquiry.

To be fully acquainted, therefore, with the idea of power or necessary connection, let us examine its impression and, in order to find the impression with greater certainty, let us search for it in all the sources from which it may possibly be derived.

When we look about us toward external objects and consider the operation of causes, we are never able, in a single instance, to discover any power or necessary connection, any quality which binds the effect to the cause and renders the one an infallible consequence of the other. We only find that the one does actually in fact follow the other. The impulse of one billiard ball is attended with motion in the second. This is the whole that appears to the *outward* senses. The mind feels no sentiment or *inward* impression from this succession of objects; consequently, there is not, in any single particular instance of cause and effect, anything which can suggest the idea of power or necessary connection.

From the first appearance of an object we never can conjecture what effect will result from it. But were the power or energy of any cause

[5] Section II. [Not included here.]

discoverable by the mind, we could foresee the effect, even without experience, and might, at first, pronounce with certainty concerning it by the mere dint of thought and reasoning.

In reality, there is no part of matter that does ever, by its sensible qualities, discover any power or energy, or give us ground to imagine that it could produce anything, or be followed by any other object, which we could denominate its effect. Solidity, extension, motion—these qualities are all complete in themselves and never point out any other event which may result from them. The scenes of the universe are continually shifting, and one object follows another in an uninterrupted succession; but the power or force which actuates the whole machine is entirely concealed from us and never discovers itself in any of the sensible qualities of body. We know that, in fact, heat is a constant attendant of flame; but what is the connection between them we have no room so much as to conjecture or imagine. It is impossible, therefore, that the idea of power can be derived from the contemplation of bodies in single instances of their operation, because no bodies ever discover any power which can be the original of this idea.[6]

Since, therefore, external objects as they appear to the senses give us no idea of power or necessary connection by their operation in particular instances, let us see whether this idea be derived from reflection on the operations of our own minds and be copied from any internal impression. It may be said that we are every moment conscious of internal power while we feel that, by the simple command of our will, we can move the organs of our body or direct the faculties of our mind. An act of volition produces motion in our limbs or raises a new idea in our imagination. This influence of the will we know by consciousness. Hence we acquire the idea of power or energy, and are certain that we ourselves and all other intelligent beings are possessed of power. This idea, then, is an idea of reflection since it arises from reflecting on the operations of our own mind and on the command which is exercised by will both over the organs of the body and faculties of the soul.

We shall proceed to examine this pretension and, first, with regard to the influence of volition over the organs of the body. This influence, we may observe, is a fact which, like all other natural events, can be known only by experience, and can never be foreseen from any apparent energy or power in the cause which connects it with the effect and renders the one an infallible consequence of the other. The motion of our body follows upon the command of our will. Of this we are every moment conscious. But the means by which this is effected, the energy by which the will performs so extraordinary an operation—of this we are so far from being immediately conscious that it must forever escape our most diligent inquiry.

For, *first,* is there any principle in all nature more mysterious than the union of soul with body, by which a supposed spiritual substance acquires such an influence over a material one that the most refined thought is able to actuate the grossest matter? Were we empowered by a secret wish to remove mountains or control the planets in their orbit, this extensive authority would not be more extraordinary, nor more beyond our comprehension. But if, by consciousness, we perceived any power or energy in the will, we must know this power; we must know its connection with the effect; we must know the secret union of soul and body, and the nature of both these substances by which the one is able to operate in so many instances upon the other.

Secondly, we are not able to move all the organs of the body with a like authority, though we cannot assign any reason, besides experience, for so remarkable a difference between one and the other. Why has the will an influence over the tongue and fingers, not over the heart or liver? This question would never embarrass us were we conscious of a power in the former case, not in the latter. We should then perceive, independent of experience, why the authority of the will over the organs of the body is circumscribed within such particular limits. Being in that case fully acquainted with the power or force by which it operates, we should also know why its influence reaches precisely to such boundaries, and no further.

[6] Mr. Locke, in his chapter of Power, says that, finding from experience that there are several new productions in matter, and concluding that there must somewhere be a power capable of producing them, we arrive at last by this reasoning at the idea of power. But no reasoning can ever give us a new, original, simple idea, as this philosopher himself confesses. This, therefore, can never be the origin of that idea.

A man suddenly struck with a palsy in the leg or arm, or who had newly lost those members, frequently endeavors, at first, to move them and employ them in their usual offices. Here he is as much conscious of power to command such limbs as a man in perfect health is conscious of power to actuate any member which remains in its natural state and condition. But consciousness never deceives. Consequently, neither in the one case nor in the other are we ever conscious of any power. We learn the influence of our will from experience alone. And experience only teaches us how one event constantly follows another, without instructing us in the secret connection which binds them together and renders them inseparable.

Thirdly, we learn from anatomy that the immediate object of power in voluntary motion is not the member itself which is moved, but certain muscles and nerves and animal spirits, and, perhaps, something still more minute and more unknown, through which the motion is successively propagated ere it reach the member itself whose motion is the immediate object of volition. Can there be a more certain proof that the power by which this whole operation is performed, so far from being directly and fully known by an inward sentiment or consciousness, is to the last degree mysterious and unintelligible? Here the mind wills a certain event; immediately another event, unknown to ourselves and totally different from the one intended, is produced. This event produces another, equally unknown, till, at last, through a long succession the desired event is produced. But if the original power were felt, it must be known; were it known, its effect must also be known, since all power is relative to its effect. And, *vice versa,* if the effect be not known, the power cannot be known nor felt. How indeed can we be conscious of a power to move our limbs when we have no such power, but only that to move certain animal spirits which, though they produce at last the motion of our limbs, yet operate in such a manner as is wholly beyond our comprehension?

We may therefore conclude from the whole, I hope, without any temerity, though with assurance, that our idea of power is not copied from any sentiment or consciousness of power within ourselves when we give rise to animal motion or apply our limbs to their proper use and office. That their motion follows the command of the will is a matter of common experience, like other natural events; but the power or energy by which this is effected, like that in other natural events, is unknown and inconceivable.[7]

Shall we then assert that we are conscious of a power or energy in our own minds when, by an act or command of our will, we raise up a new idea, fix the mind to the contemplation of it, turn it on all sides, and at last dismiss it for some other idea when we think that we have surveyed it with sufficient accuracy? I believe the same arguments will prove that even this command of the will gives us no real idea of force or energy.

First, it must be allowed that when we know a power, we know that very circumstance in the cause by which it is enabled to produce the effect, for these are supposed to be synonymous. We must, therefore, know both the cause and effect and the relation between them. But do we pretend to be acquainted with the nature of the human soul and the nature of an idea, or the aptitude of the one to produce the other? This is a real creation, a production of something out of nothing, which implies a power so great that it may seem, at first sight, beyond the reach of any being less than infinite. At least it must be owned that such a power is not felt, nor known, nor even conceivable by the mind. We only feel the event, namely, the existence of an idea consequent to a command of the will; but the manner in which this operation is performed, the power by which it is produced, is entirely beyond our comprehension.

Secondly, the command of the mind over itself

[7] It may be pretended, that the resistance which we meet with in bodies, obliging us frequently to exert our force and call up all our power, this gives us the idea of force and power. It is this *nisus* or strong endeavor of which we are conscious, that is the original impression from which this idea is copied. But, *first,* we attribute power to a vast number of objects where we never can suppose this resistance or exertion of force to take place: to the Supreme Being, who never meets with any resistance; to the mind in its command over its ideas and limbs, in common thinking and motion, where the effect follows immediately upon the will, without any exertion or summoning up of force; to inanimate matter, which is not capable of this sentiment. *Secondly,* this sentiment of an endeavor to overcome resistance has no known connection with any event: What follows it we know by experience, but could not know it *a priori.* It must, however, be confessed that the animal *nisus* which we experience, though it can afford no accurate precise idea of power, enters very much into that vulgar, inaccurate idea which is formed of it.

is limited, as well as its command over the body; and these limits are not known by reason or any acquaintance with the nature of cause and effect, but only by experience and observation, as in all other natural events and in the operation of external objects. Our authority over our sentiments and passions is much weaker than that over our ideas; and even the latter authority is circumscribed within very narrow boundaries. Will any one pretend to assign the ultimate reason of these boundaries, or show why the power is deficient in one case, not in another?

Thirdly, this self-command is very different at different times. A man in health possesses more of it than one languishing with sickness. We are more master of our thoughts in the morning than in the evening; fasting, than after a full meal. Can we give any reason for these variations except experience? Where then is the power of which we pretend to be conscious? Is there not here, either in a spiritual or material substance, or both, some secret mechanism or structure of parts upon which the effect depends, and which, being entirely unknown to us, renders the power or energy of the will equally unknown and incomprehensible?

Volition is surely an act of the mind with which we are sufficiently acquainted. Reflect upon it. Consider it on all sides. Do you find anything in it like this creative power by which it raises from nothing a new idea and, with a kind of *fiat,* imitates the omnipotence of its Maker, if I may be allowed so to speak, who called forth into existence all the various scenes of nature? So far from being conscious of this energy in the will, it requires as certain experience as that of which we are possessed to convince us that such extraordinary effects do ever result from a simple act of volition.

The generality of mankind never find any difficulty in accounting for the more common and familiar operations of nature, such as the descent of heavy bodies, the growth of plants, the generation of animals, or the nourishment of bodies by food; but suppose that in all these cases they perceive the very force or energy of the cause by which it is connected with its effect, and is forever infallible in its operation. They acquire, by long habit, such a turn of mind that upon the appearance of the cause they immediately expect, with assurance, its usual attendant, and hardly conceive it possible that any other event could result from it. It is only on the discovery of extraordinary phenomena, such as earthquakes, pestilence, and prodigies of any kind, that they find themselves at a loss to assign a proper cause and to explain the manner in which the effect is produced by it. It is usual for men, in such difficulties, to have recourse to some invisible intelligent principle as the immediate cause of that event which surprises them, and which they think cannot be accounted for from the common powers of nature. But philosophers, who carry their scrutiny a little further, immediately perceive that, even in the most familiar events, the energy of the cause is as unintelligible as in the most unusual, and that we only learn by experience the frequent conjunction of objects, without being ever able to comprehend anything like connection between them. Here, then, many philosophers think themselves obliged by reason to have recourse, on all occasions, to the same principle which the vulgar never appeal to but in cases that appear miraculous and supernatural. They acknowledge mind and intelligence to be, not only the ultimate and original cause of all things, but the immediate and sole cause of every event which appears in nature. They pretend that those objects which are commonly denominated "causes" are in reality nothing but "occasions," and that the true and direct principle of every effect is not any power or force in nature, but a volition of the Supreme Being, who wills that such particular objects should forever be conjoined with each other. Instead of saying that one billiard ball moves another by a force which it has derived from the author of nature, it is the Deity himself, they say, who, by a particular volition, moves the second ball, being determined to this operation by the impulse of the first ball, in consequence of those general laws which he has laid down to himself in the government of the universe. But philosophers, advancing still in their inquiries, discover that as we are totally ignorant of the power on which depends the mutual operation of bodies, we are no less ignorant of that power on which depends the operation of mind on body, or of body on mind; nor are we able, either from our senses or consciousness, to assign the ultimate principle in the one case more than in the other. The same ignorance, therefore, reduces them to the same conclusion. They assert that the Deity is the immediate cause of the union between soul and body, and that they are not the organs of sense which, being agitated by external objects, produce sensations in the mind; but that it is a particular volition of our omnipotent Maker which excites such a sensation in consequence of such a motion in the organ. In like manner, it is not any energy in the will that produces local motion in our members: It is God himself, who is pleased to second our will, in itself impotent, and to command that motion which we erroneously attribute to our own power and efficacy. Nor do philosophers stop at this conclusion. They sometimes extend the same inference to the mind itself in its internal operations. Our mental vision or conception of ideas is nothing but a revelation made to us by our Maker. When we voluntarily turn our thoughts to any object and raise up its image in the fancy, it is not the will which creates that idea, it is the universal Creator who discovers it to the mind and renders it present to us.

Thus, according to these philosophers, every thing is full of God. Not content with the principle that nothing exists but by his will, that nothing possesses any power but by his concession, they rob nature and all created beings of every power in order to render their dependence on the Deity still more sensible and immediate. They consider not that by this theory they diminish, instead of magnifying, the grandeur of those attributes which they affect so much to celebrate. It argues, surely, more power in the Deity to delegate a certain degree of power to inferior creatures than to produce everything by his own immediate volition. It argues more wisdom to contrive at first the fabric of the world with such perfect foresight that of itself, and by its proper operation, it may serve all the purposes of Providence than if the great Creator were obliged every moment to adjust its parts and animate by his breath all the wheels of that stupendous machine.

But if we would have a more philosophical confutation of this theory, perhaps the two following reflections may suffice:

First, it seems to me that this theory of the universal energy and operation of the Supreme Being is too bold ever to carry conviction with it to a man sufficiently apprised of the weakness of human reason and the narrow limits to which it is confined in all its operations. Though the chain of arguments which conduct to it were ever so logical, there must arise a strong suspicion, if not an absolute assurance, that it has carried us quite beyond the reach of our faculties when it leads to conclusions so extraordinary and so remote from common life and experience. We are got into fairyland long ere we have reached the last steps of our theory; and *there* we have no reason to trust our common methods of argument or to think that our usual analogies and probabilities have any authority. Our line is too short to fathom such immense abysses. And however we may flatter ourselves that we are guided, in every step which we take, by a kind of verisimilitude and experience, we may be assured that this fancied experience has no authority when we thus apply it to subjects that lie entirely out of the sphere of experience. But on this we shall have occasion to touch afterwards.[8]

Secondly, I cannot perceive any force in the arguments on which this theory is founded. We are ignorant, it is true, of the manner in which bodies operate on each other. Their force or energy is entirely incomprehensible. But are we not equally ignorant of the manner or force by which a mind, even the Supreme Mind, operates, either on itself or on body? Whence, I beseech you, do we acquire any idea of it? We have no sentiment or consciousness of this power in ourselves. We have no idea of the Supreme Being but what we learn from reflection on our own faculties. Were our ignorance, therefore, a good reason for rejecting anything, we should be led into that principle of denying all energy in the Supreme Being, as much as in the grossest matter. We surely comprehend as little the operations of the one as of the other. Is it more difficult to conceive that motion may arise from impulse than that it may arise from volition? All we know is our profound ignorance in both cases.[9]

[8] Section XII. [Not included here.]

[9] I need not examine at length the *vis inertiae* which is so much talked of in the new philosophy, and which is ascribed to matter. We find by experience that a body at rest or in motion continues forever in its present state, till put from it by some new cause; and that a body impelled takes as much motion from the impelling body as it acquires itself. These are facts. When we call this a *vis inertiae,* we only mark these facts, without pretending to have any idea of the inert power, in the same manner as, when we talk of gravity, we mean certain effects without comprehending that active power. It was never the meaning of Sir Isaac Newton to rob second causes of all force or energy, though some of his followers have endeavored to establish that theory upon his authority. On the contrary, that great philosopher had recourse to an ethereal active fluid to explain his universal attraction,

PART II

But to hasten to a conclusion of this argument, which is already drawn out to too great a length: We have sought in vain for an idea of power or necessary connection in all the sources from which we would suppose it to be derived. It appears that in single instances of the operation of bodies we never can, by our utmost scrutiny, discover anything but one event following another, without being able to comprehend any force or power by which the cause operates or any connection between it and its supposed effect. The same difficulty occurs in contemplating the operations of mind on body, where we observe the motion of the latter to follow upon the volition of the former, but are not able to observe or conceive the tie which binds together the motion and volition, or the energy, by which the mind produces this effect. The authority of the will over its own faculties and ideas is not a whit more comprehensible, so that, upon the whole, there appears not, throughout all nature, any one instance of connection which is conceivable by us. All events seem entirely loose and separate. One event follows another, but we never can observe any tie between them. They seem *conjoined,* but never *connected.* But as we can have no idea of anything which never appeared to our outward sense or inward sentiment, the necessary conclusion *seems* to be that we have no idea of connection or power at all, and that these words are absolutely without any meaning when employed either in philosophical reasonings or common life.

But there still remains one method of avoiding this conclusion, and one source which we have not yet examined. When any natural object or event is presented, it is impossible for us, by any sagacity or penetration, to discover, or even conjecture, without experience, what event will result from it, or to carry our foresight beyond that object which is immediately present to the memory and senses. Even after one instance or experiment where we have observed a particular event to follow upon another, we are not entitled to form a general rule or foretell what will happen in like cases, it being justly esteemed an unpardonable temerity to judge of the whole course of nature from one single experiment, however accurate or certain. But when one particular species of events has always, in all instances, been conjoined with another, we make no longer any scruple of foretelling one upon the appearance of the other, and of employing that reasoning which can alone assure us of any matter of fact or existence. We then call the one object "cause," the other "effect." We suppose that there is some connection between them, some power in the one by which it infallibly produces the other and operates with the greatest certainty and strongest necessity.

It appears, then, that this idea of a necessary connection among events arises from a number of similar instances which occur, of the constant conjunction of these events; nor can that idea ever be suggested by any one of these instances surveyed in all possible lights and positions. But there is nothing in a number of instances, different from every single instance, which is supposed to be exactly similar, except only that after a repetition of similar instances the mind is carried by habit, upon the appearance of one event, to expect its usual attendant and to believe that it will exist. This connection, therefore, which we *feel* in the mind, this customary transition of the imagination from one object to its usual attendant, is the sentiment or impression from which we form the idea of power or necessary connection. Nothing further is in the case. Contemplate the subjects on all sides, you will never find any other origin of that idea. This is the sole difference between one instance, from which we can never receive the idea of connection, and a number of similar instances by which it is suggested. The first time a man saw the communication of motion by impulse, as by the shock of two billiard balls, he could not pronounce that the one event was *connected,* but only that it was *conjoined* with the other. After he has observed several instances of this nature, he then pronounces them to be *connected.* What alteration has happened to give rise to this new idea of

---

though he was so cautious and modest as to allow that it was a mere hypothesis not to be insisted on without more experiments. I must confess that there is something in the fate of opinions a little extraordinary. Descartes insinuated that doctrine of the universal and sole efficacy of the Deity, without insisting on it. Malebranche and other Cartesians made it the foundation of all their philosophy. It had, however, no authority in England. Locke, Clarke, and Cudworth never so much as take notice of it, but suppose all along that matter has a real, though subordinate and derived, power. By what means has it become so prevalent among our modern metaphysicians?

connection? Nothing but that he now *feels* these events to be *connected* in his imagination, and can readily foretell the existence of one from the appearance of the other. When we say, therefore, that one object is connected with another, we mean only that they have acquired a connection in our thought and gave rise to this inference by which they become proofs of each other's existence—a conclusion which is somewhat extraordinary, but which seems founded on sufficient evidence. Nor will its evidence be weakened by any general diffidence of the understanding or skeptical suspicion concerning every conclusion which is new and extraordinary. No conclusions can be more agreeable to skepticism than such as make discoveries concerning the weakness and narrow limits of human reason and capacity.

And what stronger instance can be produced of the surprising ignorance and weakness of the understanding than the present? For surely, if there be any relation among objects which it imports us to know perfectly, it is that of cause and effect. On this are founded all our reasonings concerning matter of fact or existence. By means of it alone we attain any assurance concerning objects which are removed from the present testimony of our memory and senses. The only immediate utility of all sciences is to teach us how to control and regulate future events by their causes. Our thoughts and inquiries are, therefore, every moment employed about this relation; yet so imperfect are the ideas which we form concerning it that it is impossible to give any just definition of cause, except what is drawn from something extraneous and foreign to it. Similar objects are always conjoined with similar. Of this we have experience. Suitably to this experience, therefore, we may define a cause to be *an object followed by another, and where all the objects, similar to the first, are followed by objects similar to the second.* Or, in other words, *where, if the first object had not been, the second never had existed.* The appearance of a cause always conveys the mind, by a customary transition, to the idea of the effect. Of this also we have experience. We may, therefore, suitably to this experience, form another definition of cause and call it *an object followed by another, and whose appearance always conveys the thought to that other.* But though both these definitions be drawn from circumstances foreign to the cause, we cannot remedy this inconvenience or attain any more perfect definition which may point out that circumstance in the cause which gives it a connection with its effect. We have no idea of this connection, nor even any distinct notion what it is we desire to know when we endeavor at a conception of it. We say, for instance, that the vibration of this string is the cause of this particular sound. But what do we mean by that affirmation? We either mean *that this vibration is followed by this sound, and that all similar vibrations have been followed by similar sounds;* or, *that this vibration is followed by this sound, and that, upon the appearance of one, the mind anticipates the senses and forms immediately an idea of the other.* We may consider the relation of cause and effect in either of these two lights; but beyond these we have no idea of it.[10]

To recapitulate, therefore, the reasonings of this Section: Every idea is copied from some preceding impression or sentiment; and where

[10] According to these explications and definitions, the idea of *power* is relative as much as that of *cause;* and both have a reference to an effect, or some other event constantly conjoined with the former. When we consider the *unknown* circumstance of an object by which the degree or quantity of its effect is fixed and determined, we call that its power. And accordingly, it is allowed by all philosophers that the effect is the measure of the power. But if they had any idea of power as it is in itself, why could they not measure it in itself? The dispute, whether the force of a body in motion be as its velocity, or the square of its velocity; this dispute, I say, needed not be decided by comparing its effects in equal or unequal times, but by direct mensuration and comparison.

As to the frequent use of the words "force," "power," "energy," etc., which everywhere occur in common conversation as well as in philosophy, that is no proof that we are acquainted, in any instance, with the connecting principle between cause and effect, or can account ultimately for the production of one thing by another. These words, as commonly used, have very loose meanings annexed to them, and their ideas are very uncertain and confused. No animal can put external bodies in motion without the sentiment of a *nisus* or endeavor; and every animal has a sentiment or feeling from the stroke or blow of an external object that is in motion. These sensations, which are merely animal, and from which we can *a priori* draw no inference, we are apt to transfer to inanimate objects, and to suppose that they have some such feelings whenever they transfer or receive motion. With regard to energies, which are exerted without our annexing to them any idea of communicated motion, we consider only the constant experienced conjunction of the events; and as we *feel* a customary connection between the ideas, we transfer that feeling to the objects, as nothing is more usual than to apply to external bodies every internal sensation which they occasion.

we cannot find any impression, we may be certain that there is no idea. In all single instances of the operation of bodies or minds there is nothing that produces any impression, nor consequently can suggest any idea, of power or necessary connection. But when many uniform instances appear, and the same object is always followed by the same event, we then begin to entertain the notion of cause and connection. We then *feel* a new sentiment or impression, to wit, a customary connection in the thought or imagination between one object and its usual attendant; and this sentiment is the original of that idea which we seek for. For as this idea arises from a number of similar instances, and not from any single instance, it must arise from that circumstance in which the number of instances differ from every individual instance. But this customary connection or transition of the imagination is the only circumstance is which they differ. In every other particular they are alike. The first instance which we saw of motion, communicated by the shock of two billiard balls (to return to this obvious illustration), is exactly similar to any instance that may at present occur to us, except only that we could not at first *infer* one event from the other, which we are enabled to do at present, after so long a course of uniform experience. I know not whether the reader will readily apprehend this reasoning. I am afraid that, should I multiply words about it or throw it into a greater variety of lights, it would only become more obscure and intricate. In all abstract reasonings there is one point of view which, if we can happily hit, we shall go further toward illustrating the subject than by all the eloquence and copious expression in the world. This point of view we should endeavor to reach, and reserve the flowers of rhetoric for subjects which are more adapted to them.

IMMANUEL KANT

Introduction to *The Critique of Pure Reason**

I

Of the Difference between Pure and Empirical Cognition.

It is beyond a doubt that all our knowledge begins with experience. For by what should our faculties be roused to act, if not by objects that affect our senses, and thus partly of themselves produce impressions, partly, again, bring the understanding itself into movement, in order to compare these, to join or disjoin them, and in this manner work up such crude material of the intimations of sense into a cognition or recognition of objects which is named experience. So far as time is concerned, then, no cognition of ours precedes experience, and with experience all our knowledge begins.

But, though all our knowledge begins *with* experience, it does not follow that therefore it all derives *from* experience. For it is just possible that experience is itself a compound. It is just possible, that is, that there is in experience, besides what is due to the impression of sense, something in addition that comes from our faculties themselves (when merely acting because of impression); and in that case, it would take long practice, it may be, to enable us to distinguish the latter, and separate it from the former.

It is at least not a question to be summarily dismissed, but one that demands more particular consideration, this, to wit: whether there really be such component part of knowledge as is independent of experience and, indeed, of any im-

* Immanuel Kant, *The Critique of Pure Reason,* Introduction, Parts I-VI. Trans. J. H. Stirling (Edinburgh: Oliver, 1881). First published in German in 1781.

pression of sense whatever? Such component part of knowledge, did it exist, were alone to be truly termed *a priori;* and it would evidently stand in contradistinction to what other component part of knowledge is called empirical: the latter, namely, having its source only *a posteriori,* or in experience.

The expression *a priori,* at the same time, is not precise enough to designate the entire sense of the preceding question. For of many a mere empirical fact, we say, that we know it *a priori,* simply because we do not directly derive it from experience, but from a general rule; and this, even notwithstanding that the rule itself may be so derived. For example, we say of a man that shall have undermined his house, he might have known *a priori* that it would fall in; he had no occasion to wait for the experience of the actual event. Nevertheless, he could not have known this absolutely *a priori.* For that bodies are heavy and, consequently, fall when their supports are withdrawn—this, at least, he must have known by experience beforehand.

In what follows, therefore, we shall understand by cognitions *a priori,* not such as are independent of this or that experience, but such as are totally independent of any experience whatsoever. Opposed to these are empirical cognitions, or such as are only possible *a posteriori,* or from experience. Pure, again, are those *a priori* cognitions which are quite free from all and every empirical admixture. Thus, for example, the proposition, that all change has its cause, is an *a priori* proposition; but it is not, at the same time, *purely* such, for change is an idea which can only be derived from experience.

II

We do possess certain a priori *Cognitions, and even Common Sense is never without such.*

What is wanted here is a criterion, by means of which we may, with certainty, distinguish what is pure from what is empirical. Now experience informs us that something *is* so and so, but not that it cannot be otherwise. *Firstly,* then, should there be a proposition such that it is thought together with its necessity, then it is a judgment *a priori;* and, if underived from any other, absolutely *a priori. Secondly,* experience extends to its judgments never strict or true, but only (through induction) assumptive or comparative universality; so that, properly, it can only be said, So far as we are yet aware, there is no exception to this or that rule. Should any judgment, then, be thought in strict universality, or so, that is, that exceptions are impossible, we may be sure that that judgment is no derivative from experience, but directly *a priori.* Empirical universality, therefore, is only an arbitrary raising of validity from that which obtains in most cases to that which holds good in all, as in the proposition, for example, that all bodies are heavy. Whereas, when strict universality attaches to a judgment, such universality points to a special cognitive source, namely, to a faculty of cognition *a priori.* Necessity and strict universality, therefore, are sure criteria of *a priori* cognition, and inseparably found together. In practice, however, as it is easier, now to apply the one and now the other, it will be advisable to avail ourselves, as occasion may suggest, of either criterion separately; for, even separately, either of them is quite infallible.

Now, it is easy to show that there actually are in our knowledge such necessary and, in the strictest sense, universal (consequently pure *a priori*) judgments. Would we have an example from science, we have only to turn to any proposition in mathematics; while, as for the most ordinary common sense, there is obviously to hand, by way of instance, the proposition that every change must have a cause, where the very notion cause so manifestly implies necessity (of connexion with an effect) and strict universality (of rule), that it would be altogether lost did we derive it, like Hume, from our conjoining what simply follows with what simply precedes, through the mere habit of the experience, and the consequent simple custom of connecting ideas (where the necessity could be only subjective). Besides demonstrating the actual existence in our knowledge of principles *a priori* by a reference to fact, we might even *a priori* prove as much. We might demonstrate, that is, the indispensable necessity of such principles to the very possibility of experience. For how should there be any certainty in experience, were all the rules in it only empirical and (consequently) contingent? It were hardly possible, evidently, to allow any such rules the name of first principles. But it may suffice here to have demonstrated the fact of the possession of pure cognition on our part, together with the signs of the latter. Nay, not merely judgments, but even certain ideas, may claim for themselves an *a priori* origin. Suppose, in the case of our empirical idea of a *body,* we successively withdraw all its empirical constituents, such as colour, consistency, weight, even impenetrability, we shall still find it impossible to withdraw the space it occupied. This space will still remain when the body itself has disappeared. In like manner, if, in regard to our empirical idea of an object in general, whether corporeal or incorporeal, we withdraw all properties known to us from experience, we shall still be unable to withdraw from it those by which we think it as substance, or as attributive to substance (though this notion of substance has more determination in it than that of an object in general). We must, therefore, overborne by the necessity with which said notion forces itself upon us, admit that it has its seat *a priori* in our faculties of cognition.

III

Philosophy stands in need of a Science which shall determine the Possibility, the Principles, and the Limits of all a priori *Cognition.*

But, to go still further, it is a fact that there are cognitions which even quit the bounds of all possible experience, and actually, by means of ideas for which, so far as experience goes, no correspondent object can be found, assume to extend the range of our judgments beyond any experience whatever.

And just in these latter cognitions, transcending as they do the world of sense, and unaccompanied by experience to guide and correct them, there lie interests of reason which we hold to be of far greater consequence and loftier aim than anything or all that understanding can teach us in the domain of experience. In these cognitions, indeed, even at the risk of failure, we rather venture everything than, for any reason of doubt, or carelessness and indifference, consent to forego what is of such an import. Such unavoidable problems of pure reason's own are God, Free Will, and Immortality. The science, again, which, as well in the end it contemplates, as in all its complement of means, is alone directed to the solution of these, we name metaphysic—a science that, in its procedure, starts as yet only dogmatically; that is, having instituted no previous inquiry into sufficiency or insufficiency on the part of reason for so great an enterprise, it yet confidently undertakes completion of it.

Now, it seems no more than natural that, once we have left the solid ground of experience, we should not forthwith proceed to build, without having carefully assured ourselves, first of all, in regard to a foundation, and that, too, all the more, should we find ourselves provided only with principles which are unauthenticated, and have come to us we know not whence. It seems no more than natural, I say, that, rather than this, we should have long before started the question, How have we got to these principles, and of what extent, import, and value are they? In effect, nothing is more natural when by the word *natural* we understand what, rightly and reasonably, ought to take place; but, on the other hand, when we mean by *natural* only what usually takes place, then nothing is more natural than that any such preliminary inquiry should remain long null. For the fact is, that some of the principles in view (as the mathematical ones) possess authentication from of old, and reflect, consequently, a similar presumption on to others which may in reality be altogether different. Besides, when one is beyond experience, one is safe not to be contradicted by experience; and, eager as we are to extend our knowledge, only when so contradicted is it that we can allow ourselves a halt. But even this may be avoided, should we be but careful with our fictions; for fictions, in such circumstances, they must be. On the other hand, mathematics afford us a splendid example of success in the cognition in question. Objects and ideas, it is true, are considered there only so far as they are capable of being exhibited in objective representation. But this is easily overlooked, because said representation can itself be *a priori* given, and is, consequently, scarcely to be distinguished from a pure notion proper. Led away by such a proof of the power of reason, we can see no bounds to the extension we desire. The light dove, in feeling the resistance of the air its free flight cleaves, might very well think to itself that it would have a still better chance in a space that were void. Even so Plato, because of the narrow limits it set the understanding, forsook the world of sense; and, beyond its bounds, buoyed up on the wings of the ideas, committed himself to the blank inane of the pure intellect. He did not perceive that, with every effort, his progress was null; for foothold he had none, against which steadied, he might have exerted his strength to bring reason from the spot. It is, however, an ordinary fate of speculative reason, to complete its edifice at the soonest, and only then to examine whether the foundations are well laid or not. All manner of excuses, rather, is indulged in to comfort us in regard of their entire sufficiency, or even to prove such late, dangerous examination wholly inexpedient. What saves us during the work from any fear or suspicion, deceiving us with apparent substantiality indeed, is this. A great part, perhaps the greatest, of the business of our reason consists in the analysis of ideas which we have already formed of objects. This furnishes us with a number of cognitions which, although they are nothing more than elucidations or explanations of what is already (confusedly) implied, are still, at least in form, regarded as new: in matter or contents, not extending our notions, they explicate them. But this process furnishing, as it does, an actual *a priori* cognition, accompanied, too, by a certain safe gain, our reason interpolates unawares into this false show of extension allegations of quite another nature; foisting in with given notions other notions quite alien, and that, too, *a priori,* without our knowing how or whence these latter come, or even without any such question being ever once entertained by us. Accordingly, I shall treat directly now in the beginning of the difference between these two modes of cognition.

IV

Of the Difference between Analytic and Synthetic Judgments.

In all judgments in which the relation of a subject to a predicate is thought (affirmatives alone considered—application to negatives being afterwards easy) this relation is possible in two ways. Either the predicate B belongs to the subject A as something that (covertly) is contained in it; or B lies completely outside of the notion A, though possessing connexion with it. In the first case I call the judgment *analytic;* in the second *synthetic.* Analytic judgments (the affirmative ones) are therefore those in which the connexion of the predicate with the subject is thought through identity; synthetic, again, those in which this connexion is thought without identity. We might name them also, the former, judgments of explication; the latter, judgments of extension. The former, namely, add, in the predi-

cate, nothing to the notion of the subject, but only separate this notion into its subnotional parts, which parts are already (obscurely) thought *in* the notion. The latter, on the other hand, add to the subject a predicate which was not at all thought in it, and could not by any analysis have been extracted from it. For example, if I say, All bodies are extended, this is an analytic judgment. For, in order that I may find extension as connected with it, I need not leave what notion itself I attach to *body*. I have only to analyze it, or open my eyes to what complex I think in it, to become aware of this predicate as contained in it. The judgment, therefore, is analytic. On the other hand, if I say, All bodies are heavy, in that case the predicate is something quite different from anything I think in the mere notion of a body as such. The addition of such a predicate produces, therefore, a synthetic judgment.

Judgments of experience, as such, are all synthetic. For it were absurd to have recourse to experience for an analytic judgment, seeing that I need not go out of my notion itself to get the judgment, nor require, therefore, any testimony of experience in the case. That a body is extended is a proposition *a priori* evident, and not a judgment of experience. For, without having recourse to experience, I have already in the notion all the conditions necessary for my judgment. I have only, according to the principle of contradiction, to extract the predicate from the notion. In so acting, I become aware, also, of the necessity of the judgment, and necessity is no declaration of experience. On the other hand, although I do not include, in the notion of a body in general, the predicate heavy, still said notion (body) designates an object of experience, by a part of experience, to which part I can add other parts of the same experience, not comprehended in the first. I know the notion body already analytically, say, through the characters extension, impenetrability, figure, etc., which the notion simply implies. But now I extend my knowledge, and in once more consulting experience (from which I had derived this notion of body), I find, always conjoined with the said characters, that also of weight, which, as a predicate, therefore, I add synthetically to the notion in question. It is, therefore, on experience that the possibility is founded of the synthesis of the predicate heavy with the subject body, because, though the one is not implied in the other, still both notions, as parts of a whole (namely experience, which is itself a synthetic conjunction of perceptions), belong to each other, if only contingently.

But, in the case of *a priori* synthetic judgments, this expedient (of experience) is altogether inapplicable. If, in such reference, I am to go beyond the notion A in order to recognise another, B, as connected with it, on what do I support myself, and by what is the synthesis made possible, seeing that I have not the advantage in this case of looking about me for it in the field of experience? Let us take the proposition, All that happens has a cause. In the notion of something that happens (an effect), I think something come to be, which, therefore, had a certain time before it, etc., and from this something, as it is there before me, it is possible for me to deduce various analytic judgments. But the notion cause lies quite out of this notion. Denoting something quite different from that which happens (the effect), it is not at all implied in it. How do I come, then, to say of any fact in event something quite different from the fact itself, and to recognise the notion cause, though not contained in said fact, nevertheless as belonging to it, and that, too, necessarily? What is the unknown x on which the understanding supports itself, when it believes itself to discover from the notion A a predicate B, alien to it, but which it judges, nevertheless, to be connected with it? It cannot be experience, because the relative proposition adds the latter to the former, not only with a greater universality than experience can supply, but even with the expression of necessity, and consequently wholly *a priori* or through mere notions. Well now, the entire end and aim of our speculative cognition *a priori* concern such synthetic principles, or judgments of extension. For the analytic ones are certainly of the greatest importance and necessity, but, here with us, they are available only for the sake of that precision of ideas which is required for an accurate and complete synthesis, as an acquisition veritably new.

V

In all the Rational Theoretic Sciences, Synthetic a priori *Judgments are present as Principles.*

1. Mathematical judgments are all synthetic. This proposition seems hitherto to have escaped the observation of the anatomists of human reason—nay, to be directly opposed to all their suppositions, although it is undeniably certain, and very important in result. For, because it was found that mathematical reasonings proceed all of them on the principle of contradiction (as the nature, indeed, of apodictic certainty requires), there ensued the conviction that by means of the same principle also it was that the fundamental propositions themselves were to be seen into. In this they erred. For a synthetic proposition may certainly be understood from the principle of contradiction; still, only in this way, that another synthetic proposition is presupposed from which it may be inferred,—but never independently.

First of all, it is to be remarked that mathematical judgments as such are always *a priori,* and not empirical; for they bring with them necessity, which is not to be got from experience. Should this, however, as a general proposition, appear doubtful, I will confine it to *pure* mathematic, the very notion of which implies that it is not concerned with empirical, but only with pure *a priori* cognition.

We might be apt to think at first that the proposition $7 + 5 = 12$ is merely an analytic proposition, which follows from the notion of a sum of 7 and 5, according to the principle of contradiction. But if we look closer, we shall find that the notion of the sum of 7 and 5 implies nothing but the uniting of the two numbers into one, there being no thought, at the same time, of what this one number itself is which comprehends the two. The notion of 12 is not thought in this, that I think to myself the uniting of 7 and 5; and I may analyze my notion of such possible sum as long as I please without finding the 12 in it. We must go out of these notions, and take help from perception. We must assist ourselves, that is, by such objective representation as corresponds to one of the two numbers (say five points or the five fingers), and, so assisted, add the units of the number perceived (5), one by one, to the notion of the number thought (7). I take first the number 7; next, for the notion of the 5, I refer to my fingers as perceived; and then I add the units (which together constitute the number 5), one by one, in guidance of the representation perceived, to the number 7. In this way, for result, I see the number 12 emerge. That 7 should be added to 5, I have indeed thought in the notion of a sum 7 + 5, but not that this sum is equal to the number 12. An arithmetical proposition is, therefore, always synthetic, as we may more distinctly discern, should we assume somewhat larger numbers; in which case it will clearly appear that, let us turn and twist our notions as we may, we never can, by mere analysis of notions, and unassisted by perception, discover their sum.

Just as little is any proposition of pure geometry analytic. That the straight line between any two points is the shortest, is a synthetic proposition. For my notion of straight includes in it nothing of quantity, but only a quality. The notion shortest is wholly something adscititious, something added to it, and cannot by any analysis be derived from the notion straight line. Perception, then, must be here called in to assist, and only by its intervention is the synthesis possible.

Some few propositions which are presupposed in geometry are, it is true, really analytic and rest on the principle of contradiction. They serve, however, only as identical propositions, for the chain of the method, and not as principles. For example, it is said *a* is equal to *a,* that is, the whole is equal to itself; or *a* + *b* is greater than *a,* which is, the whole is greater than its part. And yet even these, that pass valid on the authority of mere notions, are only allowed place in mathematic because they can be exhibited in perception. What commonly leads us here to suppose that the predicate of such apodictic judgments is already contained in our notion, and that, consequently, the judgment is analytic, is solely the peculiarity of the expression. To a given notion, namely, we must think a certain predicate, and this necessity is already present with the notions. But the question is not what we must think *to* the given notion, but what we actually, though obscurely, think *in* it; and then we see that the predicate belongs to the notion, necessarily indeed, not, however, because of being thought in it, but because of a perception which must be added to it.

2. Natural philosophy possesses synthetic *a priori* judgments as principles. I will only adduce a couple of propositions in example; as that in all changes of the corporeal world the quantity of matter remains the same, or that in all communication of motion, action and reaction are always alike. In both, not only the necessity is clear, and by consequence their *a priori* origin, but also the fact that they are synthetic propositions. For in the notion of matter I do not think its permanence, but only its presence in space as filling it. That is, I actually go beyond the notion of matter in order to think *a priori to* it something that I did not think *in* it. The proposition, therefore, is not analytic, but synthetic, and yet *a priori;* so it is with the other propositions of the pure part of the science.

3. In metaphysic (though we should only regard it as a science which has been hitherto desiderated, but which, from the very nature of human reason, nevertheless, is a science indispensable), synthetic cognitions *a priori* simply *must be.* For it is not its business merely to unravel notions which we *a priori* form of things. On the contrary, the business here is to extend our *a priori* cognition; and to that we must avail ourselves of such propositions as add on something beyond the given notion, something not contained in it; and in this way, by means of synthetic *a priori* judgments alone, advance indeed so far that experience itself is unable to follow us. For example, there is the proposition, among others, that the world must have a beginning. And by this we see that metaphysic, at least in its aim, consists of pure *a priori* synthetic propositions.

VI

General Problem of Pure Reason.

It is already not a little won, if we can bring a variety of questions under the formula of a single problem. For in this way, through exact determination of it, we not only lighten to ourselves our own work, but we facilitate for everybody else as well, who will examine it, the judgment whether we have done justice to our own design or not. The problem proper of pure reason, now, is comprised in the question, How are *a priori* synthetic judgments possible?

That metaphysic, hitherto, has remained in so vacillating a condition of uncertainty and contradiction, is solely to be ascribed to the fact that we have not sooner attained to the conception of this problem, or even to that of the distinction between analytic and synthetic judgments. On the solution of this problem now, or on a satisfactory proof that the possibility it would wish demonstrated does not exist, it depends whether metaphysic shall stand or fall. David Hume, who of all philosophers came nearest to this problem, thought it not out, however, by any means determinately enough, or in its generality, but merely took his stand by the synthetic proposition of the connexion of the effect with its cause (*principium causalitatis*). Accordingly, he assumed to make out that such a proposition is, *a priori*, wholly impossible. His reasonings went to prove, indeed, that all we call metaphysic terminates in a mere delusion of a supposed insight on the part of reason, into what in effect is merely borrowed from experience, and has only taken on, through custom, the semblance of necessity. But such an allegation, subversive as it is of all pure philosophy, would never have occurred to him had he but caught sight of our problem in its universality. For he would have then been conscious that, on his argument, even pure mathematic would be impossible, inasmuch as it is a science built on *a priori* synthetic propositions—a conclusion, plainly, from which his own good sense would certainly have saved him.

In the solution of the above problem there is involved, at the same time, the possibility of an application of pure reason in foundation and completion of all the sciences in which any theoretical *a priori* cognition of objects is concerned; that is, an answer to the questions, How is pure mathematic possible? How is pure natural philosophy possible?

Of these sciences, inasmuch as they once for all are, we may certainly with propriety ask, how they are possible; for that they must be possible is demonstrated by their actuality.[1] As for metaphysic, again, we may reasonably doubt of possibility in its regard, in view, namely, of its unsatisfactory progress hitherto, as well as of the fact that, considering its essential aim, we cannot say it has, in any instance, actually been.

And yet, again, knowledge of this kind is really, in a certain sense, to be assumed as given, or metaphysic is actual after all—if not as science, then as natural capability (*metaphysica naturalis*). For human reason, not moved by any vanity of mere learning, but impelled by necessity of its very nature, strives ever irrepressibly forward towards such questions as cannot possibly be answered by any mere empirical consideration, or principles derived thence. So it is that really in all men, so soon as reason has advanced to speculation, a metaphysic of some kind always has been and always will be. And now, from the same source, we have this question also: How is metaphysic as natural capability possible? That is, how do the questions which pure reason starts for herself, and which, in some way, she *must* answer—how do these questions originate in the very nature of reason as such?

It is the fact, however, that unavoidable contradictions have always shown themselves in any attempt yet to answer these natural questions (*e.g.*, whether the world has had a beginning, or whether it exists from all eternity, etc.)? We cannot, therefore, remain satisfied with a mere natural capability for metaphysic, or with the mere faculty of reason itself, in possession of which there is always that necessity of a metaphysic of some kind, be it what it may. It must be possible, rather, to bring matters relatively to some certainty as concerns either the knowing or the not knowing of the objects in question, either the ability or the inability of reason to judge in their regard. That is, it must be possible for us either confidently to extend, or else duly limit, reason. This last question, which flows from the general problem, were rightly put thus: How is metaphysic as a science possible?

A criticism of reason leads, therefore, at last necessarily to science; while, without criticism, dogmatically to set to work with reason, results only in groundless allegations, to which others equally specious may be opposed, and the end, consequently, is scepticism.

Neither will this science be of great and forbidding extent. It is not with the objects of reason, namely, the multiplicity of which is infinite, but with reason's self, that it has to do. The problems it considers take birth in the bosom of reason only: they are not imposed upon reason by the nature of things, which are different from it, but by its own nature. Accordingly, therefore, if reason has, first of all, come perfectly to know its own powers in regard of objects which may be

[1] This may be doubted as regards a pure natural philosophy. But we have only to look to the first propositions of physic proper (empirical), as the permanence of matter in quantity, inertia, the equality of action and reaction, etc., to be convinced that they constitute a *physicam puram* (or *rationalem*), which certainly deserves to be separately established, in its whole extent, whether large or limited, as science proper.

offered in experience, it must be easy fully and surely to determine the range and extent of its desired application beyond all bounds of experience.

We may and must, therefore, regard all these previous attempts dogmatically to bring about a metaphysic as, in effect, null. For, whatever there may be of analytic in the one or the other of them, as regards the mere dissection of the notions which *a priori* attend our reason, such material is not the end and aim of, but only a preparation for, metaphysic proper. To this science it belongs, namely, to extend our synthetic *a priori* knowledge, and to that, said analytic material is inapplicable, as it merely shows what is contained in those notions, but not how we *a priori* attain to them. Accordingly, we are not enabled thereby to determine their due and valid use in regard of the objects of cognition generally. It is no great hardship to abandon such pretensions wholly, seeing that the undeniable and dogmatically inevitable contradictions of reason have long since cost every previous metaphysic all its credit. It will demand more self-reliance, in view of the difficulty within and the opposition without, to resist, in regard to a science indispensable to human reason (whose root, let us hew off whatever actual stems we may, it is impossible to tear up), discouragement from the attempt to further it, once for all at last, into a prosperous and fruitful growth, by means of another, and, to those in the past, wholly opposed method.

A. J. AYER

The A Priori*

The view of philosophy which we have adopted may, I think, fairly be described as a form of empiricism. For it is characteristic of an empiricist to eschew metaphysics, on the ground that every factual proposition must refer to sense-experience. And even if the conception of philosophizing as an activity of analysis is not to be discovered in the traditional theories of empiricists, we have seen that it is implicit in their practice. At the same time, it must be made clear that, in calling ourselves empiricists, we are not avowing a belief in any of the psychological doctrines which are commonly associated with empiricism. For, even if these doctrines were valid, their validity would be independent of the validity of any philosophical thesis. It could be established only by observation, and not by the purely logical considerations upon which our empiricism rests.

Having admitted that we are empiricists, we must now deal with the objection that is commonly brought against all forms of empiricism; the objection, namely, that it is impossible on empiricist principles to account for our knowledge of necessary truths. For, as Hume conclusively showed, no general proposition whose validity is subject to the test of actual experience can ever be logically certain. No matter how often it is verified in practice, there still remains the possibility that it will be confuted on some future occasion. The fact that a law has been substantiated in $n - 1$ cases affords no logical guarantee that it will be substantiated in the nth case also, no matter how large we take n to be. And this means that no general proposition referring to a matter of fact can ever be shown to be necessarily and universally true. It can at best be a

* From A. J. Ayer, *Language, Truth, and Logic* (London: Victor Gollancz, Ltd., 1936), pp. 71–87. Reprinted by permission of the publisher.

probable hypothesis. And this, we shall find, applies not only to general propositions, but to all propositions which have a factual content. They can none of them ever become logically certain. This conclusion, which we shall elaborate later on, is one which must be accepted by every consistent empiricist. It is often thought to involve him in complete scepticism; but this is not the case. For the fact that the validity of a proposition cannot be logically guaranteed in no way entails that it is irrational for us to believe it. On the contrary, what is irrational is to look for a guarantee where none can be forthcoming; to demand certainty where probability is all that is obtainable. We have already remarked upon this, in referring to the work of Hume. And we shall make the point clearer when we come to treat of probability, in explaining the use which we make of empirical propositions. We shall discover that there is nothing perverse or paradoxical about the view that all the "truths" of science and common sense are hypotheses; and consequently that the fact that it involves this view constitutes no objection to the empiricist thesis.

Where the empiricist does encounter difficulty is in connection with the truths of formal logic and mathematics. For whereas a scientific generalization is readily admitted to be fallible, the truths of mathematics and logic appear to everyone to be necessary and certain. But if empiricism is correct no proposition which has a factual content can be necessary or certain. Accordingly the empiricist must deal with the truths of logic and mathematics in one of the two following ways: he must say either that they are not necessary truths, in which case he must account for the universal conviction that they are; or he must say that they have no factual content, and then he must explain how a proposition which is empty of all factual content can be true and useful and surprising.

If neither of these courses proves satisfactory, we shall be obliged to give way to rationalism. We shall be obliged to admit that there are some truths about the world which we can know independently of experience; that there are some properties which we can ascribe to all objects, even though we cannot conceivably observe that all objects have them. And we shall have to accept it as a mysterious inexplicable fact that our thought has this power to reveal to us authoritatively the nature of objects which we have never observed. Or else we must accept the Kantian explanation which, apart from the epistemological difficulties which we have already touched on, only pushes the mystery a stage further back.

It is clear that any such concession to rationalism would upset the main argument of this book. For the admission that there were some facts about the world which could be known independently of experience would be incompatible with our fundamental contention that a sentence says nothing unless it is empirically verifiable. And thus the whole force of our attack on metaphysics would be destroyed. It is vital, therefore, for us to be able to show that one or other of the empiricist accounts of the propositions of logic and mathematics is correct. If we are successful in this, we shall have destroyed the foundations of rationalism. For the fundamental tenet of rationalism is that thought is an independent source of knowledge, and is moreover a more trustworthy source of knowledge than experience; indeed some rationalists have gone so far as to say that thought is the only source of knowledge. And the ground for this view is simply that the only necessary truths about the world which are known to us are known through thought and not through experience. So that if we can show either that the truths in question are not necessary or that they are not "truths about the world," we shall be taking away the support on which rationalism rests. We shall be making good the empiricist contention that there are no "truths of reason" which refer to matters of fact.

The course of maintaining that the truths of logic and mathematics are not necessary or certain was adopted by Mill. He maintained that these propositions were inductive generalizations based on an extremely large number of instances. The fact that the number of supporting instances was so very large accounted, in his view, for our believing these generalizations to be necessarily and universally true. The evidence in their favour was so strong that it seemed incredible to us that a contrary instance should ever arise. Nevertheless it was in principle possible for such generalizations to be confuted. They were highly probable, but, being inductive generalizations, they were not certain. The difference between them and the hypotheses of natural science was a difference in degree and not in kind. Experience gave us very good reason to suppose that a "truth" of mathematics or logic was true univer sally; but we were not possessed of a guarantee. For these "truths" were only empirical hypotheses which had worked particularly well in the past; and like all empirical hypotheses, they were theoretically fallible.

I do not think that this solution of the empiricist's difficulty with regard to the propositions of logic and mathematics is acceptable. In discussing it, it is necessary to make a distinction which is perhaps already enshrined in Kant's famous dictum that, although there can be no doubt that all our knowledge begins with experience, it does not follow that it all arises out of experience.[1] When we say that the truths of logic are known independently of experience, we are not of course saying that they are innate, in the sense that we are born knowing them. It is obvious that mathematics and logic have to be learned in the same way as chemistry and history have to be learned. Nor are we denying that the first person to discover a given logical or mathematical truth was led to it by an inductive procedure. It is very probable, for example, that the principle of the syllogism was formulated not before but after the validity of syllogistic reasoning had been observed in a number of particular cases. What we are discussing, however, when we say that logical and mathematical truths are known independently of experience, is not a historical question concerning the way in which these truths were originally discovered, nor a psychological question concerning the way in which each of us comes to learn them, but an epistemological question. The contention of Mill's which we reject is that the propositions of logic and mathematics have the same status as empirical hypotheses; that their validity is determined in the same way. We maintain that they are independent of experience in the sense that they do not owe their validity to empirical verification. We may come to discover them through an inductive process; but once we have apprehended them we see that they are necessarily true, that they hold good for every conceivable instance. And this serves to distinguish them from empirical generalizations. For we know that a proposition whose validity depends upon experience cannot be seen to be necessarily and universally true.

In rejecting Mill's theory, we are obliged to be somewhat dogmatic. We can do no more than state the issue clearly and then trust that his contention will be seen to be discrepant with the relevant logical facts. The following considerations may serve to show that of the two ways of dealing with logic and mathematics which are open to the empiricist, the one which Mill adopted is not the one which is correct.

The best way to substantiate our assertion that the truths of formal logic and pure mathematics are necessarily true is to examine cases in which they might seem to be confuted. It might easily happen, for example, that when I came to count what I had taken to be five pairs of objects, I found that they amounted only to nine. And if I wished to mislead people I might say that on this occasion twice five was not ten. But in that case I should not be using the complex sign "$2 \times 5 = 10$" in the way in which it is ordinarily used. I should be taking it not as the expression of a purely mathematical proposition, but as the expression of an empirical generalization, to the effect that whenever I counted what appeared to me to be five pairs of objects I discovered that they were ten in number. This generalization may very well be false. But if it proved false in a given case, one would not say that the mathematical proposition "$2 \times 5 = 10$" had been confuted. One would say that I was wrong in supposing that there were five pairs of objects to start with, or that one of the objects had been taken away while I was counting, or that two of them had coalesced, or that I had counted wrongly. One would adopt as an explanation whatever empirical hypothesis fitted in best with the accredited facts. The one explanation which would in no circumstances be adopted is that ten is not always the product of two and five.

To take another example: if what appears to be a Euclidean triangle is found by measurement not to have angles totalling 180 degrees, we do not say that we have met with an instance which invalidates the mathematical proposition that the sum of the three angles of a Euclidean triangle is 180 degrees. We say that we have measured wrongly, or, more probably, that the triangle we have been measuring is not Euclidean. And this is our procedure in every case in which a mathematical truth might appear to be confuted. We always preserve its validity by adopting some other explanation of the occurrence.

The same thing applies to the principles of formal logic. We may take an example relating to

[1] *Critique of Pure Reason,* 2nd ed., Introduction, section i.

the so-called law of excluded middle, which states that a proposition must be either true or false, or, in other words, that it is impossible that a proposition and its contradictory should neither of them be true. One might suppose that a proposition of the form "*x* has stopped doing *y*" would in certain cases constitute an exception to this law. For instance, if my friend has never yet written to me, it seems fair to say that it is neither true nor false that he has stopped writing to me. But in fact one would refuse to accept such an instance as an invalidation of the law of excluded middle. One would point out that the proposition "My friend has stopped writing to me" is not a simple proposition, but the conjunction of the two propositions "My friend wrote to me in the past" and "My friend does not write to me now": and, furthermore, that the proposition "My friend has not stopped writing to me" is not, as it appears to be, contradictory to "My friend has stopped writing to me," but only contrary to it. For it means "My friend wrote to me in the past, and he still writes to me." When, therefore, we say that such a proposition as "My friend has stopped writing to me" is sometimes neither true nor false, we are speaking inaccurately. For we seem to be saying that neither it nor its contradictory is true. Whereas what we mean, or anyhow should mean, is that neither it nor its apparent contradictory is true. And its apparent contradictory is really only its contrary. Thus we preserve the law of excluded middle by showing that the negating of a sentence does not always yield the contradictory of the proposition originally expressed.

There is no need to give further examples. Whatever instance we care to take, we shall always find that the situations in which a logical or mathematical principle might appear to be confuted are accounted for in such a way as to leave the principle unassailed. And this indicates that Mill was wrong in supposing that a situation could arise which would overthrow a mathematical truth. The principles of logic and mathematics are true universally simply because we never allow them to be anything else. And the reason for this is that we cannot abandon them without contradicting ourselves, without sinning against the rules which govern the use of language, and so making our utterances self-stultifying. In other words, the truths of logic and mathematics are analytic propositions or tautologies. In saying this we are making what will be held to be an extremely controversial statement, and we must now proceed to make its implications clear.

The most familiar definition of an analytic proposition, or judgement, as he called it, is that given by Kant. He said[2] that an analytic judgement was one in which the predicate B belonged to the subject A as something which was covertly contained in the concept of A. He contrasted analytic with synthetic judgements, in which the predicate B lay outside the subject A, although it did stand in connection with it. Analytic judgements, he explains, "add nothing through the predicate to the concept of the subject, but merely break it up into those constituent concepts that have all along been thought in it, although confusedly." Synthetic judgements, on the other hand, "add to the concept of the subject a predicate which has not been in any wise thought in it, and which no analysis could possibly extract from it." Kant gives "all bodies are extended" as an example of an analytic judgement, on the ground that the required predicate can be extracted from the concept of "body," "in accordance with the principle of contradiction"; as an example of a synthetic judgement, he gives "all bodies are heavy." He refers also to "$7 + 5 = 12$" as a synthetic judgement, on the ground that the concept of twelve is by no means already thought in merely thinking the union of seven and five. And he appears to regard this as tantamount to saying that the judgement does not rest on the principle of contradiction alone. He holds, also, that through analytic judgements our knowledge is not extended as it is through synthetic judgements. For in analytic judgements "the concept which I already have is merely set forth and made intelligible to me."

I think that this is a fair summary of Kant's account of the distinction between analytic and synthetic propositions, but I do not think that it succeeds in making the distinction clear. For even if we pass over the difficulties which arise out of the use of the vague term "concept," and the unwarranted assumption that every judgement, as well as every German or English sentence, can be said to have a subject and a predicate, there remains still this crucial defect. Kant does not give one straightforward criterion for distinguishing between analytic and synthetic propositions; he gives two distinct criteria, which

[2] *Critique of Pure Reason,* 2nd ed., Introduction, sections iv and v.

are by no means equivalent. Thus his ground for holding that the proposition "7 + 5 = 12" is synthetic is, as we have seen, that the subjective intension of "7 + 5" does not comprise the subjective intension of "12"; whereas his ground for holding that "all bodies are extended" is an analytic proposition is that it rests on the principle of contradiction alone. That is, he employs a psychological criterion in the first of these examples, and a logical criterion in the second, and takes their equivalence for granted. But, in fact, a proposition which is synthetic according to the former criterion may very well be analytic according to the latter. For, as we have already pointed out, it is possible for symbols to be synonymous without having the same intensional meaning for anyone: and accordingly from the fact that one can think of the sum of seven and five without necessarily thinking of twelve, it by no means follows that the proposition "7 + 5 = 12" can be denied without self-contradiction. From the rest of his argument, it is clear that it is this logical proposition, and not any psychological proposition, that Kant is really anxious to establish. His use of the psychological criterion leads him to think that he has established it, when he has not.

I think that we can preserve the logical import of Kant's distinction between analytic and synthetic propositions, while avoiding the confusions which mar his actual account of it, if we say that a proposition is analytic when its validity depends solely on the definitions of the symbols it contains, and synthetic when its validity is determined by the facts of experience. Thus, the proposition "There are ants which have established a system of slavery" is a synthetic proposition. For we cannot tell whether it is true or false merely by considering the definitions of the symbols which constitute it. We have to resort to actual observation of the behaviour of ants. On the other hand, the proposition "Either some ants are parasitic or none are" is an analytic proposition. For one need not resort to observation to discover that there either are or are not ants which are parasitic. If one knows what is the function of the words "either," "or," and "not," then one can see that any proposition of the form "Either p is true or p is not true" is valid, independently of experience. Accordingly, all such propositions are analytic.

It is to be noticed that the proposition "Either some ants are parasitic or none are" provides no information whatsoever about the behaviour of ants, or, indeed, about any matter of fact. And this applies to all analytic propositions. They none of them provide any information about any matter of fact. In other words, they are entirely devoid of factual content. And it is for this reason that no experience can confute them.

When we say that analytic propositions are devoid of factual content, and consequently that they say nothing, we are not suggesting that they are senseless in the way that metaphysical utterances are senseless. For, although they give us no information about any empirical situation, they do enlighten us by illustrating the way in which we use certain symbols. Thus if I say, "Nothing can be coloured in different ways at the same time with respect to the same part of itself," I am not saying anything about the properties of any actual thing; but I am not talking nonsense. I am expressing an analytic proposition, which records our determination to call a colour expanse which differs in quality from a neighbouring colour expanse a different part of a given thing. In other words, I am simply calling attention to the implications of a certain linguistic usage. Similarly, in saying that if all Bretons are Frenchmen, and all Frenchmen Europeans, then all Bretons are Europeans, I am not describing any matter of fact. But I am showing that in the statement that all Bretons are Frenchmen, and all Frenchmen Europeans, the further statement that all Bretons are Europeans is implicitly contained. And I am thereby indicating the convention which governs our usage of the words "if" and "all."

We see, then, that there is a sense in which analytic propositions do give us new knowledge. They call attention to linguistic usages, of which we might otherwise not be conscious, and they reveal unsuspected implications in our assertions and beliefs. But we can see also that there is a sense in which they may be said to add nothing to our knowledge. For they tell us only what we may be said to know already. Thus, if I know that the existence of May Queens is a relic of tree-worship, and I discover that May Queens still exist in England, I can employ the tautology "If p implies q, and p is true, q is true" to show that there still exists a relic of tree-worship in England. But in saying that there are still May Queens in England, and that the existence of May Queens is a relic of tree-worship, I have already asserted the existence in England of a relic of tree-worship. The use of the tautology does, indeed, enable me to make this concealed assertion explicit. But it does not provide me with any new knowledge, in the sense in which empirical evidence that the election of May Queens had been forbidden by law would provide me with new knowledge. If one had to set forth all the information one possessed, with regard to matters of fact, one would not write down any analytic propositions. But one would make use of analytic propositions in compiling one's encyclopedia, and would thus come to include propositions which one would otherwise have overlooked. And, besides enabling one to make one's list of information complete, the formulation of analytic propositions would enable one to make sure that the synthetic propositions of which the list was composed formed a self-consistent system. By showing which ways of combining propositions resulted in contradictions, they would prevent one from including incompatible propositions and so making the list self-stultifying. But in so far as we had actually used such words as "all" and "or" and "not" without falling into self-contradiction, we might be said already to know what was revealed in the formulation of analytic propositions illustrating the rules which govern our usage of these logical particles. So that here again we are justified in saying that analytic propositions do not increase our knowledge.

The analytic character of the truths of formal logic was obscured in the traditional logic through its being insufficiently formalized. For in speaking always of judgements, instead of propositions, and introducing irrelevant psychological questions, the traditional logic gave the impression of being concerned in some specially intimate way with the workings of thought. What it was actually concerned with was the formal relationship of classes, as is shown by the fact that all its principles of inference are subsumed in the Boolean class-calculus, which is subsumed in its turn in the propositional calculus of Russell and Whitehead.[3] Their system, expounded in *Principia Mathematica,* makes it clear that formal logic is not concerned with the properties of men's minds, much less with the properties of material objects, but simply with the possibility of combining propositions by means of logical particles into analytic propositions, and with studying the formal relationship of these analytic propositions, in virtue of which one is deducible from another. Their procedure is to exhibit the propositions of formal logic as a deductive system, based on five primitive propositions, subsequently reduced in number to one. Hereby the distinction between logical truths and principles of inference, which was maintained in the Aristotelian logic, very properly disappears. Every principle of inference is put forward as a logical truth and every logical truth can serve as a principle of inference. The three Aristotelian "laws of thought," the law of identity, the law of excluded middle, and the law of non-contradiction, are incorporated in the system, but they are not considered more important than the other analytic propositions. They are not reckoned among the premises of the system. And the system of Russell and Whitehead itself is probably only one among many possible logics, each of which is composed of tautologies as interesting to the logician as the arbitrarily selected Aristotelian "laws of thought."[4]

A point which is not sufficiently brought out by Russell, if indeed it is recognised by him at all, is that every logical proposition is valid in its own right. Its validity does not depend on its being incorporated in a system, and deduced from certain propositions which are taken as self-evident. The construction of systems of logic is useful as a means of discovering and certifying analytic propositions, but it is not in principle essential even for this purpose. For it is possible to conceive of a symbolism in which every analytic proposition could be seen to be analytic in virtue of its form alone.

The fact that the validity of an analytic proposition in no way depends on its being deducible from other analytic propositions is our justification for disregarding the question whether the propositions of mathematics are reducible to propositions of formal logic, in the way that Russell supposed.[5] For even if it is the case that the definition of a cardinal number as a class of classes similar to a given class is circular, and it is

[3] Vide Karl Menger, "Die Neue Logik," *Krise und Neuaufbau in den Exakten Wissenschaften,* pp. 94–6; and Lewis and Langford, *Symbolic Logic,* Chapter v.

[4] Vide Lewis and Langford, *Symbolic Logic,* Chapter vii, for an elaboration of this point.

[5] Vide *Introduction to Mathematical Philosophy,* Chapter ii.

not possible to reduce mathematical notions to purely logical notions, it will still remain true that the propositions of mathematics are analytic propositions. They will form a special class of analytic propositions, containing special terms, but they will be none the less analytic for that. For the criterion of an analytic proposition is that its validity should follow simply from the definition of the terms contained in it, and this condition is fulfilled by the propositions of pure mathematics.

The mathematical propositions which one might most pardonably suppose to be synthetic are the propositions of geometry. For it is natural for us to think, as Kant thought, that geometry is the study of the properties of physical space, and consequently that its propositions have factual content. And if we believe this, and also recognize that the truths of geometry are necessary and certain, then we may be inclined to accept Kant's hypothesis that space is the form of intuition of our outer sense, a form imposed by us on the matter of sensation, as the only possible explanation of our *a priori* knowledge of these synthetic propositions. But while the view that pure geometry is concerned with physical space was plausible enough in Kant's day, when the geometry of Euclid was the only geometry known, the subsequent invention of non-Euclidean geometries has shown it to be mistaken. We see now that the axioms of a geometry are simply definitions, and that the theorems of a geometry are simply the logical consequences of these definitions.[6] A geometry is not in itself about physical space; in itself it cannot be said to be "about" anything. But we can use a geometry to reason about physical space. That is to say, once we have given the axioms a physical interpretation, we can proceed to apply the theorems to the objects which satisfy the axioms. Whether a geometry can be applied to the actual physical world or not, is an empirical question which falls outside the scope of the geometry itself. There is no sense, therefore, in asking which of the various geometries known to us are false and which are true. In so far as they are all free from contradiction, they are all true. What one can ask is which of them is the most useful on any given occasion, which of them can be applied most easily and most fruitfully to an actual empirical situation. But the proposition which states that a certain application of a geometry is possible is not itself a proposition of that geometry. All that the geometry itself tells us is that if anything can be brought under the definitions, it will also satisfy the theorems. It is therefore a purely logical system, and its propositions are purely analytic propositions.

It might be objected that the use made of diagrams in geometrical treatises shows that geometrical reasoning is not purely abstract and logical, but depends on our intuition of the properties of figures. In fact, however, the use of diagrams is not essential to completely rigorous geometry. The diagrams are introduced as an aid to our reason. They provide us with a particular application of the geometry, and so assist us to perceive the more general truth that the axioms of the geometry involve certain consequences. But the fact that most of us need the help of an example to make us aware of those consequences does not show that the relation between them and the axioms is not a purely logical relation. It shows merely that our intellects are unequal to the task of carrying out very abstract processes of reasoning without the assistance of intuition. In other words, it has no bearing on the nature of geometrical propositions, but is simply an empirical fact about ourselves. Moreover, the appeal to intuition, though generally of psychological value, is also a source of danger to the geometer. He is tempted to make assumptions which are accidentally true of the patricular figure he is taking as an illustration, but do not follow from his axioms. It has, indeed, been shown that Euclid himself was guilty of this, and consequently that the presence of the figure is essential to some of his proofs.[7] This shows that his system is not, as he presents it, completely rigorous, although of course it can be made so. It does not show that the presence of the figure is essential to a truly rigorous geometrical proof. To suppose that it did would be to take as a necessary feature of all geometries what is really only an incidental defect in one particular geometrical system.

We conclude, then, that the propositions of pure geometry are analytic. And this leads us to reject Kant's hypothesis that geometry deals with the form of intuition of our outer sense. For the ground for this hypothesis was that it alone ex-

[6] Cf. H. Poincaré, *La Science et l'Hypothèse,* Part II, Chapter iii.

[7] Cf. M. Black, *The Nature of Mathematics,* p. 154.

plained how the propositions of geometry could be both true *a priori* and synthetic: and we have seen that they are not synthetic. Similarly our view that the propositions of arithmetic are not synthetic but analytic leads us to reject the Kantian hypothesis[8] that arithmetic is concerned with our pure intuition of time, the form of our inner sense. And thus we are able to dismiss Kant's transcendental æsthetic without having to bring forward the epistemological difficulties which it is commonly said to involve. For the only argument which can be brought in favour of Kant's theory is that it alone explains certain "facts." And now we have found that the "facts" which it purports to explain are not facts at all. For while it is true that we have *a priori* knowledge of necessary propositions, it is not true, as Kant supposed, that any of these necessary propositions are synthetic. They are without exception analytic propositions, or, in other words, tautologies.

We have already explained how it is that these analytic propositions are necessary and certain. We saw that the reason why they cannot be confuted in experience is that they do not make any assertion about the empirical world. They simply record our determination to use words in a certain fashion. We cannot deny them without infringing the conventions which are presupposed by our very denial, and so falling into self-contradiction. And this is the sole ground of their necessity. As Wittgenstein puts it, our justification for holding that the world could not conceivably disobey the laws of logic is simply that we could not say of an unlogical world how it would look.[9] And just as the validity of an analytic proposition is independent of the nature of the external world; so is it independent of the nature of our minds. It is perfectly conceivable that we should have employed different linguistic conventions from those which we actually do employ. But whatever these conventions might be, the tautologies in which we recorded them would always be necessary. For any denial of them would be self-stultifying.

We see, then, that there is nothing mysterious about the apodeictic certainty of logic and mathematics. Our knowledge that no observation can ever confute the proposition "$7 + 5 = 12$" depends simply on the fact that the symbolic expression "$7 + 5$" is synonymous with "12," just as our knowledge that every oculist is an eye-doctor depends on the fact that the symbol "eye-doctor" is synonymous with "oculist." And the same explanation holds good for every other *a priori* truth.

What is mysterious at first sight is that these tautologies should on occasion be so surprising, that there should be in mathematics and logic the possibility of invention and discovery. As Poincaré says: "If all the assertions which mathematics puts forward can be derived from one another by formal logic, mathematics cannot amount to anything more than an immense tautology. Logical inference can teach us nothing essentially new, and if everything is to proceed from the principle of identity, everything must be reducible to it. But can we really allow that these theorems which fill so many books serve no other purpose than to say in a round-about fashion '$A = A$'?"[10] Ponicaré finds this incredible. His own theory is that the sense of invention and discovery in mathematics belongs to it in virtue of mathematical induction, the principle that what is true for the number 1, and true for $n + 1$ when it is true for n,[11] is true for all numbers. And he claims that this is a synthetic *a priori* principle. It is, in fact, *a priori*, but is not synthetic. It is a defining principle of the natural numbers, serving to distinguish them from such numbers as the infinite cardinal numbers, to which it cannot be applied.[12] Moreover, we must remember that discoveries can be made, not only in arithmetic, but also in geometry and formal logic, where no use is made of mathematical induction. So that even if Poincaré were right about mathematical induction, he would not have provided a satisfactory explanation of the paradox that a mere body of tautologies can be so interesting and so surprising.

The true explanation is very simple. The power of logic and mathematics to surprise us depends, like their usefulness, on the limitations of our reason. A being whose intellect was infinitely powerful would take no interest in logic

[8] This hypothesis is not mentioned in the *Critique of Pure Reason*, but was maintained by Kant at an earlier date.

[9] *Tractatus Logico-Philosophicus*, 3·031.

[10] *La Science et l'Hypothèse*, Part I, Chapter i.

[11] This was wrongly stated in previous editions as "true for n when it is true for $n + 1$."

[12] Cf. B. Russell's *Introduction to Mathematical Philosophy*, Chapter iii, p. 27.

and mathematics.[13] For he would be able to see at a glance everything that his definitions implied, and, accordingly, could never learn anything from logical inference which he was not fully conscious of already. But our intellects are not of this order. It is only a minute proportion of the consequences of our definitions that we are able to detect at a glance. Even so simple a tautology as "$91 \times 79 = 7189$" is beyond the scope of our immediate apprehension. To assure ourselves that "7189" is synonymous with "91×79" we have to resort to calculation, which is simply a process of tautological transformation—that is, a process by which we change the form of expressions without altering their significance. The multiplication tables are rules for carrying out this process in arithmetic, just as the laws of logic are rules for the tautological transformation of sentences expressed in logical symbolism or in ordinary language. As the process of calculation is carried out more or less mechanically, it is easy for us to make a slip and so unwittingly contradict ourselves. And this accounts for the existence of logical and mathematical "falsehoods," which otherwise might appear paradoxical. Clearly the risk of error in logical reasoning is proportionate to the length and the complexity of the process of calculation. And in the same way,

[13] Cf. Hans Hahn, "Logik, Mathematik und Naturerkennen," *Einheitswissenschaft,* Heft II, p. 18. "Ein allwissendes Wesen braucht keine Logik und keine Mathematik."

the more complex an analytic proposition is, the more chance it has of interesting and surprising us.

It is easy to see that the danger of error in logical reasoning can be minimized by the introduction of symbolic devices, which enable us to express highly complex tautologies in a conveniently simple form. And this gives us an opportunity for the exercise of invention in the pursuit of logical enquiries. For a well-chosen definition will call our attention to analytic truths, which would otherwise have escaped us. And the framing of definitions which are useful and fruitful may well be regarded as a creative act.

Having thus shown that there is no inexplicable paradox involved in the view that the truths of logic and mathematics are all of them analytic, we may safely adopt it as the only satisfactory explanation of their *a priori* necessity. And in adopting it we vindicate the empiricist claim that there can be no *a priori* knowledge of reality. For we show that the truths of pure reason, the propositions which we know to be valid independently of all experience, are so only in virtue of their lack of factual content. To say that a proposition is true *a priori* is to say that it is a tautology. And tautologies, though they may serve to guide us in our empirical search for knowledge, do not in themselves contain any information about any matter of fact.

A. C. EWING

The A Priori and the Empirical*

MEANING OF THE DISTINCTION, 'A PRIORI' CHARACTER OF MATHEMATICS

In the theory of knowledge, the first point that confronts us is the sharp distinction between two kinds of knowledge which have been called respectively *a priori* and empirical. Most of our knowledge we obtain by observation of the external world (sense-perception) and of ourselves (introspection). This is called empirical knowledge. But some knowledge we can obtain by simply thinking. That kind of knowledge is called *a priori*. Its chief exemplifications are to be found in logic and mathematics. In order to see that $5 + 7 = 12$ we do not need to take five

* Reprinted with permission of The Macmillan Company from *The Fundamental Questions of Philosophy* (pp. 26–36) by A. C. Ewing. First published in 1951 by Routledge & Kegan Paul Ltd.

things and seven things, put them together, and then count the total number. We can know what the total number will be simply by thinking.

Another important difference between *a priori* and empirical knowledge is that in the case of the former we do not see merely that something, S, is in fact P, but that it must be P and why it is P. I can discover that a flower is yellow (or at least produces sensations of yellow) by looking at it, but I cannot thereby see why it is yellow or that it must be yellow. For anything I can tell it might equally well have been a red flower. But with a truth such as that $5 + 7 = 12$ I do not see merely that it is a fact but that it must be a fact. It would be quite absurd to suppose that $5 + 7$ might have been equal to 11 and just happened to be equal to 12, and I can see that the nature of 5 and 7 constitutes a fully adequate and intelligible reason why their sum should be 12 and not some other number. It is indeed conceivable that some of the things which make the two groups of 5 and 7 might, when they were put together, fuse like drops of water, or even vanish, so that there were no longer 12 things; but what is inconceivable is that there could *at the same time* be $5 + 7$ things of a certain kind at once in a certain place and yet less than 12 things of that kind in that place. Before some of the things fused or vanished they would be $5 + 7$ in number and also 12 in number, and after the fusion or disappearance they would be neither $5 + 7$ nor 12. When I say in this connection that something is inconceivable, I do not mean merely or primarily that we cannot conceive it—this is not a case of a mere psychological inability like the inability to understand higher mathematics. It is a positive insight: we definitely see it to be impossible that certain things could happen. This we do not see in the case of empirical propositions which are false: they are not true but might for anything we know have been true. It is even conceivable, so far as we can see, that the fundamental laws of motion might have been quite different from what they are, but we can see that there could not have been a world which contradicted the laws of arithmetic. This is expressed by saying that empirical propositions are *contingent,* but true *a priori* propositions *necessary*. What we see to be necessary is not indeed that arithmetic should apply to the universe. It is conceivable that the universe might have been constituted entirely of a homogeneous fluid, and then, since there would have been no distinction between different things, it is difficult to see how arithmetic could have applied to it. What we do see is that arithmetic must be true of whatever can be numbered at all.

We must not be misled here by the fact that in order to come to understand arithmetic we originally required examples. Once we have learnt the beginnings of arithmetic in the kindergarten with the help of examples, we do not need examples any more to grasp it, and we can see the truth of many arithmetical propositions, e.g. that $3112 + 2467 = 5579$, of which we have never had examples. We have probably never taken 3112 things and 2467 things, put them together and counted the resulting set, but we still know that this is what the result of the counting would be. If it were empirical knowledge, we could not know it without counting. The examples are needed, not to prove anything, but only in order to enable us to come to understand in the first instance what is meant by number.

In geometry we indeed stand more in need of examples than in arithmetic, though I think this is only a psychological matter. In arithmetic we only need examples at the most elementary stage, but in geometry most people need a drawn figure, or at least an image of one in their minds, to see the validity of most proofs. But we must distinguish between an illustration and the basis of a proof. If the particular figure were not merely an illustration but the basis of the theorem, the latter would have to be proved by measuring it, but a measurement with a ruler or protractor never figures in Euclid's proofs. That the proof is not really based on the figure drawn is shown by the fact that we can still follow a proof concerning the properties of right-angled triangles even if the figure used to illustrate it is so badly drawn that it is obviously not a right-angled triangle at all. Again, if geometry were empirical, it would be a very hazardous speculation from the single example before us on the blackboard to conclude that all triangles had a property. It might be an individual idiosynacrasy of some triangles and not others. These considerations should be conclusive of themselves, but we might add that recent developments in geometry have had the effect of much loosening the connection between geometrical proofs and the empirical figure. It is possible to work out non-Euclidean geometries where we cannot depend on figures.

Another important field for *a priori* knowledge is logic. The laws of logic must be known *a priori* or not at all. They certainly are not a matter for empirical observation, and the function of logical argument is just to give us conclusions which we have not discovered by observation. The argument would be superfluous if we had observed them already. We are able to make inferences because there is sometimes a logical connection between one or more propositions (the premise or premises) and another proposition, the conclusion, such that the latter must be true if the former is. Then, if we know the former, we can assert the latter on the strength of it, thus anticipating any experience. To take an example, there is a story that Mr. X., a man of high reputation and great social standing, had been asked to preside at a big social function. He was late in coming, and so a Roman Catholic priest was asked to make a speech to pass the time till his arrival. The priest told various anecdotes, including one which recorded his embarrassment when as confessor he had to deal with his first penitent and the latter confessed to a particularly atrocious murder. Shortly afterwards Mr. X. arrived, and in his own speech he said: 'I see Father —— is here. Now, though he may not recognize me, he is an old friend of mine, in fact I was his first penitent.' It is plain that such an episode would enable one to infer that Mr. X. had committed a murder without having observed the crime. The form of inference involved: The first penitent was a murderer, Mr. X. was the first penitent, therefore Mr. X. was a murderer—is of the famous kind to which logicians have given the name of *syllogism*. The importance of syllogisms has often been exaggerated, but they are as important as any kind of inference, and we cannot deny that in many cases a syllogism has given people information of which they were not in any ordinary sense aware before they used the syllogism and which they did not acquire by observation. Inference is only possible because there are special connections between the propositions involved such that one necessarily follows from others. It is a chief function of logic to study these connections, of which that expressed in the syllogism is by no means the only one.

(A *syllogism* consists of three propositions, two forming the *premises* and the other the *conclusion*. Each proposition can be expressed by a subject and predicate connected by the verb to be, the *copula,* and if we call everything which stands as either subject or predicate a *term,* there must be three and only three terms in the syllogism. The one common to the two premises is called the *middle term,* and it is on this common element that the inference depends. The other two, having been connected by means of it, occur without it in the conclusion. Thus in the usual example of the syllogism—All men are mortal, Socrates is a man, ∴ Socrates is mortal—man is the middle term connecting Socrates with mortality so that we could, even if he had not already died, know that he was mortal.)

OTHER CASES OF THE 'A PRIORI'

A priori knowledge, while most prominent in mathematics and logic, is not limited to these subjects. For instance, we can see *a priori* that the same surface cannot have two different colours all over at the same time, or that a thought cannot have a shape. Philosophers have been divided into *rationalists* and *empiricists* according to whether they stressed the *a priori* or the empirical element more. The possibility of metaphysics depends on *a priori* knowledge, for our experience is quite inadequate to enable us to make on merely empirical grounds any sweeping generalizations of the kind the metaphysician desires. The term *a priori* covers both self-evident propositions, i.e. those which are seen to be true in their own right and those which are derived by inference from propositions themselves self-evident.

THE LINGUISTIC THEORY OF THE 'A PRIORI' AND THE DENIAL THAT 'A PRIORI' PROPOSITIONS OR INFERENCES CAN GIVE NEW KNOWLEDGE

At the present time even empiricist philosophers recognize the impossibility of explaining away *a priori* propositions as merely empirical generalizations, but they are inclined to the view that *a priori* propositions and *a priori* reasoning are merely concerned with language, and so cannot tell us anything new about the real world. Thus it is said that, when we make an inference, the conclusion is just part of the premises expressed in different language.[1] If so, inference

[1] This theory is not applied to *inductive* inference.

would be of use merely for clarifying our language and would involve no real advance in knowledge. Some inferences are of this type, e.g. A is a father, therefore A is male. But are they all? That would be hard indeed to square with the *prima facie* novelty of many conclusions. Take, for instance, the proposition that the square on the hypotenuse of a right-angled triangle is equal to the sum of the squares on the other two sides. Such a proposition can be inferred from the axioms and postulates of Euclid, but it certainly does not seem to be included in their meaning.[2] Otherwise we should know it as soon as we understood the axioms and postulates. The example I gave of the murder discovered by a logical argument seems to be another case of a fact not known at all beforehand by the reasoner which is discovered by his reasoning. Extreme empiricist philosophers contend that this appearance of novelty is really illusory, and that in some sense we knew the conclusion all along; but they have never succeeded in making clear in what sense we did so. It is not enough to say that the conclusion is implicit in the premises. 'Implicit' means 'implied by', and of course a conclusion is implied by its premises, if the inference is correct at all.[3] But this admission leaves quite open the question whether or not a proposition can follow from a different one which does not contain it as part of itself; and since we obviously can by deductive inference come to know things which we did not know before in any ordinary sense of 'know', we must treat the empiricist's claim as unjustified till he had produced a clearly defined sense of 'implicit in' or 'contained in' which leaves room for that novelty in inference which we all cannot help really admitting. In any ordinary sense of 'know' the conclusion is not in the cases I have mentioned known prior to the inference, and since the premises are and indeed must be known before we know the conclusion, it is therefore in no ordinary sense of 'part' part of the premises.

It is indeed sometimes said that the premises include the conclusion in a confused form, but it is obvious that the beginner in geometry cannot be said to be aware of Pythagoras's theorem even in a confused form though he may know all the premises from which it can be deduced. Nor does awareness of the propositions that A was B's first penitent and that B's first penitent was a murderer include even confusedly the awareness that A was a murderer as long as the premises are not combined. When they are combined therefore something new appears that was not present to consciousness before in any way; there is a new discovery. We can also show by definite logical argument that the interpretation we are discussing does not enable one to avoid the admission of novelty in inference. For, what is it to know something in a confused form? It is surely to know some general attributes present in a whole but not others. To be aware of *p* even confusedly must involve discriminating some general attributes in *p*, and those are given in the premises, which are admittedly understood in some degree. If we do not discriminate any attributes, the confusion is too great for argument to be possible at all. Now it is admitted that, when we reach the conclusion, we do discriminate attributes which we did not discriminate before, even if they are alleged to have been contained in the confused whole which was present to our minds before we started inferring. It is further admitted that the conclusion follows necessarily from the premises. Therefore the general attributes which we discriminated at the time when we knew only the premises and not the conclusion must be linked with the attributes we discriminate afterwards in such a way that the latter follow necessarily from the former. So we still have to admit that sheer *a priori* inference can enable us to discover new attributes. In some cases it may take a good while to draw the inference, in other cases it may be practically instantaneous as soon as the premises are known and combined, but whether it takes a long or a short time to draw the inference cannot be relevant to the principle.

Nevertheless, the view that inference cannot yield new conclusions dies hard, and so it will not be superfluous to bring further arguments. (1) 'This has shape' admittedly follows logically

[2] It is no objection to this illustration that Euclidean geometry has not been proved true of the physical world, for the proposition in question undoubtedly follows from the premises of Euclid and therefore should on the theory we are discussing be included as part of them. What is denied by modern scientists is not that the conclusion follows from the premises, but that the premises and what follows from them are true of the world.

[3] Similarly, the phrase 'is contained in' is sometimes used just to mean 'follows from' or 'is implied by' and need not connote that the conclusion is actually part of the premises, as would be the case on the literal meaning of 'contained'.

from 'this has size' and vice versa. If the view I am criticizing were true, 'this has size' would, therefore, have to include in its meaning 'this has shape', and 'this has shape' would also have to include in its meaning 'this has size.' But this would only be possible if the two sentences meant exactly the same thing, which they obviously do not. (2) Take an argument such as—Montreal is to the north of New York, New York is to the north of Washington, therefore Montreal is to the north of Washington. If the view I am discussing is true, the conclusion is part of the premises. But it is not part of either premise by itself, otherwise both premises would not be needed. So the only way in which it could be part of both together would be if it were divisible into two propositions one of which was part of the first and the other part of the second. I defy anybody to divide it in this way. (3) The proposition 'Socrates was a philosopher' certainly entails the proposition 'if Socrates had measles some philosophers have had measles', but it cannot be that the second proposition is included in the first. For the first proposition certainly does not include the notion of measles.

What is really the same view is often expressed by saying that all *a priori* propositions are 'analytic'. A distinction has commonly been drawn between *analytic* propositions, in which the predicate is in the notion of the subject already formed before the proposition is asserted, so that the proposition gives no new information, and *synthetic* propositions in which the predicate is not so contained and which are thus capable of giving new information.[4] Analytic propositions are essentially verbal, being all true by definition, e.g. all fathers are male. As an example of a synthetic proposition we could take any proposition established by experience such as 'I am cold' or 'It is snowing', but empiricists often assert that there are no synthetic *a priori* propositions. That this view cannot be justified may be shown at once. The proposition that there are no synthetic *a priori* propositions, since it cannot be established by empirical observations, would be, if justified, itself a synthetic *a priori* proposition, and we cannot affirm it as a synthetic *a priori* proposition that there are no synthetic *a priori* propositions. We may therefore dismiss off-hand any arguments for the theory. Such arguments, whatever they were, would have to involve synthetic *a priori* propositions. Further, the view must be false if it is ever true that the conclusion of an inference is not part of its premises. For, if the proposition—S is Q—ever follows validly from—S is P, the proposition—all that is SP is SQ must be true *a priori*. But, unless the concept Q is part of the concept SP, the proposition—all that is SP is SQ—cannot be analytic. Therefore our arguments against the view that in all valid inferences the conclusion is part of the premises expressed in different language are also arguments against the view that all *a priori* propositions are analytic.

The analytic view seems plausible when we are concerned with the simplest propositions of logic and arithmetic, but we must not assume that a proposition is analytic because it is obvious. Though it may be very difficult to determine precisely where analytic propositions end and synthetic propositions begin, we cannot use this as a ground for denying the latter. It is very difficult to say precisely where blue ends and green begins, since the different shades run into each other imperceptibly, but we cannot therefore argue that all blue is really green. Taking arithmetic, even if there is a good deal of plausibility in saying that $2 + 2$ is included in the meaning of '4', there is none in saying $95 - 91$ or $\frac{216}{2} - \frac{67 + 25}{3}$ are so included. Yet, if the analytic view were true, all the infinite numerical combinations which could be seen *a priori* to be equal to 4 would have to be included in the meaning of '4'.

Some empiricists, without committing themselves to the view that all *a priori* propositions are analytic, still say these are a matter of arbitrary choice or verbal convention. They are influenced here by a modern development in the view of geometry. It used to be held that the axioms of Euclid expressed a direct insight into the nature of physical space, but this is denied by modern scientists, and the view is taken that they are arbitrary postulates which geometricians make because they are interested in what would follow *if* they were true. Whether they are true or not is then a matter of empirical fact to be decided by science. But, even if this suggests that the prem-

[4] This definition would have to be amended slightly to suit modern logicians who (I think, rightly) deny that all propositions are of the subject-predicate form, but this would not alter the principle though imparting a complication of detail with which we need not deal here.

ises of our *a priori* arguments may be arbitrary postulates, this does not make the subsequent steps arbitrary. From the postulates of Euclid it follows that the three angles of a triangle are equal to two right angles. If the original postulates are arbitrary, it is not certain that the conclusion is true of the real world; but it is still not an arbitrary matter that it follows from the postulates. The postulates may well be false, but there can be no doubt that *if* they were true the conclusions must be so, and it is in this hypothetical working out of the consequences of postulates which may not be true that pure geometry consists. The *a priori* necessity of pure geometry is not therefore in the least invalidated by modern developments. What is *a priori* is that the conclusions follow from the axioms and postulates, and this is not at all affected by the (empirical) discovery that not all the axioms and postulates exactly apply to the physical world. (Applied Euclidean geometry is possible in practice because it is an empirical fact that they approximately apply. The divergencies only show themselves when we consider unusually great velocities or distances.)

If not only the postulates but the successive stages in the inference were themselves arbitrary, we might just as well infer from the same premise that the angles of a triangle were equal to a million right angles or to none at all. All point in inference would be lost. Dictators may do a great deal, but they cannot alter the laws of logic and mathematics; these laws would not change even if by a system of intensive totalitarian education every human being were persuaded to fall in with a world dictator's whim in the matter and believe they were different from what they are. Nor can they change with alterations in language, though they may be expressed differently. That the truth of *a priori* propositions does not just depend on the nature of language can be easily seen when we consider that, even if we do not know any Fijian or Hottentot, we can know that also in these languages and not only in the languages we know the propositions $5 + 7 = 12$ must be true. It is of course true that by altering the meaning of the words we could make the proposition we expressed by '$5 + 7 = 12$' false, e.g. if I used '12' in a new sense to mean what other people mean by '11', but then it would be a different proposition. I could play the same trick with empirical propositions and say truly, e.g., that 'fire does not burn' or 'there is an elephant in this room' if I used 'burn' to mean 'drown' or 'elephant' to mean 'table'. This does not in the least impair the obviousness of the contrary propositions established by experience. Finally, as we argued above that the proposition that there can be no synthetic *a priori* propositions would itself, if justified, have to be a synthetic *a priori* proposition, so we may argue that the proposition that all *a priori* propositions are a matter of arbitrary linguistic convention would, if true, have to be itself a matter of arbitrary linguistic convention. It therefore could not be vindicated by any argument and would be merely a matter of a new usage of words arbitrarily established by the persons who assert it, since it certainly does not express the usual meaning of '*a priori* propositions'. So we must reject any attempt to explain away the *a priori* as a genuine source of new knowledge. If the attempt had succeeded, we should have had to admit that philosophy in anything like its old sense was impossible, for philosophy clearly cannot be based merely on observation.

The views we have been criticizing contain the following elements of truth. (1) *A priori* propositions can be seen to be true and the conclusions of an inference seem to follow from their premises without any further observation, provided we understand the meaning of the words used. But to say that q follows from p once we understand the meaning of the words is not to say that q is part of the meaning of the words used to express p. 'Follow from' and 'be part of' are not synonyms. (2) If q follows from p you cannot assert p and deny q without contradicting yourself, but this is only to say that in that case the denial of q implies the denial of p. It is not to say that q is part of what you assert when you assert p, unless we already assume that what is implied is always part of what implies it, i.e. beg the question at issue. (3) An *a priori* proposition cannot be fully understood without being seen to be true. It may be impossible to understand something fully without understanding something else not included in it at all, so it may still be synthetic.

People have been inclined to deny synthetic *a priori* propositions because they could not see how one characteristic could necessarily involve another, but that this could not happen would be itself a synthetic *a priori* metaphysical proposition. People have also thought that it was necessary to give some sort of explanation of *a priori* knowledge, and could not see how this could be done except in terms of language. To this I should reply that there is no reason to suppose that *a priori* knowledge requires some special explanation any more than does our ability to

attain knowledge empirically by observation. Why not take it as an ultimate fact? Human beings certainly cannot explain everything, whether there is ultimately an explanation for it or not.

CHARLES S. PEIRCE

The Pragmatic Maxim*

The principles set forth in the first part of this essay[1] lead, at once, to a method of reaching a clearness of thought of higher grade than the "distinctness" of the logicians. It was there noticed that the action of thought is excited by the irritation of doubt, and ceases when belief is attained; so that the production of belief is the sole function of thought. All these words, however, are too strong for my purpose. It is as if I had described the phenomena as they appear under a mental microscope. Doubt and Belief, as the words are commonly employed, relate to religious or other grave discussions. But here I use them to designate the starting of any question, no matter how small or how great, and the resolution of it. If, for instance, in a horse-car, I pull out my purse and find a five-cent nickel and five coppers, I decide, while my hand is going to the purse, in which way I will pay my fare. To call such a question Doubt, and my decision Belief, is certainly to use words very disproportionate to the occasion. To speak of such a doubt as causing an irritation which needs to be appeased, suggests a temper which is uncomfortable to the verge of insanity. Yet, looking at the matter minutely, it must be admitted that, if there is the least hesitation as to whether I shall pay the five coppers or the nickel (as there will be sure to be, unless I act from some previous contracted habit in the matter), though irritation is too strong a word, yet I am excited to such small mental activity as may be necessary to deciding how I shall act. Most frequently doubts arise from some indecision, however momentary, in our action. Sometimes it is not so. I have, for example, to wait in a railway-station, and to pass the time I read the advertisements on the walls. I compare the advantages of different trains and different routes which I never expect to take, merely fancying myself to be in a state of hesitancy, because I am bored with having nothing to trouble me. Feigned hesitancy, whether feigned for mere amusement or with a lofty purpose, plays a great part in the production of scientific inquiry. However the doubt may originate, it stimulates the mind to an activity which may be slight or energetic, calm or turbulent. Images pass rapidly through consciousness, one incessantly melting into another, until at last, when all is over—it may be in a fraction of a second, in an hour, or after long years—we find ourselves decided as to how we should act under such circumstances as those which occasioned our hesitation. In other words, we have attained belief.

In this process we observe two sorts of elements of consciousness, the distinction between which may best be made clear by means of an illustration. In a piece of music there are the separate notes, and there is the air. A single tone may be prolonged for an hour or a day, and it

* From Charles S. Peirce, "How to Make Our Ideas Clear," Part II. First published in *Popular Science Monthly*, XII (1878).

[1] [Part I of "How to Make Our Ideas Clear," omitted here.]

exists as perfectly in each second of that time as in the whole taken together; so that, as long as it is sounding, it might be present to a sense from which everything in the past was as completely absent as the future itself. But it is different with the air, the performance of which occupies a certain time, during the portions of which only portions of it are played. It consists in an orderliness in the succession of sounds which strike the ear at different times; and to perceive it there must be some continuity of consciousness which makes the events of a lapse of time present to us. We certainly only perceive the air by hearing the separate notes; yet we cannot be said to directly hear it, for we hear only what is present at the instant, and an orderliness of succession cannot exist in an instant. These two sorts of objects, what we are *immediately* conscious of and what we are *mediately* conscious of, are found in all consciousness. Some elements (the sensations) are completely present at every instant so long as they last, while others (like thought) are actions having beginning, middle, and end, and consist in a congruence in the succession of sensations which flow through the mind. They cannot be immediately present to us, but must cover some portion of the past or future. Thought is a thread of melody running through the succession of our sensations.

We may add that just as a piece of music may be written in parts, each part having its own air, so various systems of relationship of succession subsist together between the same sensations. These different systems are distinguished by having different motives, ideas, or functions. Thought is only one such system, for its sole motive, idea, and function is to produce belief, and whatever does not concern that purpose belongs to some other system of relations. The action of thinking may incidentally have other results; it may serve to amuse us, for example, and among *dilettanti* it is not rare to find those who have so perverted thought to the purposes of pleasure that it seems to vex them to think that the questions upon which they delight to exercise it may ever get finally settled; and a positive discovery which takes a favorite subject out of the arena of literary debate is met with ill-concealed dislike. This disposition is the very debauchery of thought. But the soul and meaning of thought, abstracted from the other elements which accompany it, though it may be voluntarily thwarted, can never be made to direct itself toward anything but the production of belief. Thought in action has for its only possible motive the attainment of thought at rest; and whatever does not refer to belief is no part of the thought itself.

And what, then, is belief? It is the demi-cadence which closes a musical phrase in the symphony of our intellectual life. We have seen that it has just three properties: First, it is something that we are aware of; second, it appeases the irritation of doubt; and, third, it involves the establishment in our nature of a rule of action, or, say for short, a *habit*. As it appeases the irritation of doubt, which is the motive for thinking, thought relaxes, and comes to rest for a moment when belief is reached. But, since belief is a rule for action, the application of which involves further doubt and further thought, at the same time that it is a stopping-place, it is also a new starting-place for thought. That is why I have permitted myself to call it thought at rest, although thought is essentially an action. The *final* upshot of thinking is the exercise of volition, and of this thought no longer forms a part; but belief is only a stadium of mental action, an effect upon our nature due to thought, which will influence future thinking.

The essence of belief is the establishment of a habit; and different beliefs are distinguished by the different modes of action to which they give rise. If beliefs do not differ in this respect, if they appease the same doubt by producing the same rule of action, then no more differences in the manner of consciousness of them can make them different beliefs, any more than playing a tune in different keys is playing different tunes. Imaginary distinctions are often drawn between beliefs which differ only in their mode of expression;—the wrangling which ensues is real enough, however. To believe that any objects are arranged among themselves as in Fig. 1 [p. 177], and to believe that they are arranged [as] in Fig. 2, are one and the same belief; yet it is conceivable that a man should assert one proposition and deny the other. Such false distinctions do as much harm as the confusion of beliefs really different, and are among the pitfalls of which we ought constantly to beware, especially when we are upon metaphysical ground. One singular deception of this sort, which often occurs, is to mistake the sensation produced by our own unclearness of thought for a character of the object we are thinking. Instead of perceiving that the obscurity is purely subjective, we fancy that we contemplate a quality of the object which is essentially mysterious; and if our conception be afterward presented to us in a clear form we do not recognize it as the same, owing to the absence of the feeling of unintelligibility. So long as this deception lasts, it obviously puts an impassable barrier in the way of perspicuous thinking; so that it equally interests the opponents of rational thought to perpetuate it, and its adherents to guard against it.

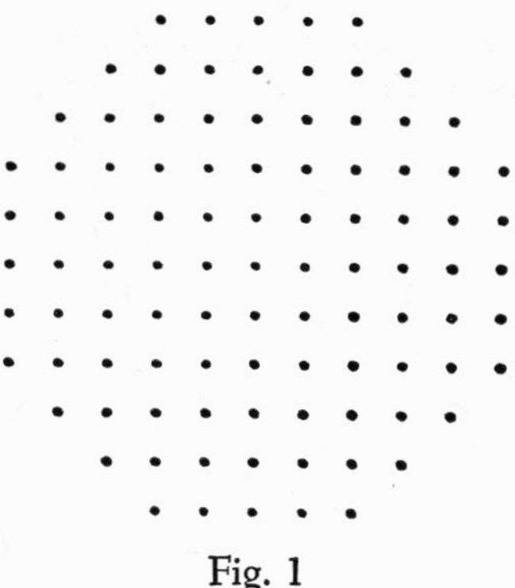

Fig. 1

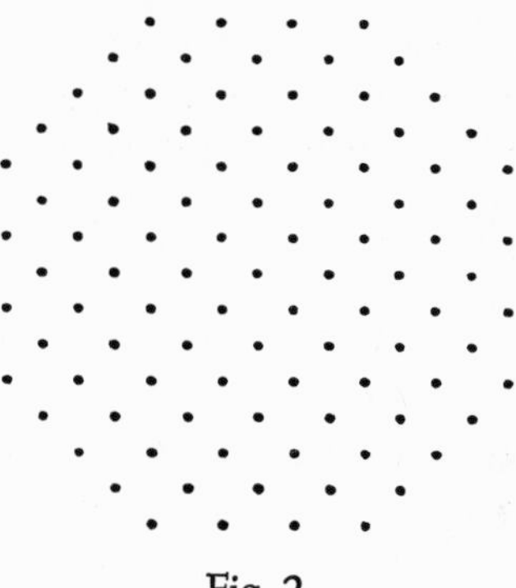

Fig. 2

Another such deception is to mistake a mere difference in the grammatical construction of two words for a distinction between the ideas they express. In this pedantic age, when the general mob of writers attend so much more to words than to things, this error is common enough. When I just said that thought is an *action,* and that it consists in a *relation,* although a person performs an action but not a relation, which can only be the result of an action, yet there was no inconsistency in what I said, but only a grammatical vagueness.

From all these sophisms we shall be perfectly safe so long as we reflect that the whole function of thought is to produce habits of action; and that whatever there is connected with a thought, but irrelevant to its purpose, is an accretion to it, but no part of it. If there be a unity among our sensations which has no reference to how we shall act on a given occasion, as when we listen to a piece of music, why we do not call that thinking. To develop its meaning, we have, therefore, simply to determine what habits it produces, for what a thing means is simply what habits it involves. Now, the identity of a habit depends on how it might lead us to act, not merely under such circumstances as are likely to arise, but under such as might possibly occur, no matter how improbable they may be. What the habit is depends on *when* and *how* it causes us to act. As for the *when,* every stimulus to action is derived from perception; as for the *how,* every purpose of action is to produce some sensible result. Thus, we come down to what is tangible and conceivably practical, as the root of every real distinction of thought, no matter how subtle it may be; and there is no distinction of meaning so fine as to consist in anything but a possible difference of practice.

To see what this principle leads to, consider in the light of it such a doctrine as that of transubstantiation. The Protestant churches generally hold that the elements of the sacrament are flesh and blood only in a tropical sense; they nourish our souls as meat and the juice of it would our bodies. But the Catholics maintain that they are literally just meat and blood; although they possess all the sensible qualities of wafer-cakes and diluted wine. But we can have no conception of wine except what may enter into a belief, either—

1. That this, that, or the other, is wine; or,
2. That wine possesses certain properties.

Such beliefs are nothing but self-notifications that we should, upon occasion, act in regard to such things as we believe to be wine according to the qualities which we believe wine to possess. The occasion of such action would be some sensible perception, the motive of it to produce some sensible result. Thus our action has exclusive reference to what affects the senses, our habit has the same bearing as our action, our belief the same as our habit, our conception the same as our belief; and we can consequently mean nothing by wine but what has certain effects, direct or indirect, upon our senses; and to talk of something as having all the sensible characters of wine, yet being in reality blood, is senseless jargon. Now, it is not my object to pursue the theological question; and having used it as a logical example I drop it, without caring to anticipate the theologian's reply. I only desire to point out how impossible it is that we should have an idea in our minds which relates to anything but conceived sensible effects of things. Our idea of anything *is* our idea of its sensible effects; and if we fancy that we have any other we deceive ourselves, and mistake a mere sensation accompanying the thought for a part of the thought itself. It is absurd to say that thought has any meaning unrelated to its only function. It is foolish for Catholics and Protestants to fancy themselves in disagreement about the elements of the sacrament, if they agree in regard to all their sensible effects, here and hereafter.

It appears, then, that the rule for attaining the third grade of clearness of apprehension is as follows: Consider what effects, that might conceivably have practical bearings, we conceive the object of our conception to have. Then, our conception of these effects is the whole of our conception of the object.

WILLIAM JAMES

Every Difference Must Make a Difference*

. . .

The Continental schools of philosophy have too often overlooked the fact that man's thinking is organically connected with his conduct. It seems to me to be the chief glory of English and Scottish thinkers to have kept the organic connection in view. The guiding principle of British philosophy has in fact been that every difference must *make* a difference, every theoretical difference somewhere issue in a practical difference, and that the best method of discussing points of theory is to begin by ascertaining what practical difference would result from one alternative or the other being true. What is the particular truth in question *known as?* In what facts does it result? What is its cash-value in terms of particular experience? This is the characteristic English way of taking up a question. In this way, you remember, Locke takes up the question of personal identity. What you mean by it is just your chain of particular memories, says he. That is the only concretely verifiable part of its significance. All further ideas about it, such as the oneness or manyness of the spiritual substance on which it is based, are therefore void of intelligible meaning; and propositions touching such ideas may be indifferently affirmed or denied. So Berkeley with his 'matter.' The cash-value of matter is our physical sensations. That is what it is known as, all that we concretely verify of its conception. That, therefore, is the whole meaning of the term 'matter'—any other pretended meaning is mere wind of words. Hume does the same thing with causation. It is known as habitual antecedence, and as tendency on our part to look for something definite to come. Apart from this practical meaning it has no significance whatever, and books about it may be committed to the flames, says Hume. Dugald Stewart and Thomas Brown, James Mill, John Mill, and Professor Bain, have followed more or less consistently the same method; and Shadworth Hodgson has used the principle with full explicitness. When all is said and done, it was English and Scotch writers, and not Kant,

* From William James, *The Varieties of Religious Experience,* Modern Library Edition, pp. 433–439. First published in 1902.

who introduced 'the critical method' into philosophy, the one method fitted to make philosophy a study worthy of serious men. For what seriousness can possibly remain in debating philosophic propositions that will never make an appreciable difference to us in action? And what could it matter, if all propositions were practically indifferent, which of them we should agree to call true or which false?

An American philosopher of eminent originality, Mr. Charles Sanders Peirce, has rendered thought a service by disentangling from the particulars of its application the principle by which these men were instinctively guided, and by singling it out as fundamental and giving to it a Greek name. He calls it the principle of *pragmatism,* and he defends it somewhat as follows:[1]

Thought in movement has for its only conceivable motive the attainment of belief, or thought at rest. Only when our thought about a subject has found its rest in belief can our action on the subject firmly and safely begin. Beliefs, in short, are rules for action; and the whole function of thinking is but one step in the production of active habits. If there were any part of a thought that made no difference in the thought's practical consequences, then that part would be no proper element of the thought's significance. To develop a thought's meaning we need therefore only determine what conduct it is fitted to produce; that conduct is for us its sole significance; and the tangible fact at the root of all our thought-distinctions is that there is no one of them so fine as to consist in anything but a possible difference of practice. To attain perfect clearness in our thoughts of an object, we need then only consider what sensations, immediate or remote, we are conceivably to expect from it, and what conduct we must prepare in case the object should be true. Our conception of these practical consequences is for us the whole of our conception of the object, so far as that conception has positive significance at all.

This is the principle of Peirce, the principle of pragmatism. Such a principle will help us on this occasion to decide, among the various attributes set down in the scholastic inventory of God's perfections, whether some be not far less significant than others.

If, namely, we apply the principle of pragmatism to God's metaphysical attributes, strictly so called, as distinguished from his moral attributes, I think that, even were we forced by a coercive logic to believe them, we still should have to confess them to be destitute of all intelligible significance. Take God's aseity, for example; or his necessariness; his immateriality; his 'simplicity' or superiority to the kind of inner variety and succession which we find in finite beings, his indivisibility, and lack of the inner distinctions of being and activity, substance and accident, potentiality and actuality, and the rest; his repudiation of inclusion in a genus; his actualized infinity; his 'personality,' apart from the moral qualities which it may comport; his relations to evil being permissive and not positive; his self-sufficiency, self-love, and absolute felicity in himself:—candidly speaking, how do such qualities as these make any definite connection with our life? And if they severally call for no distinctive adaptations of our conduct, what vital difference can it possibly make to a man's religion whether they be true or false?

For my own part, although I dislike to say aught that may grate upon tender associations, I must frankly confess that even though these attributes were faultlessly deduced, I cannot conceive of its being of the smallest consquence to us religiously that any one of them should be true. Pray, what specific act can I perform in order to adapt myself the better to God's simplicity? Or how does it assist me to plan my behavior, to know that his happiness is anyhow absolutely complete? In the middle of the century just past, Mayne Reid was the great writer of books of out-of-door adventure. He was forever extolling the hunters and field-observers of living animals' habits, and keeping up a fire of invective against the 'closet-naturalists,' as he called them, the collectors and classifiers, the handlers of skeletons and skins. When I was a boy, I used to think that a closet-naturalist must be the vilest type of wretch under the sun. But surely the systematic theologians are the closet-naturalists of the deity, even in Captain Mayne Reid's sense. What is their deduction of metaphysical attributes but a shuffling and matching of pedantic dictionary-adjectives, aloof from morals, aloof from human needs, something that might be worked out from the mere word 'God' by one of those logical machines of wood and brass which recent inge-

[1] In an article, "How to make Our Ideas Clear," in the *Popular Science Monthly* for January, 1878, vol. xii. p. 286. [This volume, p. 175]

nuity has contrived as well as by a man of flesh and blood. They have the trial of the serpent over them. One feels that in the theologians' hands, they are only a set of titles obtained by a mechanical manipulation of synonyms; verbality has stepped into the place of vision, professionalism into that of life. Instead of bread we have a stone; instead of a fish, a serpent. Did such a conglomeration of abstract terms give really the gist of our knowledge of the deity, schools of theology might indeed continue to flourish, but religion, vital religion, would have taken its flight from this world. What keeps religion going is something else than abstract definitions and systems of concatenated adjectives, and something different from faculties of theology and their professors. All these things are after-effects, secondary accretions upon those phenomena of vital conversation with the unseen divine, of which I have shown you so many instances, renewing themselves *in sœcula sœculorum* in the lives of humble private men.

So much for the metaphysical attributes of God! From the point of view of practical religion, the metaphysical monster which they offer to our worship is an absolutely worthless invention of the scholarly mind.

What shall we now say of the attributes called moral? Pragmatically, they stand on an entirely different footing. They positively determine fear and hope and expectation, and are foundations for the saintly life. It needs but a glance at them to show how great is their significance.

God's holiness, for example: being holy, God can will nothing but the good. Being omnipotent, he can secure its triumph. Being omniscient, he can see us in the dark. Being just, he can punish us for what he sees. Being loving, he can pardon too. Being unalterable, we can count on him securely. These qualities enter into connection with our life, it is highly important that we should be informed concerning them. That God's purpose in creation should be the manifestation of his glory is also an attribute which has definite relations to our practical life. Among other things it has given a definite character to worship in all Christian countries. If dogmatic theology really does prove beyond dispute that a God with characters like these exists, she may well claim to give a solid basis to religious sentiment. But verily, how stands it with her arguments?

It stands with them as ill as with the arguments for his existence. Not only do post-Kantian idealists reject them root and branch, but it is a plain historic fact that they never have converted any one who has found in the moral complexion of the world, as he experienced it, reasons for doubting that a good God can have framed it. To prove God's goodness by the scholastic argument that there is no non-being in his essence would sound to such a witness simply silly.

No! the book of Job went over this whole matter once for all and definitively. Ratiocination is a relatively superficial and unreal path to the deity: "I will lay mine hand upon my mouth; I have heard of Thee by the hearing of the ear, but now mine eye seeth Thee." An intellect perplexed and baffled, yet a trustful sense of presence—such is the situation of the man who is sincere with himself and with the facts, but who remains religious still.[2]

We must therefore, I think, bid a definitive good-by to dogmatic theology. In all sincerity our faith must do without that warrant. . . .

[2] Pragmatically, the most important attribute of God is his punitive justice. But who, in the present state of theological opinion on that point, will dare maintain that hell fire or its equivalent in some shape is rendered certain by pure logic? Theology herself has largely based this doctrine upon revelation; and, in discussing it, has tended more and more to substitute conventional ideas of criminal law for a priori principles of reason. But the very notion that this glorious universe, with planets and winds, and laughing sky and ocean, should have been conceived and had its beams and rafters laid in technicalities of criminality, is incredible to our modern imagination. It weakens a religion to hear it argued upon such a basis.

JOHN HOSPERS

What Is Explanation*

I

We are sometimes presented with a statement describing some observed fact, and when we ask 'Why?' we are presented with another statement which is said to constitute an explanation of the first. What is the relation between these two statements? What is it that makes the second statement an 'explanation' of the first? By virtue of what does it explain? Though everyone is constantly uttering statements which are supposed in one way or another to explain, few persons are at all clear about what it is that makes such statements explanations. Nor is the situation clarified when it is declared on the one hand that science explains everything and on the other hand that science never explains at all but only describes.

The question 'What is it to explain?" admits of no general answer, for the term 'to explain' covers many activities: one may explain how, and why, and whither, and whence, and how much, and many other things. Very frequently when we ask someone to explain what he has just said we are merely asking him to restate his assertion in clearer or simpler words.

In this essay I shall treat only explaining *why*. Even within this area there are some cases with which we shall not be concerned: one may explain why the angles of a Euclidean triangle must equal 180°, and this is quite different from explaining why iron rusts. The latter is an event or a process, and I shall be concerned solely with explaining why in the special context of temporal events: roughly, why did event x happen, or why do events of class X happen? The illustration from geometry is, I should prefer to say, an example of giving *reasons* rather than explanations. Another example may further illustrate the point: If you ask me to explain why I hold a certain belief, I may reply by giving *reasons* for it—statements which I take to be evidence for the belief in question. Now, if I am rational, the fact that there is good evidence for *p* may explain why I believe *p*—that is, the reason for my believing *p* may also constitute an explanation of why I believe *p*. But this may not be so: the explanation of a person's believing in a benevolent Deity may be that he wants a father-substitute or that he needs a protector in a cold harsh world; but when asked to explain why he believes in a benevolent Deity he may cite reasons, *e.g.* the Argument from Design, which may have nothing to do with *why* he holds the belief. We shall be concerned here, then, with the explanation of events, not with reasons or evidences one might cite in favour of propositions.

II

What, then, is it to explain why an event occurs? (1) It has sometimes been said that we have explained it if we have stated its *purpose*. 'Why did you walk through the snow for ten miles when you could have taken the bus?' 'Because I wanted to win a wager.' 'Why does that dog scratch at the door?' 'He's cold and he wants to get in.' When such answers are given we are inclined to feel that our question has been answered and that the event has been satisfactorily explained; and it has been explained with reference to a purpose which some sentient being(s) had in attaining a certain end. This is the most primitive conception of explanation.

* John Hospers, "What Is Explanation?" First published in the *Journal of Philosophy*, 1946. This is the revised version published in *Essays in Conceptual Analysis*, edited by Antony Flew (London: Macmillan; New York: St. Martin's Press, 1956), pp. 94–119. Reprinted by permission of the author, the *Journal of Philosophy*, The Macmillan Company, and St. Martin's Press.

People like to feel that there is a purposive explanation for everything: if not in terms of human or animal purposes, then of divine ones, or mysterious forces and powers. We tend to extend what holds true of some events to all events whatever; we know what conscious motivation is like from our own experience of it, and so we 'feel at home' with this kind of explanation.

We shall examine the scope and legitimacy of purposive explanation later in this paper. It is enough to remark here that if explanation must always be in terms of purpose, then the physical sciences do not explain anything. The properties of uranium, the rise of aeroplanes, the phenomena of magnetism are not explained in terms of any purposes at all; biologists even avoid talking about animal events such as the hen sitting on eggs in terms of purpose. However animistically the nature of explanation may at one time have been conceived, purposiveness is certainly no essential part of its meaning now. The stone is no longer held to fall because it wants to get to the centre of the earth.

(2) Another account of the nature of explanation is that an event has been explained when it has been shown to be an instance of some class of events which is already familiar to us. For example, when a person's behaviour seems strange to us, we are satisfied when it is 'explained' to us as being really impelled by the same sort of motives and desires as occur in us, and are therefore familiar to us. 'Why is he introducing the man he hates to the woman he loves?' 'Because he wants them to fall in love with each other' would not generally be accepted as an explanation, for this very reason. When we observe that a balloon ascends rather than descends, unlike most objects, and it is made clear to us that air has weight and that the gas inside the balloon weighs less than would an equal volume of air, we are satisfied; the phenomenon has been 'reduced' to something already familiar to us in everyday experience, such as a dense object sinking in water while a hollow one floats. The event is no longer unusual, strange, or unique; it has been shown to illustrate a principle with which we were already acquainted. When we want to know why gases diffuse when released into a chamber from which the air has been pumped out, the explanation offered by the kinetic theory of gases is satisfactory to us because it asserts that molecules behave *like* particles with which we are already acquainted in our everyday experience.

> Only those who have practised experimental physics know anything by actual experience about the laws of gases; they are not things which force themselves on our attention in common life, and even those who are most familiar with them never think of them out of working hours. On the other hand, the behaviour of moving solid bodies is familiar to everyone; everyone knows roughly what will happen when such bodies collide with each other or with a solid wall, though they may not know the exact dynamical laws involved in such reactions. In all our common life we are continually encountering moving bodies, and noticing their reactions; indeed, if the reader thinks about it, he will realize that whenever we are passively affected by it, a moving body is somehow involved in the transaction. Movement is just the most familiar thing in the world; it is through motion that everything and anything happens. And so by tracing a relation between the unfamiliar changes which gases undergo when their temperature or volume is altered, and the extremely familiar changes which accompany the motions and mutual reactions of solid bodies, we are rendering the former more intelligible; we are explaining them. (Norman Campbell, *What Is Science?* Dover, N.Y., p. 84.)

Professor Bridgman holds that all explanation is of this kind:

> I believe that examination will show that the essence of an explanation consists in reducing a situation to elements with which we are so familiar that we accept them as a matter of course, so that our curiosity rests (P. W. Bridgman, *The Logic of Modern Physics,* p. 37).

And yet I am sure that such a view as this must be mistaken. In the *first* place, we may seek explanations for the most familiar events as well as of those unfamiliar to us. We may ask why stones fall as well as why aeroplanes rise, and be curious for an answer equally in both cases. True, our motivation for asking the latter question is probably greater because the kind of phenomenon in question is (or was) less familiar; most people would not think to ask it about stones because the falling of stones is familiar and usual—but the question can as legitimately be asked in the one case as in the other. In the *second* place, the explanation may not be familiar at all: it may be far less familiar than the event to be explained. The discoloration of a painted kitchen wall when gas heat is used may be a familiar phenomenon to the housewife—surely more familiar than its explanation in terms of the chemical combination of sulphur in the gas fumes with elements in the paint, producing a compound that is dark in colour. Yet this is the true explanation. If the explanation is not familiar, one is tempted to say, it ought to be, as long as it is true. Surely its familiarity is irrelevant to its validity as an explanation. Familiarity is, in any case, a subjective matter—what is familiar to you may not be familiar to me; and yet the explanation, if true, is as true for me as for you.

The only grain of truth in the view that explaining is rendering familiar seems to be this: the law that does the explaining may not be familiar, *but* the fact that the phenomenon in question, such as the flight of an aeroplane, *can* be subsumed under a law—the fact that the behaviour *is* lawlike and hence predictable—tends to make it less mysterious, less like a miracle, and thus in a sense more familiar. To show that the behaviour of something is lawlike is to show it to be a part of the order of nature, and in that sense familiar, although the particular law or laws stating the uniformity may be quite unfamiliar.

In what, then, *does* explanation consist? The answer, I think, is quite simple: (3) to explain an event is simply to bring it under a law;[1] and to explain a law is to bring it under another law. It does not matter whether the law is one about purposes or not, or whether it is familiar or not; what matters is that if the explanation is to be *true* (and we surely seek true explanations, not false ones), the law invoked must be true: indeed, this is already implied in the use of the word 'law', which refers to a true, *i.e.* a really existing, uniformity of nature; if the uniformity turned out to be only imaginary, or having exceptions, we would no longer call it a law.

In saying that explanation is in terms of laws, I use the word 'law' in a wider sense than is sometimes employed: in the sense I mean, any uniformity of nature is a law. Thus, it is a law that iron rusts, and it is a law that iron is magnetic—although both of these are usually listed in textbooks as 'properties of iron' rather than as laws. In this sense, it seems to me that explaining why something occurs always involves a law. If we ask, 'Why don't the two liquids in the flask mix?' and someone answers, 'Don't you see, the one is transparent and the other is red?' this does not strike us as an explanation (*i.e.* as a true explanation) of the phenomenon, because we know of no law according to which red liquids will not mix with transparent ones. But when we are told that the red liquid is coloured water and that the transparent liquid is gasoline, we consider the phenomenon to be explained, for we hold it to be a law of nature that water and gasoline do not mix. In the sense in which I am using the word 'law', the non-mixture of water and gasoline is a law; and *only* if a law is brought in do we have an explanation of the phenomenon.

Sometimes, I should add, all we have available is a 'statistical law'—a law not of the form 'All A is B' or 'Whenever A, then B', but, *e.g.*, '75 per cent of A is B'. Can such a 'law' constitute an explanation? I should be inclined to say that it is, although we would still want an explanation of why 25 per cent of A's are *not* B's. If water did not always boil at 212° F. but did so only 75 per cent of the time, we might explain the boiling of this kettle of water by saying that its temperature had reached 212°, though we would still want an explanation of why the kettle of water next to it, which had also reached 212°, did not boil. In other words, our statistical law would still not answer the question 'Why this and not that?' and in order to answer *this* question, we would need a non-statistical law of the form, 'Under such-and-such conditions, water always boils at 212° F., but under such-and-such other conditions, it does not'. It would seem, then, that a statistical law has in turn to be explained by a non-statistical one, although of course we may not, at any given stage in the progress of science, know of any non-statistical law by which to explain the statistical one.

Another example: 'Why does Johnny have a cold?' 'Because Johnny has been playing with Roger, and Roger has a cold.' It is not a law that everyone who plays with someone who has a cold also gets a cold; the best we can do here is to state a percentage of cases in which this happens. So far as it goes, this is satisfactory; some uniformity is better than none. And yet, surely, we do not rest satisfied with this; we want to go on and ask why it sometimes happens but sometimes not. And the answer to this question would be a non-statistical law: 'People always get colds under such-and-such conditions'. Whether a statistical law can *always* be explained in terms of a non-

[1] With qualifications to be discussed later.

statistical one depends not only on our powers of discovery but upon the nature of the universe. It is certainly no *a priori* truth that nature's uniformities are all of the 100 per cent variety instead of 75 per cent.

One further qualification: We have said that we explain particular events in terms of laws, and laws in terms of wider laws. But sometimes we give at least tentative explanations of them in terms not of laws but of general *hypotheses:* if a law is a well-established statement of how nature works, a statement about nature's workings that is not well established, or perhaps not even probable but only possible, cannot be a law. And yet we can use it to explain a law. But to whatever degree the hypothesis is uncertain, to that degree the explanation is jeopardized. An explanation cannot be known to be true if it involves a hypothesis which (by the definition of 'hypothesis') is *not* known to be true. Whether the explanation is a true explanation, then, depends on the fate of the hypothesis. (In the 'higher reaches' of most sciences, where the most general laws are involved, the only explanations possible are usually those in terms of very general hypotheses.)

III

So much for a general statement of what explanation consists of. I should like now to append some comments and to answer some questions to which the above account may give rise.

1. Thus far we have been content to answer the question 'Why does A do B?' by saying 'Because all A's do B'. But there are those who say that such an answer is no explanation at all. 'To say that all gases expand when heated', says Norman Campbell (*What Is Science?* p. 80), 'is not to explain why hydrogen expands when heated; it merely leads us to ask immediately why all gases expand. An explanation which leads immediately to another question of the same kind is no explanation at all.'

I want to insist that the answer given *is* an explanation of the occurrence in question; to say 'Hydrogen is a gas, and all gases expand when heated' is a perfectly satisfactory answer to the question why hydrogen expands when heated. But it is *not,* of course, an answer to *another* question—Why do all gases expand when heated?—and this is probably the question which the person meant to ask in the first place. These questions must not be confused with each other; I believe Campbell's position is the result of this confusion. It is fatally easy to telescope (unconsciously) two questions into one, and then be dissatisfied with the answer. Distinguishing them, we get:

Question 1. Why does this gas expand when heated?

Explanation. It is hydrogen, and hydrogen expands when heated.

Question 2. Why does hydrogen expand when heated?

Explanation. Hydrogen is a gas, and all gases expand when heated.

Question 3. Why do all gases expand when heated?

Here we attempt to give an explanation in terms of the kinetic theory of gases. To criticize Answer 1 because it is not an answer to Question 2, or Answer 2 because it is not an answer to Question 3, is surely a confusion. I want to say that Answer 1 is a perfectly satisfactory explanation for the phenomenon referred to in Question 1, though of course not for those referred to in Questions 2 and 3. But there is a frequent tendency to telescope these questions and demand to Question 1 the answer to Question 3.

The situation may be illustrated in another way. If I ask, 'Why did the water-pipes in my basement burst last night?' someone may answer that it is because the basement got too cold, and another may answer that it is because water expands when it freezes, while yet another may say that we do not know the 'real explanation' unless we can state why water expands when it freezes. Here, again we must separate the questions:

Question 1. Why did the water-pipes break?

Explanation. They always do when the temperature falls to below 32°.

Question 2. Why do they break when the temperature falls . . . etc.?

Explanation. Because the water in them expands when it freezes, and the water on expanding breaks the pipes.

Question 3. Why does water expand when it freezes?

Explanation. Here we try to answer in terms of the structure of the water-molecule.

But to say that we have not explained (1) until we have explained (3) is grossly to underestimate the number of phenomena for which we do have perfectly satisfactory explanations. That is, we *do* have explanations for (1) and (2), and our having them is *not* contingent upon having an explanation for (3).

We could put our point in another way. *Logically* the answers given to each question in turn are satisfactory explanations; but *psychologically* they may not be equally satisfying, *depending on the previous knowledge of the questioner*. To the questioner who knew nothing about the relation of pipes bursting to temperature, the answer 'Because they got cold' (to the first question) would be psychologically quite satisfactory, but not to the person who already knew that it had something to do with temperature, for the question *he* meant to ask was (2) or (3). Again: If I ask why this wire conducts electricity, it is a perfectly good explanation to answer 'Because it is made of copper, and copper is a conductor of electricity'. Psychologically, however, this answer would not be equally satisfying to everyone; it *would* be to the person who knew nothing of the properties of copper (or who did not know that this wire was copper), but it would *not* be to the person who already knew the properties of copper but was really enquiring as to why copper, unlike many other substances, is a conductor of electricity.

2. Can an event have *two* explanations? Why not? Let us suppose that we want to explain an event E, and that we have a law saying that every time conditions A are fulfilled, E happens, and another law saying that every time conditions B are fulfilled, E happens. A will then be a complete explanation for the occurrence of E, and B will also be a complete explanation. Whether any such state of affairs actually occurs in the world is, of course, another question. Most of the suggested double explanations of events are in fact parts of a single explanation. Thus, for example, if we are asked to explain why the burglar committed the robbery last night, the detective may explain it in terms of his expertness at picking locks, the butler may explain it in terms of the family being out of the room, the maid may say it was because the bedroom window was open, the policeman may say it was because the night was foggy and visibility at a minimum, the sociologist may explain it in terms of the criminal's background of slum conditions, and the psychologist may explain it in terms of pseudo-aggressive impulses dating from a childhood period marked by intense family quarrels. All these explanations are probably correct enough as far as they go. It may well be that in the absence of any one of these factors the burglary would not have occurred. But these are, it would surely seem, parts and aspects of *one* complete explanation—and in explaining human actions the whole explanation may be inconceivably complex. Still, the possibility remains that in *some* cases there may be two separate and complete explanations for an occurrence; at least it cannot be ruled out *a priori*.

3. Must there be a *deductive* relation between the thing to be explained and the explanation, such that one can deduce the statement of the phenomenon to be explained from the explanation?

All copper conducts electricity.
This wire is made of copper.
Therefore, This wire conducts electricity.

Here the explanation yields the desired conclusion easily, and it is quite clear that what we have here is a genuine explanation. The question is, must all explanation conform to this model? Have we failed to give an explanation if we have failed to deduce the explanandum from the explanation?

Let us first note that in many cases, if this is required, the explanation would be bewilderingly complex, and the premises in the deduction extremely numerous. Consider the burglary example just cited. From the fact that the weather was foggy and that the man had tendencies to steal and that he had a poor background . . . etc., we cannot deduce the fact that he committed the theft. We cannot deduce it, indeed, from any set of premises known to be true. What we need for deducing it is a law, to the effect that if such-and-such conditions are fulfilled an act of this kind will always occur, and then a minor premise to the effect that these conditions were in fact fulfilled. The conditions would indeed have to be extremely numerous, and the statement of the law immensely complicated. Yet such a law is required if the desired conclusion is to be deduced.

We never in fact use a deductive model in cases like this one, and it is worthy of note that we do not deny ourselves the claim that we have explained the event because of this. What, therefore, are we to say of the deductive model as a *sine qua non* for all explanation? As I see it, we have two alternatives open to us:

(*a*) We can, in the light of such examples, scrap the deductive model entirely. We can say that often one can in fact deduce the explanandum from the explanation, but that this is not essential to explanation. We might add, as some do, that to perform the deduction is one way (the best way?) to *justify* an explanation we have put forward, but that the giving of a true explanation is not dependent on this.

(*b*) We can still insist that a complete explanation does involve the deduction, but that what we often give is in fact less than a complete explanation. We list, as in the burglary example, a few salient facts and either take the remainder as too obvious to mention or do not know what they are. But such measures are concessions of failure. The fact is that the only way to be sure of our explanation is to deduce the phenomenon in question from premises which we know to be true.

I merely wish here to state these alternatives, not to decide between them. It is, surely, a matter of how liberally or how strictly we wish to use the term 'explanation'; and, though I incline toward the second alternative, I do not wish to champion without reserve a 'puristic' account of explanation which is not in fact followed by anyone—at least anyone in the psychological and social sciences—and which, it is sometimes declared, is in practice almost useless and boringly academic.

Thus far in enquiring about the need for a deductive relationship, we have considered only the explanation of particular events: we have deduced them from two premises, one stating a law and the other stating a particular condition: 'All copper conducts electricity; this is copper, therefore this conducts electricity.' 'All water freezes at 32° F., the water in the pond went below 32° last night; therefore the water in the pond froze.' And so on. But, as we saw earlier, we not only explain particular events; we also explain *laws*. And the same question could be repeated here: is the deductive requirement necessary? There is no doubt that in the 'neat, tidy' cases it is fulfilled: for example, Kepler's laws of planetary motion can be deduced from Newton's laws of motion together with the law of gravitation; and thus the latter clearly explain the former. But is this strictly a requirement for *all* explanation of laws? Again, some would say that it is—that anything short of this is not a full explanation. Others would say that it is not—that the deductive case is only the ideal one but that explanation does not require it. For example, a law can be explained in terms of a very general theory, from which the law cannot be strictly deduced, but which will nevertheless entitle the theory to be called an explanation. (The deductivist will reply that it is not *known* to be an explanation until the acid test, *i.e.* the deduction, is performed.)

4. In any case, whether deducibility is a necessary condition of explanation or not, it is not a sufficient condition. One can deduce that this watch will not work from the premises that watches will not work if gremlins get into them and that gremlins are in fact in this watch. Yet no one would accept this as an explanation for the misbehaviour of the watch. Similarly, one might deduce it from the premises that whatever God wills happens and that God has willed the misbehaviour of this watch. One can deduce anything if one selects one's premises carefully.

One might remark at this point that it is also necessary that the premises be *true,* and that this is the required addition. I would unhesitatingly agree that the premises must indeed be true—false statements cannot form parts of true explanations (indeed, if explanation is in terms of law, and a law is a true statement of a uniformity, *i.e.* one that actually occurs, then this proviso has already been implicit in our account of explanation). But suppose we make this proviso explicit—is it enough? I do not believe so. It might be true that God wills everything that happens, but as long as we have no means of knowing this, we cannot use it as a premise in our explanation. That is, we cannot use it as an explanation unless the proposition is not only true, but is *known to be so.*

Suppose, then, that we accept this last revision—will it do the trick? I hardly think so; it still misses the main point. Let us imagine a deeply religious scientist who holds that everything that happens is the result of divine will; he may yet reject the theological explanation as an account of *why* things happen as they do. The reason is surely fairly obvious: what the scientist wishes to discover is why this happened *rather than that,* and the theological explanation will not enable him to make this discrimination: *whatever* happens, one can deduce it from the premises that God willed it to happen and that whatever He wills happens.

What condition, then, remains to be supplied? The condition seems to be a rather simple one, yet one which it is difficult to state precisely. What we have in mind is this: we want to eliminate the indiscriminate 'explanatory' power of the gremlin-hypothesis and the God-hypothesis, even though they slip through the deductive net, because they do not enable us to explain why this happens *rather than that*. 'What explains everything explains nothing.'

This *can* be put by saying that the explanation must have *predictive* value, but this is a bit misleading. For one thing, it places undue emphasis upon the future, whereas explanation of past is just as important as explanation of future; we would have, then, to use a tenseless sense of 'predict'. For another thing, there are many explanations which seem to be true but whose predictive power is minimal or at any rate difficult to see: many biological phenomena can be explained in terms of laws of mutations, for example, but it is not clear what these laws enable us to *predict*—certainly not where or when a mutation will occur or what kind it will be when it does arise.

Perhaps what we want to say can be best expressed by the simple proviso that the explanation must explain *other* phenomena than those it is invoked to explain, and yet, unlike the God-hypothesis, not just everything indiscriminately: in other words, it should explain other events (whether past, present, or future makes no difference), but it should all the same be *capable of disproof* by empirical observations, whether or not any actual empirical observations ever disprove it, it must be capable of testing. Without this condition it would not be considered an explanation in any science.

In fact all this is implicit in our requirement that an explanation be in terms of law or laws. A law is a universal proposition about all events or processes in a certain class, and if it holds for A, a member of the class (a present event), it also holds for members B, C, and D (future events); thus by the very nature of a law, laws explain more than a single event. The testability of explanations is also implicit in the concept of law, for a law is an empirical statement of a uniformity of nature, and, being contingent, it is always subject to disconfirmation by observation. Still, it is well to make the implicit explicit to show why the deductive requirement is not enough and what more is required of an explanation.

5. In evaluating the extent to which proffered explanations yield us genuine empirical knowledge (*i.e.* are real empirical laws), much care is required, for in this field the verbal booby-traps in our way are numerous and intricate.

If someone asked, 'Why is this object spherical?' and the reply were given, 'Because it's globular', everyone would recognize the answer to be trivial because it is analytic. Many so-called explanations do not give much more information than this, although even very bad ones are not usually quite as empty as this one. Even when one says that opium produces sleep because of its dormitive power, we are at least told that it is because of something within it that sleep is produced, not by some outside factor such as the atmosphere. When we ask why hydrogen combines with oxygen to form water, and are told that it is because hydrogen has an *affinity* for oxygen, again the reply is relatively empty: it tells us only that under certain conditions hydrogen does combine with oxygen but tells us nothing of why hydrogen rather than some other substances does this; but at least we know from the answer that there *is* a law relating the combination of elements to some set of conditions, though we do not yet know what this law is. And if we ask why the mother cat takes care of her kittens and fights to defend them, and are told that it is because she has a *maternal instinct,* at least we know that the activity is not a learned one—and this is indeed something—although again the answer may not give us the kind of thing we were asking for. Most explanations in terms of instinct, tendency, affinity, power, and faculty are of this next-to-worthless kind, conveying only a minimum of information, and leading us to ask a why-question of the explanation given.

Let us observe how easily the invention of a name may make us assume that an explanation has been given. If it is asked, 'Why is iron magnetic?' and we answer, 'Because iron, cobalt, and nickel are magnetic', no one would think much of this as an explanation; but the moment we give a name to the behaviour of these metals, and call them, say, 'fero-affinitive', then when someone asks why iron is magnetic, we can say, 'Why, because it's a fero-affinitive metal, that's why'. And yet no more has been said in the second case than in the first. Similarly, if we had a name for the tendency of seeds to sprout upwards to reach the surface of the ground, people would be readier to say that their tendency to rise could be *explained* by the presence of this property. Yet a name for what it does is a different thing from an explanation of why it does what it does.

Not all examples are as simple as this. When external influences tend to reduce or raise the bodily temperature of an organism, various bodily mechanisms come into play to return the temperature to normal. This is known as 'homeostasis'. So far, we simply have a name for the phenomenon, and if someone volunteered it as an *explanation* he would surely be mistaken. But now suppose a bird finds its nest partially destroyed and it sets about rebuilding it to the way it was before; we ask why, and are told, 'That's the bird's homeostatic tendency'. Now the name 'homeostasis' is no longer merely a label for the temperature-controlling mechanisms; it relates these mechanisms to a quite different thing, the bird's attempt to restore the *status quo*. In both examples there is an attempt to restore a state which has ceased to exist. Is 'homeostasis' now an explanation, or is it simply a description-in-a-nutshell, a *generalized* description, of what the organism does, without attempting to explain why?

Observe, incidentally, how easily all these so-called explanations slip through the deductive net. We can deduce the required conclusion easily: 'When organisms have homeostatic tendencies, they do so-and-so. This organism has homeostatic tendencies. Therefore, it does so-and-so.' The deductive requirement will let good and bad explanations alike slip through like water through a sieve. This shows us again that, whether necessary to explanation or not, the deducibility requirement is not sufficient.

But let us return: Is homeostasis an explanation of the organism's behaviour or not? Before we say, 'No, it isn't', let us reflect on this point: if appeal to homeostasis is simply a short way of saying that birds do this and people do that, is not the appeal to gravitation simply a short way of saying that apples do this and stars do that? And yet the Law of Gravitation is one of the most sacred of our explanatory principles. Perhaps, as Wisdom says, talking about gravitation is simply a way of saying that apples fall *and so on;* but then is not homeostasis simply a way of saying that birds rebuild their nests *and so on?*

It is, of course, incorrect to say that apples fall because of gravitation, if we mean by this that gravitation is some animistic force or pull, just as it would be wrong to say that birds behave so-and-so because of homeostasis, if we mean it to be a separate force or magnetism within birds. If we are so tempted, it is both useful and important to say that each of the explanations referred to is simply a way of saying 'this happens *and so on*'. But it is, I should think, the *extent and range* of the 'and so on' that matters here. What gives the Principle of Gravitation its remarkable explanatory power is not its appeal to an occult force but its bringing together under one formula an enormous range of diverse and complex phenomena. Because of this range, and the exactitude with which it can be applied to widely separate phenomena, the Law of Gravitation is the classical case of a law having predictive power—and it is extremely doubtful whether homeostasis possesses or ever will possess this. We rest, then, once again with this second and all-important necessary condition of explanation (the first being, at least in common opinion, the deducibility requirement): its power to explain a wide range of phenomena *other* than those it was invoked to explain.

6. No mention has thus far been made of explanation in terms of *purpose*. And yet this is the oldest concept of explanation and still the one most frequently employed by primitive peoples. And there are contexts in which we still employ the concept of purpose in giving explanations—for example, when we say that my purpose in going to the store was to do some Christmas shopping, and that this is *why* I went.

The word 'purpose' is, of course, ambiguous. (*a*) Most frequently in ordinary usage a purpose is something of which I am conscious—a conscious intent to do something. The conscious intent is not the *whole* of the purpose: part of the criterion of whether it is my purpose to do X is whether I am disposed towards doing X, whether I take steps towards X and do X if I have the chance. (*b*) Some tendencies to act are not accompanied by any state of awareness; and here psychologists speak of *un*conscious purposes. We need not stop here over the exact interpretation of this way of speaking; let us simply say that one is said to have X as his unconscious purpose if he consistently acts, without intending it, so as to bring about X. (*c*) We speak of inanimate objects as having purposes—for example, the purpose of a hammer is to drive nails. This of course is not a purpose consciously envisaged by the hammer. All we mean here is that the mechanical object *reflects* the conscious purposes of its makers. *We* had a conscious purpose in making the hammer, and thus we speak elliptically of the hammer as having that purpose. Strictly speaking, of course, the purpose is ours and not the hammer's.

In all of these cases a purpose implies a purposer, or someone to have the purpose. We do sometimes use the word 'purpose' in another sense which carries no such implication, (*d*) when we say, 'What is the purpose of the heart?' 'To pump blood through the body.' Here purpose simply means function—*i.e.* what does it *do?* what part does it play in the bodily economy? If the word 'purpose' is used here I would view it as a 'degenerate' usage—a misleading locution in which another word, 'function', would serve much better. It is true that someone, in asking the purpose of the heart, might have in mind a theological question, 'What purpose did God have in endowing us with this organ?' but if this is meant, we are back again to purpose in sense 1, in which purpose implies a purposer and the word 'purpose' refers to conscious intent—the only difference now being that it is God's intent and not ours that is in question. But this, of course, is not what medical men generally have in mind when they ask purpose-questions about parts of organisms; else every such medical question would be a disguised theological question.

Having disentangled these senses of 'purpose', let us ask about the legitimacy of purposive explanations. Briefly I think it comes to this: explanations require laws, and if there are laws *about* purposes, there is no reason why they cannot figure in some explanations just as laws about falling bodies figure in other explanations. To the extent that laws about purposes have been established, they can be used as explanations like any other laws. Unfortunately the only laws (if any) that we are in a position to make about purposes are about human ones. Explanations in terms of divine purposes cannot be employed because no laws about divine purposes have ever been established. Even explanations of biological events in terms of animal purposes is frowned upon: we do not count it an explanation if it is said that the hen sits on her eggs *in order to* hatch chicks, because we have no indication that the hen does so with this purpose in mind; even if this is true, we do not know it, and therefore we cannot use it as a law in our explanation. In the human realm alone we know that purposes exist, and only there can we therefore employ them in explanations. We can even deduce conclusions from them, thus:

People act so as to fulfill their purposes, unless prevented by external circumstances.

My purpose was to go shopping, and I was not prevented . . . etc.

Therefore, I went shopping.

This way of putting it may sound rather silly, as the deductive model often does, but at any rate a deduction can be achieved from premises which are in all probability true.

The chief mistake which people are in the habit of making with regard to purposive explanation is probably that of wanting an answer to a why-question in terms of purpose when the conditions under which a purpose-answer is legitimate are not fulfilled. People extend their questioning unthinkingly from areas in which purposive explanation is in order into areas in which it is not. Thus: 'Why did he go to New York?' 'Well, in response to impulses from certain centres in his brain, some muscles in his arms and legs started moving towards the airport and . . .' 'No, that's not what I mean. I mean, why did he go? what did he go for? what purpose did he have in view?' 'He went in order to see some operas.' Contrast this with the following: 'Why did he die?' 'Well, a bullet entered his lung, puncturing some blood vessels, and the blood filled his lung so that he couldn't breathe any more, and . . .' 'No, that's not what I mean. I mean, *why* did he die?' But here we can no longer give an answer in terms of purpose—unless, that is, our talk is rooted in a theological context and we are willing to say that, just as the first person went to New York because he wanted to see operas, so the second person died because God had some purpose (intent) in seeing to it that he was murdered. If this is what is meant, one could try to answer the question in the theistic context of divine purposes; but if this context is rejected, the why-question demanding an answer in terms of purpose is meaningless, because an answer is being demanded when the only conditions under which the question is meaningful are not fulfilled.

This point is worth emphasizing because it is so often ignored in practice. Having received answers to why-questions when these questions were meaningful and explanations could be given, people continue to use why-questions even when they no longer know what they are asking for. One need not be surprised that no answer is forthcoming to such questions. And in our discouragement with such questions we are all too prone to make a mistake ourselves and terminate an exasperating series of why-questions with a remark such as, 'That's just something we don't know,' as if it were like cases where something definite is being asked but we do not yet know the laws which explain the phenomena we are asking about. If something in the case is not known, there must be something in the case which we could fail to know. If we are to ask a meaningful question, we must know what it is that we are asking for; only then can we recognize an answer as being one when we do find it.

7. This leads us directly into an important question, How far can explanation go? We may explain an event in terms of a law, and this law in terms of other laws, and so on? but must we not finally come to a stop? The bursting of the pipes is explained by the expansion of water on freezing; let us assume that water expands on freezing because the water-molecule has such-and-such a structure; now why does the water-molecule have this structure? Perhaps this can some day be explained by reference to electron-proton arrangements within the atom, and this in turn by reference to the disposition of more minute particles (if they can be called such) yet to be discovered; but sooner or later must we not say, 'That's just the way things are—this is just an ultimate law about the universe. We can explain other things in terms of it, but it we cannot explain'? Are there ultimate laws, laws which explain but cannot even in principle be explained?

In practice we come rather quickly to laws which cannot be explained further. Laws about atomic structure are typical of such laws. Laws of psycho-physical correlation are another example. *Why* do I have a certain colour-sensation which I call red, indescribable but qualitatively different from all others, when light within a certain range of wave-length impinges upon my retina, and another indescribably different sensation which I call yellow when rays of another wave-length strike the retina? That this wave-length is correlated with this visual experience seems to be sheer 'brute fact'—a law[2] which cannot be explained in terms of anything more ultimate than itself.

At the same time, we should be careful in dismissing any uniformity we cannot explain as a 'brute fact' or 'basic law'. Many things, such as why this element has this melting-point and these spectral lines, were once considered basic and unexplainable properties of the element, but have since been explained in terms of the intramolecular structure of the element. No matter how much at a loss we may be for an explanation, we can always ask and speculate. If it had been accepted as a basic law that water starts to expand when it gets below 39° F., we would never have gone on to discover anything about the structure of the water-molecule. Fruitful scientific procedure depends on assuming that no given law is basic; if scientists did not continue always to ask the question 'Why?' the process of scientific enquiry would stop dead in its tracks.

Thus, if there *are* basic laws, it seems that we cannot know of any given law that it is one. We can know that it is *not,* by explaining it in terms of other laws; but how could we know that it *is*? Discovering basic laws is epistemologically similar to discovering uncaused events: if there are uncaused events, we can never know that there are, for all we can safely say is that we have not yet found causes for them.

One further point about basic or ultimate laws: If a law is really a basic one, any request for an explanation of it is self-contradictory. To explain a law is to place it in a context or network of wider and more inclusive laws; a basic law is by definition one of which this cannot be done; therefore to ask of an admittedly basic law that it be explained is implicitly to deny that it is basic and thus to deny the very premise of the argument. It is a request for explanation in a situation where by one's own admission no more explaining can be done.

Like so many others, this point may seem logically compelling but psychologically unsatisfying. Having heard the above argument, one may still feel inclined to ask, 'Why are the basic uniformities of the universe the way they are, and not some other way? Why should we have just *these* laws rather than other ones? I want an *explanation* of why they are as they are.' I must confess here, as an autobiographical remark, that I cannot help sharing this feeling: I want to ask why the laws of nature, being contingent, are as

[2] A law which would, to be sure, have to be qualified to take care of abnormal cases, *e.g.* colour-blindness, jaundice, etc. The genesis of colour-sensations is complex and does not depend *merely* upon the kind of light-rays entering the eye.

they are, even though I cannot conceive of what an explanation of this would be like, and even though by my own argument above the request for such an explanation is self-contradictory.[3] The fact is, as we saw above, that why-questions have had answers so many times that we tend automatically to ask them here even when they can have no answers because we have ripped them out of the only context in which they have meaning—like the situation of the child who, being told what is above the table and above the ceiling of his room and above the house and above the earth, now asks what is above the universe. The question has now gone outside the context of meaningful discourse, and so has the request for the explanation of a basic law. We should remember: to explain is to explain *in terms of something,* and if *ex hypothesi* there is no longer any something for it to be explained in terms of, then the request for an explanation is self-contradictory: it demands on the one hand that you explain X in terms of a Y while insisting simultaneously that there is no Y.

8. One sometimes encounters the complaint that science does not really explain but only describes. 'Science doesn't tell us *why* things happen,' it is said, 'it only tells us *how* things happen.' Now it does often happen that the exact intention of the user of a why-question is not very clear—as we have already seen. But in the way in which the term 'why' is most commonly used, science *does* explain why: for example, the bursting of the pipes, the formation of ice at the top of ponds rather than at the bottom, and many other phenomena, are explained by reference to the law that water expands when it freezes. (If someone says we have *not* explained why the pipes burst, then what does he mean by 'why'? What sort of thing is he asking for? What *would* answer his question? Let him state in other terms what it is that he is asking for.)

'But is not explanation after all merely description?' It is all very well to say that when we explain something we actually describe—*e.g.* stating laws of nature is describing how nature works. But this does not preclude the fact that we *are* explaining. When the question is asked why pressing the button turns on the light, we explain by describing just what goes on—currents, open and closed circuits, conduction of electricity by wires, dynamos in the power plant, and so on. But have we not in so doing explained the phenomenon about which we were asking? We have explained *by* describing, if you will; but certainly we have explained. To say that because we are describing we cannot be explaining would be like saying that because an object is red it cannot also be coloured.

9. A similar complaint is sometimes voiced against scientific explanation, that it 'explains things *away*'. Explaining something is interpreted as equivalent to explaining it away. Now the precise meaning of the phrase 'explaining away' is one which I have never been able to discover. What is one supposed to be doing when he explains something away? Surely not to declare that it does not exist! Explanation deprives us of no facts we had before. To 'explain colour' in terms of light-waves is not, of course (as should have been obvious), to take away the fact of colour-experiences. 'Thinking is nothing but the occurrence of certain neural impulses' should be changed into '*When* thinking takes place (and that it does is just as incontrovertible a fact as the neurons are), there are neural impulses.'

In the special context of beliefs, perhaps 'explaining away' may mean impugning the truth of one's conclusions. If so, there are again no grounds for fear. To 'explain away' someone's politically reactionary tendencies by saying, 'He's old, and people always get conservative when they get old', does not for a moment take away whatever truth the person's opinions may have; at most, it only exposes part of the causal genesis of his having them. And if the views of this person were 'explained away' by these biographical observations, the views of his opponent would be equally vulnerable: 'You needn't pay any attention to that young upstart, they're all hot communists when they're young'. Reference to biography may, together with laws of human nature (if any are known in this area), explain why a person held a certain belief at a certain time, but the truth or falsity of the belief is quite unaffected by this and, of course, is tested on different grounds entirely. The idea that reference to a person's mental or physical condition could 'explain away' the truth of a belief is one of the most flagrant blunders of the materialistically minded laity of our day.

[3] Explanation in terms of divine purposes again will not help: if we are told that the laws of nature are as they are because God willed it so, we can ask why He should have willed it so; and if here again an answer is given, we can once again ask a why-question of this answer.

PART 3 MIND AND ITS

To a large degree, what has come to be known as the "Mind-Body Problem" in philosophy is a product of the philosophy of René Descartes. How can things differing as radically as minds (or souls) and bodies, in Descartes's conception, be so intimately related, as they clearly are, in every human person? Bodies are solid chunks of material stuff, extended in three-dimensional space, publicly observable and measurable, possessed of a certain mass and velocity, and capable of causing things to happen, in accordance with the invariant laws of mechanics, by transmitting their impact in "collisions" with other material things. A mind, on the other hand, is directly "observable" only by the person who owns it; only he can think his thoughts, feel his emotions, suffer his pains. Although, under certain circumstances, someone else can cut open his skull and see and touch his living *brain,* there is no conceivable way for another to see or touch his mind or its beliefs, sensations, and desires. Minds, moreover, have no size or shape or spatial location, no mass, or velocity, or capacity to make impact.

Nevertheless, to common sense, it seems certain that minds and bodies do causally interact. When I will, or wish, or desire (mental events) to raise my arm, up it goes (bodily event); and when a sliver of wood penetrates my flesh (bodily event), I feel pain (mental event). It would surely seem, then, that in normal volition, mental events *cause* physical ones and, in sensation and perception, physical events *cause* mental ones. Yet how can this be? How can the mind, a mass-less, weightless, unextended thing, push up against a nerve cell and cause an impulse to be transmitted along a nerve to a muscle? And how can physical stimuli like wood slivers or even light rays penetrate a thing that has no size or location and cause it to have an experience? Isn't this as inconceivable as a collision between a physical object and a ghost? This is the kind of difficulty cited by Pierre Gassendi in his objections to Descartes's theory of the interaction between mind and body. (Gassendi was one of a number of distinguished philosophers, theologians, and scientists invited to comment on the manuscript of Descartes's *Meditations* before it was published. Their "Objections" were then forwarded to Descartes, who in turn composed "Replies," and published the whole

PLACE IN NATURE

exchange along with the original work. The whole discussion is strongly recommended to the serious student of Descartes's philosophy.)

Most important seventeenth-century philosophers, no matter how impressed in other ways by the "Cartesian philosophy" (as the philosophy of Descartes came to be called), found Descartes's theory of interaction between mind and body unacceptable. Some came, therefore, to abandon the part of Descartes's philosophy that generated the difficulty: his *Dualism,* or theory that mind and matter are distinct and independent kinds of substances, each capable of existing quite independently of the other. *Idealism* of Berkeley's sort was one alternative. *Materialism,* the theory that mind is either reducible to, or ultimately dependent on, matter, was another. Others kept a kind of dualism, but abandoned the common-sense view that mind and body do really interact causally. Some held, for example, that the wood sliver's penetration of my flesh does not *cause* me pain; rather, it is the *occasion* for God, whose infinite nature somehow encompasses both mind and matter, to cause me to feel pain, and similarly that my desire to raise my arm is simply the occasion for God's causing my arm to go up. This is the theory called *Occasionalism.* Others held the view called *Parallelism,* according to which mind and body only appear to interact because of a kind of "pre-established harmony" between their life histories. Leibniz likened this parallelism to that between two clocks that strike at the same moment, having been wound up together and each designed to keep accurate time, in causal independence of each other.

Efforts to solve the Mind-Body problem by such means are quite unnecessary, C. D. Broad argues in his spirited defense of interactionism; for, once we state and consider carefully the reasons that have been urged against causal interaction of mind and body, we can find no basis in them for denying the deliverances of common sense on this matter. C. J. Ducasse, one of our century's most distinguished proponents of dualism, also comes to the aid of the doctrine of interaction in his effort to show that a life after death is at least conceivable. If body and mind are one and the same thing, or if mind is a mere "epiphenomenon" or by-product of body, then it would follow that the disintegration of mind (soul, self) would proceed *pari passu* with the disintegration of the body. But if our minds are distinct substances, and causally efficacious in their own right, then it is at least possible that they (we) can survive the death of their (our) bodies. That survival is possible is the main conclusion for which Professor Ducasse here argues. Whether survival is an actual fact he takes to be an empirical question, for which the only available evidence is that provided by psychical research.

Gilbert Ryle, on the other hand, in one of the most discussed and influential essays in twentieth-century philosophy (Chapter I of *The Concept of Mind*), argues that the venerable conception of "the mind" as a noncorporeal *thing* operating a mechanical sort of body (or as he puts it "a ghost in the machine") is based on a radical conceptual error. It is important to take Professor Ryle at his word, however, and withhold from his view the label "materialism." He holds neither that "mind" and "body" are two names for the same thing (the "identity theory") nor that mind is a distinct but causally impotent by-product of the world charted by physics (these are the two leading versions of materialism). Indeed, it is hard to find any traditional -ism label that clearly fits Ryle's view. Perhaps the most suggestive way of putting his conception of the human person is found later in his book (p. 81) where he writes: "Men are not machines, not even ghost-ridden machines. They are men—a tautology which is sometimes worth remembering." The selection from U. T. Place is an ingenious defense of a cautiously qualified version of the "identity theory." Its conjunction with Richard B. Brandt's general statement of the difficulties involved in identity theories should provide the student with an excellent sample of the ways in which the Mind-Body problem is being discussed and debated today.

RENÉ DESCARTES

*Meditations on First Philosophy**

MEDITATION VI

Of the Existence of Material Things, and of the real distinction between the Soul and Body of Man.

Nothing further now remains but to inquire whether material things exist. And certainly I at least know that these may exist in so far as they are considered as the objects of pure mathematics, since in this aspect I perceive them clearly and distinctly. For there is no doubt that God possesses the power to produce everything that I am capable of perceiving with distinctness, and I have never deemed that anything was impossible for Him, unless I found a contradiction in attempting to conceive it clearly. Further, the faculty of imagination which I possess, and of which, experience tells me, I make use when I apply myself to the consideration of material things, is capable of persuading me of their existence; for when I attentively consider what imagination is, I find that it is nothing but a certain application of the faculty of knowledge to the body which is immediately present to it, and which therefore exists.

And to render this quite clear, I remark in the first place the difference that exists between the imagination and pure intellection [or conception]. For example, when I imagine a triangle, I do not conceive it only as a figure comprehended by three lines, but I also apprehend these three lines as present by the power and inward vision of my mind, and this is what I call imagining. But if I desire to think of a chiliagon, I certainly conceive truly that it is a figure composed of a thousand sides, just as easily as I conceive of a triangle that it is a figure of three sides only; but I cannot in any way imagine the thousand sides of a chiliagon [as I do the three sides of a triangle], nor do I, so to speak, regard them as present [with the eyes of my mind]. And although in accordance with the habit I have formed of always employing the aid of my imagination when I think of corporeal things, it may happen that in imagining a chiliagon I confusedly represent to myself some figure, yet it is very evident that this figure is not a chiliagon, since it in no way differs from that which I represent to myself when I think of a myriagon or any other many-sided figure; nor does it serve my purpose in discovering the properties which go to form the distinction between a chiliagon and other polygons. But if the question turns upon a pentagon, it is quite true that I can conceive its figure as well as that of a chiliagon without the help of my imagination; but I can also imagine it by applying the attention of my mind to each of its five sides, and at the same time to the space which they enclose. And thus I clearly recognise that I have need of a particular effort of mind in order to effect the act of imagination, such as I do not require in order to understand, and this particular effort of mind clearly manifests the difference which exists between imagination and pure intellection.

I remark besides that this power of imagination which is in one, inasmuch as it differs from the power of understanding, is in no wise a necessary element in my nature, or in [my essence, that is to say, in] the essence of my mind; for although I did not possess it I should doubtless ever remain the same as I now am, from which it appears that we might conclude that it depends on something which differs from me. And I easily conceive that if some body exists with which my mind is conjoined and united in

* From René Descartes, *Meditations on First Philosophy,* trans. Elizabeth Haldane and G. R. T. Ross (London: Cambridge University Press, 1931), Meditation VI. Reprinted by permission of the publisher.

such a way that it can apply itself to consider it when it pleases, it may be that by this means it can imagine corporeal objects; so that this mode of thinking differs from pure intellection only inasmuch as mind in its intellectual activity in some manner turns on itself, and considers some of the ideas which it possesses in itself; while in imagining it turns towards the body, and there beholds in it something conformable to the idea which it has either conceived of itself or perceived by the senses. I easily understand, I say, that the imagination could be thus constituted if it is true that body exists; and because I can discover no other convenient mode of explaining it, I conjecture with probability that body does exist; but this is only with probability, and although I examine all things with care, I nevertheless do not find that from this distinct idea of corporeal nature, which I have in my imagination, I can derive any argument from which there will necessarily be deduced the existence of body.

But I am in the habit of imagining many other things besides this corporeal nature which is the object of pure mathematics, to wit, the colours, sounds, scents, pain, and other such things, although less distinctly. And inasmuch as I perceive these things much better through the senses, by the medium of which, and by the memory, they seem to have reached my imagination, I believe that, in order to examine them more conveniently, it is right that I should at the same time investigate the nature of sense perception, and that I should see if from the ideas which I apprehend by this mode of thought, which I call feeling, I cannot derive some certain proof of the existence of corporeal objects.

And first of all I shall recall to my memory those matters which I hitherto held to be true, as having perceived them through the senses, and the foundations on which my belief has rested; in the next place I shall examine the reasons which have since obliged me to place them in doubt; in the last place I shall consider which of them I must now believe.

First of all, then, I perceived that I had a head, hands, feet, and all other members of which this body—which I considered as a part, or possibly even as the whole, of myself—is composed. Further I was sensible that this body was placed amidst many others, from which it was capable of being affected in many different ways, beneficial and hurtful, and I remarked that a certain feeling of pleasure accompanied those that were beneficial, and pain those which were harmful. And in addition to this pleasure and pain, I also experienced hunger, thirst, and other similar appetites, as also certain corporeal inclinations towards joy, sadness, anger, and other similar passions. And outside myself, in addition to extension, figure, and motions of bodies, I remarked in them hardness, heat, and all other tactile qualities, and, further, light and colour, and scents and sounds, the variety of which gave me the means of distinguishing the sky, the earth, the sea, and generally all the other bodies, one from the other. And certainly, considering the ideas of all these qualities which presented themselves to my mind, and which alone I perceived properly or immediately, it was not without reason that I believed myself to perceive objects quite different from my thought, to wit, bodies from which those ideas proceeded; for I found by experience that these ideas presented themselves to me without my consent being requisite, so that I could not perceive any object, however desirous I might be, unless it were present to the organs of sense; and it was not in my power not to perceive it, when it was present. And because the ideas which I received through the senses were much more lively, more clear, and even, in their own way, more distinct than any of those which I could of myself frame in meditation, or than those I found impressed on my memory, it appeared as though they could not have proceeded from my mind, so that they must necessarily have been produced in me by some other things. And having no knowledge of those objects excepting the knowledge which the ideas themselves gave me, nothing was more likely to occur to my mind than that the objects were similar to the ideas which were caused. And because I likewise remembered that I had formerly made use of my senses rather than my reason, and recognised that the ideas which I formed of myself were not so distinct as those which I perceived through the senses, and that they were most frequently even composed of portions of these last, I persuaded myself easily that I had no idea in my mind which had not formerly come to me through the senses. Nor was it without some reason that I believed that this body (which by a certain special right I call my own) belonged to me more properly and more strictly than any other; for in fact I could never be separated from it as from other bodies; I experienced in it and on account of it all my appetites and affections, and finally I was touched by the feeling of pain and the titillation of pleasure in its parts, and not in the parts of other bodies which were separated from it. But when I inquired, why, from some, I know not what, painful sensation, there follows sadness of mind, and from the pleasurable sensation there arises joy, or why this mysterious pinching of the stomach which I call hunger causes me to desire to eat, and dryness of throat causes a desire to drink, and so on, I could give no reason excepting that nature taught me so; for there is certainly no affinity (that I at least can understand) between the craving of the stomach and the desire to eat, any more than between the perception of whatever causes pain and the thought of sadness which arises from this perception. And in the same way it appeared to me that I had learned from nature all the other judgments which I formed regarding the objects of my senses, since I remarked that these judgments were formed in me before I had the leisure to weigh and consider any reasons which might oblige me to make them.

But afterwards many experiences little by little destroyed all the faith which I had rested in my senses; for I from time to time observed that those towers which from afar appeared to me to be round, more closely observed seemed square, and that colossal statues raised on the summit of these towers, appeared as quite tiny statues when viewed from the bottom; and so in an infinitude of other cases I found error in judgments founded on the external senses. And not only in those founded on the external senses, but even in those founded on the internal as well; for is there anything more intimate or more internal than pain? And yet I have learned from some persons whose arms or legs have been cut off, that they sometimes seemed to feel pain in the part which had been amputated, which made me think that I could not be quite certain that it was a certain member which pained me, even although I felt pain in it. And to those grounds of doubt I have lately added two others, which are very general; the first is that I never have believed myself to feel anything in waking moments which I cannot also sometimes believe myself to feel when I sleep, and as I do not think that these things which I seem to feel in sleep, proceed from objects outside of me, I do not see any reason why I should have this belief regarding objects which I seem to perceive while awake. The other was that being still ignorant, or rather supposing myself to be ignorant, of the author of my being, I saw nothing to prevent me from having been so constituted by nature that I might be deceived even in matters which seemed to me to be most certain. And as to the grounds on which I was formerly persuaded of the truth of sensible objects, I had not much trouble in replying to them. For since nature seemed to cause me to lean towards many things from which reason repelled me, I did not believe that I should trust much to the teachings of nature. And although the ideas which I receive by the senses do not depend on my will, I did not think that one should for that reason conclude that they proceeded from things different from myself, since possibly some faculty might be discovered in me—though hitherto unknown to me—which produced them.

But now that I begin to know myself better, and to discover more clearly the author of my being, I do not in truth think that I should rashly admit all the matters which the senses seem to teach us, but, on the other hand, I do not think that I should doubt them all universally.

And first of all, because I know that all things which I apprehend clearly and distinctly can be created by God as I apprehend them, it suffices that I am able to apprehend one thing apart from another clearly and distinctly in order to be certain that the one is different from the other, since they may be made to exist in separation at least by the omnipotence of God; and it does not signify by what power this separation is made in order to compel me to judge them to be different: and, therefore, just because I know certainly that I exist, and that meanwhile I do not remark that any other thing necessarily pertains to my nature or essence, excepting that I am a thinking thing, I rightly conclude that my essence consists solely in the fact that I am a thinking thing [or a substance whose whole essence or nature is to think]. And although possibly (or rather certainly, as I shall say in a moment) I possess a body with which I am very intimately conjoined, yet because, on the one side, I have a clear and distinct idea of myself inasmuch as I am only a thinking and unextended thing, and as, on the other, I possess a distinct idea of body, inasmuch as it is only an extended and unthinking thing, it is certain that this I [that is to say, my soul by which I am what I am], is entirely and absolutely distinct from my body, and can exist without it.

I further find in myself faculties employing modes of thinking peculiar to themselves, to wit, the faculties of imagination and feeling, without which I can easily conceive myself clearly and distinctly as a complete being; while, on the other hand, they cannot be so conceived apart from me, that is without an intelligent substance in which they reside, for [in the notion we have of these faculties, or, to use the language of the Schools] in their formal concept, some kind of intellection is comprised, from which I infer that they are distinct from me as its modes are from a thing. I observe also in me some other faculties such as that of change of position, the assumption of different figures and such like, which cannot be conceived, any more than can the preceding, apart from some substance to which they are attached, and consequently cannot exist without it; but it is very clear that these faculties, if it be true that they exist, must be attached to some corporeal or extended substance, and not to an intelligent substance, since in the clear and distinct conception of these there is some sort of extension found to be present, but no intellection at all. There is certainly further in me a certain passive faculty of perception, that is, of receiving and recognising the ideas of sensible things, but this would be useless to me [and I could in no way avail myself of it], if there were not either in me or in some other thing another active faculty capable of forming and producing these ideas. But this active faculty cannot exist in me [inasmuch as I am a thing that thinks] seeing that it does not presuppose thought, and also that those ideas are often produced in me without my contributing in any way to the same, and often even against my will; it is thus necessarily the case that the faculty resides in some substance different from me in which all the reality which is objectively in the ideas that are produced by this faculty is formally or eminently contained, as I remarked before. And this substance is either a body, that is, a corporeal nature in which there is contained formally [and really] all that which is objectively [and by representation] in those ideas, or it is God Himself, or some other creature more noble than body in which that same is contained eminently. But, since God is no deceiver, it is very manifest that He does not communicate to me these ideas immediately and by Himself, nor yet by the intervention of some creature in which their reality is not formally, but only eminently, contained. For since He has given me no faculty to recognise that this is the case, but, on the other hand, a very great inclination to believe [that they are sent to me or] that they are conveyed to me by corporeal objects, I do not see how He could be defended from the accusation of deceit if these ideas were produced by causes other than corporeal objects. Hence we must allow that corporeal things exist. However, they are perhaps not exactly what we perceive by the senses, since this comprehension by the senses is in many instances very obscure and confused; but we must at least admit that all things which I conceive in them clearly and distinctly, that is to say, all things which, speaking generally, are comprehended in the object of pure mathematics, are truly to be recognised as external objects.

As to other things, however, which are either particular only, as, for example, that the sun is of such and such a figure, etc., or which are less clearly and distinctly conceived, such as light, sound, pain and the like, it is certain that although they are very dubious and uncertain, yet on the sole ground that God is not a deceiver, and that consequently He has not permitted any falsity to exist in my opinion which He has not likewise given me the faculty of correcting, I may assuredly hope to conclude that I have within me the means of arriving at the truth even here. And first of all there is no doubt that in all things which nature teaches me there is some truth contained; for by nature, considered in general, I now understand no other thing that either God Himself or else the order and disposition which God has established in created things; and by my nature in particular I understand no other thing than the complexus of all the things which God has given me.

But there is nothing which this nature teaches me more expressly [nor more sensibly] than that I have a body which is adversely affected when I feel pain, which has need of food or drink when I experience the feelings of hunger and thirst, and so on; nor can I doubt there being some truth in all this.

Nature also teaches me by these sensations of pain, hunger, thirst, etc., that I am not only lodged in my body as a pilot in a vessel, but that I am very closely united to it, and so to speak so intermingled with it that I seem to compose with it one whole. For if that were not the case, when my body is hurt, I, who am merely a thinking thing, should not feel pain, for I should perceive this wound by the understanding only, just as the sailor perceives by sight when something is damaged in his vessel; and when my body has need of drink or food, I should clearly understand the fact without being warned of it by confused feelings of hunger and thirst. For all these sensations of hunger, thirst, pain, etc. are in truth none other than certain confused modes of thought which are produced by the union and apparent intermingling of mind and body.

Moreover, nature teaches me that many other bodies exist around mine, of which some are to be avoided, and others sought after. And certainly from the fact that I am sensible of different sorts of colours, sounds, scents, tastes, heat, hardness, etc., I very easily conclude that there are in the bodies from which all these diverse sense-perceptions proceed certain variations which answer to them, although possibly these are not really at all similar to them. And also from the fact that amongst these different sense-perceptions some are very agreeable to me and others disagreeable, it is quite certain that my body (or rather myself in my entirety, inasmuch as I am formed of body and soul) may receive different impressions agreeable and disagreeable from the other bodies which surround it.

But there are many other things which nature seems to have taught me, but which at the same time I have never really received from her, but which have been brought about in my mind by a certain habit which I have of forming inconsiderate judgments on things; and thus it may easily happen that these judgments contain some error. Take, for example, the opinion which I hold that all space in which there is nothing that affects [or makes an impression on] my senses is void; that in a body which is warm there is something entirely similar to the idea of heat which is in me; that in a white or green body there is the same whiteness or greenness that I perceive; that in a bitter or sweet body there is the same taste, and so on in other instances; that the stars, the towers, and all other distant bodies are of the same figure and size as they appear from far off to our eyes, etc. But in order that in this there should be nothing which I do not conceive distinctly, I should define exactly what I really understand when I say that I am taught somewhat by nature. For here I take nature in a more limited signification than when I term it the sum of all the things given me by God, since in this sum many things are comprehended which only pertain to mind (and to these I do not refer in speaking of nature) such as the notion which I have of the fact that what has once been done cannot ever be undone and an infinitude of such things which I know by the light of nature [without the help of the body]; and seeing that it comprehends many other matters besides which only pertain to body, and are no longer here contained under the name of nature, such as the quality of weight which it possesses and the like, with which I also do not deal; for in talking of nature I only treat of those things given by God to me as a being composed of mind and body. But the nature here described truly teaches me to flee from things which cause the sensation of pain, and seek after the things which communicate to me the sentiment of pleasure and so forth; but I do not see that beyond this it teaches me that from those diverse sense-perceptions we should ever form any conclusion regarding things outside of us, without having [carefully and maturely] mentally examined them beforehand. For it seems to me that it is mind alone, and not mind and body in conjunction, that is requisite to a knowledge of the truth in regard to such things. Thus, although a star makes no larger an impression on my eye than the flame of a little candle there is yet in me no real or positive propensity impelling me to believe that it is not greater than that flame; but I have judged it to be so from my earliest years, without any rational foundation. And although in approaching fire I feel heat, and in approaching it a little too near I even feel pain, there is at the same time no reason in this which could persuade me that there is in the fire something resembling this heat any more than there is in it something resembling the pain; all that I have any reason to believe from this is, that there is something in it, whatever it may be, which excites in me these sensations of heat or of pain. So also, although there are spaces in which I find nothing which excites my senses, I must not from that conclude that these spaces contain no body; for I see in this, as in other similar things, that I have been in the habit of perverting the order of nature, because these perceptions of sense having been placed within me by nature merely for the purpose of signifying to my mind what things are beneficial or hurtful to the composite whole of which it forms a part, and being up to that point sufficiently clear and distinct, I yet avail myself of them as though they were absolute rules by which I might immediately determine the essence of the bodies which are outside me, as to which, in fact, they can teach me nothing but what is most obscure and confused.

But I have already sufficiently considered how, notwithstanding the supreme goodness of God, falsity enters into the judgments I make. Only here a new difficulty is presented—one respecting those things the pursuit or avoidance of which is taught me by nature, and also respecting the internal sensations which I possess, and in which I seem to have sometimes detected error [and thus to be directly deceived by my own nature]. To take an example, the agreeable taste of some food in which poison has been intermingled may induce me to partake of the poison, and thus deceive me. It is true, at the same time, that in this case nature may be excused, for it only induces me to desire food in which I find a pleasant taste, and not to desire the poison which is unknown to it; and thus I can infer nothing from this fact, except that my nature is not omniscient, at which there is certainly no reason to be astonished, since man, being finite in nature, can only have knowledge the perfectness of which is limited.

But we not unfrequently deceive ourselves even in those things to which we are directly impelled by nature, as happens with those who when they are sick desire to drink or eat things hurtful to them. It will perhaps be said here that the cause of their deceptiveness is that their nature is corrupt, but that does not remove the difficulty, because a sick man is none the less truly God's creature than he who is in health; and it is therefore as repugnant to God's goodness for the one to have a deceitful nature as it is for the other. And as a clock composed of wheels and counter-weights no less exactly observes the laws of nature when it is badly made, and does not show the time properly, than when it entirely satisfies the wishes of its maker, and as, if I consider the body of a man as being a sort of machine so built up and composed of nerves, muscles, veins, blood and skin, that though there were no mind in it at all, it would not cease to have the same motions as at present, exception being made of those movements which are due to the direction of the will, and in consequence depend upon the mind [as opposed to those which operate by the disposition of its organs], I easily recognise that it would be as natural to this body, supposing it to be, for example, dropsical, to suffer the parchedness of the throat which usually signifies to the mind the feeling of thirst, and to be disposed by this parched feeling to move the nerves and other parts in the way requisite for drinking, and thus to augment its malady and do harm to itself, as it is natural to it, when it has no indisposition, to be impelled to drink for its good by a similar cause. And although, considering the use to which the clock has been destined by its maker, I may say that it deflects from the order of its nature when it does not indicate the hours correctly; and as, in the same way, considering the machine of the human body as having been formed by God in order to have in itself all the movements usually manifested there, I have reason for thinking that it does not follow the order of nature when, if the throat is dry, drinking does harm to the conservation of health, nevertheless I recognize at the same time that this last mode of explaining nature is very different from the other. For this is but a purely verbal characterisation depending entirely on my thought, which compares a sick man and a badly constructed clock with the idea which I have of a healthy man and a well made clock, and it is hence extrinsic to the things to which it is applied; but according to the other interpretation of the term nature I understand something which is truly found in things and which is therefore not without some truth.

But certainly although in regard to the dropsical body it is only so to speak to apply an extrinsic term when we say that its nature is corrupted, inasmuch as apart from the need to drink, the throat is parched; yet in regard to the composite whole, that is to say, to the mind or soul united to this body, it is not a purely verbal predicate, but a real error of nature, for it to have thirst when drinking would be hurtful to it. And thus it still remains to inquire how the goodness of God does not prevent the nature of man so regarded from being fallacious.

In order to begin this examination, then, I here say, in the first place, that there is a great difference between mind and body, inasmuch as body is by nature always divisible, and the mind is entirely indivisible. For, as a matter of fact, when I consider the mind, that is to say, myself inasmuch as I am only a thinking thing, I cannot distinguish in myself any parts, but apprehend myself to be clearly one and entire; and although the whole mind seems to be united to the whole body, yet if a foot, or an arm, or some other part, is separated from my body, I am aware that nothing has been taken away from my mind. And the faculties of willing, feeling, conceiving, etc. cannot be properly speaking said to be its parts, for it is one and the same mind which employs itself in willing and in feeling and understanding. But it is quite otherwise with corporeal or extended objects, for there is not one of these imaginable by me which my mind cannot easily divide into parts, and which consequently I do not recognise as being divisible; this would be sufficient to teach me that the mind or soul of man is entirely different from the body, if I had not already learned it from other sources.

I further notice that the mind does not receive the impressions from all parts of the body immediately, but only from the brain, or perhaps even from one of its smallest parts, to wit, from that in which the common sense is said to reside, which, whenever it is disposed in the same particular way, conveys the same thing to the mind, although meanwhile the other portions of the body may be differently disposed, as is testified by innumerable experiments which it is unnecessary here to recount.

I notice, also, that the nature of body is such that none of its parts can be moved by another part a little way off which cannot also be moved in the same way by each one of the parts which are between the two, although this more remote part does not act at all. As, for example, in the cord *ABCD* [which is in tension] if we pull the last part *D*, the first part *A* will not be moved in any way differently from what would be the case if one of the intervening parts B or *C* were pulled, and the last part *D* were to remain unmoved. And in the same way, when I feel pain in my foot, my knowledge of physics teaches me that this sensation is communicated by means of nerves dispersed through the foot, which, being extended like cords from there to the brain, when they are contracted in the foot, at the same time contract the inmost portions of the brain which is their extremity and place of origin, and then excite a certain movement which nature has established in order to cause the mind to be affected by a sensation of pain represented as existing in the foot. But because these nerves must pass through the tibia, the thigh, the loins, the back and the neck, in order to reach from the leg to the brain, it may happen that although their extremities which are in the foot are not affected, but only certain ones of their intervening parts [which pass by the loins or the neck], this action will excite the same movement in the brain that might have been excited there by a hurt received in the foot, in consequence of which the mind will necessarily feel in the foot the same pain as if it had received a hurt. And the same holds good of all the other perceptions of our senses.

I notice finally that since each of the movements which are in the portion of the brain by which the mind is immediately affected brings about one particular sensation only, we cannot under the circumstances imagine anything more likely than that this movement, amongst all the sensations which it is capable of impressing on it, causes mind to be affected by that one which is best fitted and most generally useful for the conservation of the human body when it is in health. But experience makes us aware that all the feelings with which nature inspires us are such as I have just spoken of; and there is therefore nothing in them which does not give testimony to the power and goodness of the God [who has produced them]. Thus, for example, when the nerves which are in the feet are violently or more than usually moved, their movement, passing through the medulla of the spine to the inmost parts of the brain, gives a sign to the mind which makes it feel somewhat, to wit, pain, as though in the foot, by which the mind is excited to do its utmost to remove the cause of the evil as dangerous and hurtful to the foot. It is true that God could have constituted the nature of man in such a way that this same movement in the brain would have conveyed something quite different to the mind; for example, it might have produced consciousness of itself either in so far as it is in the brain, or as it is in the foot, or as it is in some other place between the foot and the brain, or it might finally have produced consciousness of anything else whatsoever; but none of all this would have contributed so well to the conservation of the body. Similarly, when we desire to drink, a certain dryness of the throat is produced which moves its nerves, and by their means the internal portions of the brain; and this movement causes in the mind the sensation of thirst, because in this case there is nothing more useful to us than to become aware that we have need to drink for the conservation of our health; and the same holds good in other instances.

From this it is quite clear that, notwithstanding the supreme goodness of God, the nature of man, inasmuch as it is composed of mind and body, cannot be otherwise than sometimes a source of deception. For if there is any cause which excites, not in the foot but in some part of the nerves which are extended between the foot and the brain, or even in the brain itself, the same movement which usually is produced when the foot is detrimentally affected, pain will be experienced as though it were in the foot, and the sense will thus naturally be deceived; for since the same movement in the brain is capable of causing but one sensation in the mind, and this sensation is much more frequently excited by a cause which hurts the foot than by another existing in some other quarter, it is reasonable that it should convey to the mind pain in the foot rather than in any other part of the body. And although the parchedness of the throat does not always proceed, as it usually does, from the fact that drinking is necessary for the health of the body, but sometimes comes from quite a different cause, as is the case with dropiscal patients, it is yet much better that it should mislead on this occasion than if, on the other hand, it were always to deceive us when the body is in good health; and so on in similar cases.

And certainly this consideration is of great service to me, not only in enabling me to recognise all the errors to which my nature is subject, but also in enabling me to avoid them or to correct them more easily. For knowing that all my senses more frequently indicate to me truth than falsehood respecting the things which concern that which is beneficial to the body, and being able almost always to avail myself of many of them in order to examine one particular thing, and, besides that, being able to make use of my memory in order to connect the present with the past, and of my understanding which already has discovered all the causes of my errors, I ought no longer to fear that falsity may be found in matters every day presented to me by my senses. And I ought to set aside all the doubts of these past days as hyperbolical and ridiculous, particularly that very common uncertainty respecting sleep, which I could not distinguish from the waking state; for at present I find a very notable difference between the two, inasmuch as our memory can never connect our dreams one with the other, or with the whole course of our lives, as it unites events which happen to us while we are awake. And, as a matter of fact, if someone, while I was awake, quite suddenly appeared to me and disappeared as fast as do the images which I see in sleep, so that I could not know from whence the form came nor whither it went, it would not be without reason that I should deem it a spectre or a phantom formed by my brain [and similar to those which I form in sleep], rather than a real man. But when I perceive things as to which I know distinctly both the place from which they proceed, and that in which they are, and the time at which they appeared to me; and when, without any interruption, I can connect the perceptions which I have of them with the whole course of my life, I am perfectly assured that these perceptions occur while I am waking and not during sleep. And I ought in no wise to doubt the truth of such matters, if, after having called up all my senses, my memory, and my understanding, to examine them, nothing is brought to evidence by any one of them which is repugnant to what is set forth by the others. For because God is in no wise a deceiver, it follows that I am not deceived in this. But because the exigencies of action often oblige us to make up our minds before having leisure to examine matters carefully, we must confess that the life of man is very frequently subject to error in respect to individual objects, and we must in the end acknowledge the infirmity of our nature.

PIERRE GASSENDI

Objections to Meditation VI*

. . .

For finally you say: And although possibly (or rather certainly, as I shall say in a moment) I possess a body with which I am very intimately conjoined, yet because on the one side I have a clear and distinct idea of myself, inasmuch as I am only a thinking and not an extended thing, and on the other I possess a distinct idea of body, inasmuch as it is only an extended and not a thinking thing; it is certain that I am really distinct from my body, and can exist without it.

So this was your objective, was it? Hence, since the whole of the difficulty hinges on this, we must halt awhile, in order to see how you manage to make this position good. The principal matter here in question is the distinction between you and body. But what body do you here mean? Plainly this solid body composed of members, the body to which, without doubt, the following words refer: I possess a body connected with myself and it is certain that I am distinct from my body, etc.

But now, O Mind, there is no difficulty about this body. There would be a difficulty, if with the greater part of philosophers I were to object that you were the realisation, the perfection, the activity, the form, the appearance, or, to use a popular fashion of speech, a mode of the body. They, forsooth, do not acknowledge that you are more distinct and separable from your body than figure, or any other mode. This, too, they maintain, whether you are the entire soul, or are besides also νοῦς δυνάμει, νοῦς παθητικός, *the potential intellect, or passive intellect, as they style it. But it pleases me to deal somewhat liberally with you and consider you as though you were the* νοῦς ποιητικός, *the active intellect, nay, even as* χωριστός, *i.e. capable of separate existence, though separable in another sense than they imagined.*

For since those philosophers assigned it to all men (if not rather to all things) as something common to them and as being the source of intellectual activity on the part of the potential intellect, exactly in the same way and with the same necessity as light supplies the eye with the opportunity of seeing (whence they were wont to compare it to the light of the sun, and hence to regard it as coming from without), I myself rather consider you (as you also are quite willing I should) as a certain special intellect exercising domination in the body.

Moreover I repeat that the difficulty is not as to whether you are separable or not from this body (whence, shortly before, I hinted that it was not necessary to recur to the power of God in order to secure the separability of those things which you apprehend as separate), but from the body which you yourself are: seeing that possibly you really are a subtle body diffused within that solid one, or occupying some seat within it. But you have not yet convinced us that you are anything absolutely incorporeal. Likewise, though in the second Meditation you proclaimed that you are not a wind, nor a fire, nor a vapour, nor a breath, *do be advised of the warning I give you, that the statement thus announced has not been proved.*

You said that you did not at that point dispute about those matters; *but you have not subsequently discussed them, nor have you in any way proved that you are not a body of this kind. I had hoped that here you would make the matter good; but if you do discuss anything, if you do prove anything, your discussion and proof merely show*

* From the "Objections and Replies" published with Descartes's *Meditations* in the second edition (1642); trans. Elizabeth Haldane and G. R. T. Ross (London: Cambridge University Press, 1931), pp. 195–203. Reprinted by permission of the publisher.

that you are not the solid body, about which, as I have already said, there is no difficulty.

4. But, *you say,* I have on the one hand a clear and distinct idea of myself, in so far as I am merely a thinking thing and not extended, and on the other a distinct idea of body, in so far as it is an extended thing, but not one that thinks. *Firstly, however, in so far as the idea of body is concerned, there appears to be no need for spending much pains over it. For, if you indeed make this pronouncement about the idea of body universally, we must repeat our previous objection, namely that you have to prove that it is incompatible with the nature of body to be capable of thinking. Thus it would be a begging of the question when the problem was raised by you* as to whether you are a subtle body or not, *in a way that implied that thought is incompatible with body.*

But since you make that assertion and certainly treat only of that solid body, from which you maintain that you are separable and distinct, I do not on that account so much deny that you have an idea of yourself, as maintain that you could not possess it if you were really an unextended thing. For, I ask you, how do you think that you, an unextended subject, could receive into yourself the semblance or idea of a body which is extended? For, if such a semblance proceeds from the body, it is certainly corporeal and has parts outside of other parts, and consequently is corporeal. Or alternatively, whether or not its impression is due to some other source, since necessarily it always represents an extended body, it must still have parts and, consequently, be extended. Otherwise, if it has no parts, how will it represent parts? If it has no extension how will it represent extension? If devoid of figure, how represent an object possessing figure? If it has no position, how can it represent a thing which has upper and lower, right and left, and intermediate parts? If without variation, how represent the various colours, etc.? Therefore an idea appears not to lack extension utterly. But unless it is devoid of extension how can you, if unextended, be its subject? How will you unite it to you? How lay hold of it? How will you be able to feel it gradually fade and finally vanish away?

Next, relatively to your idea of yourself nothing is to be added to what has been already said, and especially in the second Meditation. For thence it is proved that, far from having a clear and distinct idea of yourself, you seem to be wholly without one. This is because, even though you recognise that you think, you do not know of what nature you, who think, are. Hence, since this operation alone is known to you, the chief matter is, nevertheless, hidden from you, namely, the substance which so operates. This brings up the comparison in which you may be likened to a blind man, who, on feeling heat, and being told that it proceeds from the sun, should think that he has a clear and distinct idea of the sun, inasmuch as, if anyone ask him what the sun is, he can reply: it is something which produces heat.

But, you will say, I here add not only that I am a thinking thing, *but that I am* a thing which is not extended. *But not to mention that this is asserted without proof, since it is still in question, I ask firstly: for all that have you a clear and distinct idea of yourself? You say that you are not extended; but in so doing you say what you are not, not what you are. In order to have a clear and distinct idea, or, what is the same thing, a true and genuine idea of anything, is it not necessary to know the thing itself positively, and so to speak affirmatively, or does it suffice to know that it is not any other thing? Would it not then be a clear and distinct idea of Bucephalus, if one knew of him that he was not a fly?*

But, not to urge this, my question is rather: are you not an extended thing, or are you not diffused throughout the body? I cannot tell what you will reply; for, though from the outset I recognised that you existed only in the brain, I formed that belief rather by conjecture than by directly following your opinion. I derived my conjecture from the statement which ensues, in which you assert, that you are not affected by all parts of the body, but only by the brain, or even by one of its smallest parts. *But I was not quite certain whether you were found therefore only in the brain or in a part of it, since you might be found in the whole body, but be acted on at only one part. Thus it would be according to the popular belief, which takes the soul to be diffused throughout the entire body, while yet it is in the eye alone that it has vision.*

Similarly the following words moved one to doubt: 'and, although the whole mind seems to be united to the whole body,' etc. *You indeed do not there assert that you are united with the whole of the body, but you do not deny it. Howsoever it be, with your leave let me consider you firstly as diffused throughout the whole body. Whether you are the same as the soul, or something diverse from it, I ask you, O unextended thing, what you are that are spread from head to heel, or that are coextensive with the body, that have a like number of parts corresponding to its parts? Will you say that you are therefore unextended, because you are a whole in a whole, and are wholly in every part? I pray you tell me, if you maintain this, how you conceive it. Can a single thing thus be at the same time wholly in several parts? Faith assures us of this in the case of the sacred mystery (of the Eucharist). But the question here is relative to you, a natural object, and is indeed one relative to our natural light. Can we grasp how there can be a plurality of places without there being a plurality of objects located in them? Is not a hundred more than one? Likewise, if a thing is wholly in one place, can it be in others, unless it is itself outside itself, as place is outside place? Say what you will, it will at least be obscure and uncertain whether you are wholly in any part and not rather in the various parts of the body by means of your several parts. And since it is much more evident that nothing can exist as a whole in different places, it will turn out to be still more clear that you are not wholly in the single parts of your body but merely in the whole as a whole, and that you are so by means of your parts diffused through the whole and consequently that you have extension.*

Secondly let us suppose that you are in the brain alone, or merely in some minute part of it. You perceive that the same thing is clearly an objection, since, however small that part be, it is nevertheless extended, and you are coextensive with it, and consequently are extended and have particular parts corresponding to its particular parts. Will you say that you take that part of the brain to be a point? That is surely incredible, but suppose it is a point. If it is indeed something Physical, the same difficulty remains, because such a point is extended and is certainly not devoid of parts. If it is a Mathematical point you know that it is given only by the imagination. But let it be given or let rather us feign that in the brain there is given a Mathematical point, to which you are united, and in which you exist. Now, see how useless a fiction this will turn out to be. For, if it is to be assumed, we must feign it to exist in such a way that you are at the meeting place of the nerves by which all the regions informed by the soul transmit to the brain the ideas or semblances of the things perceived by the senses. But firstly, the nerves do not all meet at one point, whether for the reason that, as the brain is continued into the spinal marrow, many nerves all over the back pass into that, or because those which extend to the middle of the head are not found to terminate in the same part of the brain. But let us assume that they all do meet; none the less they cannot all unite in a mathematical point, since they are bodies, not mathematical lines, and so able to meet in a mathematical point. And supposing we grant that they do so unite, it will be impossible for the spirits[1] which pass through these to pass out of the nerves or to enter them, as being bodies; since body cannot be in or pass through what is not a place, as the mathematical point is. But though we should allow that the animal spirits do exist in or pass through what is not a place, nevertheless you, existing as you do in a point, in which there are neither right hand parts nor left hand, neither higher nor lower, nor anything similar, cannot judge as to whence they come nor what they report.

Moreover I say the same thing of those spirits which you must transmit in order to have feeling or to report tidings[2], and in order to move. I omit that we cannot grasp how you impress a motion upon them, you who are yourself in a point, unless you are really a body, or unless you have a body by which you are in contact with them and at the same time propel them. For, if you say that they are moved by themselves, and that you only direct their motion, remember that you somewhere else denied that the body is moved by itself; *so that we must thence infer that you are the cause of that movement. Next, explain to us how such a direction can take place without some effort and so some motion on your part? How can there be effort directed towards anything, and motion on its part, without mutual contact of what moves and what is moved? How can there be contact apart from body, when (as is so clear to the natural light)*

[1] The 'animal spirits' correspond to the 'nervous impulses' of modern psychology. D. and his contemporaries believed that an actual substance passed along the nerve when it was stimulated.

[2] of the external world? Clerselier translates this passage 'proclaim or communicate feeling or movement.'

'Apart from body, naught touches or is touched[3]?'

Yet why do I delay here when it is on you that the onus rests of proving that you are unextended and hence incorporeal? But neither do I think that you will find an argument in the fact that man is popularly said to consist of soul and body, inferring that if one part is said to be body, the other must be declared not to be body. For, if you did so, you would give us an opportunity of drawing the distinction in such a way that man should be held to consist of a double body, viz. the solid one and the subtle one; and according to this scheme while the former retained the name body, the common term, the other would be given the name soul. I pass by the fact that the same thing would be said about the other animals, to which you have not granted a mind similar to your own; lucky they, if by your sanction they possess even a soul! Hence, therefore, when you conclude that you are certain that you are really distinct from your body, *you see that that would be admitted, but that it would not therefore be conceded that you were incorporeal, and not rather a species of very subtle body distinct from your grosser body.*

You add that hence you can exist apart from it. *But after being conceded the point that you can exist apart from that grosser body in the same way as an odoriferous vapour does while passing out of an apple and dispersing into the air, what do you think you have gained? Something more certainly than the above mentioned Philosophers wish to prove, who believe that you wholly perish at death itself; being as it were like a figure which on the alteration of the superficies so disappears, that it may be said to be non-existent or wholly nothing. Indeed, since you were something corporeal as well, or a fine substance, you will not be said to vanish wholly at death, or wholly to pass into nothing, but to exist by means of your dispersed parts, howsoever much, on account of being thus drawn asunder, you are not likely to think any more, and will be said to be neither a thinking thing, nor a mind, nor a soul. Yet all these objections I bring, not in order to cast doubt on the conclusion you intend to prove, but merely by way of expressing my disagreement as to the cogency of the argument set forth by you.*

5. *In connection with this, you interpose several things tending to the same conclusion, on all of which we need not insist. One thing I note, and that is that you say* that nature teaches you by the sensation of pain, hunger, thirst, etc., that you are not lodged in the body as a sailor in a ship, but that you are very closely united with it and, so to speak, intermingled with it so as to compose one whole along with it. For if that were not the case, *you say,* "when my body is hurt, I who am merely a thinking thing would not feel pain, but should perceive the wound with the mere understanding, just as the sailor perceives by sight when something is damaged in his vessel, and when my body has need of food or drink, I should clearly understand this fact, and not have the confused feelings of hunger and thirst. For all these sensations of hunger, thirst, pain, etc. are in truth none other than certain confused modes of thought which are produced by the union and apparent intermingling of mind and body."

This is indeed quite right; but it still remains to be explained, how that union and apparent intermingling, *or* confusion, *can be found in you, if you are incorporeal, unextended and indivisible. For if you are not greater than a point, how can you be united with the entire body, which is of such great magnitude? How, at least, can you be united with the brain, or some minute part in it, which (as has been said) must yet have some magnitude or extension, however small it be? If you are wholly without parts, how can you mix or appear to mix with its minute subdivisions? For there is no mixture unless each of the things to be mixed has parts that can mix with one another. Further, if you are discrete, how could you be involved with and form one thing along with matter itself? Again since conjunction or union exists between certain parts, ought there not to be a relation of similarity between parts of this sort? But what must the union of the corporeal with the incorporeal be thought to be? Do we conceive how stone and air are fused together, as in pumice stone, so as to become a fusion of uniform character? Yet the similarity between stone and air which itself is also a body, is greater than that between body and soul, or a wholly incorporeal mind. Further, ought not that union to take place by means of the closest contact? But how, as I*

[3] Tangere nec tangi sine corpore nulla potest res—a misquotation of Lucretius (*De Rerum natura* I. 305):—Tangere enim et tangi, nisi corpus nulla potest res.

said before, can that take place, apart from body? How will that which is corporeal seize upon that which is incorporeal, so to hold it conjoined with itself, or how will the incorporeal grasp the corporeal, so as reciprocally to keep it bound to itself, if in it, the incorporeal, there is nothing which it can use to grasp the other, or by which it can be grasped.

Hence, since you admit that you feel pain, I ask you how you think that you, if you are incorporeal and unextended, are capable of experiencing the sensation of pain. Thus the affection pain can only be understood as arising from some pulling asunder of bodily parts when something interferes and annuls their continuity. For example a state of pain is an unnatural state, but how can that be in an unnatural state or be affected contrary to nature, which by nature is of one sort, simple, indivisible and immutable? Again since pain is either alteration, or cannot occur without it, how can that be altered, which, being more devoid of parts than a point, cannot be altered nor can cease to be just as it is, unless it turns into nothing? I add also: since pain comes from the foot, the arm, and from other regions at the same time, ought there not to be in you various parts, in which you receive it in various ways, in order not to be confused and to regard it as being the pain of merely one part. But, in a word, the general difficulty always remains, viz. how the corporeal can have anything in common with the incorporeal, or what relationship may be established between the one and the other.

6. *I pass by the other passages in which, in a very copious and neat argument, you strive to show that something else is in existence besides yourself and God. For you deduce the conclusion that your body and its corporeal faculties exist; and likewise other bodies which despatch into your senses and into yourself the semblances of themselves, and produce the experiences of pleasure and pain, which beget in you desire and aversion.*

And from this you at length derive the following conclusion, which is, as it were, the fruit of your reasoning, in order that since all the sensations relative to the things which have to do with the welfare of the body more frequently indicate to you truth than falsehood, *you may thence infer* that you ought no longer to fear that falsity may be found in matters every day represented to you by the senses. *You say the same, consequently, about dreams,* for since they are not connected with the whole of our actions and course of life in the same way as what we experience when awake, *you thence establish the conclusion that real things* are presented to you, not in sleep, but when you are awake. Hence, *you say next,* since God is not a deceiver, it follows that you are not deceived in such matters. *This is an extremely pious statement; and so, too, you are assuredly quite in the right when you finally conclude:* that the life of man is subject to error, and that we must acknowledge the infirmity of our nature.

RENÉ DESCARTES

Reply to Gassendi*

. . . Finally it is worthy of you alone, O flesh, to think *that the idea of God, of an Angel, and of the human mind, are corporeal, or after the fashion of the corporeal, derived forsooth from the human form, and from other very subtle, simple, and imperceptible objects, such as air or aether.* For whosoever thus represents God or the mind to himself, tries to imagine a thing which is not imageable, and constructs nothing but a corporeal

* From the "Objections and Replies" published with the *Meditations;* trans. Elizabeth Haldane and G. R. T. Ross (London: Cambridge University Press, 1931), pp. 230–233. Reprinted by permission of the publishers.

idea to which he falsely assigns the name God or mind. For, in the true idea of mind, nothing is contained but thought and its attributes, of which none is corporeal.

2. In this passage you show very clearly that you rely on prejudices merely and never divest yourself of them, when you wish to make out that we suspect no falsity in matters in which we have never detected falsity; it is thus that, *when we behold a tower close at hand and touch it, we are sure that it is square,* if it appear to be square; so too when we are really awake *we cannot doubt whether we are awake or dreaming;* and so forth. Now you have no reason to think that all the things in which error can reside have been noticed by you, and it could easily be proved that you sometimes are wrong about those things which you accept as certain. But when you come round to the position at which you state, *that at least we cannot doubt that things appear as they do,* you have returned to the true path; your statement is one that I have myself made in the second Meditation. But here the question raised concerned the reality of external objects, and in what you have contributed to this there is nothing correct.

3. I shall not here delay to notice your tedious and frequent repetitions of such statements as, e.g. *that I have failed to prove certain matters,* which nevertheless I have demonstrated; *that I have treated only of the solid body,* though I have dealt with every kind of matter, even of the subtlest; etc. What opposition other than a plain denial is merited by affirmations of this kind, which are not supported by reasons? Yet incidentally I should like to discover what argument you use to prove that I have treated of solid matter rather than of that which is subtle. Have I not said: '*I possess (a body) united with myself, and it is certain that I am distinct from my body*'? And I cannot see why these words are not equally applicable to an impalpable and to a solid body; nor do I think that anyone but you could fail to see this. Apart from this, in the second Meditation I made it evident that mind could be understood as an existing substance, though we did not understand anything to exist that was wind, or fire, or vapour, or breath, or anything else of a bodily nature however impalpable and refined. I said however that at that point I did not discuss whether it was in truth distinct from every kind of body; but in the present passage I did discuss the matter and proved my assertion. But you show that you have wholly failed to comprehend the controversy by your confusion of the issue as to what may be known of the soul with the question as to that which the soul really is.

4. Here you ask, *how I think that I, an unextended subject, can receive into myself the resemblance or idea of a thing which is extended.* I reply that no corporeal resemblance can be received in the mind, but that what occurs there is the pure thinking of a thing, whether it be corporeal or equally whether it be one that is incorporeal and lacking any corporeal semblance. But as to imagination, which can only be exercised in reference to corporeal things, my opinion is that it requires the presence of a semblance which is truly corporeal, and to which the mind applies itself, without, however, its being received in the mind.

Your statement *about the idea of the sun, which a blind man can derive merely from the sun's warmth,* is easily refuted. For the blind man can have a clear and distinct idea of the sun as a source of heat although he does not possess the idea of it as a source of light. Nor is your comparison of me to that blind man just: firstly, because the act of knowledge which apprehends a thing that thinks is much more extensive than our apprehension of a thing which warms, as it is much more than that of anything else, as was shown in its proper place; secondly, because no one can prove that that idea of the sun which the blind man forms, does not contain everything which can be learned of the sun, save those who, being endowed with sight, are aware in addition of its light and figure. You, however, not only know nothing more than I do of mind, but do not even have knowledge of the very thing I recognize in it; so that in this comparison it is rather you who play the part of blind man, while I, along with the whole human race, could at most be said to be one-eyed.

In adding that *the mind is not extended,* my intention was not thereby to explain what mind is, but merely to proclaim that those people are wrong who think that it is extended. In the same way if any people affirmed *that Bucephalus was Music*[1], it would not be idle of others to deny the

[1] Descartes misread Gassendi's *musca* (fly) as musica. Cf. above, p. 197, par. 3. The mistake must have occurred when he saw Gassendi's work in MS. But in spite of the fact that *musca* appeared in the printed

statement. In good truth your subsequent attempts to prove that mind is extended because it makes use of a body which is extended, seem to employ no better reasoning than if you were to argue that because Bucephalus neighs and whinnies, and so utters sounds that are comparable with Music, it followed that Bucephalus is Music. For, though mind is united with the whole body, it does not follow that it itself is extended throughout the body, because it is not part of its notion to be extended, but merely to think. Neither does it apprehend extension by means of an extended semblance existing in it, although it images it by applying itself to a corporeal semblance which is extended, as has already been said. Finally there is no necessity for it itself to be a body although it has the power of moving body.

5. What you say at this point *relatively to the union of mind and body* is similar to what precedes. At no place do you bring an objection to my arguments; you only set forth the doubts which you think follow from my conclusions, though they arise merely from your wishing to subject to the scrutiny of the imagination matters which, by their own nature, do not fall under it. Thus when you wish to compare the union of mind and body with the mixture of two bodies, it is enough for me to reply that no such comparison ought to be set up, because the two things are wholly diverse, and we must not imagine that there are parts in mind because it is aware of parts in body. Whence do you derive the conclusion that everything which mind knows must exist in mind? If that were so, then, when it was aware of the magnitude of the earth, it would be obliged to have that object within it, and consequently would not only be extended but greater in extent than the whole world.

6. Here though you do not contradict me at all, you have nevertheless much to say; and hence the reader may discover that the number of your arguments is not to be inferred from any proportion between them and the prolixity of your words.

Up to this point we have had a discussion between mind and flesh, and, as was but natural, in many things they disagreed. But now, at the end, I catch sight of the real Gassendi, and look up to him as a man of great philosophical eminence. I salute him as a man noted for his intellectual candour and integrity of life, and shall endeavour, by employing all the courtesies which I can muster, to merit his friendship at all times. I therefore ask him not to take it amiss if, in replying to his objections, I have used a Philosophical freedom, since their entire contents caused me very great pleasure. Among other things I rejoiced that such a long and carefully composed dissertation contained nothing in opposition to my reasoning, nothing opposed even to my conclusions, to which I was not able very easily to reply.

version when the work was published, so that Descartes had the opportunity of rectifying his error, he refrained from doing so. This provoked an attack by an opponent, Revius, in *Statera Philosophiae Cartesianae,* a pamphlet published at Amsterdam in 1650.

C. D. BROAD

The Traditional Problem of Body and Mind*

In the last chapter we considered organisms simply as complicated material systems which behave in certain characteristic ways. We did not consider the fact that some organisms are animated by minds, and that all the minds of whose existence we are certain animate organisms. And we did not deal with those features in the behaviour of certain organisms which are commonly

* From C. D. Broad, *The Mind and Its Place in Nature* (London: Routledge & Kegan Paul Ltd; New York: Humanities Press Inc., 1925), pp. 95–97, 103–121. Reprinted by permission of the author and publishers.

supposed to be due to the mind which animates the organism. It is such facts as these, and certain problems to which they have given rise, which I mean to discuss in the present chapter. There is a question which has been argued about for some centuries now under the name of "Interaction"; this is the question whether minds really do act on the organisms which they animate, and whether organisms really do act on the minds which animate them. (I must point out at once that I imply no particular theory of mind or body by the word "to animate". I use it as a perfectly neutral name to express the fact that a certain mind is connected in some peculiarly intimate way with a certain body, and, under normal conditions with no other body. This is a fact even on a purely behaviouristic theory of mind; on such a view to say that the mind M animates the body B would mean that the body B, in so far as it behaves in certain ways, *is* the mind M. A body which did not act in these ways would be said not to be animated by a mind. And a different Body B′, which acted in the same general way as B, would be said to be animated by a different mind M′.)

The problem of Interaction is generally discussed at the level of enlightened common-sense; where it is assumed that we know pretty well what we mean by "mind", by "matter" and by "causation". Obviously no solution which is reached at that level can claim to be ultimate. If what we call "matter" should turn out to be a collection of spirits of low intelligence, as Leibniz thought, the argument that mind and body are so unlike that their interaction is impossible would become irrelevant. Again, if causation be nothing but regular sequence and concomitance, as some philosophers have held, it is ridiculous to regard psycho-neural parallelism and interaction as mutually exclusive alternatives. For interaction will mean no more than parallelism, and parallelism will mean no less than interaction. Nevertheless I am going to discuss the arguments here at the common-sense level, because they are so incredibly bad and yet have imposed upon so many learned men.

We start then by assuming a developed mind and a developed organism as two distinct things, and by admitting that the two are now intimately connected in some way or other which I express by saying that "this mind *animates* this organism". We assume that bodies are very much as enlightened common-sense believes them to be; and that, even if we cannot define "causation", we have some means of recognising when it is present and when it is absent. The question then is: "Does a mind ever act on the body which it animates, and does a body ever act on the mind which animates it?" The answer which common-sense would give to both questions is: "Yes, certainly." On the face of it my body acts on my mind whenever a pin is stuck into the former and a painful sensation thereupon arises in the latter. And, on the face of it, my mind acts on my body whenever a desire to move my arm arises in the former and is followed by this movement in the latter. Let us call this common-sense view "Two-sided Interaction". Although it seems so obvious it has been denied by probably a majority of philosophers and a majority of physiologists. So the question is: "Why should so many distinguished men, who have studied the subject, have denied the apparently obvious fact of Two-sided Interaction?"

ARGUMENTS AGAINST INTERACTION

. . . There are, so far as I know, two [scientific arguments against two-sided interaction]. One is supposed to be based on the physical principle of the Conservation of Energy, and on certain experiments which have been made on human bodies. The other is based on the close analogy which is said to exist between the structures of the physiological mechanism of reflex action and that of voluntary action. I will take them in turn.

(1) *The Argument from Energy.* It will first be needful to state clearly what is asserted by the principle of the Conservation of Energy. It is found that, if we take certain material systems, *e.g.*, a gun, a cartridge, and a bullet, there is a certain magnitude which keeps approximately constant throughout all their changes. This is called "Energy". When the gun has not been fired it and the bullet have no motion, but the explosive in the cartridge has great chemical energy. When it has been fired the bullet is moving very fast and has great energy of movement. The gun, though not moving fast in its recoil, has also great energy of movement because it is very massive. The gases produced by the explosion have some energy of movement

and some heat-energy, but much less chemical energy than the unexploded charge had. These various kinds of energy can be measured in common units according to certain conventions. To an innocent mind there seems to be a good deal of "cooking" at this stage, *i.e.*, the conventions seem to be chosen and various kinds and amounts of concealed energy seem to be postulated in order to make the principle come out right at the end. I do not propose to go into this in detail, for two reasons. In the first place, I think that the conventions adopted and the postulates made, though somewhat suggestive of the fraudulent company-promoter, can be justified by their coherence with certain experimental facts, and that they are not simply made *ad hoc*. Secondly, I shall show that the Conservation of Energy is absolutely irrelevant to the question at issue, so that it would be waste of time to treat it too seriously in the present connexion. Now it is found that the total energy of all kinds in this system, when measured according to these conventions, is approximately the same in amount though very differently distributed after the explosion and before it. If we had confined our attention to a part of this system and *its* energy this would not have been true. The bullet, *e.g.*, had no energy at all before the explosion and a great deal afterwards. A system like the bullet, the gun, and the charge, is called a "Conservative System"; the bullet alone, or the gun and the charge, would be called "Non-conservative Systems". A conservative system might therefore be defined as one whose total energy is redistributed, but not altered in amount, by changes that happen within it. Of course a given system might be conservative for some kinds of change and not for others.

So far we have merely defined a "Conservative System", and admitted that there are systems which, for some kinds of change at any rate, answer approximately to our definition. We can now state the Principle of the Conservation of Energy in terms of the conceptions just defined. The principle asserts that every material system is either itself conservative, or, if not, is part of a larger material system which is conservative. We may take it that there is good inductive evidence for this proposition.

The next thing to consider is the experiments on the human body. These tend to prove that a living body, with the air that it breathes and the food that it eats, forms a conservative system to a high degree of approximation. We can measure the chemical energy of the food given to a man, and that which enters his body in the form of Oxygen breathed in. We can also, with suitable apparatus, collect, measure and analyse the air breathed out, and thus find its chemical energy. Similarly, we can find the energy given out in bodily movement, in heat, and in excretion. It is alleged that, on the average, whatever the man may do, the energy of his bodily movements is exactly accounted for by the energy given to him in the form of food and of Oxygen. If you take the energy put in in food and Oxygen, and subtract the energy given out in waste-products, the balance is almost exactly equal to the energy put out in bodily movements. Such slight differences as are found are as often on one side as on the other, and are therefore probably due to unavoidable experimental errors. I do not propose to criticise the interpretation of these experiments in detail, because, as I shall show soon, they are completely irrelevant to the problem of whether mind and body interact. But there is just one point that I will make before passing on. It is perfectly clear that such experiments can tell us only what happens on the average over a long time. To know whether the balance was accurately kept at very moment we should have to kill the patient at each moment and analyse his body so as to find out the energy present then in the form of stored-up products. Obviously we cannot keep on killing the patient in order to analyse him, and then reviving him in order to go on with the experiment. Thus it would seem that the results of the experiment are perfectly compatible with the presence of quite large excesses or defects in the total bodily energy at certain moments, provided that these average out over longer periods. However, I do not want to press this criticism; I am quite ready to accept for our present purpose the traditional interpretation which has been put on the experiments.

We now understand the physical principle and the experimental facts. The two together are generally supposed to prove that mind and body cannot interact. What precisely is the argument, and is it valid? I imagine that the argument, when fully stated, would run somewhat as follows: "I will to move my arm, and it moves. If the volition has anything to do with causing the movement we might expect energy to flow from my mind to my body. Thus the energy of my body ought to receive a measurable increase, not accounted for by the food that I eat and the Oxygen that I breathe. But no such physically unaccountable increases of bodily energy are found. Again, I tread on a tin-tack, and a painful sensation arises in my mind. If treading on the tack has anything to do with causing the sensation we might expect energy to flow from my body to my mind. Such energy would cease to be measurable. Thus there ought to be a noticeable decrease in my bodily energy, not balanced by increases anywhere in the physical system. But such unbalanced decreases of bodily energy are not found." So it is concluded that the volition has nothing to do with causing my arm to move, and that treading on the tack has nothing to do with causing the painful sensation.

Is this argument valid? In the first place it is important to notice that the conclusion does not follow from the Conservation of Energy and the experimental facts alone. The real premise is a tacitly assumed proposition about causation; viz., that, if a change in A has anything to do with causing a change in B, energy must leave A and flow into B. This is neither asserted nor entailed by the Conservation of Energy. What *it* says is that, *if* energy leaves A, it must appear in something else, say B; so that A and B together form a conservative system. Since the Conservation of Energy is not itself the premise for the argument against Interaction, and since it does not entail that premise, the evidence for the Conservation of Energy is not evidence against Interaction. Is there any independent evidence for the premise? We may admit that it *is* true of many, though not of all, transactions within the physical realm. But there are cases where it is not true even of purely physical transactions; and, even if it were always true in the physical realm, it would not follow that it must also be true of transphysical causation. Take the case of a weight swinging at the end of a string hung from a fixed point. The total energy of the weight is the same at all positions in its course. It is thus a conservative system. But at every moment the direction and velocity of the weight's motion are different, and the proportion between its kinetic and its potential energy is constantly changing. These changes are caused by the pull of the string, which acts in a different direction at each different moment. The string makes no difference to the total energy of the weight; but it makes all the difference in the world to the particular way in which the weight moves and the particular way in which the energy is distributed between the potential and the kinetic forms. This is evident when we remember that the weight would begin to move in an utterly different course if at any moment the string were cut.

Here, then, we have a clear case even in the physical realm where a system is conservative but is continually acted on by something which affects its movement and the distribution of its total energy. Why should not the mind act on the body in this way? If you say that you can see how a string can affect the movement of a weight, but cannot see how a volition could affect the movement of a material particle, you have deserted the scientific argument and have gone back to one of the philosophical arguments. Your real difficulty is either that volitions are so very unlike movements, or that the volition is in your mind whilst the movement belongs to the physical realm. And we have seen how little weight can be attached to these objections.

The fact is that, even in purely physical systems, the Conservation of Energy does not explain what changes will happen or when they will happen. It merely imposes a very general limited condition on the changes that are possible. The fact that the system composed of bullet, charge, and gun, in our earlier example, is conservative does not tell us that the gun ever will be fired, or when it will be fired if at all, or what will cause it to go off, or what forms of energy will appear if and when it does go off. The change in this case is determined by pulling the trigger. Likewise the mere fact that the human body and its neighbourhood form a conservative system does not explain any particular bodily movement; it does not explain why I ever move at all, or why I sometimes write, sometimes walk, and sometimes swim. To explain the happening of these particular movements at certain times it seems to be essential to take into account the volitions which happen from time to time in my mind; just as it is essential to take the string into account to explain the particular behaviour of the weight, and to take the trigger into account to explain the going off of the gun at a certain moment. The difference between the gun-system and the body-system is that a little energy does flow into the former when the trigger is pulled, whilst it is alleged that none does so when a volition starts a bodily movement. But there is not even this amount of difference between the body-system and the swinging weight.

Thus the argument from energy has no tendency to disprove Two-sided Interaction. It has gained a spurious authority from the august name of the Conservation of Energy. But this impressive principle proves to have nothing to do with the case. And the real premise of the argument is not self-evident, and is not universally true even in purely intra-physical transactions. In the end this scientific argument has to lean on the old philosophic arguments; and we have seen that these are but bruised reeds. Nevertheless, the facts brought forward by the argument from energy do throw some light on the *nature* of the interaction between mind and body, assuming this to happen. They do suggest that all the energy of our bodily actions comes out of and goes back into the physical world, and that minds neither add energy to nor abstract it from the latter. What they do, if they do anything, is to determine that at a given moment so much energy shall change from the chemical form to the form of bodily movement; and they determine this, so far as we can see, without altering the total amount of energy in the physical world.

(2) *The Argument from the Structure of the Nervous System.* There are purely reflex actions, like sneezing and blinking, in which there is no reason to suppose that the mind plays any essential part. Now we know the nervous structure which is used in such acts as these. A stimulus is given to the outer end of an effect nerve; some change or other runs up this nerve, crosses a synapsis between this and an afferent nerve, travels down the latter to a muscle, causes the muscle to contract, and so produces a bodily movement. There seems no reason to believe that the mind plays any essential part in this process. The process may be irreducibly vital, and not merely physico-chemical; but there seems no need to assume anything more than this. Now it is said that the whole nervous system is simply an immense complication of interconnected nervous arcs. The result is that a change which travels inwards has an immense number of alternative paths by which it may travel outwards. Thus the reaction to a given stimulus is no longer one definite movement, as in the simple reflex. Almost any movement may follow any stimulus according to the part which the afferent disturbance happens to take. This path will depend on the relative resistance of the various synapses at the time. Now a variable response to the same stimulus is characteristic of deliberate as opposed to reflex action.

These are the facts. The argument based on them runs as follows. It is admitted that the mind has nothing to do with the causation of purely reflex actions. But the nervous structure and the nervous processes involved in deliberate action do not differ in kind from those involved in reflex action; they differ only in degree of complexity. The variability which characterises deliberate action is fully explained by the variety of alternative paths and the variable resistances of the synapses. So it is unreasonable to suppose that the mind has any more to do with causing deliberate actions than it has to do with causing reflex actions.

I think that this argument is invalid. In the first place I am pretty sure that the persons who use it have before their imagination a kind of picture of how mind and body must interact if they interact at all. They find that the facts do not answer to this picture, and so they conclude that there is no interaction. The picture is of the following kind. They think of the mind as sitting somewhere in a hole in the brain, surrounded by telephones. And they think of the efferent disturbance as coming to an end at one of these telephones and there affecting the mind. The mind is then supposed to respond by sending an efferent impulse down another of these telephones. As no such hole, with efferent nerves stopping at its walls and afferent nerves starting from them, can be found, they conclude that the mind can play no part in the transaction. But another alternative is that this picture of how the mind must act if it acts at all is wrong. To put it shortly, the mistake is to confuse a gap in an explanation with a spatio-temporal gap, and to argue from the absence of the latter to the absence of the former.

The interactionist's contention is simply that there is a gap in any purely physiological explanation of deliberate action; *i.e.,* that all such explanations fail to account completely for the facts because they leave out one necessary condition. It does not follow in the least that there must be a spatio-temporal breach of continuity in the physiological conditions, and that the missing condition must fill this gap in the way in which the movement of a wire fills the spatio-temporal interval between the pulling of a bell-handle and the ringing of a distant bell. To assume this is to make the mind a kind of physical object, and to make its action a kind of mechanical action. Really, the mind and its actions are not literally in Space at all, and the time which is occupied by the mental event is no doubt *also* occupied by some part of the physiological process. Thus I am inclined to think that much of the force which this argument actually exercises on many people is simply due to the presupposition about the *modus operandi* of interaction, and that it is greatly weakened when this presupposition is shown to be a mere prejudice due to our limited power of envisaging unfamiliar alternative possibilities.

We can, however, make more detailed objections to the argument than this. There is a clear introspective difference between the mental accompaniment of voluntary action and that of reflex action. What goes on in our minds when we decide with difficulty to get out of a hot bath on a cold morning is obviously extremely different from what goes on in our minds when we sniff pepper and sneeze. And the difference is qualitative; it is not a mere difference of complexity. This difference has to be explained somehow; and the theory under discussion gives no plausible explanation of it. The ordinary view that, in the latter case, the mind is not acting on the body at all; whilst, in the former, it is acting on the body in a specific way, does at least make the introspective difference between the two intelligible.

Again, whilst it is true that deliberate action differs from reflex action in its greater variability of response to the same stimulus, this is certainly not the whole or the most important part of the difference between them. The really important difference is that, in deliberate action, the response is varied *appropriately* to meet the special circumstances which are supposed to exist at the time or are expected to arise later; whilst reflex action is not varied in this way, but is blind and almost mechanical. The complexity of the nervous system explains the *possibility* of variation; it does not in the least explain why the alternative which actually takes place should as a rule be appropriate and not merely haphazard. And so again it seems as if some factor were in operation in deliberate action which is not present in reflex action; and it is reasonable to suppose that this factor is the volition in the mind.

It seems to me that this second scientific argument has no tendency to disprove interaction; but that the facts which it brings forward do tend to suggest the particular form which interaction probably takes if it happens at all. They suggest that what the mind does to the body in voluntary action, if it does anything, is to lower the resistance of certain synapses and to raise that of others. The result is that the nervous current follows such a course as to produce the particular movement which the mind judges to be appropriate at the time. On such a view the difference between reflex, habitual, and deliberate actions for the present purpose becomes fairly plain. In pure reflexes the mind cannot voluntarily affect the resistance of the synapses concerned, and so the action takes place in spite of it. In habitual action it deliberately refrains from interfering with the resistance of the synapses, and so the action goes on like a complicated reflex. But it *can* affect these resistances if it wishes, though often only with difficulty; and it is ready to do so if it judges this to be expedient. Finally, it may lose the power altogether. This would be what happens when a person becomes a slave to some habit, such as drug-taking.

I conclude that, at the level of enlightened common-sense at which the ordinary discussion of Interaction moves, no good reason has been produced for doubting that the mind acts on the body in volition, and that the body acts on the mind in sensation. The philosophic arguments are quite inconclusive; and the scientific arguments, when properly understood, are quite compatible with Two-sided Interaction. At most they suggest certain conclusions as to the form which interaction probably takes if it happens at all.

DIFFICULTIES IN THE DENIAL OF INTERACTION

I propose now to consider some of the difficulties which would attend the denial of Interaction, still keeping the discussion at the same common-sense level. If a man denies the action of body on mind he is at once in trouble over the causation of new sensations. Suppose that I suddenly tread on an unsuspected tin-tack. A new sensation suddenly comes into my mind. This is an event, and it presumably has some cause. Now, however carefully I introspect and retrospect, I can find no other mental event which is adequate to account for the fact that just that sensation has arisen at just that moment. If I reject the common-sense view that treading on the tack is an essential part of the cause of the sensation, I must suppose either that it is uncaused, or that it is caused by other events in my mind which I cannot discover by introspection or retrospection, or that it is caused telepathically by other finite minds or by God. Now enquiry of my neighbours would show that it is not caused telepathically by any event in their minds which they can introspect or remember. Thus anyone who denies the action of body on mind, and admits that sensations have causes, must postulate either (*a*) immense numbers of unobservable states in his own mind; or (*b*) as many unobservable states in his neighbours' minds, together with telepathic action; or (*c*) some non-human spirit together with telepathic action. I must confess that the difficulties which have been alleged against the action of body on mind seem to be mild compared with those of the alternative hypotheses which are involved in the denial of such action.

The difficulties which are involved in the denial of the action of mind on body are at first sight equally great; but I do not think that they turn out to be so serious as those which are involved in denying the action of body on mind. The *prima facie* difficulty is this. The world contains many obviously artificial objects, such as books, bridges, clothes, etc. We know that, if we go far enough back in the history of their production, we always do in fact come on the actions of some human body. And the minds connected with these bodies did design the objects in question, did will to produce them, and did believe that they were initiating and guiding the physical process by means of these designs and volitions. If it be true that the mind does not act on the body, it follows that the designs and volitions in the agents' minds did not in fact play any part in the production of books, bridges, clothes, etc. This appears highly paradoxical. And it is an easy step from it to say that anyone who denies the action of mind on body must admit that books, bridges, and other such objects *could* have been produced even though there had been no minds, no thought of these objects and no desire for them. This consequence seems manifestly absurd to common-sense, and it might be argued that it reflects its absurdity back on the theory which entails it.

The man who denies that mind can act on body might deal with this difficulty in two ways: (1) He might deny that the conclusion *is* intrinsically absurd. He might say that human bodies are extraordinarily complex physical objects, which probably obey irreducible laws of their own, and that we really do not know enough about them to set limits to what their unaided powers could accomplish. This is the line which Spinoza took. The conclusion, it would be argued, *seems* absurd only because the state of affairs which it contemplates is so very unfamiliar. We find it difficult to imagine a body like ours without a mind like ours; but, if we could get over this defect in our powers of imagination, we might have no difficulty in admitting that such a body could do all the things which our bodies do. I think it must be admitted that the difficulty is not so great as that which is involved in denying the action of body on mind. There we had to postulate *ad hoc* utterly unfamiliar entities and modes of action; here it is not certain that we should have to do this.

(2) The other line of argument would be to say that the alleged consequence does not necessarily follow from denying the action of mind on body. I assume that both parties admit that causation is something more than mere *de facto* regularity of sequence and concomitance. If they do not, of course the whole controversy between them becomes futile; for there will certainly be causation between mind and body and between body and mind, in the only sense in which there is causation anywhere. This being presupposed, the following kind of answer is logically possible. When I say that B could not have happened unless A had happened, there are two alternative possibilities. (*a*) A may itself be an indispensable link in any chain of causes which ends up with B. (*b*) A may not itself be a link in any chain of causation which ends up with B. But there may be an indispensible link *a* in any such chain of causation, and A may be a necessary accompaniment or sequent of *a*. These two possibilities may be illustrated by diagrams. (*a*) is represented by the figure below:—

$A_0 \longrightarrow A \longrightarrow A_1 \longrightarrow A_2 \longrightarrow B$

The two forms of (*b*) are represented by the two figures below:—

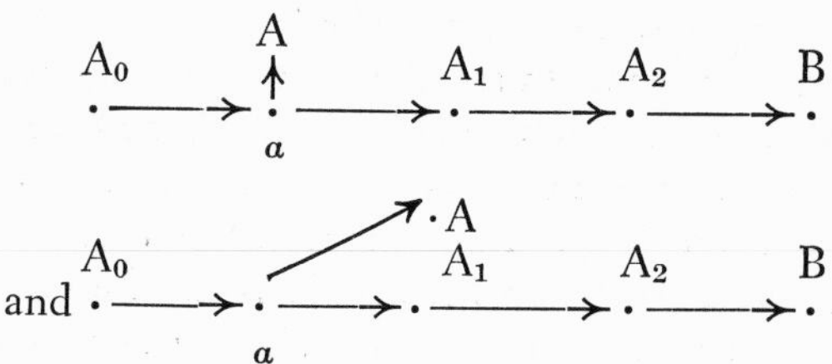

Evidently, if B cannot happen unless *a* precedes, and if *a* cannot happen without A accompanying or immediately following it, B will not be able to happen unless A precedes it. And yet A will have had no part in causing B. It will be noticed that, on this view, *a* has a complex effect AA_1, of which a certain part, viz., A_1 is sufficient by itself to produce A_2 and ultimately B. Let us apply this abstract possibility to our present problem. Suppose that B is some artificial object, like a book or a bridge. If we admit that this could not have come into existence unless a certain design and volition had existed in a certain mind, we could interpret the facts in two ways. (*a*) We could hold that the design and volition are themselves an indispensable link in the chain of causation which ends in the production of a bridge or a book. This is the common view, and it requires us to admit the action of mind on body. (*b*) We might hold that the design and the volition are not themselves a link in the chain of causation which ends in the production of the artificial object; but that they are a necessary accompaniment or sequent of something which is an indispensable link in this chain of causation. On this view the chain consists wholly of physical events; but one of these physical events (viz., some event in the brain) has a complex consequent. One part of this consequent is purely physical, and leads by purely physical causation to the ultimate production of a bridge or a book. The other is purely mental, and consists of a certain design and volition in the mind which animates the human body concerned. If this has any consequences they are purely mental. Each part of this complex consequent follows with equal necessity; this particular brain-state could no more have existed without such and such a mental state accompanying or following it than it could have existed without such and such a bodily movement following it. If we are willing to take some such view as this, we can admit that certain objects could not have existed unless there had been designs of them and desires for them; and yet we could consistently deny that these desires and designs have any effect on the movements of our bodies.

It seems to me then that the doctrine which I will call "One-sided Action of Body on Mind" is logically possible; *i.e.*, a theory which accepts the action of body on mind but denies the action of mind on body. But I do not see the least reason to accept it, since I see no reason to deny that mind acts on body in volition. One-sided Action has, I think, generally been held in the special form called "Epiphenomenalism." I take this doctrine to consist of the following four propositions: (1) Certain bodily events cause certain mental events. (2) No mental event plays any part in the causation of any bodily event. (3) No mental event plays any part in the causation of any other mental event. Consequently (4) all mental events are caused by bodily events and by them only. Thus Epiphenomenalism is just One-sided Action of Body on Mind, together with a special theory about the nature and structure of mind. This special theory does not call for discussion here, where I am dealing only with the relations between minds and bodies, and am not concerned with a detailed analysis of mind. . . .

ARGUMENTS IN FAVOUR OF INTERACTION

The only arguments *for* One-sided Action of Body on Mind or for Parallelism are the arguments *against* Two-sided Interaction; and these, as we have seen, are worthless. Are there any arguments in favour of Two-side Interaction? I have incidentally given two which seem to me to have considerable weight. In favour of the action of mind on body is the fact that we seem to be immediately aware of a causal relation when we voluntarily try to produce a bodily movement, and that the arguments to show that this cannot be true are invalid. In favour of the action of body on mind are the insuperable difficulties which I have pointed out in accounting for the happening of new sensations on any other hypothesis. There are, however, two other arguments which have often been thought to prove the action of mind on body. These are (1) an evolutionary argument, first used, I believe, by William James; and (2) the famous "telegram argument." They both seem to me to be quite obviously invalid.

(1) The evolutionary argument runs as follows: It is a fact, which is admitted by persons who deny Two-sided Interaction, that minds increase in complexity and power with the growth in complexity of the brain and nervous system. Now, if the mind makes no difference to the actions of the body, this development on the mental side is quite unintelligible from the point of view of natural selection. Let us imagine two animals whose brains and nervous systems were of the same degree of complexity; and suppose, if possible, that one had a mind and the other had none. If the mind makes no difference to the behaviour of the body the chance of survival and of leaving descendants will clearly be the same for the two animals. Therefore natural selection will have no tendency to favour the evolution of mind which has actually taken place. I do not think that there is anything in this argument. Natural selection is a purely negative process; it simply tends to eliminate individuals and species which have variations unfavourable to survival. Now, by hypothesis, the possession of a mind is not *unfavourable* to survival; it simply makes no difference. Now it may be that the existence of a mind of such and such a kind is an inevitable consequence of the existence of a brain and nervous system of such and such a degree of complexity. Indeed we have seen that some such view is essential if the opponent of Two-sided Interaction is to answer the common-sense objection that artificial objects could not have existed unless there had been a mind which designed and desired them. On this hypothesis there is no need to invoke natural selection twice over, once to explain the evolution of the brain and nervous system, and once to explain the evolution of the mind. If natural selection will account for the evolution of the brain and nervous system, the evolution of the mind will follow inevitably, even though it adds nothing to the survival-value of the organism. The plain fact is that natural selection does not account for the origin or for the growth in complexity of anything whatever; and therefore it is no objection to any particular theory of the relations of mind and body that, if it were true, natural selection would not explain the origin and development of mind.

(2) The "telegram argument" is as follows:

Suppose there were two telegrams, one saying "Our son has been killed", and the other saying: "Your son has been killed". And suppose that one or other of them was delivered to a parent whose son was away from home. As physical stimuli they are obviously extremely alike, since they differ only in the fact that the letter "Y" is present in one and absent in the other. Yet we know that the reaction of the person who received the telegram might be very different according to which one he received. This is supposed to show that the reactions of the body cannot be wholly accounted for by bodily causes, and that the mind must intervene causally in some cases. Now I have very little doubt that the mind does play a part in determining the action of the recipient of the telegram; but I do not see why this argument should prove it to a person who doubted or denied it. If two very similar stimuli are followed by two very different results, we are no doubt justified in concluding that these stimuli are not the complete causes of the reactions which follow them. But of course it would be admitted by every one that the receipt of the telegram is not the complete cause of the recipient's reaction. We all know that his brain and nervous system play an essential part in any reaction that he may make to the stimulus. The question then is whether the minute structure of his brain and nervous system, including in this the supposed traces left by past stimuli and past reactions, is not enough to account for the great difference in his behaviour on receiving two very similar stimuli. Two keys may be very much alike, but one may fit a certain lock and the other may not. And, if the lock be connected with the trigger of a loaded gun, the results of "stimulating" the system with one or other of the two keys will be extremely different. We know that the brain and nervous system are very complex, and we commonly suppose that they contain more or less permanent traces and linkages due to past stimuli and reactions. If this be granted, it is obvious that two very similar stimuli may produce very different results, simply because one fits in with the internal structure of the brain and nervous system whilst the other does not. And I do not see how we can be sure that anything more is needed to account for the mere difference of reaction adduced by the "telegram argument."

C. J. DUCASSE

Is Life after Death Possible?*

The question whether human personality survives death is sometimes asserted to be one upon which reflection is futile. Only empirical evidence, it is said, can be relevant, since the question is purely one of fact.

But no question is purely one of fact until it is clearly understood; and this one is, on the contrary, ambiguous and replete with tacit assumptions. Until the ambiguities have been removed and the assumptions critically examined, we do not really know just what it is we want to know when we ask whether a life after death is possible. Nor, therefore, can we tell until then what bearing on this question various facts empirically known to us may have.

To clarify its meaning is chiefly what I now propose to attempt. I shall ask first why a future life is so generally desired and believed in. Then I shall state, as convincingly as I can in the time available, the arguments commonly advanced to prove that such a life is impossible. After that, I shall consider the logic of these arguments, and show that they quite fail to establish the impossibility. Next, the tacit but arbitrary assumption, which makes them nevertheless appear convincing, will be pointed out. . . .

Let us turn to the first of these tasks.

WHY MAN DESIRES LIFE AFTER DEATH

To begin with, let us note that each of us here has been alive and conscious at all times in the past which he can remember. It is true that sometimes our bodies are in deep sleep, or made inert by anesthetics or injuries. But even at such times we do not experience unconsciousness in ourselves, for to experience it would mean being conscious of being unconscious, and this is a contradiction. The only experience of unconsciousness in ourselves we ever have is, not experience of total unconsciousness, but of unconsciousness *of this or that;* as when we report: "I am not conscious of any pain," or "of any bell-sound," or "of any difference between those two colors," etc. Nor do we ever experience unconsciousness in another person, but only the fact that, sometimes, some or all of the ordinary activities of his body cease to occur. That consciousness itself is extinguished at such times is thus only a hypothesis which we construct to account for certain changes in the behavior of another person's body or to explain in him or in ourselves the eventual lack of memories relating to the given period.

Being alive and conscious is thus, with all men, a lifelong experience and habit; and conscious life is therefore something they naturally—even if tacitly—expect to continue. As J. B. Pratt has pointed out, the child takes the continuity of life for granted. It is the fact of death that has to be taught him. But when he has learned it, and the idea of a future life is then put explicitly before his mind, it seems to him the most natural thing in the world.[1]

The witnessing of death, however, is a rare experience for most of us, and, because it breaks so sharply into our habits, it forces on us the question whether the mind, which until then was manifested by the body now dead, continues somehow to live on, or, on the contrary, has become totally extinct. This question is commonly phrased as concerning "the immortality of

* C. J. Ducasse, "Some Questions concerning Survival after Death," *Newsletter of the Parapsychology Foundation,* Vol. 3, No. 1, Jan.–Feb. 1956. This paper is a slight extension of Professor Ducasse's Foerster Lecture (at the University of California, Berkeley, May 1947) entitled "Is a Life after Death Possible?" The concluding section has been omitted. Reprinted by permission of the author, the University of California Press, and the Parapsychology Foundation.

[1] J. B. Pratt, *The Religious Consciousness,* p. 225.

the soul," and immortality, strictly speaking, means survival forever. But assurance of survival for some considerable period—say a thousand, or even a hundred, years—would probably have almost as much present psychological value as would assurance of survival strictly forever. Most men would be troubled very little by the idea of extinction at so distant a time—even less troubled than is now a healthy and happy youth by the idea that he will die in fifty or sixty years. Therefore, it is survival for some time, rather than survival specifically forever, that I shall alone consider.

The craving for continued existence is very widespread. Even persons who believe that death means complete extinction of the individual's consciousness often find comfort in various substitute conceptions of survival. They may, for instance, dwell on the continuity of the individual's germ plasm in his descendants. Or they find solace in the thought that, the past being indestructible, their individual life remains eternally an intrinsic part of the history of the world. Also—and more satisfying to one's craving for personal importance—there is the fact that since the acts of one's life have effects, and these in turn further effects, and so on, therefore what one has done goes on forever influencing remotely, and sometimes greatly, the course of future events.

Gratifying to one's vanity, too, is the prospect that, if the achievements of one's life have been great or even only conspicuous, or one's benefactions or evil deeds have been notable, one's name may not only be remembered by acquaintances and relatives for a little while, but may live on in recorded history. But evidently survival in any of these senses is but a consolation prize—but a thin substitute for the continuation of conscious individual life, which may not be a fact, but which most men crave nonetheless.

The roots of this craving are certain desires which death appears to frustrate. For some, the chief of these is for reunion with persons dearly loved. For others, whose lives have been wretched, it is the desire for another chance at the happiness they have missed. For others yet, it is desired for further opportunity to grow in ability, knowledge or character. Often, there is also the desire, already mentioned, to go on counting for something in the affairs of men. And again, a future life for oneself and others is often desired in order that the redressing of the many injustices of this life shall be possible. But it goes without saying that, although desires such as these are often sufficient to cause belief in a future life, they constitute no evidence at all that it is a fact.

In this connection, it may be well to point out that, although both the belief in survival and the belief in the existence of a god or gods are found in most religions, nevertheless there is no necessary connection between the two beliefs. No contradiction would be involved in supposing either that there is a God but no life after death or that there is a life after death but no God. The belief that there is a life after death may be tied to a religion, but it is no more intrinsically religious than would be a belief that there is life on the planet Mars. The after-death world, if it exists, is just another region or dimension of the universe.

But although belief in survival of death is natural and easy and has always been held in one form or another by a large majority of mankind, critical reflection quickly brings forth a number of apparently strong reasons to regard that belief as quite illusory. Let us now review them.

THE ARGUMENTS AGAINST SURVIVAL

There are, first of all, a number of facts which definitely suggest that both the existence and the nature of consciousness wholly depend on the presence of a functioning nervous system. It is pointed out, for example, that wherever consciousness is observed, it is found associated with a living and functioning body. Further, when the body dies, or the head is struck a heavy blow, or some anesthetic is administered, the familiar outward evidences of consciousness terminate, permanently or temporarily. Again, we know well that drugs of various kinds—alcohol, caffein, opium, heroin, and many others—cause specific changes at the time in the nature of a person's mental states. Also, by stimulating in appropriate ways the body's sense organs, corresponding states of consciousness—namely, the various kinds of sensations—can be caused at will. On the other hand, cutting a sensory nerve immediately eliminates a whole range of sensations.

Again, the contents of consciousness, the mental powers, or even the personality, are modified in characteristic ways when certain regions of the brain are destroyed by disease or injury or are disconnected from the rest by such an operation as prefrontal lobotomy. And that the nervous system is the indispensable basis of mind is further suggested by the fact that, in the evolutionary scale, the degree of intelligence of various species of animals keeps pace closely with the degree of development of their brain.

That continued existence of mind after death is impossible has been argued also on the basis of theoretical considerations. It has been contended, for instance, that what we call states of consciousness—or more particularly, ideas, sensations, volitions, feelings, and the like—are really nothing but the minute physical or chemical events which take place in the tissues of the brain. For, it is urged, it would be absurd to suppose that an idea or a volition, if it is not itself a material thing or process, could cause material effects such as contractions of muscles.

Moreover, it is maintained that the possibility of causation of a material event by an immaterial, mental cause is ruled out *a priori* by the principle of the conservation of energy; for such causation would mean that an additional quantity of energy suddenly pops into the nervous system out of nowhere.

Another conception of consciousness, which is more often met with today than the one just mentioned, but which also implies that consciousness cannot survive death, is that "consciousness" is only the name we give to certain types of behavior, which differentiate the higher animals from all other things in nature. According to this view, to say, for example, that an animal is conscious of a difference between two stimuli means nothing more than that it responds to each by different behavior. That is, the difference of *behavior* is what consciousness of difference between the stimuli *consists in;* and is not, as is commonly assumed, only the behavioral *sign* of something mental and not public, called "consciousness that the stimuli are different."

Or again, consciousness, of the typically human sort called thought, is identified with the typically human sort of behavior called speech; and this, again not in the sense that speech *expresses* or *manifests* something different from itself, called "thought," but in the sense that speech—whether uttered or only whispered—*is* thought itself. And obviously, if thought, or any mental activity, is thus but some mode of behavior of the living body, the mind cannot possibly survive death.

Still another difficulty confronting the hypothesis of survival becomes evident when one imagines in some detail what survival would have to include in order to satisfy the desires which cause man to crave it. It would, of course, have to include persistence not alone of consciousness, but also of personality; that is, of the individual's character, acquired knowledge, cultural skills and interests, memories, and awareness of personal identity. But even this would not be enough, for what man desires is not bare survival, but to go on living in some objective way. And this means to go on meeting new situations and, by exerting himself to deal with them, to broaden and deepen his experience and develop his latent capacities.

But it is hard to imagine this possible without a body and an environment for it, upon which to act and from which to receive impressions. And, if a body and an environment were supposed, but not material and corruptible ones, then it is paradoxical to think that, under such radically different conditions, a given personality could persist.[2]

To take a crude but telling analogy, it is past belief that, if the body of any one of us were suddenly changed into that of a shark or an octopus, and placed in the ocean, his personality could, for more than a very short time, if at all, survive intact so radical a change of environment and of bodily form.

THE ARGUMENTS EXAMINED

Such, in brief, are the chief reasons commonly advanced for holding that survival is impossible. Scrutiny of them, however, will, I think, reveal that they are not as strong as they first seem and far from strong enough to show that there can be no life after death.

Let us consider first the assertion that "thought," or "consciousness," is but another name for subvocal speech, or for some other form of behavior, or for molecular processes in the tissues of the brain. As Paulsen and others have

[2] Cf. Gardner Murphy, "Difficulties Confronting the Survival Hypothesis," *Journal of the American Society for Psychical Research* for April, 1945, p. 72; Corliss Lamont, *The Illusion of Immortality* (New York, 1935), pp. 26ff.

pointed out,[3] no evidence ever is or can be offered to support that assertion, because it is in fact but a disguised proposal to make the words "thought," "feeling," "sensation," "desire," and so on, denote facts quite different from those which these words are commonly employed to denote. To say that those words are but other names for certain chemical or behavioral events is as grossly arbitrary as it would be to say that "wood" is but another name for glass, or "potato" but another name for cabbage. What thought, desire, sensation, and other mental states are like, each of us can observe directly by introspection; and what introspection reveals is that they do not in the least resemble muscular contraction, or glandular secretion, or any other known bodily events. No tampering with language can alter the observable fact that thinking is one thing and muttering quite another; that the feeling called anger has no resemblance to the bodily behavior which usually goes with it; or that an act of will is not in the least like anything we find when we open the skull and examine the brain. Certain mental events are doubtless connected in some way with certain bodily events, but they are not those bodily events themselves. The connection is not identity.

This being clear, let us next consider the arguments offered to show that mental processes, although not identical with bodily processes, nevertheless depend on them. We are told, for instance, that some head injuries, or anesthetics, totally extinguish consciousness for the time being. As already pointed out, however, the strict fact is only that the usual bodily signs of consciousness are then absent. But they are also absent when a person is asleep; and yet, at the same time, dreams, which are states of consciousness, may be occurring.

It is true that when the person concerned awakens, he often remembers his dreams, whereas the person that has been anesthetized or injured has usually no memories relating to the period of apparent blankness. But this could mean that his consciousness was, for the time, dissociated from its ordinary channels of manifestation, as was reported of the co-conscious personalities of some of the patients of Dr. Morton Prince.[4] Moreover, it sometimes occurs that a

[3] F. Paulsen, *Introduction to Philosophy* (trans. by F. Thilly, 2d ed.), pp. 82–83.

[4] *My Life as a Dissociated Personality*, edited by Morton Prince (Boston: Badger).

person who has been in an accident reports lack of memories not only for the period during which his body was unresponsive but also for a period of several hours *before* the accident, during which he had given to his associates all the ordinary external signs of being conscious as usual.

But, more generally, if absence of memories relating to a given period proved unconsciousness for that period, this would force us to conclude that we were unconscious during the first few years of our lives, and indeed have been so most of the time since; for the fact is that we have no memories whatever of most of our days. That we are alive and conscious on any long past specific date is, with only a few exceptions, not something we actually remember, but only something which we infer must be true.

EVIDENCE FROM PSYCHICAL RESEARCH

Another argument advanced against survival was, it will be remembered, that death must extinguish the mind, since all manifestations of it then cease. But to assert that they invariably then cease is to ignore altogether the considerable amount of evidence to the contrary, gathered over many years and carefully checked by the Society for Psychical Research. This evidence, which is of a variety of kinds, has been reviewed by Professor Gardner Murphy in an article published in the Journal of the Society.[5] He mentions first the numerous well-authenticated cases of apparition of a dead person to others as yet unaware that he had died or even been ill or in danger. The more strongly evidential cases of apparition are those in which the apparition conveys to the person who sees it specific facts until then secret. An example would be that of the apparition of a girl to her brother nine years after her death, with a conspicuous scratch on her cheek. Their mother then revealed to him that she herself had made that scratch accidentally while preparing her daughter's body for burial, but that she had then at once covered it with powder and never mentioned it to anyone.

Another famous case is that of a father whose apparition some time after death revealed to one of his sons the existence and location of an unsus-

[5] "An Outline of Survival Evidence," *Journal of the American Society for Psychical Research* for January, 1945.

pected second will, benefiting him, which was then found as indicated. Still another case would be the report by General Barter, then a subaltern in the British Army in India, of the apparition to him of a lieutenant he had not seen for two or three years. The lieutenant's apparition was riding a brown pony with black mane and tail. He was much stouter than at their last meeting, and, whereas formerly clean-shaven, he now wore a peculiar beard in the form of a fringe encircling his face. On inquiry the next day from a person who had known the lieutenant at the time he died, it turned out that he had indeed become very bloated before his death; that he had grown just such a beard while on the sick list; and that he had some time before bought and eventually ridden to death a pony of that very description.

Other striking instances are those of an apparition seen simultaneously by several persons. It is on record that an apparition of a child was perceived first by a dog, that the animal's rushing at it, loudly barking, interrupted the conversation of the seven persons present in the room, thus drawing their attention to the apparition, and that the latter then moved through the room for some fifteen seconds, followed by the barking dog.[6]

Another type of empirical evidence of survival consists of communications, purporting to come from the dead, made through the persons commonly called sensitives, mediums, or automatists. Some of the most remarkable of these communications were given by the celebrated American medium, Mrs. Piper, who for many years was studied by the Society for Psychical Research, London, with the most elaborate precautions against all possibility of fraud. Twice, particularly, the evidences of identity supplied by the dead persons who purportedly were thus communicating with the living were of the very kinds, and of the same precision and detail, which would ordinarily satisfy a living person of the identity of another living person with whom he was not able to communicate directly, but only through an intermediary, or by letter or telephone.[7]

Again, sometimes the same mark of identity of a dead person, or the same message from him, or complementary parts of one message, are obtained independently from two mediums in different parts of the world.

Of course, when facts of these kinds are recounted, as I have just done, only in abstract summary, they make little if any impression upon us. And the very word "medium" at once brings to our minds the innumerable instances of demonstrated fraud perpetrated by charlatans to extract money from the credulous bereaved. But the modes of trickery and sources of error, which immediately suggest themselves to us as easy, natural explanations of the seemingly extraordinary facts, suggest themselves just as quickly to the members of the research committees of the Society for Psychical Research. Usually, these men have had a good deal more experience than the rest of us with the tricks of conjurers and fraudulent mediums, and take against them precautions far more strict and ingenious than would occur to the average sceptic.[8]

But when, instead of stopping at summaries, one takes the trouble to study the detailed, original reports, it then becomes evident that they cannot all be just laughed off; for to accept the hypothesis of fraud or mal-observation would often require more credulity than to accept the facts reported.

To *explain* those facts, however, is quite another thing. Only two hypotheses at all adequate to do so have yet been advanced. One is that the communications really come, as they purport to do, from persons who have died and have survived death. The other is the hypothesis of telepathy—that is, the supposition, itself startling enough, that the medium is able to gather information directly from the minds of others, and that this is the true source of the information

[6] The documents obtained by the Society for Psychical Research concerning this case, that of the lieutenant's apparation, and that of the girl with the scratch, are reproduced in Sir Ernest Bennett's *Apparitions and Haunted Houses* (London: Faber and Faber, 1945), pp. 334–337, 28–35, and 145–150 respectively.

[7] A summary of some of the most evidential facts may be found in the book by M. Sage, entitled *Mrs. Piper and the Society for Psychical Research* (New York: Scott-Thaw Co., 1904); others of them are related in some detail in Sir Oliver Lodge's *The Survival of Man*, Sec. IV (New York, Moffat, Yard and Co., 1909) and in A. M. Robbins' *Both Sides of the Veil*, Part II (Boston: Sherman, French, and Co., 1909). The fullest account is in the *Proceedings of the Society for Psychical Research*.

[8] Cf. H. Carrington, *The Physical Phenomena of Spiritualism, Fraudulent and Genuine* (Small, Maynard & Co., Boston, 1908).

communicated. To account for all the facts, however, this hypothesis has to be stretched very far, for some of them require us to suppose that the medium can tap the minds even of persons far away and quite unknown to him, and can tap even the subconscious part of their minds.

Diverse highly ingenious attempts have been made to devise conditions that would rule out telepathy as a possible explanation of the communications received; but some of the most critical and best-documented investigators still hold that it has not yet been absolutely excluded. Hence, although some of the facts recorded by psychical research constitute, prima facie, strong empirical evidence of survival, they cannot be said to establish it beyond question. But they do show that we need to revise rather radically in some respects our ordinary ideas of what is and is not possible in nature.

CAN MENTAL STATES CAUSE BODILY EVENTS?

Let us now turn to another of the arguments against survival. That states of consciousness entirely depend on bodily processes, and therefore cannot continue when the latter have ceased, is proved, it is argued, by the fact that various states of consciousness—in particular, the several kinds of sensations—can be caused at will by appropriately stimulating the body.

Now, it is very true that sensations and some other mental states can be so caused; but we have just as good and abundant evidence that mental states can cause various bodily events. John Laird mentions, among others, the fact that merely willing to raise one's arm normally suffices to cause it to rise; that a hungry person's mouth is caused to water by the idea of food; that feelings of rage, fear or excitement cause digestion to stop; that anxiety causes changes in the quantity and quality of the milk of a nursing mother; that certain thoughts cause tears, pallor, blushing or fainting; and so on.[9] The evidence we have that the relation is one of cause and effect is exactly the same here as where bodily processes cause mental states.

It is said, of course, that to suppose something non-physical, such as thought, to be capable of causing motion of a physical object, such as the body, is absurd. But I submit that if the heterogeneity of mind and matter makes this absurd, then it makes equally absurd the causation of mental states by stimulation of the body. Yet no absurdity is commonly found in the assertion that cutting the skin causes a feeling of pain, or that alcohol, caffein, bromides, and other drugs, cause characteristic states of consciousness. As David Hume made clear long ago, no kind of causal connection is intrinsically absurd. Anything might cause anything; and only observation can tell us what in fact can cause what.

Somewhat similar remarks would apply to the allegation that the principle of the conservation of energy precludes the possibility of causation of a physical event by a mental event. For if it does, then it equally precludes causation in the converse direction, and this, of course, would leave us totally at a loss to explain the occurrence of sensations. But, as Keeton and others have pointed out,[10] that energy is conserved is not something observation has revealed or could reveal, but only a postulate—a defining postulate for the notion of an "isolated physical system."

That is, conservation of energy is something one has to have if, but only if, one insists on conceiving the physical world as wholly self-contained, independent, isolated. And just because the metaphysics which the natural sciences tacitly assume does insist on so conceiving the physical world, this metaphysics compels them to save conservation by postulations *ad hoc* whenever dissipation of energy is what observation reveals. It postulates, for instance, that something else, which appears at such times but was not until then regarded as energy, is energy too, but it is then said, "in a different form."

Furthermore, as Broad has emphasized, all that the principle of conservation requires is that when a quantity Q of energy disappears at one place in the physical world an equal quantity of it should appear at some other place there. And the supposition that, in some cases, what causes it to disappear here and appear there is some mental event, such perhaps as a volition, does not violate at all the supposition that energy is conserved.[11]

[9] John Laird, *Our Minds and Their Bodies* (London, 1925), pp. 16–19.

[10] M. T. Keeton, "Some Ambiguities in the Theory of the Conservation of Energy," *Philosophy of Science*, Vol. 8, No. 3, July 1941.

[11] C. D. Broad, *The Mind and Its Place in Nature*, pp. 103ff. [This volume, pp. 209ff.]

A word, next, on the parallelism between the degree of development of the nervous systems of various animals and the degree of their intelligence. This is alleged to prove that the latter is the product of the former. But the facts lend themselves equally well to the supposition that, on the contrary, an obscurely felt need for greater intelligence in the circumstances the animal faced was what brought about the variations which eventually resulted in a more adequate nervous organization.

In the development of the individual, at all events, it seems clear that the specific, highly complex nerve connections which become established in the brain and cerebellum of, for instance, a skilled pianist are the results of his will over many years to acquire the skill.

We must not forget in this context that there is a converse, equally consistent with the facts, for the theory, called epiphenomenalism, that mental states are related to the brain much as the halo is to the saint, that is, as effects but never themselves as causes. The converse theory, which might be called hypophenomenalism, and which is pretty well that of Schopenhauer, is that the instruments which the various mechanisms of the body constitute are the objective products of obscure cravings for the corresponding powers; and, in particular, that the organization of the nervous system is the effect and material isomorph of the variety of mental functions exercised at a given level of animal or human existence.

THE INITIAL ASSUMPTION BEHIND THE ARGUMENTS AGAINST SURVIVAL

We have now scrutinized all but the last of the reasons mentioned earlier for rejecting the possibility of survival, and we have found them all logically weak. Before examining the one which remains, it will be useful for us to pause a moment and inquire why so many of the persons who advance those reasons nevertheless think them convincing.

It is, I believe, because these persons approach the question of survival with a certain unconscious metaphysical bias. It derives from a particular initial assumption which they tacitly make. It is that *to be real is to be material.* And to be material, of course, is to be some process or part of the perceptually public world, that is, of the world we all perceive by means of our so-called five senses.

Now the assumption that to be real is to be material is a useful and appropriate one for the purpose of investigating the material world and of operating upon it; and this purpose is a legitimate and frequent one. But those persons, and most of us, do not realize that the validity of that assumption is strictly relative to that specific purpose. Hence they, and most of us, continue making the assumption, and it continues to rule judgment, even when, as now, the purpose in view is a different one, for which the assumption is no longer useful or even congruous.

The point is all-important here and therefore worth stressing. Its essence is that the conception of the nature of reality that proposes to define the real as the material is not the expression of an observable fact to which everyone would have to bow, but is the expression only of a certain direction of interest on the part of the persons who so define reality—of interest, namely, which they have chosen to center wholly in the material, perceptually public world. This specialized interest is of course as legitimate as any other, but it automatically ignores all the facts, commonly called facts of mind, which only introspection reveals. And that specialized interest is what alone compels persons in its grip to employ the word "mind" to denote, instead of what it commonly does denote, something else altogether, namely, the public behavior of bodies that have minds.

Only so long as one's judgment is swayed unawares by that special interest do the logically weak arguments against the possibility of survival, which we have examined, seem strong.

It is possible, however, and just as legitimate, as well as more conducive to a fair view of our question, to center one's interest at the start on the facts of mind as introspectively observable, ranking them as most real in the sense that they are the facts the intrinsic nature of which we mostly directly experience, the facts which we most certainly know to exist; and moreover, that they are the facts without the experiencing of which we should not know any other facts whatever—such, for instance, as those of the material world.

The sort of perspective one gets from this point of view is what I propose now to sketch briefly.

For one thing, the material world is then seen to be but one among other objects of our consciousness. Moreover, one becomes aware of the crucially important fact that it is an object postulated rather than strictly given. What this means may be made clearer by an example. Suppose that, perhaps in a restaurant we visit for the first time, an entire wall is occupied by a large mirror and we look into it without realizing that it is a mirror. We then perceive, in the part of space beyond it, various material objects, notwithstanding that in fact they have no existence there at all. A certain set of the vivid color images which we call visual sensations was all that was strictly given to us, and these we construed, automatically and instantaneously, but nonetheless erroneously, as signs or appearances of the existence of certain material objects at a certain place.

Again, and similarly, we perceive in our dreams various objects which at the time we take as physical but which eventually we come to believe were not so. And this eventual conclusion, let it be noted, is forced upon us not because we then detect that something, called "physical substance," was lacking in those objects, but only because we notice, as we did not at the time, that their behavior was erratic—incoherent with their ordinary one. That is, their appearance was a *mere* appearance, deceptive in the sense that it did not then predict truly, as ordinarily it does, their later appearances. This, it is important to notice, is the *only* way in which we ever discover that an object we perceive was not really physical, or was not the particular sort of physical object we judged it to be.

These two examples illustrate the fact that our perception of physical objects is sometimes erroneous. But the essential point is that, even when it is veridical instead of erroneous, *all* that is literally and directly given to our minds is still only *some set of sensations*. These, on a given occasion, may be only color sensations; but they often include also tactual sensations, sounds, odors, and so on. It is especially interesting, however, to remark here in passing that, with respect to almost all the many thousands of persons and other "physical" objects we have perceived in a life time, *vivid color images* were the only data our perceiving strictly had to go by; so that, if the truth should happen to have been that those objects, like ghosts or images in a mirror, were actually intangible—that is, were *only* color images—we should never have discovered that this was the fact. For all we *directly* know, it *may* have been the fact!

To perceive a physical object, then, instead of merely experiencing passively certain sensations (something which perhaps hardly ever occurs), is always to *interpret*, that is, to *construe*, given sensations as signs of, and appearances to us of, a postulated something other than themselves, which we believe is causing them in us and is capable of causing in us others of specific kinds. We believe this because we believe that our sensations too must have some cause, and we find none for them among our other mental states.

Such a postulated extramental something we call "a physical object." We say that we observe physical objects, and this is true. But it is important for the present purpose to be clear that we "observe" them never in any more direct or literal manner than is constituted by the process of interpretive postulation just described—never, for example, in the wholly direct and literal manner in which we are able to observe our sensations themselves and our other mental states.

That perception of a physical object is thus always the product of two factors—one, a set of sensations simply given to us, and the other an act of interpretation of these, performed by us—is something which easily escapes notice and has even been denied. This, however, is only because the interpretive act is almost always automatic, instantaneous, and correct—like, for instance, that of thinking of the meaning of any familiar word we hear. But that an interpretive act does occur is forced on our attention when, in a particular case, we discover that we misconstrued the meaning of the sensations. Or, again, the interpretive act is noticeable when, because the sensations are too scant and therefore ambiguous, we catch ourselves hesitating between two or more possible interpretations of them and say that we are not sure what object it is we see.

"OUR OWN" BODIES

To complete the sketch of the view of the universe obtained when we conceive ourselves primarily as minds rather than primarily as bodies, attention must now be directed to a particular one of the objects which, in the sense described, we perceive in the world external to our minds. This especially interesting object is the one we call "our own body"; and the question we must now ask is: How do we identify it among the thousands of human bodies we perceive? What peculiarities mark it from all others and make us call it our own?

One of them, of course, is that we never directly see certain parts of it; for instance, most of its back, or any part of its head except a certain aspect of its nose and orbital arch. This aspect, moreover, we always see when it is illuminated if we see anything at all.

But there are four other and more important peculiarities which mark a human body as our own. One is that it is the only physical object we can directly cause to move by a mere act of will. This statement, however, probably needs to be slightly qualified, since the results of the many experiments at Duke University and elsewhere have provided strong evidence of the reality of the so-called psychokinetic effect (as well as of clairvoyance).[12] These experiments appear to show that it is sometimes possible for a human volition to cause directly at least minute alterations in the behavior of physical objects other than one's own body. If so, we could then conceive a willed motion of our own body as simply a psychokinetic effect in maximum degree. It is well to remember in this connection that causation, directly by an act of will, of some alteration in the behavior of a molecule, is neither more nor less intrinsically intelligible, nor *a priori* more probable or improbable, when the molecule happens to be part of a brain than when it happens instead to be part of a physical object of some other kind, such as a piece of wood or a stone.

Another of the marks of the body we call our own is that it is the only one the stimulation of which causes directly in us sensations of the corresponding kinds. This statement, too, may turn out to need slight qualification if full confirmation should be obtained that vivid images are sometimes received by the mind *directly* from physical objects or events, that is, received without intermediary stimulation of the sense organs of one's body.

Cases of this kind would be examples of what is meant by clairvoyance as distinguished from telepathy, and if the reality of it can be regarded as firmly established, then sensation could be viewed as a special instance of clairvoyance, and the sense organs, together with the corresponding nerves and brain regions, as specialized transmitters, which, like microscopes, magnify what they transmit, but transmit at all only what occurs at relatively short distances and in circumstances of special kinds. Here, as before, we should not forget that it is neither more nor less intelligible or probable *a priori* that a color experience, for example, should have for its immediate cause a molecular event in the visual cortex of the brain, than a molecular event in some physical object other than the brain or even the body.[13]

Besides the two marks just mentioned, there are two others likewise peculiar to the body we call our own. They are less obvious to casual observation, but quite as important theoretically. And they, too, consist of unique capacities in respect to causation, but causation now of changes in the structure, instead of only the states, of conscious mind and of brain.

One of them is that the body we call our own is the only one in which certain mutilations of the brain ever directly cause specific alterations in the dispositions or capacities our mind manifests. An example would be the effects upon the mind of the brain operation called prefrontal lobotomy, mentioned earlier. It notably alters the conscious personality.

The other mark relates to causation in the converse direction: the body we call our own is the only one in which certain elaborate connections among the nerve cells in the association areas of the brain can be directly caused by a mental event—for instance, by that mental event which consists of a firm and persistent volition to acquire some particular bodily skill, such as skill to play a given musical instrument.

[12] For a summary of these experiments, see J. B. Rhine's book *The Reach of the Mind* (New York, 1947).

[13] It is interesting to note that essentially the same suggestion as that made above—that voluntary activity is a special case of psychokinesis, and sensory perception a special case of clairvoyance—was independently made and developed by R. H. Thouless and B. P. Wiesner in an article, "The Psi Processes in Normal and 'Paranormal' Psychology" (*Procs. Soc. for Psychical Research*, December 1947), where they wrote: "The hypothesis we wish to suggest is that, in normal thinking and perceiving I am in the same sort of relation to what is going on in the sensory part of my brain and nervous system as that of the successful clairvoyant to some external event, and that this relation is established by the same means," and "We suggest also that there is a similar identity of relation in normal motor control of the body on the one hand and the 'paranormal' process of psychokinesis on the other" (pp. 180–181).

These remarks have been intended to provide a perspective by virtue of which the relation of body to mind can be observed without the distortion otherwise imposed by the tacit assumption we mentioned, which is commonly made, but which has validity and relevance strictly limited to the purpose of studying and controlling the material world. That enlarged and fairer perspective, I now submit, makes clear that no paradox at all is really involved in the supposition that some forms of consciousness may exist independently of connection with animal or human bodies; and, therefore, that survival is at least theoretically possible. . . .

GILBERT RYLE

Descartes's Myth*

THE OFFICIAL DOCTRINE

There is a doctrine about the nature and place of minds which is so prevalent among theorists and even among laymen that it deserves to be described as the official theory. Most philosophers, psychologists and religious teachers subscribe, with minor reservations, to its main articles and, although they admit certain theoretical difficulties in it, they tend to assume that these can be overcome without serious modifications being made to the architecture of the theory. It will be argued here that the central principles of the doctrine are unsound and conflict with the whole body of what we know about minds when we are not speculating about them.

The official doctrine, which hails chiefly from Descartes, is something like this. With the doubtful exceptions of idiots and infants in arms every human being has both a body and a mind. Some would prefer to say that every human being is both a body and a mind. His body and his mind are ordinarily harnessed together, but after the death of the body his mind may continue to exist and function.

Human bodies are in space and are subject to the mechanical laws which govern all other bodies in space. Bodily processes and states can be inspected by external observers. So a man's bodily life is as much a public affair as are the lives of animals and reptiles and even as the careers of trees, crystals and planets.

But minds are not in space, nor are their operations subject to mechanical laws. The workings of one mind are not witnessable by other observers; its career is private. Only I can take direct cognisance of the states and processes of my own mind. A person therefore lives through two collateral histories, one consisting of what happens in and to his body, the other consisting of what happens in and to his mind. The first is public, the second private. The events in the first history are events in the physical world, those in the second are events in the mental world.

It has been disputed whether a person does or can directly monitor all or only some of the episodes of his own private history; but, according to the official doctrine, of at least some of these episodes he has direct and unchallengeable cognisance. In consciousness, self-consciousness and introspection he is directly and authentically apprised of the present states and operations of his mind. He may have great or small uncertainties about concurrent and adjacent episodes in the physical world, but he can have none about at least part of what is momentarily occupying his mind.

It is customary to express this bifurcation of his two lives and of his two worlds by saying that the things and events which belong to the physical

* Gilbert Ryle, *The Concept of Mind* (London: The Hutchinson Publishing group; New York: Barnes and Noble, 1949), pp. 11–24. Reprinted by permission of the author and publishers.

world, including his own body, are external, while the workings of his own mind are internal. This antithesis of outer and inner is of course meant to be construed as a metaphor, since minds, not being in space, could not be described as being spatially inside anything else, or as having things going on spatially inside themselves. But relapses from this good intention are common and theorists are found speculating how stimuli, the physical sources of which are yards or miles outside a person's skin, can generate mental responses inside his skull, or how decisions framed inside his cranium can set going movements of his extremities.

Even when 'inner' and 'outer' are construed as metaphors, the problem how a person's mind and body influence one another is notoriously charged with theoretical difficulties. What the mind wills, the legs, arms and the tongue execute; what affects the ear and the eye has something to do with what the mind perceives; grimaces and smiles betray the mind's moods and bodily castigations lead, it is hoped, to moral improvement. But the actual transactions between the episodes of the private history and those of the public history remain mysterious, since by definition they can belong to neither series. They could not be reported among the happenings described in a person's autobiography of his inner life, but nor could they be reported among those described in some one else's biography of that person's overt career. They can be inspected neither by introspection nor by laboratory experiment. They are theoretical shuttlecocks which are forever being bandied from the physiologist back to the psychologist and from the psychologist back to the physiologist.

Underlying this partly metaphorical representation of the bifurcation of a person's two lives there is a seemingly more profound and philosophical assumption. It is assumed that there are two different kinds of existence or status. What exists or happens may have the status of physical existence, or it may have the status of mental existence. Somewhat as the faces of coins are either heads or tails, or somewhat as living creatures are either male or female, so, it is supposed, some existing is physical existing, other existing is mental existing. It is a necessary feature of what has physical existence that it is in space and time; it is a necessary feature of what has mental existence that it is in time but not in space. What has physical existence is composed of matter, or else is a function of matter; what has mental existence consists of consciousness, or else is a function of consciousness.

There is thus a polar opposition between mind and matter, an opposition which is often brought out as follows. Material objects are situated in a common field, known as 'space', and what happens to one body in one part of space is mechanically connected with what happens to other bodies in other parts of space. But mental happenings occur in insulated fields, known as 'minds', and there is, apart maybe from telepathy, no direct causal connection between what happens in one mind and what happens in another. Only through the medium of the public physical world can the mind of one person make a difference to the mind of another. The mind is its own place and in his inner life each of us lives the life of a ghostly Robinson Crusoe. People can see, hear and jolt one another's bodies, but they are irremediably blind and deaf to the workings of one another's minds and inoperative upon them.

What sort of knowledge can be secured of the workings of a mind? On the one side, according to the official theory, a person has direct knowledge of the best imaginable kind of the workings of his own mind. Mental states and processes are (or are normally) conscious states and processes, and the consciousness which irradiates them can engender no illusions and leaves the door open for no doubts. A person's present thinkings, feelings and willings, his perceivings, rememberings and imaginings are intrinsically 'phosphorescent'; their existence and their nature are inevitably betrayed to their owner. The inner life is a stream of consciousness of such a sort that it would be absurd to suggest that the mind whose life is that stream might be unaware of what is passing down it.

True, the evidence adduced recently by Freud seems to show that there exist channels tributary to this stream, which run hidden from their owner. People are actuated by impulses the existence of which they vigorously disavow; some of their thoughts differ from the thoughts which they acknowledge; and some of the actions which they think they will to perform they do not really will. They are thoroughly gulled by some of their own hypocrisies and they successfully ignore facts about their mental lives which on the official theory ought to be patent to them. Holders of the official theory tend, however, to maintain that anyhow in normal circumstances a person must be directly and authentically seized of the present state and workings of his own mind.

Besides being currently supplied with these alleged immediate data of consciousness, a person is also generally supposed to be able to exercise from time to time a special kind of perception, namely inner perception, or introspection. He can take a (non-optical) 'look' at what is passing in his mind. Not only can he view and scrutinize a flower through his sense of sight and listen to and discriminate the notes of a bell through his sense of hearing; he can also reflectively or introspectively watch, without any bodily organ of sense, the current episodes of his inner life. This self-observation is also commonly supposed to be immune from illusion, confusion or doubt. A mind's reports of its own affairs have a certainty superior to the best that is possessed by its reports of matters in the physical world. Sense-perceptions can, but consciousness and introspection cannot, be mistaken or confused.

On the other side, one person has no direct access of any sort to the events of the inner life of another. He cannot do better than make problematic inferences from the observed behaviour of the other person's body to the states of mind which, by analogy from his own conduct, he supposes to be signalised by that behaviour. Direct access to the workings of a mind is the privilege of that mind itself; in default of such privileged access, the workings of one mind are inevitably occult to everyone else. For the supposed arguments from bodily movements similar to their own to mental workings similar to their own would lack any possibility of observational corroboration. Not unnaturally, therefore, an adherent of the official theory finds it difficult to resist this consequence of his premisses, that he has no good reason to believe that there do exist minds other than his own. Even if he prefers to believe that to other human bodies there are harnessed minds not unlike his own, he cannot claim to be able to discover their individual characteristics, or the particular things that they undergo and do. Absolute solitude is on this showing the ineluctable destiny of the soul. Only our bodies can meet.

As a necessary corollary of this general scheme there is implicitly prescribed a special way of construing our ordinary concepts of mental powers and operations. The verbs, nouns and adjectives, with which in ordinary life we describe the wits, characters and higher-grade performances of the people with whom we have do, are required to be construed as signifying special episodes in their secret histories, or else as signifying tendencies for such episodes to occur. When someone is described as knowing, believing or guessing something, as hoping, dreading, intending or shirking something, as designing this or being amused at that, these verbs are supposed to denote the occurrence of specific modifications in his (to us) occult stream of consciousness. Only his own privileged access to this stream in direct awareness and introspection could provide authentic testimony that these mental-conduct verbs were correctly or incorrectly applied. The onlooker, be he teacher, critic, biographer or friend, can never assure himself that his comments have any vestige of truth. Yet it was just because we do in fact all know how to make such comments, make them with general correctness and correct them when they turn out to be confused or mistaken, that philosophers found it necessary to construct their theories of the nature and place of minds. Finding mental-conduct concepts being regularly and effectively used, they properly sought to fix their logical geography. But the logical geography officially recommended would entail that there could be no regular or effective use of these mental-conduct concepts in our descriptions of, and prescriptions for, other people's minds.

THE ABSURDITY OF THE OFFICIAL DOCTRINE

Such in outline is the official theory. I shall often speak of it, with deliberate abusiveness, as 'the dogma of the Ghost in the Machine'. I hope to prove that it is entirely false, and false not in detail but in principle. It is not merely an assemblage of particular mistakes. It is one big mistake and a mistake of a special kind. It is, namely, a category-mistake. It represents the facts of mental life as if they belonged to one logical type or category (or range of types or categories), when they actually belong to another. The dogma is therefore a philosopher's myth. In attempting to explode the myth I shall probably be taken to be denying well-known facts about the mental life of human beings, and my plea that I aim at doing nothing more than rectify the logic of mental-conduct concepts will probably be disallowed as mere subterfuge.

I must first indicate what is meant by the phrase 'Category-mistake'. This I do in a series of illustrations.

A foreigner visiting Oxford or Cambridge for the first time is shown a number of colleges, libraries, playing fields, museums, scientific departments and administrative offices. He then asks 'But where is the University? I have seen where the members of the Colleges live, where the Registrar works, where the scientists experiment and the rest. But I have not yet seen the University in which reside and work the members of your University.' It has then to be explained to him that the University is not another collateral institution, some ulterior counterpart to the colleges, laboratories and offices which he has seen. The University is just the way in which all that he has already seen is organized. When they are seen and when their co-ordination is understood, the University has been seen. His mistake lay in his innocent assumption that it was correct to speak of Christ Church, the Bodleian Library, the Ashmolean Museum *and* the University, to speak, that is, as if 'the University' stood for an extra member of the class of which these other units are members. He was mistakenly allocating the University to the same category as that to which the other institutions belong.

The same mistake would be made by a child witnessing the march-past of a division, who, having had pointed out to him such and such battalions, batteries, squadrons, etc., asked when the division was going to appear. He would be supposing that a division was a counterpart to the units already seen, partly similar to them and partly unlike them. He would be shown his mistake by being told that in watching the battalions, batteries and squadrons marching past he had been watching the division marching past. The march-past was not a parade of battalions, batteries, squadrons *and* a division; it was a parade of the battalions, batteries and squadrons *of* a division.

One more illustration. A foreigner watching his first game of cricket learns what are the functions of the bowlers, the batsmen, the fielders, the umpires and the scorers. He then says 'But there is no one left on the field to contribute the famous element of team-spirit. I see who does the bowling, the batting and the wicket-keeping; but I do not see whose role it is to exercise *esprit de corps*.' Once more, it would have to be explained that he was looking for the wrong type of thing. Team-spirit is not another cricketing-operation supplementary to all of the other special tasks. It is, roughly, the keenness with which each of the special tasks is performed, and performing a task keenly is not performing two tasks. Certainly exhibiting team-spirit is not the same thing as bowling or catching, but nor is it a third thing such that we can say that the bowler first bowls *and* then exhibits team-spirit or that a fielder is at a given moment *either* catching *or* displaying *esprit de corps*.

These illustrations of category-mistakes have a common feature which must be noticed. The mistakes were made by people who did not know how to wield the concepts *University, division* and *team-spirit*. Their puzzles arose from inability to use certain items in the English vocabulary.

The theoretically interesting category-mistakes are those made by people who are perfectly competent to apply concepts, at least in the situations with which they are familiar, but are still liable in their abstract thinking to allocate those concepts to logical types to which they do not belong. An instance of a mistake of this sort would be the following story. A student of politics has learned the main differences between the British, the French and the American Constitutions, and has learned also the differences and connections between the Cabinet, Parliament, the various Ministries, the Judicature and the Church of England. But he still becomes embarrassed when asked questions about the connections between the Church of England, the Home Office and the British Constitution. For while the Church and the Home Office are institutions, the British Constitution is not another institution in the same sense of that noun. So inter-institutional relations which can be asserted or denied to hold between the Church and the Home Office cannot be asserted or denied to hold between either of them and the British Constitution. 'The British Constitution' is not a term of the same logical type as 'the Home Office' and 'the Church of England'. In a partially similar way, John Doe may be a relative, a friend, an enemy or a stranger to Richard Roe; but he cannot be any of these things to the Average Taxpayer. He knows how to talk sense in certain sorts of discussions about the Average Taxpayer, but he is baffled to say why he could not come across him in the street as he can come across Richard Roe.

It is pertinent to our main subject to notice that, so long as the student of politics continues to think of the British Constitution as a counterpart to the other institutions, he will tend to describe it as a mysteriously occult institution; and so long as John Doe continues to think of the Average Taxpayer as a fellow-citizen, he will tend to think of him as an elusive insubstantial man, a ghost who is everywhere yet nowhere.

My destructive purpose is to show that a family of radical category-mistakes is the source of the double-life theory. The representation of a person as a ghost mysteriously ensconced in a machine derives from this argument. Because, as is true, a person's thinking, feeling and purposive doing cannot be described solely in the idioms of physics, chemistry and physiology, therefore they must be described in counterpart idioms. As the human body is a complex organised unit, so the human mind must be another complex organised unit, though one made of a different sort of stuff and with a different sort of structure. Or, again, as the human body, like any other parcel of matter, is a field of causes and effects, so the mind must be another field of causes and effects, though not (Heaven be praised) mechanical causes and effects.

THE ORIGIN OF THE CATEGORY-MISTAKE

One of the chief intellectual origins of what I have yet to prove to be the Cartesian category-mistake seems to be this. When Galileo showed that his methods of scientific discovery were competent to provide a mechanical theory which should cover every occupant of space, Descartes found in himself two conflicting motives. As a man of scientific genius he could not but endorse the claims of mechanics, yet as a religious and moral man he could not accept, as Hobbes accepted, the discouraging rider to those claims, namely that human nature differs only in degree of complexity from clockwork. The mental could not be just a variety of the mechanical.

He and subsequent philosophers naturally but erroneously availed themselves of the following escape-route. Since mental-conduct words are not to be construed as signifying the occurrence of mechanical processes, they must be construed as signifying the occurrence of non-mechanical processes; since mechanical laws explain movements in space as the effects of other movements in space, other laws must explain some of the non-spatial workings of minds as the effects of other non-spatial workings of minds. The difference between the human behaviours which we describe as intelligent and those which we describe as unintelligent must be a difference in their causation; so, while some movements of human tongues and limbs are the effects of mechanical causes, others must be the effects of non-mechanical causes, i.e. some issue from movements of particles of matter, others from workings of the mind.

The differences between the physical and the mental were thus represented as differences inside the common framework of the categories of 'thing', 'stuff', 'attribute', 'state', 'process', 'change', 'cause' and 'effect'. Minds are things, but different sorts of things from bodies; mental processes are causes and effects, but different sorts of causes and effects from bodily movements. And so on. Somewhat as the foreigner expected the University to be an extra edifice, rather like a college but also considerably different, so the repudiators of mechanism represented minds as extra centres of causal processes, rather like machines but also considerably different from them. Their theory was a para-mechanical hypothesis.

That this assumption was at the heart of the doctrine is shown by the fact that there was from the beginning felt to be a major theoretical difficulty in explaining how minds can influence and be influenced by bodies. How can a mental process, such as willing, cause spatial movements like the movements of the tongue? How can a physical change in the optic nerve have among its effects a mind's perception of a flash of light? This notorious crux by itself shows the logical mould into which Descartes pressed his theory of the mind. It was the self-same mould into which he and Galileo set their mechanics. Still unwittingly adhering to the grammar of mechanics, he tried to avert disaster by describing minds in what was merely an obverse vocabulary. The workings of minds had to be described by the mere negatives of the specific descriptions given to bodies; they are not in space, they are not motions, they are not modifications of matter, they are not accessible to public observation. Minds are not bits of clockwork, they are just bits of not-clockwork.

As thus represented, minds are not merely ghosts harnessed to machines, they are themselves just spectral machines. Though the human body is an engine, it is not quite an ordinary engine, since some of its workings are governed by another engine inside it—this interior governor-engine being one of a very special sort. It is invisible, inaudible and it has no size or weight. It cannot be taken to bits and the laws it obeys are not those known to ordinary engineers. Nothing is known of how it governs the bodily engine.

A second major crux points the same moral. Since, according to the doctrine, minds belong to the same category as bodies and since bodies are rigidly governed by mechanical laws, it seemed to many theorists to follow that minds must be similarly governed by rigid non-mechanical laws. The physical world is a deterministic system, so the mental world must be a deterministic system. Bodies cannot help the modifications that they undergo, so minds cannot help pursuing the careers fixed for them. *Responsibility, choice, merit* and *demerit* are therefore inapplicable concepts —unless the compromise solution is adopted of saying that the laws governing mental processes, unlike those governing physical processes, have the congenial attribute of being only rather rigid. The problem of the Freedom of the Will was the problem how to reconcile the hypothesis that minds are to be described in terms drawn from the categories of mechanics with the knowledge that higher-grade human conduct is not of a piece with the behaviour of machines.

It is an historical curiosity that it was not noticed that the entire argument was broken-backed. Theorists correctly assumed that any sane man could already recognise the differences between, say, rational and non-rational utterances or between purposive and automatic behaviour. Else there would have been nothing requiring to be salved from mechanism. Yet the explanation given presupposed that one person could in principle never recognise the difference between the rational and the irrational utterances issuing from other human bodies, since he could never get access to the postulated immaterial causes of some of their utterances. Save for the doubtful exception of himself, he could never tell the difference between a man and a Robot. It would have to be conceded, for example, that, for all that we can tell, the inner lives of persons who are classed as idiots or lunatics are as rational as those of anyone else. Perhaps only their overt behaviour is disappointing; that is to say, perhaps 'idiots' are not really idiotic, or 'lunatics' lunatic. Perhaps, too, some of those who are classed as sane are really idiots. According to the theory, external observers could never know how the overt behaviour of others is correlated with their mental powers and processes and so they could never know or even plausibly conjecture whether their applications of mental-conduct concepts to these other people were correct or incorrect. It would then be hazardous or impossible for a man to claim sanity or logical consistency even for himself, since he would be debarred from comparing his own performances with those of others. In short, our characterisations of persons and their performances as intelligent, prudent and virtuous or as stupid, hypocritical and cowardly could never have been made, so the problem of providing a special causal hypothesis to serve as the basis of such diagnoses would never have arisen. The question, 'How do persons differ from machines?' arose just because everyone already knew how to apply mental-conduct concepts before the new causal hypothesis was introduced. This causal hypothesis could not therefore be the source of the criteria used in those applications. Nor, of course, has the causal hypothesis in any degree improved our handling of those criteria. We still distinguish good from bad arithmetic, politic from impolitic conduct and fertile from infertile imaginations in the ways in which Descartes himself distinguished them before and after he speculated how the applicability of these criteria was compatible with the principle of mechanical causation.

He had mistaken the logic of his problem. Instead of asking by what criteria intelligent behaviour is actually distinguished from non-intelligent behaviour, he asked 'Given that the principle of mechanical causation does not tell us the difference, what other causal principle will tell it us?' He realised that the problem was not one of mechanics and assumed that it must therefore be one of some counterpart to mechanics. Not unnaturally psychology is often cast for just this role.

When two terms belong to the same category, it is proper to construct conjunctive propositions embodying them. Thus a purchaser may say that he bought a left-hand glove and a right-hand glove, but not that he bought a left-hand glove, a right-hand glove and a pair of gloves. 'She came home in a flood of tears and a sedan-chair' is a well-known joke based on the absurdity of conjoining terms of different types. It would have been equally ridiculous to construct the disjunction 'She came home either in a flood of tears or else in a sedan-chair'. Now the dogma of the Ghost in the Machine does just this. It maintains that there exist both bodies and minds; that there occur physical processes and mental processes; that there are mechanical causes of corporeal movements and mental causes of corporeal movements. I shall argue that these and other analogous conjunctions are absurd; but, it must be noticed, the argument will not show that either of the illegitimately conjoined propositions is absurd in itself. I am not, for example, denying that there occur mental processes. Doing long division is a mental process and so is making a joke. But I am saying that the phrase 'there occur mental processes' does not mean the same sort of thing as 'there occur physical processes', and, therefore, that it makes no sense to conjoin or disjoin the two.

If my argument is successful, there will follow some interesting consequences. First, the hallowed contrast between Mind and Matter will be dissipated, but dissipated not by either of the equally hallowed absorptions of Mind by Matter or of Matter by Mind, but in quite a different way. For the seeming contrast of the two will be shown to be as illegitimate as would be the contrast of 'she came home in a flood of tears' and 'she came home in a sedan-chair'. The belief that there is a polar opposition between Mind and Matter is the belief that they are terms of the same logical type.

It will also follow that both Idealism and Materialism are answers to an improper question. The 'reduction' of the material world to mental states and processes, as well as the 'reduction' of mental states and processes to physical states and processes, presuppose the legitimacy of the disjunction 'Either there exist minds or there exist bodies (but not both)'. It would be like saying, 'Either she bought a left-hand and a right-hand glove or she bought a pair of gloves (but not both)'.

It is perfectly proper to say, in one logical tone of voice, that there exist minds and to say, in another logical tone of voice, that there exist bodies. But these expressions do not indicate two different species of existence, for 'existence' is not a generic word like 'coloured' or 'sexed'. They indicate two different senses of 'exist', somewhat as 'rising' has different senses in 'the tide is rising', 'hopes are rising', and 'the average age of death is rising'. A man would be thought to be making a poor joke who said that three things are now rising, namely the tide, hopes and the average age of death. It would be just as good or bad a joke to say that there exist prime numbers and Wednesdays and public opinions and navies; or that there exist both minds and bodies. In the succeeding chapters I try to prove that the official theory does rest on a batch of category-mistakes by showing that logically absurd corollaries follow from it. The exhibition of these absurdities will have the constructive effect of bringing out part of the correct logic of mental-conduct concepts.

HISTORICAL NOTE

It would not be true to say that the official theory derives solely from Descartes' theories, or even from a more widespread anxiety about the implications of seventeenth century mechanism. Scholastic and Reformation theology had schooled the intellects of the scientists as well as of the laymen, philosophers and clerics of that age. Stoic-Augustinian theories of the will were embedded in the Calvinist doctrines of sin and grace; Platonic and Aristotelian theories of the intellect shaped the orthodox doctrines of the immortality of the soul. Descartes was reformulating already prevalent theological doctrines of the soul in the new syntax of Galileo. The theologian's privacy of conscience became the philosopher's privacy of consciousness, and what had been the bogy of Predestination reappeared as the bogy of Determinism.

It would also not be true to say that the two-worlds myth did no theoretical good. Myths often do a lot of thoeretical good, while they are still new. One benefit bestowed by the para-mechanical myth was that it partly superannuated the then prevalent para-political myth. Minds and their Faculties had previously been described by analogies with political superiors and political subordinates. The idioms used were those of ruling, obeying, collaborating and rebelling. They survived and still survive in many ethical and some epistemological discussions. As, in physics, the new myth of occult Forces was a scientific improvement on the old myth of Final Causes, so, in anthropological and psychological theory, the new myth of hidden operations, impulses and agencies was an improvement on the old myth of dictations, deferences and disobediences.

U. T. PLACE

Is Consciousness a Brain Process*

INTRODUCTION

The view that there exists a separate class of events, mental events, which cannot be described in terms of the concepts employed by the physical sciences no longer commands the universal and unquestioning acceptance amongst philosophers and psychologists which it once did. Modern physicalism, however, unlike the materialism of the seventeenth and eighteenth centuries, is behaviouristic. Consciousness of this view is either a special type of behaviour, "sampling" or "running-back-and-forth" behaviour as Tolman (*Purposive Behaviour in Animals and Men*, Berkeley, University of California Press, 1932, p. 206) has it, or a disposition to behave in a certain way, an itch, for example, being a temporary propensity to scratch. In the case of cognitive concepts like "knowing," "believing," "understanding," "remembering" and volitional concepts like "wanting" and "intending," there can be little doubt, I think, that an analysis in terms of dispositions to behave is fundamentally sound (See Ryles's *Concept of Mind* and Wittgenstein's *Philosophical Investigations*). On the other hand, there would seem to be an intractable residue of concepts clustering around the notions of consciousness, experience, sensation and mental imagery, where some sort of inner process story is unavoidable. It is possible, of course, that a satisfactory behaviouristic account of this conceptual residuum will ultimately be found. For our present purposes, however, I shall assume that this cannot be done and that statements about pains and twinges, about how things look, sound and feel, about things dreamed of or pictured in the mind's eye, are statements referring to events and processes which are in some sense private or internal to the individual of whom they are predicated. The question I wish to raise is whether in making this assumption we are inevitably committed to a dualist position in which sensations and mental images form a separate category of processes over and above the physical and physiological processes with which they are known to be correlated. I shall argue that an acceptance of inner processes does not entail dualism and that the thesis that consciousness is a process in the brain cannot be dismissed on logical grounds.

THE "IS" OF DEFINITION AND THE "IS" OF COMPOSITION

I want to stress from the outset that in defending the thesis that consciousness is a process in the brain, I am not trying to argue that when we describe our dreams, fantasies and sensations we are talking about processes in our brains. That is, I am not claiming that statements about sensations and mental images are reducible to or analysable into statements about brain processes, in the way in which "cognition statements" are analysable into statements about behaviour. To say that statements about consciousness are statements about brain processes is manifestly false. This is shown (*a*) by the fact that you can describe your sensations and mental imagery without knowing anything about your brain processes or even that such things exist, (*b*) by the fact that statements about one's consciousness and statements about one's brain processes are verified in entirely different ways and (*c*) by the fact that there is nothing self-contradictory about the statment "X has a pain but there is nothing

* U. T. Place, "Is Consciousness a Brain Process?" *British Journal of Psychology*, XLVII, Part I (February 1956), 44–50. Reprinted by permission of the author and the editor of the *British Journal of Psychology*.

going on in his brain." What I do want to assert, however, is that the statement, "consciousness is a process in the brain," although not necessarily true, is not necessarily false. "Consciousness is a process in the brain," in my view is neither self-contradictory nor self-evident; it is a reasonable scientific hypothesis, in the way that the statement, "lightning is a motion of electric charges," is a reasonable scientific hypothesis.

The all but universally accepted view that an assertion of identity between consciousness and brain processes can be ruled out on logical grounds alone, derives, I suspect, from a failure to distinguish between what we may call the "is" of definition and the "is" of composition. The distinction I have in mind here is the difference between the function of the word "is" in statements like, "a square is an equilateral rectangle," "red is a colour," "to understand an instruction is to be able to act appropriately under the appropriate circumstances," and its function in statements like, "his table is an old packing case," "her hat is a bundle of straw tied together with string," "a cloud is a mass of water droplets or other particles in suspension." These two types of "is" statement have one thing in common. In both cases it makes sense to add the qualification "and nothing else." In this they differ from those statements in which the "is" is an "is" of predication; the statements, "Toby is eighty years old and nothing else," "her hat is red and nothing else" or "giraffes are tall and nothing else," for example, are nonsense. This logical feature may be described by saying that in both cases both the grammatical subject and the grammatical predicate are expressions which provide an adequate characterization of the state of affairs to which they both refer.

In another respect, however, the two groups of statements are strikingly different. Statements like, "a square is an equilateral rectangle," are necessary statements which are true by definition. Statements like, "his table is an old packing case," on the other hand, are contingent statements which have to be verified by observation. In the case of statements like, "a square is an equilateral rectangle" or, "red is a colour," there is a relationship between the meaning of the expression forming the grammatical predicate and the meaning of the expression forming the grammatical subject, such that whenever the subject expression is applicable the predicate must also be applicable. If you can describe something as red then you must also be able to describe it as coloured. In the case of statements like, "his table is an old packing case," on the other hand, there is no such relationship between the meanings of the expressions "his table" and "old packing case"; it merely so happens that in this case both expressions are applicable to and at the same time provide an adequate characterization of the same object. Those who contend that the statement, "consciousness is a brain process," is logically untenable base their claim, I suspect, on the mistaken assumption that if the meanings of two statements or expressions are quite unconnected, they cannot both provide an adequate characterization of the same object or state of affairs: if something is a state of consciousness, it cannot be a brain process, since there is nothing self-contradictory in supposing that someone feels a pain when there is nothing happening inside his skull. By the same token we might be led to conclude that a table cannot be an old packing case, since there is nothing self-contradictory in supposing that someone has a table, but is not in possession of an old packing case.

THE LOGICAL INDEPENDENCE OF EXPRESSIONS AND THE ONTOLOGICAL INDEPENDENCE OF ENTITIES

There is, of course, an important difference between the table/packing-case case and the consciousness/brain-process case in that the statement, "his table is an old packing case," is a particular proposition which refers only to one particular case, whereas the statement, "consciousness is a process in the brain" is a general or universal proposition applying to all states of consciousness whatever. It is fairly clear, I think, that if we lived in a world in which all tables without exception were packing cases, the concepts of "table" and "packing case" in our language would not have their present logically independent status. In such a world a table would be a species of packing case in much the same way that red is a species of colour. It seems to be a rule of language that whenever a given variety of object or state of affairs has two characteristics or sets of characteristics, one of which is unique to the variety of object or state of affairs in question, the expression used to refer to the characteristic or set of characteristics which defines the variety of object or state of affairs in question will always entail the expression used to refer to the other characteristic or set of characteristics. If this rule admitted of no exception it would follow that any expression which is logically independent of another expression which uniquely characterizes a given variety of object or state of affairs, must refer to a characteristic or set of characteristics which is not normally or necessarily associated with the object or state of affairs in question. It is because this rule applies almost universally, I suggest, that we are normally justified in arguing from the logical independence of two expressions to the ontological independence of the states of affairs to which they refer. This would explain both the undoubted force of the argument that consciousness and brain processes must be independent entities because the expressions used to refer to them are logically independent and, in general, the curious phenomenon whereby questions about the furniture of the universe are often fought and not infrequently decided merely on a point of logic.

The argument from the logical independence of two expressions to the ontological independence of the entities to which they refer, breaks down in the case of brain processes and consciousness, I believe, because this is one of a relatively small number of cases where the rule stated above does not apply. These exceptions are to be found, I suggest, in those cases where the operations which have to be performed in order to verify the presence of the two sets of characteristics inhering in the object or state of affairs in question can seldom if ever be performed simultaneously. A good example here is the case of the cloud and the mass of droplets or other particles in suspension. A cloud is a large semi-transparent mass with a fleecy texture suspended in the atmosphere whose shape is subject to continual and kaleidoscopic change. When observed at close quarters, however, it is found to consist of a mass of tiny particles, usually water droplets, in continuous motion. On the basis of this second observation we conclude that a cloud is a mass of tiny particles and nothing else. But there is no logical connexion in our language between a cloud and a mass of tiny particles; there is nothing self-contradictory in talking about a cloud which is not composed of tiny particles in suspension. There is no contradiction involved in supposing that clouds consist of a dense mass of fibrous tissue; indeed, such a consistency seems to be implied by many of the functions performed by clouds in fairy stories and mythology. It is clear from this that the terms "cloud" and "mass of tiny particles in suspension" mean quite different things. Yet we do not conclude from this that there must be two things, the mass of particles in suspension and the cloud. The reason for this, I suggest, is that although the characteristics of being a cloud and being a mass of tiny particles in suspension are invariably associated, we never make the observations necessary to verify the statement "that is a cloud" and those necessary to verify the statement "this is a mass of tiny particles in suspension" at one and the same time. We can observe the micro-structure of a cloud only when we are enveloped by it, a condition which effectively prevents us from observing those characteristics which from a distance lead us to describe it as a cloud. Indeed, so disparate are these two experiences that we use different words to describe them. That which is a cloud when we observe it from a distance becomes a fog or mist when we are enveloped by it.

WHEN ARE TWO SETS OF OBSERVATIONS OBSERVATIONS OF THE SAME EVENT?

The example of the cloud and the mass of tiny particles in suspension was chosen because it is one of the few cases of a general proposition involving what I have called the "is" of composition which does not involve us in scientific technicalities. It is useful because it brings out the connexion between the ordinary everyday cases of the "is" of composition like the table/packing case example and the more technical cases, like "lightning is a motion of electric charges," where the analogy with the consciousness/brain process case is most marked. The limitation of the cloud/tiny particles in suspension case is that it does not bring out sufficiently clearly the crucial problem of how the identity of the states of affairs referred to by the two expressions is established. In the cloud case the fact that something is a cloud and the fact that something is a mass of tiny particles in suspension are both verified by the normal processes of visual observation. It is arguable, moreover, that the identity of the entities referred to by the two expressions is established by the continuity between the two sets of observations as the observer moves towards or away from the cloud. In the case of brain processes and consciousness there is no such continuity between the two sets of observations involved. A closer introspective scrutiny will never reveal the passage of nerve impulses over a thousand synapses in the way that a closer scrutiny of a cloud will reveal a mass of tiny particles in suspension. The operations required to verify statements about consciousness and statements about brain processes are fundamentally different.

To find a parallel for this feature we must examine other cases where an identity is asserted between something whose occurrence is verified by the ordinary processes of observation and something whose occurrence is established by special scientific procedures. For this purpose I have chosen the case where we say that lightning is a motion of electric charges. As in the case of consciousness, however closely we scrutinize the lightning we shall never be able to observe the electric charges, and just as the operations for determining the nature of one's state of consciousness are radically different from those involved in determining the nature of one's brain processes, so the operations for determining the occurrence of lightning are radically different from those involved in determining the occurrence of a motion of electric charges. What is it, therefore, that leads us to say that the two sets of observations are observations of the same event? It cannot be merely the fact that the two sets of observations are systematically correlated such that whenever there is lightning there is always a motion of electric charges. There are innumerable cases of such correlations where we have no temptation to say that the two sets of observations are observations of the same event. There is a systematic correlation, for example, between the movement of the tides and the stages of the moon, but this does not lead us to say that records of tidal levels are records of the moon's stages or vice versa. We speak rather of a causal connexion between two independent events or processes.

The answer here seems to be that we treat the two sets of observations as observations of the same event, in those cases where the technical scientific observations set in the context of the appropriate body of scientific theory provide an immediate explanation of the observations made by the man in the street. Thus we conclude that lightning is nothing more than a motion of electric charges, because we know that a motion of electric charges through the atmosphere, such as occurs when lightning is reported, gives rise to the type of visual stimulation which would lead an observer to report a flash of lightning. In the moon/tide case, on the other hand, there is no such direct causal connexion between the stages of the moon and the observations made by the man who measures the height of the tide. The causal connexion is between the moon and the tides, not between the moon and the measurement of the tides.

THE PHYSIOLOGICAL EXPLANATION OF INTROSPECTION AND THE PHENOMENOLOGICAL FALLACY

If this account is correct, it should follow that in order to establish the identity of consciousness and certain processes in the brain, it would be necessary to show that the introspective observations reported by the subject can be accounted for in terms of processes which are known to have occurred in his brain. In the light of this suggestion it is extremely interesting to find that when a physiologist as distinct from a philosopher finds it difficult to see how consciousness could be a process in the brain, what worries him is not any supposed self-contradiction involved in such an assumption, but the apparent impossibility of accounting for the reports given by the subject of his conscious processes in terms of the known properties of the central nervous system. Sir Charles Sherrington has posed the problem as follows: "The chain of events stretching from the sun's radiation entering the eye to, on the one hand, the contraction of the pupillary muscles, and on the other, to the electrical disturbances in the brain-cortex are all straightforward steps in a sequence of physical 'causation,' such as, thanks to science, are intelligible. But in the second serial chain there follows on, or attends, the stage of brain-cortex reaction an event or set of events quite inexplicable to us, which both as to themselves and as to the causal tie between them and what preceded them science does not help us; a set of events seemingly incommensurable with any of the events leading up to it. The self 'sees' the sun; it senses a two-dimensional disc of brightness, located in the 'sky,' this last a field of lesser brightness, and overhead shaped as a rather flattened dome, coping the self and a hundred other visual things as well. Of hint that this is within the head there is none. Vision is saturated with this strange property called 'projection,' the unargued inference that what it sees is at a 'distance' from the seeing 'self.' Enough has been said to stress that in the sequence of events a step is reached where a physical situation in the brain leads to a psychical, which, however, contains no hint of the brain or any other bodily part. . . . The supposition has to be, it would seem, two continuous series of events, one physico-chemical, the other psychical, and at times interaction between them" (Sir Charles Sherrington in the Foreword to a new edition of *The Integrative Action of the Central Nervous System* [Cambridge University Press: Cambridge, 1947], pp. xx–xxi).

Just as the physiologist is not likely to be impressed by the philosopher's contention that there is some self-contradiction involved in supposing consciousness to be a brain process, so the philosopher is unlikely to be impressed by the considerations which lead Sherrington to conclude that there are two sets of events, one physico-chemical, the other psychical. Sherrington's argument, for all its emotional appeal, depends on a fairly simple logical mistake, which is unfortunately all too frequently made by psychologists and physiologists and not infrequently in the past by the philosophers themselves. This logical mistake, which I shall refer to as the "phenomenological fallacy," is the mistake of supposing that when the subject describes his experience, when he describes how things look, sound, smell, taste or feel to him, he is describing the literal properties of objects and events on a peculiar sort of internal cinema or television screen, usually referred to in the modern psychological literature as the "phenomenal field." If we assume, for example, that when a subject reports a green after-image he is asserting the occurrence inside himself of an object which is literally green, it is clear that we have on our hands an entity for which there is no place in the world of physics. In the case of the green after-image there is no green object in the subject's environment corresponding to the description that he gives. Nor is there anything green in his brain; certainly there is nothing which could have emerged when he reported the appearance of the green after-image. Brain processes are not the sort of things to which colour concepts can be properly applied.

The phenomenological fallacy on which this argument is based depends on the mistaken assumption that because our ability to describe things in our environment depends on our consciousness of them, our descriptions of things are primarily descriptions of our conscious experience and only secondarily, indirectly and inferentially descriptions of the objects and events in our environments. It is assumed that because we recognize things in our environment by their look, sound, smell, taste and feel, we begin by describing their phenomenal properties, i.e., the properties of the looks, sounds, smells, tastes and feels which they produce in us, and infer their real properties from their phenomenal properties. In fact, the reverse is the case. We begin by learning to recognize the real properties of things in our environment. We learn to recognize them, of course, by their look, sound, smell, taste and feel; but this does not mean that we have to learn to describe the look, sound, smell, taste and feel of things before we can describe the things themselves. Indeed, it is only after we have learnt to describe the things in our environment that we can learn to describe our consciousness of them. We describe our conscious experience not in terms of the mythological "phenomenal properties" which are supposed to inhere in the mythological "objects" in the mythological "phenomenal field," but by reference to the actual physical properties of the concrete physical objects, events and processes which normally, though not perhaps in the present instance, give rise to the sort of conscious experience which we are trying to describe. In other words when we describe the after-images as green, we are not saying that there is something, the after-image, which is green, we are saying that we are having the sort of experience which we normally have when, and which we have learnt to describe as, looking at a green patch of light.

Once we rid ourselves of the phenomenological fallacy we realize that the problem of explaining introspective observations in terms of brain processes is far from insuperable. We realize that there is nothing that the introspecting subject says about his conscious experiences which is inconsistent with anything the physiologist might want to say about the brain processes which cause him to describe the environment and his consciousness of that environment in the way he does. When the subject describes his experience by saying that a light which is in fact stationary, appears to move, all the physiologist or physiological psychologist has to do in order to explain the subject's introspective observations, is to show that the brain process which is causing the subject to describe his experience in this way, is the sort of process which normally occurs when he is observing an actual moving object and which therefore normally causes him to report the movement of an object in his environment. Once the mechanism whereby the individual describes what is going on in his environment has been worked out, all that is required to explain the individual's capacity to make introspective observations is an explanation of his ability to discriminate between those cases where his normal habits of verbal description are appropriate to the stimulus situation and those cases where they are not and an explanation of how and why, in those cases where the appropriateness of his normal descriptive habits is in doubt, he learns to issue his ordinary descriptive protocols preceded

by a qualificatory phrase like "it appears," "seems," "looks," "feels," etc.

I am greatly indebted to my fellow-participants in a series of informal discussions on this topic which took place in the Department of Philosophy, University of Adelaide, in particular to Mr. C. B. Martin for his persistent and searching criticism of my earlier attempts to defend the thesis that consciousness is a brain process, to Prof. D. A. T. Gasking, of the University of Melbourne, for clarifying many of the logical issues involved and to Prof. J. J. C. Smart for moral support and encouragement in what often seemed a lost cause.

R I C H A R D B. B R A N D T

Doubts about the Identity Theory*

I

It is useful to stipulate the meaning of *"is a particular mental (phenomenal) fact"* as follows: *"F is a particular mental fact"* is to mean the same as *"F is temporal, and something is directly aware of F."* We can add, if we like, "And it is causally impossible for more than one thing to be directly aware of *F*." The concept of direct awareness may be taken to be sufficiently familiar. An example of a mental fact is that, if I thump the table, here and now there is a thumping sound. If a particular is wholly a constituent of a mental fact, we can call it a "mental particular," or a "mental event."

The phrase I suggest we may wish to add may need to be complicated if it is true that, in the case of split personalities, we must say that there are two things, both of which are directly aware of the same fact; conceivably, evidence for telepathy may lead in the same direction. For it is not true that, as some have thought, we can show that it is *logically* impossible for two persons to be directly aware of the same fact; the most we can say is that no one can demonstrate that he is directly aware of another person's mental events, as distinct from being directly aware of a numerically different fact, similar to and causally connected with the former.

Some would object to the foregoing proposal for the reason that it implies that some things—especially the look of physical objects—must be classified as mental, although ordinary language does not so classify them. Ordinary language calls "mental" only facts or things which we naturally regard as experiences or states or activities of ourselves—such events as thinking, remembering, noticing, attending, having an emotion, and being in pain. But the look of a tree would never be so-classified by ordinary language. Hence our definition is at best far too broad.

There is an adequate rejoinder to this objection. To begin, the expression "is a mental fact" is hardly a term of ordinary language, so we do not mislead if, for purposes of philosophy, we stipulate a meaning for it in any way that is

* From *Dimensions of Mind,* ed. Sidney Hook (New York: New York University Press, 1960). Reprinted by permission of the author and publisher.

useful. Further, there are good reasons for classifying things like the look of trees along with remembering, etc., as our definition proposes to do. For the look of trees is part of the subject-matter of the psychological theory of perception, not of the science of physics. It obeys certain psychological laws, such as size-constancy, and color-constancy. Moreover, the look of a tree is conditioned by the brain state of the observer, and is structured by his past experience; very probably nothing at all like it occurs except when a complex nervous system is present. So, although doubtless there are some reasons for refusing to classify the look of a tree with remembering, there are many reasons for doing so.

II

Let us now consider the things which qualify as mental facts or particulars. Among them are color patches, sounds, pains, thoughts, stabs of anxiety, memory images, and daydreams. We should notice, however, that it need not follow logically from the fact that something is a color patch, sound, pain, etc., that it is a mental fact in the above sense. We are apt to think of these kinds of things as "phenomenal qualities" and to speak of words which describe them as "phenomenal language." This way of thinking, however, is apt to be misleading. What is true is that we learn the use of such terms through being directly aware of what they designate, and we use them mostly to talk about situations of which at least someone is directly aware. But there is no formal contradiction in saying that there is a sound, or a pain, etc., which is not a mental event—is not observed by anybody—although, perhaps, in *some* sense it is meaningless to talk of such, since we know how to confirm the occurrence of such things only as they occur in the experience of persons. Philosophers who have supposed that colors are in inanimate nature, and that it is only an external relation for them sometimes to be objects of awareness, were not contradicting themselves although doubtless they had only aesthetic preference as a reason for what they said.

III

Some philosophers have held that mental facts or particulars are *identical* with physical facts or particulars. What might this mean?

One thing that might be meant is this: Suppose we had a description of some of these things, a true and complete description—perhaps, for instance, "There is a stabbing pain," or "There is a pinkish image in the center of this visual field"; suppose also we had the vocabulary of physics and chemistry—all the terms which are needed for giving a complete description of the inanimate world (presumably this vocabulary would consist of the basic terms of physics and chemistry, words like "velocity," "mass," "energy," "ion," "electron," and so forth); we might then hold that any description of a mental fact could be put in the vocabulary of physics and chemistry, in sentences *synonymous* with our "mental language" description. The claim that this is so may be called the logical-identity theory.

It would be agreed, I think, that the logical-identity theory is false. Given belief in Ps, a person who understood the language might doubt whether Ph; certainly he would not be contradicting himself if he asserted that Ps and denied Ph. One way of showing this is to point out that a blind man might well understand "Ph" but fail to understand "Ps" if "Ps" happened to be about visual facts; and it would not be merely that he could not be taught the meaning of "Ps" by ostensive means. He obviously would lack the *concept*, the *proposition*, which would not be the case if "Ph" were really synonymous with "Ps."

IV

Sophisticated contemporary advocates of an identity theory, such as Professor Feigl and Professor Köhler, do not support the logical-identity theory. In order to understand what they do advocate, let us first formulate what we may call the correspondence hypothesis. This hypothesis is the view that for every distinguishable class of mental fact or event, there is a distinct set (perhaps with only one member, if nature is simple) of types of brain state, such that if, and only if, there is a brain event of this set, there will be an associated mental fact of the corresponding kind. In other words, the occurrence of some one of a set of distinct types of brain state is a necessary and sufficient condition for a certain kind of associated mental fact. There are, of course, brain states which have no corresponding mental facts, e.g., those of a person who is sound asleep, or many microscopic events in the brain of a waking man (e.g., the pulsations in the blood vessels in the brain have no representation in experience).

A consequence of this view is that in a sense there can be a physiological explanation of every mental event, provided brain states are instances of deterministic laws. That is, on this view brain states must be predictable on the basis of information only about their physical antecedents, and, given the predicted brain state, one can always predict the corresponding mental event by looking up, in a telephone-book-like directory, the kind of mental state which corresponds to the predicted type of brain state. One might question whether, on this theory, it "must" be that brain states can be predicted on the basis of information about physical antecedents only, given merely that they are instances of "deterministic laws." Thus, the interactionist theory might be proposed as an alternative, that we must have information about some prior mental events in order to predict the occurrence of at least some brain states—so that, while brain states may be instances of deterministic laws, they are not instances of purely physical laws. But this suggestion would be mistaken. For, according to the correspondence hypothesis, since some one physical state or disjunctive set of physical states always corresponds to a mental state, causal laws always *can* be formulated so that their antecedents refer only to brain states, and information about mental states is in principle unnecessary.

Do identity-theorists adopt the correspondence hypothesis? In a sense they do, except that they do not construe the hypothesis so as to imply that the facts or events which correspond are numerically different from one another. They hold that correspondence is the case because the corresponding entities are really identical. Note, incidentally, that they could not hold that some type of brain event is merely the *sufficient* condition of any given type of mental fact or event. For they hold that mental facts are identical with distinct and circumscribed facts about the brain, whereas one can include anything one wishes in the *sufficient* conditions of something. (If *B* is a sufficient condition of *A*, then *B* and *C*, where *C* is anything you please, is also a sufficient condition of *A*.)

V

The identity theory goes beyond the correspondence theory in asserting that every mental event is *identical* with some physical event, or more particularly, with some brain state. For instance, it holds that the fact that there is a stabbing pain now in A's experience is the *very same fact* as the fact that there is (let us suppose) an S-excitation in his thalamus (the corresponding physical fact). It holds that, although "is a stabbing pain" and "is an S-excitation in the thalamus" do not *mean the same*, nevertheless it so happens that they refer to the same thing. It is very like the fact that "This is garnet-colored" asserts the same fact as "This has the color of transparent almandite" although the two sentences do not *mean* the same. The same universal is named by the expression "garnet-colored" and identified by the description "the color of transparent almandite," and both statements say that something is an instance of that universal. The identity of reference, however, is an empirical fact which one must ascertain by observing transparent almandite. Similarly, "stabbing pain" and "S-excitation in the thalamus" refer to the same thing. There are, of course, differences between the two cases. There are simple tests which establish conclusively that a given object is transparent almandite) and direct inspection assures us that a sample of this stone has the color we designate by "garnet"—and that the same is true of all observed examples. On the other hand, we have at most only probabilistic observation indicators of an S-excitation in the thalamus, and we cannot inspect either our pain and note that it is an S-excitation in the thalamus, or our thalamus and note that some state of it is a stabbing pain.

Suppose a person, with these differences in view, tried to collect his thoughts about whether "There is a stabbing pain" and "There is an S-excitation in the thalamus" do refer to one and the same fact. What might he say? Let us suppose he means by "x is identical with y" that there is no property which x has which y has not, and vice versa; and let us suppose that he uses this expression in the same way, whether he is talking of individual things, or universal, or facts.

VI

Let us list some grounds for doubt.

(A) It is logically possible that interactionism is true—that we in principle need information about prior mental states in order to predict either brain states or mental states. If this is the case, the correspondence hypothesis, as we have seen, is false; and if the correspondence hypothesis is false, then *a fortiori* the identity theory is false. Now there is nothing absurd about interactionism in this sense, nor has it been shown to be mistaken.

(B) The identity theory is a stronger theory than the correspondence hypothesis. There is no empirical evidence for it beyond the evidence for the correspondence hypothesis. Unless there are other advantages in the identity theory, we are in a better-entrenched position to support the correspondence theory and leave open questions of identity, refraining from commitment.

(C) The correspondence hypothesis, we saw, in theory makes mental events predictable, and in this sense explainable, by physical laws. That is, according to it brain states are predictable by physical laws, and since it is (*ex hypothesi*) a fact that certain physical states are correlated with the occurrence of certain mental states, the prediction of the brain state will also make possible the prediction of the correlated mental state. The apparatus for the prediction of mental states will then include (a) laws for predicting brain states, and (b) correlation laws, perhaps rather like a telephone book and quite unlike equations, connecting specific kinds of brain state with specific kinds of mental state.

What difference would it make if we adopted the identity theory? Only that in the correlation laws we should remove the signs of material equivalence (≡) and replace them by identity signs (=). There is no further theoretical gain. It is not as if the identity theory permitted compressing many correlation laws into one general law—as Newton's theory made possible for the description of motion—as compared with the correspondence hypothesis. If physical brain-theory enables us to predict that at a certain time a person's brain state will be Ph, then, despite the identity theory, we must still consult our good old correlation rules to find out what the corresponding psychological state will be.

The theoretical gain in the identity theory, then, is trivial.

This conclusion may be disputed. It may be urged that the identity theory allows us to substitute, for the idea that a stabbing pain and an S-excitation of the thalamus are different but causally related, the much simpler idea that there is only one thing described or known in two ways. As a result, it may be suggested we can simplify our ontology, not only with respect to the number of different kinds of fact, but with respect to the number of laws of nature (since laws causally connecting these different things are no longer required).

But where is the simplification in ontology? There are still all the distinct types of property mentioned in books on physics and chemistry. Moreover, there are still things like pains, colors, sounds, smells, etc., they are what they are and cannot be made to disappear by any alchemy. The only simplification is the disappearance, as a property distinct from a stabbing pain, of the property of being an S-excitation of the thalamus (and so on for the particular physical properties correlated with other brain states). This is a very doubtful boon. Nor do any laws disappear. The physical laws which predict an S-excitation of the thalamus presumably are general laws needed elsewhere in physics or chemistry. Nor do we dispense with the correlation laws, for wherever previously we moved from some state K to an S-excitation of the thalamus and from there via a correlation law to a stabbing pain, now we must move from state K directly to a stabbing pain, and this law will be irreducible. One might suggest that at least we no longer have two widely separated kinds of substance on our hands, a mental and a physical. We need not dispute this, but we still have electrons and velocity and spatial position and mass and colors and smells and pains and emotions. There is nothing missing from the new list of kinds of thing that was present on the old list, unless it be the transcendental ego, but the transcendental ego is not an entity currently in dispute.

(D) What would it *mean* to say that the reference or designation of "is a stabbing pain" and "is an S-excitation in the thalamus" are one and the same? We may suppose there is no difficulty about the fact referred to by "is a stabbing pain"; we know how to pick out, in our own experience, just the fact that would fit this description, and to distinguish it from other facts of experience. But "is an S-excitation in the thalamus" is a theoretical term in science which is partly an *uninterpreted* term. It has no explicit definition in terms of observables. It gains whatever meaning it has from the fact that there are commitments in asserting that something has this property, because of the theoretical postulates of our system of science, and because of the "dictionary rules" which connect some of the predicates of our theoretical system with observation predicates. But while use of this theoretical predicate commits us in various directions, it is not explicitly definable in terms of these commitments (see C. G. Hempel, "The Theoretician's Dilemma," *Univ. of Minnesota Studies in the Philosophy of Science,* II [1958], 84–85). In what sense, then, may we say that some fact in nature is designated or referred to by a partly uninterpreted predicate? And is there then a clear sense in which we can say that this uninterpreted term, and the observation predicate "is a stabbing pain" have the same reference?

(E) It may be argued that the foregoing objection carries purism to an extreme; the same argument, it may be said, would prove that the scientist ought never to identify a given temperature of a gas with a given mean kinetic energy of its constituent particles, that the scientist should never identify magnetism with certain micro-structures and processes involving electron spins, and that the scientist should not say that the disease of general paresis, formerly defined by certain symptoms, is the very same disease as that now identified by the presence of spirochetes. If the foregoing objection were correct, it may be said, science should in each case content itself with asserting a correlation. But in fact it has felt free to do more, to say that temperature really *is* just mean kinetic energy of molecules, and so on.

Is the parallel exact? Let us consider the parallel with temperature, even though there is some reason for rejecting the identification of temperature with mean kinetic molecular energy.

It is important to note that there is excellent reason for regarding all molar physical objects as aggregates of micro-objects, evidence all the way from observations of Brownian motion to the subtlest triumphs of atomic theory. We have reason, therefore, to suppose in advance that temperature is identical with some fact about molecular atomic behavior. Moreover, it can be successfully construed in this way. There is a micro-theory of the behavior of mercury in thermometers; there is a micro-theory of heat-conduction. The whole theoretical structure fits together to give a coherent account of heat-phenomena of great generality and fine predictive force. Moreover, it does not make sense to say there is merely a *correlation* of molar physical facts and this molecular theory. What it is for there to be a thermometer, according to the theory, is for there to be a certain structure of particles; there is no place in the world for two thermometers, the micro-thermometer and the macro-thermometer. The atomic theory is all-encompassing in the physical world; it leaves no room for micro-objects *and* correlated macro-objects; the whole point is that a macro-object is a complex micro-structure and nothing more. There *is,* of course, room for the *perception* of these objects, and that is a very different story.

There is not similar compulsion to identify stabbing pains with states of the brain. There is not even necessity to locate them in the brain at all: one can adopt conventions about location of mental events which have this result, or one can decide to say that an event is where its necessary and sufficient conditions are, but in either case there is not forceful *evidence* which supports the principle. Even if one does decide to locate them in the brain, it is possible to hold that the brain-volume contains *both* physical events *and* these other events, and to deny that they are one and the same thing. (One might say they are aspects of something else, a fundamental substance, but to say this is only to introduce more mysteries.) Moreover, in the case of stabbing pains, it is not possible to hold that the micro-picture is the real picture, that perceptual appearances are only a coarse duplication, for in this case we are dealing with the perceptual appearances themselves, which cannot very well be a coarse duplicate of themselves.

Furthermore, it seems likely that mental events have properties that are discrepant with the properties of the correlated physical processes, and hence cannot be the same. Suppose I am looking at the sky, and all I see is a homogeneous blue expanse. The identity theory, however, tells me that this homogeneous blue expanse is the very same fact as a vast pattern of electrical discharges between tiny wires, three dimensional in character, and perhaps occupying an ellipsoidal volume of the brain. Can this identification be accepted? Of course, one can hope to pick out a corresponding brain feature which has not got properties discrepant with those of the corresponding mental event. But one cannot go forever on hopes.

PART 4 DETERMINISM,

Determinism is the theory that all events, including human actions and choices, are, without exception, totally determined. What does it mean to say that an event is "totally determined"? To this question various answers have been given, which for our present purposes we can take to be roughly equivalent. To say that a past event, E, was totally determined, is to say:

(1) E was completely caused.

(2) There were antecedent sufficient conditions for E; that is, conditions such that given their occurrence E *had to* occur.

(3) It was causally necessary that E occur.

(4) Given what preceded it, it was inevitable that E take place.

(5) E is subsumable under a universal law of nature; that is, the occurrence of E was deducible from a description of the conditions that obtained before its occurrence and certain universal laws.

(6) The occurrence of E is subject in principle to scientific explanation.

(7) The occurrence of E was in principle predictable.

(8) There are circumstances and laws which, if they had been known, would have made it possible for one to predict the occurrence and exact nature of E.

Indeterminism can be defined as the logical contradictory of determinism; namely, the theory that some events are not determined. Most (but by no means all) of those who have espoused indeterminism have held that the events that are not determined are human actions.

There are a number of common-sense considerations that should at least incline a reflective person toward determinism. Many of these are stated with unsurpassed force and clarity in David Hume's "Liberty and Necessity," included here. Common sense, however, is not all of one mind about determinism, for it clearly recognizes that sometimes human beings do things "of their own free will"; that is, in circumstances when they might very well have done something else instead. Yet this indisputable common-

FREEDOM, AND RESPONSIBILITY

sense truth seems hard to reconcile with determinism, which seems to imply that every event that occurs is the only one that could have occurred in the circumstances. This in turn seems to imply that no matter what I did a moment ago, I *could not have done otherwise*—which, in turn, seems to say that I *had* to do what I did, that I was not a free agent. Moreover, my ability to do otherwise, most of us would agree, is a necessary condition of praise or blame, reward or punishment—in short, for my *being responsible.* Therefore, if determinism cannot be reconciled with the ability to do otherwise, it follows that it cannot be reconciled with moral responsibility either. But we do hold people responsible for what they do (indeed, some say we *must* hold people responsible); therefore (some have argued), so much the worse for determinism. Such is the common-sense case against determinism.

Common sense, however, is no more pleased with indeterminism. We do generally expect that there is an answer to be discovered to any query of the form "Why did this happen rather than some other thing?" and the reply "It just happened, that's all" inevitably leaves us unsatisfied. If we drop a stone and, to our astonishment, it rises straight up in the air instead of falling, we won't rest content with the "explanation" that "it was just one of those things—a totally random chance occurrence without rhyme or reason." Nor are we likely to accept "chance" as an account of how human actions come about, for not only does that seem to make them all arbitrary and unintelligible; it also seems to destroy the intimate bond between a person and his actions that is required by judgments of moral responsibility. Yet just insofar as a person's action was uncaused, just so far does it seem to have occurred "without rhyme or reason," as a "matter of pure chance." In the words of one determinist: "In proportion as an act of volition starts of itself without cause it is exactly, so far as the freedom of the individual is concerned, as if it had been thrown into his mind from without—'suggested to him by a freakish demon.' "[1]

[1] R. E. Hobart, "Free-Will as Involving Determinism and Inconceivable without It," *Mind,* 43, 1934.

Common sense thus is tied up in knots. It looks with little favor either on determinism or indeterminism in respect to human actions. Yet since these two theories are defined as logical contradictories, one of them *must* be true. The plight of common sense thus takes the form of a *dilemma;* that is, an argument of the form

1. If P is true, then Q is true;
2. If not-P is true, then Q is true;
3. Either P is true or not-P is true;
4. Therefore, Q is true (where Q is something repugnant or antecedently unacceptable).

The dilemma of determinism can be stated thus:

1. If determinism is true, we can never do other than we do; hence, we are never responsible for what we do.
2. If indeterminism is true, then some events—namely all human actions—are random, hence not free; hence, we are never responsible for what we do.
3. Either determinism is true or else indeterminism is true.
4. Therefore, we are never responsible for what we do.

There are several ways we might try to escape being gored by the "horns of the dilemma," but one way is *not* open to us. We may not deny the third premise; for, given our definitions of "determinism" and "indeterminism," it amounts simply to the statement that either determinism is true or else it is not—surely an innocuous claim! We are, in short, not able in this case to get "between the horns of the dilemma" by denying its disjunctive premise.

We are thus left with three possibilities. We can deny the first premise and hold that determinism is, after all, perfectly compatible with free will and responsibility; or we can deny the second premise and hold that an act can be both free and intelligible, and hence responsible, though it was not traceable to determining causes outside the actor himself; or finally we can accept the entire argument just as it stands and argue on independent grounds that its conclusion is not so "repugnant" nor so "antecedently unacceptable" as it seems on first appearance. (Actually, the third kind of approach is more often taken by determinists who accept the first premise and therefore the conclusion than by indeterminists who accept the second premise and therefore the conclusion.)

The first way of attempting to resolve the dilemma is often called "soft determinism"; but that label is unfortunate, bringing with it pejorative associations of "tender mindedness." Perhaps "reconciling determinism" would be a better name, for this theory is, after all, the conjunction of two theses: (1) that determinism is true, and (2) that determinism is compatible with free will and responsibility. Reconciling determinism was the view of Thomas Hobbes, John Locke, and John Stuart Mill, and is represented here by the selections from David Hume and the contemporary English philosopher A. J. Ayer (also in Part Five by the selection from the contemporary American philosopher Charles L. Stevenson). Common to all these philosophers is the view that the key phrase "he could have done otherwise" is properly understood as hypothetical, meaning roughly "he would have done otherwise *if* he had so chosen (intended, wished)." In this hypothetical sense, I could have done otherwise than I did, even if determinism is true. I just wrote the word "true," but *if* I had chosen to write another word (say "right") instead, I would have done so (providing nobody had intervened with a gun or knife to prevent me), and this is true even though I was determined to choose to write "true." In short, if I can do what I choose, I am free, according to this theory, in the only sense of "free" used in ordinary parlance and in ascriptions of responsibility, and it matters not whether my choice itself was causally determined.

Reconciling determinists often take great pains to distinguish the determinism they espouse from a theory called *Fatalism,* which they reject. To say of an event that it was fated to happen is to say more than that it was causally determined. It is to say that it would have happened no matter what the person involved might have done to avoid it. In this sense all of us are fated to die (at some time or other); but only a fatalist would say that a person is fated from birth to die at a definite place and at a definite time. A determinist would admit that it was determined that Abraham Lincoln die in Washington in 1865; but to say that it was *fated* that he so die is to imply, among other things, that even had Lincoln tried to shoot himself in Springfield, Illinois, in 1850, or even had he not gone to the theater on the fatal night, somehow he would have met the same fate he in fact met, in Washington, D.C., in 1865. That *all* events are so fated is a doctrine with strange mystic overtones, and has rarely been defended by philosophers.[2]

The second way of attempting to resolve the dilemma is to deny that an uncaused act would be a random event "without rhyme or reason." This approach, discussed in the BBC symposium included here, is found in the writings of Aristotle and the Scottish philosopher Thomas Reid (1710–1796), among others, and is represented in one form here by the selection from the contemporary Scottish philosopher C. A. Campbell. Proponents of this view, often called *Libertarianism,* remind us that human actions, unlike other events in nature, are subject to a special kind of explanation in terms of the actor's *reasons* for acting. An uncaused action, done deliberately for some reason, would be a perfectly intelligible one, and adequately explained by an account of its reasons, on this view. The libertarian denies both theses of the reconciling determinist; and the article of Campbell's must be understood to be, in large part, a reply to views like those of Hume and Ayer.

The compatibility of free will and determinism is also denied by those who respond to the dilemma in the third way. The non-reconciling determinists (sometimes called "hard determinists"), however, instead of abandoning determinism as the libertarians do, jettison free will and moral responsibility instead, thus embracing the conclusion of the dilemma, instead of trying to avoid it. Non-reconciling determinism was the view of Spinoza and Arthur Schopenhauer, among others, and is represented here by the selection from John Hospers.

The brief essay by Roderick M. Chisholm puts the logical form of our problem into clearer focus. Chisholm's terse statement of the shortcomings of all the attempted solutions also serves to indicate the difficulty of this problem, which, of all the venerable riddles of philosophy, is perhaps the one that has the most immediate practical urgency.

[2] One outstanding exception to this generalization is Richard Taylor. See his *Metaphysics* (Englewood Cliffs, N.J.: Prentice-Hall, Inc., 1963), Chapter 5.

GEOFFREY J. WARNOCK, PETER F. STRAWSON, AND JAMES F. THOMSON

Determinism*

Geoffrey J. Warnock. 'Determinism' has meant so many different things to different people that perhaps it will be better to avoid asking straight out what it is. We should only find ourselves with a long list of not very clear theses. A list of that sort would be an interesting place to start a discussion from, but compiling the list and explaining the items would leave us no time for discussion of it. So I suggest we ask instead: How do people become determinists? What motives or reasons draw them in this direction?

J. F. Thomson. Isn't it often that determinism of some kind seems to be enjoined by a scientific way of looking at human beings? Suppose you are an experimental psychologist. Then you may very well say: 'For my purposes, a human being is just something with an input and an output. And I am interested in discovering what correlations hold between input and output. Now the output at a given moment doesn't depend simply on the input then or immediately preceding. This is a fact of everyday observation. So I suppose that it depends on, at most, the input then and the state of the organism; the latter depending on, at most, past inputs, past outputs, and perhaps innate factors. But this means that the organism's output—what you call the man's behaviour, how he responds to a situation—is completely determined by (*a*) what happens to him and (*b*) how he is.'

* From *Freedom and the Will,* ed. D. F. Pears (London: Macmillan; New York: St. Martin's Press, 1963), pp. 48–68. Reprinted by permission of the publishers.

P. F. Strawson. And this picture completely leaves out and ignores choice.

J. F. T. It leaves it out. It doesn't deny it.

P. F. S. But you, quite naturally, made your experimentalist say: 'For my purposes.' This is surely important. If he had said: 'A human being is just something with an input and an output, that would have been a statement, a thesis, but it would almost certainly turn out to be either blatantly false or quite trivially true, because true by definition. But your experimentalist, I think, isn't asserting a thesis or not one about his subject-matter. He is saying that it is convenient to start off with a certain kind of model. He wants, for his own professional purposes, to regard human beings and their behavior in a certain light. He certainly needn't say that this is the only way of regarding them; and obviously it isn't.

J. F. T. Yes, I think that is quite right. What I described could be called an engineer's way of looking at human beings.

G. J. W. But now doesn't this mean that the kind of 'determinism' you hinted at isn't a philosophical thesis either?

J. F. T. Well, I agree that if it is one, then it's very difficult to see just what thesis it is or what would count as a refutation of it. Our imaginary psychologist says that what the organism does at any given moment is uniquely determined by the situation it is in—or, perhaps, by how it 'sees' that situation, and also by the state of the organism. It seems that 'determined' here has something like its mathematical meaning, as when we say that the volume of a sphere is uniquely determined by its radius. The volume is a function of the radius—a function of just one variable. So we should ask, just what are the variables on which the behaviour is held to depend? Since these aren't in fact specified, there isn't really a determinate thesis to discuss. It isn't enough to say that how a man behaves depends on something; you have to be able to say on what it depends.

G. J. W. And if the psychologist were actually to list some measurable quantities and then say that behaviour is some function of these and these alone, what he says might well be wrong—I mean untrue in a quite straightforward way.

P. F. S. Exactly. Whereas if he doesn't, if what the relevant variables are is left completely open, they might be anything—for example, they might for all that has been said, include variables connected somehow with acts of choice.

J. F. T. So it now seems that this kind of determinism is either not a thesis at all, or is a thesis so vague and ill-defined as not to be really discussable. Perhaps we should say that it is the form of a thesis.

P. F. S. Yes, but all the same you were right in implying that it must have seemed much more than this to many people. And we shan't have answered Warnock's original questions until we have seen why.

G. J. W. Yes, there is still the question why some form of determinism is so often taken for granted.

J. F. T. Well, I suppose that we are inclined to extrapolate from particular examples of success in explaining and predicting human behaviour.

G. J. W. How do you mean? I might explain your behaviour to a friend in a quite satisfactory way simply by telling him what your own acknowledged reasons were for acting in the way you did. Or again, I might succeed in telling him correctly what your future course of action was going to be, simply by quoting your own statement of your intentions. These would be, wouldn't they, 'particular examples of success in explanation and prediction of human behaviour.' But it's hard to see how any amount of 'extrapolation' from such examples as these could lead one to determinism.

P. F. S. Would you really say that you were 'predicting' Thomson's behaviour when you merely reproduced his own statement of his intentions?

G. J. W. I don't see why not. I shouldn't

merely be passing his statement on. I should be committing myself to the belief that he would actually do what he said he would do. In any case, even if the word 'prediction' isn't quite right for this kind of case, the word 'explanation' seems perfectly satisfactory for the other kind.

J. F. T. But it wasn't either of these kinds of case that I had in mind. It seems, on the face of it, that there are two quite different and contrasting ways in which human actions can be explained; and similarly two quite different and contrasting ways in which we can come to hold beliefs about what men's future courses of action are going to be. One of these ways in each case essentially involves going by a man's acknowledged reasons or disclosed intentions. Insincerity and unforeseen obstacles apart, these are simply accepted as explanations of what was done or as statements of what will be done. The other way of coming to hold such beliefs is sharply contrasted with this. Acknowledged reasons and declared intentions either play no part at all, or play quite a different part. They are not accepted as the answers to our questions. At the most, they are treated as additional bits of the evidence in the light of which we frame our own answers. It was explanations of this kind which I had in mind when I said what I did say about extrapolation from successes.

P. F. S. If I understand you, you're suggesting two things: first, that the thesis of determinism is simply that the whole field of human action could be covered by explanation and predictions of your second kind; and, second, that particular examples of success in this kind of explanation and prediction incline us, or some of us, to think that the thesis may be true.

J. F. T. Well, for the moment, yes.

G. J. W. I'm afraid I'm not altogether clear. Is the suggestion that, if the second kind of explanation or prediction is available, the first somehow lapses or doesn't count, or embodies an illusion? Are the two kinds of explanation opposed? If you can explain an action of mine in the second way, does this mean that my giving my reason for it is no explanation at all? If you can predict an action of mine in the second way, does this mean that I am under an illusion in thinking that I decided to do it for certain reasons, that I was carrying out such-and-such an intention in doing it?

J. F. T. Well, it certainly seems that sometimes these consequences follow. We dismiss some reasons as rationalizations. But I don't think that the determinist—my determinist—has to claim that these consequences necessarily, or even usually, follow. Won't his point simply be that, on the hypothesis in question, we should be able adequately to explain and predict human actions without, as it were, taking anything on trust from the agent?

G. J. W. If this is all his point is, it doesn't seem to me to be enough to make him a determinist. When I rely on a man's announced intentions, I don't have to be taking anything on trust from him. I may simply know that he is not a man to misrepresent his intentions, or to change his mind unless his knowledge of the circumstances changes. Quite apart from announced intentions, I might very well be able to explain a man's actions and to predict, within rough limits, what he will do in important situations, without taking anything on trust from him, simply because I know him very well. Knowing him, I know what sort of reasons weigh with him, what sort of decisions he may be expected to make. This doesn't mean that the reasons don't really weigh with him, that he doesn't really make the decisions. And since it doesn't, I see nothing determinist at all in this possibility.

P. F. S. But I don't think this possibility can be quite what Thomson had in mind, though I agree it seems to be covered by the concessive form of words he adopted. When you spoke of knowing a man well, you were thinking, and indeed you spoke, of knowing what sort of reasons weighed with him, what sort of decisions he might be expected to make. This is what we mean, or part of what we mean, by knowing a man's character. But suppose we had a different and deeper kind of knowledge. Suppose we were able to give a complete explanation, in terms of factors that didn't themselves include a man's reasons or decisions, of the fact that the reasons that weighed with a man did weigh with him. Then, in a sense, we could still admit that a man's action was explained by the reasons he gave for it; that these were his reasons. And this was the point of Thomson's concessions. But the fact that those reasons weighed with him would, by this hypothesis, be completely explained by factors of a quite different kind. And if an explanation of this second kind were available, the availability of the explanation of the first kind might seem to be a matter of smaller significance than it currently does. For we should have, as it were, two stages of explanation. There would be the question: 'Why did he act as he did?' answered by mentioning, among other things, the reasons that weighed with him. Then there would be the question: 'Why did those reasons weigh with him?' answered by mentioning only factors which were not reasons for him at all. If now we put the first question again—'Why did he act as he did?'—we might well feel that we could give a complete answer to it simply by mentioning the factors referred to in the answer to the second question, together with a description of the stimuli the man was exposed to. The sense of the word 'Why?' will have changed, of course, just because, in the answer to it, we no longer mention the man's reasons. This is not to say that he didn't have those reasons. Only now it will not seem so important that he had them.

G. J. W. That sounds more like determinism to me. But it also sounds enormously hypothetical. Is there any reason at all to suppose that one kind of explanation could be undermined in this way by the other?

P. F. S. Well, if you mean 'Could one kind of explanation ever be undermined by the other?' the answer surely is 'Yes'. Suppose that someone is, habitually, painfully shrinking and hesitant about entering a room full of strangers. We ask why. Well, his reason, the reason he gives, is just that to go into a room full of strangers frightens him; the situation just strikes him as frightening. But of course we want to know why he is frightened. Now the answer to this question, let's assume, is some fact about his early upbringing—some fact of which he may be completely unaware, so that it would not figure in the explanation given by him. Now, surely in this case, the fact about his early upbringing would quite naturally and properly be taken as the explanation of his odd behaviour; the explanation he gives, that he finds the situation frightening, would be regarded as having, by comparison, no explanatory force.

J. F. T. Yes, but I suppose the question Warnock had in mind was not whether this displacing of one type of explanation by the other ever occurs, but whether there is the slightest reason to suppose that it might occur universally, in absolutely every case.

G. J. W. Yes, that was what seemed to me enormously doubtful. And I think I can explain why. You said earlier, you remember, that probably what inclines some people to accept a general determinist thesis is a simple propensity to generalize from examples of success in explaining and predicting human behaviour. But now, if we see what kind of explanation and prediction the determinist needs, doesn't there seem to be an objection in principle to generalizing from the examples of success? You see, the sort of behaviour Strawson mentioned in his example—excessive hesitancy about entering a crowded room—is abnormal behaviour; and this is just why the example suited his book. The reason the man gives—that the situation frightens him—is quite easily undermined as the explanation of his behaviour just because normal people are not frightened in this situation; so of course we have to look for a further explanation of his abnormality. Now I strongly suspect that our successes—successes of the kind that the determinist needs—are all achieved in this field of abnormal behaviour—typically psychotic and neurotic behaviour, and some kinds of criminal and generally anti-social behaviour. But if so, to generalize on the basis of these successes would be to propound the obviously absurd thesis that all human behaviour is abnormal.

J. F. T. Neat, but unconvincing.

G. J. W. Well, what's wrong with it?

J. F. T. Well, what worries me about it is really, I think, a general point about explanation. It's broadly true, isn't it, for fairly obvious reasons, that what we tend to have an interest in explaining is abnormality, deviation from the normally expected course of events. When things go as we expect them to, we don't raise any questions—it's when something odd happens that we look round for an explanation. But of course that doesn't mean that the normal course of events can't be explained. When aeroplanes crash, we want to know why, we look for an explanation; when they don't crash no questions are asked. But of course there is a reason why aeroplanes usually stay up in the air and come down safely—that they do this depends, furthermore, on factors of exactly the same kind as those we invoke to explain why they sometimes crash. So the thesis you nearly presented as obviously ridiculous could be put in a quite sensible way—not as the thesis that all human behaviour is abnormal, but as the thesis that all human behaviour could in principle be explained in the same way as some kinds of abnormal behaviour can in fact be explained already. And that makes perfectly good sense.

P. F. S. But wait a moment. In making this general point about explanation, I think you're ignoring the special difficulty about human behaviour (as I think Warnock did too). People, unlike aeroplanes, often have reason for what they do, and often can say what their reasons are. Well, wasn't the significant feature of the example I produced, not just that this man's neurotic behaviour was abnormal (as Warnock said), but that the reason he gave for it was plainly inadequate? He is frightened, as he tells us—but by something which just isn't really frightening. It's not just that normal people aren't frightened of going into rooms full of people, but that there is no reason to be frightened. And that is why the reason he gives 'It frightens me' is regarded as having no, or insufficient, explanatory force, and is accordingly displaced by explaining how he came to be afflicted with baseless fright in this situation.

G. J. W. All right, but I don't retract my point; I amend it. The position seems to be that the reasons people give for what they do are sometimes undermined by explanations of the other kind—which explain, in fact, why they are such as to be influenced by the reasons they give—but this second kind of explanation displaces or undermines the first kind in those cases in which (and precisely because) the reasons these people give are not good or adequate reasons for behaving as they do. But if so, to erect a general determinist thesis by generalizing on the basis of these cases still looks absurd: because it seems to imply the obvious falsehood that the reasons people give for what they do are never good reasons, and never have explanatory force.

J. F. T. But no, surely this isn't what the determinist is committed to saying. (I think I can now amend the point I made before.) It's admitted, or anyway it seems to be, that sometimes, when the reasons people give for what they do are very bad or inadequate reasons, we can further explain how they came to be influenced by such reasons—and in doing this we shall normally mention factors of a quite different kind from any they do give or could give, as their reasons; for instance, facts about their early upbringing, or perhaps about their physiological make-up. Now surely the determinist is not committed to saying that the reasons people give for what they do are never good reasons; but only that whether the reasons they give are good or bad, there will always be a further explanation of the fact that those reasons weighed with them. And is there anything patently absurd in that suggestion?

P. F. S. No, I don't think it's patently absurd. But isn't it in some danger of turning out to be rather trivial? As the thesis stands, it contains too many blank cheques, so to speak, for one to be sure what it amounts to. We have to ask, surely, what kind of 'further explanation' is envisaged here. For example, if someone has, and avows, a perfectly good reason for something that he does, it is, I suppose, some sort of further explanation of his behaviour to say that he is quite an intelligent person, whose upbringing and background and present circumstances are perfectly normal and satisfactory, so that he is, in short, a rational man—the sort of man who tends to adopt good reasons as his reasons for doing things. But then two questions arise: first, it seems to me highly doubtful whether a 'further explanation' of this kind lends any support to any thesis that could aptly be called determinism—the points that add up to his being a rational man may explain his behaviour, but why should we say that they determine it? And, secondly, surely a 'further explanation' to the general effect that someone is a rational man has no tendency to undermine the explanation he himself gives of his own behaviour. Just the contrary, in fact; if the reasons he gives are good reasons, the fact that he is a rational man strengthens the view that the good reasons he gives do really explain his behaviour. So—either the 'further explanations' which the determinist claims could always be given do not (always) undermine explanations of the kind the agent himself gives in giving his reasons, or the determinist must have in mind some special sort of further explanation, something different from the kind of thing I mentioned just now.

J. F. T. Well, he won't, I think, have in mind the kind of 'further explanation' you've just mentioned. If 'being rational' comes in, it will come in because he is someone who sets himself certain ideals, prides himself on—or even makes a thing of—rationality, and then this latter fact—supposing it to be one—will be put down to parental influence or something like that. But before we ask what kind of further explanation the determinist does envisage as being available in all cases, I think we ought to retrace our steps a little and ask what we mean by one kind of reason undermining another. I think you, Warnock, had in mind that the existence of the 'outside' kind of explanation (call it a B-explanation) would typically undermine the agent's own explanation (call this an A-explanation) in cases where the reasons given by the agent were not good ones. Hence you said that determinism as a general thesis seemed to imply 'the obvious falsehood that the reasons people give for what they do are never good reasons'. But surely there is quite a different way in which the existence of a B-explanation might undermine or discredit an A-explanation; it might tend to show that the reasons given by the agent, whether adequate or inadequate, weren't really his reasons, or weren't all of them.

P. F. S. I think what you're now calling attention to isn't, or isn't only, an obscurity in the notion of undermining; it's a general difficulty about A-explanations. If we ask someone why he did something, he may reply by 'giving his reasons'—or by 'giving the reasons'. In the former case, what is in question is, roughly, whether what he did was a reasonable thing to do; he will aim to show that it was, and to do this by telling us of good reasons for doing it. And his standpoint here is that of an agent who is, or wants to be thought, reasonable and responsible. But in the second case, he is not concerned with the reasonableness of the action, but only with explaining it.

G. J. W. Is this distinction as clear as you suggest? Take 'I hit her because she was becoming hysterical'. That she was hysterical is here put forward as showing that an action was reasonable and justified. But it also explains it in a quite straightforward way.

P. F. S. But I think all that matters for our purposes is that we can distinguish two ways in which such a statement might be attacked. It might be attacked, first by denying that she was becoming hysterical, or by denying that this is the right way of handling someone who is becoming hysterical. Or, quite differently, it might be met with the suggestion that it doesn't correctly or doesn't completely state the agent's motive. For example, it might be suggested that although she was becoming hysterical and although this was the best way of handling the situation, the man in question hit her partly because he wanted to or because it gave him pleasure.

J. F. T. Exactly. And the reason I wanted to draw this distinction is that it enables us to see that determinism needn't have the absurd consequence that Warnock mentioned, that no reasons are really good reasons. The consequence that would presumably remain—that many and perhaps all of the assessments we make of our own motives, and our statements about how we came to do the things we did, are at best incomplete and partial—this consequence doesn't seem absurd, at least to me.

P. F. S. But I still don't see just how every such statement could turn out to be 'incomplete'. And this brings us back to the question I asked: what sort of further explanations does the determinist envisage being available in every case?

G. J. W. Your question is a pressing one, I think. It's now generally recognized that behind, or besides, acknowledged reasons there sometimes lie unacknowledged reasons—generally of a less reputable kind—of which the agent may not be wholly conscious or of which he may be wholly unconscious. But, first, it would seem difficult to generalize this thesis without trouble; and, second, and more important, it is hard to see that it offers even limited support to determinism. When a man is brought to acknowledge an unacknowledged reason as his, he certainly sees his action in a different light; but not as an action for which he can disclaim responsibility.

J. F. T. Perhaps the would-be determinist might look altogether elsewhere for his further explanations. What about this? All human action is ultimately a matter of physical movement, of movement of parts of the body, including, of course, the organs of speech. All such movements may be completely explained as the consequences of events within the body, of the kind studied in physiology and neurophysiology. And all these events may themselves be completely explained, in terms of physical laws, as the result of physical stimuli acting upon a body of a certain physical constitution. Is this deterministic enough for you?

G. J. W. You would agree that you describe at best a programme rather than an achievement?

J. F. T. Certainly. But not an absurd one.

P. F. S. I think you must agree too, that it's a

different sort of programme from the one you initially mentioned. Initially you spoke of finding explanations of why certain reasons weighed with a man, in the light of which we might be inclined to think of his action as wholly explained by factors which were not reasons for him. The reasons were to be first explained, then by-passed. But the new programme doesn't even mention reasons. It just envisages physical explanations of physical movements.

J. F. T. Yes. I said, I think, that the would-be determinist might look altogether elsewhere for his further explanations.

P. F. S. I think the new programme is rather a lot to take on at this stage. But my first reactions are these. First, and concessively, it seems to me pure folly for any philosopher to declare, about any scientific aim that can intelligibly be stated, that that aim is in principle unattainable for philosophical reasons. But I think that what you said wasn't simply the statement of an intelligible scientific programme. It began with the purely philosophical remark that all human action is ultimately a matter of movement of parts of the body. It is this which makes me suspicious. I agree that we might, for some purposes, describe a particular bit of human behaviour in terms of 'moving parts'. But I don't agree that such descriptions would be adequate to the concept of human action. So long as we are the sort of creatures we are, the possible availability of descriptions of particular bits of human behaviour in these terms wouldn't dispense us from the need to see and interpret human actions in terms of a quite different set of concepts. The first sort of descriptions might indeed all find a place in, or under, physical explanatory laws of the kind you envisage. But the second and indispensable sort could find no such place. They belong to a different kind of vocabulary and call for a place in a wholly different dimension of explanation.

J. F. T. But this sounds like a mere evasion. Wouldn't they just be the same events under different names? If I completely explain an event under one name, calling it a different name doesn't mean that I haven't completely explained it.

G. J. W. Isn't Strawson's point precisely that it wouldn't be simply a matter of different names for, or descriptions of, the same event? The two names, as you call them, belong to wholly different systems of classification. Unless those systems of classification exhibited a kind of correlation which we can be quite sure they won't exhibit, then however much neuro-physiology advances, no interesting thesis of determinism can be based on that advance. There may be as complete a system as you like of physical laws of movements of bodily parts; but there will still be no physical laws of human action.

J. F. T. But I'm afraid this still sounds to me like a mere evasion. You seem to me to be saying that the thesis that all movements of bodily parts might be brought under a system of physical laws is, in a sense, not interesting, for the reason that the system (if we can call it such) within which we employ the concepts of human action is, and would remain, a quite different system. Well, that can scarcely be denied. But aren't you also assuming that these systems are not just different, but also independent?

P. F. S. How do you mean?

J. F. T. Well, you seem to me to be suggesting that we now have a way of talking about, and a way of seeing, human behaviour (bringing in such ideas as those of reasons, intentions, choices, decisions and responsibility)—and that it would just make no difference to this whether or not it were also possible to explain all bodily movements completely in physical terms.

P. F. S. Well, what difference would it make?

J. F. T. I'm sure you'd really agree, anyway, that it isn't just obvious that it wouldn't make any. What about this, for instance (though I'm talking pretty vaguely here)—mightn't one say that our current way of thinking and talking about human action tacitly makes a claim (which, by most people, is tacitly conceded) to being indispensable to the explanation of what goes on in the world, so far at least as human beings are concerned in what goes on? That is, isn't it perhaps taken for granted that where human beings are involved, what goes on can neither be predicted, nor explained, without employing the notions of reasoning, choosing, deciding and the rest. But your thesis denies this, at any rate; and that's quite enough to make it far from uninteresting.

P. F. S. I really must disagree with you about this. You speak of 'what goes on, where human beings are concerned'. But what does go on? Certainly, bodily parts move. Equally certainly, people do things. The blanket expression, 'what goes on', conceals the fact that there are no effective correlations between the two vocabularies for talking about what goes on, the vocabulary of human action and the vocabulary of physical science. If, for example, every case of someone's telling a lie were an instance of one physically specifiable class of sets of physical movements (and vice versa), and every case of someone's jilting his girl friend were an instance of another such class (and vice versa), then the reign of law in the field of physical movements would mean that lying and jilting could be deterministically explained. There would, as far as lying and jilting were concerned, be physical laws of human action as well as physical laws of physical movement. But there is no question of any such correlations ever being established. And it's no good saying that every description of a type of human action must in fact be correlated with some disjunction or other of descriptions in purely physical terms. This would be a pointless piece of logic, which could never be the basis of a scientific theory of human action, and could never yield deterministic explanations of human action.

J. F. T. Well, I think I must disagree with you in turn. First, if we assume, as it were, unlimited success in physical explanation of physical movements, then it's by no means clear to me that people in general would find your point about absence of correlations an adequate defence against determinism. To many this defence will seem rather like surrender. And, second, why are you so sure that 'effective correlations', as you call them, can't be established? This sounds like a piece of dogmatism, on a matter which should be left to scientific investigation.

P. F. S. On the first point—I can't help it if people are confused. And on the second—I don't think it is a matter for scientific investigation, but for philosophical argument.

G. J. W. I'm afraid it's too late to pursue this disagreement any further. I think perhaps we ought to try to summarize what's emerged so far. We've referred to more than one type of thesis as deterministic, or possibly deterministic, and I think we ought to end by listing and distinguishing them. The thesis we've just been discussing might be labelled 'physical determinism'. This was the thesis that human behaviour, at least in so far as it consists in movements of bodily parts, might be brought under a system of purely physical laws. This was agreed to be a programme, not an achievement. But there seems to be room for disagreement as to whether even the fulfilment of the programme would establish what might be called a physical determinism of human action. Perhaps, for this, some other conditions would need to be fulfilled. And there seems to be room for disagreement about whether they could be fulfilled.

J. F. T. What we were discussing earlier, of course, was something quite different from this—it could be called psychological determinism.

G. J. W. Yes—but it's important to notice that we actually considered two possibilities, both broadly 'psychological' I suppose, but different. The first was the thesis that explanations of human behaviour in terms of the agent's own reasons could always be supplemented by explanations, in quite different terms, of the fact that those reasons weighed with him; and what we chiefly discussed here was whether, and, if so, in what sense, this kind of supplementary explanation could properly be regarded as undermining, by-passing, or somehow displacing the other kind. Then Thomson mentioned the rather different thesis that the reasons an agent gives for his action might be held to be always incomplete—that he always has further, unacknowledged, perhaps unconscious reasons (or motives). What I said about this, you remember, and I still think rightly, is that, although no doubt it is a somehow worrying thesis, it is very doubtful whether it should be called a species of determinism; and also very doubtful whether it could plausibly, or even reasonably, be put forward as true of all human behaviour.

P. F. S. But that last remark, of course, applies to any kind of determinism which is really a thesis, and not just a programme. Perhaps the clearest point of all is that no such thesis worth taking seriously is known to be true.

J. F. T. Or false.

RODERICK M. CHISHOLM

Responsibility and Avoidability*

Edwards and Hospers[1] hold that there is an important sense in which we may be said *not* to be morally responsible for any of our acts or choices. I propose the following as an explicit formulation of their reasoning:

1. If a choice is one we could not have avoided making, then it is one for which we are not morally responsible.
2. If we make a choice under conditions such that, given those conditions, it is (causally but not logically) impossible for the choice not to be made, then the choice is one we could not have avoided making.
3. Every event occurs under conditions such that, given those conditions, it is (causally but not logically) impossible for that event not to occur.
4. The making of a choice is the occurrence of an event.
5. We are not morally responsible for any of our choices.

If we wish to reject the conclusion (5)—and for most of us (5) is difficult to accept—we must reject at least one of the premises.

Premise (1), I think, may be interpreted as a logical truth. If a man is responsible for what he did, then we may say, "He *could* have done

* From *Determinism and Freedom in the Age of Modern Science,* ed. Sidney Hook (New York: New York University Press, 1960), pp. 145–147. Reprinted by permission of the author and publisher.

[1] [Paul Edwards and John Hospers each wrote articles included in the same volume as that in which this article appeared.]

otherwise." And if we may say, "He couldn't help it," then he is not responsible for what he did.

Many philosophers would deny (2), substituting a weaker account of *avoidability*. A choice is avoidable, they might say, provided only it is such that, *if* the agent had reflected further, or had reflected on certain things on which in fact he did not reflect, he would *not* have made the choice. To say of a choice that it "could *not* have been avoided," in accordance with this account, would be to say that, even if the agent *had* reflected further, on anything you like, he would all the same have made the choice. But such conditional accounts of *avoidability* ("An act or choice is avoidable provided only it is such that, *if* the agent were to do so-and-so, the act or choice would not occur") usually have this serious defect: the antecedent clause ("if the agent were to do so-and-so") refers to some act or choice, or to the failure to perform some act or to make some choice; hence we may ask, concerning the occurrence or nonoccurrence of this act or choice, whether or not *it* is avoidable. Thus one who accepted (5) could say that, if the agent's failure to reflect further was itself unavoidable, his choice was also unavoidable. And no such conditional account of *avoidability* seems adequate to the use of "avoidable" and "unavoidable" in questions and statements such as these.

If we accept a conditional account of avoidability, we may be tempted to say, of course, that it would be a *misuse* of "avoidable" to ask whether the nonoccurrence of the antecedent event ("the agent does so-and-so") is avoidable. But the philosopher who accepts (5) may well insist that, since the antecedent clause refers to an act or a choice, the use of "avoidable" in question is *not* a misuse.

What, then, if we were to deny (3)? Suppose that some of our choices do not satisfy (3)—that when they are made they are *not* made under any conditions such that it is (causally) impossible (though logically possible) for them not to be made. If there are choices of this sort, then they are merely fortuitous or capricious. And if they are merely fortuitous or capricious, if they "just happen," then, I think, we may say with Blanshard that we are *not* morally responsible for them. Hence denying (3) is not the way to avoid (5).

We seem confronted, then, with a dilemma: either our choices have sufficient causal conditions or they do not; if they do have sufficient causal conditions they are not avoidable; if they do not, they are fortuitous or capricious; and therefore, since our choices are either unavoidable or fortuitous, we are not morally responsible for them.

There are philosophers who believe that by denying the rather strange-sounding premise (4) we can escape the dilemma. Insisting on something like "the primacy of practical reason," they would say that since we are certain that (5) is false we must construct a metaphysical theory about the self, a theory denying (4) and enabling us to reconcile (3) and the denial of (5). I say "metaphysical" because it seems to be necessary for the theory to replace (4) by sentences using such terms as "active power," "the autonomy of the will," "prime mover," or "higher levels of causality"—terms designating something to which we apparently need not refer when expressing the conclusions of physics and the natural sciences. But I believe we cannot know whether such theories enable us to escape our dilemma. For it seems impossible to conceive what the relation is that, according to these theories, holds between the "will," "self," "mover," or "active power," on the one hand, and the bodily events this power is supposed to control, on the other—the relation between the "activities" of the self and the events described by physics.

I am dissatisfied, then, with what philosophers have proposed as alternatives to premises (1) through (4) above, but since I feel certain that (5) is false I also feel certain that at least one of the premises is false.

DAVID HUME

Liberty and Necessity*

PART I

It might reasonably be expected, in questions which have been canvassed and disputed with great eagerness since the first origin of science and philosophy, that the meaning of all the terms, at least, should have been agreed upon among the disputants, and our inquiries, in the course of two thousand years, been able to pass from words to the true and real subject of the controversy. For how easy may it seem to give exact definitions of the terms employed in reasoning, and make these definitions, not the mere sound of words, the object of future scrutiny and examination? But if we consider the matter more narrowly, we shall be apt to draw a quite opposite conclusion. From this circumstance alone, that a controversy has been long kept on foot and remains still undecided, we may presume that there is some ambiguity in the expression, and that the disputants affix different ideas to the terms employed in the controversy. For as the faculties of the mind are supposed to be naturally alike in every individual—otherwise nothing could be more fruitless than to reason or dispute together—it were impossible, if men affix the same ideas to their terms, that they could so long form different opinions of the same subject, especially when they communicate their views and each party turn themselves on all sides in search of arguments which may give them the victory over their antagonists. It is true, if men attempt the discussion of questions which lie entirely beyond the reach of human capacity, such as those concerning the origin of worlds or the economy of the intellectual system or region of spirits, they may long beat the air in their fruitless contests and never arrive at any determinate conclusion. But if the question regard any subject of common life and experience, nothing, one would think, could preserve the dispute so long undecided, but some ambiguous expressions which keep the antagonists still at a distance and hinder them from grappling with each other.

This has been the case in the long-disputed question concerning liberty and necessity, and to so remarkable a degree that, if I be not much mistaken, we shall find that all mankind, both learned and ignorant, have always been of the same opinion with regard to this subject, and that a few intelligible definitions would immediately have put an end to the whole controversy. I own that this dispute has been so much canvassed on all hands, and has led philosophers into such a labyrinth of obscure sophistry, that it is no wonder if a sensible reader indulge his ease so far as to turn a deaf ear to the proposal of such a question from which he can expect neither instruction nor entertainment. But the state of the argument here proposed may, perhaps, serve to renew his attention, as it has more novelty, promises at least some decision of the controversy, and will not much disturb his ease by any intricate or obscure reasoning.

I hope, therefore, to make it appear that all men have ever agreed in the doctrine both of necessity and of liberty, according to any reasonable sense which can be put on these terms, and that the whole controversy has hitherto turned merely upon words. We shall begin with examining the doctrine of necessity.

It is universally allowed that matter, in all its operations, is actuated by a necessary force, and that every natural effect is so precisely determined by the energy of its cause that no other effect, in such particular circumstances, could

* From David Hume, *An Inquiry concerning Human Understanding*, Section 8. First published in 1748.

possibly have resulted from it. The degree and direction of every motion is, by the laws of nature, prescribed with such exactness that a living creature may as soon arise from the shock of two bodies, as motion, in any other degree or direction than what is actually produced by it. Would we, therefore, form a just and precise idea of *necessity,* we must consider whence that idea arises when we apply it to the operation of bodies.

It seems evident that, if all the scenes of nature were continually shifted in such a manner that no two events bore any resemblance to each other, but every object was entirely new, without any similitude to whatever had been seen before, we should never, in that case, have attained the least idea of necessity or of a connection among these objects. We might say, upon such a supposition, that one object or event has followed another, not that one was produced by the other. The relation of cause and effect must be utterly unknown to mankind. Inference and reasoning concerning the operations of nature would, from that moment, be at an end; and the memory and senses remain the only canals by which the knowledge of any real existence could possibly have access to the mind. Our idea, therefore, of necessity and causation arises entirely from the uniformity observable in the operations of nature, where similar objects are constantly conjoined together, and the mind is determined by custom to infer the one from the appearance of the other. These two circumstances form the whole of that necessity which we ascribe to matter. Beyond the constant *conjunction* of similar objects and the consequent *inference* from one to the other, we have no notion of any necessity of connection.

If it appear, therefore, that all mankind have ever allowed, without any doubt or hesitation, that these two circumstances take place in the voluntary actions of men and in the operations of mind, it must follow that all mankind have ever agreed in the doctrine of necessity, and that they have hitherto disputed merely for not understanding each other.

As to the first circumstance, the constant and regular conjunction of similar events, we may possibly satisfy ourselves by the following considerations. It is universally acknowledged that there is a great uniformity among the actions of men, in all nations and ages, and that human nature remains still the same in its principles and operations. The same motives always produce the same actions; the same events follow from the same causes. Ambition, avarice, self-love, vanity, friendship, generosity, public spirit—these passions, mixed in various degrees and distributed through society, have been, from the beginning of the world, and still are, the source of all the actions and enterprises which have ever been observed among mankind. Would you know the sentiments, inclinations, and course of life of the Greeks and Romans? Study well the temper and actions of the French and English: you cannot be much mistaken in transferring to the former *most* of the observations which you have made with regard to the latter. Mankind are so much the same, in all times and places, that history informs us of nothing new or strange in this particular. Its chief use is only to discover the constant and universal principles of human nature by showing men in all varieties of circumstances and situations, and furnishing us with materials from which we may form our observations and become acquainted with the regular springs of human action and behavior. These records of wars, intrigues, factions, and revolutions are so many collections of experiments by which the politician or moral philosopher fixes the principles of his science, in the same manner as the physician or natural philosopher becomes acquainted with the nature of plants, minerals, and other external objects, by the experiments which he forms concerning them. Nor are the earth, water, and other elements examined by Aristotle and Hippocrates more like to those which at present lie under our observation than the men described by Polybius and Tacitus are to those who now govern the world.

Should a traveler, returning from a far country, bring us an account of men wholly different from any with whom we were ever acquainted, men who were entirely divested of avarice, ambition, or revenge, who knew no pleasure but friendship, generosity, and public spirit, we should immediately, from these circumstances, detect the falsehood and prove him a liar with the same certainty as if he had stuffed his narration with stories of centaurs and dragons, miracles and prodigies. And if we would explode any forgery in history, we cannot make use of a more convincing argument than to prove that the actions ascribed to any person are directly contrary to the course of nature, and that no human motives, in such circumstances, could ever induce him to such a conduct. The veracity of Quintus Curtius is as much to be suspected when he describes the supernatural courage of Alexander by which he was hurried on singly to attack multitudes, as when he describes his supernatural force and activity by which he was able to resist them. So readily and universally do we acknowledge a uniformity in human motives and actions as well as in the operations of body.

Hence, likewise, the benefit of that experience acquired by long life and a variety of business and company, in order to instruct us in the principles of human nature and regulate our future conduct as well as speculation. By means of this guide we mount up to the knowledge of men's inclinations and motives from their actions, expressions, and even gestures, and again descend to the interpretation of their actions from our knowledge of their motives and inclinations. The general observations, treasured up by a course of experience, give us the clue of human nature and teach us to unravel all its intricacies. Pretexts and appearances no longer deceive us. Public declarations pass for the specious coloring of a cause. And though virtue and honor be allowed their proper weight and authority, that perfect disinterestedness, so often pretended to, is never expected in multitudes and parties, seldom in their leaders, and scarcely even in individuals of any rank or station. But were there no uniformity in human actions, and were every experiment which we could form of this kind irregular and anomalous, it were impossible to collect any general observations concerning mankind, and no experience, however accurately digested by reflection, would ever serve to any purpose. Why is the aged husbandman more skillful in his calling than the young beginner, but because there is a certain uniformity in the operation of the sun, rain, and earth toward the production of vegetables, and experience teaches the old practitioner the rules by which this operation is governed and directed?

We must not, however, expect that this uniformity of human actions should be carried to such a length as that all men, in the same circumstances, will always act precisely in the same manner, without making any allowance for the diversity of characters, prejudices, and opinions. Such a uniformity, in every particular, is found in no part of nature. On the contrary, from observing the variety of conduct in different men we are enabled to form a greater variety of maxims which still suppose a degree of uniformity and regularity.

Are the manners of men different in different ages and countries? We learn thence the great force of custom and education, which mold the human mind from its infancy and form it into a fixed and established character. Is the behavior and conduct of the one sex very unlike that of the other? It is thence we become acquainted with the different characters which nature has impressed upon the sexes, and which she preserves with constancy and regularity. Are the actions of the same person much diversified in the different periods of his life from infancy to old age? This affords room for many general observations concerning the gradual change of our sentiments and inclinations, and the different maxims which prevail in the different ages of human creatures. Even the characters which are peculiar to each individual have a uniformity in their influence, otherwise our acquaintance with the persons, and our observations of their conduct, could never teach us their dispositions or serve to direct our behavior with regard to them.

I grant it possible to find actions which seem to have no regular connection with any known motives and are exceptions to all the measures of conduct which have ever been established for the government of men. But if we could willingly know what judgment should be formed of such irregular and extraordinary actions, we may consider the sentiments commonly entertained with regard to those irregular events which appear in the course of nature and the operations of eternal objects. All causes are not conjoined to their usual effects with like uniformity. An artificer who handles only dead matter may be disappointed of his aim, as well as the politician who directs the conduct of sensible and intelligent agents.

The vulgar, who take things according to their first appearance, attribute the uncertainty of events to such an uncertainty in the causes as makes the latter often fail of their usual influence, though they meet with no impediment in their operation. But philosophers, observing that almost in every part of nature there is contained a vast variety of springs and principles which are hid by reason of their minuteness or remoteness, find that it is at least possible the contrariety of events may not proceed from any contingency in the cause but from the secret operation of contrary causes. This possibility is converted into certainty by further observation, when they remark that, upon an exact scrutiny, a contrariety of effects always betrays a contrariety of causes and proceeds from their mutual opposition. A peasant can give no better reason for the stopping of any clock or watch than to say that it does not commonly go right. But an artist easily perceives that the same force in the spring or pendulum has always the same influence on the wheels, but fails of its usual effect perhaps by reason of a grain of dust which puts a stop to the whole movement. From the observation of several parallel instances philosophers form a maxim that the connection between all causes and effects is equally necessary, and that its seeming uncertainty in some instances proceeds from the secret opposition of contrary causes.

Thus, for instance, in the human body, when the usual symptoms of health or sickness disappoint our expectation, when medicines operate not with their wonted powers, when irregular events follow from any particular cause, the philosopher and physician are not surprised at the matter, nor are ever tempted to deny, in general, the necessity and uniformity of those principles by which the animal economy is conducted. They know that a human body is a mighty complicated machine, that many secret powers lurk in it which are altogether beyond our comprehension, that to us it must often appear very uncertain in its operations, and that, therefore, the irregular events which outwardly discover themselves can be no proof that the laws of nature are not observed with the greatest regularity in its internal operations and government.

The philosopher, if he be consistent, must apply the same reasonings to the actions and volitions of intelligent agents. The most irregular and unexpected resolutions of men may frequently be accounted for by those who know every particular circumstance of their character and situation. A person of an obliging disposition gives a peevish answer; but he has the toothache, or has not dined. A stupid fellow discovers an uncommon alacrity in his carriage; but he has met with a sudden piece of good fortune. Or even when an action, as sometimes happens, cannot be particularly accounted for, either by the person himself or by others, we know, in general, that the characters of men are to a certain degree inconstant and irregular. This is, in a manner, the constant character of human nature, though it be applicable, in a more particular manner, to some persons who have no fixed rule for their conduct, but proceed in a continual course of caprice and inconstancy. The internal principles and motives may operate in a uniform manner, notwithstanding these seeming irregularities—in the same manner as the winds, rains, clouds, and other variations of the weather are supposed to be governed by steady principles, though not easily discoverable by human sagacity and inquiry.

Thus it appears not only that the conjunction between motives and voluntary actions is as regular and uniform as that between the cause and effect in any part of nature, but also that this regular conjunction has been universally acknowledged among mankind and has never been the subject of dispute either in philosophy or common life. Now, as it is from past experience that we draw all inferences concerning the future, and as we conclude that objects will always be conjoined together which we find to have always been conjoined, it may seem superfluous to prove that this experienced uniformity in human actions is a source whence we draw *inferences* concerning them. But in order to throw the argument into a greater variety of lights, we shall also insist, though briefly, on this latter topic.

The mutual dependence of men is so great in all societies that scarce any human action is entirely complete in itself or is performed without some reference to the actions of others, which are requisite to make it answer fully the intention of the agent. The poorest artificer who labors alone expects at least the protection of the magistrate to insure him the enjoyment of the fruits of his labor. He also expects that when he carries his goods to market and offers them at a reasonable price, he shall find purchasers and shall be able, by the money he acquires, to engage others to supply him with those commodities which are requisite for his subsistence. In proportion as men extend their dealings and render their intercourse with others more complicated, they always comprehend in their schemes of life a greater variety of voluntary actions which they expect, from the proper motives, to co-operate with their own. In all these conclusions they take their measures from past experience, in the same manner as in their reasonings concerning external objects, and firmly believe that men, as well as all the elements, are to continue in their operations the same that they have ever found them. A manufacturer reckons upon the labor of his servants for the execution of any work as much as upon the tools which he employs, and would be equally surprised were his expectations disappointed. In short, this experimental inference and reasoning concerning the actions of others enters so much into human life that no man, while awake, is ever a moment without employing it. Have we not reason, therefore, to affirm that all mankind have always agreed in the doctrine of necessity, according to the foregoing definition and explication of it?

Nor have philosophers ever entertained a different opinion from the people in this particular. For, not to mention that almost every action of their life supposes that opinion, there are even few of the speculative parts of learning to which it is not essential. What would become of *history* had we not a dependence on the veracity of the historian according to the experience which we have had of mankind? How could *politics* be a science if laws and forms of government had not a uniform influence upon society? Where would be the foundation of *morals* if particular characters had no certain or determinate power to produce particular sentiments, and if these sentiments had no constant operation on actions? And with what pretense could we employ our *criticism* upon any poet or polite author if we could not pronounce the conduct and sentiments of his actors either natural or unnatural to such characters and in such circumstances? It seems almost impossible, therefore, to engage either in science or action of any kind without acknowledging the doctrine of necessity, and this *inference* from motives to voluntary action, from characters to conduct.

And, indeed, when we consider how aptly *natural* and *moral* evidence link together and form only one chain of argument, we shall make no scruple to allow that they are of the same nature and derived from the same principles. A prisoner who has neither money nor interest discovers the impossibility of his escape as well when he considers the obstinacy of the jailer as the walls and bars with which he is surrounded, and in all attempts for his freedom chooses rather to work upon the stone and iron of the one than upon the inflexible nature of the other. The same prisoner, when conducted to the scaffold, foresees his death as certainly from the constancy and fidelity of his guards as from the operation of the ax or wheel. His mind runs along a certain train of ideas: the refusal of the soldiers to consent to his escape; the action of the executioner; the separation of the head and body; bleeding, convulsive motions, and death. Here is a connected chain of natural causes and voluntary actions, but the mind feels no difference between them in passing from one link to another, nor is less certain of the future event than if it were connected with the objects present to the memory or senses by a train of causes cemented together by what we are pleased to call a "physical" necessity. The same experienced union has the same effect on the mind, whether the united objects be motives, volition, and actions, or figure and motion. We may change the names of things, but their nature and their operation on the understanding never change.

Were a man whom I know to be honest and opulent, and with whom I lived in intimate friendship, to come into my house, where I am surrounded with my servants, I rest assured that he is not to stab me before he leaves it in order to rob me of my silver standish; and I no more suspect this event than the falling of the house itself, which is new and solidly built and founded.—*But he may have been seized with a sudden and unknown frenzy.*—So may a sudden earthquake arise, and shake and tumble my house about my ears. I shall, therefore, change the suppositions. I shall say that I know with certainty that he is not to put his hand into the fire and hold it there till it be consumed. And this event I think I can foretell with the same assurance as that, if he throw himself out of the window and meet with no obstruction, he will not remain a moment suspended in the air. No suspicion of an unknown frenzy can give the least possibility to the former event which is so contrary to all the known principles of human nature. A man who at noon leaves his purse full of gold on the pavement at Charing Cross may as well expect that it will fly away like a feather as that he will find it untouched an hour after. Above one-half of human reasonings contain inferences of a similar nature, attended with more or less degrees of certainty, proportioned to our experience of the usual conduct of mankind in such particular situations.

I have frequently considered what could possibly be the reason why all mankind, though they have ever, without hesitation, acknowledged the doctrine of necessity in their whole practice and reasoning, have yet discovered such a reluctance to acknowledge it in words, and have rather shown a propensity, in all ages, to profess the contrary opinion. The matter, I think, may be accounted for after the following manner. If we examine the operations of body and the production of effects from their causes, we shall find that all our faculties can never carry us further in our knowledge of this relation than barely to observe that particular objects are *constantly conjoined* together, and that the mind is carried, by a *customary transition,* from the appearance of the one to the belief of the other. But though this conclusion concerning human ignorance be the result of the strictest scrutiny of this subject, men still entertain a strong propensity to believe that they penetrate further into the powers of nature and perceive something like a necessary connection between the cause and the effect. When, again, they turn their reflections toward the operations of their own minds and *feel* no such connection of the motive and the action, they are thence apt to suppose that there is a difference between the effects which result from material force and those which arise from thought and intelligence. But being once convinced that we know nothing further of causation of any kind than merely the *constant conjunction* of objects and the consequent *inference* of the mind from one to another, and finding that these two circumstances are universally allowed to have place in voluntary actions, we may be more easily led to own the same necessity common to all causes. And though this reasoning may contradict the systems of many philosophers in ascribing necessity to the determinations of the will, we shall find, upon reflection, that they dissent from it in words only, not in their real sentiments. Necessity, according to the sense in which it is here taken, has never yet been rejected, nor can ever, I think, be rejected by any philosopher. It may only, perhaps, be pretended that the mind can perceive in the operations of matter some further connection between the cause and effect, and a connection that has not place in the voluntary actions of intelligent beings. Now, whether it be so or not can only appear upon examination, and it is incumbent on these philosophers to make good their assertion by defining or describing that necessity and pointing it out to us in the operations of material causes.

It would seem, indeed, that men begin at the wrong end of this question concerning liberty and necessity when they enter upon it by examining the faculties of the soul, the influence of the understanding, and the operations of the will. Let them first discuss a more simple question, namely, the question of body and brute unintelligent matter, and try whether they can there form any idea of causation and necessity, except that of a constant conjunction of objects and subsequent inference of the mind from one to another. If these circumstances form, in reality, the whole of that necessity which we conceive in matter, and if these circumstances be also universally acknowledged to take place in the operations of the mind, the dispute is at an end; at least, must be owned to be thenceforth merely verbal. But as long as we will rashly suppose that we have some further idea of necessity and causation in the operations of external objects, at the same time that we can find nothing further in the voluntary actions of the mind, there is no possibility of bringing the question to any determinate issue while we proceed upon so erroneous a supposition. The only method of undeceiving us is to mount up higher, to examine the narrow extent of science when applied to material causes, and to convince ourselves that all we know of them is the constant conjunction and inference above mentioned. We may, perhaps, find that it is with difficulty we are induced to fix such narrow limits to human understanding, but we can afterwards find no difficulty when we come to apply this doctrine to the actions of the will. For as it is evident that these have a regular conjunction with motives and circumstances and character, and as we always draw inferences from one to the other, we must be obliged to acknowledge in words that necessity which we have already avowed in every deliberation of our lives and in every step of our conduct and behavior.[1]

[1] The prevalence of the doctrine of liberty may be accounted for from another cause, viz., a false sensation, or seeming experience, which we have, or may have, of liberty or indifference in many of our actions.

But to proceed in this reconciling project with regard to the question of liberty and necessity—the most contentious question of metaphysics, the most contentious science—it will not require many words to prove that all mankind have ever agreed in the doctrine of liberty as well as in that of necessity, and that the whole dispute, in this respect also, has been hitherto merely verbal. For what is meant by liberty when applied to voluntary actions? We cannot surely mean that actions have so little connection with motives, inclinations, and circumstances that one does not follow with a certain degree of uniformity from the other, and that one affords no inference by which we can conclude the existence of the other. For these are plain and acknowledged matters of fact. By liberty, then, we can only mean *a power of acting or not acting according to the determinations of the will;* that is, if we choose to remain at rest, we may; if we choose to move, we also may. Now this hypothetical liberty is universally allowed to belong to everyone who is not a prisoner and in chains. Here then is no subject of dispute.

Whatever definition we may give of liberty, we should be careful to observe two requisite circumstances: *first,* that it be consistent with plain matter of fact; *secondly,* that it be consistent with itself. If we observe these circumstances and render our definition intelligible, I am persuaded that all mankind will be found of one opinion with regard to it.

It is universally allowed that nothing exists without a cause of its existence, and that chance, when strictly examined, is a mere negative word and means not any real power which has anywhere a being in nature. But it is pretended that some causes are necessary, some not necessary. Here then is the advantage of definitions. Let anyone *define* a cause without comprehending, as a part of the definition, a *necessary connection* with its effect, and let him show distinctly the origin of the idea expressed by the definition, and I shall readily give up the whole controversy. But if the foregoing explication of the matter be received, this must be absolutely impracticable. Had not objects a regular conjunction with each other, we should never have entertained any notion of cause and effect; and this regular conjunction produces that inference of the understanding which is the only connection that we can have any comprehension of. Whoever attempts a definition of cause exclusive of these circumstances will be obliged either to employ unintelligible terms or such as are synonymous to the term which he endeavors to define.[2] And if the definition above mentioned be admitted, liberty, when opposed to necessity, not to constraint, is the same thing with chance, which is universally allowed to have no existence.

PART II

There is no method of reasoning more common, and yet none more blamable, than in philo-

The necessity of any action, whether of matter or of mind, is not, properly speaking, a quality in the agent but in any thinking or intelligent being who may consider the action; and it consists chiefly in the determination of his thoughts to infer the existence of that action from some preceding objects; as liberty, when opposed to necessity, is nothing but the want of that determination, and a certain looseness or indifference which we feel in passing, or not passing, from the idea of one object to that of any succeeding one. Now we may observe that though, in *reflecting* on human actions, we seldom feel such a looseness or indifference, but are commonly able to infer them with considerable certainty from their motives, and from the disposition of the agent; yet it frequently happens that, in *performing* the actions themselves, we are sensible of something like it; and as all resembling objects are readily taken for each other, this has been employed as a demonstrative and even intuitive proof of human liberty. We feel that our actions are subject to our will on most occasions, and imagine we feel that the will itself is subject to nothing, because, when by a denial of it we are provoked to try, we feel that it moves easily every way, and produces an image of itself (or a "velleity," as it is called in the schools), even on that side on which it did not settle. This image, or faint motion, we persuade ourselves, could at that time have been completed into the thing itself, because, should that be denied, we find upon a second trial that at present it can. We consider not that the fantastical desire of showing liberty is here the motive of our actions. And it seems certain that however we may imagine we feel a liberty within ourselves, a spectator can commonly infer our actions from our motives and character; and even where he cannot, he concludes in general that he might, were he perfectly acquainted with every circumstance of our situation and temper, and the most secret springs of our complexion and disposition. Now this is the very essence of necessity, according to the foregoing doctrine.

[2] Thus, if a cause be defined, *that which produces anything,* it is easy to observe that *producing* is synonymous to *causing*. In like manner, if a cause be defined, *that by which anything exists,* this is liable to the same objection. For what is meant by these words, *"by which"*? Had it been said that a cause is *that* after which *anything constantly exists,* we should have understood the terms. For this is, indeed, all we know of the matter. And this constancy forms the very essence of necessity, nor have we any other idea of it.

sophical disputes to endeavor the refutation of any hypothesis by a pretense of its dangerous consequences to religion and morality. When any opinion leads to absurdity, it is certainly false; but it is not certain that an opinion is false because it is of dangerous consequence. Such topics, therefore, ought entirely to be forborne as serving nothing to the discovery of truth, but only to make the person of an antagonist odious. This I observe in general, without pretending to draw any advantage from it. I frankly submit to an examination of this kind, and shall venture to affirm that the doctrines both of necessity and liberty, as above explained, are not only consistent with morality, but are absolutely essential to its support.

Necessity may be defined two ways, conformably to the two definitions of *cause* of which it makes an essential part. It consists either in the constant conjunction of like objects or in the inference of the understanding from one object to another. Now necessity, in both these senses (which, indeed, are at bottom the same), has universally, though tacitly, in the schools, in the pulpit, and in common life been allowed to belong to the will of man, and no one has ever pretended to deny that we can draw inferences concerning human actions, and that those inferences are founded on the experienced union of like actions, with like motives, inclinations, and circumstances. The only particular in which anyone can differ is that either perhaps he will refuse to give the name of necessity to this property of human actions—but as long as the meaning is understood I hope the word can do no harm—or that he will maintain it possible to discover something further in the operations of matter. But this, it must be acknowledged, can be of no consequence to morality or religion, whatever it may be to natural philosophy or metaphysics. We may here be mistaken in asserting that there is no idea of any other necessity or connection in the actions of the body, but surely we ascribe nothing to the actions of the mind but what everyone does and must readily allow of. We change no circumstance in the received orthodox system with regard to the will, but only in that with regard to material objects and causes. Nothing, therefore, can be more innocent at least than this doctrine.

All laws being founded on rewards and punishments, it is supposed, as a fundamental principle, that these motives have a regular and uniform influence on the mind and both produce the good and prevent the evil actions. We may give to this influence what name we please; but as it is usually conjoined with the action, it must be esteemed a *cause* and be looked upon as an instance of that necessity which we would here establish.

The only proper object of hatred or vengeance is a person or creature endowed with thought and consciousness; and when any criminal or injurious actions excite that passion, it is only by their relation to the person, or connection with him. Actions are, by their very nature, temporary and perishing; and where they proceed not from some *cause* in the character and disposition of the person who performed them, they can neither redound to his honor if good, nor infamy if evil. The actions themselves may be blamable; they may be contrary to all the rules of morality and religion; but the person is not answerable for them and, as they proceeded from nothing in him that is durable and constant and leave nothing of that nature behind them, it is impossible he can, upon their account, become the object of punishment or vengeance. According to the principle, therefore, which denies necessity and, consequently, causes, a man is as pure and untainted, after having committed the most horrid crime, as at the first moment of his birth, nor is his character anywise concerned in his actions, since they are not derived from it; and the wickedness of the one can never be used as a proof of the depravity of the other.

Men are not blamed for such actions as they perform ignorantly and casually, whatever may be the consequences. Why? But because the principles of these actions are only momentary and terminate in them alone. Men are less blamed for such actions as they perform hastily and unpremeditately than for such as proceed from deliberation. For what reason? But because a hasty temper, though a constant cause or principle in the mind, operates only by intervals and infects not the whole character. Again, repentance wipes off every crime if attended with a reformation of life and manners. How is this to be accounted for? But by asserting that actions render a person criminal merely as they are proofs of criminal principles in the mind; and when, by an alteration of these principles, they cease to be just proofs, they likewise cease to be criminal. But, except upon the doctrine of necessity, they never were just proofs, and consequently never were criminal.

It will be equally easy to prove, and from the same arguments, that *liberty,* according to that definition above mentioned, in which all men agree, is also essential to morality, and that no human actions, where it is wanting, are susceptible of any moral qualities or can be the objects of approbation or dislike. For as actions are objects of our moral sentiment so far only as they are indications of the internal character, passions, and affections, it is impossible that they can give rise either to praise or blame where they proceed not from these principles, but are derived altogether from external violence.

I pretend not to have obviated or removed all objections to this theory with regard to necessity and liberty. I can forsee other objections derived from topics which have not here been treated of. It may be said, for instance, that if voluntary actions be subjected to the same laws of necessity with the operations of matter, there is a continued chain of necessary causes, preordained and predetermined, reaching from the Original Cause of all to every single volition of every human creature. No contingency anywhere in the universe, no indifference, no liberty. While we act, we are at the same time acted upon. The ultimate Author of all our volitions is the Creator of the world, who first bestowed motion on this immense machine and placed all beings in that particular position whence every subsequent event, by an inevitable necessity, must result. Human actions, therefore, either can have no moral turpitude at all, as proceeding from so good a cause, or if they have any turpitude, they must involve our Creator in the same guilt, while he is acknowledged to be their ultimate cause and Author. For as a man who fired a mine is answerable for all the consequences, whether the train he employed be long or short, so, wherever a continued chain of necessary causes is fixed, that Being, either finite or infinite, who produces the first is likewise the author of all the rest and must both bear the blame and acquire the praise which belong to them. Our clear and unalterable ideas of morality establish this rule upon unquestionable reasons when we examine the consequences of any human action; and these reasons must still have greater force when applied to the volitions and intentions of a Being infinitely wise and powerful. Ignorance or impotence may be pleaded for so limited a creature as man, but those imperfections have no place in our Creator. He foresaw, he ordained, he intended all those actions of men which we so rashly pronounce criminal. And we must, therefore, conclude either that they are not criminal or that the Deity, not man, is accountable for them. But as either of these positions is absurd and impious, it follows that the doctrine from which they are deduced cannot possibly be true, as being liable to all the same objections. An absurd consequence, if necessary, proves the original doctrine to be absurd in the same manner as criminal actions render criminal the original cause if the connection between them be necessary and inevitable.

This objection consists of two parts, which we shall examine separately:

First, that if human actions can be traced up, by a necessary chain, to the Deity, they can never be criminal, on account of the infinite perfection of that Being from whom they are derived, and who can intend nothing but what is altogether good and laudable. Or, *secondly,* if they be criminal, we must retract the attribute of perfection which we ascribe to the Deity and must acknowledge him to be the ultimate author of guilt and moral turpitude in all his creatures.

The answer to the first objection seems obvious and convincing. There are many philosophers who, after an exact scrutiny of the phenomena of nature, conclude that the WHOLE, considered as one system, is, in every period of its existence, ordered with perfect benevolence; and that the utmost possible happiness will, in the end, result to all created beings without any mixture of positive or absolute ill and misery. Every physical ill, say they, makes an essential part of this benevolent system, and could not possibly be removed, by even the Deity himself, considered as a wise agent, without giving entrance to greater ill or excluding greater good which will result from it. From this theory some philosophers, and the ancient Stoics among the rest, derived a topic of consolation under all afflictions, while they taught their pupils that those ills under which they labored were in reality goods to the universe, and that to an enlarged view which could comprehend the whole system of nature every event became an object of joy and exultation. But though this topic be specious and sublime, it was soon found in practice weak and ineffectual.

You would surely more irritate than appease a man lying under the racking pains of the gout by preaching up to him the rectitude of those general laws which produced the malignant humors in his body and led them through the proper canals to the sinews and nerves, where they now excite such acute torments. These enlarged views may, for a moment, please the imagination of a speculative man who is placed in ease and security, but neither can they dwell with constancy on his mind, even though undisturbed by the emotions of pain or passion, much less can they maintain their ground when attacked by such powerful antagonists. The affections take a narrower and more natural survey of their object and, by an economy more suitable to the infirmity of human minds, regard alone the beings around us, and are actuated by such events as appear good or ill to the private system.

The case is the same with *moral* as with *physical* ill. It cannot reasonably be supposed that those remote considerations which are found of so little efficacy with regard to the one will have a more powerful influence with regard to the other. The mind of man is so formed by nature that, upon the appearance of certain characters, dispositions, and actions, it immediately feels the sentiment of approbation or blame; nor are there any emotions more essential to its frame and constitution. The characters which engage our approbation are chiefly such as contribute to the peace and security of human society, as the characters which excite blame are chiefly such as tend to public detriment and disturbance; whence it may reasonably be presumed that the moral sentiments arise, either mediately or immediately, from a reflection on these opposite interests. What though philosophical meditations establish a different opinion or conjecture that everything is right with regard to the whole, and that the qualities which disturb society are, in the main, as beneficial, and are as suitable to the primary intention of nature, as those which more directly promote its happiness and welfare? Are such remote and uncertain speculations able to counterbalance the sentiments which arise from the natural and immediate view of the objects? A man who is robbed of a considerable sum, does he find his vexation for the loss anywise diminished by these sublime reflections? Why, then, should his moral resentment against the crime be supposed incompatible with them? Or why should not the acknowledgment of a real distinction between vice and virtue be reconcilable to all speculative systems of philosophy, as well as that of a real distinction between personal beauty and deformity? Both these distinctions are founded in the natural sentiments of the human mind; and these sentiments are not to be controlled or altered by any philosophical theory or speculation whatsoever.

The *second* objection admits not of so easy and satisfactory an answer, nor is it possible to explain distinctly how the Deity can be the immediate cause of all the actions of men without being the author of sin and moral turpitude. These are mysteries which mere natural and unassisted reason is very unfit to handle; and whatever system she embraces, she must find herself involved in inextricable difficulties, and even contradictions, at every step which she takes with regard to such subjects. To reconcile the indifference and contingency of human actions with prescience or to defend absolute decrees, and yet free the Deity from being the author of sin, has been found hitherto to exceed all the power of philosophy. Happy, if she be thence sensible of her temerity, when she pries into these sublime mysteries, and, leaving a scene so full of obscurities and perplexities, return with suitable modesty to her true and proper province, the examination of common life, where she will find difficulties enough to employ her inquiries without launching into so boundless an ocean of doubt, uncertainty, and contradiction.

A. J. AYER

Freedom and Necessity*

When I am said to have done something of my own free will it is implied that I could have acted otherwise; and it is only when it is believed that I could have acted otherwise that I am held to be morally responsible for what I have done. For a man is not thought to be morally responsible for an action that it was not in his power to avoid. But if human behaviour is entirely governed by causal laws, it is not clear how any action that is done could ever have been avoided. It may be said of the agent that he would have acted otherwise if the causes of his action had been different, but they being what they were, it seems to follow that he was bound to act as he did. Now it is commonly assumed both that men are capable of acting freely, in the sense that is required to make them morally responsible, and that human behaviour is entirely governed by causal laws: and it is the apparent conflict between these two assumptions that gives rise to the philosophical problem of the freedom of the will.

Confronted with this problem, many people will be inclined to agree with Dr. Johnson: 'Sir, we *know* our will is free, and *there's* an end on't'. But, while this does very well for those who accept Dr. Johnson's premiss, it would hardly convince anyone who denied the freedom of the will. Certainly, if we do know that our wills are free, it follows that they are so. But the logical reply to this might be that since our wills are not free, it follows that no one can know that they are: so that if anyone claims, like Dr. Johnson, to know that they are, he must be mistaken. What is evident, indeed, is that people often believe themselves to be acting freely; and it is to this 'feeling' of freedom that some philosophers appeal when they wish, in the supposed interests of morality, to prove that not all human action is causally determined. But if these philosophers are right in their assumption that a man cannot be acting freely if his action is causally determined, then the fact that someone feels free to do, or not to do, a certain action does not prove that he really is so. It may prove that the agent does not himself know what it is that makes him act in one way rather than another: but from the fact that a man is unaware of the causes of his action, it does not follow that no such causes exist.

So much may be allowed to the determinist; but his belief that all human actions are subservient to causal laws still remains to be justified. If, indeed, it is necessary that every event should have a cause, then the rule must apply to human behaviour as much as to anything else. But why should it be supposed that every event must have a cause? The contrary is not unthinkable. Nor is the law of universal causation a necessary presupposition of scientific thought. The scientist may try to discover causal laws, and in many cases he succeeds; but sometimes he has to be content with statistical laws, and sometimes he comes upon events which, in the present state of his knowledge, he is not able to subsume under any law at all. In the case of these events he assumes that if he knew more he would be able to discover some law, whether causal or statistical, which would enable him to account for them. And this assumption cannot be disproved. For however far he may have carried his investigation, it is always open to him to carry it further; and it is always conceivable that if he carried it further he would discover the connection which had hitherto escaped him. Nevertheless, it is also

* A. J. Ayer, "Freedom and Necessity," in *Philosophical Essays* (London: Macmillan; New York: St. Martin's Press, 1954), pp. 271–284. Reprinted by permission of the author and St. Martin's Press, Inc., The Macmillan Company of Canada, Ltd., and Macmillan & Co. Ltd. First published in *Polemic*, 5 (1946).

conceivable that the events with which he is concerned are not systematically connected with any others: so that the reason why he does not discover the sort of laws that he requires is simply that they do not obtain.

Now in the case of human conduct the search for explanations has not in fact been altogether fruitless. Certain scientific laws have been established; and with the help of these laws we do make a number of successful predictions about the ways in which different people will behave. But these predictions do not always cover every detail. We may be able to predict that in certain circumstances a particular man will be angry, without being able to prescribe the precise form that the expression of his anger will take. We may be reasonably sure that he will shout, but not sure how loud his shout will be, or exactly what words he will use. And it is only a small proportion of human actions that we are able to forecast even so precisely as this. But that, it may be said, is because we have not carried our investigations very far. The science of psychology is still in its infancy and, as it is developed, not only will more human actions be explained, but the explanations will go into greater detail. The ideal of complete explanation may never in fact be attained: but it is theoretically attainable. Well, this may be so: and certainly it is impossible to show *a priori* that it is not so: but equally it cannot be shown that it is. This will not, however, discourage the scientist who, in the field of human behaviour, as elsewhere, will continue to formulate theories and test them by the facts. And in this he is justified. For since he has no reason *a priori* to admit that there is a limit to what he can discover, the fact that he also cannot be sure that there is no limit does not make it unreasonable for him to devise theories, nor, having devised them, to try constantly to improve them.

But now suppose it to be claimed that, so far as men's actions are concerned, there is a limit: and that this limit is set by the fact of human freedom. An obvious objection is that in many cases in which a person feels himself to be free to do, or not to do, a certain action, we are even now able to explain, in causal terms, why it is that he acts as he does. But it might be argued that even if men are sometimes mistaken in believing that they act freely, it does not follow that they are always so mistaken. For it is not always the case that when a man believes that he has acted freely we are in fact able to account for his action in causal terms. A determinist would say that we should be able to account for it if we had more knowledge of the circumstances, and had been able to discover the appropriate natural laws. But until those discoveries have been made, this remains only a pious hope. And may it not be true that, in some cases at least, the reason why we can give no causal explanation is that no causal explanation is available; and that this is because the agent's choice was literally free, as he himself felt it to be?

The answer is that this may indeed be true, inasmuch as it is open to anyone to hold that no explanation is possible until some explanation is actually found. But even so it does not give the moralist what he wants. For he is anxious to show that men are capable of acting freely in order to infer that they can be morally responsible for what they do. But if it is a matter of pure chance that a man should act in one way rather than another, he may be free but he can hardly be responsible. And indeed when a man's actions seem to us quite unpredictable, when, as we say, there is no knowing what he will do, we do not look upon him as a moral agent. We look upon him rather as a lunatic.

To this it may be objected that we are not dealing fairly with the moralist. For when he makes it a condition of my being morally responsible that I should act freely, he does not wish to imply that it is purely a matter of chance that I act as I do. What he wishes to imply is that my actions are the result of my own free choice: and it is because they are the result of my own free choice that I am held to be morally responsible for them.

But now we must ask how it is that I come to make my choice. Either it is an accident that I choose to act as I do or it is not. If it is an accident, then it is merely a matter of chance that I did not choose otherwise; and if it is merely a matter of chance that I did not choose otherwise, it is surely irrational to hold me morally responsible for choosing as I did. But if it is not an accident that I choose to do one thing rather than another, then presumably there is some causal explanation of my choice: and in that case we are led back to determinism.

Again, the objection may be raised that we are not doing justice to the moralist's case. His view is not that it is a matter of chance that I choose to act as I do, but rather that my choice depends upon my character. Nevertheless he holds that I can still be free in the sense that he requires; for it is I who am responsible for my character. But in what way am I responsible for my character? Only, surely, in the sense that there is a causal connection between what I do now and what I have done in the past. It is only this that justifies the statement that I have made myself what I am: and even so this is an over-simplification, since it takes no account of the external influences to which I have been subjected. But, ignoring the external influences, let us assume that it is in fact the case that I have made myself what I am. Then it is still legitimate to ask how it is that I have come to make myself one sort of person rather than another. And if it be answered that it is a matter of my strength of will, we can put the same question in another form by asking how it is that my will has the strength that it has and not some other degree of strength. Once more, either it is an accident or it is not. If it is an accident, then by the same argument as before, I am not morally responsible, and if it is not an accident we are led back to determinism.

Furthermore, to say that my actions proceed from my character or, more colloquially, that I act in character, is to say that my behaviour is consistent and to that extent predictable: and since it is, above all, for the actions that I perform in character that I am held to be morally responsible, it looks as if the admission of moral responsibility, so far from being incompatible with determinism, tends rather to presuppose it. But how can this be so if it is a necessary condition of moral responsibility that the person who is held responsible should have acted freely? It seems that if we are to retain this idea of moral responsibility, we must either show that men can be held responsible for actions which they do not do freely, or else find some way of reconciling determinism with the freedom of the will.

It is no doubt with the object of effecting this reconciliation that some philosophers have defined freedom as the consciousness of necessity. And by so doing they are able to say not only that a man can be acting freely when his action is causally determined, but even that his action must be causally determined for it to be possible for him to be acting freely. Nevertheless this definition has the serious disadvantage that it gives to the word 'freedom' a meaning quite different from any that it ordinarily bears. It is indeed obvious that if we are allowed to give the word 'freedom' any meaning that we please, we can find a meaning that will reconcile it with determinism: but this is no more a solution of our present problem than the fact that the word 'horse' could be arbitrarily used to mean what is ordinarily meant by 'sparrow' is a proof that horses have wings. For suppose that I am compelled by another person to do something 'against my will'. In that case, as the word 'freedom' is ordinarily used, I should not be said to be acting freely: and the fact that I am fully aware of the constraint to which I am subjected makes no difference to the matter. I do not become free by becoming conscious that I am not. It may, indeed, be possible to show that my being aware that my action is causally determined is not incompatible with my acting freely: but it by no means follows that it is in this that my freedom consists. Moreover, I suspect that one of the reasons why people are inclined to define freedom as the consciousness of necessity is that they think that if one is conscious of necessity one may somehow be able to master it. But this is a fallacy. It is like someone's saying that he wishes he could see into the future, because if he did he would know what calamities lay in wait for him and so would be able to avoid them. But if he avoids the calamities then they don't lie in the future and it is not true that he foresees them. And similarly if I am able to master necessity, in the sense of escaping the operation of a necessary law, then the law in question is not necessary. And if the law is not necessary, then neither my freedom nor anything else can consist in my knowing that it is.

Let it be granted, then, that when we speak of reconciling freedom with determinism we are using the word 'freedom' in an ordinary sense. It still remains for us to make this usage clear: and perhaps the best way to make it clear is to show what it is that freedom, in this sense, is contrasted with. Now we began with the assumption that freedom is contrasted with causality: so that a man cannot be said to be acting freely if his action is causally determined. But this assumption has led us into difficulties and I now wish to suggest that it is mistaken. For it is not, I think, causality that freedom is to be contrasted with, but constraint. And while it is true that being constrained to do an action entails being caused to do it, I shall try to show that the converse does not hold. I shall try to show that from the fact that my action is causally determined it does not necessarily follow that I am constrained to do it: and this is equivalent to saying that it does not necessarily follow that I am not free.

If I am constrained, I do not act freely. But in what circumstances can I legitimately be said to be constrained? An obvious instance is the case in which I am compelled by another person to do what he wants. In a case of this sort the compulsion need not be such as to deprive one of the power of choice. It is not required that the other person should have hypnotized me, or that he should make it physically impossible for me to go against his will. It is enough that he should induce me to do what he wants by making it clear to me that, if I do not, he will bring about some situation that I regard as even more undesirable than the consequences of the action that he wishes me to do. Thus, if the man points a pistol at my head I may still choose to disobey him: but this does not prevent its being true that if I do fall in with his wishes he can legitimately be said to have compelled me. And if the circumstances are such that no reasonable person would be expected to choose the other alternative, then the action that I am made to do is not one for which I am held to be morally responsible.

A similar, but still somewhat different, case is that in which another person has obtained an habitual ascendancy over me. Where this is so, there may be no question of my being induced to act as the other person wishes by being confronted with a still more disagreeable alternative: for if I am sufficiently under his influence this special stimulus will not be necessary. Nevertheless I do not act freely, for the reason that I have been deprived of the power of choice. And this means that I have acquired so strong a habit of obedience that I no longer go through the process of deciding whether or not to do what the other person wants. About other matters I may still deliberate; but as regards the fulfillment of this other person's wishes, my own deliberations have ceased to be a causal factor in my behaviour. And it is in this sense that I may be said to be constrained. It is not, however, necessary that such constraint should take the form of subservience to another person. A kleptomaniac is not a free agent, in respect of his stealing, because he does not go through any process of deciding whether or not to steal. Or rather, if he does go through such a process, it is irrelevant to his behaviour. Whatever he resolved to do, he would steal all the same. And it is this that distinguishes him from the ordinary thief.

But now it may be asked whether there is any essential difference between these cases and those in which the agent is commonly thought to be free. No doubt the ordinary thief does go through a process of deciding whether or not to steal, and no doubt it does affect his behaviour. If he resolved to refrain from stealing, he could carry his resolution out. But if it be allowed that his making or not making this resolution is causally determined, then how can he be any more free than the kleptomaniac? It may be true that unlike the kleptomaniac he could refrain from stealing if he chose: but if there is a cause, or set of causes, which necessiate his choosing as he does, how can he be said to have the power of choice? Again, it may be true that no one now compels me to get up and walk across the room: but if my doing so can be causally explained in terms of my history or my environment, or whatever it may be, then how am I any more free than if some other person had compelled me? I do not have the feeling of constraint that I have when a pistol is manifestly pointed at my head; but the chains of causation by which I am bound are no less effective for being invisible.

The answer to this is that the cases I have mentioned as examples of constraint do differ from the others: and they differ just in the ways that I have tried to bring out. If I suffered from a compulsion neurosis, so that I got up and walked across the room, whether I wanted to or not, or if I did so because somebody else compelled me, then I should not be acting freely. But if I do it now, I shall be acting freely, just because these conditions do not obtain; and the fact that my action may nevertheless have a cause is, from this point of view, irrelevant. For it is not when my action has any cause at all, but only when it has a special sort of cause, that it is reckoned not to be free.

But here it may be objected that, even if this distinction corresponds to ordinary usage, it is still very irrational. For why should we distinguish, with regard to a person's freedom, between the operations of one sort of cause and those of another? Do not all causes equally necessitate?

And is it not therefore arbitrary to say that a person is free when he is necessitated in one fashion but not when he is necessitated in another?

That all causes equally necessitate is indeed a tautology, if the word 'necessitate' is taken merely as equivalent to 'cause': but if, as the objection requires, it is taken as equivalent to 'constrain' or 'compel', then I do not think that this proposition is true. For all that is needed for one event to be the cause of another is that, in the given circumstances, the event which is said to be the effect would not have occurred if it had not been for the occurrence of the event which is said to be the cause, or *vice versa,* according as causes are interpreted as necessary, or sufficient, conditions: and this fact is usually deducible from some causal law which states that whenever an event of the one kind occurs then, given suitable conditions, an event of the other kind will occur in a certain temporal or spatio-temporal relationship to it. In short, there is an invariable concomitance between the two classes of events; but there is no compulsion, in any but a metaphorical sense. Suppose, for example, that a psycho-analyst is able to account for some aspect of my behaviour by referring it to some lesion that I suffered in my childhood. In that case, it may be said that my childhood experience, together with certain other events, necessitates my behaving as I do. But all that this involves is that it is found to be true in general that when people have had certain experiences as children, they subsequently behave in certain specifiable ways; and my case is just another instance of this general law. It is in this way indeed that my behaviour is explained. But from the fact that my behaviour is capable of being explained, in the sense that it can be subsumed under some natural law, it does not follow that I am acting under constraint.

If this is correct, to say that I could have acted otherwise is to say, first, that I should have acted otherwise if I had so chosen; secondly, that my action was voluntary in the sense in which the actions, say, of the kleptomaniac are not; and thirdly, that nobody compelled me to choose as I did: and these three conditions may very well be fulfilled. When they are fulfilled, I may be said to have acted freely. But this is not to say that it was a matter of chance that I acted as I did, or, in other words, that my action could not be explained. And that my actions should be capable of being explained is all that is required by the postulate of determinism.

If more than this seems to be required it is, I think, because the use of the very word 'determinism' is in some degree misleading. For it tends to suggest that one event is somehow in the power of another, whereas the truth is merely that they are factually correlated. And the same applies to the use, in this context, of the word 'necessity' and even of the word 'cause' itself. Moreover, there are various reasons for this. One is the tendency to confuse causal with logical necessitation, and so to infer mistakenly that the effect is contained in the cause. Another is the uncritical use of a concept of force which is derived from primitive experiences of pushing and striking. A third is the survival of an animistic conception of causality, in which all causal relationships are modelled on the example of one person's exercising authority over another. As a result we tend to form an imaginative picture of an unhappy effect trying vainly to escape from the clutches of an overmastering cause. But, I repeat, the fact is simply that when an event of one type occurs, an event of another type occurs also, in a certain temporal or spatio-temporal relation to the first. The rest is only metaphor. And it is because of the metaphor, and not because of the fact, that we come to think that there is an antithesis between causality and freedom.

Nevertheless, it may be said, if the postulate of determinism is valid, then the future can be explained in terms of the past: and this means that if one knew enough about the past one would be able to predict the future. But in that case what will happen in the future is already decided. And how then can I be said to be free? What is going to happen is going to happen and nothing that I do can prevent it. If the determinist is right, I am the helpless prisoner of fate.

But what is meant by saying that the future course of events is already decided? If the implication is that some person has arranged it, then the proposition is false. But if all that is meant is that it is possible, in principle, to deduce it from a set of particular facts about the past, together with the appropriate general laws, then, even if this is true, it does not in the least entail that I am the helpless prisoner of fate. It does not even entail that my actions make no difference to the future: for they are causes as well as effects; so that if they were different their consequences would be different also. What it does entail is that my behaviour can be predicted: but to say that my behaviour can be predicted is not to say that I am acting under constraint. It is indeed true that I cannot escape my destiny if this is taken to mean no more than that I shall do what I shall do. But this is a tautology, just as it is a tautology that what is going to happen is going to happen. And such tautologies as these prove nothing whatsoever about the freedom of the will.

JOHN HOSPERS

Free Will and Psychoanalysis*

O Thou, who didst with pitfall and with gin
Beset the Road I was to wander in,
Thou wilt not with Predestined Evil round
Enmesh, and then impute my Fall to Sin!
—Edward FitzGerald,
The Rubaiyat of Omar Khayyam

. . . It is extremely common for nonprofessional philosophers and iconoclasts to deny that human freedom exists, but at the same time to have no clear idea of what it is that they are denying to exist. The first thing that needs to be said about the free-will issue is that any meaningful term must have a meaningful opposite: if it is meaningful to assert that people are not free, it must be equally meaningful to assert that people *are* free, whether this latter assertion is in fact true or not. Whether it is true, of course, will depend on the meaning that is given the weasel-word "free." For example, if freedom is made dependent on indeterminism, it may well be that human freedom is nonexistent. But there seem to be no good grounds for asserting such a dependence, especially since lack of causation is the furthest thing from people's minds when they call an act free. Doubtless there are other senses that can be given to the word "free"—such as "able to do anything we want to do"—in which no human beings are free. But the first essential point about which the denier of freedom must be clear is *what* it is that he is denying. If one knows what it is like for people not to be free, one must know what it *would* be like for them to *be* free.

Philosophers have advanced numerous senses of "free" in which countless acts performed by human beings can truly be called free acts. The most common conception of a free act is that according to which an act is free if and only if it is a *voluntary* act. But the word "voluntary" does not always carry the same meaning. Sometimes to call an act voluntary means that we can do the act *if* we choose to do it: in other words, that it is physically and psychologically possible for us to do it, so that the occurrence of the act follows upon the decision to do it. (One's decision to raise his arm is in fact followed by the actual raising of his arm, unless he is a paralytic; one's decision to pluck the moon from the sky is not followed by the actual event.) Sometimes a voluntary act is conceived (as by G. E. Moore[1]) as an act which would not have occurred if, just beforehand, the agent had chosen not to perform it. But these senses are different from the sense in which a voluntary act is an act resulting from

* John Hospers, "Meaning and Free Will," *Philosophy and Phenomenological Research,* X (1950), 313–330, reprinted by permission of the author and the editor. The selection appearing here is the abridged version printed as "Free Will and Psychoanalysis" in Wilfred Sellars and John Hospers, eds., *Readings in Ethical Theory* (New York: Appleton Century-Crofts, 1952), pp. 560–575. For a later discussion of the problem of this paper and one more in accord with the author's present views, see Professor Hospers' *Human Conduct* (New York: Harcourt, Brace & World, 1961), pp. 493–524.

[1] *Ethics,* pp. 15–16.

deliberation, or perhaps merely from *choice.* For example, there are many acts which we could have avoided, if we had chosen to do so, but which we nevertheless did not *choose* to perform, much less *deliberate* about them. The act of raising one's leg in the process of taking a step while out for a walk, is one which a person could have avoided by choosing to, but which, after one has learned to walk, takes place automatically or semi-automatically through habit, and thus is not the result of choice. (One may have chosen to take the walk, but not to take this or that step while walking.) Such acts are free in Moore's sense but are not free in the sense of being deliberate. Moreover, there are classes of acts of the same general character which are not even covered by Moore's sense: sudden outbursts of feeling, in some cases at least, could not have been avoided by an immediately preceding volition, so that if these are to be included under the heading of voluntary acts, the proviso that the act could have been avoided by an immediately preceding volition must be amended to read "could have been avoided by a volition or series of volitions by the agent *at some time in the past*"—such as the adoption of a different set of habits in the agent's earlier and more formative years.

(Sometimes we call *persons,* rather than their acts, free. S. Stebbing, for example, declares that one should never call acts free, but only the doers of the acts.[2] But the two do not seem irreconcilable: can we not speak of a *person* as free *with respect to a certain act* (never just free in general) if that *act* is free—whatever we may then go on to mean by saying that an act is free? Any statement about a free act can then be translated into a statement about the doer of the act.)

Now, no matter in which of the above ways we may come to define "voluntary," there are still acts which are voluntary *but which we would be very unlikely to think of as free.* Thus, when a person submits to the command of an armed bandit, he may do so voluntarily in every one of the above senses: he may do so as a result of choice, even of deliberation, and he could have avoided doing it by willing not to—he could, instead, have refused and been shot. The man who reveals a state secret under torture does the same: he could have refused and endured more torture. Yet such acts, and persons in respect of such acts, are not generally called free. We say that they were performed *under compulsion,* and if an act is performed under compulsion we do not call it free. We say, "He wasn't free because he was forced to do as he did," though of course his act was voluntary.

This much departure from the identification of free acts with voluntary acts almost everyone would admit. Sometimes, however, it would be added that this is all the departure that can be admitted. According to Moritz Schlick, for example,

> Freedom means the opposite of compulsion; a man is *free* if he does not act under *compulsion,* and he is compelled or unfree when he is hindered from without in the realization of his natural desires. Hence he is unfree when he is locked up, or chained, or when someone forces him at the point of a gun to do what otherwise he would not do. This is quite clear, and everyone will admit that the everyday or legal notion of the lack of freedom is thus correctly interpreted, and that a man will be considered quite free . . . if no such external compulsion is exerted upon him.[3]

Schlick adds that the entire vexed free-will controversy in philosophy is so much wasted ink and paper, because compulsion has been confused with causality and necessity with uniformity. If the question is asked whether every event is caused, the answer is doubtless yes; but if it is whether every event is compelled, the answer is clearly no. Free acts are uncompelled acts, not uncaused acts. Again, when it is said that some state of affairs (such as water flowing downhill) is necessary, if "necessary" means "compelled," the answer is no; if it means merely that it always happens that way, the answer is yes: universality of application is confused with compulsion. And this, according to Schlick, is the end of the matter.

Schlick's analysis is indeed clarifying and helpful to those who have fallen victim to the confusions he exposes—and this probably includes most persons in their philosophical growing-pains. But *is* this the end of the matter? Is it true that all acts, though caused, are free as long as they are not compelled in the sense which he specifies? May it not be that, while the

[2] *Philosophy and the Physicists,* p. 212.

[3] *The Problems of Ethics,* Rynin translation, p. 150.

identification of "free" with "uncompelled" is acceptable, the area of compelled acts is vastly greater than he or most other philosophers have ever suspected? (Moore is more cautious in this respect than Schlick; while for Moore an act is free if it is voluntary in the sense specified above, he thinks there may be another sense in which human beings, and human acts, are not free at all.[4]) We remember statements about human beings being pawns of their early environment, victims of conditions beyond their control, the result of causal influences stemming from their parents, and the like, and we ponder and ask, "Still, are we really free?" Is there not something in what generations of sages have said about man being fettered? Is there not perhaps something too facile, too sleight-of-hand, in Schlick's cutting of the Gordian knot? For example, when a metropolitan newspaper headlines an article with the words "Boy Killer is Doomed Long before He Is Born,"[5] and then goes on to describe how a twelve-year-old boy has been sentenced to prison for the murder of a girl, and how his parental background includes records of drunkenness, divorce, social maladjustment, and paresis, are we still to say that his act, though voluntary and assuredly *not* done at the point of a gun, is free? The boy has early displayed a tendency toward sadistic activity to hide an underlying masochism and "prove that he's a man"; being coddled by his mother only worsens this tendency, until, spurned by a girl in his attempt on her, he kills her—not simply in a fit of anger, but calculatingly, deliberately. Is he free in respect of his criminal act, or for that matter in most of the acts of his life? Surely to ask this question is to answer it in the negative. Perhaps I have taken an extreme case; but it is only to show the superficiality of the Schlick analysis the more clearly. Though not everyone has criminotic tendencies, everyone has been molded by influences which in large measure at least determine his present behavior; he is literally the product of these influences, stemming from periods prior to his "years of discretion," giving him a host of character traits that he cannot change now even if he would. So obviously does what a man is depend upon how a man comes to be, that it is small wonder that philosophers and sages have considered man far indeed from being the master of his fate. It is not as if man's will were standing high and serene above the flux of events that have molded him; it is itself caught up in this flux, itself carried along on the current. An act is free when it is determined by the man's character, say moralists; but what if the most decisive aspects of his character were already irrevocably acquired before he could do anything to mold them? What if even the degree of will power available to him in shaping his habits and disciplining himself now to overcome the influence of his early environment is a factor over which he has no control? What are we to say of this kind of "freedom?" Is it not rather like the freedom of the machine to stamp labels on cans when it has been devised for just that purpose? Some machines can do so more efficiently than others, but only because they have been better constructed.

It is not my purpose here to establish this thesis in general, but only in one specific respect which has received comparatively little attention, namely, the field referred to by psychiatrists as that of unconscious motivation. In what follows I shall restrict my attention to it because it illustrates as clearly as anything the points I wish to make.

Let me try to summarize very briefly the psychoanalytic doctrine on this point.[6] The conscious life of the human being, including the conscious decisions and volitions, is merely a mouthpiece for the unconscious—not directly for the enactment of unconscious drives, but of the compromise between unconscious drives and unconscious reproaches. There is a Big Three behind the scenes which the automaton called the conscious personality carries out: the id, an "eternal gimme," presents its wish and demands its immediate satisfaction; the super-ego says no to the wish immediately upon presentation, and the

[4] *Ethics,* Chapter 6, pp. 217ff.

[5] *New York Post,* Tuesday, May 18, 1948, p. 4.

[6] I am aware that the theory presented below is not accepted by all practicing psychoanalysts. Many non-Freudians would disagree with the conclusions presented below. But I do not believe that this fact affects my argument, as long as the concept of unconscious motivation is accepted. I am aware, too, that much of the language employed in the following descriptions is animistic and metaphorical; but as long as I am presenting a view I would prefer to "go the whole hog" and present it in its most dramatic form. The theory can in any case be made clearest by the use of such language, just as atomic theory can often be made clearest to students with the use of models.

unconscious ego, the mediator between the two, tries to keep peace by means of compromise.[7]

To go into examples of the functioning of these three "bosses" would be endless; psychoanalytic case books supply hundreds of them. The important point for us to see in the present context is that *it is the unconscious that determines what the conscious impulse and the conscious action shall be.* Hamlet, for example, had a strong Oedipus wish, which was violently counteracted by super-ego reproaches; these early wishes were vividly revived in an unusual adult situation in which his uncle usurped the coveted position from Hamlet's father and won his mother besides. This situation evoked strong strictures on the part of Hamlet's super-ego, and it was this that was responsible for his notorious delay in killing his uncle. A dozen times Hamlet could have killed Claudius easily; but everytime Hamlet "decided" not to: a free choice, moralists would say—but no, listen to the super-ego: "What you feel such hatred toward your uncle for, what you are plotting to kill him for, is precisely the crime which you yourself desire to commit: to kill your father and replace him in the affections of your mother. Your fate and your uncle's are bound up together." This paralyzes Hamlet into inaction. Consciously all he knows is that he is unable to act; this conscious inability he rationalizes, giving a different excuse each time.[8]

We have always been conscious of the fact that we are not masters of our fate in every respect—that there are many things which we cannot do, that nature is more powerful than we are, that we cannot disobey laws without danger of reprisals, etc. We have become "officially" conscious, too, though in our private lives we must long have been aware of it, that we are not free with respect to the emotions that we feel—whom we love or hate, what types we admire, and the like. More lately still we have been reminded that there are unconscious motivations for our basic attractions and repulsions, our compulsive actions or inabilities to act. But what is not welcome news is that our very acts of volition, and the entire train of deliberations leading up to them, are but façades for the expression of unconscious wishes, or rather, unconscious compromises and defenses.

A man is faced by a choice: shall he kill another person or not? Moralists would say, here is a free choice—the result of deliberation, an action consciously entered into. And yet, though the agent himself does not know it, and has no awareness of the forces that are at work within him, his choice is already determined for him: his conscious will is only an instrument, a slave, in the hands of a deep unconscious motivation which determines his action. If he has a great deal of what the analyst calls "free-floating guilt," he will not; but if the guilt is such as to demand immediate absorption in the form of self-damaging behavior, this accumulated guilt will have to be discharged in some criminal action. The man himself does not know what the inner clockwork is; he is like the hands on the clock, thinking they move freely over the face of the clock.

A woman has married and divorced several husbands. Now she is faced with a choice for the next marriage: shall she marry Mr. A, or Mr. B, or nobody at all? She may take considerable time to "decide" this question, and her decision may appear as a final triumph of her free will. Let us assume that A is a normal, well-adjusted, kind, and generous man, while B is a leech, an impostor, one who will become entangled constantly in quarrels with her. If she belongs to a certain classifiable psychological type, she will inevitably choose B, and she will do so even if her previous husbands have resembled B, so that one would think that she "had learned from experience." Consciously, she will of course "give the matter due consideration," etc., etc. To the psychoanalyst all this is irrelevant chaff in the wind—only a camouflage for the inner workings about which she knows nothing consciously. If she is of a certain kind of masochistic strain, as exhibited in her previous set of symptoms, she *must* choose B: her super-ego, always out to maximize the torment in the situation, seeing what dazzling possibilities for self-damaging behavior are promised by the choice of B, compels her to make the choice she does, and even to conceal the real basis of the choice behind an elaborate façade of rationalizations.

A man is addicted to gambling. In the service

[7] This view is very clearly developed in Edmund Bergler, *Divorce Won't Help,* especially Chapter I.

[8] See *The Basic Writings of Sigmund Freud,* Modern Library Edition, p. 310. (In *The Interpretation of Dreams.*) Cf. also the essay by Ernest Jones, "A Psycho-analytical Study of Hamlet."

of his addiction he loses all his money, spends what belongs to his wife, even sells his property and neglects his children. For a time perhaps he stops; then, inevitably, he takes it up again. The man does not know that he is a victim rather than an agent; or, if he sometimes senses that he is in the throes of something-he-knows-not-what, he will have no inkling of its character and will soon relapse into the illusion that he (his conscious self) is freely deciding the course of his own actions. What he does not know, of course, is that he is still taking out on his mother the original lesion to his infantile narcissism, getting back at her for her fancied refusal of his infantile wishes—and this by rejecting everything identified with her, namely education, discipline, logic, common sense, training. At the roulette wheel, almost alone among adult activities, chance—the opposite of all these things—rules supreme; and his addiction represents his continued and emphatic reiteration of his rejection of Mother and all she represents to his unconscious.

This pseudo-aggression of his is of course masochistic in its effects. In the long run he always loses; he can never quit while he is winning. And far from playing in order to win, rather one can say that his losing is a *sine qua non* of his psychic equilibrium (as it was for example with Dostoyevsky): guilt demands punishment, and in the ego's "deal" with the super-ego the super-ego has granted satisfaction of infantile wishes in return for the self-damaging conditions obtaining. Winning would upset the neurotic equilibrium.[9]

A man has wash-compulsion. He must be constantly washing his hands—he uses up perhaps 400 towels a day. Asked why he does this, he says, "I need to, my hands are dirty"; and if it is pointed out to him that they are not really dirty, he says "They feel dirty anyway, I feel better when I wash them." So once again he washes them. He "freely decides" every time; he feels that he must wash them, he deliberates for a moment perhaps, but always ends by washing them. What he does not see, of course, are the invisible wires inside him pulling him inevitably to do the thing he does: the infantile id-wish concerns preoccupation with dirt, the super-ego charges him with this, and the terrified ego must respond, "No, I don't like dirt, see how clean I like to be, look how I wash my hands!"

Let us see what further "free acts" the same patient engages in (this is an actual case history): he is taken to a concentration camp, and given the worst of treatment by the Nazi guards. In the camp he no longer chooses to be clean, does not even try to be—on the contrary, his choice is now to wallow in filth as much as he can. All he is aware of now is a disinclination to be clean, and every time he must choose he chooses not to be. Behind the scenes, however, another drama is being enacted: the super-ego, perceiving that enough torment is being administered from the outside, can afford to cease pressing its charges in this quarter—the outside world is doing the torturing now, so the super-ego is relieved of the responsibility. Thus the ego is relieved of the agony of constantly making terrified replies in the form of washing to prove that the super-ego is wrong. The defense no longer being needed, the person slides back into what is his natural predilection anyway, for filth. This becomes too much even for the Nazi guards: they take hold of him one day, saying "We'll teach you how to be clean!" drag him into the snow, and pour bucket after bucket of icy water over him until he freezes to death. Such is the end-result of an original id-wish, caught in the machinations of a destroying super-ego.

Let us take, finally, a less colorful, more everyday example. A student at a university, possessing wealth, charm, and all that is usually considered essential to popularity, begins to develop the following personality-pattern: although well taught in the graces of social conversation, he always makes a *faux pas* somewhere, and always in the worst possible situation; to his friends he makes cutting remarks which hurt deeply—and always apparently aimed in such a way as to hurt the most: a remark that would not hurt A but would hurt B he invariably makes to B rather than to A, and so on. None of this is conscious. Ordinarily he is considerate of people, but he contrives always (unconsciously) to impose on just those friends who would resent it most, and at just the times when he should know that he should not impose: at 3 o'clock in the morning, without forewarning, he phones a friend in a

[9] See Edmund Bergler's article on the pathological gambler in *Diseases of the Nervous System* (1943). Also "Suppositions about the Mechanism of Criminosis," *Journal of Criminal Psychopathology* (1944) and "Clinical Contributions to the *Psychogenesis of Alcohol Addiction*," *Quarterly Journal of Studies on Alcohol*, 5: 434 (1944).

near-by city demanding to stay at his apartment for the weekend; naturally the friend is offended, but the person himself is not aware that he has provoked the grievance ("common sense" suffers a temporary eclipse when the neurotic pattern sets in, and one's intelligence, far from being of help in such a situation, is used in the interest of the neurosis), and when the friend is cool to him the next time they meet, he wonders why and feels unjustly treated. Aggressive behavior on his part invites resentment and aggression in turn, but all that he consciously sees is others' behavior towards him—and he considers himself the innocent victim of an unjustified "persecution."

Each of these acts is, from the moralist's point of view, free: he chose to phone his friend at 3 a.m.; he chose to make the cutting remark that he did, etc. What he does not know is that an ineradicable masochistic pattern has set in. His unconscious is far more shrewd and clever than is his conscious intellect; it sees with uncanny accuracy just what kind of behavior will damage him most, and unerringly forces him into that behavior. Consciously, the student "doesn't know why he did it"—he gives different "reasons" at different times, but they are all, once again, rationalizations cloaking the unconscious mechanism which propels him willy-nilly into actions that his "common sense" eschews.

The more of this sort of thing one observes, the more he can see what the psychoanalyst means when he talks about *the illusion of freedom.* And the more of a psychiatrist one becomes, the more he is overcome with a sense of what an illusion this free-will can be. In some kinds of cases most of us can see it already: it takes no psychiatrist to look at the epileptic and sigh with sadness at the thought that soon this person before you will be as one possessed, not the same thoughtful intelligent person you knew. But people are not aware of this in other contexts, for example when they express surprise at how a person whom they have been so good to could treat them so badly. Let us suppose that you help a person financially or morally or in some other way, so that he is in your debt; suppose further that he is one of the many neurotics who unconsciously identify kindness with weakness and aggression with strength, then he will unconsciously take your kindness to him as weakness and use it as the occasion for enacting some aggression against you. He can't help it, he may regret it himself later; still, he will be driven to do it. If we gain a little knowledge of psychiatry, we can look at him with pity, that a person otherwise so worthy should be so unreliable—but we will exercise realism too, and be aware that there are some types of people that you cannot be good to in "free" acts of their conscious volition, they will use your own goodness against you.

Sometimes the persons themselves will become dimly aware that "something behind the scenes" is determining their behavior. The divorcee will sometimes view herself with detachment, as if she were some machine (and indeed the psychoanalyst does call her a "repeating-machine"): "I know I'm caught in a net, that I'll fall in love with this guy and marry him and the whole ridiculous merry-go-round will start all over again."

We talk about free will, and we say, for example, the person is free to do so-and-so if he can do so *if* he wants to—and we forget that his wanting to is itself caught up in the stream of determinism, that unconscious forces drive him into the wanting or not wanting to do the thing in question. The analogy of the puppet whose motions are manipulated from behind by invisible wires, or better still, by springs inside, is a telling one at almost every point.

And the glaring fact is that it all started so early, before we knew what was happening. The personality-structure is inelastic after the age of five, and comparatively so in most cases after the age of three. Whether one acquires a neurosis or not is determined by that age—and just as involuntarily as if it had been a curse of God. If, for example, a masochistic pattern was set up, under pressure of hyper-narcissism combined with real or fancied infantile deprivation, then the masochistic snowball was on its course downhill long before we or anybody else knew what was happening, and long before anyone could do anything about it. To speak of human beings as "puppets" in such a context is no idle metaphor, but a stark rendering of a literal fact: only the psychiatrist knows what puppets people really are; and it is no wonder that the protestations of philosophers that "the act which is the result of a volition, a deliberation, a conscious decision, is free" leave these persons, to speak mildly, somewhat cold.

But, one may object, all the states thus far described have been abnormal, neurotic ones.

The well-adjusted (normal) person at least is free.

Leaving aside the question of how clearly and on what grounds one can distinguish the neurotic from the normal, let me use an illustration of a proclivity that everyone would call normal, namely, the decision of a man to support his wife and possibly a family, and consider briefly its genesis, according to psychoanalytic accounts.[10]

Every baby comes into the world with a full-fledge case of megalomania—interested only in himself, acting as if believing that he is the center of the universe and that others are present only to fulfill his wishes, and furious when his own wants are not satisfied immediately no matter for what reason. Gratitude, even for all the time and worry and care expended on him by the mother, is an emotion entirely foreign to the infant, and as he grows older it is inculcated in him only with the greatest difficulty; his natural tendency is to assume that everything that happens to him is due to himself, except for denials and frustrations, which are due to the "cruel, denying" outer world, in particular the mother; and that he owes nothing to anyone, is dependent on no one. This omnipotence-complex, or illusion of non-dependence, has been called the "autarchic fiction." Such a conception of the world is actually fostered in the child by the conduct of adults, who automatically attempt to fulfill the infant's every wish concerning nourishment, sleep, and attention. The child misconceives causality and sees in these wish-fulfillments not the results of maternal kindness and love, but simply the result of his own omnipotence.

This fiction of omnipotence is gradually destroyed by experience, and its destruction is probably the deepest disappointment of the early years of life. First of all, the infant discovers that he is the victim of organic urges and necessities: hunger, defecation, urination. More important, he discovers that the maternal breast, which he has not previously distinguished from his own body (he has not needed to, since it was available when he wanted it), is not a part of himself after all, but of another creature upon whom he is dependent. He is forced to recognize this, e.g., when he wants nourishment and it is at the moment not present; even a small delay is most damaging to the "autarchic fiction." Most painful of all is the experience of weaning, probably the greatest tragedy in every baby's life, when his dependence is most cruelly emphasized; it is a frustrating experience because what he wants is no longer there at all; and if he has been able to some extent to preserve the illustion of non-dependence heretofore, he is not able to do so now—it is plain that the source of his nourishment is not dependent on him, but he on it. The shattering of the autarchic fiction is a great disillusionment to every child, a tremendous blow to his ego which he will, in one way or another, spend the rest of his life trying to repair. How does he do this?

First of all, his reaction to frustration is anger and fury; and he responds by kicking, biting, etc., the only ways he knows. But he is motorically helpless, and these measures are ineffective, and only serve to emphasize his dependence the more. Moreover, against such responses of the child the parental reaction is one of prohibition, often involving deprivation of attention and affection. Generally the child soon learns that this form of rebellion is profitless, and brings him more harm than good. He wants to respond to frustration with violent aggression, and at the same time learns that he will be punished for such aggression, and that in any case the latter is ineffectual. What face-saving solution does he find? Since he must "face facts," since he must in any case "conform" if he is to have any peace at all, he tries to make it seem as if he himself is the source of the commands and prohibitions: the *external* prohibitive force is *internalized*—and here we have the origin of conscience. By making the prohibitive agency seem to come from within himself, the child can "save face"—as if saying, "The prohibition comes from within me, not from outside, so I'm not subservient to external rule, I'm only obeying rules I've set up myself," thus to some extent saving the autarchic fiction, and at the same time avoiding unpleasant consequences directed against himself by complying with parental commands.

Moreover, the boy[11] has unconsciously never

[10] E.g., Edmund Bergler, *The Battle of the Conscience,* Chapter I.

[11] The girl's development after this point is somewhat different. Society demands more aggressiveness of the adult male, hence there are more super-ego strictures on tendencies toward passivity in the male; accordingly his defenses must be stronger.

forgiven the mother for his dependence on her in early life, for nourishment and all other things. It has upset his illusion of non-dependence. These feelings have been repressed and are not remembered; but they are acted out in later life in many ways—e.g., in the constant deprecation man has for woman's duties such as cooking and housework of all sorts ("All she does is stay home and get together a few meals, and she calls that work"), and especially in the man's identification with the mother in his sex experiences with women. By identifying with someone one cancels out in effect the person with whom he identifies—replacing that person, unconsciously denying his existence, and the man, identifying with his early mother, playing the active rôle in "giving" to his wife as his mother has "given" to him, is in effect the denial of his mother's existence, a fact which is narcissistically embarrassing to his ego because it is chiefly responsible for shattering his autarchic fiction. In supporting his wife, he can unconsciously deny that his mother gave to him, and that he was dependent on her giving. Why is it that the husband plays the provider, and wants his wife to be dependent on no one else, although twenty years before he was nothing but a parasitic baby? This is a face-saving device on his part: he can act out the reasoning "See, I'm not the parasitic baby, on the contrary I'm the provider, the giver." His playing the provider is a constant face-saving device, to deny his early dependence which is so embarrassing to his ego. It is no wonder that men generally dislike to be reminded of their babyhood, when they were dependent on woman.

Thus we have here a perfectly normal adult reaction which is unconsciously motivated. The man "chooses" to support a family—and his choice is as unconsciously motivated as anything could be. (I have described here only the "normal" state of affairs, uncomplicated by the well-nigh infinite number of variations that occur in actual practice.)

Now, what of the notion of responsibility? What happens to it on our analysis?

Let us begin with an example, not a fictitious one. A woman and her two-year-old baby are riding on a train to Montreal in mid-winter. The child is ill. The woman wants badly to get to her destination. She is, unknown to herself, the victim of a neurotic conflict whose nature is irrelevant here except for the fact that it forces her to behave aggressively toward the child, partly to spite her husband whom she despises and who loves the child, but chiefly to ward off super-ego charges of masochistic attachment. Consciously she loves the child, and when she says this she says it sincerely, but she must behave aggressively toward it nevertheless, just as many children love their mothers but are nasty to them most of the time in neurotic pseudo-aggression. The child becomes more ill as the train approaches Montreal; the heating system of the train is not working, and the conductor pleads with the woman to get off the train at the next town and get the child to a hospital at once. The woman refuses. Soon after, the child's condition worsens, and the mother does all she can to keep it alive, without, however, leaving the train, for she declares that it is absolutely necessary that she reach her destination. But before she gets there the child is dead. After that, of course, the mother grieves, blames herself, weeps hysterically, and joins the church to gain surcease from the guilt that constantly overwhelms her when she thinks of how her aggressive behavior has killed her child.

Was she responsible for her deed? In ordinary life, after making a mistake, we say, "Chalk it up to experience." Here we should say, "Chalk it up to the neurosis." *She* could not help it if her neurosis forced her to act this way—she didn't even know what was going on behind the scenes, her conscious self merely acted out its assigned part. This is far more true than is generally realized: criminal actions in general are not actions for which their agents are responsible; the agents are passive, not active—they are victims of a neurotic conflict. Their very hyper-activity is unconsciously determined.

To say this is, of course, not to say that we should not punish criminals. Clearly, for our own protection, we must remove them from our midst so that they can no longer molest and endanger organized society. And, of course, if we use the word "responsible" in such a way that justly to hold someone responsible for a deed is by definition identical with being justified in punishing him, then we can and do hold people responsible. But this is like the sense of "free" in which free acts are voluntary ones. It does not go deep enough. In a deeper sense we cannot hold the person responsible: we can hold his neurosis responsible, but *he is not responsible for his neurosis,* particularly since the age at which its onset was inevitable was an age before he could even speak.

The neurosis is responsible—but isn't the neurosis a part of *him?* We have been speaking all the time as if the person and his unconscious were two separate beings; but isn't he one personality, including conscious and unconscious departments together?

I do not wish to deny this. But it hardly helps us here; for what people want when they talk about freedom, and what they hold to when they champion it, is the idea that the *conscious* will is the master of their destiny. "I am the master of my fate, I am the captain of my soul"—and they surely mean their conscious selves, the self that they can recognize and search and introspect. Between an unconscious that willy-nilly determines your actions, and an external force which pushes you, there is little if anything to choose. The unconscious is just *as if* it were an outside force; and indeed, psychiatrists will assert that the inner Hitler (your super-ego) can torment you far more than any external Hitler can. Thus the kind of freedom that people want, the only kind they will settle for, is precisely the kind that psychiatry says they cannot have.

Heretofore it was pretty generally thought that, while we could not rightly blame a person for the color of his eyes or the morality of his parents, or even for what he did at the age of three, or to a large extent what impulses he had and whom he fell in love with, one *could* do so for other of his adult activities, particularly the acts he performed voluntarily and with premeditation. Later this attitude was shaken. Many voluntary acts came to be recognized, at least in some circles, as compelled by the unconscious. Some philosophers recognized this too—Ayer[12] talks about the kleptomaniac being unfree, and about a person being unfree when another person exerts a habitual ascendancy over his personality. But this is as far as he goes. The usual examples, such as the kleptomaniac and the schizophrenic, apparently satisfy most philosophers, and with these exceptions removed, the rest of mankind is permitted to wander in the vast and alluring fields of freedom and responsibility. So far, the inroads upon freedom left the vast majority of humanity untouched; they began to hit home when psychiatrists began to realize, though philosophers did not, that the domination of the conscious by the unconscious extended, not merely to a few exceptional individuals, but to all human beings, that the "big three behind the scenes" are not respecters of persons, and dominate us all, even including that *sanctum sanctorum* of freedom, our conscious will. To be sure, the domination by the unconscious in the case of "normal" individuals is somewhat more benevolent than the tyranny and despotism exercised in neurotic cases, and therefore the former have evoked less comment; but the principle remains in all cases the same: the unconscious is the master of every fate and the captain of every soul.

We speak of a machine turning out good products most of the time but every once in a while it turns out a "lemon." We do not, of course, hold the product responsible for this, but the machine, and via the machine, its maker. Is it silly to extend to inanimate objects the idea of responsibility? Of course. But is it any less so to employ the notion in speaking of human creatures? Are not the two kinds of cases analogous in countless important ways? Occasionally a child turns out badly too, even when his environment and training are the same as that of his brothers and sisters who turn out "all right." He is the "bad penny." His acts of rebellion against parental discipline in adult life (such as the case of the gambler, already cited) are traceable to early experiences of real or fancied denial of infantile wishes. Sometimes the denial has been real, though many denials are absolutely necessary if the child is to grow up to observe the common decencies of civilized life; sometimes, if the child has an unusual quantity of narcissism, every event that occurs is interpreted by him as a denial of his wishes, and nothing a parent could do, even granting every humanly possible wish, would help. In any event, the later neurosis can be attributed to this. Can the person himself be held responsible? Hardly. If he engages in activities which are a menace to society, he must be put into prison, of course, but responsibility is another matter. The time when the events occurred which rendered his neurotic behavior inevitable was a time long before he was capable of thought and decision. As an adult, he is a victim of a world he never made—only this world is inside him.

What about the children who turn out "all

[12] A. J. Ayer, "Freedom and Necessity," *Polemic* (September–October 1946), pp. 40–43. [This volume, pp. 267–72.]

right?" All we can say is that "it's just lucky for them" that what happened to their unfortunate brother didn't happen to them; *through no virtue of their own* they are not doomed to the life of unconscious guilt, expiation, conscious depression, terrified ego-gestures for the appeasement of a tyrannical super-ego, that he is. The machine turned them out with a minimum of damage. But if the brother cannot be blamed for his evils, neither can they be praised for their good; unless, of course, we should blame people for what is not their fault, and praise them for lucky accidents.

We all agree that machines turn out "lemons," we all agree that nature turns out misfits in the realm of biology—the blind, the crippled, the diseased; but we hesitate to include the realm of the personality, for here, it seems, is the last retreat of our dignity as human beings. Our ego can endure anything but this; this island at least must remain above the encroaching flood. But may not precisely the same analysis be made here also? Nature turns out psychological "lemons" too, in far greater quantities than any other kind; and indeed all of us are "lemons" in some respect or other, the difference being one of degree. Some of us are lucky enough not to have a gambling-neurosis or criminotic tendencies or masochistic mother-attachment or overdimensional repetition-compulsion to make our lives miserable, but most of our actions, those usually considered the most important, are unconsciously dominated just the same. And, if a neurosis may be likened to a curse of God, let those of us, the elect, who are enabled to enjoy a measure of life's happiness without the hell-fire of neurotic guilt, take this, not as our own achievement, but simply for what it is—a gift of God.

Let us, however, quit metaphysics and put the situation schematically in the form of a deductive argument.

1. An occurrence over which we had no control is something we cannot be held responsible for.

2. Events E, occurring during our babyhood, were events over which we had no control.

3. Therefore events E were events which we cannot be held responsible for.

4. But if there is something we cannot be held responsible for, neither can we be held responsible for something that inevitably results from it.

5. Events E have as inevitable consequence Neurosis N, which in turn has as inevitable consequence Behavior B.

6. Since N is the inevitable consequence of E and B is the inevitable consequence of N, B is the inevitable consequence of E.

7. Hence, not being responsible for E, we cannot be responsible for B.

In Samuel Butler's Utopian satire *Erewhon* there occurs the following passage, in which a judge is passing sentence on a prisoner:

> It is all very well for you to say that you came of unhealthy parents, and had a severe accident in your childhood which permanently undermined your constitution; excuses such as these are the ordinary refuge of the criminal; but they cannot for one moment be listened to by the ear of justice. I am not here to enter upon curious metaphysical questions as to the origin of this or that—questions to which there would be no end were their introduction once tolerated, and which would result in throwing the only guilt on the tissues of the primordial cell, or on the elementary gases. There is no question of how you came to be wicked, but only this—namely, are you wicked or not? This has been decided in the affirmative, neither can I hesitate for a single moment to say that it has been decided justly. You are a bad and dangerous person, and stand branded in the eyes of your fellow countrymen with one of the most heinous known offenses.[13]

As moralists read this passage, they may perhaps nod with approval. But the joke is on them. The sting comes when we realize what the crime is for which the prisoner is being sentenced: namely, consumption. The defendant is reminded that during the previous year he was sentenced for aggravated bronchitis, and is warned that he should profit from experience in the future. Butler is employing here his familiar method of presenting some human tendency (in this case, holding people responsible for what isn't their fault) to a ridiculous extreme and thereby reducing it to absurdity.

Assuming the main conclusions of this paper to be true, is there any room left for freedom?

This, of course, all depends on what we mean by "freedom." In the senses suggested at the beginning of this paper, there are countless free

[13] Samuel Butler, *Erewhon* (Modern Library edition), p. 107.

acts, and unfree ones as well. When "free" means "uncompelled," and only external compulsion is admitted, again there are countless free acts. But now we have extended the notion of compulsion to include determination by unconscious forces. With this sense in mind, our question is, "With the concept of compulsion thus extended, and in the light of present psychoanalytic knowledge, is there any freedom left in human behavior?"

If practicising psychoanalysts were asked this question, there is little doubt that their answer would be along the following lines: they would say that they were not accustomed to using the term "free" at all, but that if they had to suggest a criterion for distinguishing the free from the unfree, they would say that a person's freedom is present *in inverse proportion to his neuroticism;* in other words, the more his acts are determined by a *malevolent* unconscious, the less free he is. Thus they would speak of *degrees* of freedom. They would say that as a person is cured of his neurosis, he becomes more free—free to realize capabilities that were blocked by the neurotic affliction. The psychologically well-adjusted individual is in this sense comparatively the most free. Indeed, those who are cured of mental disorders are sometimes said to have *regained their freedom:* they are freed from the tyranny of a malevolent unconscious which formerly exerted as much of a domination over them as if they had been the abject slaves of a cruel dictator.

But suppose one says that a person is free only to the extent that his acts are *not unconsciously determined at all,* be they unconscious benevolent *or* malevolent? If this is the criterion, psychoanalysts would say, most human behavior cannot be called free at all: our impulses and volitions having to do with our basic attitudes toward life, whether we are optimists or pessimists, tough-minded or tender-minded, whether our tempers are quick or slow, whether we are "naturally self-seeking" or "naturally benevolent" (and *all the acts consequent upon these things*), what things annoy us, whether we take to blondes or brunettes, old or young, whether we become philosophers or artists or businessmen—all this has its basis in the unconscious. If people generally call most acts free, it is not because they believe that compelled acts should be called free, it is rather through not knowing how large a proportion of our acts actually are compelled. Only the comparatively "vanilla-flavored" aspects of our lives—such as our behavior toward people who don't really matter to us—are exempted from this rule.

These, I think, are the two principal criteria for distinguishing freedom from the lack of it which we might set up on the basis of psychoanalytic knowledge. Conceivably we might set up others. In every case, of course, it remains trivially true that "it all depends on how we choose to use the word." The facts are what they are, regardless of what words we choose for labeling them. But if we choose to label them in a way which is not in accord with what human beings, however vaguely, have long had in mind in applying these labels, as we would be doing if we labeled as "free" many acts which we know as much about as we now do through modern psychoanalytic methods, then we shall only be manipulating words to mislead our fellow creatures.

C. A. CAMPBELL

Is "Free Will" a Pseudo-Problem?*

I

In the days when the Verifiability Principle was accepted by its devotees as a secure philosophical truth, one could understand, though one might not agree with, the sweeping claim that many of the traditional problems of philosophy had been shown to be mere 'pseudo-problems'. It was easy to see how, given the Principle's validity, most of the leading questions which agitated our forefathers in metaphysics, in

* C. A. Campbell, "Is 'Free Will' a Pseudo-Problem?" *Mind,* LX (1951), 441–465. Reprinted by permission of the author and the editor of *Mind.*

ethics, and in theology, automatically become nonsensical questions. What is perplexing, however, is that despite the pretty generally acknowledged deterioration in the Principle's status to that of a convenient methodological postulate, the attitude to these same questions seems to have changed but little. To admit that the Verifiability Principle is not an assured truth entails the admission that a problem can no longer be dismissed as meaningless simply on the ground that it cannot be stated in a way which satisfies the Principle. Whether or not a problem is meaningless is now something that can only be decided after critical examination of the particular case on its own individual merits. But the old antipathies seem in large measure to have survived the disappearance of their logical basis. One gets the impression that for at least many thinkers with Positivist sympathies the 'liquidation' of a large, if unspecified, group of traditional philosophic problems is still established fact. If that impression is mistaken, well and good. One may then hope for an early recrudescence of interest in certain problems that have too long suffered the consequences of an unhappy *tabu*. If the impression is correct, a real service would be done to philosophy if it were plainly stated which of the traditional problems are still regarded as pseudo-problems, and what are the reasons, old or new, for passing this sentence upon them. The smoke of old battles, perhaps understandably, darkens the philosophic air, to the considerable inconvenience of all concerned.

Fortunately, however, the obscurity complained of is not totally unrelieved. We do know of one traditional problem that is definitely on the black list of the *avant garde*—the problem of 'Free Will': and we do have pretty adequate information about the reasons which have led to its being placed thereon. This, so far as it goes, is satisfactory. A plain obligation now lies upon philosophers who still believe that 'Free Will' is a genuine problem to explain just where, in their opinion, the case for the prosecution breaks down. To discharge this obligation is the main purpose of the present paper.

There will be a clear advantage in making our start from the *locus classicus* of the 'pseudo-problem' theory, if *locus classicus* there be. And I think that there must be something of the sort. At any rate, the casual, and indeed slightly bored, tones in which so many contemporary philosophers allude to the traditional problem, and their contentment to indicate in only a sketchy manner the reasons why it no longer exists, strongly suggest that *somewhere* the matter has in their eyes been already effectively settled. At least one important 'document in the case' is, I suspect, Chapter VII of Moritz Schlick's *Problems of Ethics,* first published in 1931. This chapter, the title of which is 'When is a Man Responsible?' and the first section of which bears the heading 'The Pseudo-problem of Freedom of the Will', presents in concentrated form, but with some show of systematic argument, most of the considerations upon which later writers appear to rely. It will be worth our while, therefore, to try to see just why Professor Schlick is so sure (and he is *very* sure indeed) that 'Free Will', as traditionally formulated, is a pseudo-problem, begotten by mere confusion of mind.

II

I shall first summarise, as faithfully as I can, what I take to be the distinctive points in Schlick's argument.

The traditional formulation of the problem, Schlick points out, is based on the assumption that to have 'free will' entails having a will that is, at least sometimes, exempt from causal law. It is traditionally supposed, quite rightly, that moral responsibility implies freedom in *some* sense: and it is supposed, also quite rightly, that this sense is one which is incompatible with compulsion. But because it is further supposed, quite *wrongly,* that to be subject to causal or natural law is to be subject to compulsion, the inference is drawn that the free will implied in moral responsibility is incompatible with causal continuity. The ultimate root of the error, Schlick contends, lies in a failure to distinguish between two different kinds of Law, one of which does indeed 'compel', but the other of which does *not.*[1] There are, first, *pre*scriptive laws, such as the laws imposed by civil authority, which presume contrary desires on the part of those to whom they are applied; and these may fairly be said to exercise 'compulsion'. And there are, secondly, *de*scriptive laws, such as the laws which the sciences seek to formulate; and these merely state what does as a matter of fact always happen. It is perfectly clear

[1] *Problems of Ethics,* Ch. VIII. Section 2. (All references are to the English translation by David Rynin, published in New York in 1939.)

that the relation of the latter, the natural, causal laws, to human willing is radically different from the 'compulsive' relation of prescriptive laws to human willing, and that it is really an absurdity to talk of a species of natural law like, say, psychological laws, *compelling* us to act in this or that way. The term 'compulsion' is totally inept where, as in this case, there are no contrary desires. But the traditional discussions of Free Will, confusing descriptive with prescriptive laws, fallaciously assume 'compulsion' to be ingredient in Law as such, and it is contended accordingly that moral freedom, since it certainly implies absence of compulsion, implies also exemption from causal law.

It follows that the problem of Free Will, as traditionally stated, is a mere pseudo-problem. The statement of it in terms of exemption from causal law rests on the assumption that causal law involves 'compulsion'. And this assumption is demonstrably false. Expose the muddle from which it arises and the so-called 'problem' in its traditional form disappears.

But is it quite certain that the freedom which moral responsibility implies is no more than 'the absence of compulsion'? This is the premise upon which Schlick's argument proceeds, but Schlick is himself well aware that it stands in need of confirmation from an analysis of the notion of moral responsibility. Otherwise it might be maintained that although 'the absence of compulsion' has been shown not to entail a contra-causal type of freedom, there is nevertheless some *other* condition of moral responsibility that *does* entail it. Accordingly Schlick embarks now upon a formal analysis of the nature and conditions of moral responsibility designed to show that the *only* freedom implied by moral responsibility is freedom from compulsion. It was a trifle ambitious, however, even for a master of compression like Professor Schlick, to hope to deal satisfactorily in half a dozen very brief pages with a topic which has been so extensively debated in the literature of moral philosophy: and I cannot pretend that I find what he has to say free from obscurity. But to the best of my belief what follows does reproduce the gist of Schlick's analysis.

What precisely, Schlick asks, does the term 'moral responsibility' mean in our ordinary linguistic usage?[2] He begins his answer by insisting upon the close connexion for ordinary usage between 'moral responsibility' and *punishment* (strictly speaking, punishment and *reward:* but for convenience Schlick virtually confines the discussion to punishment, and we shall do the same). The connexion, as Schlick sees it, is this. In ordinary practice our concern with the responsibility for an act (he tells us) is with a view to determining *who is to be punished for it.* Now punishment is (I quote) 'an educative measure'. It is 'a means to the formation of motives, which are in part to prevent the wrong-doer from repeating the act (reformation), and in part to prevent others from committing a similar act (intimidation)'.[3] When we ask, then, 'Who in a given case is to be punished?'—which is the same as the question 'Who is responsible?'—what we are really wanting to discover is some agent in the situation upon whose motives we can bring to bear the appropriate educative influences, so that in similar situations in future his strongest motive will impel him to refrain from, rather than to repeat, the act. 'The question of who is responsible' Schlick sums up, 'is . . . a matter only of knowing who is to be punished or rewarded, in order that punishment and reward function as such—be able to achieve their goal'.[4] It is not a matter, he expressly declares, of trying to ascertain what may be called the 'original instigator' of the act. That might be a great-grand-parent, from the consequence of whose behaviour vicious tendencies have been inherited by a living person. Such 'remote causes' as this are irrelevant to questions of punishment (and so to questions of moral responsibility), 'for in the first place their actual contribution cannot be determined, and in the second place they are generally out of reach'.[5]

It is a matter for regret that Schlick has not rounded off his discussion, as one had hoped and expected he would, by formulating a precise definition of moral responsibility in terms of what he has been saying. I think, however, that the conclusion to which his argument leads could be not unfairly expressed in some such way as this: 'We say that a man is morally responsible for an act if his motives for bringing about the act are such as we can affect favourably in respect of his future behaviour by the educative influences of reward and punishment'.

Given the truth of this analysis of moral re-

[2] *Loc. cit.*, Ch. VII, Section 5.

[3] *Ibid.*, p. 152.

[4] *Ibid.*, p. 153.

[5] *Ibid.*, p. 153.

sponsibility, Schlick's contention follows logically enough that the only freedom that is required for moral responsibility is freedom from compulsion. For what are the cases in which a man's motives are *not* capable of being favourably affected by reward and punishment?—the cases in which, that is, according to Schlick's analysis, we do *not* deem him morally responsible? The only such cases, it would seem, are those in which a man is subjected to some form of external constraint which prevents him from acting according to his 'natural desires'. For example, if a man is compelled by a pistol at his breast to do a certain act, or induced to do it by an externally administered narcotic, he is not 'morally responsible'; or not, at any rate, in so far as punishment would be impotent to affect his motives in respect of his future behaviour. External constraint in one form or another seems to be the sole circumstance which absolves a man from moral responsibility. Hence we may say that freedom from external constraint is the only sort of freedom which an agent must possess in order to be morally responsible. The 'contra-causal' sort of freedom which so many philosophers and others have supposed to be required is shown by a true analysis of moral responsibility to be irrelevant.

This completes the argument that 'Free Will', as traditionally formulated, is a pseudo-problem. The only freedom implied by moral responsibility is freedom from compulsion; and as we have rid ourselves of the myth that subjection to causal law is a form of compulsion, we can see that the only compulsion which absolves from moral responsibility is the external constraint which prevents us from translating our desires into action. The true meaning of the question 'Have we free will?' thus becomes simply 'Can we translate our desires into action?' And this question does not constitute a 'problem' at all, for the answer to it is not in doubt. The obvious answer is 'Sometimes we can, sometimes we can't, according to the specific circumstances of the case'.

III

Here, then, in substance is Schlick's theory. Let us now examine it.

In the first place, it is surely quite unplausible to suggest that the common assumption that moral freedom postulates some breach of causal continuity arises from a confusion of two different types of law. Schlick's distinction between descriptive and prescriptive law is, of course, sound. It was no doubt worth pointing out, too, that descriptive laws cannot be said to 'compel' human behaviour in the same way as prescriptive laws do. But it seems to me evident that the usual reason why it is held that moral freedom implies some breach of causal continuity, is not a belief that causal laws 'compel' as civil laws 'compel', but simply the belief that the admission of unbroken causal continuity entails a *further* admission which is directly incompatible with moral responsibility; *viz.* the admission that no man could have acted otherwise than he in fact did. Now it may, of course, be an error thus to assume that a man is not morally responsible for an act, a fit subject for moral praise and blame in respect of it, unless he could have acted otherwise than he did. Or, if *this* is not an error, it may still be an error to assume that a man could not have acted otherwise than he did, in the sense of the phrase that is crucial for moral responsibility, without there occurring some breach of causal continuity. Into these matters we shall have to enter very fully at a later stage. But the relevant point at the moment is that these (not *prima facie* absurd) assumptions about the conditions of moral responsibility have very commonly, indeed normally, been made, and that they are entirely adequate to explain why the problem of Free Will finds its usual formulation in terms of partial exemption from causal law. Schlick's distinction between prescriptive and descriptive laws has no bearing at all upon the truth or falsity of these assumptions. Yet if these assumptions are accepted, it is (I suggest) really inevitable that the Free Will problem should be formulated in the way to which Schlick takes exception. Recognition of the distinction upon which Schlick and his followers lay so much stress can make not a jot of difference.

As we have seen, however, Schlick does later proceed to the much more important business of disputing these common assumptions about the conditions of moral responsibility. He offers us an analysis of moral responsibility which flatly contradicts these assumptions; an analysis according to which the only freedom demanded by morality is a freedom which is compatible with Determinism. If this analysis can be sustained, there is certainly no problem of 'Free Will' in the traditional sense.

But it seems a simple matter to show that

Schlick's analysis is untenable. Let us test it by Schlick's own claim that it gives us what we mean by 'moral responsibility' in ordinary linguistic usage.

We do not ordinarily consider the lower animals to be morally responsible. But *ought* we not to do so if Schlick is right about what we mean by moral responsibility? It is quite possible, by punishing the dog who absconds with the succulent chops designed for its master's luncheon, favourably to influence its motives in respect of its future behaviour in like circumstances. If moral responsibility is to be linked with punishment as Schlick links it, and punishment conceived as a form of education, we should surely hold the dog morally responsible? The plain fact, of course, is that we don't. We don't, because we suppose that the dog 'couldn't help it': that its action (unlike what we usually believe to be true of human beings) was simply a link in a continuous chain of causes and effects. In other words, we do commonly demand the contra-causal sort of freedom as a condition of moral responsibility.

Again, we do ordinarily consider it proper, in certain circumstances, to speak of a person no longer living as morally responsible for some present situation. But *ought* we to do so if we accept Schlick's essentially 'forward-looking' interpretation of punishment and responsibility? Clearly we cannot now favourably affect the dead man's motives. No doubt they could *at one time* have been favourably affected. But that cannot be relevant to our judgment of responsibility if, as Schlick insists, the question of who is responsible 'is a matter only of knowing who is to be punished or rewarded'. Indeed he expressly tells us, as we saw earlier, that in asking this question we are not concerned with a 'great-grand-parent' who may have been the 'original instigator', because, for one reason, this 'remote cause' is 'out of reach'. We cannot bring the appropriate educative influence to bear upon it. But the plain fact, of course, is that we do frequently assign moral responsibility for present situations to persons who have long been inaccessible to any punitive action on our part. And Schlick's position is still more paradoxical in respect of our apportionment of responsibility for occurrences in the distant past. Since in these cases there is no agent whatsoever whom we can favourably influence by punishment, the question of moral responsibility here should have no meaning for us. But of course it has. Historical writings are studded with examples.

Possibly the criticism just made may seem to some to result from taking Schlick's analysis too much *au pied de la lettre*. The absurd consequences deduced, it may be said, would not follow if we interpreted Schlick as meaning that a man is morally responsible where his motive is such as can *in principle* be favourably affected by reward or punishment—whether or not we who pass the judgment are in a position to take such action. But with every desire to be fair to Schlick, I cannot see how he could accept this modification and still retain the essence of his theory. For the essence of his theory seems to be that moral responsibility has its whole meaning and importance for us in relation to our potential control of future conduct in the interests of society. (I agree that it is hard to believe that anybody *really* thinks this. But it is perhaps less hard to believe to-day than it has ever been before in the history of modern ethics.)

Again, we ordinarily consider that, in certain circumstances, the *degree* of a man's moral responsibility for an act is affected by considerations of his inherited nature, or of his environment, or of both. It is our normal habit to 'make allowances' (as we say) when we have reason to believe that a malefactor had a vicious heredity, or was nurtured in his formative years in a harmful environment. We say in such cases 'Poor chap, he is more to be pitied than blamed. We could scarcely expect him to behave like a decent citizen with *his* parentage or upbringing.' But this extremely common sort of judgment has no point at all if we mean by moral responsibility what Schlick says that we mean. On *that* meaning the degree of a man's moral responsibility must presumably be dependent upon the degree to which we can favourably affect his future motives, which is quite another matter. Now there is no reason to believe that the motives of a man with a bad heredity or a bad upbringing are either less or more subject to educative influence than those of his more fortunate fellows. Yet it is plain matter of fact that we do commonly consider the degree of a man's moral responsibility to be affected by these two factors.

A final point. The extremity of paradox in Schlick's identification of the question 'Who is morally blameworthy?' with the question 'Who is to be punished?' is apt to be partially concealed from us just because it is our normal habit to include in the meaning of 'punishment' an element of 'requital for moral transgression' which Schlick expressly denies to it. On that account we commonly think of 'punishment', in its strict sense, as implying moral blameworthiness in the person punished. But if we remember to mean by punishment what Schlick means by it, a purely 'educative measure', with no retributive ingredients, his identification of the two questions loses such plausibility as it might otherwise have. For clearly we often think it proper to 'punish' a person, in *Schlick's* sense, where we are not at all prepared to say that the person is morally blameworthy. We may even think him morally commendable. A case in point would be the unmistakably sincere but muddleheaded person who at the cost of great suffering to himself steadfastly pursues as his 'duty' a course which, in our judgment is fraught with danger to the common weal. We should most of us feel entitled, in the public interest, to bring such action to bear upon the man's motives as might induce him to refrain in future from his socially injurious behaviour: in other words, to inflict upon him what Schlick would call 'punishment'. But we should most of us feel perfectly clear that in so 'punishing' this misguided citizen we are not proclaiming his moral blameworthiness for moral wickedness.

Adopting Schlick's own criterion, then, looking simply 'to the manner in which the concept is used',[6] we seem bound to admit that constantly people do assign moral responsibility where Schlick's theory says they shouldn't, don't assign moral responsibility where Schlick's theory says they should, and assign degrees of moral responsibility where on Schlick's theory there should be no difference in degree. I think we may reasonably conclude that Schlick's account of what we mean by moral responsibility breaks down.

The rebuttal of Schlick's arguments, however, will not suffice of itself to refute the pseudo-problem theory. The indebtedness to Schlick of most later advocates of the theory may be conceded; but certainly it does not comprehend all of significance that they have to say on the problem. There are recent analyses of the conditions of moral responsibility containing sufficient new matter, or sufficient old matter in a more precise and telling form, to require of us now something of a fresh start. In the section which follows I propose to consider some representative samples of these analyses—all of which, of course, are designed to show that the freedom which moral responsibility implies is not in fact a contra-causal type of freedom.

But before reopening the general question of the nature and conditions of moral responsibility there is a *caveat* which it seems to me worth while to enter. The difficulties in the way of a clear answer are not slight; but they are apt to seem a good deal more formidable than they really are because of a common tendency to consider in unduly close association two distinct questions: the question 'Is a contra-causal type of freedom implied by moral responsibility?' and the question 'Does a contra-causal type of freedom anywhere exist?'. It seems to me that many philosophers (and I suspect that Moritz Schlick is among them) begin their enquiry with so firm a conviction that the contra-causal sort of freedom nowhere exists, that they find it hard to take very seriously the possibility that it is *this* sort of freedom that moral responsibility implies. For they are loth to abandon the commonsense belief that moral responsibility itself is something real. The implicit reasoning I take to be this. Moral responsibility is real. If moral responsibility is real, the freedom implied in it must be a fact. But contra-causal freedom is not a fact. Therefore contra-causal freedom is not the freedom implied in moral responsibility. I think we should be on our guard against allowing this or some similar train of reasoning (whose premises, after all, are far from indubitable) to seduce us into distorting what we actually find when we set about a direct analysis of moral responsibility and its conditions.

IV

The pseudo-problem theorists usually, and naturally, develop their analysis of moral responsibility by way of contrast with a view which, while it has enjoyed a good deal of philosophic support, I can perhaps best describe as the common view. It will be well to remind ourselves, therefore, of the main features of this view.

So far as the *meaning*, as distinct from the *conditions*, of moral responsibility is concerned, the common view is very simple. If we ask our-

[6] *Loc. cit.*, Ch. VII, Section 5, p. 151.

selves whether a certain person is morally responsible for a given act (or it may be just 'in general'), what we are considering, it would be said, is whether or not that person is a fit subject upon whom to pass moral judgment; whether he can fittingly be deemed morally good or bad, morally praiseworthy or blameworthy. This does not take us any great way: but (*pace* Schlick) so far as it goes it does not seem to me seriously disputable. The really interesting and controversial question is about the *conditions* of moral responsibility, and in particular the question whether freedom of a contra-causal kind is among these conditions.

The answer of the common man to the latter question is that it most certainly *is* among the conditions. Why does he feel so sure about this? Not, I argued earlier, because the common man supposes that causal law exercises 'compulsion' in the sense that prescriptive laws do, but simply because he does not see how a person can be deemed morally praiseworthy or blameworthy in respect of an act which he could not help performing. From the stand-point of moral praise and blame, he would say—though not necessarily from other stand-points—it is a matter of indifference whether it is by reason of some external constraint or by reason of his own given nature that the man could not help doing what he did. It is quite enough to make moral praise and blame futile that in either case there were no genuine alternatives, no open possibilities, before the man when he acted. He could not have acted otherwise than he did. And the common man might not unreasonably go on to stress the fact that we all, even if we are linguistic philosophers, do in our actual practice of moral judgment appear to accept the common view. He might insist upon the point alluded to earlier in this paper, that we do all, in passing moral censure, 'make allowances' for influences in a man's hereditary nature or environmental circumstances which we regard as having made it more than ordinarily difficult for him to act otherwise than he did: the implication being that if we supposed that the man's heredity and environment made it not merely very *difficult* but actually *impossible* for him to act otherwise than he did, we could not properly assign moral blame to him at all.

Let us put the argument implicit in the common view a little more sharply. The moral 'ought' implies 'can'. If we say that A morally ought to have done X, we imply that in our opinion, he could have done X. But we assign moral blame to a man only for failing to do what we think he morally ought to have done. Hence if we morally blame A for not having done X, we imply that he could have done X even though in fact he did not. In other words, we imply that A could have acted otherwise than he did. And that means that we imply, as a necessary condition of a man's being morally blameworthy, that he enjoyed a freedom of a kind not compatible with unbroken causal continuity.

V

Now what is it that is supposed to be wrong with this simple piece of argument?—For, of course, it must be rejected by all these philosophers who tell us that the traditional problem of Free Will is a mere pseudo-problem. The argument looks as though it were doing little more than reading off necessary implications of the fundamental categories of our moral thinking. One's inclination is to ask 'If one is to think morally at all, how else than this *can* we think?'.

In point of fact, there is pretty general agreement among the contemporary critics as to what is wrong with the argument. Their answer in general terms is as follows. No doubt A's moral responsibility does imply that he could have acted otherwise. But this expression 'could have acted otherwise' stands in dire need of analysis. When we analyse it, we find that it is not, as is so often supposed, simple and unambiguous, and we find that in *some* at least of its possible meanings it implies *no* breach of causal continuity between character and conduct. Having got this clear, we can further discern that only in one of these *latter* meanings is there any compulsion upon our moral thinking to assert that if A is morally blameworthy for an act, A 'could have acted otherwise than he did'. It follows that, contrary to common belief, our moral thinking *does not* require us to posit a contra-causal freedom as a condition of moral responsibility.

So much of importance obviously turns upon the validity or otherwise of this line of criticism that we must examine it in some detail and with express regard to the *ipsissima verba* of the critics.

In the course of a recent article in MIND,[7] entitled 'Free Will and Moral Responsibility', Mr. Nowell Smith (having earlier affirmed his belief that 'the traditional problem has been solved') explains very concisely the nature of the confusion which, as he thinks, has led to the demand for a contra-causal freedom. He begins by frankly recognising that "It is evident that one of the necessary conditions of moral action is that the agent 'could have acted otherwise'" and he adds "it is to this fact that the Libertarian is drawing attention".[8] Then, after showing (unexceptionably, I think) how the relationship of 'ought' to 'can' warrants the proposition which he has accepted as evident, and how it induces the Libertarian to assert the existence of action that is 'uncaused', he proceeds to point out, in a crucial passage, the nature of the Libertarian's error:

> The fallacy in the argument (he contends) lies in supposing that when we say 'A could have acted otherwise' we mean that A, *being what he was and being placed in the circumstances in which he was placed,* could have done something other than what he did. But in fact we never do mean this.[9]

What then *do* we mean here by 'A could have acted otherwise'? Mr. Nowell Smith does not tell us in so many words, but the passage I have quoted leaves little doubt how he would answer. What we really mean by the expression, he implies, is not a *categorical* but a *hypothetical* proposition. We mean 'A could have acted otherwise, *if he did not happen to be what he in fact was,* or *if he were placed in circumstances other than those in which he was in fact placed*'. Now, *these* propositions, it is easy to see, are in no way incompatible with acceptance of the causal principle in its full rigour. Accordingly the claim that our fundamental moral thinking obliges us to assert a contra-causal freedom as a condition of moral responsibility is disproved.

Such is the 'analytical solution' of our problem offered (with obvious confidence) by one able philosopher of to-day, and entirely representative of the views of many other able philosophers. Yet I make bold to say that its falsity stares one in the face. It seems perfectly plain that the hypothetical propositions which Mr. Nowell Smith proposes to substitute for the categorical proposition cannot express 'what we really mean' in this context by 'A could have acted otherwise', for the simple reason that these hypothetical propositions have no bearing whatsoever upon the question of the moral responsibility of *A*. And it is *A* whose moral responsibility we are talking about—a definite person *A* with a definitive character and in a definitive set of circumstances. What conceivable significance could it have for our attitude to A's responsibility to know that someone with a *different* character (or *A* with a different character, if that collocation of words has any meaning), or A in a different set of circumstances from those in which A as we are concerned with him was in fact placed, 'could have acted otherwise'? No doubt this supposititious being *could* have acted otherwise than the definitive person A acted. But the point is that where we are reflecting, as we are supposed in this context to be reflecting, upon the question of *A*'s moral responsibility, our interest in this supposititious being is precisely *nil.*

The two hypothetical propositions suggested in Mr. Nowell Smith's account of the matter do not, however, exhaust the speculations that have been made along these lines. Another very common suggestion by the analysts is that what we really mean by 'A could have acted otherwise' is 'A could have acted otherwise *if he had willed, or chosen, otherwise*'. This was among the suggestions offered by G. E. Moore in the well-known chapter on Free Will in his *Ethics.* It is, I think, the suggestion he most strongly favoured: though it is fair to add that neither about this nor about any other of his suggestions is Moore in the least dogmatic. He does claim, for, I think, convincing reasons, that "we *very often* mean by 'could' merely 'would, *if* so-and-so had chosen'".[10] And he concludes "I must confess that I cannot feel certain that this may not be all that we usually mean and understand by the assertion that we have Free Will".[11]

This third hypothetical proposition appears to enjoy also the support of Mr. C. L. Stevenson. Mr. Stevenson begins the chapter of *Ethics and Language* entitled 'Avoidability-Indeterminism' with the now familiar pronouncement of his School that 'controversy about freedom and determinism of the will . . . presents no perma-

[7] January, 1948.
[8] *Loc. cit.*, p. 49.
[9] *Loc. cit.*, p. 49.
[10] *Ethics*, p. 212.
[11] *Loc. cit.*, p. 217.

nent difficulty to ethics, being largely a product of confusions'. A major confusion (if I understand him rightly) he takes to lie in the meaning of the term 'avoidable', when we say 'A's action was avoidable'—or, I presume, 'A could have acted otherwise'. He himself offers the following definition of 'avoidable'—" 'A's action was avoidable' has the meaning of 'If A had made a certain choice, which in fact he did not make, his action would not have occurred' ".[12] This I think we may regard as in substance identical with the suggestion that what we really mean by 'A could have acted otherwise' is 'A could have acted otherwise *if* he had chosen (or willed) otherwise'. For clarity's sake we shall here keep to this earlier formulation. In either formulation the special significance of the third hypothetical proposition, as of the two hypothetical propositions already considered, is that it is compatible with strict determinism. If this be indeed all that we mean by the 'freedom' that conditions moral responsibility, then those philosophers are certainly wrong who hold that moral freedom is of the contra-causal type.

Now this third hypothetical proposition does at least possess the merit, not shared by its predecessors, of having a real relevance to the question of moral responsibility. If, *e.g.* A had promised to meet us at 2 P.M., and he chanced to break his leg at 1 P.M., we should not blame him for his failure to discharge his promise. For we should be satisfied that he *could not* have acted otherwise, even if he had so chosen; or *could not,* at any rate, in a way which would have enabled him to meet us at 2 P.M. The freedom to translate one's choice into action, which we saw earlier is for Schlick the *only* freedom required for moral responsibility, is without doubt *one* of the conditions of moral responsibility.

But it seems easy to show that this third hypothetical proposition does not exhaust what we mean, and *some*times is not even *part* of what we mean, by the expression 'could have acted otherwise' in its moral context. Thus it can hardly be even part of what we mean in the case of that class of wrong actions (and it is a large class) concerning which there is really no question whether the agent could have acted otherwise, *if* he had chosen otherwise. Take lying, for example. Only in some very abnormal situation could it occur to one to doubt whether A, whose power of speech was evinced by his telling a lie, was in a position to tell what he took to be the truth *if* he had so chosen. Of *course* he was. Yet it still makes good sense for one's moral thinking to ask whether A, when lying, 'could have acted otherwise': and we still require an affirmative answer to this question if A's moral blameworthiness is to be established. It seems apparent, therefore, that in this class of cases at any rate one does *not* mean by 'A could have acted otherwise', 'A could have acted otherwise *if* he had so chosen'.

What then *does* one mean in this class of cases by 'A could have acted otherwise'? I submit that the expression is taken in its simple, categorical meaning, without any suppressed 'if' clause to qualify it. Or perhaps, in order to keep before us the important truth that it is only as expressions of *will* or *choice* that acts are of moral import, it might be better to say that a condition of A's moral responsibility is that he could have *chosen* otherwise. We saw that there is no real question whether A who told a lie could have acted otherwise *if* he had chosen otherwise. But there is a very real question, at least for any person who approaches the question of moral responsibility at a tolerably advanced level of reflexion, about whether A could have *chosen* otherwise. Such a person will doubtless be acquainted with the claims advanced in some quarters that causal law operates universally: or/and with the theories of some philosophies that the universe is throughout the expression of a single supreme principle; or/and with the doctrines of some theologians that the world is created, sustained and governed by an Omniscient and Omnipotent Being. Very understandably such world-views awaken in him doubts about the validity of his first, easy, instinctive assumption that there are genuinely open possibilities before a man at the moment of moral choice. It thus becomes for him a real question whether a man could have chosen otherwise than he actually did, and, in consequence, whether man's moral responsibility is really defensible. For how can a man be morally responsible, he asks himself, if his choices, like all other events in the universe, could not have been otherwise than they in fact were? It is precisely against the background of world-views such as these that for reflective people the problem of moral responsibility normally arises.

[12] *Ethics and Language,* p. 298.

Furthermore, to the man who has attained this level of reflexion, it will in *no* class of cases be a sufficient condition of moral responsibility for an act that one could have acted otherwise *if* one had chosen otherwise—not even in these cases where there *was* some possibility of the operation of 'external constraint'. In these cases he will, indeed expressly recognise freedom from external constraint as a *necessary condition*, but not as a *sufficient* condition. For he will be aware that, even granted *this* freedom, it is still conceivable that the agent had no freedom to choose otherwise than he did, and he will therefore require that the latter sort of freedom be added if moral responsibility for the act is to be established.

I have been contending that, for persons at a *tolerably advanced level of reflexion,* 'A could have acted otherwise', as a condition of A's moral responsibility, means 'A could have chosen otherwise'. The qualification italicised is of some importance. The unreflective or unsophisticated person, the ordinary 'man in the street', who does not know or much care what scientists and theologians and philosophers have said about the world, sees well enough that A is morally responsible only if he could have acted otherwise, but in his intellectual innocence he will, very probably, envisage nothing capable of preventing A from having acted otherwise except some material impediment—like the broken leg in the example above. Accordingly, for the unreflective person, 'A could have acted otherwise, as a condition of moral responsibility, *is* apt to mean no more than 'A could have acted otherwise *if* he had so chosen'.

It would appear, then, that the view now favoured by many philosophers, that the freedom required for moral responsibility is merely freedom from external constraint, is a view which they share only with the less reflective type of layman. Yet it should be plain that on a matter of this sort the view of the unreflective person is of little value by comparison with the view of the reflective person. There are some contexts, no doubt, in which lack of sophistication is an asset. But this is not one of them. The question at issue here is as to the kind of impediments which might have prevented a man from acting otherwise than he in fact did: and on this question knowledge and reflexion are surely prerequisites of any answer that is worth listening to. It is simply on account of the limitations of his mental vision that the unreflective man interprets the expression 'could have acted otherwise', in its context as a condition of moral responsibility, solely in terms of external constraint. He has failed (as yet) to reach the intellectual level at which one takes into account the implications for moral choices of the world-views of science, religion, and philosophy. If on a matter of this complexity the philosopher finds that his analysis accords with the utterances of the uneducated he has, I suggest, better cause for uneasiness than for self-congratulation.

This concludes the main part of what it seems to me necessary to say in answer to the pseudo-problem theorists. My object so far has been to expose the falsity of those innovations (chiefly Positivist) in the way of argument and analysis which are supposed by many to have made it impossible any longer to formulate the problem of Free Will in the traditional manner. My contention is that, at least so far as these innovations are concerned, the simple time-honoured argument still holds from the nature of the moral ought to the conclusion that moral responsibility implies a contra-causal type of freedom. The attempts to avoid that conclusion by analysing the proposition 'A could have acted otherwise' (acknowledged to be implied in *some* sense in A's moral responsibility) into one or other of certain hypothetical propositions which are compatible with unbroken causal continuity, break down hopelessly when tested against the touchstone of actual moral thinking. It is, I think, not necessary to defend the procedure of testing hypotheses in the ethical field by bringing to bear upon them our actual moral thinking. If there is any other form of test applicable, I should be much interested to learn what it is supposed to be. Certainly 'logical analysis' *per se* will not do. That has a function, but a function that can only be ancillary. For what we are seeking to know is the meaning of the expression 'could have acted otherwise' not *in the abstract,* but in the context of the question of man's *moral responsibility.* Logical analysis *per se* is impotent to give us this information. It can be of value only in so far as it operates within the orbit of 'the moral consciousness'. One may admit, with some qualifications, that on a matter of this sort the moral consciousness without logical analysis is blind: but it seems to me to be true without any qualification whatsoever that, on the same problem, logical analysis without the moral consciousness is empty.

VI

There are times when what seems to a critic the very strength of his case breeds mistrust in the critic's own mind. I confess that in making the criticisms that have preceded I have not been altogether free from uncomfortable feelings of this kind. For the arguments I have criticised, and more particularly the analyses of the conditions of moral responsibility, seem to me to be in many cases quite desperately unplausible. Such a state of affairs ought, I think, to give the critic pause. The thought must at least enter his mind (unless he be a total stranger to modesty) that perhaps, despite his best efforts to be fair, he has after all misrepresented what his opponents are saying. No doubt a similar thought will enter, and perhaps find lodgment in, the minds of many readers.

In this situation there is, however, one course by which the critic may reasonably hope to allay these natural suspicions. He should consider whether there may not be certain predisposing influences at work, extrinsic to the specific arguments, which could have the effect of blinding the proponents of these arguments to their intrinsic demerits. If so, he need not be too much disquieted by the seeming weakness of the case against him. For it is a commonplace that, once in the grip of general prepossessions, even very good philosophers sometimes avail themselves of very bad arguments.

Actually, we can, I think, discern at least two such influences operating powerfully in the case before us. One is sympathy with the general tenets of Positivism. The other is the conviction already alluded to, that man does not in fact possess a contra-causal type of freedom; whence follows a strong presumption that no such freedom is necessary to moral responsibility.

About the first of these influences I propose to say very little. I wish merely to indicate how strict adherence to Positivist tenets precludes one in principle from understanding moral responsibility as the ordinary man understands it, and how Positivists are therefore bound, when they attempt to define the conditions of moral responsibility, to say things that seem monstrously unplausible.

That the Positivist—who has certainly not been drawn initially to this way of philosophising by reflexion upon the phenomena of the moral life—should approach the problems of ethical analysis with certain strong prepossessions, is only to be expected. The most crucial of these is that (non-tautologous) statements in this field, as in every other field, can have no meaning—or at any rate no cognitive meaning —unless they are, at least in principle, sensibly verifiable. The consequence of that prepossession must be to close the mind in advance, more or less absolutely according to the extent to which the Verifiability principle is maintained as unshakeable dogma, against the common view of the moral ought—which happens also to be the view in terms of which the problem of moral responsibility historically and habitually arises. For on this view the moral ought as apprehended by the moral consciousness is most certainly an object neither of 'outer' nor of 'inner' sense. One need not wonder, therefore, that the Positivist should recommend analyses of the conditions of moral responsibility, such as the hypothetical propositions offered as the meaning of the expression 'could have acted otherwise', which to anyone who understands the moral ought in the ordinary way seem little short of fantastic. By an *a priori* prejudice he has effectively debarred himself from appreciating what ordinary men mean by moral obligation and moral responsibility. I cannot forbear adding that in view of the doom which has so swiftly attended the very various attempts so far made to define moral obligation in Positivist terms, the case for at least a temporary suspension of belief in Positivist pre-suppositions in the ethical field would appear to be a strong one.

Of far wider and more permanent interest, in my judgment, is the second of the 'predisposing influences'—the conviction that there just *is* no contra-causal freedom such as is commonly alleged to be a condition of moral responsibility. A natural desire to 'save' moral responsibility issues, logically enough, in attempts to formulate its conditions in a manner compatible with unbroken causal continuity. The consequent analyses may be, as I have urged, very unsatisfactory. But there is no doubt that the conviction that motivates the analysis is supported by reasons of great weight: well-known arguments that are the property of no particular school and which most of us learned in our philosophical cradles. A very brief summary of what I take to be the most influential of these arguments will suffice for the comments I wish to make upon them.

A contra-causal freedom, it is argued, such as is implied in the 'categorical' interpretation of the proposition 'A could have chosen otherwise than he did', posits a breach of causal continuity between a man's character and his conduct. Now apart from the general presumption in favour of the universality of causal law, there are special reasons for disallowing the breach that is here alleged. It is the common assumption of social intercourse that our acquaintances will act 'in character'; that their choices will exhibit the 'natural' response of their characters to the given situation. And this assumption seems to be amply substantiated, over a wide range of conduct, by the actual success which attends predictions made on this basis. Where there should be, on the contra-causal hypothesis, chaotic variability, there is found in fact a large measure of intelligible continuity. Moreover, what is the alternative to admitting that a person's choices flow from his character? Surely just that the so-called 'choice' is not *that person's* choice at all: that, relatively to the person concerned, it is a mere 'accident'. Now we cannot really believe this. But if it *were* the case, it would certainly not help to establish *moral* freedom, the freedom required for *moral* responsibility. For clearly a man cannot be morally responsible for an act which does not express his own choice but is, on the contrary, attributable simply to chance.

These are clearly considerations worthy of all respect. It is not surprising if they have played a big part in persuading people to respond sympathetically to the view that 'Free Will', in its usual contra-causal formulation, is a pseudo-problem. A full answer to them is obviously not practicable in what is little more than an appendix to the body of this paper; but I am hopeful that something can be said, even in a little space, to show that they are very far from being as conclusive against a contra-causal freedom as they are often supposed to be.

To begin with the less troublesome of the two main objections indicated—the objection that the break in causal continuity which free will involves is inconsistent with the predictability of conduct on the basis of the agent's known character. All that is necessary to meet this objection, I suggest, is the frank recognition, which is perfectly open to the Libertarian, that there is a wide area of human conduct, determinable on clear general principles, within which free will does not effectively operate. The most important of these general principles (I have no space to deal here with the others) has often enough been stated by Libertarians. Free will does not operate in these practical situations in which no conflict arises in the agent's mind between what he conceives to be his 'duty' and what he feels to be his 'strongest desire'. It does not operate here because there just is no occasion for it to operate. There is no reason whatever why the agent should here even contemplate choosing any course other than that prescribed by his strongest desire. In all such situations, therefore, he naturally wills in accordance with strongest desire. But his 'strongest desire' is simply the specific *ad hoc* expression of that system of conative and emotive dispositions which we call his 'character'. In all such situations, therefore, whatever may be the case elsewhere, his will is in effect determined by his character as so far formed. Now when we bear in mind that there are an almost immeasurably greater number of situations in a man's life that conform to *this* pattern than there are situations in which an agent is aware of a conflict between strongest desire and duty, it is apparent that a Libertarianism which accepts the limitation of free will to the *latter* type of situation is not open to the stock objection on the score of 'predictability'. For there still remains a vast area of human behaviour in which prediction on the basis of known character may be expected to succeed: an area which will accommodate without difficulty, I think, all these empirical facts about successful prediction which the critic is apt to suppose fatal to Free Will.

So far as I can see, such a delimitation of the field of effective free will denies to the Libertarian absolutely nothing which matters to him. For it is precisely that small sector of the field of choices which our principle of delimitation still leaves open to free will—the sector in which strongest desire clashes with duty—that is crucial for moral responsibility. It is, I believe, with respect to such situations, and in the last resort to such situations alone, that the agent himself recognises that moral praise and blame are appropriate. They are appropriate, according as he does or does not 'rise to duty' in the face of opposing desires; always granted, that is, that he is free to choose between these courses as genuinely open possibilities. If the reality of freedom be conceded *here,* everything is conceded that the Libertarian has any real interest in securing.

But, of course, the most vital question is, can the reality of freedom be conceded even here? In particular, can the standard objection be met which we stated, that if the person's choice does not, in these situations as elsewhere, flow from his *character,* then it is not *that person's* choice at all.

This is, perhaps, of all the objections to a contra-causal freedom, the one which is generally felt to be the most conclusive. For the assumption upon which it is based, *viz.* that no intelligible meaning can attach to the claim that an act which is not an expression of the self's *character* may nevertheless be the *self's* act, is apt to be regarded as self-evident. The Libertarian is accordingly charged with being in effect an *In*determinist, whose 'free will', in so far as it does not flow from the agent's character, can only be a matter of 'chance'. Has the Libertarian—who invariably repudiates this charge and claims to be a *Self*-determinist—any way of showing that, contrary to the assumption of his critics, we *can* meaningfully talk of an act as the self's act even though, in an important sense, it is not an expression of the self's 'character'?

I think that he has. I want to suggest that what prevents the critics from finding a meaning in this way of talking is that they are looking for it in the wrong way; or better, perhaps, with the wrong orientation. They are looking for it from the stand-point of the *external observer;* the stand-point proper to, because alone possible for, apprehension of the physical world. Now from the external stand-point we may observe processes of change. But one thing which, by common consent, *cannot* be observed from without is *creative activity.* Yet—and here lies the crux of the whole matter—it is precisely creative activity which we are trying to understand when we are trying to understand what is traditionally designated by 'free will'. For if there should be an act which is genuinely the self's act and is nevertheless not an expression of its character, such an act, in which the self 'transcends' its character as so far formed, would seem to be essentially of the nature of creative activity. It follows that to look for a meaning in 'free will' from the external stand-point is absurd. It is to look for it in a way that ensures that it will not be found. Granted that a creative activity of any kind is at least *possible* (and I know of no ground for its *a priori* rejection), there is one way, and one way only, in which we can hope to apprehend it, and that is from the *inner* stand-point of direct participation.

It seems to me therefore, that if the Libertarian's claim to find a meaning in a 'free' will which is genuinely the self's will, though not an expression of the self's character, is to be subjected to any test that is worth applying, that test must be undertaken from the inner stand-point. We ought to place ourselves imaginatively at the stand-point of the agent engaged in the typical moral situation in which free will is claimed, and ask ourselves whether from *this* stand-point the claim in question does or does not have meaning for us. That the appeal must be to introspection is no doubt unfortunate. But he would be a very doctrinaire critic of introspection who declined to make use of it when in the nature of the case no other means of apprehension is available. Everyone must make the introspective experiment for himself: but I may perhaps venture to report, though at this late stage with extreme brevity, what I at least seem to find when I make the experiment myself.

In the situation of moral conflict, then, I (as agent) have before my mind a course of action X, which I believe to be my duty; and also a course of action Y, incompatible with X, which I feel to be that which I most strongly desire. Y is, as it is sometimes expressed, 'in the line of least resistance' for me—the course which I am aware I should take if I let my purely desiring nature operate without hindrance. It is the course towards which I am aware that my *character,* as so far formed, naturally inclines me. Now, as actually engaged in this situation, I find that I cannot help believing that I *can* rise to duty and choose X; the 'rising to duty' being effected by what is commonly called 'effort of will'. And I further find, if I ask myself just what it is I am believing when I believe that I 'can' rise to duty, that I cannot help believing that it lies with me here and now, quite absolutely, which of two genuinely open possibilities I adopt; whether, that is, I make the effort of will and choose X, or, on the other hand, let my desiring nature, my character as so far formed, 'have its way', and choose Y, the course 'in the line of least resistance'. These beliefs may, of course, be illusory, but that is not at present in point. For the present argument all that matters is whether beliefs of this sort are in fact discoverable in the moral agent in the situation of 'moral temptation'. For my own part, I cannot doubt the introspective evidence that they are.

Now here is the vital point. No matter which course, X or Y, I choose in this situation, I cannot doubt, *qua* practical being engaged in it, that my choice is *not* just the expression of my formed character, and yet *is* a choice made by my *self*. For suppose I make the effort and choose X (my 'duty'). Since my very purpose in making the 'effort' is to enable me to act against the existing 'set' of desire, which is the expression of my character as so far formed, I cannot possibly regard the act itself as the expression of my *character*. On the other hand, introspection makes it equally clear that I am certain that it is *I* who choose; that the act is not an 'accident', but is genuinely *my* act. Or suppose that I choose Y (the end of 'strongest desire'). The course chosen here is, it is true, in conformity with my 'character'. But since I find myself unable to doubt that I *could* have made the effort and chosen X, I cannot possibly regard the choice of Y as *just* the expression of my character. Yet here again I find that I cannot doubt that the choice is *my* choice, a choice for which *I* am justly to be blamed.

What this amounts to is that I *can* and *do* attach meaning, *qua* moral agent, to an act which is not the self's character and yet is genuinely the self's act. And having no good reason to suppose that other persons have a fundamentally different mental constitution, it seems to me probable that anyone else who undertakes a similar experiment will be obliged to submit a similar report. I conclude, therefore, that the argument against 'free will' on the score of its 'meaninglessness' must be held to fail. 'Free Will' does have meaning; though, because it is of the nature of a creative activity, its meaning is discoverable only in an intuition of the practical consciousness of the participating agent. To the agent making a moral choice in the situation where duty clashes with desire, his 'self' is known to him as a creatively active self, a self which declines to be identified with his 'character' as so formed. Not, of course, that the self's character—let it be added to obviate misunderstanding—either is, or is supposed by the agent to be, devoid of bearing upon his choices, even in the 'sector' in which free will is held to operate. On the contrary, such a bearing is manifest in the empirically verifiable fact that we find it 'harder' (as we say) to make the effort of will required to 'rise to duty' in proportion to the extent that the 'dutiful' course conflicts with the course to which our character as so far formed inclines us. It is only in the polemics of the critics that a 'free' will is supposed to be incompatible with recognising the bearing of 'character' upon choice.

"But what" (it may be asked) "of the all-important question of the *value* of this 'subjective certainty'? Even if what you say is sound as 'phenomenology', is there any reason to suppose that the conviction on which you lay so much stress is in fact *true?*" I agree that the question is important; far more important, indeed, than is always realised, for it is not always realised that the only direct evidence there *could* be for a creative activity like 'free will' is an intuition of the practical consciousness. But this question falls outside the purview of the present paper. The aim of the paper has not been to offer a constructive defence of free will. It has been to show that the problem as traditionally posed is a real, and not a pseudo, problem. A serious threat to that thesis, it was acknowledged, arises from the apparent difficulty of attaching meaning to an act which is not the expression of the self's character and yet *is* the self's own act. The object of my brief phenomenological analysis was to provide evidence that such an act *does* have meaning for us in the one context in which there is any sense in *expecting* it to have meaning.

VII

My general conclusion is, I fear, very unexciting. It is merely that it is an error to suppose that the 'Free Will' problem, when correctly formulated, turns out not to be a 'problem' at all. Labouring to reinstate an old problem is dull work enough. But I am disposed to think that the philosophic situation to-day calls for a good deal more dull work of a similar sort.

PART 5 RESPONSIBILITY,

This section carries the discussion of Part Four into the realm of moral philosophy. All parties to the discussion agree that in order for a man to be held morally responsible for his past action, he must have been able to do other than he did. Put more tersely: Avoidability is a necessary condition of responsibility. We saw in Part Four that there are two senses of "avoidable." In the *categorical sense,* to say that an act is avoidable is to say that there were no antecedent conditions (causes) sufficient for its occurrence. In the *hypothetical sense,* to say that an act is avoidable is to say that *if* the actor had chosen (or perhaps, intended) to do otherwise, he would have done otherwise (nothing would have stopped him). Avoidability in the hypothetical sense is perfectly compatible with determinism; avoidability in the categorical sense, by definition, is not. Now the question arises: In which of the senses of "avoidable" —the categorical sense, the hypothetical sense, or both—is it true that a man can be held responsible for his action only if it is avoidable?

Perhaps responsibility, in the relevant sense, is best understood as a kind of *liability* to responsive actions of various kinds by other people. Thus, to be responsible for a past action is to be properly subject (that is, liable) to credit, praise, or reward if the act was in some special way a good one; or to blame, censure, or punishment if it was an evil one. Most of the essays included here are concerned with responsibility as liability to criminal punishment or to moral blame. Essentially, they inquire: Under what conditions are criminal punishment and/or moral blame reasonable and justified? This in turn takes us to the larger questions: What are blame and punishment all about? What are their functions, their aims, their justifying rationales?

A vast amount has been written on the aims and justification of criminal punishment (probably because, as a political institution devoted to the infliction of pain on human beings, it has never sat easily on the conscience of civilized man), and insofar as blame can be construed as "a kind of verbally mediated punishment,"[1] the various traditional theories of the nature and justification of punishment find

[1] C. L. Stevenson, *Ethics and Language* (New Haven: Yale University Press, 1944), p. 307.

BLAME, AND PUNISHMENT

their counterparts in discussions of blame. These theories can be classified very roughly as follows:

1. *Utilitarian Theories.* These theories hold that punishment is at best a necessary evil, justifiable if and only if the good of its consequences (its "social utility") outweighs its own immediate and intrinsic evil. Punishment is pain or deprivation inflicted on a person (presumably a wrongdoer) for the sake of such future goods as correction or reform of the offender, protection of society against other offenses by the same offender, and (especially) deterrence of other would-be offenders by backing up the threat of retribution.

2. *The Retributive Theory.* This theory is not to be confused with the theory (discussed below) that vindictive satisfaction in the mind of the beholder is the ultimate justification of punishment, for its proponents have been among the leading enemies of vengeance. (Some confusion about this matter is no doubt caused by the inconstant terminology used by philosophers. McTaggart, for example, in his essay in this section, uses the term "vindictive theory" for what is here called the retributive theory.) In the words of one of its critics, the retributive theory holds that "the primary justification of punishment is always to be found in the fact that an offense has been committed which deserves punishment, not in any future advantage to be gained by its infliction."[2] Two versions of the theory should be distinguished: a *moralistic version,* which maintains that the proper function of punishment is to inflict on the offender the pain "called for" or deserved by the moral gravity of his offense; and a *legalistic version,* which holds that the justification of punishment is always to be found in the fact that a rule has been broken, for the violation of which a certain penalty is specified—whether or not the offender incurs any moral guilt.

3. *Vengeance Theories.* Vengeance theories make much of the unhappy fact that, when harmful wrongs are committed, there is among men a widespread and natural

[2] A. C. Ewing, *The Morality of Punishment* (London: Kegan Paul, 1929), p. 13.

lust for vengeance. Such theories are of three different kinds. The *escape-valve version,* associated with the names of James Fitzjames Stephen and Oliver Wendell Holmes, Jr., holds that legal punishment is an orderly outlet for aggressive feelings, which would otherwise demand satisfaction in socially disruptive ways. This, of course, is a variant of the utilitarian theory. The *hedonistic version* finds the justification of punishment in the pleasure it gives people (particularly the victim of the crime and his loved ones) to see the criminal suffer for his crime. Few philosophers have held this odious version of the utilitarian theory, though perhaps Lotze, Bentham, and Gabriel DeTarde come close to it. Finally, the *romantic version* of the theory, very popular among the uneducated, holds that the justification of punishment is to be found in the emotions of hate and anger it expresses, these emotions being those allegedly felt by all normal or right-thinking people. This theory is called "romantic" because, like any theory labeled romantic, it holds that certain emotions and the actions they inspire are self-certifying, needing no further justification.

Erewhon, the imaginary land of Samuel Butler's novel, is "nowhere" misspelled backwards, and since it is a slightly distorted mirror image of Butler's own Victorian England, or our own time, with almost everything "put backwards," it is aptly named. The prevailing Erewhonian practice in respect to moral delinquency is very much the same as our own practice in respect to physical illness: delinquents are "treated" and often "cured" by "straighteners." But the Erewhonian treatment of the physically ill is the same as our treatment of the morally delinquent: the sick are severely reprobated and punished. The aim of the wily satirist is to get his readers to see that the Erewhonians are neither more nor less rational than we are, all told; that *any* society that makes a fundamental distinction between disease and crime is cruelly inconsistent. The reformers, or "malcontents," in Erewhon also have their mirrored counterparts among our own moral philosophers. Substitute "crime" for the words "illness" and "consumption" in the following passage, and it becomes an accurate statement of the views of many utilitarian philosophers about punishment:

> The malcontents . . . assert that illness is the inevitable result of certain antecedent causes, which, in the great majority of cases, were beyond the control of the individual, and that therefore a man is only guilty for being in a consumption in the same way as rotten fruit is guilty for having gone rotten.

We may, of course, be driven to cutting out rotten spots or throwing away rotten fruit, just as we must, in difficult cases, incarcerate, flog, or even hang, rotten men, but in neither case is self-righteous moralizing appropriate.

Note how naturally a utilitarian account of punishment fits a deterministic world view. Indeed, determinism, in the quoted passage, is cited as a reason for holding a utilitarian theory. The Erewhonians themselves seem to be determinists, and this drives them to find some justifying myth to support their harsh standards of responsibility for illness. Their myth of the unborn invites comparison both with the Christian doctrine of original sin and Oriental doctrines of pre-existence. The reasoning of the Erewhonians, put in terms of morality rather than illness, seems to be as follows. It would be unfair to hold a person responsible for his evil ways if the causes of his character can be traced back ultimately to his parents, his earliest influences, his genes, etc. Indeed, if determinism is true, one's parents cannot help having the characters *they* have, and so on back in time. Therefore, if responsibility is to be reasonable, a person somehow must have created or chosen his own character. But to do this he would have to exist before he was born. Hence, the myth of the unborn. Aristotle, in the selection that opens this section, has a much more plausible account of the way in which one can be said to have chosen his own character, and also a famous argument to show that most of us are in fact responsible for the characters we have.

The moralistic version of the retributive theory is given its classic statement in the passage from Immanuel Kant included here. The great Russian novelist Fyodor Dostoevsky, in an account of his own experiences in a nineteenth-century Siberian prison camp, points out the difficulties of making punishment fit the moral gravity of the offense; he cites inevitable inequalities of moral guilt in the commission of the same crime and inequalities of suffering from the same punishment. Oliver Wendell Holmes also argues against the retributive theory, calling the intuition of fittingness between moral evil and suffering merely "vengeance in disguise." The satisfaction of vengeance for Holmes, however, is a proper function of criminal law. The German philosopher G. W. F. Hegel (1770–1831) is often listed in the textbooks as a proponent of the retributive theory; but this is a misinterpretation, according to J. E. McTaggart in his subtle essay included here. Punishment of the wicked is not an end in itself, according to McTaggart's Hegel; rather, it serves to bring the criminal to repentance for his crime. This is not to be confused with the utilitarian theory that society "reforms" a criminal in punishing him by a kind of intimidation; for this, Hegel insists, would be to use the criminal as a mere means to society's ends. If McTaggart is right, we need a new pigeonhole to accommodate Hegel's theory.

J. D. Mabbott boldly announces that he is going to defend a retributive theory of punishment. Mabbott's retributivism, however, is the legalistic kind, and has no more in common with Kant than with utilitarianism. M. R. Glover's critical reply to Professor Mabbott was published in the issue of *Mind* following that in which Mabbott's article appeared. John Rawls's very influential discussion of punishment, using some arguments foreshadowed in Mabbott's article, attempts to work out a compromise between legalistic retributivism and utilitarianism. Charles L. Stevenson, a reconciling determinist, defends a utilitarian theory of blame, and is criticized in turn by David Braybrooke. The final article in this section, by Elizabeth Beardsley, is also concerned with blame (and praise). By distinguishing between the various "perspectives" from which judgments of praise and blame are made, she goes a long way toward settling the question whether praise and blame can be reasonable, if determinism should happen to be true.

A R I S T O T L E

Conditions of Responsibility for Action*

BOOK TWO

This book is the first of a series (II–V) dealing with the moral virtues. But first we have to ask what moral virtue or goodness is. It is a confirmed disposition to act rightly, the disposition being itself formed by a continuous series of right actions.

CHAPTER ONE

Virtue, then, is of two kinds, intellectual and moral. Of these the intellectual is in the main indebted to teaching for its production and growth, and this calls for time and experience. Moral goodness, on the other hand, is the child of habit, from which it has got its very name, ethics being derived from *ethos*, 'habit', by a slight alteration in the quantity of the *e*. This is an indication that none of the moral virtues is implanted in us by Nature, since nothing that Nature creates can be taught by habit to change the direction of its development. For instance a stone, the natural tendency of which is to fall down, could never, however often you threw it up in the air, be trained to go in that direction. No more can you train fire to burn downwards. Nothing in fact, if the law of its being is to behave in one way, can be habituated to behave in another. The moral virtues, then, are produced in us neither *by* Nature nor *against* Nature. Nature, indeed, prepares in us the ground for their reception, but their complete formation is the product of habit.

Consider again these powers or faculties with which Nature endows us. We acquire the ability to use them before we do use them. The senses provide us with a good illustration of this truth. We have not acquired the sense of sight from repeated acts of seeing, or the sense of hearing from repeated acts of hearing. It is the other way round. We had these senses before we used them, we did not acquire them as a result of using them. But the moral virtues we do acquire by first exercising them. The same is true of the arts and crafts in general. The craftsman has to learn how to make things, but he learns in the process of making them. So men become builders by building, harp players by playing the harp. By a similar process we become just by performing just actions, temperate by performing temperate actions, brave by performing brave actions. Look at what happens in political societies—it confirms our view. We find legislators seeking to make good men of their fellows by making good behaviour habitual with them. That is the aim of every law-giver, and when he is unable to carry it out effectively, he is a failure; nay, success or failure in this is what makes the difference between a good constitution and a bad.

Again, the creation and the destruction of any virtue are effected by identical causes and identical means; and this may be said, too, of every art. It is as a result of playing the harp that harpers become good or bad in their art. The same is true of builders and all other craftsmen. Men will become good builders as a result of building well, and bad builders as a result of building badly. Otherwise what would be the use of having anyone to teach a trade? Craftsmen would all be born either good or bad. Now this holds also of the virtues. It is in the course of our dealings with our fellow-men that we become just or unjust. It is our behaviour in a crisis and our habitual reactions to danger that make us brave or cowardly, as it may be. So with our desires and passions. Some men are made temperate and

* Aristotle, *The Nicomachean Ethics*, trans. (with notes in italics) J. A. K. Thomson (Harmondsworth: Penguin Books, 1955), Book Two, Chapters 1–5; Book three, Chapters 1, 5. Reprinted by permission of George Allen & Unwin Ltd.

gentle, others profligate and passionate, the former by conducting themselves in one way, the latter by conducting themselves in another, in situations in which their feelings are involved. We may sum it all up in the generalization, 'Like activities produce like dispositions'. This makes it our duty to see that our activities have the right character, since the differences of quality in them are repeated in the dispositions that follow in their train. So it is a matter of real importance whether our early education confirms us in one set of habits or another. It would be nearer the truth to say that it makes a very great difference indeed, in fact all the difference in the world.

If, then, everything depends upon the way in which we act, clearly it is incumbent on us to inquire what this way is, never forgetting that we must not look for the precision attainable in the exact sciences.

CHAPTER TWO

Since the branch of philosophy on which we are at present engaged differs from the others in not being a subject of merely intellectual interest—I mean we are not concerned to know what goodness essentially is, but how we are to become good men, for this alone gives the study its practical value—we must apply our minds to the solution of the problems of conduct. For, as I remarked, it is our actions that determine our dispositions.

Now that when we act we should do so according to the right principle, is common ground and I propose to take it as a basis of discussion.[1] But we must begin with the admission that any theory of conduct must be content with an outline without much precision in details. We noted this when I said at the beginning of our discussion of this part of our subject that the measure of exactness of statement in any field of study must be determined by the nature of the matter studied. Now matters of conduct and considerations of what is to our advantage have no fixity about them any more than matters affecting our health. And if this be true of moral philosophy as a whole, it is still more true that the discussion of particular problems in ethics admits of no exactitude. For they do not fall under any science or professional tradition, but those who are following some line of conduct are forced in every collocation of circumstances to think out for themselves what is suited to these circumstances, just as doctors and navigators have to do in their different *métiers*. We can do no more than give our arguments, inexact as they necessarily are, such support as is available.

After this reminder Aristotle proceeds to lay down a proposition or generalization which is cardinal in his system of ethics. Excess of deficiency in his actions impairs the moral quality of the agent.

Let us begin with the following observation. It is in the nature of moral qualities that they can be destroyed by deficiency on the one hand and excess on the other. We can see this in the instances of bodily health and strength.[2] Physical strength is destroyed by too much and also by too little exercise. Similarly health is ruined by eating and drinking either too much or too little, while it is produced, increased, and preserved by taking the right quantity of drink and victuals. Well, it is the same with temperance, courage, and the other virtues. The man who shuns and fears everything and can stand up to nothing becomes a coward. The man who is afraid of nothing at all, but marches up to every danger, becomes foolhardy. In the same way the man who indulges in every pleasure without refraining from a single one becomes incontinent. If, on the other hand, a man behaves like the Boor in comedy and turns his back on every pleasure, he will find his sensibilities becoming blunted. So also temperance and courage are destroyed both by excess and deficiency, and they are kept alive by observance of the mean.

Our virtues are employed in the same kinds of action as established them.

Let us go back to our statement that the virtues are produced and fostered as a result, and by the agency, of actions of the same quality as effect their destruction. It is also true that after the virtues have been formed they find expression in actions of that kind. We may see this in a

[1] There will be an opportunity later of considering what is meant by this formula, in particular what is meant by 'the right principle' and how, in its ethical aspect, it is related to the moral virtues.

[2] If we are to illustrate the material, it must be by concrete images.

concrete instance—bodily strength. It results from taking plenty of nourishment and going in for hard training, and it is the strong man who is best fitted to cope with such conditions. So with the virtues. It is by refraining from pleasures that we become temperate, and it is when we have become temperate that we are most able to abstain from pleasures. Or take courage. It is by habituating ourselves to make light of alarming situations and to confront them that we become brave, and it is when we have become brave that we shall be most able to face an alarming situation.

There is one way of discovering whether we are in full possession of a virtue or not. We possess it if we feel pleasure in its exercise; indeed, it is just with pleasures and pains that virtue is concerned.

CHAPTER THREE

We may use the pleasure (or pain) that accompanies the exercise of our dispositions as an index of how far they have established themselves. A man is temperate who abstaining from bodily pleasures finds this abstinence pleasant; if he finds it irksome, he is intemperate. Again, it is the man who encounters danger gladly, or at least without painful sensations, who is brave; the man who has these sensations is a coward. In a word, moral virtue has to do with pains and pleasures. There are a number of reasons for believing this. (1) Pleasure has a way of making us do what is disgraceful; pain deters us from doing what is right and fine. Hence the importance—I quote Plato—of having been brought up to find pleasure and pain in the right things. True education is just such a training. (2) The virtues operate with actions and emotions, each of which is accompanied by pleasure or pain. This is only another way of saying that virtue has to do with pleasures and pains. (3) Pain is used as an instrument of punishment. For in her remedies Nature works by opposites, and pain can be remedial. (4) When any disposition finds its complete expression it is, as we noted, in dealing with just those things by which it is its nature to be made better or worse, and which constitute the sphere of its operations. Now when men become bad it is under the influence of pleasures and pains when they seek the wrong ones among them, or seek them at the wrong time, or in the wrong manner, or in any of the wrong forms which such offences may take; and in seeking the wrong pleasures and pains they shun the right. This has led some thinkers to identify the moral virtues with conditions of the soul in which passion is eliminated or reduced to a minimum. But this is to make too absolute a statement—it needs to be qualified by adding that such a condition must be attained 'in the right manner and at the right time' together with the other modifying circumstances.

So far, then, we have got this result. Moral goodness is a quality disposing us to act in the best way when we are dealing with pleasures and pains, while vice is one which leads us to act in the worst way when we deal with them.

The point may be brought out more clearly by some other considerations. (5) There are three kinds of things that determine our choice in all our actions—the morally fine, the expedient, the pleasant; and three that we shun—the base, the harmful, the painful. Now in his dealings with all of these it is the good man who is most likely to go right, and the bad man who tends to go wrong, and that most notably in the matter of pleasure. The sensation of pleasure is felt by us in common with all animals, accompanying everything we choose, for even the fine and the expedient have a pleasurable effect upon us. (6) The capacity for experiencing pleasure has grown in us from infancy as part of our general development, and human life, being dyed in grain with it, receives therefrom a colour hard to scrape off. (7) Pleasure and pain are also the standards by which with greater or less strictness we regulate our considered actions. Since to feel pleasure and pain rightly or wrongly is an important factor in human behaviour, it follows that we are primarily concerned with these sensations. (8) Heraclitus says it is hard to fight against anger, but it is harder still to fight against pleasure. Yet to grapple with the harder has always been the business, as of art, so of goodness, success in a task being proportionate to its difficulty. This gives us another reason for believing that morality and statesmanship must concentrate on pleasures and pains, seeing it is the man who deals rightly with them who will be good, and the man who deals with them wrongly who will be bad.

Here, then, are our conclusions. (*a*) Virtue is concerned with pains and pleasures. (*b*) The actions which produce virtue are identical in character with those which increase it. (*c*) These actions differently performed destroy it. (*d*) The actions which produced it are identical with those in which it finds expression.

Aristotle now meets an obvious objection: How can a man perform (say) just actions unless he is already just?

CHAPTER FOUR

A difficulty, however, may be raised as to what we mean when we say that we must perform just actions if we are to become just, and temperate actions if we are to be temperate. It may be argued that, if I do what is just and temperate, I am just and temperate already, exactly as, if I spell words or play music correctly, I must already be literate or musical. This I take to be a false analogy, even in the arts. It is possible to spell a word right by accident or because somebody tips you the answer. But you will be a scholar only if your spelling is done as a scholar does it, that is thanks to the scholarship in your own mind. Nor will the suggested analogy with the arts bear scrutiny. A work of art is good or bad in itself—let it possess a certain quality, and that is all we ask of it. But virtuous actions are not done in a virtuous—a just or temperate—way merely because *they* have the appropriate quality. The *doer* must be in a certain frame of mind when he does them. Three conditions are involved. (1) The agent must act in full consciousness of what he is doing. (2) He must 'will' his action, and will it for its own sake. (3) The act must proceed from a fixed and unchangeable disposition. Now these requirements, if we except mere knowledge, are not counted among the necessary qualifications of an artist. For the acquisition of virtue, on the other hand, knowledge is of little or no value, but the other requirements are of immense, of sovran, importance, since it is the repeated performance of just and temperate actions that produces virtue. Actions, to be sure, are *called* just and temperate when they are such as a just or temperate man would do. But the doer is just or temperate not because he does such things but when he does them in the way of just and temperate persons. It is therefore quite fair to say that a man becomes just by the performance of just, and temperate by the performance of temperate, actions; nor is there the smallest likelihood of a man's becoming good by any other course of conduct. It is not, however, a popular line to take, most men preferring theory to practice under the impression that arguing about morals proves them to be philosophers, and that in this way they will turn out to be fine characters. Herein they resemble invalids, who listen carefully to all the doctor says but do not carry out a single one of his orders. The bodies of such people will never respond to treatment—nor will the souls of such 'philosophers'.

It is now time to produce a formal definition of virtue. In the Aristotelian system this means stating its genus and differentia—that is to say, the class of things to which it belongs and the point or points which distinguish it from other members of the class.

CHAPTER FIVE

We now come to the formal definition of virtue. Note first, however, that the human soul is conditioned in three ways. It may have (1) feelings, (2) capacities, (3) dispositions; so virtue must be one of these three. By 'feelings' I mean desire, anger, fear, daring, envy, gratification, friendliness, hatred, longing, jealousy, pity and in general all states of mind that are attended by pleasure or pain. By 'capacities' I mean those faculties in virtue of which we may be described as capable of the feelings in question—anger, for instance, or pain, or pity. By 'dispositions' I mean states of mind in virtue of which we are well or ill disposed in respect of the feelings concerned. We have, for instance, a bad disposition where angry feelings are concerned if we are disposed to become excessively or insufficiently angry, and a good disposition in this respect if we consistently feel the due amount of anger, which comes between these extremes. So with the other feelings.

Now, neither the virtues nor the vices are feelings. We are not spoken of as good or bad in respect of our feelings but of our virtues and vices. Neither are we praised or blamed for the way we feel. A man is not praised for being frightened or angry, nor is he blamed just for being angry; it is for being angry in a particular way. But we *are* praised and blamed for our virtues and vices. Again, feeling angry or frightened is something we can't help, but our virtues are in a manner expressions of our will; at any rate there is an element of will in their formation. Finally, we are said to be 'moved' when our feelings are affected, but when it is a question of moral goodness or badness we are not said to be 'moved' but to be 'disposed' in a particular way. A similar line of reasoning will prove that the virtues and vices are not capacities either. We are not spoken of as good or bad, nor are we praised or blamed, merely because we are *capable* of feeling. Again, what capacities we have, we have by nature; but it is not nature that makes us good or bad. . . . So, if the virtues are neither feelings nor capacities, it remains that they must be dispositions. . . .

We have now to state the 'differentia' of virtue. Virtue is a disposition; but how are we to distinguish it from other dispositions? We may say that it is such a disposition as enables the good man to perform his function well. And he performs it well when he avoids the extremes and chooses the mean in actions and feelings. . . .

BOOK THREE

Aristotle now approaches the question of moral responsibility, so important in modern ethics. It never occurred to him to doubt the freedom of the will, but he is as much alive as any modern thinker to the fact—and the importance of the fact—that our acts are not all voluntary. In the following chapter he distinguishes between the degrees of their voluntariness.

CHAPTER ONE

We have found that moral excellence or virtue has to do with feelings and actions. These may be voluntary or involuntary. It is only to the former that we assign praise or blame, though when the involuntary are concerned we may find ourselves ready to condone and on occasion to pity. It is clearly, then, incumbent on the student of moral philosophy to determine the limits of the voluntary and involuntary. Legislators also find such a definition useful when they are seeking to prescribe appropriate rewards and punishments.

Actions are commonly regarded as involuntary when they are performed (*a*) under compulsion, (*b*) as the result of ignorance. An act, it is thought, is done under compulsion when it originates in some external cause of such a nature that the agent or person subject to the compulsion contributes nothing to it. Such a situation is created, for example, when a sea captain is carried out of his course by a contrary wind or by men who have got him in their power. But the case is not always so clear. One might have to consider an action performed for some fine end or through fear of something worse to follow. For example, a tyrant who had a man's parents or children in his power might order him to to do something dishonourable on condition that, if the man did it, their lives would be spared; otherwise not. In such cases it might be hard to say whether the actions are voluntary or not. A similar difficulty is created by the jettison of cargo in a storm. When the situation has no complications you never get a man voluntarily throwing away his property. But if it is to save the life of himself and his mates, any sensible person will do it. Such actions partake of both qualities, though they look more like voluntary than involuntary acts. For at the time they are performed they are the result of a deliberate choice between alternatives, and when an action is performed the end or object of that action is held to be the end it had at the moment of its performance. It follows that the terms 'voluntary' and 'involuntary' should be used with reference to the time when the acts were being performed. Now in the imaginary cases we have stated the acts are voluntary. For the movement of the limbs instrumental to the action originates in the agent himself, and when this is so it is in a man's own power to act or not to act. Such actions therefore are voluntary. But they are so only in the special circumstances; otherwise of course they would be involuntary. For nobody would choose to do anything of the sort purely for its own sake. Occasionally indeed the performance of such actions is held to do a man credit. This happens when he submits to some disgrace or pain as the only way of achieving some great or splendid result. But if his case is just the opposite he is blamed, for it shows a degraded nature to submit to humiliations with only a paltry object in view, or at any rate not a high one. But there are also cases which are thought to merit, I will not say praise, but condonation. An example is provided when a man does something wrong because he is afraid of torture too severe for flesh and blood to endure. Though surely there are some things which a man cannot be compelled to do—which he will rather die than do, however painful the mode of death. Such a deed is matricide; the reasons which 'compelled' Alcmaeon in Euripides' play to kill his mother carry their absurdity on the face of them. Yet it is not always easy to make up our minds what is our best course in choosing one of two alternatives—such and such an action instead of such and such another—or in facing one penalty instead of another. Still harder is it to stick to our decision when made. For, generally speaking, the consequences we expect in such imbroglios are painful, and what we are forced to do far from honourable. Then we get praised or blamed according as we succumb to the compulsion or resist it.

What class of actions, then, ought we to distinguish as 'compulsory'? It is arguable that the bare description will apply to any case where the cause of the action is found in things external to the agent when he contributes nothing to the result. But it may happen that actions, though, abstractly considered, involuntary, are deliberately chosen at a given time and in given circumstances in preference to a given alternative. In that case, their origin being in the agent, these actions must be pronounced voluntary in the particular circumstances and because they are preferred to their alternatives. In themselves they are involuntary, yet they have more of the voluntary about them, since conduct is a sequence of particular acts, and the particular things done in the circumstances we have supposed are voluntary. But when it comes to saying which of two alternative lines of action should be preferred—then difficulties arise. For the differences in particular cases are many.

If it should be argued that pleasurable and honourable things exercise constraint upon us from without, and therefore actions performed under their influence are compulsory, it may be replied that this would make every action compulsory. For we all have some pleasurable or honourable motive in everything we do. Secondly, people acting under compulsion and against their will find it painful, whereas those whose actions are inspired by the pleasurable and the honourable find that these actions are accompanied by pleasure. In the third place it is absurd to accuse external influences instead of ourselves when we fall an easy prey to such inducements and to lay the blame for all dishonourable deeds on the seductions of pleasure, while claiming for ourselves credit for any fine thing we have done. It appears, then, that an action is compulsory only when it is caused by something external to itself which is not influenced by anything contributed by the person under compulsion.

Then there are acts done through ignorance. Any act of this nature is other than voluntary, but it is involuntary only when it causes the doer subsequent pain and regret. For a man who has been led into some action by ignorance and yet has no regrets, while he cannot be said to have been a voluntary agent—he did not know what he was doing—nevertheless cannot be said to have acted involuntarily, since he feels no compunction. We therefore draw a distinction. (*a*) When a man who has done something as the result of ignorance is sorry for it, we take it that he has acted involuntarily. (*b*) When such a man is not sorry, the case is different and we shall have to call him a 'non-voluntary' agent. For it is better that he should have a distinctive name in order to mark the distinction. Note, further, that there is evidently a difference between acting *in consequence* of ignorance and acting *in* ignorance. When a man is drunk or in a passion his actions are not supposed to be the result of ignorance but of one or other of these conditions. But, as he does not realize what he is doing, he is acting *in* ignorance. To be sure every bad man is ignorant of what he ought to do and refrain from doing, and it is just this ignorance that makes people unjust and otherwise wicked. But when we use the word 'involuntary' we do not apply it in a case where the agent does not know what is for his own good. For involuntary acts are not the consequence of ignorance when the ignorance is shown in our choice of ends; what does result from such ignorance is a completely vicious condition. No, what I mean is not general ignorance—which is what gives ground for censure—but particular ignorance, ignorance that is to say of the particular circumstances or the particular persons concerned. In such cases there may be room for pity and pardon, because a man who acts in ignorance of such details is an involuntary agent. It will therefore no doubt be well to define the nature and determine the number of these particular circumstances. They are (1) the agent, (2) the act; (3) that which is the object or within the range of the act. Sometimes we must add (4) the instrument (e.g. a tool), (5) the effect or result (e.g. when a man's life is saved), (6) the manner (e.g. gently or roughly). Now nobody in his right mind could be ignorant of *all* these circumstances. Obviously he cannot be ignorant of (1) the agent—how can he fail to know himself? But a man may fail to know (2) what he is doing, as when people say that a remark 'escaped' them or that they did not know they were betraying secrets. (A good instance is that of Aeschylus' supposed revelation of the Mysteries.) Or like the man who was accused of killing another with a catapult, you might say you only wanted to show him how the thing worked. Then (3) you might mistake, say, your son for an enemy, like Merope in the play, or (4) take a naked spear instead of one with the button on, or a lump of rock in mistake for a pumice stone, or (5) you might be the death of a man with a medicine which you hoped would save his life, or (6) hit your antagonist a blow when you only meant to grip his hand, as in 'open' wrestling. Seeing then that there is the possibility of ignorance in any of these special circumstances, one who has acted in ignorance of any one of them is considered to have acted involuntarily, especially if it was the most important of them that he did not know, which by general agreement are (2) the act and (3) the effect of the act.

An involuntary act being one performed under compulsion or as the result of ignorance, a voluntary act would seem to be one of which the origin or efficient cause lies in the agent, he knowing the particular circumstances in which he is acting. I believe it to be an error to say that acts occasioned by anger or desire are involuntary. For in the first place if we maintain this we shall have to give up the view that any of the lower animals, or even children, are capable of voluntary action. In the second place, when we act from desire or anger are none of our actions voluntary? Or are our fine actions voluntary, our ignoble actions involuntary? It is an absurd distinction, since the agent is one and the same person. It is surely paradoxical to describe as 'involuntary' acts inspired by sentiments which we quite properly desire to have. There are some things at which we *ought* to feel angry, and others which we *ought* to desire—health, for instance, and the acquisition of knowledge. Thirdly, people assume that what is involuntary must be painful and what falls in with our own wishes must be pleasant. Fourthly, what difference is there in point of voluntariness between wrong actions which are calculated and wrong actions which are done on impulse? Both are to be avoided; and the further reflection suggests itself, that the irrational emotions are no less typically human than our considered judgement. Whence it follows that actions inspired by anger or desire are equally typical of the human being who performs them. Therefore to classify these actions as 'involuntary' is surely a very strange proceeding. . . .

The question is now raised whether it is at all times in our power to be good and to do the right. The answer is yes. And it is also in our power at all times to be vicious.

CHAPTER FIVE

Since then it is the end that is the object of our wishing, and the means to the end that is the object of our deliberating and choosing, the actions which deal with means must be done by choice and must be voluntary. Now when the virtues are exercised it is upon means. So virtue also is attainable by our own exertions. And so is vice. For what it lies in our power to do, it lies in our power not to do; when we can say 'no', we can say 'yes'. If, then, it is in our power to perform an action when it is right, it will be equally in our power to refrain from performing it when it is wrong; and if it lies with us to refrain from doing a thing when that is right, it will also lie with us to do it when that is wrong. But if it is in our power to do the right or the wrong thing, and equally in our power to refrain from doing so; and if doing right or wrong is, as we saw, the same as being good or bad ourselves, we must conclude that it depends upon ourselves whether we are to be virtuous or vicious. The words

> To sin and suffer—that offends us still:
> But who is ever blest against his will?

must be regarded as a half-truth. It is true that no one is blest against his will, but untrue that wickedness is involuntary. Otherwise we shall have to deny the truth of what we have just been saying and maintain that a man is not the originator of his own actions, of which he might be described as the begetter. But if he demonstrably is so, and we cannot trace our actions to any other springs than those which are found within ourselves, then actions which have such an origin are themselves within our control and are voluntary. In support of this conclusion it seems possible to call in evidence the practice of both private individuals and of legislators. For they inflict pains and penalties for misbehaviour, except in cases where the offender is not held responsible, because he has acted from ignorance or under duress. On the other hand they bestow honours on those who have done some fine action. Their motive in the first case is to stop evil practices, in the second to encourage the well-doer. Now nobody encourages us to do things which it is not in our power to do and which are not voluntary. It does not help at all to be made to believe that there is no such thing as getting hot, or feeling pain or anger, and so on. We shall feel them all the same. We even find that the circumstance that an offence was committed out of ignorance is made a reason for punishment when the offender is held responsible for his ignorance, as is shown, for instance, by the sentence in a case where the accused had been drunk. It may then be doubled on the ground that the offence originated with the offender, since it was open to him to refrain from getting drunk and his drunkenness was responsible for his not knowing what he was doing when he committed the offence. We punish people, too, for breaking the law through ignorance of some point in it which it was their business to know and which they could have known without much trouble. And punishment follows also when the ignorance is thought to have been due to carelessness, it being held that the guilty party need not have shown this ignorance. He should have noticed what he was doing—it was his duty to notice. You may say that very likely he could not help it, he is just that sort of man. But there is an answer to that. Such people have only themselves to blame for having acquired a character like that by their loose living, just as they have only themselves to blame for being unjust, if they make a practice of unjust behaviour, or intemperate, if they spend their time in drinking or other forms of dissipation. It is their persistent activities in certain directions that make them what they are. This is well illustrated by the behaviour of men who are training for some competition or performance: they devote their whole time to the appropriate exercises. The man, then, must be a perfect fool who is unaware that people's characters take their bias from the steady direction of their activities. If a man, well aware of what he is doing, behaves in such a way that he is bound to become unjust, we can only say that he is voluntarily unjust.

Again, while we cannot fairly argue that when a man behaves unjustly he does not wish to be unjust, or that when he plunges into dissipation he has no wish to be dissipated, it is by no means true that he can stop being unjust or dissolute merely by wishing it. You might as well expect a sick man to get better by wishing it. Yet the illness may be voluntary in the sense that it has been caused by loose living and neglecting the doctor's orders. There was a time when he need not have been ill; but once he let himself go, the opportunity was lost. When once you have thrown a stone, it is gone for good and all. Still it lay with yourself to let it lie instead of picking it up and throwing it; the origin of the act was in you. Similarly it was open to the dishonest and dissolute fellow to avoid becoming such a character; so that his original action was voluntary. But once he is hardened in vice the possibility of reforming disappears. Nor is it only vices of character that are voluntary. It is not rare to find bodily defects which are so too. Doubtless nobody blames a man for being born ugly, but we do blame those who lose their looks from want of exercise and neglect of hygiene. We may have the same feeling when a man's physique is weakened or impaired. Thus blindness is not an object of censure but of compassion when it is the result of a congenital defect or an illness or a blow. But if it is the result of alcoholic poisoning or general debauchery, then no one has any sympathy with the blind man. It comes to this. Physical defects which could have been avoided are blamed, but not those which a man cannot help and for which he is therefore not responsible. But, this granted, we must be held responsible for moral failings which are generally reprobated.

But someone may say, 'We all aim at what appears to us to be good, but over this appearance we have no control. How the end appears is determined by the character of the individual. Now one of two things. Either the individual is in a manner responsible for his moral character or he is not. If he is, he will also be in a manner responsible for the way in which the end—that is the good—appears to him. If he is not, then none of us will be responsible for his own misdeeds. The wrongdoer will be acting wrongly because he is ignorant of the true end and thinks that by such wrongdoing he will attain the highest good.

That he should aim at the end in this fashion is not a matter of his own choosing. We must be born with an eye for a moral issue which will enable us to form a correct judgement and choose what is truly good. A man who has this natural gift is one of Nature's favourites, and such an endowment is one of the greatest and noblest in the world. It is something that cannot be acquired or learned; and if a man possesses it just as it was when it was bestowed upon him at birth, he will have all the native gifts and graces in their genuine and fullest form.' But if this be a sound argument, how will it be possible to maintain that virtue is more voluntary than vice? To the good and the bad man alike the end presents and establishes itself in the same way, whatever that may be, whether an instinctive process or not; and whatever they do, they do it somehow with reference to the end as they see it. One is driven then to hold one of two positions. Either (*a*) the view one takes of the end—whatever that view may be—is not imposed on us by Nature but is partly due to oneself. Or (*b*) the end is given by Nature but virtue is voluntary, because the virtuous man does voluntarily whatever he has left himself to do in order to attain his end. In either case vice will be just as voluntary as virtue. For the free agency of the bad man is just as important for his conduct as the free agency of the good man for his, even if we agree that it does not appear in the bad man's choice of an end. So if we say that the virtues are voluntary, then our vices are voluntary too. The cases are identical. . . .

Our dispositions, however, have a different kind of voluntariness from that of our actions. We are masters of an action of ours from start to finish, and it is present to our minds at every stage, so that we know what we are doing. But with dispositions it is otherwise. Their beginning is something we can control, but as they develop step by step the stages of their development elude our observation—it is like the progress of a disease. They are, however, voluntary in the sense that it was originally in our power to exercise them for good or for evil.

SAMUEL BUTLER

Erewhon*

CURRENT OPINIONS

This is what I gathered. That in that country if a man falls into ill health, or catches any disorder, or fails bodily in any way before he is seventy years old, he is tried before a jury of his countrymen, and if convicted is held up to public scorn and sentenced more or less severely as the case may be. There are subdivisions of illness into crimes and misdemeanours as with offences amongst ourselves—a man being punished very heavily for serious illness, while failure of eyes or hearing in one over sixty-five, who has had good health hitherto, is dealt with by fine only, or imprisonment in default of payment. But if a man forges a cheque, or sets his house on fire, or robs with violence from the person, or does any other such things as are criminal in our own country, he is either taken to a hospital and most carefully tended at the public expense, or if he is in good circumstances, he lets it be known to all his friends that he is suffering from a severe fit of immorality, just as we do when we are ill, and they come and visit him with great solicitude, and inquire with interest how it all came about, what symptoms first showed themselves, and so forth—questions which he will answer with perfect unreserve; for bad conduct, though considered no less deplorable than illness with our-

* From Chapters 10, 12, 18, 19. *Erewhon* was first published in 1872.

selves, and as unquestionably indicating something seriously wrong with the individual who misbehaves, is nevertheless held to be the result of either pre-natal or post-natal misfortune.

The strange part of the story, however, is that though they ascribe moral defects to the effect of misfortune either in character or surroundings, they will not listen to the plea of misfortune in cases that in England meet with sympathy and commiseration only. Ill luck of any kind, or even ill treatment at the hands of others, is considered an offence against society, inasmuch as it makes people uncomfortable to hear of it. Loss of fortune, therefore, or loss of some dear friend on whom another was much dependent, is punished hardly less severely than physical delinquency. . . .

MALCONTENTS

I confess that I felt rather unhappy when I got home, and thought more closely over the trial[1] that I had just witnessed. For the time I was carried away by the opinion of those among whom I was. They had no misgivings about what they were doing. There did not seem to be a person in the whole court who had the smallest doubt but that all was exactly as it should be. This universal unsuspecting confidence was imparted by sympathy to myself, in spite of all my training in opinions so widely different. So it is with most of us: that which we observe to be taken as a matter of course by those round us, we take as a matter of course ourselves. And after all, it is our duty to do this, save upon grave occasion.

But when I was alone, and began to think the trial over, it certainly did strike me as betraying a strange and untenable position. Had the judge said that he acknowledged the probable truth, namely, that the prisoner was born of unhealthy parents, or had been starved in infancy, or had met with some accidents which had developed consumption; and had he then gone on to say that though he knew all this, and bitterly regretted that the protection of society obliged him to inflict additional pain on one who had suffered so much already, yet that there was no help for it, I could have understood the position, however mistaken I might have thought it. The judge was fully persuaded that the infliction of pain upon the weak and sickly was the only means of preventing weakness and sickliness from spreading, and that ten times the suffering now inflicted upon the accused was eventually warded off from others by the present apparent severity. I could therefore perfectly understand his inflicting whatever pain he might consider necessary in order to prevent so bad an example from spreading further and lowering the Erewhonian standard; but it seemed almost childish to tell the prisoner that he could have been in good health, if he had been more fortunate in his constitution, and been exposed to less hardships when he was a boy.

I write with great diffidence, but it seems to me that there is no unfairness in punishing people for their misfortunes, or rewarding them for their sheer good luck; it is the normal condition of human life that this should be done, and no right-minded person will complain of being subjected to the common treatment. There is no alternative open to us. It is idle to say that men are not responsible for their misfortunes. What is responsibility? Surely to be responsible means to be liable to have to give an answer should it be demanded, and all things which live are responsible for their lives and actions should society see fit to question them through the mouth of its authorized agent.

What is the offence of a lamb that we should rear it, and tend it, and lull it into security, for the express purpose of killing it? Its offence is the misfortune of being something which society wants to eat, and which cannot defend itself. This is ample. Who shall limit the right of society except society itself? And what consideration for the individual is tolerable unless society be the gainer thereby? Wherefore should a man be so richly rewarded for having been the son of a millionaire, were it not clearly provable that the common welfare is thus better furthered? We cannot seriously detract from a man's merit in having been the son of a rich father without imperilling our own tenure of things which we do not wish to jeopardize; if this were otherwise we should not let him keep his money for a single hour; we would have it ourselves at once. For property *is* robbery, but then, we are all robbers or would-be robbers together, and have found it essential to organize our thieving, as we have

[1] [The trial referred to here is that of a man convicted of consumption. See the quotation in John Hospers' article, p. 281.]

found it necessary to organize our lust and our revenge. Property, marriage, the law; as the bed to the river, so rule and convention to the instinct; and woe to him who tampers with the banks while the flood is flowing.

But to return. Even in England a man on board a ship with yellow fever is held responsible for his mischance, no matter what his being kept in quarantine may cost him. He may catch the fever and die; we cannot help it; he must take his chance as other people do; but surely it would be desperate unkindness to add contumely to our self-protection, unless, indeed, we believe that contumely is one of our best means of self-protection. Again, take the case of maniacs. We say that they are irresponsible for their actions, but we take good care, or ought to take good care, that they shall answer to us for their insanity, and we imprison them in what we call an asylum (that modern sanctuary!) if we do not like their answers. This is a strange kind of irresponsibility. What we ought to say is that we can afford to be satisfied with a less satisfactory answer from a lunatic than from one who is not mad, because lunacy is less infectious than crime.

We kill a serpent if we go in danger by it, simply for being such and such a serpent in such and such a place; but we never say that the serpent has only itself to blame for not having been a harmless creature. Its crime is that of being the thing which it is: but this is a capital offence, and we are right in killing it out of the way, unless we think it more danger to do so than to let it escape; nevertheless we pity the creature, even though we kill it.

But in the case of him whose trial I have described above, it was impossible that any one in the court should not have known that it was but by an accident of birth and circumstances that he was not himself also in a consumption; and yet none thought that it disgraced them to hear the judge give vent to the most cruel truisms about him. The judge himself was a kind and thoughtful person. He was a man of magnificent and benign presence. He was evidently of an iron constitution, and his face wore an expression of the maturest wisdom and experience; yet for all this, old and learned as he was, he could not see things which one would have thought would have been apparent even to a child. He could not emancipate himself from, nay, it did not even occur to him to feel, the bondage of the ideas in which he had been born and bred.

So was it also with the jury and bystanders; and—most wonderful of all—so was it even with the prisoner. Throughout he seemed fully impressed with the notion that he was being dealt with justly: he saw nothing wanton in his being told by the judge that he was to be punished, not so much as a necessary protection to society (although this was not entirely lost sight of), as because he had not been better born and bred than he was. But this led me to hope that he suffered less than he would have done if he had seen the matter in the same light that I did. And, after all, justice is relative.

I may here mention that only a few years before my arrival in the country, the treatment of all convicted invalids had been much more barbarous than now, for no physical remedy was provided, and prisoners were put to the severest labour in all sorts of weather, so that most of them soon succumbed to the extreme hardships which they suffered; this was supposed to be beneficial in some ways, inasmuch as it put the country to less expense for the maintenance of its criminal class; but the growth of luxury had induced a relaxation of the old severity, and a sensitive age would no longer tolerate what appeared to be an excess of rigour, even towards the most guilty; moreover, it was found that juries were less willing to convict, and justice was often cheated because there was no alternative between virtually condemning a man to death and letting him go free; it was also held that the country paid in recommittals for its over-severity; for those who had been imprisoned even for trifling ailments were often permanently disabled by their imprisonment; and when a man had been once convicted, it was probable that he would seldom afterwards be off the hands of the country.

These evils had long been apparent and recognized; yet people were too indolent, and too indifferent to suffering not their own, to bestir themselves about putting an end to them, until at last a benevolent reformer devoted his whole life to effecting the necessary changes. He divided all illnesses into three classes—those affecting the head, the trunk, and the lower limbs—and obtained an enactment that all diseases of the head, whether internal or external, should be treated with laudanum, those of the body with castor oil, and those of the lower limbs with an embrocation of strong sulphuric acid and water.

It may be said that the classification was not sufficiently careful, and that the remedies were ill chosen; but it is a hard thing to initiate any reform, and it was necessary to familiarize the public mind with the principle, by inserting the thin end of the wedge first: it is not, therefore, to be wondered at that among so practical a people there should still be some room for improvement. The mass of the nation are well pleased with existing arrangements, and believe that their treatment of criminals leaves little or nothing to be desired; but there is an energetic minority who hold what are considered to be extreme opinions, and who are not at all disposed to rest contented until the principle lately admitted has been carried further.

I was at some pains to discover the opinions of these men, and their reasons for entertaining them. They are held in great odium by the generality of the public, and are considered as subverters of all morality whatever. The malcontents, on the other hand, assert that illness is the inevitable result of certain antecedent causes, which, in the great majority of cases, were beyond the control of the individual, and that therefore a man is only guilty for being in a consumption in the same way as rotten fruit is guilty for having gone rotten. True, the fruit must be thrown on one side as unfit for man's use, and the man in a consumption must be put in prison for the protection of his fellow-citizens; but these radicals would not punish him further than by loss of liberty and a strict surveillance. So long as he was prevented from injuring society, they would allow him to make himself useful by supplying whatever of society's wants he could supply. If he succeeded in thus earning money, they would have him made as comfortable in prison as possible, and would in no way interfere with his liberty more than was necessary to prevent him from escaping, or from becoming more severely indisposed within the prison walls; but they would deduct from his earnings the expenses of his board, lodging, surveillance, and half those of his conviction. If he was too ill to do anything for his support in prison, they would allow him nothing but bread and water, and very little of that.

They say that society is foolish in refusing to allow itself to be benefited by a man merely because he has done it harm hitherto, and that objection to the labour of the diseased classes is only protection in another form. It is an attempt to raise the natural price of a commodity by saying that such and such persons, who are able and willing to produce it, shall not do so, whereby every one has to pay more for it.

Besides, so long as a man has not been actually killed he is our fellow-creature, though perhaps a very unpleasant one. It is in a great degree the doing of others that he is what he is, or in other words, the society which now condemns him is partly answerable concerning him. They say that there is no fear of any increase of disease under these circumstances; for the loss of liberty, the surveillance, the considerable and compulsory deduction from the prisoner's earnings, the very sparing use of stimulants (of which they would allow but little to any, and none to those who did not earn them), the enforced celibacy, and above all, the loss of reputation among friends, are in their opinion as ample safeguards to society against a general neglect of health as those now resorted to. A man, therefore (so they say), should carry his profession or trade into prison with him if possible; if not, he must earn his living by the nearest thing to it that he can; but if he be a gentleman born and bred to no profession, he must pick oakum, or write art criticisms for a newspaper.

These people say further, that the greater part of the illness which exists in their country is brought about by the insane manner in which it is treated.

They believe that illness is in many cases just as curable as the moral diseases which they see daily cured round them, but that a great reform is impossible till men learn to take a juster view of what physical obliquity proceeds from. Men will hide their illnesses as long as they are scouted on its becoming known that they are ill; it is the scouting, not the physic, which produces the concealment; and if a man felt that the news of his being in ill-health would be received by his neighbours as a deplorable fact, but one as much the result of necessary antecedent causes as though he had broken into a jeweller's shop and stolen a valuable diamond necklace—as a fact which might just as easily have happened to themselves, only that they had the luck to be better born or reared; and if they also felt that they would not be made more uncomfortable in the prison than the protection of society against infection and the proper treatment of their own disease actually demanded, men would give themselves up to the police as readily on perceiving that they had taken smallpox, as they go now to the straightener when they feel that they are on the point of forging a will, or running away with somebody else's wife.

But the main argument on which they rely is that of economy: for they know that they will sooner gain their end by appealing to men's pockets, in which they have generally something of their own, than to their heads, which contain for the most part little but borrowed or stolen property; and also, they believe it to be the readiest test and the one which has most to show for itself. If a course of conduct can be shown to cost a country less, and this by no dishonourable saving and with no indirectly increased expenditure in other ways, they hold that it requires a good deal to upset the arguments in favour of its being adopted, and whether rightly or wrongly I cannot pretend to say, they think that the more medicinal and humane treatment of the diseased of which they are the advocates would in the long run be much cheaper to the country: but I did not gather that these reformers were opposed to meeting some of the more violent forms of illness with the cat-of-nine-tails, or with death; for they saw no effectual way of checking them; they would therefore both flog and hang, but they would do so pitifully.

I have perhaps dwelt too long upon opinions which can have no possible bearing upon our own, but I have not said the tenth part of what these would-be reformers urged upon me. I feel, however, that I have sufficiently trespassed upon the attention of the reader. . . .

BIRTH FORMULAE

I heard what follows not from Arowhena, but from Mr. Nosnibor and some of the gentlemen who occasionally dined at the house: they told me that the Erewhonians believe in pre-existence; and not only this (of which I will write more fully in the next chapter), but they believe that it is of their own free act and deed in a previous state that they come to be born into this world at all. They hold that the unborn are perpetually plaguing and tormenting the married of both sexes, fluttering about them incessantly, and giving them no peace either of mind or body until they have consented to take them under their protection. If this were not so (this at least is what they urge), it would be a monstrous freedom for one man to take with another, to say that he should undergo the chances and changes of this mortal life without any option in the matter. No man would have any right to get married at all, inasmuch as he can never tell what frightful misery his doing so may entail forcibly upon a being who cannot be unhappy as long as he does not exist. They feel this so strongly that they are resolved to shift the blame on to other shoulders; and have fashioned a long mythology as to the world in which the unborn people live, and what they do, and arts and machinations to which they have recourse in order to get themselves into our own world. But of this more anon: what I would relate here is their manner of dealing with those who do come.

It is a distinguishing peculiarity of the Erewhonians that when they profess themselves to be quite certain about any matter, and avow it as a base on which they are to build a system of practise, they seldom quite believe in it. If they smell a rat about the precincts of a cherished institution, they will always stop their noses to it *if* they can.

This is what most of them did in this matter of the unborn, for I cannot (and never could) think that they seriously believed in their mythology concerning pre-existence: they did and they did not; they did not know themselves what they believed; all they did know was that it was a disease not to believe as they did. The only thing of which they were quite sure was that it was the pestering of the unborn which caused them to be brought into this world, and that they would not have been here if they would have only let peaceable people alone.

It would be hard to disprove this position, and they might have a good case if they would only leave it as it stands. But this they will not do; they must have assurance doubly sure; they must have the written word of the child itself as soon as it is born, giving the parents indemnity from all responsibility on the score of its birth, and asserting its own pre-existence. They have therefore devised something which they call a birth formula—a document which varies in words according to the caution of parents, but is much the same practically in all cases; for it has been the business of the Erewhonian lawyers during many ages to exercise their skill in perfecting it and providing for every contingency.

These formulae are printed on common paper at a moderate cost for the poor; but the rich have them written on parchment and handsomely bound, so that the getting up of a person's birth formula is a test of his social position. They commence by setting forth, That whereas A. B. was a member of the kingdom of the unborn, where he was well provided for in every way, and had no cause of discontent, etc., etc., he did of his own wanton depravity and restlessness conceive a desire to enter into this present world; that thereon having taken the necessary steps as set forth in laws of the unborn kingdom, he did with malice aforethought set himself to plague and pester two unfortunate people who had never wronged him, and who were quite contented and happy until he conceived this base design against their peace; for which wrong he now humbly entreats their pardon.

He acknowledges that he is responsible for all physical blemishes and deficiencies which may render him answerable to the laws of his country; that his parents have nothing whatever to do with any of these things; and that they have a right to kill him at once if they be so minded, though he entreats them to show their marvellous goodness and clemency by sparing his life. If they will do this, he promises to be their most obedient and abject creature during his earlier years, and indeed all his life, unless they should see fit in their abundant generosity to remit some portion of his service hereafter. And so the formula continues, going sometimes into very minute details, according to the fancies of family lawyers, who will not make it any shorter than they can help.

The deed being thus prepared, on the third or fourth day after the birth of the child, or as they call it, the "final importunity," the friends gather together, and there is a feast held, where they are all very melancholy—as a general rule, I believe, quite truly so—and make presents to the father and mother of the child in order to console them for the injury which has just been done them by the unborn.

By and by the child himself is brought down by his nurse, and the company begin to rail upon him, upbraiding him for his impertinence, and asking him what amends he proposes to make for the wrong that he has committed, and how he can look for care and nourishment from those who have perhaps already been injured by the unborn on some ten or twelve occasions; for they say of people with large families, that they have suffered terrible injuries from the unborn; till at last, when this has been carried far enough, some one suggests the formula, which is brought out and solemnly read to the child by the family straightener. This gentleman is always invited on these occasions, for the very fact of intrusion into a peaceful family shows a depravity on the part of the child which requires his professional services.

On being teased by the reading and tweaked by the nurse, the child will commonly begin to cry, which is reckoned a good sign, as showing a consciousness of guilt. He is thereon asked, Does he assent to the formula? on which, as he still continues crying and can obviously make no answer, some one of the friends comes forward and undertakes to sign the document on his behalf, feeling sure (so he says) that the child would do it if he only knew how, and that he will release the present signer from his engagement on arriving at maturity. The friend then inscribes the signature of the child at the foot of the parchment, which is held to bind the child as much as though he had signed it himself.

Even this, however, does not fully content them, for they feel a little uneasy until they have got the child's own signature after all. So when he is about fourteen, these good people partly bribe him by promises of greater liberty and good things, and partly intimidate him through their great power of making themselves actively unpleasant to him, so that though there is a show of freedom made, there is really none; they also use the offices of the teachers in the Colleges of Unreason, till at last, in one way or another, they take very good care that he shall sign the paper by which he professes to have been a free agent in coming into the world, and to take all the responsibility of having done so on to his own shoulders. And yet, though this document is obviously the most important which any one can sign in his whole life, they will have him do so at an age when neither they nor the law will for many a year allow any one else to bind him to the smallest obligation, no matter how righteously he may owe it, because they hold him too young to know what he is about, and do not consider it fair that he should commit himself to anything that may prejudice him in after years.

I own that all this seemed rather hard, and not of a piece with the many admirable institutions existing among them. I once ventured to say a part of what I thought about it to one of the Professors of Unreason. I did it very tenderly, but his justification of the system was quite out of my comprehension. I remember asking him whether he did not think it would do harm to a lad's principles, by weakening his sense of the sanctity of his word and of truth generally, that he should be led into entering upon a solemn declaration as to the truth of things about which all that he can certainly know is that he knows nothing—whether, in fact, the teachers who so led him, or who taught anything as a certainty of which they were themselves uncertain, were not earning their living by impairing the truth-sense of their pupils (a delicate organisation mostly), and by vitiating one of their most sacred instincts.

The Professor, who was a delightful person, seemed greatly surprised at the view which I took, but it had no influence with him whatsoever. No one, he answered, expected that the boy either would or could know all that he said he knew; but the world was full of compromises; and there was hardly any affirmation which would bear being interpreted literally. Human language was too gross a vehicle of thought—thought being incapable of absolute translation. He added, that as there can be no translation from one language into another which shall not scant the meaning somewhat, or enlarge upon it, so there is no language which can render thought without a jarring and a harshness somewhere—and so forth; all of which seemed to come to this in the end, that it was the custom of the country, and that the Erewhonians were a conservative people; that the boy would have to begin compromising sooner or later, and this was part of his education in the art. It was perhaps to be regretted that compromise should be as necessary as it was; still it was necessary, and the sooner the boy got to understand it the better for himself. But they never tell this to the boy.

From the book of their mythology about the unborn I made the extracts which will form the following chapter.

THE WORLD OF THE UNBORN

. . . Having waded through many chapters . . . I came at last to the unborn themselves, and found that they were held to be souls pure and simple, having no actual bodies, but living in a sort of gaseous yet more or less anthropomorphic existence, like that of a ghost; they have thus neither flesh nor blood nor warmth. Nevertheless they are supposed to have local habitations and cities wherein they dwell, though these are as unsubstantial as their inhabitants; they are even thought to eat and drink some thin ambrosial sustenance, and generally to be capable of doing whatever mankind can do, only after a visionary ghostly fashion as in a dream. On the other hand, as long as they remain where they are they never die—the only form of death in the unborn world being the leaving it for our own. They are believed to be extremely numerous, far more so than mankind. They arrive from unknown planets, full grown, in large batches at a time; but they can only leave the unborn world by taking the steps necessary for their arrival here—which is, in fact, by suicide.

They ought to be an exceedingly happy people, for they have no extremes of good or ill fortune; never marrying, but living in a state much like that fabled by the poets as the primitive condition of mankind. In spite of this, however, they are incessantly complaining; they know that we in this world have bodies, and indeed they know everything else about us, for they move among us whithersoever they will, and can read our thoughts, as well as survey our actions at pleasure. One would think that this should be enough for them; and most of them are indeed alive to the desperate risk which they will run by indulging themselves in that body with "sensible warm motion" which they so much desire; nevertheless, there are some to whom the *ennui* of a disembodied existence is so intolerable that they will venture anything for a change; so they resolve to quit. The conditions which they must accept are so uncertain, that none but the most foolish of the unborn will consent to them; and it is from these, and these only, that our own ranks are recruited.

When they have finally made up their minds to leave, they must go before the magistrate of the nearest town, and sign an affidavit of their desire to quit their then existence. On their having done this, the magistrate reads them the conditions which they must accept, and which are so long that I can only extract some of the principal points, which are mainly the following:

First, they must take a potion which will destroy their memory and sense of identity; they must go into the world helpless, and without a will of their own; they must draw lots for their dispositions before they go, and take them, such as they are, for better or worse—neither are they to be allowed any choice in the matter of the body which they so much desire; they are simply allotted by chance, and without appeal, to two people whom it is their business to find and pester until they adopt them. Who these are to be, whether rich or poor, kind or unkind, healthy or diseased, there is no knowing; they have, in fact, to entrust themselves for many years to the care of those for whose good constitution and good sense they have no sort of guarantee.

It is curious to read the lectures which the wiser heads give to those who are meditating a change. They talk with them as we talk with a spendthrift, and with about as much success.

"To be born," they say, "is a felony—it is a capital crime, for which sentence may be executed at any moment after the commission of the offence. You may perhaps happen to live for some seventy or eighty years, but what is that compared with the eternity you now enjoy? And even though the sentence were commuted, and you were allowed to live on for ever, you would in time become so terribly weary of life that execution would be the greatest mercy to you.

"Consider the infinite risk; to be born of wicked parents and trained in vice! to be born of silly parents, and trained to unrealities! of parents who regard you as a sort of chattel or property, belonging more to them than to yourself! Again, you may draw utterly unsympathetic parents, who will never be able to understand you, and who will do their best to thwart you (as a hen when she has hatched a duckling), and then call you ungrateful because you do not love them; or, again, you may draw parents who look upon you as a thing to be cowed while it is still young, lest it should give them trouble hereafter by having wishes and feelings of its own.

"In later life, when you have been finally allowed to pass muster as a full member of the world, you will yourself become liable to the

pesterings of the unborn—and a very happy life you may be led in consequence! for we solicit so strongly that a few only—nor these the best—can refuse us; and yet not to refuse is much the same as going into partnership with half a dozen different people about whom one can know absolutely nothing beforehand—not even whether one is going into partnership with men or women, nor with how many of either. Delude not yourself with thinking that you will be wiser than your parents. You may be an age in advance of those whom you have pestered, but unless you are one of the great ones you will still be an age behind those who will in their turn pester you.

"Imagine what it must be to have an unborn quartered upon you, who is of an entirely different temperament and disposition to your own; nay, half a dozen such, who will not love you though you have stinted yourself in a thousand ways to provide for their comfort and well-being—who will forget all your self-sacrifice, and of whom you may never be sure that they are not bearing a grudge against you for errors of judgement into which you may have fallen, though you had hoped that such had been long since atoned for. Ingratitude such as this is not uncommon, yet fancy what it must be to bear! It is hard upon the duckling to have been hatched by a hen, but is it not also hard upon the hen to have hatched the duckling?

"Consider it again, we pray you, not for our sake but for your own. Your initial character you must draw by lot; but whatever it is, it can only come to a tolerably successful development after long training; remember that over that training you will have no control. It is possible, and even probable, that whatever you may get in after life which is of real pleasure and service to you, will have to be won in spite of, rather than by the help of, those whom you are now about to pester, and that you will only win your freedom after years of a painful struggle in which it will be hard to say whether you have suffered most injury, or inflicted it.

"Remember also, that if you go into the world you will have free will; that you will be obliged to have it; that there is no escaping it; that you will be fettered to it during your whole life, and must on every occasion do that which on the whole seems best to you at any given time, no matter whether you are right or wrong in choosing it. Your mind will be a balance for considerations, and your action will go with the heavier scale. How it shall fall will depend upon the kind of scales which you may have drawn at birth, the bias which they will have obtained by use, and the weight of the immediate considerations. If the scales were good to start with, and if they have not been outrageously tampered with in childhood, and if the combinations into which you enter are average ones, you may come off well; but there are too many 'ifs' in this, and with the failure of any one of them your misery is assured. Reflect on this, and remember that should the ill come upon you, you will have yourself to thank, for it is your own choice to be born, and there is no compulsion in the matter. . . .

IMMANUEL KANT

The Right of Punishing*

The Right of administering Punishment, is the Right of the Sovereign as the Supreme Power to inflict pain upon a Subject on account of a Crime committed by him. The Head of the State cannot therefore be punished; but his supremacy may be withdrawn from him. Any Transgression of the public law which makes him who commits it incapable of being a Citizen, constitutes a *Crime,* either simply as a private Crime (*crimen*), or also as a *public* Crime (*crimen publicum*). Private crimes are dealt with by a Civil Court; Public Crimes by a Criminal Court.—Embezzlement or peculation of money or goods entrusted in trade, Fraud in purchase or sale, if done before the eyes of the party who suffers, are Private Crimes. On the other hand, Coining false money or forging Bills of Exchange, Theft, Robbery, etc., are Public Crimes, because the Commonwealth, and not merely some particular individual, is endangered thereby. Such Crimes may be divided into those of a *base* character (*indolis abjectæ*) and those of a *violent* character (*indolis violentiœ*).

Judicial or Juridical Punishment (*pœna forensis*) is to be distinguished from Natural Punishment (*pœna naturalis*), in which Crime as Vice punishes itself, and does not as such come within the cognizance of the Legislator. Juridical Punishment can never be administered merely as a means for promoting another Good either with regard to the Criminal himself or to Civil Society, but must in all cases be imposed only because the individual on whom it is inflicted *has committed a Crime.* For one man ought never to be dealt with merely as a means subservient to the purpose of another, nor be mixed up with the subjects of Real Right. Against such treatment his Inborn Personality has a Right to protect him, even although he may be condemned to lose his Civil Personality. He must first be found guilty and *punishable,* before there can be any thought of drawing from his Punishment any benefit for himself or his fellow-citizens. The Penal Law is a Categorical Imperative; and woe to him who creeps through the serpent-windings of Utilitarianism to discover some advantage that may discharge him from the Justice of Punishment, or even from the due measure of it, according to the Pharisaic maxim: 'It is better that *one* man should die than that the whole people should perish.' For if Justice and Righteousness perish, human life would no longer have any value in the world.—What, then, is to be said of such a proposal as to keep a Criminal alive who has been condemned to death, on his being given to understand that if he agreed to certain dangerous experiments being performed upon him, he

* From Immanuel Kant, *The Philosophy of Law,* trans. W. Hastie (Edinburgh, 1887), pp. 194–201. First published in 1797.

would be allowed to survive if he came happily through them? It is argued that Physicians might thus obtain new information that would be of value to the Commonweal. But a Court of Justice would repudiate with scorn any proposal of this kind if made to it by the Medical Faculty; for Justice would cease to be Justice, if it were bartered away for any consideration whatever.

But what is the mode and measure of Punishment which Public Justice takes as its Principle and Standard? It is just the Principle of Equality, by which the pointer of the Scale of Justice is made to incline no more to the one side than the other. It may be rendered by saying that the undeserved evil which any one commits on another, is to be regarded as perpetrated on himself. Hence it may be said: 'If you slander another, you slander yourself; if you steal from another, you steal from yourself; if you strike another, you strike yourself; if you kill another, you kill yourself.' This is the Right of RETALIATION (*jus talionis*); and properly understood, it is the only Principle which in regulating a Public Court, as distinguished from mere private judgment, can definitely assign both the quality and the quantity of a just penalty. All other standards are wavering and uncertain; and on account of other considerations involved in them, they contain no principle conformable to the sentence of pure and strict Justice. It may appear, however, that difference of social status would not admit the application of the Principle of Retaliation, which is that of 'Like with Like.' But although the application may not in all cases be possible according to the letter, yet as regards the effect it may always be attained in practice, by due regard being given to the disposition and sentiment of the parties in the higher social sphere. Thus a pecuniary penalty on account of a verbal injury, may have no direct proportion to the injustice of slander; for one who is wealthy may be able to indulge himself in this offence for his own gratification. Yet the attack committed on the honour of the party aggrieved may have its equivalent in the pain inflicted upon the pride of the aggressor, especially if he is condemned by the judgment of the Court, not only to retract and apologize, but to submit to some meaner ordeal, as kissing the hand of the injured person. In like manner, if a man of the highest rank has violently assaulted an innocent citizen of the lower orders, he may be condemned not only to apologize but to undergo a solitary and painful imprisonment, whereby, in addition to the discomfort endured, the vanity of the offender would be painfully affected, and the very shame of his position would constitute an adequate Retaliation after the principle of 'Like with Like.' But how then would we render the statement: 'If you *steal* from another, you steal from yourself'? In this way, that whoever steals anything makes the property of all insecure; he therefore robs himself of all security in property, according to the Right of Retaliation. Such a one has nothing, and can acquire nothing, but he has the Will to live; and this is only possible by others supporting him. But as the State should not do this gratuitously, he must for this purpose yield his powers to the state to be used in penal labour; and thus he falls for a time, or it may be for life, into a condition of slavery.—But whoever has committed Murder, must *die*. There is, in this case, no juridical substitute or surrogate, that can be given or taken for the satisfaction of Justice. There is no *Likeness* or proportion between Life, however painful, and Death; and therefore there is no Equality between the crime of Murder and the retaliation of it but what is judicially accomplished by the execution of the Criminal. His death, however, must be kept free from all maltreatment that would make the humanity suffering in his Person loathsome or abominable. Even if a Civil Society resolved to dissolve itself with the consent of all its members—as might be supposed in the case of a People inhabiting an island resolving to separate and scatter themselves throughout the whole world—the last Murderer lying in the prison ought to be executed before the resolution was carried out. This ought to be done in order that every one may realize the desert of his deeds, and that bloodguiltiness may not remain upon the people; for otherwise they might all be regarded as participators in the murder as a public violation of Justice.

The Equalization of Punishment with Crime, is therefore only possible by the cognition of the Judge extending even to the penalty of Death, according to the Right of Retaliation. This is manifest from the fact that it is only thus that a Sentence can be pronounced over all criminals proportionate to their internal *wickedness;* as may be seen by considering the case when the punishment of Death has to be inflicted, not on account of a murder, but on account of a political crime that can only be punished capitally. A hypothetical case, founded on history, will illustrate this. In the last Scottish Rebellion there were various participators in it—such as Balmerino and others—who believed that in taking part in the Rebellion they were only discharging their duty to the House of Stuart; but there were also others who were animated only by private motives and interests. Now, suppose that the Judgment of the Supreme Court regarding them had been this: that every one should have liberty to choose between the punishment of Death or Penal Servitude for life. In view of such an alternative, I say that the Man of Honour would choose Death, and the Knave would choose servitude. This would be the effect of their human nature as it is; for the honourable man values his Honour more highly than even Life itself, whereas a Knave regards a Life, although covered with shame, as better in his eyes than not to be. The former is, without gainsaying, less guilty than the other; and they can only be proportionately punished by death being inflicted equally upon them both; yet to the one it is a mild punishment when his nobler temperament is taken into account, whereas it is a hard punishment to the other in view of his baser temperament. But, on the other hand, were they all equally condemned to Penal Servitude for life, the honourable man would be too severely punished, while the other, on account of his baseness of nature, would be too mildly punished. In the judgment to be pronounced over a number of criminals united in such a conspiracy, the best Equalizer of Punishment and Crime in the form of public Justice is Death. And besides all this, it has never been heard of, that a Criminal condemned to death on account of a murder has complained that the Sentence inflicted on him more than was right and just; and any one would treat him with scorn if he expressed himself to this effect against it. Otherwise it would be necessary to admit that although wrong and injustice are not done to the Criminal by the Law, yet the Legislative Power is not entitled to administer this mode of Punishment; and if it did so, it would be in contradiction with itself.

However many they may be who have committed a murder, or have even commanded it, or acted as art and part in it, they ought all to suffer death; for so Justice wills it, in accordance with the Idea of the juridical Power as founded on the universal Laws of Reason. But the number of the Accomplices (*correi*) in such a deed might happen to be so great that the State, in resolving to be without such criminals, would be in danger of soon also being deprived of subjects. But it will not thus dissolve itself, neither must it return to the much worse condition of Nature, in which there would be no external Justice. Nor, above all, should it deaden the sensibilities of the People by the spectacle of Justice being exhibited in the mere carnage of a slaughtering bench. In such circumstances the Sovereign must always be allowed to have it in his power to take the part of the Judge upon himself as a case of Necessity,—and to deliver a Judgment which, instead of the penalty of death, shall assign some other punishment to the Criminals, and thereby preserve a multitude of the People. The penalty of Deportation is relevant in this connection. Such a form of Judgment cannot be carried out according to a public law, but only by an authoritative act of the royal Prerogative, and it may only be applied as an act of grace in individual cases.

Against these doctrines, the Marquis Beccaria has given forth a different view. Moved by the compassionate sentimentality of a humane feeling, he has asserted that all Capital Punishment is wrong in itself and unjust. He has put forward this view on the ground that the penalty of death could not be contained in the original Civil Contract; for, in that case, every one of the People would have had to consent to lose his life if he murdered any of his fellow-citizens. But, it is argued, such a consent is impossible, because no one can thus dispose of his own life.—All this is mere sophistry and perversion of Right. No one undergoes Punishment because he has willed to be punished, but because he has willed *a punishable Action;* for it is in fact no Punishment when any one experiences what he wills, and it is impossible for any one to *will* to be punished. To say, 'I *will* to be punished, if I murder any one,' can mean nothing more than, 'I submit myself along with all the other citizens to the Laws;' and if there are any Criminals among the People, these Laws will include Penal Laws. The individual who, as a Co-legislator, enacts *Penal Law,* cannot possibly be the same Person who, as a Subject, is punished according to the Law; for, *quâ* Criminal, he cannot possibly be regarded as having a voice in the Legislation, the Legislator being rationally viewed as just and holy. If any one, then, enact a Penal Law against himself as a Criminal, it must be the pure juridically law-giving Reason (*homo noumenon*), which subjects him as one capable of crime, and consequently as another Person (*homo phenomenon*), along with all the others in the Civil Union, to this Penal Law. In other words, it is not the People taken distributively, but the Tribunal of public Justice, as distinct from the Criminal, that prescribes Capital Punishment; and it is not to be viewed as if the Social Contract contained the Promise of all the individuals to allow themselves to be punished, thus disposing of themselves and their lives. For if the Right to punish must be grounded upon a promise of the wrongdoer, whereby he is to be regarded as being willing to be punished, it ought also to be left to him to find himself deserving of the Punishment; and the Criminal would thus be his own Judge. The chief error (πρῶτον ψεῦδος) of this sophistry consists in regarding the judgment of the Criminal himself, necessarily determined by his Reason, that he is under obligation to undergo the loss of his life, as a judgment that must be grounded on a resolution of his *Will* to take it away himself; and thus the execution of the Right in question is represented as united in one and the same person with the adjudication of the Right.

FYODOR DOSTOEVSKY

Prison Life in Siberia*

That same evening, before the closing of the barracks, when it was already dark, I walked to the side of the palisade. A heavy feeling of sadness weighed upon my soul. During all the time that I passed in the convict prison I never felt myself so miserable as on that evening, though the first day is always the hardest, whether at hard labour or in the prison. One thought in particular had left me no respite since my deportation—a question insoluble then and insoluble now. I reflected on the inequality of the punishments inflicted for the same crimes. Often, indeed, one crime cannot be compared even approximately to another. Two murderers kill a man under circumstances which in each case are minutely examined and weighed. They each receive the same punishment; and yet by what an abyss are their two actions separated! One has committed a murder for a trifle—for an onion. He has killed on the high-road a peasant who was passing, and found on him an onion, and nothing else.

"Well, I was sent to hard labour for a peasant who had nothing but an onion!"

"Fool that you are! an onion is worth a kopeck. If you had killed a hundred peasants you would have had a hundred kopecks, or one rouble." The above is a prison joke.

Another criminal has killed a debauchee who was oppressing or dishonouring his wife, his sister, or his daughter.

A third, a vagabond, half dead with hunger, pursued by a whole band of police, was defending his liberty, his life. He is to be regarded as on an equality with the brigand who assassinates children for his amusement, for the pleasure of feeling their warm blood flow over his hands, of seeing them shudder in a last bird-like palpitation beneath the knife which tears their flesh!

They will all alike be sent to hard labour; though the sentence will perhaps not be for the same number of years. But the variations in the punishment are not very numerous, whereas different kinds of crimes may be reckoned by

* From Fyodor Dostoevsky, *The House of the Dead,* trans. H. Sutherland Edwards (London: J. M. Dent; New York: E. P. Dutton, Everyman's Library, 1912), pp. 57–60. Reprinted by permission of the publishers.

thousands. As many characters, so many crimes.

Let us admit that it is impossible to get rid of this first inequality in punishment, that the problem is insoluble, and that in connection with penal matters it is the squaring of the circle. Let all that be admitted; but even if this inequality cannot be avoided, there is another thing to be thought of—the consequences of the punishment. Here is a man who is wasting away like a candle; there is another one, on the contrary, who had no idea before going into exile that there could be such a gay, such an idle life, where he would find a circle of such agreeable friends. Individuals of this latter class are to be found in the convict prison.

Now take a man of heart, of cultivated mind, and of delicate conscience. What he feels kills him more certainly than the material punishment. The judgment which he himself pronounces on his crime is more pitiless than that of the most severe tribunal, the most Draconian law. He lives by the side of another convict, who has not once reflected on the murder he is expiating, during the whole time of his sojourn in the convict prison. He, perhaps, even considers himself innocent. Are there not, also, poor devils who commit crimes in order to be sent to hard labour, and thus to escape the liberty which is much more painful than confinement? A man's life is miserable, he has never, perhaps, been able to satisfy his hunger. He is worked to death in order to enrich his master. In the convict prison his work will be less severe, less crushing. He will eat as much as he wants, better than he could ever have hoped to eat, had he remained free. On holidays he will have meat, and fine people will give him alms, and his evening's work will bring him in some money. And the society one meets with in the convict prison, is that to be counted for nothing? The convicts are clever, wide-awake people, who are up to everything. The new arrival can scarcely conceal the admiration he feels for his companions in labour. He has seen nothing like it before, and he will consider himself in the best company possible.

Is it possible that men so differently situated can feel in an equal degree the punishment inflicted? But why think about questions that are insoluble? The drum beats, let us go back to barracks.

J. ELLIS McTAGGART

Hegel's Theory of Punishment*

. . . Of late years we have almost given up the defence of vindictive punishment, both in law and education, though it is still retained in theology by those who accept the doctrine that punishment may be eternal. The ordinary view of the use of punishment in law is, I take it, that its main object is deterrent—to prevent crime by making the possible criminal frightened at the punishment which will follow. Its preventive use—of checking crime by restraining or removing persons who have already proved themselves criminals—is also considered important, but in a lesser degree. Finally, if the state *can* reform the criminal while punishing him, it considers itself bound to try; but the primary object of criminal justice, I think, is held to be the protection of the innocent rather than the improvement of the guilty, and therefore the discouragement of crime is taken as of more importance than the reform of the criminal. . . .

We have now seen what the ordinary view of punishment is. My object is to consider what relation to this ordinary view is held by Hegel's

* J. Ellis McTaggart, "Hegel's Theory of Punishment," *International Journal of Ethics,* VI (1896), 482–502.

theory of punishment, as expressed in his "Philosophy of Law." It has often been said that he supports vindictive punishment. And, at first sight, it looks very much as if he did. He deals with this subject in the ninety-ninth and subsequent paragraphs of his book on the "Philosophy of Law," and there he expressly says that it is superficial to regard punishment as protective to society, or as deterring, or as improving the criminal. If it is not protective or threatening, we must surrender the theories which we have called the preventive and the deterrent. If it is not improving, we must give up the reformatory theory. Hegel does not deny that punishment may deter, prevent, or improve, and he does not deny that this will be an additional advantage. But he says that none of these are the chief object of punishment, and none of them express its real nature. It would seem, therefore, that he must intend to advocate vindictive punishment. And this is confirmed by the fact that he expressly says the object of punishment is not to do "this or that" good.

Nevertheless, I believe that Hegel had not the slightest intention of advocating what we have called vindictive punishment. For he says, beyond the possibility of a doubt, that in punishment the criminal is to be treated as a moral being,—that is, one who is potentially moral, however immoral he may be in fact, and one in whom this potential morality must be called into actual existence. He complains that in the deterrent theory we treat a man like a dog to whom his master shows a whip, and not as a free being. He says that the criminal has a right to be punished, which indicates that the punishment is in a sense for his sake. And, still more emphatically, "in punishment the offender is honored as a rational being, since the punishment is looked on as his right."[1]

Now this is incompatible with the view that Hegel is here approving of vindictive punishment. For he says that a man is only to be punished because he is a moral being, and that it would be an injury to him not to punish him. The vindictive theory knows nothing of all this. It inflicts pain on a man, not for his ultimate good, but because, as it says, he has deserved to suffer pain. And, on Hegel's theory, punishment depends on the recognition of the criminal's rational and moral nature, so that, in his phrase, it is an honor as well as a disgrace. Nothing of the sort exists for vindictive punishment. It does not care whether the sinner can or will do good in the future. It punishes him because he has done wrong in the past. If we look at the doctrine of hell,—which is a pure case of vindictive punishment,—we see that it is possible to conceive punishment of this sort when the element of a potential moral character has entirely disappeared, for I conceive that the supporters of this doctrine would deny the possibility of repentance, since they deny the possibility of pardon.

What, then, is Hegel's theory? It is, I think, briefly this. In sin, man rejects and defies the moral law. Punishment is pain inflicted on him because he has done this, and in order that he may, by the fact of his punishment, be forced into recognizing as valid the law which he rejected in sinning, and so repent of his sin—really repent, and not merely be frightened out of doing it again.

Thus the object of punishment is that the criminal should repent of his crime, and by so doing realize the moral character, which has been temporarily obscured by his wrong action, but which is, as Hegel asserts, really his truest and deepest nature. At first sight this looks very much like the reformatory theory of punishment, which Hegel has rejected. But there is a great deal of difference between them. The reformatory theory says that we ought to reform our criminals *while* we are punishing them. Hegel says that punishment itself tends to reform them. The reformatory theory wishes to pain criminals as little as possible, and improve them as much as possible. Hegel's theory says that it is the pain which will improve them, and therefore, although it looks on pain in itself as an evil, is by no means particularly anxious to spare it, since it holds that through the pain the criminals will be raised, and that we have therefore no right to deny it to them.

When Hegel says, therefore, as we saw above, that the object of punishment is not to effect "this or that good," we must not, I think, take him to mean that we do not look for a good result from punishment. We must rather interpret him to mean that it is not in consequence of some *accidental* good result that punishment is to be defended, but that, for the criminal, punishment is inherently good. This use of "this or that" to express an accidental or contingent good seems in

[1] *Philosophy of Law,* Sections 99 and 100.

accordance with Hegel's usual style. And we must also remember that Hegel, who hated many things, hated nothing more bitterly than sentimental humanitarianism, and that he was in consequence more inclined to emphasize his divergence from a reformatory theory of punishment, than his agreement with it. . . .

It is not impossible that we may find out that the world has been acting on the Hegelian view for many ages, but as an explicit theory it has found little support. We all recognize that a man can be frightened into or out of a course of action by punishment. We all recognize that a man can sometimes be reformed by influences applied while he is being punished. But can he ever be reformed simply by punishment? Reform and repentance involve that he should either see that something was wrong which before he thought was right, or else that the intensity of his moral feelings should be so strengthened that he is enabled to resist a temptation, to which before he yielded. And why should punishment help him to do either of these things?

There is a certain class of people in the present day who look on all punishment as essentially degrading. They do not, in their saner moods, deny that there may be people for whom it is necessary. But they think that, if any one requires punishment, he proves himself to be uninfluenced by moral motives, and only to be governed by fear, which they declare to be degrading. (It is curious, by the way, that this school is rather fond of the idea that people should be governed by rewards rather than punishments. It does not seem easy to understand why it is less degrading to be bribed into virtue than to be frightened away from vice.) They look on all punishment as implying deep degradation in some one,—if it is justified, the sufferer must be little better than a brute; if it is not justified, the brutality is in the person who inflicts it.

This argument appears to travel in a circle. Punishment, they say, is degrading, therefore it can work no moral improvement. But this begs the question. For if punishment could work a moral improvement, it would not degrade but elevate. The humanitarian argument alternately proves that punishment can only intimidate because it is brutalizing, and that it is brutalizing because it can only intimidate. The real reason, apparently, of the foregone conviction which tries to justify itself by this confusion, is an unreasoning horror of the infliction of pain which has seized on many very excellent and disinterested people. That pain is an evil cannot be denied. It may, perhaps, be reasonably asserted that it is the ultimate evil. But to assert that it is always wrong to inflict it is equivalent to a declaration that there is no moral difference between a dentist and a wife-beater. No one can deny that the infliction of pain may in the long run increase happiness—as in the extraction of an aching tooth. If pain, in spite of its being evil *per se*, can thus be desirable as a means, the general objection to pain as a moral agent would seem to disappear also.

Of course, there is nothing in simple pain, as such, which can lead to repentance. If I get into a particular train, and break my leg in a collision, that cannot make me repent my action in going by the train, though it will very possibly make me regret it. For the pain in this case was not a punishment. It came, indeed, because I got into the train, but not because I had done wrong in getting into the train.

Hegel's theory is that punishment, that is, pain inflicted because the sufferer had previously done wrong, may lead to repentance for the crime which caused the punishment. We have now to consider whether this is true. Our thesis is not that it always produces repentance—which, of course, is not the case—but that there is something in its nature as punishment which tends to produce repentance. And this, as we have seen, is not a common theory of punishment. "Men do not," says George Eliot in "Felix Holt," (Chap. 41,)—"men do not become penitent and learn to abhor themselves by having their backs cut open with the lash; rather, they learn to abhor the lash." That the principle expressed here is one which often operates, cannot be denied. Can we so far limit its application that Hegel's theory shall also be valid?

We have so far defined punishment as pain inflicted because the sufferer has done wrong. But, looking at it more closely, we should have to alter this definition, which is too narrow, and does not include cases of unjust or mistaken punishment. To bring these in we must say that it is pain inflicted because the person who inflicts it thinks that the person who suffers it has done wrong. Repentance, again, is the realization by the criminal, with sufficient vividness to govern future action, that he has done wrong. Now is there anything in the nature of punishment to cause the conviction in the mind of the judge to be reproduced in the mind of the culprit? If so, punishment will tend to produce repentance.

I submit that this is the case under certain conditions. When the culprit recognizes the punishing authority as one which embodies the moral law, and which has a right to enforce it, then punishment may lead to repentance, but not otherwise.

Let us examine this a little more closely. A person who suffers punishment may conceive the authority which inflicts it as distinctly immoral in its tendencies. In this case, of course, he will not be moved to repent of his action. The punishment will appear to him unjust, the incurring of the punishment will present itself in the light of a duty, and he will consider himself not as a criminal, but as a martyr. On the other hand, if the punishment causes him to change his line of action, this, his convictions being as we have supposed, will not be repentance, but cowardice.

Or again, he may not regard it as distinctly immoral—as punishing him for what it is his duty to do, but he may regard it as non-moral—as punishing him for what he had a right, though not a duty, to do. In this case, too, punishment will not lead to repentance. He will not regard himself as a martyr, but he will be justified in regarding himself as a very badly-treated individual. If the punishment does cause him to abstain from such action in future, it will not be the result of repentance, but of prudence. He will not have come to think it wrong, but he may think it not worth the pain it will bring on him.

If, however, he regards the authority which punishes him as one which expresses, and which has a right to express, the moral law, his attitude will be very different. He will no longer regard his punishment either as a martyrdom or as an injury. On the contrary, he will feel that it is the proper consequence of his fault. And to feel this, and to be able to accept it as such, is surely repentance.

But it may be objected that this will lead to a dilemma. The punishment cannot have this moral effect on us unless it comes from an authority which we recognize as expressing the moral law, and therefore valid for us. But if we recognize this, how did we ever come to commit the sin, which consists in a defiance of the moral law? Does not the existence of the sin itself prove that we are not in that submissive position to the moral law, and to the power which is enforcing it, which alone can make the punishment a purification?

I do not think this is the case. It is, in the first place, quite possible for a recognition of the moral law to exist which is not sufficiently strong to prevent our violating it at the suggestion of our passions or our impulses, but which is yet strong enough, when the punishment follows, to make us recognize the justice of the sentence. After all, most cases of wrong-doing, which can be treated as criminal, are cases of this description, in which a man defies a moral law which he knows to be binding, because the temptations to violate it are at that moment too strong for his desire to do what he knows to be right. In these cases the moral law is, indeed, recognized,—for the offender knows he is doing wrong,—but not recognized with sufficient strength; for, if it was, he would abstain from doing wrong. And, therefore, the moral consciousness is strong enough to accept the punishment as justly incurred, though it was not strong enough to prevent the offender from incurring it. In this case, the significance of the punishment is that it tends to produce that vividness in the recognition of the moral law, which the occurrence of the offence shows to have been previously wanting. The pain and coercion involved in punishment present the law with much greater impressiveness than can, for the mass of people, be gained from a mere admission that the law is binding. On the other hand, the fact that the pain coincides with that intellectual recognition, on the part of the offender, that the law is binding, prevents the punishment having a merely intimidating effect, and makes it a possible stage in a moral advance.

Besides these cases of conscious violation of a moral law, there are others where men sincerely believe in a certain principle, and yet systematically fail to see that it applies in certain cases, not because they really think these cases are exceptions, but because indolence or prejudice has prevented them from ever applying their general principle to those particular instances. Thus there have been nations who conscientiously believed murder to be sinful, and yet fought duels with a good conscience. If pressed, they would have admitted duels to be attempts to murder. But no one ever did press them, and they never pressed themselves. As soon as a set of reformers arose, who did press the question, duels were found to be indefensible, and disappeared. So for many years the United States solemnly affirmed the right of all men to liberty, while slavery was legally recognized. Yet they would not have denied that slaves were men.

When such cases occur with a single individual, punishment might here, also, lead to repentance. For it was only possible to accept the general law, and reject the particular application, by ignoring the unanswerable question, Why do not you in this case practise what you preach? Now, you *can* ignore a question, but you cannot ignore a punishment, if it is severe enough. You cannot put it on one side; you must either assert that it is unjust, or admit that it is just. And in the class of cases we have now been considering, we have seen that when the question is once asked, it must condemn the previous line of action. Here, therefore, punishment may lead to repentance.

A third case is that in which the authority is recognized, but in which it is not known beforehand that it disapproved of the act for which the punishment is awarded. Here, therefore, there is no difficulty in seeing that recognition of the authority is compatible with transgression of the law, because the law is not known till after it has been transgressed. It may, perhaps, be doubted whether it is strictly correct to say in this case that punishment may lead to repentance, since there is no wilful fault to repent, as the law was, by the hypothesis, not known, at the time it was broken. The question is, however, merely verbal. There is no doubt that in such cases the punishment, coming from an authority accepted as moral, may lead a man to see that he has done wrong, though not intentionally, may lead him to regret it and to avoid it in future. Thus, at any rate, a moral advance comes from the punishment, and it is of no great importance whether we grant or deny it the name of repentance.

It may be objected, however, that punishment in the two last cases we have mentioned would be totally unjust. We ought to punish, it may be said, only those acts which were known by their perpetrators at the time when they did them to be wrong. And therefore we have no right to punish a man for any offence, which he did not know to be an offence, whether because he did not know of the existence of the law, or because he did not apply it to the particular case.

I do not think, however, that on examination we can limit the proper application of punishment to cases of conscious wrong-doing, plausible as such a restriction may appear at first sight. We must remember, in the first place, that not to know a moral law may be a sign of greater moral degradation than would be implied in its conscious violation. If a man really believed that he was morally justified in treating the lower animals without any consideration, he would not be consciously doing wrong by torturing them. But we should, I think, regard him as in a lower moral state than a man who was conscious of his duty to animals, though he occasionally disregarded it in moments of passion. Yet the latter in these moments would be consciously doing wrong. A man who could see nothing wrong in cowardice would be surely more degraded than a man who recognized the duty of courage, though he sometimes failed to carry it out. Thus, I submit, even if punishment were limited to cases of desert, there would be no reason to limit it to cases of conscious wrong-doing, since the absence of the consciousness of wrong-doing may itself be a mark of moral defect.

But we may, I think, go further. There seems no reason why we should inquire about any punishment, whether the criminal deserved it or not. For such a question really brings us, if we press it far enough, back to the old theory of vindictive punishment, which few of us, I suppose, would be prepared to advocate. On any other theory a man is to be punished, not to avenge the past evil, but to secure some future good. Of course, a punishment is only to be inflicted for a fault, for the effect of all punishment is to discourage the repetition of the action punished, and that would not be desirable unless the action was wrong. But to inquire into how far the criminal is to be blamed for his action seems irrelevant. If he has done wrong, and if the punishment will cure him, he has, as Hegel expresses it, a right to his punishment. If a dentist is asked to take out an aching tooth, he does not refuse to do so, on the ground that the patient did not deliberately cause the toothache, and that therefore it would be unjust to subject him to the pain of the extraction. And to refuse a man the chance of a moral advance—when the punishment appears to afford one—seems equally unreasonable.

Indeed, any attempts to measure punishment by desert gets us into hopeless difficulties. If we suppose that every man is equally responsible for every action which is not done under physical compulsion, we ignore the effect of inherited character, of difference of education, of difference of temptation, and, in fact, most of the important circumstances. Punishments measured out on such a system may, perhaps, be defended on the ground of utility, but certainly not on the ground of desert. On the other hand, if we endeavored to allow for different circumstances in fixing punishments, we should have no punishments at all. That a man commits an offence in given circumstances is due to his character, and, even if we allowed a certain amount of indeterminate free-will, we could never know that a change in the circumstances would not have saved him from the crime, so that we could never say that it was his own fault.

The only alternative seems to be to admit that we punish, not to avenge evil, but to restore or produce good, whether for society or the criminal. And on this principle we very often explicitly act. For example, we do not punish high treason because we condemn the traitors, who are often moved by sincere, though perhaps mistaken, patriotism. We punish it because we believe that they would, in fact, though with the best intentions, do harm to the state. Nor do parents, I suppose, punish young children for disobedience, on the ground that it is their own fault that they were not born with the habit of obedience developed. They do it, I should imagine, because punishment is the most effective way of teaching them obedience, and because it is desirable, for their own sakes, that they should learn it.

We must now return to the cases in which punishment can possibly produce repentance, from which we have been diverted by the question as to whether the punishment inflicted in the second and third cases could be considered just. There is a fourth and last case. In this the authority which inflicts the punishment was, before its infliction, recognized, indeed, theoretically and vaguely, as embodying the moral law, and therefore as being a valid authority. But the recognition was so languid and vague that it was not sufficient to prevent disobedience to the authority's commands. This, it will be seen, is rather analogous to the second case. There the law was held so vaguely that the logical applications of it were never made. Here the authority is recognized, but not actively enough to influence conduct. It is scarcely so much that the criminal recognizes it, as that he is not prepared to deny it.

Here the effect of punishment may again be repentance. For punishment renders it impossible any longer to ignore the authority, and it is, by the hypothesis, only by ignoring it that it can be disobeyed. The punishment clearly proves that the authority is in possession of the power. If it is pressed far enough, there are only two alternatives—to definitely rebel, and declare the punishment to be unjust, or to definitely submit and to acknowledge it to be righteous. The first is here impossible, for the criminal, by the hypothesis, is not prepared definitely to reject the authority. There remains therefore only the second.

Perhaps the best example of this state of things may be found in the attitude of the lower boys of a public school towards the authority of the masters. Their conviction that this is a lawful and valid authority does not influence them to so great an extent as to produce spontaneous and invariable obedience. But it is, I think, sufficient to prevent them from considering the enforcement of obedience by punishment unjust, except in the cases where their own code of morality comes explicitly in conflict with the official code—cases which are not very frequent. In fact, almost all English school systems would break down completely, if they trusted to their punishments being severe enough to produce obedience by fear. That they do not break down would seem important evidence that punishment can produce other effects than intimidation, unless, indeed, any ingenious person should suggest that they could get on without punishment altogether.

We have now seen that when punishment is able to fulfil the office which Hegel declares to be its highest function,—that of producing repentance,—it does so by emphasizing some moral tie which the offender was all along prepared to admit, although it was too faint or incomplete to prevent the fault. Thus it essentially works on him as, at any rate potentially, a moral agent, and thus, as Hegel expresses it, does him honor. It is no contradiction of this, though it may appear so at first sight, to say that a punishment has such an effect only by the element of disgrace which all deserved punishment contains. Here it differs from deterrent punishment. A punishment deters from the repetition of the offence, not because it is a punishment, but because it is painful. An unpleasant consequence which followed the act, not as the result of moral condemnation, but as a merely natural effect, would have the same deterrent result. A man is equally frightened by pain, whether he recognizes it as just or not. And so a punishment may deter from crime quite as effectually when it is not recognised as just, and consequently produces no feeling of disgrace. But a punishment cannot lead to repentance unless it is recognized as the fitting consequence of a moral fault, and it is this recognition which makes a punishment appear disgraceful.

It seems to be a fashionable theory at present that it is both cruel and degrading to attempt to emphasize the element of disgrace in punishment, especially in the education of children. We are recommended to trust principally to rewards, and, if we should be unhappily forced to inflict pain, we must represent it rather as an inconvenience which it would be well to avoid for the future, than as a punishment for an offence which deserved it. And for this reason all punishments, which proclaim themselves to be such, are to be avoided.

I must confess that it is the modern theory which seems to me the degrading one. To attempt to influence by the pleasures of rewards and by the pain element in punishment, implies that the person to be influenced is governed by pleasure and pain. On the other hand, to trust to the fact that his punishment will appear to him a disgrace implies that he is to some degree influenced by a desire to do right; for, if not, he would feel no disgrace in a punishment for doing wrong. And on the whole it would seem that the latter view of a child's nature is the more hopeful and the less degrading of the two.

There seems to be in this argument a confusion between degradation and disgrace. A man is degraded by anything which lowers his moral nature. A punishment which did this would of course stand condemned. But he is disgraced by being made conscious of a moral defect. And to become conscious of a defect is not to incur a new one. It is rather the most hopeful chance of escaping from the old one. It can scarcely be seriously maintained that, if a fault has been committed, the offender is further degraded by being ashamed of it.

This confusion seems to be at the root of the discussion as to whether the corporal punishment of children is degrading. There is no doubt that it expresses, more unmistakably and emphatically than any substitute that has been proposed for it, the fact that it is a punishment. It follows that, unless the offender is entirely regardless of the opinions of the authority above him, that it is more calculated than other punishments to cause a feeling of disgrace. But, supposing it to be inflicted on the right occasions, this is surely the end of punishment. That it produces any degradation is entirely a separate assertion, which demands a separate proof—a demand which it would be difficult to gratify.

But although a punishment must, to fulfil its highest end, be disgraceful, it does not follow that we can safely trust to the disgrace involved in the offence itself as a punishment,—a course which is sometimes recommended. The aim of punishment is rather to produce repentance, and, as a means to it, disgrace. If we contented ourselves with using as a punishment whatever feeling of disgrace arose independently in the culprit's mind, the result would be that we should only affect those who were already conscious of their fault, and so required punishment least, while those who were impenitent, and so required it most, would escape altogether. We require, therefore, a punishment which will produce disgrace where it is not, not merely utilize it where it is. Otherwise we should not only distribute our punishments precisely in the wrong fashion, but we should also offer a premium on callousness and impenitence. As a matter of prudence, it is as well to make sure that the offender, even if he refuses to allow his punishment to be profitable to him, shall, at any rate, find it painful.

And in this connection we must also remember that the feeling of disgrace which ensues on punishment need be nothing more introspective or morbid than a simple recognition that the punishment was deserved. On the other hand, an attempt to influence any one—especially children—by causing them to reflect on the disgrace involved in the fault itself, must lead to a habitual self-contemplation, the results of which are not unlikely to be both unwholesome to the penitent and offensive to his friends.

I have thus endeavored to show that there are certain conditions under which punishment can perform the work which Hegel assigns to it. The question then arises, When are these conditions realized? We find the question of punishment prominent in jurisprudence and in education. It is found also in theology, in so far as the course of the world is so ordered as to punish sin. Now it seems to me that Hegel's view of punishment cannot properly be applied in jurisprudence, and that his chief mistake regarding it lay in supposing that it could.

In the first place, the paramount object of punishment from the point of view of the state ought, I conceive, to be the prevention of crime and not the reformation of the criminal. The interests of the innocent are to be preferred to those of the guilty—for there are more of them, and they have on the whole a better claim to be considered. And the deterrent effect of punishment is far more certain than its purifying effect. (I use the word purifying to describe the effect of which Hegel treats. It is, I fear, rather stilted, but the word reformatory, which would be more suitable, has by common consent been appropriated to a different theory.) We cannot, indeed, eradicate crime, but experience has shown that by severe and judicious punishment we can diminish it to an enormous extent. On the other hand, punishment can only purify by appealing to the moral nature of the criminal. This may be always latent, but is sometimes far too latent for us to succeed in arousing it. Moreover, the deterrent effect of a punishment acts not only on the criminal who suffers it, but on all who realize that they will suffer it if they commit a similar offence. The purifying influence can act only on those who suffer the punishment. For these reasons it would appear that if the state allows its attention to be distracted from the humble task of frightening criminals from crime, by the higher ambition of converting them to virtue, it is likely to fail in both, and so in its fundamental object of diminishing crime.

And in addition there seems grave reason to doubt whether, in a modern state, the crimes dealt with and the attitude of the criminal to the state are such that punishment can be expected to lead to repentance. The crimes which a state has to deal with may be divided into two classes. The first and smaller class is that in which the state, for its own welfare, endeavors to suppress by punishment conduct which is actuated by conscientious convictions of duty. Examples may be found in high treason and breaches of the law relating to vaccination. Now in these cases the criminal has deliberately adopted a different view of his duty to that entertained by the state. He is not likely, therefore, to be induced to repent of his act by a punishment which can teach him nothing except that he and the state disagree in their views of his duty—which he knew before. His punishment may appear to him to be unjust persecution, or may be accepted as the inevitable result of difference of opinion, but can never be admitted by him as justly deserved by his action, and cannot therefore change the way in which he regards that action.

In the second, and much larger, class of criminal offences, the same result happens, though from very different reasons. The average criminal, convicted of theft or violence, is, no doubt, like all of us, in his essential nature, a distinctly moral being. And, even in action, the vast majority of such criminals are far from being totally depraved. But, by the time a man has become subject to the criminal law for any offence, he has generally become so far callous, with regard to that particular crime, that his punishment will not bring about his repentance. The average burglar may clearly learn from his sentence that the state objects to burglary. He might even, if pressed, admit that the state was from an objective point of view more likely to be right than he was. But, although he may have a sincere abhorrence of murder, he is probably in a condition when the disapproval of the state of his offences with regard to property will rouse no moral remorse in him. In such a case repentance is not possible. Punishment can, under the circumstances I have mentioned above, convince us that we have done wrong. But it cannot inspire us with the desire to do right. The existence of this is assumed when we punish with a view to the purification of an offender, and it is for this reason that the punishment, as Hegel says, honors him. Where the desire to do right is, at any rate as regards one field of action, hopelessly dormant, punishment must fall back on its lower office of intimidation. And this would happen with a large proportion of those offences which are dealt with by the criminal law.

Many offences, no doubt,—especially those committed in a moment of passion, or by persons till then innocent,—are not of this sort, but do coexist with a general desire to do right, which has been overpowered by a particular temptation. Yet I doubt if, at the present day, repentance in such cases would be often the result of punishment by the state. If the criminal's independent moral will was sufficiently strong, he would, when the particular temptation was removed, repent without the aid of punishment. If it was not sufficiently strong, I doubt if the punishment would much aid it. The function of punishment, as we have seen, in this respect, was to enforce on the offender the disapproval with which his action was considered by an authority, whom he regarded as expressing the moral law. But why should the modern citizen regard the state as expressing the moral law? He does not regard it as something above and superior to himself, as the ancient citizen regarded his city, as the child regards his parent, or the religious man his God. The development of individual conscience and responsibility has been too great for such an attitude. The state is now for him an aggregate of men like himself. He regards obedience to it, within certain limits, as a duty. But this is because matters which concern the whole community are matters on which the whole community is entitled to speak. It does not rest on any belief that the state can become for the individual the interpreter of the moral law, so that his moral duty lies in conforming his views to its precepts. Not only does he not feel bound, but he does not feel entitled, to surrender in this way his moral independence. He must determine for himself what he is himself to hold as right and wrong. The result of this is that if he sees for himself that his action was wrong, he will repent without waiting for the state to tell him so, and, if he does not see it for himself, the opinion of the state will not convince him. I do not assert that there are no cases in which a man finds himself in the same childlike relation to the state as was possible in classical times, but they are too few to be of material importance. And except in such cases we cannot expect the punishments of jurisprudence to have a purifying effect.

Hegel's mistake, in applying his conception of punishment to criminal law, resulted from his high opinion of the state as against the individual citizen. The most significant feature of all his writings on the metaphysics of society is the low place that he gives to the conscience and opinions of the individual. He was irritated—not without cause, though with far less cause than we have to-day—at the follies of the writers who see nothing in morality but conscientious convictions, or "the good will." It would almost seem, according to some exponents of these views, that it is entirely unimportant, from a moral point of view, what you do, if only you can manage to persuade yourself that you are doing right. But he did not lay enough emphasis on the fact that, though the approval of conscience does not carry you very far, by itself, towards a satisfactory system of morality, yet that *without* the approval of the individual conscience no modern system of morality can be satisfactory. As between adult human beings, it has become in modern times impossible for one man to yield up his conscience into the hands of any other man or body of men. A child, while it is young enough to be treated entirely as a child, can and ought to find its morality in the commands of others. And those who believe in a divine revelation, will naturally endeavor to place themselves in an attitude of entire submission to what appears to them to be the divine will, whether manifested through books or through some specially favored organization of men. But a man is not a child, and the state is not God, and the surrender of our consciences to the control of others has become impossible. A man may indeed accept the direction of a teacher whom he has chosen,—even accept it implicitly. But then this is by virtue of his own act of choice. We cannot now accept any purely outward authority as having, of its own right, the power of deciding for us on matters of right and wrong.

Hegel, indeed, in the "Phänomenologie des Geistes," points out that the highest realization of the state—that in which it is the universal which completely sums up the individuals which compose it—may be considered as being in the past or the future, but not in the present. But when he comes to deal with the state in detail he seems to forget this. Sometimes he appears to think of the classical state as not yet passed away. The ancient state did indeed endeavor to stand in the same relation to its citizens as the father to the child, or even as God to man, as is indicated by the very close connection which existed in the ancient world between religion and patriotism. But to attempt to bring this idea into the modern world is to ignore the enormous development of the idea of individuality, which accompanied, whether as cause or effect, the rise of Christianity, and was marked by the increasing prominence of the ideas of immortality and conscience. The individual began then to claim the right of relating himself directly to the highest realities of the universe—and, among others, to duty. He insisted on judging for himself. The state could be no longer the unquestioned judge of right and wrong; it could now itself be judged and condemned by the individual on moral grounds. It had still a claim to obedience, but not to unquestioning veneration. Nor is there anything inconsistent with this in the authority—perhaps as strong as that of the classical state—which the church exercised during the middle ages. For the church was regarded as a supernaturally commissioned authority. It could never have held its position, if it had been looked on as an assembly of mere men. And in the course of years it became evident that even the church's claim to unquestioning veneration could not stand before the demand of the individual, to have everything justified at the tribunal of his own spirit.

From another point of view, Hegel may be said to have supposed that the ideal state had already come, when it was still far in the future. Indeed, we may go farther and say that, by the time the state had become ideal, it would have long ceased to be a state. No doubt Hegel looked forward, and by his philosophical system was justified in looking forward, to an ultimate ideal unity which should realize all, and far more than all, that the classical state had ever aimed at. He contemplated a universal so thoroughly realized in every individual that the most complete unity of the whole should be compatible with the most complete self-development of the parts. But before this last and highest development of reality could be reached, we should have to leave behind us altogether the world of matter and time, which would be incompatible with such a complete perfection of spirit. Still more would it be impossible in a stage of development in which external government and criminal justice still existed. And to encourage the actual state, as we see it in the world to-day, to assume functions justified only in the far past or in the indefinitely remote future, is disastrous both in theory and practice. No part of Hegel's teaching has been productive of more confusion than his persistent attempt to identify the kingdom of Prussia with the kingdom of Heaven.

The result, then, to which we have come is as follows. Hegel's view of the operation of punishment is one which is correct under certain circumstances. And when punishment has this function, it is fulfilling its highest end, since only in this manner does it succeed in really eradicating the fault which caused it. But this function is one which it scarcely ever succeeds in performing at present, when administered in the course of criminal law, and which it is not more likely to succeed in performing in the future.

This does not, however, render it unimportant. For, although it is disappearing in jurisprudence, it is persistent and important in education. There is not the same need in education as in law that punishment shall be deterrent at all cost. The ordinary offences of children are not very dangerous to the structure of society, and we can therefore turn our attention, without much risk, rather to curing them than to suppressing them. And, as a general rule, the decisions of the elder world are tacitly accepted by the younger as righteous. In cases where the authority who inflicts the punishment, or the law upon which it is inflicted, are explicitly rejected as unjust by the offender, we cannot hope that punishment will be more than deterrent. But such cases are infrequent, and, in spite of the efforts of reformers, there is good reason to hope they will remain so. For it is a fact, which, though often forgotten, cannot well be denied, that children are born young, and remain so for some years,—a fact which has some significance.

So, too, in theology. In so far as any person conceives the universe as arranged by a virtue-loving God with a view, among other things, to the promotion of virtue, the effect of any event which he looks on as a divinely inflicted punishment may be, for him, purifying.

If one had the time—and the courage—some interesting, though not, I think, revolutionary, conclusions with regard to practice, and particularly to education, might be deduced from these premises. We might point out, for example, that rewards and punishments cannot properly be considered, as they often are, to be purely correlative methods of exerting influence, but that, under certain circumstances, punishment may have a moral effect to which there is nothing analogous in reward.

Again, it is not uncommonly held that "men may rise on stepping-stones of their dead selves to higher things," and that a repented sin may sometimes place the sinner on a higher level than that of his original innocence. And if we are to hold, also, that punishment may produce repentance, we might even be led to the conclusion that a fault and its punishment, taken together, may not only cancel one another, but, in some circumstances, be a positive good. And this might lead us to see some justification for institutions and practices which have been prospering lately without much theoretical defence. We might, for example, believe that it was not a reproach to a system of education that it rested largely on punishment. We might believe that it was not to be regretted that a child should require punishment—provided, of course, that there was a reasonable chance of his getting it. We might believe that it was not desirable, either to try to turn boys into jelly-fish, for fear they should break rules, or to abolish all discipline, that there might be no rules to break. We might even deny that we should gain much by reconstituting the public schools of England on the model either of a Jesuit seminary or a kindergarten.——But I perceive that at this point I have become hopelessly reactionary, and I wish that I could think that it was only at this point that I had become hopelessly tedious.

OLIVER WENDELL HOLMES, JR.

The Criminal Law*

. . . The desire for vengeance imports an opinion that its object is actually and personally to blame. It takes an internal standard, not an objective or external one, and condemns its victim by that. The question is whether such a standard is still accepted either in this primitive form, or in some more refined development, as is commonly supposed, and as seems not impossible, considering the relative slowness with which the criminal law has improved.

It certainly may be argued, with some force, that it has never ceased to be one object of punishment to satisfy the desire for vengeance. The argument will be made plain by considering those instances in which, for one reason or another, compensation for a wrong is out of the question.

Thus an act may be of such a kind as to make indemnity impossible by putting an end to the principal sufferer, as in the case of murder or manslaughter.

Again, these and other crimes, like forgery, although directed against an individual, tend to make others feel unsafe, and this general insecurity does not admit of being paid for.

Again, there are cases where there are no means of enforcing indemnity. In Macaulay's draft of the Indian Penal Code, breaches of contract for the carriage of passengers, were made criminal. The palanquin-bearers of India were too poor to pay damages, and yet had to be trusted to carry unprotected women and children through wild and desolate tracts, where their desertion would have placed those under their charge in great danger.

In all these cases punishment remains as an alternative. A pain can be inflicted upon the

* From Oliver Wendell Holmes, Jr., *The Common Law* (Boston: Little, Brown, 1881), pp. 40–51.

wrong-doer, of a sort which does not restore the injured party to his former situation, or to another equally good, but which is inflicted for the very purpose of causing pain. And so far as this punishment takes the place of compensation, whether on account of the death of the person to whom the wrong was done, the indefinite number of persons affected, the impossibility of estimating the worth of the suffering in money, or the poverty of the criminal, it may be said that one of its objects is to gratify the desire for vengeance. The prisoner pays with his body.

The statement may be made stronger still, and it may be said, not only that the law does, but that it ought to, make the gratification of revenge an object. This is the opinion, at any rate, of two authorities so great, and so opposed in other views, as Bishop Butler and Jeremy Bentham.[1] Sir James Stephen says, "The criminal law stands to the passion of revenge in much the same relation as marriage to the sexual appetite."[2]

The first requirement of a sound body of law is, that it should correspond with the actual feelings and demands of the community, whether right or wrong. If people would gratify the passion of revenge outside of the law, if the law did not help them, the law has no choice but to satisfy the craving itself, and thus avoid the greater evil of private retribution. At the same time, this passion is not one which we encourage, either as private individuals or as law-makers. Moreover, it does not cover the whole ground. There are crimes which do not excite it, and we should naturally expect that the most important purposes of punishment would be coextensive with the whole field of its application. It remains to be discovered whether such a general purpose exists, and if so what it is. Different theories still divide opinion upon the subject.

It has been thought that the purpose of punishment is to reform the criminal; that it is to deter the criminal and others from committing similar crimes; and that it is retribution. Few would now maintain that the first of these purposes was the only one. If it were, every prisoner should be released as soon as it appears clear that he will never repeat his offence, and if he is incurable he should not be punished at all. Of course it would be hard to reconcile the punishment of death with this doctrine.

[1] Butler, *Sermons,* VIII. Bentham, *Theory of Legislation* (Principles of Penal Code, Part 2, ch. 16), Hildreth's tr., p. 309.

[2] *General View of the Criminal Law of England,* p. 99.

The main struggle lies between the other two. On the one side is the notion that there is a mystic bond between wrong and punishment; on the other, that the infliction of pain is only a means to an end. Hegel, one of the great expounders of the former view, puts it, in his quasi mathematical form, that, wrong being the negation of right, punishment is the negation of that negation, or retribution. Thus the punishment must be equal, in the sense of proportionate to the crime, because its only function is to destroy it. Others, without this logical apparatus, are content to rely upon a felt necessity that suffering should follow wrong-doing.

It is objected that the preventive theory is immoral, because it overlooks the ill-desert of wrong-doing, and furnishes no measure of the amount of punishment, except the lawgiver's subjective opinion in regard to the sufficiency of the amount of preventive suffering.[3] In the language of Kant, it treats man as a thing, not as a person; as a means, not as an end in himself. It is said to conflict with the sense of justice, and to violate the fundamental principle of all free communities, that the members of such communities have equal rights to life, liberty, and personal security.[4]

In spite of all this, probably most English-speaking lawyers would accept the preventive theory without hesitation. As to the violation of equal rights which is charged, it may be replied that the dogma of equality makes an equation between individuals only, not between an individual and the community. No society has ever admitted that it could not sacrifice individual welfare to its own existence. If conscripts are necessary for its army, it seizes them, and marches them, with bayonets in their rear, to death. It runs highways and railroads through old family places in spite of the owner's protest, paying in this instance the market value, to be sure, because no civilized government sacrifices the citizen more than it can help, but still sacrificing his will and his welfare to that of the rest.[5]

If it were necessary to trench further upon the field of morals, it might be suggested that the dogma of equality applied even to individuals only within the limits of ordinary dealings in the

[3] Wharton, *Crim. Law* (8th ed.), § 8, n. 1.

[4] *Ibid.,* § 7.

[5] Even the law recognizes that his is a sacrifice. *Commonwealth* v. *Sawin,* 2 Pick. (Mass.) 547, 549.

common run of affairs. You cannot argue with your neighbor, except on the admission for the moment that he is as wise as you, although you may by no means believe it. In the same way, you cannot deal with him, where both are free to choose, except on the footing of equal treatment, and the same rules for both. The ever-growing value set upon peace and the social relations tends to give the law of social being the appearance of the law of all being. But it seems to me clear that the *ultima ratio,* not only *regum,* but of private persons, is force, and that at the bottom of all private relations, however tempered by sympathy and all the social feelings, is a justifiable self-preference. If a man is on a plank in the deep sea which will only float one, and a stranger lays hold of it, he will thrust him off if he can. When the state finds itself in a similar position, it does the same thing.

The considerations which answer the argument of equal rights also answer the objections to treating man as a thing, and the like. If a man lives in society, he is liable to find himself so treated. The degree of civilization which a people has reached, no doubt, is marked by their anxiety to do as they would be done by. It may be the destiny of man that the social instincts shall grow to control his actions absolutely, even in anti-social situations. But they have not yet done so, and as the rules of law are or should be based upon a morality which is generally accepted, no rule founded on a theory of absolute unselfishness can be laid down without a breach between law and working beliefs.

If it be true, as I shall presently try to show, that the general principles of criminal and civil liability are the same, it will follow from that alone that theory and fact agree in frequently punishing those who have been guilty of no moral wrong, and who could not be condemned by any standard that did not avowedly disregard the personal peculiarities of the individuals concerned. If punishment stood on the moral grounds which are proposed for it, the first thing to be considered would be those limitations in the capacity for choosing rightly which arise from abnormal instincts, want of education, lack of intelligence, and all the other defects which are most marked in the criminal classes. I do not say that they should not be, or at least I do not need to for my argument. I do not say that the criminal law does more good than harm. I only say that it is not enacted or administered on that theory.

There remains to be mentioned the affirmative argument in favor of the theory of retribution, to the effect that the fitness of punishment following wrong-doing is axiomatic, and is instinctively recognized by unperverted minds. I think that it will be seen, on self-inspection, that this feeling of fitness is absolute and unconditional only in the case of our neighbors. It does not seem to me that any one who has satisfied himself that an act of his was wrong, and that he will never do it again, would feel the least need or propriety, as between himself and an earthly punishing power alone, of his being made to suffer for what he had done, although, when third persons were introduced, he might, as a philosopher, admit the necessity of hurting him to frighten others. But when our neighbors do wrong, we sometimes feel the fitness of making them smart for it, whether they have repented or not. The feeling of fitness seems to me to be only vengeance in disguise, and I have already admitted that vengeance was an element, though not the chief element, of punishment.

But, again, the supposed intuition of fitness does not seem to me to be coextensive with the thing to be accounted for. The lesser punishments are just as fit for the lesser crimes as the greater for the greater. The demand that crime should be followed by its punishment should therefore be equal and absolute in both. Again, a *malum prohibitum* is just as much a crime as a *malum in se*. If there is any general ground for punishment, it must apply to one case as much as to the other. But it will hardly be said that, if the wrong in the case just supposed consisted of a breach of the revenue laws, and the government had been indemnified for the loss, we should feel any internal necessity that a man who had thoroughly repented of his wrong should be punished for it, except on the ground that his act was known to others. If it was known, the law would have to verify its threats in order that others might believe and tremble. But if the fact was a secret between the sovereign and the subject, the sovereign, if wholly free from passion, would undoubtedly see that punishment in such a case was wholly without justification.

On the other hand, there can be no case in which the law-maker makes certain conduct criminal without his thereby showing a wish and purpose to prevent that conduct. Prevention would accordingly seem to be the chief and only universal purpose of punishment. The law threatens certain pains if you do certain things, intending thereby to give you a new motive for not doing them. If you persist in doing them, it has to inflict the pains in order that its threats may continue to be believed.

If this is a true account of the law as it stands, the law does undoubtedly treat the individual as a means to an end, and uses him as a tool to increase the general welfare at his own expense. It has been suggested above, that this course is perfectly proper; but even if it is wrong, our criminal law follows it, and the theory of our criminal law must be shaped accordingly.

Further evidence that our law exceeds the limits of retribution, and subordinates consideration of the individual to that of the public well-being, will be found in some doctrines which cannot be satisfactorily explained on any other ground.

The first of these is, that even the deliberate taking of life will not be punished when it is the only way of saving one's own. This principle is not so clearly established as that next to be mentioned; but it has the support of very great authority.[6] If that is the law, it must go on one of two grounds, either that self-preference is proper in the case supposed, or that, even if it is improper, the law cannot prevent it by punishment, because a threat of death at some future time can never be a sufficiently powerful motive to make a man choose death now in order to avoid the threat. If the former ground is adopted, it admits that a single person may sacrifice another to himself, and *a fortiori* that a people may. If the latter view is taken, by abandoning punishment when it can no longer be expected to prevent an act, the law abandons the retributive and adopts the preventive theory.

The next doctrine leads to still clearer conclusions. Ignorance of the law is no excuse for breaking it. This substantive principle is sometimes put in the form of a rule of evidence, that every one is presumed to know the law. It has accordingly been defended by Austin and others, on the ground of difficulty of proof. If justice requires the fact to be ascertained, the difficulty of doing so is no ground for refusing to try. But every one

[6] Cf. 1 East, P. C. 294; *United States* v. *Holmes*, 1 Wall, Jr. 1; 1 Bishop, *Crim. Law*, §§ 347–349, 845 (6th ed.); 4 Bl. Comm. 31.

must feel that ignorance of the law could never be admitted as an excuse, even if the fact could be proved by sight and hearing in every case. Furthermore, now that parties can testify, it may be doubted whether a man's knowledge of the law is any harder to investigate than many questions which are gone into. The difficulty, such as it is, would be met by throwing the burden of proving ignorance on the lawbreaker.

The principle cannot be explained by saying that we are not only commanded to abstain from certain acts, but also to find out that we are commanded. For if there were such a second command, it is very clear that the guilt of failing to obey it would bear no proportion to that of disobeying the principal command if known, yet the failure to know would receive the same punishment as the failure to obey the principal law.

The true explanation of the rule is the same as that which accounts for the law's indifference to a man's particular temperament, faculties, and so forth. Public policy sacrifices the individual to the general good. It is desirable that the burden of all should be equal, but it is still more desirable to put an end to robbery and murder. It is no doubt true that there are many cases in which the criminal could not have known that he was breaking the law, but to admit the excuse at all would be to encourage ignorance where the law-maker has determined to make men know and obey, and justice to the individual is rightly outweighed by the larger interests on the other side of the scales.

If the foregoing arguments are sound, it is already manifest that liability to punishment cannot be finally and absolutely determined by considering the actual personal unworthiness of the criminal alone. That consideration will govern only so far as the public welfare permits or demands. And if we take into account the general result which the criminal law is intended to bring about, we shall see that the actual state of mind accompanying a criminal act plays a different part from what is commonly supposed.

For the most part, the purpose of the criminal law is only to induce external conformity to rule. All law is directed to conditions of things manifest to the senses. And whether it brings those conditions to pass immediately by the use of force, as when it protects a house from a mob by soldiers, or appropriates private property to public use, or hangs a man in pursuance of a judicial sentence, or whether it brings them about mediately through men's fears, its object is equally an external result. In directing itself against robbery or murder, for instance, its purpose is to put a stop to the actual physical taking and keeping of other men's goods, or the actual poisoning, shooting, stabbing, and otherwise putting to death of other men. If those things are not done, the law forbidding them is equally satisfied, whatever the motive.

Considering this purely external purpose of the law together with the fact that it is ready to sacrifice the individual so far as necessary in order to accomplish that purpose, we can see more readily than before that the actual degree of personal guilt involved in any particular transgression cannot be the only element, if it is an element at all, in the liability incurred. So far from its being true, as is often assumed, that the condition of a man's heart or conscience ought to be more considered in determining criminal than civil liability, it might almost be said that it is the very opposite of truth. For civil liability, in its immediate working, is simply a redistribution of an existing loss between two individuals; and it will be argued in the next Lecture that sound policy lets losses lie where they fall, except where a special reason can be shown for interference. The most frequent of such reasons is, that the party who is charged has been to blame.

It is not intended to deny that criminal liability, as well as civil, is founded on blameworthiness. Such a denial would shock the moral sense of any civilized community; or, to put it another way, a law which punished conduct which would not be blameworthy in the average member of the community would be too severe for that community to bear. It is only intended to point out that, when we are dealing with that part of the law which aims more directly than any other at establishing standards of conduct, we should expect there more than elsewhere to find that the tests of liability are external, and independent of the degree of evil in the particular person's motives or intentions. The conclusion follows directly from the nature of the standards to which conformity is required. These are not only external, as was shown above, but they are of general application. They do not merely require that every man should get as near as he can to the best conduct possible for him. They require him at his own peril to come up to a certain height. They take no account of incapacities, unless the weakness is so marked as to fall into well-known exceptions, such as infancy or madness. They assume that every man is as able as every other to behave as they command. If they fall on any one class harder than on another, it is on the weakest. For it is precisely to those who are most likely to err by temperament, ignorance, or folly, that the threats of the law are the most dangerous.

The reconciliation of the doctrine that liability is founded on blameworthiness with the existence of liability where the party is not to blame, will be worked out more fully in the next Lecture. It is found in the conception of the average man, the man of ordinary intelligence and reasonable prudence. Liability is said to arise out of such conduct as would be blameworthy in him. But he is an ideal being, represented by the jury when they are appealed to, and his conduct is an external or objective standard when applied to any given individual. That individual may be morally without stain, because he has less than ordinary intelligence or prudence. But he is required to have those qualities at his peril. If he has them, he will not, as a general rule, incur liability without blameworthiness. . . .

J. D. MABBOTT

Punishment*

I propose in this paper to defend a retributive theory of punishment and to reject absolutely all utilitarian considerations from its justification. I feel sure that this enterprise must arouse deep suspicion and hostility both among philosophers (who must have felt that the retributive view is the only moral theory except perhaps psychological hedonism which has been definitely destroyed by criticism) and among practical men (who have welcomed its steady decline in our penal practice).

The question I am asking is this. Under what circumstances is the punishment of some particular person justified and why? The theories of reform and deterrence which are usually considered to be the only alternatives to retribution involve well-known difficulties. These are considered fully and fairly in Dr. Ewing's book *The Morality of Punishment,* and I need not spend long over them. The central difficulty is that both would on occasion justify the punishment of an innocent man, the deterrent theory if he were believed to have been guilty by those likely to commit the crime in future, and the reformatory theory if he were a bad man though not a criminal. To this may be added the point against the deterrent theory that it is the threat of punishment and not punishment itself which deters, and that when deterrence seems to depend on actual punishment, to implement the threat, it really depends on publication and may be achieved if men believe that punishment has occurred even if in fact it has not. As Bentham saw, for a Utilitarian apparent justice is everything, real justice is irrelevant.

Dr. Ewing and other moralists would be inclined to compromise with retribution in the face of the above difficulties. They would admit that one fact and one fact only can justify the punishment of this man, and that is a *past* fact, that he has committed a crime. To this extent reform and deterrence theories, which look only to the consequences, are wrong. But they would add that retribution can determine only *that* a man should be punished. It cannot determine how or how much, and here reform and deterrence may come in. Even Bradley, the fiercest retributionist of modern times, says "Having once the right to punish we may modify the punishment according to the useful and the pleasant, but these are external to the matter; they cannot give us a right to punish and nothing can do that but criminal desert." Dr. Ewing would maintain that the whole estimate of the amount and nature of a punishment may be effected by considerations of reform and deterrence. It seems to me that this is a surrender which the upholders of retribution dare not make. As I said above, it is publicity and not punishment which deters, and the publicity though often spoken of as "part of a man's punishment" is no more part of it than his arrest or his detention prior to trial, though both these may be also unpleasant and bring him into disrepute. A judge sentences a man to three years's imprisonment not to three years *plus* three columns in the press. Similarly with reform. The visit of the prison chaplain is not part of a man's punishment nor is the visit of Miss Fields or Mickey Mouse.

The truth is that while punishing a man and punishing him justly, it is possible to deter others, and also to attempt to reform him, and if these additional goods are achieved the total state of affairs is better than it would be with the just punishment alone. But reform and deterrence are not modifications of the punishment, still less reasons for it. A parallel may be found in the case

* J. D. Mabbott, "Punishment," *Mind,* XLVIII (1939), 152–167. Reprinted by permission of the editor of *Mind.*

of tact and truth. If you have to tell a friend an unpleasant truth you may do all you can to put him at his ease and spare his feelings as much as possible, while still making sure that he understands your meaning. In such a case no one would say that your offer of a cigarette beforehand or your apology afterwards are modifications of the truth still less reasons for telling it. You do not tell the truth in order to spare his feelings, but having to tell the truth you also spare his feelings. So Bradley was right when he said that reform and deterrence were "external to the matter," but therefore wrong when he said that they may "modify the punishment." Reporters are admitted to our trials so that punishments may become public and help to deter others. But the punishment would be no less just were reporters excluded and deterrence not achieved. Prison authorities may make it possible that a convict may become physically or morally better. They cannot ensure either result; and the punishment would still be just if the criminal took no advantage of their arrangements and their efforts failed. Some moralists see this and exclude these "extra" arrangements for deterrence and reform. They say that it must be the punishment *itself* which reforms and deters. But it is just my point that the punishment *itself* seldom reforms the criminal and never deters others. It is only "extra" arrangements which have any chance of achieving either result. As this is the central point of my paper, at the cost of laboured repetition I would ask the upholders of reform and deterrence two questions. Suppose it could be shown that a particular criminal had not been improved by a punishment and also that no other would-be criminal had been deterred by it, would that prove that the punishment was unjust? Suppose it were discovered that a particular criminal had lived a much better life after his release and that many would-be criminals believing him to have been guilty were influenced by his fate, but yet that the "criminal" was punished for something he had never done, would these excellent results prove the punishment just?

It will be observed that I have throughout treated punishment as a purely legal matter. A "criminal" means a man who has broken a law, not a bad man; an "innocent" man is a man who has not broken the law in connection with which he is being punished, though he may be a bad man and have broken other laws. Here I dissent from most upholders of the retributive theory —from Hegel, from Bradley, and from Dr. Ross. They maintain that the essential connection is one between punishment and moral or social wrong-doing.

My fundamental difficulty with their theory is the question of *status*. It takes two to make a punishment, and for a moral or social wrong I can find no punisher. We may be tempted to say when we hear of some brutal action "that ought to be punished"; but I cannot see how there can be duties which are nobody's duties. If I see a man ill-treating a horse in a country where cruelty to animals is not a legal offence, and I say to him "I shall now punish you," he will reply, rightly, "What has it to do with you? Who made you a judge and a ruler over me?" I may have a duty to try to stop him and one way of stopping him may be to hit him, but another way may be to buy the horse. Neither the blow nor the price is a punishment. For a moral offence, God alone has the *status* necessary to punish the offender; and the theologians are becoming more and more doubtful whether even God has a duty to punish wrong-doing.

Dr. Ross would hold that not all wrong-doing is punishable, but only invasion of the rights of others; and in such a case it might be thought that the injured party had a right to punish. His right, however, is rather a right to reparation, and should not be confused with punishment proper.

This connection, on which I insist, between punishment and crime, not between punishment and moral or social wrong, alone accounts for some of our beliefs about punishment, and also meets many objections to the retributive theory as stated in its ordinary form. The first point on which it helps us is with regard to retrospective legislation. Our objection to this practice is unaccountable on reform and deterrence theories. For a man who commits a wrong before the date on which a law against it is passed, is as much in need of reform as a man who commits it afterwards; nor is deterrence likely to suffer because of additional punishments for the same offence. But the orthodox retributive theory is equally at a loss here, for if punishment is given for moral wrong-doing or for invasion of the rights of others, that immorality or invasion existed as certainly before the passing of the law as after it.

My theory also explains, where it seems to me

all others do not, the case of punishment imposed by an authority who believes the law in question is a bad law. I was myself for some time disciplinary officer of a college whose rules included a rule compelling attendance at chapel. Many of those who broke this rule broke it on principle. I punished them. I certainly did not want to reform them; I respected their characters and their views. I certainly did not want to drive others into chapel through fear of penalties. Nor did I think there had been a wrong done which merited retribution. I wished I could have believed that I would have done the same myself. My position was clear. They had broken a rule; they knew it and I knew it. Nothing more was necessary to make punishment proper.

I know that the usual answer to this is that the judge enforces a bad law because otherwise law in general would suffer and good laws would be broken. The effect of punishing good men for breaking bad laws is that fewer bad men break good laws.

[*Excursus on Indirect Utilitarianism.* The above argument is a particular instance of a general utilitarian solution of all similar problems. When I am in funds and consider whether I should pay my debts or give the same amount to charity, I must choose the former because repayment not only benefits my creditor (for the benefit to him might be less than the good done through charity) but also upholds the general credit system. I tell the truth when a lie might do more good to the parties directly concerned, because I thus increase general trust and confidence. I keep a promise when it might do more immediate good to break it, because indirectly I bring it about that promises will be more readily made in future and this will outweigh the immediate loss involved. Dr. Ross has pointed out that the effect on the credit system of my refusal to pay a debt is greatly exaggerated. But I have a more serious objection of principle. It is that in all these cases the indirect effects do not result from my wrong action—my lie or defalcation or bad faith—but from the publication of these actions. If in any instance the breaking of the rule were to remain unknown then I could consider only the direct or immediate consequences. Thus in my "compulsory chapel" case I could have considered which of my culprits were law-abiding men generally and unlikely to break any other college rule. Then I could have sent for each of these separately and said "I shall let you off if you will tell no one I have done so." By these means the general keeping of rules would not have suffered. Would this course have been correct? It must be remembered that the proceedings need not deceive everybody. So long as they deceive would-be law-breakers the good is achieved.

As this point is of crucial importance and as it has an interest beyond the immediate issue, and gives a clue to what I regard as the true general nature of law and punishment, I may be excused for expanding and illustrating it by an example or two from other fields. Dr. Ross says that two men dying on a desert island would have duties to keep promises to each other even though their breaking them would not affect the future general confidence in promises at all. Here is certainly the same point. But as I find that desert-island morality always rouses suspicion among ordinary men I should like to quote two instances from my own experience which also illustrate the problem.

(i) A man alone with his father at his death promises him a private and quiet funeral. He finds later that both directly and indirectly the keeping of this promise will cause pain and misunderstanding. He can see no particular positive good that the quiet funeral will achieve. No one yet knows that he has made the promise nor need anyone ever know. Should he therefore act as though it had never been made?

(ii) A college has a fund given to it for the encouragement of a subject which is now expiring. Other expanding subjects are in great need of endowment. Should the authorities divert the money? Those who oppose the diversion have previously stood on the past, the promise. But one day one of them discovers the "real reason" for this slavery to a dead donor. He says "We must consider not only the value of this money for these purposes, since on all direct consequences it should be diverted at once. We must remember the effect of this diversion on the general system of benefactions. We know that benefactors like to endow special objects, and this act of ours would discourage such benefactors in future and leave learning worse off." Here again is the indirect utilitarian reason for choosing the alternative which direct utilitarianism would reject. But the immediate answer to this from the most ingenious member of the opposition was crushing and final. He said, "Divert the money but keep it dark." This is obviously correct. It is not the act of diversion which would diminish the stream of benefactions but the news of it reaching the ears of benefactors. Provided that no possible benefactor got to hear of it no indirect loss would result. But the justification of our action would depend entirely on the success of the measures for "keeping it dark." I remember how I felt and how others felt that whatever answer was right this result was certainly wrong. But it follows that indirect utilitarianism is wrong in all such cases. For its argument can always be met by "Keep it dark."]

The view, then, that a judge upholds a bad law in order that law in general should not suffer is indefensible. He upholds it simply because he has no right to dispense from punishment.

The connection of punishment with law-breaking and not with wrong-doing also escapes moral objections to the retributive theory as held by Kant and Hegel or by Bradley and Ross. It is asked how we can measure moral wrong or balance it with pain, and how pain can wipe out moral wrong. Retributivists have been pushed into holding that pain *ipso facto* represses the worse self and frees the better, when this is contrary to the vast majority of observed cases. But if punishment is not intended to measure or balance or negate moral wrong then all this is beside the mark. There is the further difficulty of reconciling punishment with repentance and with forgiveness. Repentance is the reaction morally appropriate to moral wrong and punishment added to remorse is an unnecessary evil. But if punishment is associated with law-breaking and not with moral evil the punisher is not entitled to consider whether the criminal is penitent any more than he may consider whether the law is good. So, too, with forgiveness. Forgiveness is not appropriate to law-breaking. (It is noteworthy that when, in divorce cases, the law has to recognize forgiveness it calls it "condonation," which is symptomatic of the difference of attitude.) Nor is forgiveness appropriate to moral evil. It is appropriate to personal injury. No one has any right to forgive me except the person I have injured. No judge or jury can do so. But the person I have injured has no right to punish me. Therefore there is no clash between punishment and forgiveness since these two duties do not fall on the same person nor in connection with the same characteristic of my act. (It is the weakness of vendetta that it tends to confuse this clear line, though even there it is only by personifying the family that the injured party and the avenger are identified. Similarly we must guard against the plausible fallacy of personifying society and regarding the criminal as "injuring society," for then once more the old dilemma about forgiveness would be insoluble.) A clergyman friend of mine catching a burglar red-handed was puzzled about his duty. In the end he ensured the man's punishment by information and evidence, and at the same time showed his own forgiveness by visiting the man in prison and employing him when he came out. I believe any "good Christian" would accept this as representing his duty. But obviously if the punishment is thought of as imposed *by* the victim or *for* the injury or immorality then the contradiction with forgiveness is hopeless.

So far as the question of the actual punishment of any individual is concerned this paper could stop here. No punishment is morally retributive or reformative or deterrent. Any criminal punished for any one of these reasons is certainly unjustly punished. The only justification for punishing any man is that he has broken a law.

In a book which has already left its mark on prison administration I have found a criminal himself confirming these views. *Walls Have Mouths,* by W. F. R. Macartney, is prefaced, and provided with appendices to each chapter, by Compton Mackenzie. It is interesting to notice how the novelist maintains that the proper object of penal servitude should be reformation,[1] whereas the prisoner himself accepts the view I have set out above. Macartney says "To punish a man is to treat him as an equal. To be punished *for an offence against rules* is a sane man's right."[2] It is striking also that he never uses "injustice" to describe the brutality or provocation which he experienced. He makes it clear that there were only two types of prisoner who were *unjustly* imprisoned, those who were insane and not responsible for the acts for which they were punished[3] and those who were innocent and had broken no law.[4] It is irrelevant, as he rightly observes, that some of these innocent men were,

[1] p. 97.
[2] p. 165. My italics.
[3] pp. 165–166.
[4] p. 298.

like Steinie Morrison, dangerous and violent characters, who on utilitarian grounds might well have been restrained. That made their punishment no whit less unjust.[5] To these general types may be added two specific instances of injustice. First, the sentences on the Dartmoor mutineers. "The Penal Servitude Act . . . lays down specific punishments for mutiny and incitement to mutiny, which include flogging. . . . Yet on the occasion of the only big mutiny in an English prison, men are not dealt with by the Act specially passed to meet mutiny in prison, but are taken out of gaol and tried under an Act expressly passed to curb and curtail the Chartists —a revolutionary movement."[6] Here again the injustice does not lie in the actual effect the sentences are likely to have on the prisoners (though Macartney has some searching suggestions about that also) but in condemning men for breaking a law they did not break and not for breaking the law they did break. The second specific instance is that of Coulton, who served his twenty years and then was brought back to prison to do another eight years and to die. This is due to the "unjust order that no lifer shall be released unless he has either relations or a job to whom he can go: and it is actually suggested that this is really for the lifer's own good. Just fancy, you admit that the man in doing years upon years in prison had expiated his crime: but, instead of releasing him, you keep him a further time—perhaps another three years—because you say he has nowhere to go. Better a ditch and hedge than prison! True, there are abnormal cases who want to stay in prison, but Lawrence wanted to be a private soldier, and men go into monasteries. Because occasionally a man wants to stay in prison, must every lifer who has lost his family during his sentence (I was doing only ten years and I lost all my family) be kept indefinitely in gaol after he has paid his debt?"[7] Why is it unjust? Because he has paid his debt. When that is over it is for the man himself to decide what is for his own good. Once again the reform and utilitarian arguments are summarily swept aside. Injustice lies not in bad treatment or treatment which is not in the man's own interest, but in restriction which, according to the law, he has not merited.

It is true that Macartney writes, in one place, a paragraph of general reflection on punishment in which he confuses, as does Compton Mackenzie, retribution with revenge and in which he seems to hold that the retributive theory has some peculiar connection with private property. "Indeed it is difficult to see how, in society as it is to-day constituted, a humane prison system could function. All property is sacred, although the proceeds of property may well be reprehensible, therefore any offence against property is sacrilege and must be punished. Till a system eventuates which is based not on exploitation of man by man and class by class, prisons must be dreadful places, but at least there might be an effort to ameliorate the more savage side of the retaliation, and this could be done very easily."[8] The alternative system of which no doubt he is thinking is the Russian system described in his quotations from *A Physician's Tour in Soviet Russia,* by Sir James Purves-Stewart, the system of "correctional colonies" providing curative "treatment" for the different types of criminal.[9] There are two confusions here, to one of which we shall return later. First, Macartney confuses the retributive system with the punishment of one particular type of crime, offences against property, when he must have known that the majority of offenders against property do not find themselves in Dartmoor or even in Wandsworth. After all his own offence was not one against property—it was traffic with a foreign Power—and it was one for which in the classless society of Russia the punishment is death. It is surely clear that a retributive system may be adopted for any class of crime. Secondly, Macartney confuses injustice within a penal system with the wrongfulness of a penal system. When he pleads for "humane prisons" as if the essence of the prison should be humanity, or when Compton Mackenzie says the object of penal servitude should be reform, both of them are giving up punishment altogether, not altering it. A Russian "correctional colony," if its real object is curative treatment, is no more a "prison" than is an isolation hospital or a lunatic asylum. To this distinction between abolishing injustice in punishment and abolishing punishment altogether we must now turn.

It will be objected that my original question "Why ought X to be punished?" is an illegiti-

[5] p. 301.
[6] p. 255.
[7] p. 400.
[8] pp. 166, 167.
[9] p. 229.

mate isolation of the issue. I have treated the whole set of circumstances as determined. X is a citizen of a state. About his citizenship, whether willing or unwilling, I have asked no questions. About the government, whether it is good or bad, I do not enquire. X has broken a law. Concerning the law, whether it is well-devised or not, I have not asked. Yet all these questions are surely relevant before it can be decided whether a particular punishment is just. It is the essence of my position that none of these questions is relevant. Punishment is a corollary of law-breaking by a member of the society whose law is broken. This is a static and an abstract view but I see no escape from it. Considerations of utility come in on two quite different issues. Should there be laws, and what laws should there be? As a legislator I may ask what general types of action would benefit the community, and, among these, which can be "standardized" without loss, or should be standardized to achieve their full value. This, however, is not the primary question since particular laws may be altered or repealed. The choice which is the essential *prius* of punishment is the choice that there should be laws. The choice is not Hobson's. Other methods may be considered. A government might attempt to standardize certain modes of action by means of advice. It might proclaim its view and say "Citizens are requested" to follow this or that procedure. Or again it might decide to deal with each case as it arose in the manner most effective for the common welfare. Anarchists have wavered between these two alternatives and a third —that of doing nothing to enforce a standard of behaviour but merely giving arbitrational decisions between conflicting parties, decisions binding only by consent.

I think it can be seen without detailed examination of particular laws that the method of law-making has its own advantages. Its orders are explicit and general. It makes behaviour reliable and predictable. Its threat of punishment may be so effective as to make punishment unnecessary. It promises to the good citizen a certain security in his life. When I have talked to business men about some inequity in the law of liability they have usually said "Better a bad law than no law, for then we know where we are."

Someone may say I am drawing an impossible line. I deny that punishment is utilitarian; yet now I say that punishment is a corollary of law and we decide whether to have laws and which laws to have on utilitarian grounds. And surely it is only this corollary which distinguishes law from good advice or exhortation. This is a misunderstanding. Punishment is a corollary not of law but of law-breaking. Legislators do not choose to punish. They hope no punishment will be needed. Their laws would succeed even if no punishment occurred. The criminal makes the essential choice: he "brings it on himself." Other men obey the law because they see its order is reasonable, because of inertia, because of fear. In this whole area, and it may be the major part of the state, law achieves its ends without punishment. Clearly, then, punishment is not a corollary of law.

We may return for a moment to the question of amount and nature of punishment. It may be thought that this also is automatic. The law will include its own penalties and the judge will have no option. This, however, is again an initial choice of principle. If the laws do include their own penalties then the judge has no option. But the legislature might adopt a system which left complete or partial freedom to the judge, as we do except in the case of murder. Once again, what are the merits (regardless of particular laws, still more of particular cases) of fixed penalties and variable penalties? At first sight it would seem that all the advantages are with the variable penalties; for men who have broken the same law differ widely in degree of wickedness and responsibility. When, however, we remember that punishment is not an attempt to balance moral guilt this advantage is diminished. But there are still degrees of responsibility; I do not mean degrees of freedom of will but, for instance, degrees of complicity in a crime. The danger of allowing complete freedom to the judicature in fixing penalties is not merely that it lays too heavy a tax on human nature but that it would lead to the judge expressing in his penalty the degree of his own moral aversion to the crime. Or he might tend on deterrent grounds to punish more heavily a crime which was spreading and for which temptation and opportunity were frequent. Or again on deterrent grounds he might "make examples" by punishing ten times as heavily those criminals who are detected in cases in which nine out of ten evade detection. Yet we should revolt from all such punishments if they involved punishing theft more heavily than blackmail or negligence more heavily than premeditated assault. The death penalty for sheep-stealing might have been defended on such deterrent grounds. But we should dislike equating sheep-stealing with murder. Fixed penalties enable us to draw these distinctions between crimes. It is not that we can say how much imprisonment is right for a sheep-stealer. But we can grade crimes in a rough scale and penalties in a rough scale, and keep our heaviest penalties for what are socially the most serious wrongs regardless of whether these penalties will reform the criminal or whether they are exactly what deterrence would require. The compromise of laying down maximum penalties and allowing judges freedom below these limits allows for the arguments on both sides.

To return to the main issue, the position I am defending is that it is essential to a legal system that the infliction of a particular punishment should *not* be determined by the good *that particular punishment* will do either to the criminal or to "society." In exactly the same way it is essential to a credit system that the repayment of a particular debt should not be determined by the good that particular payment will do. One may consider the merits of a legal system or of a credit system, but the acceptance of either involves the surrender of utilitarian considerations in particular cases as they arise. This is in effect admitted by Ewing in one place where he says "It is the penal system as a whole which deters and not the punishment of any individual offender."[10]

To show that the choice between a legal system and its alternatives is one we do and must make, I may quote an early work of Lenin in which he was defending the Marxist tenet that the state is bound to "wither away" with the establishment of a classless society. He considers the possible objection that some wrongs by man against man are not economic and therefore that the abolition of classes would not *ipso facto* eliminate crime. But he sticks to the thesis that these surviving crimes should not be dealt with by law and judicature. "We are not Utopians and do not in the least deny the possibility and inevitability of excesses by *individual persons,* and equally the need to suppress such excesses. But for this no special machine, no special instrument of repression is needed. This will be done by the armed nation itself as simply and as readily as any crowd of civilized people even in modern society parts a pair of combatants or does not allow a woman to be outraged."[11] This alternative to law and punishment has obvious demerits. Any injury not committed in the presence of the crowd, any wrong which required skill to detect or pertinacity to bring home would go untouched. The lynching mob, which is Lenin's instrument of justice, is liable to error and easily deflected from its purpose or driven to extremes. It must be a mob, for there is to be no "machine." I do not say that no alternative machine to ours could be devised but it does seem certain that the absence of all "machines" would be intolerable. An alternative machine might be based on the view that "society" is responsible for all criminality, and a curative and protective system developed. This is the system of Butler's "Erewhon" and something like it seems to be growing up in Russia except for cases of "sedition."

We choose, then, or we acquiesce in and adopt the choice of others of, a legal system as one of our instruments for the establishment of the conditions of a good life. This choice is logically prior to and independent of the actual punishment of any particular persons or the passing of any particular laws. The legislators choose particular laws within the framework of this predetermined system. Once again a small society may illustrate the reality of these choices and the distinction between them. A Headmaster launching a new school must explicitly make both decisions. First, shall we have any rules at all? Second, what rules shall we have? The first decision is a genuine one and one of great importance. Would it not be better to have an "honour" system, by which public opinion in each house or form dealt with any offence? (This is the Lenin method.) Or would complete freedom be better? Or should he issue appeals and advice? Or should he personally deal with each malefactor individually, as the case arises, in the way most likely to improve his conduct? I can well imagine an idealistic Headmaster attempting to run a school with one of these methods or with a combination of several of them and therefore without punishment. I can even imagine that with a small school

[10] A. C. Ewing, *The Morality of Punishment* (London: Routledge and Kegan Paul, Ltd., 1929), p. 66.

[11] *The State and Revolution* (Eng. trans.), p. 93. Original italics.

of, say, twenty pupils all open to direct personal psychological pressure from authority and from each other, these methods involving no "rules" would work. The pupils would of course grow up without two very useful habits, the habit of having some regular habits and the habit of obeying rules. But I suspect that most Headmasters, especially those of large schools, would either decide at once, or quickly be driven, to realize that some rules were necessary. This decision would be "utilitarian" in the sense that it would be determined by consideration of consequences. The question "what rules?" would then arise and again the issue is utilitarian. What action must be regularized for the school to work efficiently? The hours of arrival and departure, for instance, in a day school. But the one choice which is now no longer open to the Headmaster is whether he shall punish those who break the rules. For if he were to try to avoid this he would in fact simply be returning to the discarded method of appeals and good advice. Yet the Headmaster does not decide to punish. The pupils make the decision there. He decides actually to have rules and to threaten, but only hypothetically, to punish. The one essential condition which makes actual punishment just is a condition he *cannot* fulfil—namely that a rule should be broken.

I shall add a final word of consolation to the practical reformer. Nothing that I have said is meant to counter any movement for "penal reform" but only to insist that none of these reforms have anything to do with punishment. The only type of reformer who can claim to be reforming the system of punishment is a follower of Lenin or of Samuel Butler who is genuinely attacking the *system* and who believes there should be no laws and no punishments. But our great British reformers have been concerned not with punishment but with its accessories. When a man is sentenced to imprisonment he is not sentenced also to partial starvation, to physical brutality, to pneumonia from damp cells and so on. And any movement which makes his food sufficient to sustain health, which counters the permanent tendency to brutality on the part of his warders, which gives him a dry or even a light and well-aired cell, is pure gain and does not touch the theory of punishment. Reformatory influences and prisoners' aid arrangements are also entirely unaffected by what I have said. I believe myself that it would be best if all such arrangements were made optional for the prisoner, so as to leave him in these cases a freedom of choice which would make it clear that they are not part of his punishment. If it is said that every such reform lessens a man's punishment, I think that is simply muddled thinking which, if it were clear, would be mere brutality. For instance, a prisoners' aid society is said to lighten his punishment, because otherwise he would suffer not merely imprisonment but also unemployment on release. But he was sentenced to imprisonment, not imprisonment *plus* unemployment. If I promise to help a friend and through special circumstances I find that keeping my promise will involve upsetting my day's work, I do not say that I really promised to help him and to ruin my day's work. And if another friend carries on my work for me I do not regard him as carrying out part of my promise, nor as stopping me from carrying it out myself. He merely removes an indirect and regrettable consequence of my keeping my promise. So with punishment. The Prisoners' Aid Society does not alter a man's punishment nor diminish it, but merely removes an indirect and regrettable consequence of it. And anyone who thinks that a criminal cannot make this distinction and will regard all the inconvenience that comes to him as punishment, need only talk to a prisoner or two to find how sharply they resent these wanton additions to a punishment which by itself they will accept as just. Macartney's chapter on "Food" in the book quoted above is a good illustration of this point, as are also his comments on Clayton's administration. "To keep a man in prison for many years at considerable expense and then to free him charged to the eyes with uncontrollable venom and hatred generated by the treatment he has received in gaol, does not appear to be sensible." Clayton "endeavoured to send a man out of prison in a reasonable state of mind. 'Well, I've done my time. They were not too bad to me. Prison is prison and not a bed of roses. Still they didn't rub it in. . . .'"[12] This "reasonable state of mind" is one in which a prisoner on release feels he has been punished but not *additionally* insulted or ill-treated. I feel convinced that penal reformers would meet with even more support if they were clear that they were *not* attempting to alter the system of punishment but to give its

[12] p. 152.

victims "fair play." We have no more right to starve a convict than to starve an animal. We have no more right to keep a convict in a Dartmoor cell "down which the water trickles night and day"[13] than we have to keep a child in such a place. If our reformers really want to alter the system of punishment, let them come out clearly with their alternative and preach, for instance, that no human being is responsible for any wrong-doing, that all the blame is on society, that curative or protective measures should be adopted, forcibly if necessary, as they are with infection or insanity. Short of this let them admit that the essence of prison is deprivation of liberty for the breaking of law, and that deprivation of food or of health or of books is unjust. And if our sentimentalists cry "coddling of prisoners," let us ask them also to come out clearly into the open and incorporate whatever starvation and disease and brutality they think necessary *into the sentences they propose.*[14] If it is said that some prisoners will prefer such reformed prisons, with adequate food and aired cells, to the outer world, we may retort that their numbers are probably not greater than those of the masochists who like to be flogged. Yet we do not hear the same "coddling" critics suggest abolition of the lash on the grounds that some criminals may like it. Even if the abolition from our prisons of all maltreatment other than that imposed by law results in a few down-and-outs breaking a window (as O. Henry's hero did) to get a night's lodging, the country will lose less than she does by her present method of sending out her discharged convicts "charged with venom and hatred" because of the additional and uncovenanted "rubbing it in" which they have received.

I hope I have established both the theoretical importance and the practical value of distinguishing between penal reform as we know and approve it—that reform which alters the accompaniments of punishment without touching its essence—and those attacks on punishment itself which are made not only by reformers who regard criminals as irresponsible and in need of treatment, but also by every judge who announces that he is punishing a man to deter others or to protect society, and by every juryman who is moved to his decision by the moral baseness of the accused rather than by his legal guilt.

[13] *Op. cit.*, p. 258.

[14] "One of the minor curiosities of jail life was that they quickly provided you with a hundred worries which left you no time or energy for worrying about your sentence, long or short. . . . Rather as if you were thrown into a fire with spikes in it, and the spikes hurt you so badly that you forget about the fire. But then your punishment would *be* the spikes not the fire. Why did they pretend it was only the fire, when they knew very well about the spikes?" (From *Lifer* by Jim Phelan, p. 40.)

M. R. GLOVER

Mr. Mabbott on Punishment*

I find it hard to see that Mr. Mabbott in his article on punishment (*Mind*, No. 190, April 1939) has really adduced any ethical arguments that establish the retributive theory; and the considerations he brings forward are mainly logical and legal.

The logical point seems to be that the very definition of law involves punishment for its infringement, so that once you have law instead of advice or request, punishment is logically entailed; in fact, the question whether punishment should be enforced does not arise, because it has been settled already; Mr. Mabbott illustrated this from his own experience of administering a college rule of compulsory chapel. This view

* M. R. Glover, "Mr. Mabbott on Punishment," *Mind*, XLVIII (1939), 488–501. Reprinted by permission of the editor of *Mind*.

implies that it cannot be right to be illogical. This, of course, is the basis of Kant's moral theory; and Hobbes seems to have had the same conviction very strongly; he maintained that voluntary law-breaking was "somewhat like to that which in the disputation of scholars is called absurdity" (III, 119, Laird's reference). It does not seem clear to me that it can never be right to be illogical. I realise that the force of this opinion must be lessened by the fact that I belong to the weaker and notoriously illogical sex; but the opinion is not confined to my sex. I am told that my great-great-uncle, serving on a jury to try a boy for sheep-stealing, refused to give the verdict "guilty" and delayed the jury for an indefinite time until out of fatigue they agreed with him, although he and they and everybody else were convinced that the boy had stolen the sheep. Because the penalty was death. It is illogical to serve on a jury instead of suffering whatever the penalty may be for refusing to serve, and then not fulfil the juryman's oath to give a true verdict. But if this deliberate illogicality is the best way to get an iniquitous law altered it might be right. It is true that if everybody everywhere held themselves at liberty to be illogical, in the sense of breaking their oaths and promises, society would break down; but no sensible person would universalise the rule "break your promises"; the rule "keep your promises" might be used as rules are used in medical practice, as principles of extremely general application, which it is your duty occasionally and at your peril to break.

Secondly, Mr. Mabbott argues that punishment has nothing to do with moral wrong-doing but only with law-breaking. But if law-breaking and wrong-doing were quite distinct, I cannot see why it would be necessary to find any moral justification whatever for punishment for law-breaking, any more than for prescribing a penalty for foot-faulting at tennis.[1]

But is this momentous separation of law and morals really intended? It would, as it seems to me, imply that the whole of political activity, which is the field of law, was exempt from moral considerations. Mr. Mabbott's point, I imagine, is that laws in general have a moral basis, inasmuch as no society can live without rules, but that it is not necessary that all particular regulations should have a justification of their own in moral feeling; indeed that every real society maintains and accepts some rules whose function is to keep alive the sense of corporate order, but which taken in themselves have no moral significance. This seems to be true, but it is notorious that there is a limit to people's capacity to respect meaningless or silly regulations.[2]

If we are not prepared to divorce law and politics, those who make laws have to ask themselves both the general question, whether it is right for a man or for society to impose suffering on another human being in the interests of order, and also whether particular laws are justified. Mr. Mabbott wants to remove the real responsibility for imposing suffering from the legislator on the ground that "Punishment is the corollary not of law but of law-breaking. Legislators do not choose to punish. They hope punishment will not be needed. Their laws would succeed even if no punishment took place. The criminal makes the essential choice, he brings it on himself" (page 161). When a headmaster has decided to have rules prescribing punishments for certain offences, "the headmaster does not decide to punish. He decides actually to have certain rules and to threaten, but only hypothetically, to punish. The one essential condition which makes actual punishment just, is a condition he cannot fulfil, namely that a rule should be broken". It does not appear to me that the makers of laws and rules can be exonerated from the moral responsibility for the punishment; it seems to me as though I were to say, "I shall turn out a dangerous bull into a field, and if people trespass in order to pick fritillaries and get hurt, it is their look-out, I do not make them trespass". A railway company that decides to build a level crossing may claim that people will get hurt there only if they drive faster than they ought to drive, or cross without looking; nevertheless, the railway company always

[1] Nevertheless I should myself maintain that any human activity may become a matter of moral significance, even sport; and that there might be moral considerations involved in the rules of a game, *e.g.* over the question of body-line bowling.

[2] *e.g.*, 'Solicitor' in his book *English Justice* asserts that the law of England is greatly brought into contempt in the poorer parts of London, because the laws that prescribe where you may bet, and where you may not, appear to rest on no moral considerations whatever. And it is commonly held that Prohibition in the U.S.A. caused a formidable outbreak of lawlessness, because very respectable people refused to obey a law that seemed to them to interfere with liberty without moral grounds.

feels that it ought to take responsibility and try to save people from actualising by their own action, the only condition that can make an accident possible, by building gates. The farmer who owns the bull, the railway company and the legislator are all in the position of doing something that entails suffering for other people under certain conditions: they cannot escape the moral obligation of considering whether it is right for them to take a decision that contains this possibility.

The early Christian Fathers were very doubtful whether the coercion of one man by another with the threat of violence in the name of government was right; they thought it was a condition of affairs by no means ideal but necessitated by the Fall. Mr. Mabbott seems to me to settle this ancient question too easily by reference to the opinions of headmasters and criminals. The moral judgment of a criminal that he or another deserved to suffer is not one that I would accept without criticism; a criminal is at least as likely as anybody else to have a defective moral sensibility. Headmasters, like other men, are under a constant temptation to save time, and choose the most convenient way of achieving their estimable purposes. But the most convenient is not necessarily the most moral either for them or states; it might be right to take a lot more trouble in order to train boys by another method. This is beginning to be recognised in the case of the training of small infants. Certain methods which teach babies not to expect that their mothers will come if they cry, are very convenient for mothers; they can leave the baby alone and get on with their jobs; the baby either gets into a habit of constant hopeless crying (to the distraction of the neighbours) or gives it up as useless; some psychologists nowadays assert that these methods may do the child harm. Most mothers would agree that if this is really the case they must abandon this convenient system, and adopt one that will give them more trouble.

It is obviously possible to produce a utilitarian justification of punishment, on the ground that we do not at present know any other way of securing the order which is the necessary basis of the common good life. But this would not justify punishment if we did know another way; and the Russian experiment in curative treatment may bring a better way to light.

In Mr. Mabbott's view, however, the utilitarian argument does not stand alone, because punishment is right in itself apart from its results, as retribution. His chief ground seems to be: (1) That we all recognise that it is wrong for an innocent man to suffer, as though it followed from this that it is right for the guilty to do so; (2) That if the utility of deterrence were all that were at stake, a system of well-chosen lies would do as well as actual punishment, and since we should not approve of such lying, we are compelled really to punish. I contest both these arguments.

(1) The conviction that it is not right for the innocent to suffer does not entail the logical corollary that the guilty should; it might be right that neither should. But I would suggest that it is not really established that it is invariably more morally wrong for the innocent to suffer than for the alternative state of affairs to ensue. When I was in the North-West Frontier Province of India a few years ago, I formed the impression that the vendetta continued to flourish there partly because the Government were handicapped in their administration by their difficulty in securing any evidence upon which to convict known murderers; anyone who gave such evidence destined himself to be the next victim of the vendetta; so a large proportion of accused murderers got off. The opinion was therefore widely held among the people that the Government would not punish for murder, and the responsibility, which they felt very heavily, lay with the private family. It appears to me thinkable that in such a case the right thing to do would be so to alter the law of the province that a man could be made to suffer the death penalty on grounds nearer to those of Oriental law; *e.g.*, upon the conviction of the judge, not necessarily grounded on evidence given in public, that a man is guilty. The chance of an innocent man suffering might be a lesser evil than the inability of the Government to give security to anybody and to protect the lives of the people. (I believe this would be felt by the people of the province to be a great improvement on the present system which they do not at all admire or understand.)

(2) An obvious answer to the unsatisfactoriness of alleging that punishment has taken place when it has not, is that such lies cannot be efficient for very long. The unwillingness to break promise with the dead seems to me not to

be a parallel because it involves another feeling altogether. I believe we value candour and good faith between persons for its own sake; and we feel that as long as we are keeping faith with the dead a certain relation with them, which is of value to us, persists and they are not wholly separated from us. Anyway the fact that lies about punishment may be wrong does not show that punishment itself is right.

The question whether there is a rightness in retribution itself, apart from its consequences, seems to me still uncertain; I think it is a matter on which our moral sensibility has no certain deliverance to make. I find myself that there are people on whom I would choose to inflict suffering if I could, in retribution for what they have done, and their suffering would seem to me fitting and proper. But I imagine most people find that when it actually lies with them to inflict pain, on someone they know and in some degree care for, in retribution (for instance to give pain by saying something, that is not expected to make them any better, in retribution for wrong they have done in causing such pain to others), we do not wish, at least in cold blood, to take this course. It would do no good, we say. Whether either of these sentiments constitutes moral insight I do not know. But it may be remarked that those whom we agree to regard as "the best and wisest and the most just" have not shown any sign of desire that there should be retribution upon those who have done them desperate wrong.

JOHN RAWLS

Punishment*

In this paper I want to show the importance of the distinction between justifying a practice[1] and justifying a particular action falling under it, and I want to explain the logical basis of this distinction and how it is possible to miss its significance. While the distinction has frequently been made,[2] and is now becoming commonplace, there remains the task of explaining the tendency either to overlook it altogether, or to fail to appreciate its importance.

To show the importance of the distinction I am going to defend utilitarianism against those objections which have traditionally been made

* From John Rawls, "Two Concepts of Rules," Part I, *Philosophical Review,* LXIV (1955), 3–13. Reprinted by permission of the author and *The Philosophical Review*.

[1] I use the word "practice" throughout as a sort of technical term meaning any form of activity specified by a system of rules which defines offices, roles, moves, penalties, defenses, and so on, and which gives the activity its structure. As examples one may think of games and rituals, trials and parliaments.

[2] The distinction is central to Hume's discussion of justice in *A Treatise of Human Nature,* bk. III, pt. II, esp. secs. 2–4. It is clearly stated by John Austin in the second lecture of *Lectures on Jurisprudence* (4th ed.; London, 1873), I, 116ff. (1st ed., 1832). Also it may be argued that J. S. Mill took it for granted in *Utilitarianism;* on this point cf. J. O. Urmson, "The Interpretation of the Moral Philosophy of J. S. Mill," *Philosophical Quarterly,* vol. III (1953). In addition to the arguments given by Urmson there are several clear statements of the distinction in *A System of Logic* (8th ed.; London, 1872), bk. VI, ch. xii pars. 2, 3, 7. The distinction is fundamental to J. D. Mabbott's important paper, "Punishment," *Mind,* n.s., vol. XLVIII (April, 1939). More recently the distinction has been stated with particular emphasis by S. E. Toulmin in *The Place of Reason in Ethics* (Cambridge, 1950), see esp. ch. xi, where it plays a major part in his account of moral reasoning. Toulmin doesn't explain the basis of the distinction, nor how one might overlook its importance, as I try to in this paper, and in my review of his book (*Philosophical Review,* vol. LX [October, 1951]), as some of my criticisms show, I failed to understand the force of it. See also H. D. Aiken, "The Levels of Moral Discourse," *Ethics,* vol. LXII (1952), A. M. Quinton, "Punishment," *Analysis,* vol. XIV (June, 1954), and P. H. Nowell-Smith, *Ethics* (London, 1954), pp. 236–239, 271–273.

against it in connection with punishment and the obligation to keep promises. I hope to show that if one uses the distinction in question then one can state utilitarianism in a way which makes it a much better explication of our considered moral judgments than these traditional objections would seem to admit.[3] Thus the importance of the distinction is shown by the way it strengthens the utilitarian view regardless of whether that view is completely defensible or not. . . .

The subject of punishment, in the sense of attaching legal penalties to the violation of legal rules, has always been a troubling moral question.[4] The trouble about it has not been that people disagree as to whether or not punishment is justifiable. Most people have held that, freed from certain abuses, it is an acceptable institution. Only a few have rejected punishment entirely, which is rather surprising when one considers all that can be said against it. The difficulty is with the justification of punishment: various arguments for it have been given by moral philosophers, but so far none of them has won any sort of general acceptance; no justification is without those who detest it. I hope to show that the use of the aforementioned distinction enables one to state the utilitarian view in a way which allows for the sound points of its critics.

For our purposes we may say that there are two justifications of punishment. What we may call the retributive view is that punishment is justified on the grounds that wrongdoing merits punishment. It is morally fitting that a person who does wrong should suffer in proportion to his wrongdoing. That a criminal should be punished follows from his guilt, and the severity of the appropriate punishment depends on the depravity of his act. The state of affairs where a wrongdoer suffers punishment is morally better than the state of affairs where he does not; and it is better irrespective of any of the consequences of punishing him.

What we may call the utilitarian view holds that on the principle that bygones are bygones and that only future consequences are material to present decisions, punishment is justifiable only by reference to the probable consequences of maintaining it as one of the devices of the social order. Wrongs committed in the past are, as such, not relevant considerations for deciding what to do. If punishment can be shown to promote effectively the interest of society it is justifiable, otherwise it is not.

I have stated these two competing views very roughly to make one feel the conflict between them: one feels the force of *both* arguments and one wonders how they can be reconciled. From my introductory remarks it is obvious that the resolution which I am going to propose is that in this case one must distinguish between justifying a practice as a system of rules to be applied and enforced, and justifying a particular action which falls under these rules; utilitarian arguments are appropriate with regard to questions about practices, while retributive arguments fit the application of particular rules to particular cases.

We might try to get clear about this distinction by imagining how a father might answer the question of his son. Suppose the son asks, "Why was *J* put in jail yesterday?" The father answers, "Because he robbed the bank at *B*. He was duly tried and found guilty. That's why he was put in jail yesterday." But suppose the son had asked a different question, namely, "Why do people put other people in jail?" Then the father might answer, "To protect good people from bad people" or "To stop people from doing things that would make it uneasy for all of us; for otherwise we wouldn't be able to go to bed at night and sleep in peace." There are two very different questions here. One question emphasizes the proper name: it asks why *J* was punished rather than someone else, or it asks what he was punished for. The other question asks why we have the institution of punishment: why do people punish one another rather than, say always forgiving one another?

Thus the father says in effect that a particular man is punished, rather than some other man, because he is guilty, and he is guilty because he broke the law (past tense). In his case the law looks back, the judge looks back, the jury looks back, and a penalty is visited upon him for some-

[3] On the concept of explication see the author's paper, *Philosophical Review,* vol. LX (April, 1951).

[4] While this paper was being revised, Quinton's appeared; footnote 2 supra. There are several respects in which my remarks are similar to his. Yet as I consider some further questions and rely on somewhat different arguments, I have retained the discussion of punishment and promises together as two test cases for utilitarianism.

thing he did. That a man is to be punished, and what his punishment is to be, is settled by its being shown that he broke the law and that the law assigns that penalty for the violation of it.

On the other hand we have the institution of punishment itself, and recommend and accept various changes in it, because it is thought by the (ideal) legislator and by those to whom the law applies that, as a part of a system of law impartially applied from case to case arising under it, it will have the consequence, in the long run, of furthering the interests of society.

One can say, then, that the judge and the legislator stand in different positions and look in different directions: one to the past, the other to the future. The justification of what the judge does, *qua* judge, sounds like the retributive view; the justification of what the (ideal) legislator does, *qua* legislator, sounds like the utilitarian view. Thus both views have a point (this is as it should be since intelligent and sensitive persons have been on both sides of the argument); and one's initial confusion disappears once one sees that these views apply to persons holding different offices with different duties, and situated differently with respect to the system of rules that make up the criminal law.[5]

One might say, however, that the utilitarian view is more fundamental since it applies to a more fundamental office, for the judge carries out the legislator's will so far as he can determine it. Once the legislator decides to have laws and to assign penalties for their violation (as things are there must be both the law and the penalty) an institution is set up which involves a retributive conception of particular cases. It is part of the concept of the criminal law as a system of rules that the application and enforcement of these rules in particular cases should be justifiable by arguments of a retributive character. The decision whether or not to use law rather than some other mechanism of social control, and the decision as to what laws to have and what penalties to assign, may be settled by utilitarian arguments; but if one decides to have laws then one has decided on something whose working in particular cases is retributive in form.[6]

The answer, then, to the confusion engendered by the two views of punishment is quite simple: one distinguishes two offices, that of the judge and that of the legislator, and one distinguishes their different stations with respect to the system of rules which make up the law; and then one notes that the different sorts of considerations which would usually be offered as reasons for what is done under the cover of these offices can be paired off with the competing justifications of punishment. One reconciles the two views by the time-honored device of making them apply to different situations.

But can it really be this simple? Well, this answer allows for the apparent intent of each side. Does a person who advocates the retributive view necessarily advocate, as an *institution*, legal machinery whose essential purpose is to set up and preserve a correspondence between moral turpitude and suffering? Surely not.[7] What retributionists have rightly insisted upon is that no man can be punished unless he is guilty, that is, unless he has broken the law. Their fundamental criticism of the utilitarian account is that, as they interpret it, it sanctions an innocent person's being punished (if one may call it that) for the benefit of society.

On the other hand, utilitarians agree that punishment is to be inflicted only for the violation of law. They regard this much as understood from the concept of punishment itself.[8] The point of the utilitarian account concerns the institution as a system of rules: utilitarianism seeks to limit its use by declaring it justifiable only if it can be

[5] Note the fact that different sorts of arguments are suited to different offices. One way of taking the differences between ethical theories is to regard them as accounts of the reasons expected in different offices.

[6] In this connection see Mabbott, *op cit.*, pp. 163–164.

[7] On this point see Sir David Ross, *The Right and the Good* (Oxford, 1930), pp. 57–60.

[8] See Hobbes's definition of punishment in *Leviathan*, ch. xxviii; and Bentham's definition in *The Principle of Morals and Legislation*, ch. xii, par. 36, ch. xv, par. 28, and in *The Rationale of Punishment*, (London, 1830), bk. I, ch. i. They could agree with Bradley that: "Punishment is punishment only when it is deserved. We pay the penalty, because we owe it, and for no other reason; and if punishment is inflicted for any other reason whatever than because it is merited by wrong, it is a gross immorality, a crying injustice, an abominable crime, and not what it pretends to be." *Ethical Studies* (2nd ed.; Oxford, 1927), pp. 26–27. Certainly by definition it isn't what it pretends to be. The innocent can only be punished by mistake; deliberate "punishment" of the innocent necessarily involves fraud.

shown to foster effectively the good of society. Historically it is a protest against the indiscriminate and ineffective use of the criminal law.[9] It seeks to dissuade us from assigning to penal institutions the improper, if not sacrilegious, task of matching suffering with moral turpitude. Like others, utilitarians want penal institutions designed so that, as far as humanly possible, only those who break the law run afoul of it. They hold that no official should have discretionary power to inflict penalties whenever he thinks it for the benefit of society; for on utilitarian grounds an institution granting such power could not be justified.[10]

The suggested way of reconciling the retributive and the utilitarian justifications of punishment seems to account for what both sides have wanted to say. There are, however, two further questions which arise, and I shall devote the remainder of this section to them.

First, will not a difference of opinion as to the proper criterion of just law make the proposed reconciliation unacceptable to retributionists? Will they not question whether, if the utilitarian principle is used as the criterion, it follows that those who have broken the law are guilty in a way which satisfies their demand that those punished deserve to be punished? To answer this difficulty, suppose that the rules of the criminal law are justified on utilitarian grounds (it is only for laws that meet his criterion that the utilitarian can be held responsible). Then it follows that the actions which the criminal law specifies as offenses are such that, if they were tolerated, terror and alarm would spread in society. Consequently, retributionists can only deny that those who are punished deserve to be punished if they deny that such actions are wrong. This they will not want to do.

The second question is whether utilitarianism doesn't justify too much. One pictures it as an engine of justification which, if consistently adopted, could be used to justify cruel and arbitrary institutions. Retributionists may be supposed to concede that utilitarians *intend* to reform the law and to make it more humane; that utilitarians do not *wish* to justify any such thing as punishment of the innocent; and that utilitarians may appeal to the fact that punishment presupposes guilt in the sense that by punishment one understands an institution attaching penalties to the infraction of legal rules, and therefore that it is logically absurd to suppose that utilitarians in justifying *punishment* might also have justified punishment (if we may call it that) of the innocent. The real question, however, is whether the utilitarian, in justifying punishment, hasn't used arguments which commit him to accepting the infliction of suffering on innocent persons if it is for the good of society (whether or not one calls this punishment). More generally, isn't the utilitarian committed in principle to accepting many practices which he, as a morally sensitive person, wouldn't want to accept? Retributionists are inclined to hold that there is no way to stop the utilitarian principle from justifying too much except by adding to it a principle which distributes certain rights to individuals. Then the amended criterion is not the greatest benefit of society *simpliciter,* but the greatest benefit of society subject to the constraint that no one's rights may be violated. Now while I think that the classical utilitarians proposed a criterion of this more complicated sort, I do not want to argue that point here.[11] What I want to show is that there is *another* way of preventing the utilitarian principle from justifying too much, or at least of making it much less likely to do so: namely, by stating utilitarianism in a way which accounts for the distinction between the justification of an institution and the justification of a particular action falling under it.

[9] Cf. Leon Radzinowicz, *A History of English Criminal Law: The Movement for Reform 1750–1833* (London, 1948), esp. ch. xi on Bentham.

[10] Bentham discusses how corresponding to a punitory provision of a criminal law there is another provision which stands to it as an antagonist and which needs a name as much as the punitory. He calls it, as one might expect, the *anaetiosostic,* and of it he says: "The punishment of guilt is the object of the former one: the preservation of innocence that of the latter." In the same connection he asserts that it is never thought fit to give the judge the option of deciding whether a thief (that is, a person whom he believes to be a thief, for the judge's belief is what the question must always turn upon) should hang or not, and so the law writes the provision: "The judge shall not cause a thief to be hanged unless he have been duly convicted and sentenced in course of law" (*The Limits of Jurisprudence Defined,* ed. C. W. Everett [New York, 1945], pp. 238–239).

[11] By the classical utilitarians I understand Hobbes, Hume, Bentham, J. S. Mill, and Sidgwick.

I begin by defining the institution of punishment as follows: a person is said to suffer punishment whenever he is legally deprived of some of the normal rights of a citizen on the ground that he has violated a rule of law, the violation having been established by trial according to the due process of law, provided that the deprivation is carried out by the recognized legal authorities of the state, that the rule of law clearly specifies both the offense and the attached penalty, that the courts construe statutes strictly, and that the statute was on the books prior to the time of the offense.[12] This definition specifies what I shall understand by punishment. The question is whether utilitarian arguments may be found to justify institutions widely different from this and such as one would find cruel and arbitrary.

This question is best answered, I think, by taking up a particular accusation. Consider the following from Carritt:

> . . . the utilitarian must hold that we are justified in inflicting pain always and only to prevent worse pain or bring about greater happiness. This, then, is all we need to consider in so-called punishment, which must be purely preventive. But if some kind of very cruel crime becomes common, and none of the criminals can be caught, it might he highly expedient, as an example, to hang an innocent man, if a charge against him could be so framed that he were universally thought guilty; indeed this would only fail to be an ideal instance of utilitarian 'punishment' because the victim himself would not have been so likely as a real felon to commit such a crime in the future; in all other respects it would be perfectly deterrent and therefore felicific.[14]

Carritt is trying to show that there are occasions when a utilitarian argument would justify taking an action which would be generally condemned; and thus that utilitarianism justifies too much. But the failure of Carritt's argument lies in the fact that he makes no distinction between the justification of the general system of rules which constitutes penal institutions and the justification of particular applications of these rules to particular cases by the various officials whose job it is to administer them. This becomes perfectly clear when one asks who the "we" are of whom Carritt speaks. Who is this who has a sort of absolute authority on particular occasions to decide that an innocent man shall be "punished" if everyone can be convinced that he is guilty? Is this person the legislator, or the judge, or the body of private citizens, or what? It is utterly crucial to know who is to decide such matters, and by what authority, for all of this must be written into the rules of the institution. Until one knows these things one doesn't know what the institution is whose justification is being challenged; and as the utilitarian principle applies to the institution one doesn't know whether it is justifiable on utilitarian grounds or not.

Once this is understood it is clear what the countermove to Carritt's argument is. One must describe more carefully what the *institution* is which his example suggests, and then ask oneself whether or not it is likely that having this institution would be for the benefit of society in the long run. One must not content oneself with the vague thought that, when it's a question of *this* case, it would be a good thing if *somebody* did something even if an innocent person were to suffer.

Try to imagine, then, an institution (which we may call "telishment") which is such that the officials set up by it have authority to arrange a trial for the condemnation of an innocent man whenever they are of the opinion that doing so would be in the best interests of society. The discretion of officials is limited, however, by the rule that they may not condemn an innocent man to undergo such an ordeal unless there is, at the time, a wave of offenses similar to that with which they charge him and telish him for. We may imagine that the officials having the discretionary authority are the judges of the higher courts in consultation with the chief of police, the minister of justice, and a committee of the legislature.

Once one realizes that one is involved in setting up an *institution*, one sees that the hazards are very great. For example, what check is there on the officials? How is one to tell whether or not their actions are authorized? How is one to limit the risks involved in allowing such systematic deception? How is one to avoid giving anything short of complete discretion to the authorities to telish anyone they like? In addition to these considerations, it is obvious that people will come

[12] All these features of punishment are mentioned by Hobbes; cf. *Leviathan*, ch. xxviii.

[13] *Ethical and Political Thinking* (Oxford, 1947), p. 65.

to have a very different attitude towards their penal system when telishment is adjoined to it. They will be uncertain as to whether a convicted man has been punished or telished. They will wonder whether or not they should feel sorry for him. They will wonder whether the same fate won't at any time fall on them. If one pictures how such an institution would actually work, and the enormous risks involved in it, it seems clear that it would serve no useful purpose. A utilitarian justification for this institution is most unlikely.

It happens in general that as one drops off the defining features of punishment one ends up with an institution whose utilitarian justification is highly doubtful. One reason for this is that punishment works like a kind of price system: by altering the prices one has to pay for the performance of actions it supplies a motive for avoiding some actions and doing others. The defining features are essential if punishment is to work in this way; so that an institution which lacks these features, e.g., an institution which is set up to "punish" the innocent, is likely to have about as much point as a price system (if one may call it that) where the prices of things change at random from day to day and one learns the price of something after one has agreed to buy it.[14]

If one is careful to apply the utilitarian principle to the institution which is to authorize particular actions, then there is *less* danger of its justifying too much. Carritt's example gains plausibility by its indefiniteness and by its concentration on the particular case. His argument will only hold if it can be shown that there are utilitarian arguments which justify an institution whose publicly ascertainable offices and powers are such as to permit officials to exercise that kind of discretion in particular cases. But the requirement of having to build the arbitrary features of the particular decision into the institutional practice makes the justification much less likely to go through.

[14] The analogy with the price system suggests an answer to the question how utilitarian considerations insure that punishment is proportional to the offense. It is interesting to note that Sir David Ross, after making the distinction between justifying a penal law and justifying a particular application of it, and after stating that utilitarian considerations have a large place in determining the former, still holds back from accepting the utilitarian justification of punishment on the grounds that justice requires that punishment be proportional to the offense, and that utilitarianism is unable to account for this. Cf. *The Right and the Good,* pp. 61–62. I do not claim that utilitarianism can account for this requirement as Sir David might wish, but it happens, nevertheless, that if utilitarian considerations are followed penalties will be proportional to offenses in this sense: the order of offenses according to seriousness can be paired off with the order of penalties according to severity. Also the absolute level of penalties will be as low as possible. This follows from the assumption that people are rational (i.e., that they are able to take into account the "prices" the state puts on actions), the utilitarian rule that a penal system should provide a motive for preferring the less serious offense, and the principle that punishment as such is an evil. All this was carefully worked out by Bentham in *The Principles of Morals and Legislation,* chs. xiii–xv.

CHARLES L. STEVENSON

Ethical Judgments and Avoidability*

1

In the essay entitled "The Emotive Meaning of Ethical Terms"[1] I have pointed out that ethical statements are used to influence people, that they change or intensify people's attitudes, rather than describe what these attitudes already are. The influence is mediated not by some occult property which the ethical terms mean, but simply by their *emotive* meaning, which fits them for use in suggestion.

In the present essay we must put this analysis to an important test. We must see whether it permits us to make intelligible the relationship between ethical judgments and the "freedom" of the will.

Our question arises from such commonplace instances as the following: A. "You ought not to have done that." B. "But I simply couldn't help it!" It is clear that if A believes B, he will immediately withdraw his ethical judgment. No one feels comfortable about judging a man for actions which he "couldn't help," or which, in other words, he was not "free" to alter. But why? What relation is there between "you ought not to have done it" and "I couldn't help it" which permits the one to be a generally accepted *reason* for rejecting the other? This is our central question. A great part of our attention, however, will be devoted to a preliminary question: What does "I couldn't help it" *mean,* when used to oppose an ethical judgment?

* Charles L. Stevenson, "Ethical Judgments and Avoidability," *Mind,* Vol. 47 (1938). Reprinted by permission of the author and the editor of *Mind.* Printed here is the revised version from Professor Stevenson's *Facts and Values* (New Haven and London: Yale University Press, 1963), pp. 138–152.

[1] *Mind,* Vol. 46 (1937).

2

Instead of the awkward expressions, "I couldn't help it" and "I was not free to do otherwise," it will be more convenient to use the expression "my action was not avoidable." Our preliminary task, then, will be to define the word "avoidable."

Since the main difficulties about avoidability arise when we speak of actions which occurred in the past, we can simplify matters by defining the word for such contexts only. The definition is as follows:

"A's action was avoidable" means *if A had made a certain choice, which in fact he did not make, then his action would not have occurred.*

We shall see that this definition is acceptable, at least in general outline. It is by no means surprising or novel. Hobbes gave the same definition and was partly anticipated by Aristotle.[2] But modern theorists, even though well acquainted with the definition, frequently reject it. It is thought to be relevant and important elsewhere, of course, but of no importance in making clear what sort of avoidability is presupposed by an ethical judgment. Since we shall accept a definition which is often deliberately rejected, we must carefully test it for the ethical contexts here in question to make sure that our departure from current trends of thought is not mistaken.

For example: An army officer has failed to win a battle. His commander tells him that he ought not to have failed. He replies that his failure was

[2] *Leviathan,* pt. 2, ch. 21 (a more detailed discussion will be found in Hobbes' *The Questions Concerning Liberty, Necessity, and Chance*); *Nicomachean Ethics,* bk. 3, ch. 1.

unavoidable. We must determine whether the circumstances under which the commander would accept this reply would be the same, regardless of whether he understood "avoidable" in a common sense way or in accordance with the definition.

Suppose that the officer had been confronted with overwhelming odds. The commander would then acknowledge, in common sense fashion, that the officer's failure was not avoidable. Nor would it be, according to the definition. It is not true, as "avoidability" in the defined sense would require, that if the officer had chosen differently the failure would have been prevented. It would have occurred no matter what the officer had chosen.

Suppose that the failure was due not to overwhelming odds but only to the officer's leading his men into a needlessly exposed position. The commander would then say that the failure was avoidable. And so it would be, according to the definition. For if the officer had chosen differently—if he had chosen to keep his men in a less exposed position—the failure would have been prevented.

Suppose, as before, that the failure was due to the officer's leading his men to a needlessly exposed position. And suppose that the officer insisted, contrary to the commander's contention, that the failure was *not* avoidable, giving the following argument: "I acknowledge that if I had chosen to keep my men away from the exposed position I should have prevented the failure. But I *couldn't choose* to do so. There were causes operating that made me choose just as I did. My choice, my actions, and the resulting failure were an inevitable outcome of natural law. Hence the failure was unavoidable." The commander would not listen for a moment but would dismiss the argument as ridiculous. And so he would be entitled to do, if he used "avoidable" in the defined sense. An "avoidable" action, according to the definition, is one that would not have resulted *if* (contrary to fact) a different choice had been made. Now clearly, what would have resulted if a man had chosen differently has nothing to do with whether or not his actual choice was determined. Similarly, the fact that rivers would have been lower if there had been less rain has nothing to do with whether or not the actual amount of rainfall was determined. According to the definition, then, arguments that seek to prove unavoidability by reference to determinism are to be dismissed as ridiculous, just as the commander would dismiss them.

In these three cases the proposed definition has proved consonant with common usage. There are other examples which will require us to revise the definition, but since these bring in nothing that will invalidate what is immediately to follow, they can be neglected until later on (Section 5).

A more important point now arises. The definition must do more than retain the customary denotation of "avoidable." It must also permit us to answer our central question. It must enable us to explain why avoidable acts alone are open to ethical judgment.

We shall soon see that the definition permits an extremely simple answer to this question. And yet this is generally denied. Theorists have repeatedly objected to the definition on the ground that it makes impossible any answer whatsoever. The objection has in part been anticipated by our army officer, in the last of the above cases, but in order to be safely rid of it, let us summarize it more fully:

"It is utterly beside the point," the objection proceeds, "to speculate about impossibilities. The proposed definition leads us to do this; but if avoidability is to be related to ethical judgments, it must deal only with the results of choices that were *possible,* granted the actual laws and causes that were operating. Suppose that a man's choice and his consequent actions were rigidly determined. He would then be a victim of circumstances, a victim of whatever hereditary and environmental factors produced the choice. It would be absurd to hold him responsible. It would be doubly absurd to "prove" him responsible by pointing out that his action was "avoidable" in the defined sense—by pointing out, in effect, that *if* his heredity and environment had yielded a different choice, his action would not have occurred. This conditional assertion, however true, leaves him no less a victim of circumstances in the *actual* case, hence not responsible, not open to judgment. The definition fails to make the relationship between avoidability and ethical judgments in any way intelligible. Indeed, no definition will succeed in this respect unless it refers to indeterminism; for only acts proceeding from choices that were not causally inevitable can sanely be considered open to judgment."

The last part of this objection is easily refuted. Reference to indeterminism, which the objection considers salutary, will throw no light on the difficulty. If a man's choice was not determined, it was theoretically unpredictable. The man himself could not have foreseen his choice nor taken any steps to prevent it. It would not have sprung from his personality but from nothing at all. He would still be a victim, not of natural forces, but of chance. What room is there here for an ethical judgment?[3]

The more destructive part of the objection is equally at fault. The contrary-to-fact conditions which occur in the definition of "avoidable" are by no means irrelevant. If they seem to be it is because of the confusion that Essay II sought to correct—a confusion about the meaning of ethical terms. The paradox which the objection attributes to the definition of "avoidable" is in fact due to a faulty analysis, tacitly presupposed, of the meanings of "right," "wrong," and "ought." If we dispel this confusion the plausibility of the objection will vanish.

3

Let us recall, then, that ethical judgments have a quasi-imperative force because of their emotive meaning. They influence people's attitudes, rather than describe what these attitudes already are.

Our chief purpose in influencing people's attitudes, obviously enough, is to lead them to *act* in a way which they otherwise would not. We tell a boy that he ought not to eat a green apple in order to keep him from eating it. Our purpose is much the same when we make ethical judgments of something which has already been done. If the boy has eaten the green apple, we tell him that he ought not have done so. We are not, to be sure, trying to do anything about that particular action, which is past and gone. But we are trying to prevent similar actions in the future. The emotive meaning of "ought" greatly assists us. It enables us to build up in the boy an adverse attitude to his act, making him recall it, say, with an unpleasant feeling of guilt. The feeling becomes associated not with the past act alone but with all others like it. It deters the boy from eating any more green apples. (We usually add to our ethical judgment the remark, "see that you don't do it again," and repeat our ethical judgment after the apple has made the boy ill, when his pain makes it easier to build up unpleasant associations with the action. These subsidiary devices, to say nothing of all forms of punishment, serve the same purpose as ethical judgments, although they operate in a different way.)

Other cases are only slightly more complicated. We often make ethical judgments of characters from a novel. By building up in the hearer, through ethical judgments, an adverse attitude to an imaginary character, we prevent the hearer from taking this character as a model for his own subsequent conduct.

When the purpose of modifying actions is not consciously present, it is latent. In other words, if a person is reminded that such a purpose will not be served by the ethical judgment he is making, he will acknowledge that he is wasting his time in making it. (This is not true for certain uses of the ethical terms; but since these have no relation to avoidability, we need not consider them.)

It will be clear, then, that *ethical judgments look mainly to the future.* Even when they are made of past or imaginary acts, they still serve a dynamic purpose—that of discouraging (or encouraging) similar acts later on.

It is precisely here that ethical judgments become related to avoidability. Ethical judgments are used to modify actions of the kind judged. But the kind of action which can be modified in this way is limited. Judgments often induce men to give money to charity but never make men add a cubit to their stature. If we tell a man that he ought to give to charity, our judgment may serve its purpose. If we tell him that he ought to add to his stature, our judgment will not serve its purpose. Since we are unwilling to talk aimlessly we confine our ethical judgments to actions of the first sort, to those which ethical judgments are likely to modify. But only avoidable acts, in the sense defined, are likely to be modified by ethical judgment. Hence only they are judged. Such, in brief, is the answer to our central question.

We must consider more carefully, however, why ethical judgments control avoidable acts

[3] It is not necessary to develop this point, since it has been made time and again by others. For a particularly clear treatment see C. D. Broad, *Determinism, Indeterminism and Libertarianism* (Cambridge, 1934).

alone. Let us return to the example about the army officer:

Suppose that the officer's failure was avoidable—that a different choice of his would have prevented it. From this it follows, granted uniformity of nature, that failure will in fact be prevented, in any future cases of the same sort, if the officer then makes the requisite choice. Of course no future cases will be of exactly the same sort as the past one, but some may be roughly so. It is *probable* that the officer will not fail if he is led to choose differently in these cases. The officer will be led to choose differently, quite possibly, by the quasi-imperative force of the commander's ethical judgment. A judgment of his past failure will make him ashamed of himself and induce him to choose differently in any roughly similar case that may arise. In this way the ethical judgment will diminish the probability of future failures. To generalize: a judgment of an avoidable act is likely to control actions of the kind judged.

Suppose, however, that the failure was unavoidable. By steps of reasoning like those above it follows that failure will probably occur, in future cases of roughly the same sort, even if the officer chooses differently. An ethical judgment will not serve, therefore, to prevent failures. It will exert its influence only through the mediating step of controlling the officer's choice, and this will not be enough. To generalize: a judgment of an unavoidable act will not control actions of the kind judged.

The relation between "you ought not to have done that" and "it was unavoidable" now loses its aura of mystery. The latter statement is recognized as a *reason* for giving up the former because it shows, if true, that the former will not serve its purpose. The relationship is not logical but psychological. It is a psychological fact that people are unwilling to make purposeless ethical judgments.

The following analogy may be helpful: A says, "please open the window." B replies, "I can't; it is built into the window frame." B's statement may properly be called a "reason" which is psychologically related to A's imperative. It leads A to withdraw the imperative as useless in serving any purpose. In a similar way the statement "it was unavoidable" leads a person to stop making an ethical judgment.

These considerations introduce no unusual features into ethical methodology. In the essay "The Emotive Meaning of Ethical Terms" we saw that empirically verifiable reasons, when used to support or oppose an ethical judgment, are always related to the judgment psychologically.[4] This is to be expected. A man uses an ethical judgment in order to exert an influence. He can be "refuted" only by being led to exert a different kind of influence or else to exert no influence at all. Empirical reasons change his beliefs about the consequences or effectiveness of his influence, and in this manner *may* change the kind of influence which he afterwards exerts. Whether or not the reasons will effect this change depends upon the man's temperament. It so happens that men are temperamentally much alike in being unwilling to judge unavoidable actions. The close relationship between avoidability and ethical judgments depends upon this psychological fact.

The answer to our central question has now been given, at least in outline. Very little of it is new. The definition of "avoidable" is a familiar one, and even the explanation of how avoidability is related to ethical judgments is familiar, not in connection with the present problem, but in analogous cases presented by theories of punishment. Preventive and reformatory theories have long made clear that punishment of unavoidable acts serves no purpose. All that has been overlooked is that ethical judgments, being used dynamically, have also a preventive and reformatory function. Theorists have been blinded to this obvious fact by their neglect of emotive meanings.

Let us now digress a little and decide whether ethics need concern itself about the indeterminism of the will.

It is clear that ethical judgments do not presuppose indeterminism. They presuppose only avoidability, which depends solely upon the re-

[4] This generalization may at first seem too broad. If a man said "go away and stay here" we should object to his imperative for a logical reason. May we not object to ethical judgments, then, for a logical reason? Yes, but our reason *would* be logical, not an *empirically verifiable* one logically related to the judgment. It would therefore constitute no exception to the generalization.

There are exceptions, but quite trivial ones. Should a man make some very curious ethical judgment, we might reply, "come, you don't feel so yourself." According to Essay II this would be an empirical reason logically related to the judgment.

sults of choice not upon the absence of its causes.

It would seem, rather, that ethics presupposes determinism. Ethical judgments must control actions through the mediating step of controlling a man's choice. If the man's choice were not determined it would not be controlled in this manner, or in any manner. Ethical judgments would be powerless to influence people's conduct. Is not determinism necessary to provide ethical judgments with any function?

A moment's reflection will show that this is not strictly the case. We must presuppose at least a "partial" determinism but need not necessarily presuppose a "complete" determinism. The meaning of these terms will be clear from the following example: The motion of the sun would be called "partially" determined if, from an exhaustive knowledge of laws and circumstances, we could predict that it would rise tomorrow at some time between five and six o'clock, say, but could not predict more specifically than this. It would be "completely" determined if we could predict that it would rise, say, at exactly five fifteen. Now ethics presupposes only the partial determination of a man's choice, for this still permits his choice to be influenced by an ethical judgment. Our judgment could not lead him to do exactly what we wanted, but it could lead him roughly in that direction.

Partial determinism is a trivial assumption, too obvious to deserve proof. The only point of dispute has been about whether choice is completely determined or only partially so. Since either alternative is compatible with our explanation of how ethical judgments are related to avoidability, we may conclude that the dispute about determinism is irrelevant to ethics, so far as it deals with general presuppositions.

Why have so many theorists *thought* that ethics presupposed indeterminism? One reason, as has been intimated, is that they overlooked the quasi-imperative force of ethical judgments. They did not see that ethical judgments look to the future. Instead, then, of placing the connection between avoidability and ethical judgments in the future—instead of seeing that avoidable acts alone will subsequently be controlled by judgment—they looked to the past for a connection. Quite naturally, they could find an explanation only by making *choice* a mystery, as if it were somehow alterable even when it was irrevocably in the past. Some began to talk of indeterminism, and others, seeing that this really did not help, became unintelligibly metaphysical.

Perhaps an equally important reason for the confusion lies in the emotional state of mind from which ethical judgments proceed. The purpose of modifying actions, which attends an ethical judgment, is usually latent. Our introspectable state of mind may at times be one of indignation, fear, or even blind hatred. These emotions often help us to attain our latent purpose by giving our ethical judgment a forceful spontaneity. If we pause to consider the causes of the act judged, our feelings become stultified. Our ethical judgment becomes less convincing. What we are inclined to do, instead of finding causes, is to invent fictions, which strengthen our feelings by giving them semi-poetic expression. We pretend that the action came, without more remote causal antecedents, from the man we are judging himself. He is "just naturally mean." His conduct has nothing to do with social pressure or an unfortunate childhood. He dimly reminds us of the villain in an old-fashioned melodrama. Fictions of indeterminism, which give our feelings a more ready point of focus, are sometimes indispensable to the effectiveness of our ethical judgment. This may be an important source of error. How easy it would be to confuse these fictions, so prominent in consciousness, with the propositional meaning of the judgment. One might readily be tempted to say that the pre-supposition of indeterminism is found in the very "meaning" of ethical statements themselves. Perhaps theorists have been led in this way to give indeterminism an entirely unwarranted importance. . . .

5

Several deliberate oversimplifications were made in Sections 2 and 3 which must now be corrected. The main simplification occurs in the definition of "avoidable." Let us see, by example, how the definition must be changed.

Suppose that our army officer would have prevented the failure only if he had given his men vigorous encouragement. He would not have had sufficient energy to encourage them unless he had had an extremely strong desire to do so. He would not, at the time, have had so strong a desire. Under these circumstances we should have to acknowledge, according to the definition, that the failure was "unavoidable." The officer would not have prevented it merely by *choosing* to encourage his men. He would have needed, as well, a strong desire to succeed in doing so, which he would not have had. A different choice alone would have been unavailing. And yet, although the failure was "unavoidable" according to our definition, it would not be called so by the commander, who would find no occasion for withholding ethical judgment.

In order to be more conventional the definition must be given as follows: "A's action was avoidable" has the same meaning as "if A had chosen a certain different alternative, and if he had had a particularly strong interest in bringing about what he chose, then his action would have been prevented." ("Interest" is here used, following R. B. Perry, to mean any kind of desire, aversion, etc.)

This new definition leaves the relationship between avoidability and ethical judgments essentially the same. In the above example the commander sees that failure may not occur in the future, other circumstances being roughly similar, if he can make the officer have a stronger desire to encourage his men. The commander's ethical judgment will serve to build up such a desire. It is likely to serve its purpose of preventing future failures.

We may now correct an unsound assumption made in Section 3. The main contention there was that avoidable acts alone are judged because they alone may be controlled by judgment. This required the assumption that ethical judgments control actions only through the mediating step of controlling a man's choice, for "avoidable" was then defined in terms of *choice* only. But at present "avoidable" is defined with reference to interests as well as choice. Hence we may replace the unsound assumption by the correct one: Ethical judgments control actions not only by modifying a man's choice, but in a more general way by intensifying his interests.

The definition of "avoidable" is still too simple, however, as may be seen from the following example:

A man is progressively becoming addicted to opium. At first we say that his taking it is "avoidable," but as he grows more and more addicted to it, we say that it is "less and less avoidable," until at last we say that it is "unavoidable." Our definition fails to provide a meaning for "less avoidable." It fails further in requiring us to say that the man's taking opium never becomes "unavoidable"; for at any time it remains the case that if he chose to stop, and desired to with *enough* strength, he would stop.

The definition is easily qualified: The stronger a man's interest must be in order to prevent the action, the "less avoidable" his action becomes. When it must be extremely strong the action ceases to be called "avoidable." These qualifications complicate our problem only very slightly. The less avoidable a man's action is, the more difficult it is for us to build up his interest in a way that would modify the action. Hence we parallel the decreasing avoidability by becoming increasingly more hesitant to make an ethical judgment. A low degree of avoidability becomes unavoidability when the intensity of the required interest becomes greater than any which our ethical judgment can build up. Judgment of avoidable acts still depends upon the probability of controlling the acts by judgment.

The example of the opium user raises a further question: If his action was avoidable, just when must the choice and interest have had to occur in order to have prevented it? Immediately before the action, or at *any previous* time? If we place no restriction on the time (and the definition does not) then his taking opium *was* avoidable even when he was in the last stages of the habit; for if he had chosen to stop taking it from the very beginning, even with a very slight interest in stopping, he would not have taken it thereafter.

The following qualification will suffice: When the conditions that existed at the time when the choice and interest would have prevented the action, and that were essential no less than the choice and interest in preventing the action, were of a sort that will not even roughly occur again, then the action is not called "avoidable." This obviously takes care of the above case. The opium user will never again be at the beginning stages of his habit if he is now in the last stages. The reasons for suspending judgment are equally obvious. If the beginning stages will not recur, and if they, no less than the effects of ethical judgment, will be essential to prevent his action, then his action cannot be controlled by ethical judgment.

We must next consider some more complicated cases. A man is sometimes excused from ethical judgment, though by no means always, because of his ignorance. If the failure of our army officer, for instance, would have been prevented by a certain choice, but if he had no reason to forsee that it would, even on the basis of excellent knowledge of the circumstances confronting him, his commander would probably make no adverse ethical judgment.

We need not trouble to decide whether this case requires us to revise the definition. It will be sufficient to see why the officer would not be judged. This is clear enough. A judgment would spur the officer on to make some change in his later procedure. The only significant change that he could make would be to acquire more knowledge thereafter. A judgment of the failure, then, would be tantamount, so far as its effective imperative force is concerned, to the judgment "you ought not to have been so ignorant." By hypothesis, however, the officer had taken great care in acquiring knowledge. Perhaps a certain amount of ignorance was unavoidable (in the sense as above qualified). Perhaps it was avoidable only to a low degree. Perhaps it was "avoidable only at too great a cost." (In other words, if the officer had taken steps to acquire more knowledge, he would have had to neglect something else and hence would have brought on even greater disaster.) For any of these reasons[5] the commander might suspend judgment of the failure. Judgment would make no desired change.

We have been assuming throughout that ethical judgments have no other purpose than to control actions of the kind judged. It is important to note that there are many exceptions to this. For example: A, whose social position is rivaled by that of B, makes many adverse ethical judgments of B's actions whenever he is talking to B's friends. His purpose is not to control these actions but rather to increase his own prestige by decreasing that of his rival. In general, an ethical judgment of a man's actions may be used to alter the man's social position. As in the preceding cases, however, such judgments usually serve no purpose when the actions judged are unavoidable. A will not induce B's friends to give B's social position to someone else unless someone else would have acted in a way more to their liking. If B's actions were unavoidable this would *usually* not be the case.

Yet the matter is not always so simple. Suppose B has become so strongly addicted to alcohol that his taking it is now unavoidable. A might then judge B's conduct, and with effect, even though the conduct was unavoidable. The reason is clear. A's judgment will be tantamount in its imperative force to the combined judgment and reason "we ought not to give B a pre-eminent social position because he is a drunkard." In this form the judgment is of an avoidable act (our giving B a pre-eminent social position) and has the purpose of controlling actions of the kind judged. The latter judgment is not strictly identical with the former; hence the former constitutes a genuine exception to our previous account. But the reader will doubtless see for himself how a perfectly accurate account would have to proceed.

A final remark is pertinent, to summarize and extend what has been in question throughout the essay. We have asked the question "why, as a matter of fact, are ethical judgments commonly limited to avoidable acts?" We have found that this is because ethical judgments of unavoidable acts would serve no purpose. Apart from definitions our inquiry has been psychological. We have not asked the question "*ought* ethical judgments to be limited to avoidable acts?" This is an entirely different question. It is an ethical question, not a psychological question relevant to ethics.

In order to distinguish the latter question from

[5] The last of the reasons I have mentioned is more interesting than it may seem, for it reminds us of an ambiguity. If we temporarily use "avoidable-I" to preserve the sense discussed above, we may describe the ambiguity as one arising from the possibility of using the term "avoidable-II," where to say that an action is unavoidable-II is a way of saying that it is avoidable-I but only at too great a cost.

Suppose, for instance, that a man became ill and consequently broke an appointment with a friend. Was his breaking the appointment unavoidable? It may have been avoidable-I, since he could perhaps have kept the appointment in spite of his illness. But even so the man may say, and honestly, that his breaking the appointment was unavoidable—i.e. unavoidable-II, and thus avoidable but only at too great a cost.

The example can be related to the withholding of blame in this way. What was unavoidable-I, we may assume, was a situation in which the man had either to break the appointment or to endanger his health quite seriously. Given these alternatives he chose what he considered the lesser evil. And his friend withholds blame, presumably, not because the man's *breaking the appointment* was unavoidable-I, but because he feels that the man, given the alternatives open to him, *should* have broken the appointment rather than endanger his health. We have in the end, then, a case where blame is withheld from a perfectly obvious reason: the man is felt to have done nothing wrong.

the former, it may be well briefly to answer it. I answer, without hesitation, that ethical judgments *ought* to be so limited. It must be understood that this statement is essentially persuasive. I use it in order to influence people to disapprove of judging unavoidable acts. My purpose is to induce people to *continue* to judge avoidable acts alone, as they now usually do. In order to make my influence permanent I shall have to support it by reasons. The main reason is this: judgments of unavoidable acts do not serve their purpose. It so happens, in this case, that the causal explanation of why people now do restrict their judgments to avoidable acts, and the reason why they ought to, coincide. Perhaps this reason will be insufficient to make permanent my influence. Perhaps the reader has very curious purposes or approves of acting in a purposeless fashion. I should then have to point out other matters of fact, which might more successfully direct his approval in the way I wish. But I trust that in the present case this will not be necessary.

D A V I D B R A Y B R O O K E

Professor Stevenson, Voltaire, and the Case of Admiral Byng*

I

In one of the later and less discussed chapters of *Ethics and Language,*[1] Professor Stevenson offers a plausible explanation of our normal practice of withholding moral judgments in cases of unavoidable actions. He maintains that the reason why we do not normally make moral judgments in such cases is that they will not be effective in controlling anyone's future conduct, either the agent's or our audience's or our own. Stevenson recognizes that we sometimes do pronounce judgments on unavoidable actions; but in these instances the judgments, he says, are merely impulsive; they "do no more than symptomize the speaker's blind emotions."[2] Moreover, Stevenson regards these instances as "relatively infrequent";[3] he thinks that habit restricts most people most of the time to making moral judgments only when there is a possibility of their being useful in the control of someone's future conduct.

Although this is a plausible theory, I do not think that it is a correct one; and while I don't have any argument that will knock down Stevenson's position, I think that I can set it tottering. Stevenson's conception of the function of ethical discourse (which he has done so much to illuminate) is in important respects defective; and I think that the present topic reveals a major point of inadequacy more clearly than any other.

To illustrate the ineffectiveness of making moral judgments of unavoidable actions (and likewise of unavoidable failures to act), Stevenson invites us to consider the case of an army officer who has failed to win an engagement. If the officer's failure was avoidable, then, Stevenson holds, his commander can expect to achieve something by censuring him. For the commander's "judgment of the officer's past failure will

* David Braybrooke, "Professor Stevenson, Voltaire, and the Case of Admiral Byng," Parts I and IV, *Journal of Philosophy*, LIII (1956), 787–792, 795–796. Reprinted by permission of the author and the *Journal of Philosophy*.

[1] Chap. XIV (pp. 298–318): "Avoidability; Indeterminism." [A development of the earlier essay of Stevenson's that is included here.]

[2] *Ibid.*, p. 308.

[3] *Ibid.*, p. 308.

make the officer ashamed of himself, and induce him to modify his choice in any roughly similar case that may arise. To generalize: a judgment of an avoidable act is likely to control actions of the kind judged."[4]

If the failure was unavoidable, however, "the officer having been confronted with overwhelming odds," then "an ethical judgment will *not* serve to prevent subsequent failure."[5] A wise commander will refrain from judgment, since judgment would not help control the future actions either of the defeated officer or of other subordinates. "The precedent established by judging an *un*avoidable act would carry over, for the most part, to *other* unavoidable acts. It would be an *ineffective* warning to the rest of his officers, terrifying them about matters which they were powerless to control."[6] If the defeated officer keeps his head in the face of such a rebuke, and does not let indignation sway him, the humiliation that he has suffered "would scarcely lead him to resign his commission; for knowing that the failure was unavoidable, he would have little or no reason to suppose that his successor could do better in preventing failures, and so would find resignation pointless."[7]

The naïveté of this last remark is rather touching. Stevenson clearly thinks better of his fellow men, including his hypothetical commander, than they ordinarily deserve. If the junior officer has no reason to expect that the commander will reform and in the future pronounce moral judgments only on Stevensonian principles, would it not be prudent for him to resign now, or get himself transferred, before by some bad chance he has another unavoidable failure and suffers worse disgrace?

Even if there are visible signs that the commander will henceforth refrain from judgment in cases where pronouncing judgments would be ineffective in controlling anyone's future conduct—which would be one way of living up to Stevensonian standards—it does not follow that the junior officer has no reason to dread his commander's judgment of some further unavoidable failure. For is it not mere unconsidered moral optimism to suppose, as Stevenson does, that unjust judgments are ineffective ones? A shrewd and unscrupulous commander might follow a deliberate policy of rebuking and punishing his subordinates for *all* failures, avoidable or not.

We may recall the case of Admiral Byng, about which Voltaire was so generously excited two hundred years ago. Byng had commanded the British fleet in an engagement with the French off Minorca in the year 1756; and, though he had not been defeated, he had not, in the opinion of the English public and his superiors, kept up the fight long enough, and the French fleet had therefore escaped. Byng was brought home and court-martialed; for "failing to do his utmost against the enemy," condemned to death; and shot, in spite of the pleas of many persons, among them the Duc de Richelieu, who had commanded the French army on Minorca and who was persuaded to intervene by the initiative of Voltaire. There is an ironic description of Byng's execution in Chapter 23 of *Candide*, which includes the famous line, "Dans ce pays-ci il est bon de tuer de temps en temps un amiral pour encourager les autres."[8]

The motives of Byng's judges, and of the King, who refused him pardon, were no doubt very complicated. But it does not seem in the least fantastic to suggest that among them was the thought that this savage punishment would cause other commanders to redouble their efforts to avoid failures. In other words, Voltaire's comment may not have been merely ironical; it may have been (even if only inadvertently) descriptive. And the policy described may have had definite chances of success. Is it not very possible that a man will strive harder to avoid failure if he knows that no excuse will be accepted for not succeeding?

Another instance of former British naval justice, slightly earlier than the case of Byng, suggests even more clearly that a policy of accepting no excuses for failures was sometimes practiced specifically in regard to unavoidable actions. In 1745 the Royal Navy had made an example of Baker Philipps, a young officer who had been so unlucky as to be left in command of a defeated ship. Philipps had been second lieutenant in the 44-gun ship *Anglesea*. On patrol the 29th of March, 1744, an approaching ship was sighted;

[4] P. 303.
[5] P. 304.
[6] P. 306.
[7] P. 306.

[8] A thorough account of Byng's misfortunes is given in Julian S. Corbett, *England in the Seven Years' War*, London, 1907, Vol. I, Chap. V.

the captain of the *Anglesea* judged that it was English and went below to dine. He was wrong. The ship was not English, it was French—the 60-gun *Apollon*—and it came up and poured a broadside into the *Anglesea* from a distance of less than a hundred yards. Surprised, and badly damaged, the *Anglesea* could not return an effective fire of its own. The *Apollon* fired a second crushing broadside, which killed the captain and the master of the *Anglesea*. Since the first lieutenant had been left ashore sick, Philipps was now in command; and seeing that further defense of the ship was hopeless, he surrendered it.

When he returned to England in an exchange of prisoners, Philipps was very harshly dealt with; he was court-martialed and executed for "neglect of duty." It was generally felt that he had been done an injustice; but the admirals may have thought that his disgrace and death would be a salutary lesson to other junior officers notwithstanding.[9]

I agree with Stevenson that an adverse ethical judgment addressed to the man whose action is judged is a sort of punishment, and may have the preventive and reformative uses of other sorts of punishment.[10] But it is at least possible that other sorts of punishment, even the most drastic, are effective in controlling future conduct when they are imposed for unavoidable actions; and I think it is also possible that adverse ethical judgments might be effective in the same circumstances: conceivably, they might be made deliberately, "pour encourager les autres."

Capital punishment, inflicted for an unavoidable action, may well seem so outrageous a penalty that most people would perhaps be reluctant to admit that it could be anything but self-defeating. Certainly one can readily imagine situations in which it would not stimulate officers to be more efficient and aggressive, or result in fewer ships surrendered, but instead so demoralize an officer corps as to incapacitate it for action of any kind. However, there are other situations in which the general intimidation and demoralization of subordinates may be precisely the effect wanted by the authorities; there are, after all, despotic societies as well as democratic ones. If we consider the amazing adaptability that human beings have demonstrated in such intensely despotic societies as those temporarily established in concentration camps, or the success obtained by the rulers of the Soviet Union with a system of punishment that evidently few men escape once they are accused of a lapse, however substantial their excuse, we shall not, I think, find the question of effectiveness so obvious, even for the most drastic punishments. I am not arguing that people are made happier or society more harmonious by inflicting drastic punishments for unavoidable actions; I am merely suggesting that there may be circumstances in which such punishments will successfully reduce the frequency of acts that are not wanted by the policy-makers and increase the frequency of acts that are wanted.[11]

Whether or not drastic punishments would be effective in controlling future conduct if they are imposed for unavoidable actions, milder punishments might be; and this possibility suffices for my argument. It is fairly standard practice in the Army to allow no excuses at all for minor putative lapses: late returning from pass; absence from formation; dirty equipment; etc. Of course, men are not shot for these things; though they used to be beaten. Working on similar principles, a Dean of Women who accepted no excuses from girls who failed to return to their dormitory by midnight might have many fewer cases of lateness to deal with than a more tolerant and popular person.

[9] Philipps' case is referred to in the *Britannica* article on Byng; for a succinct account of it see the article on Philipps in *The Dictionary of National Biography*.

[10] Stevenson, *op. cit.*, p. 307. Moral judgments like other punishments may be *just* or *unjust*. The phrase, "an adverse ethical judgment addressed to the man whose action is judged," might serve as a definition of a "reprimand," which is clearly, and in the United States Army even officially, a variety of punishment. (Of course we can blame people or disapprove of their actions without *telling* anyone; and judgments that we make but keep to ourselves are not punishments.)

[11] A society may be politically stable and economically productive without being either happy or harmonious. It has sometimes been said of the Soviet system, which persists in spite of frequent changes in its administrative elite, that in contrast to comfortable bourgeois societies it offers more people a chance to exercise power, though it denies them any security of tenure; while in bourgeois societies, promotion is slower, and most capable people never rise above relatively very subordinate jobs. Systematic insecurity in the jobs just below the highest has for the rulers of the Soviet Union the special advantage of preventing the formation of a continuous organized opposition. On this point, *cf.* Hannah Arendt, *The Origins of Totalitarianism*, New York, 1951, pp. 408–409.

In the use of any system of rewards and punishments we may suppose that the social authorities wish to encourage certain kinds of conduct and to discourage certain other kinds. Now, they may choose to punish all actions of a given sort, whether or not the action was in any particular case avoidable.[12] For instance, they may cause to be punished all cases of one man's being on another's property without the owner's explicit previous permission. Such a policy may have variable effects upon the frequency of trespass; upon respect shown for private property in other connections; upon general law-abidingness. Is it not a real question whether this policy, which might be said to risk injustice with the hope of reducing crime, would be less effective in encouraging the sort of conduct the authorities wished to encourage than an alternative policy, which perhaps risked crime in order to reduce injustice?

Of course it is a real question; and it is an empirical question, which I cannot pretend to decide *a priori.* Stevenson's position involves a number of empirical questions that neither he nor I can settle without producing a great deal of carefully elaborated factual evidence. Where is Stevenson's evidence? As far as I can see, he has not collected any; and therefore his confidence that he has solved the problem why we do not normally make moral judgments of unavoidable actions is, I think, premature. . . .

IV

My arguments on this apparently small and specialized topic do not reach the main body of Stevenson's doctrine; nor are they intended to. Stevenson teaches that the locutions of ethical discourse have only two properties generally in common: they are instruments for controlling future conduct; and they are simultaneously outlets for feelings or attitudes. I think this a useful and correct doctrine so far as it goes. But it is a doctrine that is easily distorted by prejudices (in other connections very laudable) that like Stevenson's favor calm and reasonable detachment in the practice of ethics; for this doctrine combined with these prejudices may easily lead to the position, to which they lead Stevenson, that the only rational consideration governing the use of ethical judgments is their efficiency in controlling future conduct. The offense that limitation to this consideration alone would give to our sense of justice fails to force itself upon Stevenson's attention because the same prejudices lead him to assume a world and society in which, apart from occasional lapses into "blind emotion," men can usually be counted upon to make ethical judgments calmly and reasonably, avoiding the resentments and reproaches of injustice if they can; a world, moreover, in which men never react to judgments that are unjust because they imply responsibility for unavoidable actions by conforming their future conduct more closely to the desires of their judges.

Let us call ethical judgments of actions that are not themselves instances of making ethical judgments "normative"; and ethical judgments of actions that *are* instances of making ethical judgments "bi-normative." Stevenson explicitly disavows, in *Ethics and Language,* any pretensions to "*judging* ethical methods" himself, and this is a perfectly proper restriction to impose on his work. But the conventions that govern normative judgments do fall within Stevenson's chosen subject-matter; and these cannot be accurately described if the role of bi-normative judgments in their formation is disregarded. Efficiency is not the only consideration in the use of ethical judgments, any more than it is the only consideration in our use of rewards and punishments generally. It is subordinate in the practice of conscientious judges to bi-normative considerations; and just as we shall not (as I think) understand what reasons lead men to withhold ethical judgments in cases of unavoidable actions, so we may expect that our conception of the nature and functioning of ethical discourse will not be adequate, until we have looked into the bi-normative consideration of *justice.*

[12] I am assuming that the action can be described as belonging to a sort of action that is sometimes avoidable and sometimes not. . . .

ELIZABETH L. BEARDSLEY

Determinism and Moral Perspectives*

Can determinists find a satisfactory rationale for moral praise and blame? On this question, determinists themselves have long been divided. Although the affirmative answer has enjoyed the status of a majority opinion, the negative answer has at times found very effective support. The force of the negative answer emerges clearly in certain recent writings, in which writers sympathetic to determinism vigorously defend the thesis that determinism removes from the concepts of moral praiseworthiness and blameworthiness all legitimate application whatsoever.[1]

The negative answer to the question posed here is unsatisfactory, I think; but in some ways it is preferable to the affirmative answer as the latter is usually given and supported. In this paper, I shall argue that judgments of moral praise and blame, affirmative as well as negative, can be made within the framework of determinism, provided that we accept a more complex account of these judgments and their foundations than is ordinarily supplied or assumed. I shall maintain that judgments concerning the presence or absence of moral praiseworthiness and blameworthiness are made from several different standpoints, which I shall call "moral perspectives." My primary purpose is to show how an understanding of these perspectives and their relations can contribute substantially toward relieving the tension widely felt (even by some who are reluctant to admit it) to exist between determinism and certain of our basic ethical concepts.

The terms "praise" and "blame" will be used here with the meaning of "moral praise" and "moral blame." Praise and blame will be treated as correlative concepts such that, for everything that is said about one, a corresponding statement about the other could be made, though it will usually be unnecessary to make it. The term "affirmative judgment of praise" will be used to refer to any explicit attribution of praiseworthiness to a person. A "negative judgment of praise" is an explicit denial that a person is praiseworthy. The general term "judgment of praise" will refer indifferently to either an affirmative or a negative judgment of praise, and similarly for "judgment of blame." Judgments of praise and blame will be treated here as assertions which are true or false, and not as acts which may be useful or useless to perform.

DETERMINIST VIEWS OF PRAISE AND BLAME

Before discussing judgments of praise and blame, it will be helpful to consider briefly cer-

* Elizabeth L. Beardsley, "Determinism and Moral Perspectives," *Philosophy and Phenomenological Research,* XXI, (1960), 1–20. Reprinted with permission.

[1] See Paul Edwards, "Hard and Soft Determinism," and John Hospers, "What Means This Freedom?", both in Sidney Hook, *Determinism and Freedom* (New York University Press, 1958); also W. I. Matson, "On the Irrelevance of Free-will to Moral Responsibility," *Mind,* Vol. LXV (1956), pp. 489–497. Although these writers frame their argument more explicitly in terms of the concept of moral responsibility than in terms of moral praiseworthiness and blameworthiness, the application to the latter concepts is clear. Matson's chief thesis, that libertarianism can validate the concept of moral responsibility no more successfully than determinism can, will not be dealt with in the present paper; the part of his article which bears most directly on what I shall have to say is found in sections 2 and 3.

tain moral judgments of a different kind. The standpoint from which we affirm or deny that acts are objectively right or wrong I shall call the "perspective of objective rightness or wrongness." A judgment of objective rightness or wrongness is a judgment made about an act, not an agent; and it does not carry with it any implication about the praiseworthiness or blameworthiness of an agent. Statements like "Smith's act was objectively right, but he deserves no praise for it" not only are self-consistent, but are often true; objectively right acts can be committed inadvertently, or from reprehensible motives.

The judgment that an act is objectively right furnishes insufficient evidence for a judgment that its agent is praiseworthy, because certain key facts concerning the causal antecedents of the right act remain to be supplied. The objective rightness or wrongness of an act does not depend in any way on its causal antecedents, but on other considerations, such as its consequences (for teleologists), or its harmony with the will of God, moral rules, or the like (for formalists). It is therefore appropriate to call this perspective a "non-causal" one, for it takes no account of whether an act had causal antecedents of one kind rather than another, or indeed had completely determining causal antecedents at all.

Most philosophers, I think, would agree that the use of the moral perspective of objective rightness or wrongness presents no particular problem for the determinist. It is true that certain libertarians have apparently seen something profoundly incongruous in the application of any normative predicates at all to the constituent parts of a determined universe; but this line of thought has persuaded so few that it may be disregarded.

Much less harmony prevails among philosophers who have reflected on the relation between determinism and the concepts of moral praise and blame. Libertarians, of course, maintain that because the truth of determinism would invalidate affirmative judgments of praise and blame, determinism is false, and criteria for praiseworthiness and blameworthiness must include the requirement that an agent should have performed his act "freely." Though determinists are united in rejecting the conclusion of the libertarian argument as false, they differ sharply concerning the acceptability of the conditional premise.

Among leading determinists who believe that valid affirmative judgments of praise and blame can be made, a fairly clear account of the criteria for praiseworthiness and blameworthiness seems to have emerged. I shall call those who subscribe to this account "Group I determinists." Details of the account vary, but a substantial area of agreement remains. It is commonly held that if an agent has acted wrongly, without external constraint ("voluntarily"), without ignorance of relevant facts, and from a motive or because of a trait that is undesirable, then, and only then, the agent deserves blame for his act.[2] Similar conditions are held to govern praiseworthiness.[3]

Group I determinists deny that there is anything here to conflict with the truth of determinism. They point out that those who make judgments of praise and blame must indeed attend to several key factors among the causal conditions that produced the acts whose agents are judged. But any *other* causal conditions that may have been present, and, in particular, antecedents of antecedents, are to be completely disregarded. Moral praisers and blamers, on this view, are simply not concerned with the nature, or even the existence, of such additional factors. Determinism is thus fully compatible with attributions of praiseworthiness and blameworthiness.[4]

To determinists of a second group—"Group II determinists"—this account seems seriously oversimplified.[5] They contend that the same reasoning which leads us to withhold praise and blame from agents whose acts were committed involuntarily will, when combined with the thesis of determinism, lead on inexorably to the conclu-

[2] I have found the presentation of this general position by P. H. Nowell-Smith in *Ethics* (London, 1954), particularly helpful here.

[3] Note that the terms "blameworthy" and "praiseworthy" have not been defined here and that no definitions of these terms will be offered in this paper.

[4] Many would argue, of course, that determinism is much more than merely "compatible" with these judgments, since we cannot speak of an agent's act as "his" act or as arising "from" a motive or trait, unless determinism is assumed to be true. This argument will be deliberately set aside here.

[5] My distinction between "Group I" and "Group II" determinism is plainly very similar to Edwards' distinction between "soft" and "hard" determinism. See Edwards, *op. cit.*, and also Edwards and Pap, *A Modern Introduction to Philosophy* (Free Press, 1957), p. 380.

sion that no one ever deserves praise or blame for anything. They are haunted by the knowledge that many of the causal antecedents of acts have not been investigated by those who mete out praise and blame on the grounds specified above; and most particularly they are haunted by the knowledge that not all of the causal antecedents of voluntary acts are voluntary acts. Thus they come to believe that no distinction between "voluntary" and "involuntary" acts that a determinist can consistently make can sustain the moral weight that it must bear if we are to judge men praiseworthy or blameworthy. How, they ask, could we ever be justified in blaming or praising someone for a voluntary act and not an involuntary one, when we know full well that even the voluntary act can be traced back to causes—environmental or hereditary—belonging to a world the agent never made?

I believe that there are elements of truth in each of these brands of determinism, and I shall try to show that this is the case.

THE PERSPECTIVE OF MORAL WORTH

Surely there is no doubt that the conditions for praiseworthiness and blameworthiness set forth in the Group I determinist's account do in fact constitute one important and familiar standard according to which we make judgments of praise and blame. It is highly convenient to introduce a special term for the characteristic of moral value that may be said to belong to an agent who has performed an act that meets the conditions specified. I shall say that an agent has "positive moral worth" if and only if he has acted rightly, voluntarily, with knowledge of relevant facts, and from a desire that is bad in its situation.[6] The term "moral worth" will be used to refer to either positive or negative moral worth indifferently, and the standard by which agents are judged to have moral worth (positive or negative) will be called the "standard of moral worth." Elsewhere[7] I have discussed certain features of the concept of moral worth in some detail, and have indicated how conditions for the presence of degrees of moral worth may be set up.

A "judgment of moral worth," which may be affirmative or negative, is a judgment in which moral worth is asserted to be present or absent. We must of course distinguish between a negative judgment of positive moral worth ("Agent A is not morally worthy for act A") and an affirmative judgment of negative moral worth ("Agent Y is morally unworthy for his act B").

I shall call the standpoint from which we make judgments of moral worth the "perspective of moral worth." This is plainly not a wholly non-causal perspective, as is the perspective of objective rightness or wrongness. Because *some* (a strictly limited set) of the circumstances causally relevant to the performance of an act are taken into account when the moral worth of its agent is being judged, this perspective may accurately be called a "causally limited" perspective. The factors taken into account in making judgments from this moral perspective will be termed the "worth-determining" factors.

Group II determinists are likely to feel that the introduction of the term "moral worth" is unobjectionable, and perhaps even useful, provided that judgments of moral worth are not held to imply judgments of praise or blame. Thinkers of this group may be disposed to admit that human beings do indeed have a strong psychological tendency to experience positive feelings when confronted by the gestalt agent-performing-act-under-conditions-for-positive-moral-worth, and to experience negative feelings when confronted by the corresponding negative gestalt. They may contend that, since these feelings cannot be rationally justified, human beings had better try to eliminate them from their psyches as soon as possible. The fact that there is no reason to believe that this has ever been accomplished is not likely to daunt them. In any case, the important point, for the Group II determinist, is that we should avoid the confusion of believing that persons who happen to form part of the pleasant or unpleasant gestalts just mentioned deserve praise or blame for what they do. Because the crucial distinction between voluntary and involuntary acts is bound to collapse in the end, no

[6] I prefer to formulate this last condition in terms of a "desire" rather than of a "trait," because we sometimes make judgments of this kind without having sufficient evidence to ascertain the presence of a trait; but this point is not of central importance here.

[7] "Moral Worth and Moral Credit," *The Philosophical Review,* Vol. LXVI (1957), pp. 304–328. In the present treatment I have left the term "moral worth" undefined, and I have also introduced it here to refer to an attribute of agents who are praiseworthy or blameworthy *for* acts rather than to refer to an attribute of acts themselves.

one ever deserves praise or blame. Perhaps judgments of praise and blame *are* made from the perspective of moral worth, but they *should* not be.[8]

To this the Group I determinist will reply that, since the conditions for "moral worth" were originally taken directly from an analysis of conditions for praiseworthiness and blameworthiness, it is highly arbitrary, to say the very least, to attempt to purge judgments of moral worth of all association with judgments of praise and blame. Moreover, he will continue, the assertion that human beings have "feelings" which are merely "positive" or "negative," when they encounter persons exhibiting positive or negative moral worth, is decidedly misleading. The "feelings" referred to consists of definite reactions of a specific sort, to which are added, for most moral judges, quite explicit reflective convictions. Human beings feel—and reserve—a very special kind of approval and disapproval for those members of their species who perform acts that have certain salient features. Furthermore, the majority of those who have reflected on the matter seem to have been convinced that approval and disapproval of this special kind are reactions to which the persons in question have a morally justified claim. It is this claim which is put forth in affirmative judgments of praise and blame. In view of these considerations, a heavy burden of proof rests on the Group II determinist, who proposes to eliminate from moral discourse all affirmative judgments of praise and blame. This burden, the Group I determinist charges, has not been effectively sustained.

The Group I determinist will go on to admit readily that, among those features which an act must have if its agent is to merit praise or blame, the requirement that it be voluntary is indeed crucial. But, he will say, to establish voluntariness we need examine only certain of the immediate causal ancestors of an act.[9] Considerations about more remote causal forebears are as irrelevant here as information about a man's grandparents would be if proffered in reply to a query about his parents. Therefore it is the case, not only that we *do* make judgments of praise and blame from the perspective of moral worth, but that this procedure is entirely legitimate, and is not threatened by determinism. Thus, concludes the Group I determinist, the problem of praise and blame has been solved.

The Group I determinist may seem, on the face of it, to have had the better of the argument in the exchange just described. He is right, I think, in maintaining that judgments of praise and blame, affirmative as well as negative, have an extremely strong claim to be retained in moral discourse. He is right, also, in insisting that the distinction between voluntary and involuntary acts which is needed for affirmative judgments of praise and blame can be made by determinists. Finally, he is right in holding that what has been called here the "standard of moral worth" is the standard on which many affirmative and negative judgments of praise and blame are based.

Where the Group I determinist is wrong is in his tacit assumption that *all* judgments of moral praise and blame are made from the perspective of moral worth, and that when a man has been judged praiseworthy or blameworthy from this perspective there is nothing more to say about his moral claim to be praised or blamed for the act under consideration. The truth, as I shall go on to try to show, is much less simple than this. There is indeed a network of causes stretching out in all directions, far beyond the worth-determining factors on which the Group I determinists so resolutely fix their minds. Moreover, these other causal factors are by no means without moral significance. We cannot hope to set up a genuinely effective defense against the Group II determinist's harsh view of what that significance is, unless some other way of doing justice to these additional causal factors can be found.

THE PERSPECTIVE OF MORAL CREDIT

I want now to examine a second moral perspective from which we appraise agents. It is

[8] It is convenient to speak of the point at issue between the Group I and Group II determinists as concerned primarily with the validity of *affirmative* judgments of praise and blame; and I occasionally do this. But it should be understood that the Group II determinist in fact equally denies the validity of any *negative* judgment of praise (or blame) which is made with the assumption that the class of persons who deserve praise (or blame) is not vacuous.

[9] If it should be said that so-called "voluntary" acts are not *really* voluntary after all, the Group I determinist would reply in the fashion of Flew, in the latter's discussion of the expression "acting freely." See A. Flew, "Divine Omnipotence and Human Freedom," in Flew and Macintyre, *New Essays in Philosophical Theology* (Macmillan, 1955), pp. 149–151.

necessary to explain the operation of this perspective somewhat more fully than was the case for moral worth, because it has received little attention from ethical theorists.

When we examine our affirmative and negative judgments of praise and blame, we find that many are made by the standard of moral worth; but we also find, I think, that many are not. A second standard of appraisal often comes into operation after a judgment based on moral worth has been made, when we go on to ask further questions about the individual situation of an agent who has performed an act for which he is judged morally worthy or unworthy. Here individual circumstances which facilitated or hampered the performance of the act are taken into account. What we do, that is, is to investigate factors which made the performance of a certain act by a certain agent particularly "easy" or "difficult" for *him*. On the basis of this information, a further judgment of praise or blame is made.

How do we ascertain that the performance of act A by agent X was "easy" or "difficult"? Not by endeavoring to estimate the intensity of his subjective feelings of effort. What is needed here is an objective correlate;[10] and this, I think, is provided by the concept of circumstances *favorable* or *unfavorable* to the performance of a certain act, i.e., circumstances in whose presence the performance of such an act is either more or less likely to occur than it is in their absence. Given that an act is one for which its agent has positive or negative moral worth, a judgment is made to the effect that the balance of known circumstances causally relevant to the performance of that act was favorable or unfavorable. We try to decide, that is, whether, in view of all the things we know about him, it was antecedently probable that a certain act should have been performed by its agent. If an agent has performed an act for which he has positive moral worth, and if it was antecedently improbable that he should have performed this act, then he is praiseworthy by our new standard as well as by the standard of moral worth. We say that such an act was performed "in spite of obstacles" or "against odds." Similar remarks, of course, could be made regarding blameworthiness as judged by this new standard; and it is convenient at times, though somewhat unidiomatic, to speak of an act for which an agent is morally unworthy and which was antecedently improbable as having also been performed "against odds."

To those who deny that the performance against odds of an act for which the agent is morally worthy or unworthy earns for that agent special praise or blame the only answer can be an invitation to look again, more closely, at the moral appraisals we all make. Evidence confirming the view defended here can be found on all sides. For example, it was maintained not long ago by Auxiliary Bishop Joseph M. Marling of the Roman Catholic Church that the presence of severe neurosis in certain Catholic saints could be admitted, since it not only did not detract from their saintliness, but actually contributed to it, in that a neurosis constitutes a serious obstacle to the achivement of spiritual perfection.[11]

There are strong reasons, I think, for maintaining that the criteria for moral appraisals now being examined constitute a standard separate and distinct from the standard of moral worth. The alternative "single-standard" view (the belief that both sets of criteria can be combined into one complex standard) appears to be widely, though casually, held; but I think it is mistaken. My reasons for this conclusion have been given elsewhere.[12]

By our second standard, then, an agent X is praiseworthy for his act A to some degree if and only if: (1) X has positive moral worth to some degree for A, and (2) X's situation at the time of performing A included among the known circumstances a preponderance or balance of circumstances (other than the amount of "effort" put forth by the agent) which are reasonably judged to be unfavorable to the performance of the act. Similar conditions govern the presence of blameworthiness as judged by this second standard. Agents who perform acts under the conditions for praiseworthiness just specified will be said to have "positive moral credit" for their acts. Like moral worth, moral credit may be present in either a positive or a negative form. A "judgment

[10] There will not, however, be an exact correlation between felt intensity of effort and the criterion proposed.

[11] See *Time*, Vol. LXVIII (August 27, 1956), for an account of an address by Auxiliary Bishop Joseph M. Marling of Kansas City, Mo., to the Guild of Catholic Psychiatrists.

[12] E. L. Beardsley, *op. cit.*, especially pp. 309–315.

of moral credit" is an assertion or denial that an agent possesses positive or negative moral credit.[13]

The moral perspective from which judgments of moral credit are made may be called the "perspective of moral credit," and judgments of praise and blame based on the moral credit standard may also be said to be made from this perspective. In order to judge from the perspective of moral credit, we investigate the causal antecedents of an act more extensively than is done for judgments made from the perspective of moral worth. Any instance of any kind of factor which can reasonably be judged to be an unfavorable or favorable circumstance for a given kind of act is potentially a "credit-determining" factor for any agent performing an act of that kind, even though in common practice, to be sure, not all potential credit-determining factors are investigated before judgments are made. The perspective of moral credit, accordingly, may be called a "causally extended" perspective, as compared with our causally limited perspective of moral worth, and our noncausal perspective of objective rightness or wrongness.

Judgments made from the perspective of moral credit supplement judgments made from the perspective of moral worth. They do not supplant them, any more than judgments about the objective rightness or wrongness of acts are supplanted by judgments about the moral worth of their agents. The latter are selfcontained judgments, perfectly satisfactory and significant in their own right. Nevertheless, the perspective of moral credit does set limits to the perspective of moral worth, in that it is important for those who make judgments by the moral worth standard to remember that such judgments do not give us the whole moral truth about an agent. Even when we do not actually go on to ascertain the moral credit-rating of an agent to whom we ascribe positive or negative moral worth, we must bear in mind that further questions along such lines *could* be asked. Judgments of praise and blame made from the perspective of moral worth will be made less dogmatically, with less show of finality, by those who understand that there is another moral perspective from which an individual can be judged. But those who make judgments from the perspective of moral credit must not forget the importance of the perspective of moral worth. Judges who constantly focus their attention on the "ease" or "difficulty" with which something was accomplished need to be reminded at times, to look at the quality of the moral accomplishment itself. Neither of these two moral perspectives can be said to be superior to the other.

It seems clear that the use of the perspective of moral credit is fully compatible with determinism.[14] And the identification of this new standpoint of moral appraisal as a separate moral perspective lends needed strength to the philosophical position of determinism, principally by revealing it to be less dogmatic and impersonal than it is often taken to be. In a more detailed treatment of these matters, the advantages to determinism of recognizing judgments of praise and blame based on moral credit could be explained more fully.

In the end, however, the convinced Group II determinist will always reply that the effort to set up a perspective of moral credit cannot salvage judgments of praise and blame. He will maintain that judgments of praise and blame based on moral credit are ultimately no more compatible with determinism than are judgments of praise and blame based on moral worth.[15] As before, he may look tolerantly, or even benevolently, on the procedure of setting up a "perspective of moral credit," just so long as judgments of praise and blame are kept out of the picture. Again his reaction springs from his awareness of additional causal factors, this time of causal factors lying behind those taken into account from the perspective of moral credit. The Group II determinist will say that, although those who make judgments based on moral credit may make extensive inquiries into the factors causally relevant to hu-

[13] See *ibid.* for a detailed discussion of the concept of moral credit and its relation to moral worth. Here I leave "moral credit" undefined, and use it to refer to an attribute of agents rather than of acts.

[14] It may be said, I think correctly, that the account of moral credit given here actually presupposes a determinist position, since reliable causal generalizations about human behavior underlie the estimates of probability on which judgments of moral credit, in large part, depend.

[15] I disregard here the fact that the Group II determinist would also say that the perspective of moral credit inherits what he takes to be the deficiencies of the perspective of moral worth, since judgments of moral worth are presupposed by judgments of moral credit.

man acts, sooner or later, because of the limits of time or energy or human knowledge, they must bring their investigations to a close. And when they do, they will not have told the whole causal story; and the part that will remain untold will invalidate judgments of praise and blame made from this moral perspective.

I believe that this charge can be answered, but I want to show first how it might be supported. Let us consider a comparison between two individuals, Jones and Smith. Jones has performed an act having a high degree of positive moral worth in spite of very unfavorable circumstances, whereas Smith, confronted by essentially the same kind of circumstances and placed in a very similar situation, has performed an act having a much lower degree of positive moral worth. It is clear that Jones possesses a higher degree of positive moral credit for his act than does Smith for his,[16] since the circumstances and situation constitute greater obstacles for Jones' act than for Smith's.

Now, no matter how strong our psychological tendency to feel a greater admiration for the achievement of Jones, such an attitude, the Group II determinist would claim, is not justifiable. For moral credit is ascribed on the basis of finding that a preponderance of the *known* circumstances in an agent's situation was unfavorable to the performance of a given act. Judgments of moral credit deal with acts whose performance was improbable; nevertheless, they deal with acts that *were* performed, events that *happened*. If determinism is true, these happenings were caused. Therefore for each act for which an agent possesses moral credit there must exist also a cluster of one or more unknown circumstances causally relevant to the performance of the act, and a preponderance of *these* circumstances must have been favorable, rather than unfavorable. It is all very well, then, to judge that Jones performed under great odds an act for which he is morally worthy; but such a judgment is superficial and unstable. For, if determinism is true, these vaunted "odds" disappear upon examination; and Jones is seen to have done only what the causal factors in his situation, unknown as well as known, brought forth. So did Smith, and so do we all. How then can praise and blame by the standard of moral credit be justified?

It is evident that this reasoning is too cogent to be set aside. At the close of the preceding section, it was asserted that the causal factors not dealt with in judgments of moral worth were nevertheless morally significant, and would have to be taken care of in some other way. Many of these "left-over" causal factors have now been shown to provide a basis for judgments of praise and blame made from a second moral perspective, the perspective of moral credit. But the Group II determinist now reminds us that behind even the credit-determining factors lie still others, and that these too have a moral significance that cannot be lightly dismissed. His interpretation of the moral significance of this most distant range of causal factors is, as we have seen, simply that they invalidate all affirmative judgments of praise and blame. In the remainder of this paper, I shall try to show that another interpretation is possible, and that it is to be preferred.

THE PERSPECTIVE OF ULTIMATE MORAL EQUALITY

In the course of our discussion, we have now sorted out three groups of factors causally relevant to human behavior: worth-determining factors, credit-determining factors, and what may be called "ultimate" causal factors, which are simply those factors that are left out of account when we make judgments based on moral worth and moral credit. If determinism is true, we may be said to know, for any given act, *that* there are ultimate causal factors. But we do not know *what* they are: if we did know they would take their place among the potential credit-determining factors for the act in question. It is strange that this shadowy group of unknown circumstances should be morally so significant; but I think that there is no doubt that their moral significance is real.

When we are mindful of the existence of the ultimate causal factors, we look at human beings and their acts in a special way. This was brought out by the example of Jones and Smith. When we look at persons in this special way, they are seen to be equals, as far as their claims to moral praise and blame are concerned, or, rather, they are seen to have passed beyond any point at

[16] On degrees of praiseworthiness by the standard of moral credit, see E. L. Beardsley, *op. cit.*, p. 319.

which discriminations of praiseworthiness or blameworthiness are applicable. Seen in this way, all men are members of a moral or spiritual democracy. This is a realm lying behind our distinctions of moral worth and moral credit, a realm in which each is simply the person he is. When we take into account the full range of factors causally relevant to human acts, we must regard human beings as a flock without goats and without sheep.

I propose to say that this special way of looking at persons, in the light of the existence of ultimate causal factors for their behavior, constitutes another moral perspective. This I shall call the "perspective of ultimate moral equality." From this perspective we look at persons and their acts in the widest possible causal contexts, contexts without limits of any kind. Therefore we may call this a "causally unlimited" perspective. As a moral perspective it is, of course, strikingly different in some respects from the others that we have examined. Judgments made from the perspective of moral worth and the perspective of moral credit are judgments of discrimination. This is obvious in the case of comparative judgments, but it is also true of noncomparative ones. Our interest in knowing that X possesses positive moral worth for his honest act, and Y negative moral credit for his cowardly one, stems in large part from the fact that there are honest acts whose agents do not possess positive moral worth, and cowardly acts whose agents earn no negative moral credit. Judgments of praise and blame based on moral worth and moral credit are answers to questions which can in principle be answered either affirmatively or negatively.

This is not true of judgments made from the perspective of ultimate moral equality. Here all are on the same moral footing: none has any ultimate claim to praise or blame, and the judgments made from this perspective are all negative. No matter what acts a person has performed, all that we can say of him from this final moral perspective is that he deserves no praise for what he has done, or that he deserves no blame.

The statement "X is not ultimately praiseworthy for A" is a negative judgment of praise made from the perspective of ultimate moral equality, whereas "Y is not ultimately blameworthy for B" is a negative judgment of blame made from the same perspective. Judgments of praise and blame made from this perspective will here be limited in scope to persons whose acts have earned for them moral worth or moral credit. That is to say, the statement "X is not ultimately praiseworthy for A" will be permissible if and only if A is an act for which X possesses either positive moral worth or positive moral credit. And the truth-condition for this statement can be stated very briefly: the statement is true if and only if A has ultimate causes. Similarly, "Y is not ultimately blameworthy for B" is permissible if and only if B is an act for which Y possesses negative moral worth or negative moral credit, and true if and only if B has ultimate causes.

But, if determinism is true, we know of any event that it has ultimate causes, and we know this without any specific investigation. The behavior of all men is causally determined, and the nature of what we have called the "ultimate" causes is equally unknown in each case. This eradication of all distinctions in the causal status of acts erases all distinctions in the moral status of their agents. Therefore in one way it can never be news that Brown does not ultimately deserve praise for his kind deed, or that Robinson does not ultimately deserve blame for his unkind one.

In another way, however, these assertions *are* news, and important news. The fact that Brown and Robinson are ultimately moral equals is a vital part of the whole moral truth about them. Compare the situation for a factual account.[17] In factual descriptions of human beings we are interested in the qualities in which they differ, to be sure; but we are also interested in the qualities in which they are alike. For some purposes, and in some contexts, the similarities may be legitimately disregarded; but this does not mean that they can always be left out of account. Sometimes they are more significant than the differences, and they are never more significant than they become when we are in danger of assuming that the differences tell the whole factual story. So it is with moral appraisals of human beings. For the whole moral story, judgments of praise

[17] By this manner of speaking I do not mean to rule out the possibility that a naturalistic account of the meaning of basic ethical terms can be given.

and blame based on moral worth and moral credit need to be supplemented by judgments made from the perspective of ultimate moral equality.

Because this is true, we are justified in regarding the perspective of ultimate moral equality as a genuinely "moral" perspective, even though it eradicates moral discriminations. The knowledge that when persons are viewed in relation to the ultimate causal factors of their behavior moral discriminations no longer apply to them is a piece of moral knowledge, at least in being knowledge about moral matters. It is curious that as we go from a causally limited perspective to a causally extended one we increase our power to make moral discriminations, whereas when we come to a causally unlimited perspective these moral discriminations stop altogether. But the knowledge that this is so is moral knowledge, and it has important bearings on the rest of our moral knowledge.

The relation that holds between the perspective of ultimate moral equality and the other moral perspectives from which judgments of praise and blame are made is analogous in certain ways to the relation between the perspective of moral credit and that of moral worth. Judgments based on moral credit, as we have seen, set limits to judgments based on moral worth. Similarly, the knowledge that human beings can be viewed from a perspective which will show them to be morally equal will remind those who make judgments based on moral worth and moral credit that these judgments of moral inequality do not tell the whole story about the individuals being judged. This knowledge, in turn, will affect the attitudes of those who have it: they will regard themselves and each other with more tolerance than before. Feelings of admiration, contempt, guilt, and pride, will all be experienced more moderately by those who know that no man is ever the *first* cause of evil or good deeds, or *finally* responsible for winning or losing when confronted by moral odds. But this is not to say that such feelings will not be experienced at all, or that they should not be.

For the perspective of ultimate moral equality cannot give us the whole truth about the praiseworthiness and blameworthiness of human beings either. The fact that X has negative moral worth for his act, or that Y has positive moral credit for his, is not cancelled by saying that X does not ultimately deserve blame, or that Y does not ultimately deserve praise. We value in a special way those whose acts meet the standards of moral worth and moral credit, and this is something that we cannot change. As Spinoza saw, it is true—even in a determined universe—that "we desire to form for ourselves an idea of man upon which we may look as a model of human nature."[18] The idea of a man who performs a right act voluntarily, knowingly, and from a good desire, and the idea of a man who, when confronted by odds, can still do these things—these *are* the models we have formed. Conformity to these patterns is what we regard as worthy of praise, and deviation from them in certain ways is what we regard as worthy of blame. We cannot feel about persons who thus conform or deviate as we do about animals or inanimate objects which measure up or fail to measure up to certain other standards. All this being so, judgments of praise and blame based on moral worth and moral credit are not only legitimate but vitally necessary parts of moral discourse. They are answers to questions that we cannot help asking.

The full moral truth about a man and his act, then, might run as follows: that he deserves a low degree of praise for it by the standard of moral worth, a high degree of praise for it by the standard of moral credit, and ultimately no praise for it when he is judged from the perspective of ultimate moral equality. There is no reason why the three statements cannot be true simultaneously. Also, these perspectives seem to be genuinely coordinate, and complementary: we need them all. And, if we distinguish between moral perspectives, we shall be able to avoid the doubling of metaphysical perspectives which Kant found necessary in order to reconcile causality and morality. It is easier to regard a man as blameworthy from one point of view but not from another than to say that his act is both caused and uncaused.

The acquiring of moral wisdom, at least as far as moral appraisals are concerned, does not consist only in learning how to make sound judgments from each moral perspective. It consists

[18] B. Spinoza, *Ethics* (Oxford Press, 4th ed., 1930), p. 179.

also in learning under what circumstances each of the moral perspectives should be used—a large and fundamental problem that cannot be dealt with here.[19] Here let us note only that most of the questions about the praiseworthiness and blameworthiness of human beings that are actually asked are questions to which the appropriate answer is a judgment based on moral worth or one based on moral credit. Writers on ethics[20] have pointed out that we feel something peculiarly objectionable in an attempt by a wrongdoer to exculpate himself on the ground that all his acts were caused and therefore he deserves no blame. Here an inquiry into his blameworthiness is launched from one moral perspective and a reply is made from another. But moral perspectives, however coordinate, are certainly not interchangeable. Questions about praiseworthiness or blameworthiness should be answered from the perspective from which they are asked, whenever it is possible to tell what this is. Sometimes it will be appropriate, and even very desirable, to add to this answer a judgment made from another moral perspective; but often it will not be. Particular caution must be exercised in advancing judgments made from the perspective of ultimate moral equality. These are illuminating, and even inspiring, when made in the right context, and by those who know how to make accurate discriminations by the standards of moral worth and moral credit. Otherwise they are apt to seem shallow, and somehow sentimental, or cheap.[21]

SOME OBJECTIONS AND REPLIES

The account which has been given of the perspective of ultimate moral equality and its relation to our other perspectives of praise and blame seems likely to arouse objections from all sides. Three of these appear to me to be particularly striking, and in this concluding section I shall try to reply briefly to each one in turn.

(1) The first objection that I shall consider is one that will be raised by Group II determinists. Some of what has been said in the preceding will presumably be acceptable to members of this group; but they will want to know how it can be maintained that the perspective of ultimate moral equality is merely *one* of several perspectives from which agents are appraised. It is rather *the* moral perspective, which, because of its special nature, invalidates all others. It is superior to the others because it is broader in its scope. This is the only perspective that is causally unlimited, the only one from which we view acts in the context of *all* their causes, unknown as well as known. And since we are seeing more broadly, it follows that we are seeing more accurately.

The answer here must be that it is not clear that this does follow. Do we see "better" from a height that takes in a large part of the surrounding territory? The only reply can be "Yes and no." Details which are not seen from a height spring back into view when we climb back down and look at objects in the context of a smaller part of their surroundings; and things which looked alike from above manifest striking differences when seen from a position farther down. In this case, one standpoint does not reveal the "real nature" of the objects better than another one does.

But we must not be lured into pressing our optical metaphor of "perspectives" too far. In any case, the Group II determinist may wish to support his basic contention—that the perspective of ultimate moral equality has a privileged status—in another way. He may claim that it will be impossible, psychologically, for those who have viewed persons from the perspective of ultimate moral equality to go on making the same old judgments of praise and blame from other perspectives. How, he will ask, can we throw ourselves into the task of sorting the worthy from the unworthy, the creditable from the discreditable, when we know that from another stand-

[19] One important question to consider in this connection is whether it is ever justifiable to employ the perspective of ultimate moral equality when thinking of one's own future acts and their moral status. Some reflections which bear on this question (though they are not expressed in the language of the present paper) are offered by H. Fingarette in his interesting article "Psychoanalytic Perspectives on Moral Guilt and Responsibility: a Re-Evaluation," *Philosophy and Phenomenological Research,* Vol. XVI (1955–1956), pp. 18–29.

[20] See, for example, Nowell-Smith, *op. cit.,* pp. 297–300.

[21] Judgments made from the perspective of ultimate moral equality are most effective when directed to individuals whose moral credit has been ascertained, as well as their moral worth. If we go directly from the perspective of moral worth to the perspective of ultimate moral equality without passing through the perspective of moral credit, it appears that something important has been left out.

point these distinctions will disappear altogether? Will not the view from every perspective but that of ultimate moral equality take on the aspect of something unreal, a mirage without power to deceive for more than a moment?

Part of the answer here is that we cannot, indeed, make moral discriminations in exactly the "same old" way, and that we cannot "throw ourselves" into the sorting and grading processes with quite the zeal of those who have never seen human beings as ultimate moral equals. The difference, however, will be in the quality and intensity of the emotions accompanying judgments of praise and blame based on moral worth and moral credit. The judgments themselves will go on being made; human acts will go on being looked at in causal contexts of varying scope. Our models of human nature, in short, will go on being used. To see whether it is psychologically possible to return from the perspective of ultimate moral perspectives, no determinist needs to look farther than his own experience. It is in truth not possible to do anything else.

(2) A second objection is likely to be raised by certain libertarians. It is the charge that our so-called "perspective of ultimate moral equality" is ignoble and degrading. Such a perspective, it will be said, affords a particularly deplorable example of the levelling tendency which seeks to destroy standards of merit in all areas. Plato's charge against political democracy—that it makes equals of unequals—applies a thousandfold to the "moral democracy" that is claimed to be visible from this distorting perspective. The moral world is hierarchical to the core; to remove the sheep and the goats from the moral landscape is to destroy it. So runs this second charge.

The answer to it divides into two parts. The first point to be made is that moral discriminations have not been permanently eradicated. Viewed from the other moral perspectives (which, as we have seen, are not eliminated by the perspective of ultimate moral equality), the moral landscape swims back into our ken with sheep and goats intact. Morevoer, it is sometimes more appropriate to look at the moral world in this way.

But some will feel that this part of the answer is not enough: that it is wrong *ever* to see all persons as moral equals. Now even though one may be deeply convinced that the perspective of ultimate moral equality, far from being ignoble, is—when appropriately used—exalted and inspiring, it is not altogether easy to know how to argue for this conviction. One may point to the increase in compassion, tolerance, equanimity, that come to those who know how to look at themselves and each other on occasion from the perspective of ultimate moral equality. But it may conceivably be said in reply that these are regarded as benefits only by persons who are antecedently convinced that determinism is, as a matter of fact, true. This reply is not without force. That portion of Spinoza's defense of determinism which shows "what service to our own lives a knowledge of this doctrine is" has not lost its power to move determinists; but what power do his words have over others? If all our acts go back to ultimate causes, then we should indeed look at all human beings with compassion and tolerance; but what if they do not? Libertarians may contend that compassion and tolerance are not spiritual goods if these attitudes are directed toward humans who, because they have misused their freedom, simply do not deserve to be pitied or tolerated. And equanimity in the face of moral iniquity is nothing but extreme moral callousness, particularly unforgivable, it will be said, when the wrongdoer is oneself.

It may prove impossible to disabuse some extreme libertarians of their conviction that human beings should never be regarded as being all morally equal. But it is hard to believe that most people, whatever their metaphysical beliefs, will not find something to which they can respond positively in the attitudes engendered by the perspective of ultimate moral equality. The making of all our judgments of praise and blame with less finality, less assurance that they represent the whole truth, must seem to many an end to be welcomed.[22] Religious teachings which have kept before our eyes the view from something like the perspective of ultimate moral equality ("There but for the grace of God go I") have performed a great service for our moral outlook.[23]

[22] This end is particularly desirable for those more sweeping judgments in which persons are praised or blamed, not for specified acts, but for their whole characters. Space limitations have precluded the consideration of such judgments here; but their treatment forms an important part of a more detailed examination of moral perspectives.

[23] Note that, even though the grace of God may be

(3) Finally, I want to take note of the contention—in which those of all metaphysical persuasions will doubtless heartily concur—that this account of praise and blame is simply too complicated to be acceptable. How could the average unspeculative mortal ever find his way among such a bewildering variety of moral perspectives? How could he ever make a judgment of praise or blame?

In reply to these questions, two points must be made. First, a single moral judgment arrived at from a single moral perspective is not necessarily made more complicated by the present account than by other accounts.[24] But, secondly, it must be admitted that difficulties do arise when a moral judge is asked to remember that other moral perspectives exist and set limits to the one that he is using at any given time, and when he is asked, as he sometimes must be, to decide on the moral perspective that should be used in a particular situation. We have seen that moral wisdom, on the present view, consists not merely in the ability to make correct moral appraisals from a single perspective, but also in the ability to correlate the perspectives, and, on occasion, to choose among them.

It may well be that few attain this kind of wisdom, yet it is by no means clear that it cannot be attained by unspeculative persons. Perhaps such persons can and do make concrete judgments of moral praise and blame in a balanced and large-minded way, keeping the various relevant considerations in due proportion, and governing their own attitudes accordingly, despite a lack of any grasp of a theoretical basis for what they are doing. But, if it should turn out that we cannot really evade the conclusion that the present account makes moral wisdom harder for an unspeculative person to attain, this conclusion would not necessarily vitiate the account. Why should it not be the case that moral wisdom demands considerable resources of intellect as well as of character?

In this paper, I have been arguing that the question with which we began, "Can determinists find a rationale for moral praise and blame?", can be answered affirmatively. I have tried to show, however, that the unrecognized assumption behind the typical and influential affirmative answers that have been given—the assumption that judgments of praise and blame are made from a single moral perspective—is mistaken. I have maintained that those determinists who give a negative answer to our original question have caught sight of some important truths that the others have missed. In the end, however, with their attempts to set up the perspective of ultimate moral equality as the sole valid perspective for judgments of praise and blame, they have fallen into the same fundamental error as the others. One group eternally confronts the other with the question "How can you deny that human beings can be said to be praiseworthy and blameworthy, in view of the fact that they commit acts that are right or wrong, and at the same time done voluntarily, knowingly, and from good or bad desires?" To which the second group incessantly hurls back a question of its own: "How can you assert that human beings can be said to be praiseworthy or blameworthy, in view of the fact that their acts, like all other events, are wholly subject to causal laws, and must be traced back, in the end, to factors wholly beyond the agents' control?" The account given here, which may be called the "theory of multiple moral perspectives," is designed to help put an end to this durable impasse. I have tried to show that the first group is speaking from the perspective of moral worth, while the second replies from the perspective of ultimate moral equality. Both perspectives are valid; but each perspective is incomplete.

Three moral perspectives are necessary, I have contended, if we are to tell the whole about the praiseworthiness and blameworthiness of human beings. One of these, the perspective of ultimate moral equality, takes form as a consequence of assuming determinism to be true; but its adoption is not without moral and spiritual benefits.

---

regarded as being "freely" given, in so far as it is held to constitute a causal determinant of human action, it is treated as essentially similar to what have here been called "ultimate causes." Of considerable interest for further study would be a comparison of the perspective of ultimate moral equality—here described in purely naturalistic terms—with such religious concepts as "equality in the sight of God."

[24] Indeed, the distinction between moral worth and moral credit makes it possible to give a simpler account of the judgments made by each standard than the account which proponents of the single standard view would have to give if their position were adequately worked out.

The other perspectives can be exhibited in an examination of judgments of praise and blame conducted quite independently of any determinist assumptions; and we can then see that determinism is—at the very least—fully compatible with the use of these moral perspectives. It seems to me that considerable work remains to be done in clarifying and refining these concepts and principles, and in exploring their implications in many directions. But if the claims made here are in essentials justified, it follows that determinists need not feel that old familiar uneasiness when confronted by the concepts of moral praise and blame. On the contrary, it may be that we stand here on solid ground.

PART 6 SELF-LOVE AND

Suppose you find a wallet containing $5,000 in cash. Surely the morally right thing to do (at least according to the prevailing moral code) would be to return it to its owner. But would this truly be the most reasonable course of action? Think of what you have to gain: an expression of gratitude, some small satisfaction at having done your duty (mixed with nagging doubts that you are a fool), and *maybe* a small reward. Now compare these benefits with what you have to lose—namely, the $5,000 itself—and it would seem that the losses involved in doing your "duty" (if that's what it is) far outweigh the gains. (Perhaps the example might be still more convincing if the money belonged not to a private person but to a great corporation or the federal government.) Now, looking at the matter in this way, wouldn't you be a fool to return the money? Isn't it *unreasonable,* indeed profoundly contrary to reason, voluntarily to choose a loss in preference to a gain for oneself? And yet this is what morality seems continually to require of us: that we put the interests of other people ahead of our own. How, then, can it be reasonable to be moral?

One line of reply to this challenge immediately suggests itself. Not to return the property of others is tantamount to stealing it. If other people ever were to find out that you are, in effect, a thief, their opinion of you (to put it mildly) would drop drastically, and your reputation might never fully recover. Moreover, if the authorities were to make this discovery about you, the consequences might be still worse. Of course, chances are good that no one would ever find out, but even so, you would have to live in continued anxiety and fear; and even if you got over that, you might become just a bit bolder in the face of subsequent temptations, until finally your very success betrays you, and you are found out. The idea that it ever can *pay* to do what is morally wrong, in short, is always a miscalculation.

Glaucon and Adeimantus, two characters in Plato's dialogue *The Republic,* are not satisfied with this kind of answer. That there are advantages in having the reputation of being moral and upright (or "just" as they would put it) is perfectly

THE CLAIMS OF MORALITY

evident; what they wish to learn from Socrates is whether there are corresponding advantages in really being, as opposed to merely seeming, morally upright. If it is reasonable to be honest only *because* dishonesty doesn't pay, then, it would seem, it is reasonable to be honest only *when* dishonesty doesn't pay; and the ideally wise man would be he who is able to have the "best of both worlds," by seeming, but not really being, moral. Socrates' answer to the challenge of Glaucon and Adeimantus is developed in considerable detail in *The Republic,* and is too long to be included here. It is given an accurate summary, however, in the first selection from the historian W. E. H. Lecky (1838–1903), though without its elaborate supporting argument.

Much of the literature of moral philosophy, from Plato's *Republic* to the present, consists of arguments designed to show that there is a necessary and invariant connection between duty and self-interest. Many of the greatest moralists have found it unthinkable that it could ever truly profit a man in the long run to be immoral. Whatever else morality may be, these writers argue, it must be something reasonable. Yet surely, they go on, it cannot be reasonable deliberately to act contrary to one's own interest. Hence, it follows that the dictates of morality (assumed to be reasonable) never do require sacrifice of self-interest, appearances to the contrary. Many of the great systems of moral theory, then, are designed to account for this conclusion.

The Oxford moralist H. A. Prichard (1871–1947), in the selection included here, argues that this traditional philosophical undertaking is misguided and unnecessary. There can be only one theoretical motive, he believes, for insisting, in the teeth of common sense, that morality always pays, and that is the conviction, which he thinks Socrates shares with the Sophists, that a desire for one's own happiness or well-being is, ultimately, the only human motive. If no normal person can be moved to do anything except by an appeal to his own good, then men can be induced to act morally only by being persuaded that it is not contrary to their true interests to do so, that their interests and the claims of morality necessarily coincide. Prichard (whose views, incidentally, fall neatly under Lecky's fourth heading) rejects this theory of human motivation, and is able therefore to hold that it is both possible and reasonable to do the right thing, even on those occasions when there is nothing to be gained—or even a great deal to be lost—by doing so.

The theory that human beings are so constituted by nature that they are incapable of desiring or pursuing anything but their own well-being as an end in itself is called *psychological egoism.* Genuinely disinterested acts of benevolence, on this view, do not exist, although persons sometimes appear to be acting unselfishly when they take the interests of other people to be means to the promotion of their own good. This theory of motivation should be distinguished from the doctrine called *ethical egoism,* which, as its name indicates, is not a theory about how men in fact act, but rather a moral doctrine stating how they ought to act. One ought to pursue one's own well-being, it urges, and only one's own well-being, as an end in itself. One might expect that any *psychological* egoist, insofar as he bothered with ethics at all, would be an *ethical* egoist, for if there is only one thing we *can* pursue, it can hardly be true that there is some other thing we *ought* to pursue. Most psychological egoists, however, have sought some way to reconcile necessarily selfish motivation with the unselfish and even self-sacrificing conduct required by morality. Human beings were to Bernard Mandeville (1670–1733) incorrigibly greedy, conceited, and vainglorious; yet these very vices can be motives, he argued, for the noblest conduct. "The moral virtues," he concludes, "are the political offspring which flattery begot upon pride."

Psychological egoism is represented in this section by Mandeville's bold essay and also by the doctrines of various Seventeenth and Eighteenth Century writers summarized in the second selection from Lecky. The Eleventh Sermon of Bishop Joseph Butler (1692–1752) is often said to be the definitive refutation of psychological egoism (yet Butler is no more friendly to the view that self-interest and duty must, or even often, conflict), and the brief but incisive selections from Austin Duncan-Jones, of the University of Birmingham, England, and the late Frank C. Sharp of the University of Wisconsin, expose subtle errors commonly committed in arguments *for* psychological egoism. Brian Medlin, of the University of Queensland, Australia, while skeptical of the power of reason generally to prove or disprove ultimate ethical principles, claims that one form of ethical egoism (that "everyone should look after his own interests regardless of the interests of others") can be conclusively refuted. W. D. Falk, of the University of North Carolina, is by no means an ethical egoist, but his eloquent essay argues that purely self-regarding directives must be included in the list of valid precepts by which the man of moral wisdom lives his life.

PLATO

The Immoralists' Challenge*

With these words I was thinking that I had made an end of the discussion; but the end, in truth, proved to be only a beginning. For Glaucon, who is always the most pugnacious of men, was dissatisfied at Thrasymachus' retirement; he wanted to have the battle out. So he said to me: Socrates, do you wish really to persuade us, or only to seem to have persuaded us, that to be just is always better than to be unjust?

Steph.

Socrates, Glaucon.

I should wish really to persuade you, I replied, if I could.

Then you certainly have not succeeded. Let me ask you now:—How would you arrange goods—are there not some which we welcome for their own sakes, and independently of their consequences, as, for example, harmless pleasures and enjoyments, which delight us at the time, although nothing follows from them?

The threefold division of goods.

I agree in thinking that there is such a class, I replied.

Is there not also a second class of goods, such as knowledge, sight, health, which are desirable not only in themelves, but also for their results?

Certainly, I said.

And would you not recognize a third class, such as gymnastic, and the care of the sick, and the physician's art; also the various ways of money-making—these do us good but we regard them as disagreeable; and no one would choose them for their own sakes, but only for the sake of some reward or result which flows from them?

There is, I said, this third class also. But why do you ask?

Because I want to know in which of the three classes you would place justice?

In the highest class, I replied,—among those goods which he who would be happy desires both for their own sake and for the sake of their results.

Then the many are of another mind; they think that justice is to be reckoned in the troublesome class, among goods which are to be pursued for the sake of rewards and of reputation, but in themselves are disagreeable and rather to be avoided.

I know, I said, that this is their manner of thinking, and that this was the thesis which Thrasymachus was maintaining just now, when he censured justice and praised injustice. But I am too stupid to be convinced by him.

I wish, he said, that you would hear me as well as him, and then I shall see whether you and I agree. For Thrasymachus seems to me, like a snake, to have been charmed by your voice sooner than he ought to have been; but to my mind the nature of justice and injustice have not yet been made clear. Setting aside their rewards and results, I want to know what they are in themselves, and how they inwardly work in the soul. If you please, then, I will revive the argument of Thrasymachus. And first I will speak of the nature and origin of justice according to the common view of them. Secondly, I will show that all men who practise justice do so against their will, of necessity, but not as a good. And thirdly, I will argue that there is reason in this view, for the life of the unjust is after all better far than the life of the just—if what they say is true, Socrates, since I myself am not of their opinion. But still I acknowledge that I am perplexed when I hear the voices of Thrasymachus and myriads of others dinning in my ears; and, on the other hand, I have never yet

Three heads of the argument:—1. The nature of justice: 2. Justice a necessity, but not a good: 3. The reasonableness of this notion.

* From Plato, *The Republic*, ii. 357A–367E, trans. B. Jowett.

heard the superiority of justice to injustice maintained by any one in a satisfactory way. I want to hear justice praised in respect of itself; then I shall be satisfied, and you are the person from whom I think that I am most likely to hear this; and therefore I will praise the unjust life to the utmost of my power, and my manner of speaking will indicate the manner in which I desire to hear you too praising justice and censuring injustice. Will you say whether you approve of my proposal?

Indeed I do; nor can I imagine any theme about which a man of sense would oftener wish to converse.

I am delighted, he replied, to hear you say so, and shall begin by speaking, as I proposed, of the nature and origin of justice.

Justice a compromise between doing and suffering evil.

They say that to do injustice is, by nature, good; to suffer injustice, evil; but that the evil is greater than the good. And so when men have both done and suffered injustice and have had experience of both, not being able to avoid the one and obtain the other, they think that they had better agree among themselves to have neither; hence there arise laws and mutual covenants; and that which is ordained by law is termed by them lawful and just. This they affirm to be the origin and nature of justice;—it is a mean or compromise, between the best of all, which is to do injustice and not be punished, and the worst of all, which is to suffer injustice without the power of retaliation; and justice, being at a middle point between the two, is tolerated not as a good, but as the lesser evil, and honoured by reason of the inability of men to do injustice. For no man who is worthy to be called a man would ever submit to such an agreement if he were able to resist; he would be mad if he did. Such is the received account, Socrates, of the nature and origin of justice.

Glaucon.

Now that those who practise justice do so involuntarily and because they have not the power to be unjust will best appear if we imagine something of this kind: having given both to the just and the unjust power to do what they will, let us watch and see whither desire will lead them; then we shall discover in the very act the just and unjust man to be proceeding along the same road, following their interest, which all natures deem to be their good, and are only diverted into the path of justice by the force of law. The liberty which we are supposing may be most completely given to them in the form of such a power as is said to have been possessed by Gyges the ancestor of Croesus the Lydian.

The story of Gyges.

According to the tradition, Gyges was a shepherd in the service of the king of Lydia; there was a great storm, and an earthquake made an opening in the earth at the place where he was feeding his flock. Amazed at the sight, he descended into the opening, where, among other marvels, he beheld a hollow brazen horse, having doors, at which he stooping and looking in saw a dead body of stature, as appeared to him, more than human, and having nothing on but a gold ring; this he took from the finger of the dead and reascended. Now the shepherds met together, according to custom, that they might send their monthly report about the flocks to the king; into their assembly he came having the ring on his finger, and as he was sitting among them he chanced to turn the collet of the ring inside his hand, when instantly he became invisible to the rest of the company and they began to speak of him as if he were no longer present. He was astonished at this, and again touching the ring he turned the collet outwards and reappeared; he made several trials of the ring, and always with the same result—when he turned the collet inwards he became invisible, when outwards he reappeared. Whereupon he contrived to be chosen one of the messengers who were sent to the court; where as soon as he arrived he seduced the queen, and with her help conspired against the king and slew him, and took the kingdom.

The application of the story of Gyges.

Suppose now that there were two such magic rings, and the just put on one of them and the unjust the other; no man can be imagined to be of such an iron nature that he would stand fast in justice. No man would keep his hands off what was not his own when he could safely take what he liked out of the market, or go into houses and lie with any one at his pleasure, or kill or release from prison whom he would, and in all respects be like a God among men. Then the actions of the just would be as the actions of the unjust; they would both come at last to the same point. And this we may truly affirm to be a great proof that a man is just, not willingly or because he thinks that justice is any good to him individually, but of necessity, for wherever any one thinks that he can safely be unjust, there he is unjust. For all men believe in their hearts that injustice is far more profitable to the individual than justice, and he who argues as I have been supposing, will say that they are right. If you could imagine any one obtaining this power of becoming invisible, and never doing any wrong or touching what was another's, he would be thought by the lookers-on to be a most wretched idiot, although they would praise him to one another's faces, and keep up appearances with one another from a fear that they too might suffer injustice. Enough of this.

Now, if we are to form a real judgment of the life of the just and unjust, we must isolate them; there is no other way; and how is the isolation to be effected? I answer: Let the unjust man be entirely unjust, and the just man entirely just; nothing is to be taken away from either of them, and both are to be perfectly furnished for the work of their respective lives. First, let the unjust be like other distinguished masters of craft; like the skilful pilot or physician, who knows intuitively his own powers and keeps within their limits, and who, if he fails at any point, is able to recover himself. So let the unjust make his unjust attempts in the right way, and lie hidden if he means to be great in his injustice (he who is found out is nobody): for the highest reach of injustice is: to be deemed just when you are not. Therefore I say that in the perfectly unjust man we must assume the most perfect injustice; there is to be no deduction, but we must allow him, while doing the most unjust acts, to have acquired the greatest reputation for justice. If he have taken a false step he must be able to recover himself; he must be one who can speak with effect, if any of his deeds come to light, and who can force his way where force is required by his courage and strength, and command of money and friends. And at his side let us place the just man in his nobleness and simplicity, wishing, as Aeschylus says, to be and not to seem good. There must be no seeming, for if he seem to be just he will be honoured and rewarded, and then we shall not know whether he is just for the sake of justice or for the sake of honours and rewards; therefore, let him be clothed in justice only, and have no other covering; and he must be imagined in a state of life the opposite of the former. Let him be the best of men, and let him be thought the worst; then he will have been put to the proof; and we shall see whether he will be affected by the fear of infamy and its consequences. And let him continue thus to the hour of death; being just and seeming to be unjust. When both have reached the uttermost extreme, the one of justice and the other of injustice, let judgment be given which of them is the happier of the two.

The unjust to be clothed with power and reputation.

The just to be unclothed of all but his virtue.

Socrates, Glaucon.

Heavens! my dear Glaucon, I said, how energetically you polish them up for the decision, first one and then the other, as if they were two statues.

I do my best, he said. And now that we know what they are like there is no difficulty in tracing out the sort of life which awaits either of them. This I will proceed to describe; but as you may think the description a little too coarse, I ask you to suppose, Socrates, that the words which follow are not mine.—Let me put them into the mouths of the eulogists of injustice: They will tell you that the just man who is thought unjust will be scourged, racked, bound—will have his eyes burnt out; and, at last, after suffering every kind of evil, he will be impaled: Then he will understand that he ought to seem only, and not to be, just; the words of Aeschylus may be more truly spoken of the unjust than of the just. For the unjust is pursuing a reality; he does not live with a view to appearances—he wants to be really unjust and not to seem only:—

The just man will learn by each experience that he ought to seem and not to be just.

> His mind has a soil deep and fertile,
> Out of which spring his prudent counsels.[1]

In the first place, he is thought just, and therefore bears rule in the city; he can marry whom he will, and give in marriage to whom he will; also he can trade and deal where he likes, and always to his own advantage, because he has no misgivings about injustice; and at every contest, whether in public or private, he gets the better of his antagonists, and gains at their expense, and is rich, and out of his gains he can benefit his friends, and harm his enemies;

The unjust who appears just will attain every sort of prosperity.

[1] *Seven against Thebes,* 574.

moreover, he can offer sacrifices, and dedicate gifts to the gods abundantly and magnificently, and can honour the gods or any man whom he wants to honour in a far better style than the just, and therefore he is likely to be dearer than they are to the gods. And thus, Socrates, gods and men are said to unite in making the life of the unjust better than the life of the just.

I was going to say something in answer to Glaucon, when Adeimantus, his brother, interposed: Socrates, he said, you do not suppose that there is nothing more to be urged?

Why, what else is there? I answered.

The strongest point of all has not been even mentioned, he replied.

Well, then, according to the proverb, 'Let brother help brother'—if he fails in any part do you assist him; although I must confess that Glaucon has already said quite enough to lay me in the dust, and take from me the power of helping justice.

Adeimantus takes up the argument. Justice is praised and injustice blamed, but only out of regard to their consequences.

Nonsense, he replied. But let me add something more: There is another side to Glaucon's argument about the praise and censure of justice and injustice, which is equally required in order to bring out what I believe to be his meaning. Parents and tutors are always telling their sons and their wards that they are to be just; but why? not for the sake of justice, but for the sake of character and reputation; in the hope of obtaining for him who is reputed just some of those offices, marriages, and the like which Glaucon has enumerated among the advantages accruing to the unjust from the reputation of justice. More, however, is made of appearances by this class of persons than by the others; for they throw in the good opinion of the gods, and will tell you of a shower of benefits which the heavens, as they say, rain upon the pious; and this accords with the testimony of the noble Hesiod and Homer, the first of whom says, that the gods make the oaks of the just—

To bear acorns at their summit, and bees in the middle;
And the sheep are bowed down with the weight of their fleeces.[2]

and many other blessings of a like kind are provided for them. And Homer has a very similar strain; for he speaks of one whose fame is—

As the fame of some blameless king who, like a god,
Maintains justice; to whom the black earth brings forth
Wheat and barley, whose trees are bowed with fruit,
And his sheep never fail to bear, and the sea gives him fish.[3]

The rewards and punishments of another life.

Still grander are the gifts of heaven which Musaeus and his son[4] vouchsafe to the just; they take them down into the world below, where they have the saints lying on couches at a feast, everlastingly drunk, crowned with garlands; their idea seems to be that an immortality of drunkenness is the highest meed of virtue. Some extend their rewards yet further; the posterity, as they say, of the faithful and just shall survive to the third and fourth generation. This is the style in which they praise justice. But about the wicked there is another strain; they bury them in a slough in Hades, and make them carry water in a sieve; also while they are yet living they bring them to infamy, and inflict upon them the punishments which Glaucon described as the portion of the just who are reputed to be unjust; nothing else does their invention supply. Such is their manner of praising the one and censuring the other.

Men are always repeating that virtue is painful and vice pleasant.

Once more, Socrates, I will ask you to consider another way of speaking about justice and injustice, which is not confined to the poets, but is found in prose writers. The universal voice of mankind is always declaring that justice and virtue are honourable, but grievous and toilsome; and that the pleasures of vice and injustice are easy of attainment, and are only censured by law and opinion. They say also that honesty is for the most part less profitable than dishonesty; and they are quite ready to call wicked men happy, and to honour them both in public and private when they are rich or in any other way influential, while they despise and overlook those who may be weak and poor, even though acknowledging them to be

[2] Hesiod, *Works and Days*, 230.

[3] Homer, *Od.* xix. 109.

[4] Eumolpus.

better than the others. But most extraordinary of all is their mode of speaking about virtue and the gods: they say that the gods apportion calamity and misery to many good men, and good and happiness to the wicked. And mendicant prophets go to rich men's doors and persuade them that they have a power committed to them by the gods of making an atonement for a man's own or his ancestor's sins by sacrifices or charms, with rejoicings and feasts; and they promise to harm an enemy, whether just or unjust, at a small cost; with magic arts and incantations binding heaven, as they say, to execute their will. And the poets are the authorities to whom they appeal, now smoothing the path of vice with words of Hesiod:—

> Vice may be had in abundance without trouble; the way is smooth and her dwelling-place is near. But before virtue the gods have set toil,[5]

and a tedious and uphill road: then citing Homer as a witness that the gods may be influenced by men; for he also says:—

> The gods, too, may be turned from their purpose; and men pray to them and avert their wrath by sacrifices and soothing entreaties, and by libations and the odour of fat, when they have sinned and transgressed.[6]

They are taught that sins may be easily expiated.

And they produce a host of books written by Musaeus and Orpheus, who were children of the Moon and the Muses—that is what they say—according to which they perform their ritual, and persuade not only individuals, but whole cities, that expiations and atonements for sin may be made by sacrifices and amusements which fill a vacant hour, and are equally at the service of the living and the dead; the latter sort they call mysteries, and they redeem us from the pains of hell, but if we neglect them no one knows what awaits us.

The effects of all this upon the youthful mind.

He proceeded: And now when the young hear all this said about virtue and vice, and the way in which gods and men regard them, how are their minds likely to be affected, my dear Socrates,—those of them, I mean, who are quickwitted, and, like bees on the wing, light on every flower, and from all that they hear are prone to draw conclusions as to what manner of persons they should be and in what way they should walk if they would make the best of life? Probably the youth will say to himself in the words of Pindar—

> Can I by justice or by crooked ways of deceit ascend a loftier tower which may be a fortress to me all my days?

For what men say is that, if I am really just and am not also thought just, profit there is none, but the pain and loss on the other hand are unmistakable. But if, though unjust, I acquire the reputation of justice, a heavenly life is promised to me. Since then, as philosophers prove, appearance tyrannizes over truth and is lord of happiness, to appearance I must devote myself. I will describe around me a picture and shadow of virtue to be the vestibule and exterior of my house; behind I will trail the subtle and crafty fox, as Archilochus, greatest of sages, recommends. But I hear some one exclaiming that the concealment of wickedness is often difficult; to which I answer, Nothing great is easy. Nevertheless, the argument indicates this, if we would be happy, to be the path along which we should proceed. With a view to concealment we will establish secret brotherhoods and political clubs. And there are professors of rhetoric who teach the art of persuading courts and assemblies; and so, partly by persuasion and partly by force, I shall make unlawful gains and not be punished. Still I hear a voice saying that the gods cannot be deceived, neither can they be compelled. But what if there are no gods? or, suppose them to have no care of human things—why in either case should we mind about concealment? And even if there are gods, and they do care about us, yet we know of them only from tradition and the genealogies of the poets; and these are the very persons who say that they may be influenced and turned by 'sacrifices and soothing entreaties and by offerings.' Let us be consistent then, and believe both or neither. If the poets speak truly, why then we had better be unjust, and offer of the fruits of injustice; for if we are just, although we may escape the vengeance of heaven, we shall lose the gains of injustice; but, if we are unjust,

The existence of the gods is only known to us through the poets who likewise assure us that they may be bribed and that they are very ready to forgive.

[5] Hesiod, *Works and Days*, 287.
[6] Homer, *Iliad*, ix. 493.

we shall keep the gains, and by our sinning and praying, and praying and sinning, the gods will be propitiated, and we shall not be punished. 'But there is a world below in which either we or our posterity will suffer for our unjust deeds.' Yes, my friend, will be the reflection, but there are mysteries and atoning deities, and these have great power. That is what mighty cities declare; and the children of the gods, who were their poets and prophets, bear a like testimony.

All this, even if not absolutely true, affords great excuse for doing wrong.

On what principle, then, shall we any longer choose justice rather than the worst injustice? when, if we only unite the latter with a deceitful regard to appearances, we shall fare to our mind both with gods and men, in life and after death, as the most numerous and the highest authorities tell us. Knowing all this, Socrates, how can a man who has any superiority of mind or person or rank or wealth, be willing to honour justice; or indeed to refrain from laughing when he hears justice praised? And even if there should be some one who is able to disprove the truth of my words, and who is satisfied that justice is best, still he is not angry with the unjust, but is very ready to forgive them, because he also knows that men are not just of their own free will; unless, peradventure, there be some one whom the divinity within him may have inspired with a hatred of injustice, or who has attained knowledge of the truth—but no other man. He only blames injustice who, owing to cowardice or age or some weakness, has not the power of being unjust. And this is proved by the fact that when he obtains the power, he immediately becomes unjust as far as he can be.

The cause of all this, Socrates, was indicated by us at the beginning of the argument, when my brother and I told you how astonished we were to find that of all the professing panegyrists of justice—beginning with the ancient heroes of whom any memorial has been preserved to us, and ending with the men of our own time—no one has ever blamed injustice or praised justice except with a view to the glories, honours, and benefits which flow from them. No one has ever adequately described either in verse or prose the true essential nature of either of them abiding in the soul, and invisible to any human or divine eye; or shown that of all the things of a man's soul which he has within him, justice is the greatest good, and injustice the greatest evil. Had this been the universal strain, had you sought to persuade us of this from our youth upwards, we should not have been on the watch to keep one another from doing wrong, but every one would have been his own watchman, because afraid, if he did wrong, of harbouring in himself the greatest of evils. I dare say that Thrasymachus and others would seriously hold the language which I have been merely repeating, and words even stronger than these about justice and injustice, grossly, as I conceive, perverting their true nature. But I speak in this vehement manner, as I must frankly confess to you, because I want to hear from you the opposite side; and I would ask you to show not only the superiority which justice has over injustice, but what effect they have on the possessor of them which makes the one to be a good and the other an evil to him. And please, as Glaucon requested of you, to exclude reputations; for unless you take away from each of them his true reputation and add on the false, we shall say that you do not praise justice, but the appearance of it; we shall think that you are only exhorting us to keep injustice dark, and that you really agree with Thrasymachus in thinking that justice is another's good and the interest of the stronger, and that injustice is a man's own profit and interest, though injurious to the weaker. Now as you have admitted that justice is one of that highest class of goods which are desired indeed for their results, but in a far greater degree for their own sakes—like sight or hearing or knowledge or health, or any other real and natural and not merely conventional good—I would ask you in your praise of justice to regard one point only: I mean the essential good and evil which justice and injustice work in the possessors of them. Let others praise justice and censure injustice, magnifying the rewards and honours of the one and abusing the other; that is a manner of arguing which, coming from them, I am ready to tolerate, but from you who have spent your whole life in the consideration of this question, unless I hear the contrary from your own lips, I expect something better. And therefore, I say, not only prove to us that justice is better than injustice, but show what they either of them do to the possessor of them, which makes the one to be a good and the other an evil, whether seen or unseen by gods and men.

Men should be taught that justice is in itself the greatest good and injustice the greatest evil.

W. E. H. LECKY

Ancient Views on the Relation between Duty and Self-Interest*

The reader will probably have gathered from the last chapter that there are four distinct motives which moral teachers may propose for the purpose of leading men to virtue. They may argue that the disposition of events is such that prosperity will attend a virtuous life, and adversity a vicious one—a proposition they may prove by pointing to the normal course of affairs, and by asserting the existence of a special Providence in behalf of the good in the present world, and of rewards and punishments in the future. As far as these latter arguments are concerned, the efficacy of such teaching rests upon the firmness with which certain theological tenets are held, while the force of the first considerations will depend upon the degree and manner in which society is organised, for there are undoubtedly some conditions of society in which a perfectly upright life has not even a general tendency to prosperity. The peculiar circumstances and dispositions of individuals will also influence largely the way in which they receive such teaching, and, as Cicero observed, 'what one utility has created, another will often destroy.'

They may argue, again, that vice is to the mind what disease is to the body, and that a state of virtue is in consequence a state of health. Just as bodily health is desired for its own sake, as being the absence of a painful, or at least displeasing state, so a well-ordered and virtuous mind may be valued for its own sake, and independently of all the external good to which it may lead, as being a condition of happiness; and a mind distracted by passion and vice may be avoided, not so much because it is an obstacle in the pursuit of prosperity, as because it is in itself essentially painful and disturbing. This conception of virtue and vice as states of health or sickness, the one being in itself a good and the other in itself an evil, was a fundamental proposition in the ethics of Plato.[1] It was admitted, but only to a subsidiary place, by the Stoics, and has passed more or less into all the succeeding systems. It is especially favourable to large and elevating conceptions of self-culture, for it leads men to dwell much less upon isolated acts of virtue or vice than upon the habitual condition of mind from which they spring.

It is possible, in the third place, to argue in favour of virtue by offering as a motive that sense of pleasure which follows the deliberate performance of a virtuous act. This emotion is a distinct and isolated gratification following a distinct action, and may therefore be easily separated from that habitual placidity of temper which results from the extinction of vicious and perturbing impulses. It is this theory which is implied in the

* W. E. H. Lecky, *History of European Morals from Augustus to Charlemagne* (New York: George Braziller, 1955), Vol. I, pp. 178–181. First published in 1869.

[1] Mr. Grote gives the following very clear summary of Plato's ethical theory, which he believes to be original:—'Justice is in the mind a condition analogous to good health and strength in the body. Injustice is a condition analogous to sickness, corruption, impotence in the body. . . . To possess a healthy body is desirable for its consequences as a means towards other constituents of happiness, but it is still more desirable in itself as an essential element of happiness *per se*, i.e., the negation of sickness, which would of itself make us miserable. . . . In like manner, the just mind blesses the possessor twice: first and chiefly by bringing to him happiness in itself; next, also, as it leads to ulterior happy results. The unjust mind is a curse to its possessor in itself and apart from results, though it also leads to ulterior results which render it still more a curse to him.'—Grote's *Plato*, vol. iii p. 131. According to Plutarch, Aristo of Chio defined virtue as 'the health of the soul.' (*De Virtute Morali.*)

common exhortations to enjoy 'the luxury of doing good,' and though especially strong in acts of benevolence, in which case sympathy with the happiness created intensifies the feeling, this pleasure attends every kind of virtue.

These three motives of action have all this common characteristic, that they point as their ultimate end to the happiness of the agent. The first seeks that happiness in external circumstances; the second and third in psychological conditions. There is, however, a fourth kind of motive which may be urged, and which is the peculiar characteristic of the intuitive school of moralists and the stumbling-block of its opponents. It is asserted that we are so constituted that the notion of duty furnishes in itself a natural motive of action of the highest order, wholly distinct from all the refinements and modifications of self-interest. The coactive force of this motive is altogether independent of surrounding circumstances, and of all forms of belief. It is equally true for the man who believes and for the man who rejects the Christian faith, for the believer in a future world and for the believer in the mortality of the soul. It is not a question of happiness or unhappiness, of reward or punishment, but of a generically different nature. Men feel that a certain course of life is the natural end of their being, and they feel bound, even at the expense of happiness, to pursue it. They feel that certain acts are essentially good and noble, and others essentially base and vile, and this perception leads them to pursue the one and to avoid the other, irrespective of all considerations of enjoyment.

H. A. PRICHARD

Duty and Interest*

In seeking a subject for an inaugural lecture, I have tried to find one which, without raising too technical issues, is near enough to every one to be of general interest and yet would be considered by philosophers still sufficiently controversial to deserve consideration. This subject I hope I have found in the relation between duty and interest. The topic is, of course, well worn. Nevertheless anyone who considers it closely will find that it has not the simple and straightforward character which at first sight it appears to possess.

A general but not very critical familiarity with the literature of Moral Philosophy might well lead to the remark that much of it is occupied with attempts either to prove that there is a necessary connexion between duty and interest or in certain cases even to exhibit the connexion as something self-evident. And the remark, even if not strictly accurate, plainly has some truth in it. It might be said in support that Plato's treatment of justice in the *Republic* is obviously such an attempt, and that even Aristotle in the *Ethics* tries to do the same thing, disguised and weak though his attempt may be. . . .

When we read the attempts referred to we naturally cannot help in a way wishing them to succeed; and we might express our wish in the form that we should all like to be able to believe that honesty is the best policy. At the same time we also cannot help feeling that somehow they are out of place, so that the real question is not so much whether they are successful, but whether they ought ever to have been made. And my object is to try to justify our feeling of dissatisfaction by considering what these attempts really

* H. A. Prichard, *Duty and Interest* (Oxford: Clarendon Press, 1928), pp. 4–21, 24–25. Reprinted by permission of The Clarendon Press, Oxford. Prichard's more developed views on this and related subjects can be found in his *Moral Obligation, Essays and Lectures* (Oxford: Clarendon Press, 1949), especially in the title essay, written in 1937.

amount to, and more especially what they amount to in view of the ideas which have prompted them. . . .

One preliminary remark is necessary. It must not be assumed that what are thus grouped together as attempts either to prove or to exhibit the self-evidence of a connexion between duty and interest are properly described by this phrase, or even that they are all attempts to do one and the same thing. And in particular I shall try to show that the attempts so described really consist of endeavours, based on mutually inconsistent presuppositions, to do one or another of three different things.

On a casual acquaintance with the *Republic*, we should probably say without hesitation that, apart from its general metaphysics, what it is concerned with is justice and injustice, and that, with regard to justice and injustice, its main argument is an elaborate attempt, continued to the end of the book, to show in detail that if we look below the surface and consider what just actions really consist in and also the nature of the soul, and, to a minor degree, the nature of the world in which we have to act, it will become obvious, in spite of appearance to the contrary, that it is by acting justly that we shall really gain or become happy.

Further, if we were to ask ourselves, 'What are Plato's words for right and wrong?'—and plainly the question is fair—we should have in the end to give as the true answer what at first would strike us as a paradox. We should have to allow that Plato's words for right and wrong are not to be found in such words as χρὴ ['one must'] or δεῖ ['one ought'] and their contraries, as in χρὴ δίκαιον εἶναι ['one ought to be just'] or ὅντινα τρόπον χρὴ ζῆν, ['in whatever manner one ought to live'], where the subject is implied by the context to be τὸν μέλλοντα μακάριον ἔσεσθαι ['he who would be happy or blessed'] but in δίκαιον ['just'] and ἄδικον ['unjust'] themselves. When he says of some action that it is δίκαιον, that is his way of saying that it is right, or a duty, or an act which we are morally bound to do. When he says that it is ἄδικον, that is his way of saying that it is wrong. And in the sense in which we use the terms 'justice' and 'injustice', it is less accurate to describe what Plato is discussing as justice and injustice than as right and wrong. Our previous statement, therefore, might be put in the form that Plato is mainly occupied in the *Republic* with attempting to show it is by doing our duty, or what we are morally bound to do, that we shall become happy.

This is the account of his object which we are more particularly inclined to give if we chiefly have in mind what Socrates in the fourth Book is made to offer as the solution of the main problem. But this solution is preceded by an elaborate statement of the problem itself, put into the mouth of Glaucon and Adeimantus; and if we consider this statement closely, we find ourselves forced to make a substantial revision of this account of Plato's object. Glaucon and Adeimantus make it quite clear that whatever it is that they are asking Socrates to show about what they refer to as justice, their object in doing so is to obtain a refutation of what may be called the Sophistic theory of morality. Consequently, if we judge by what Glaucon and Adeimantus say, whatever Plato is trying to prove must be something which Plato would consider as affording a refutation of the Sophistic theory. But what is this theory as represented by Plato? It almost goes without saying that in the first instance men's attitude towards matters of right and wrong is an unquestioning one. However they have come to do so, and in particular whether their doing so is due to teaching or not, they think, and think without having any doubt, that certain actions are right and that certain others are wrong. No doubt in special cases, they may be doubtful; but, as regards some actions, they have no doubt at all, though to say this is not the same as to say that they are certain. But there comes a time when men are stirred out of this unquestioning frame of mind; and in particular the Sophists, as Plato represents them, were thus stirred by the reflection that the actions which men in ordinary life thought right, such as paying a debt, helping a friend, obeying the government, however they differed in other respects, at least agreed in bringing directly a definite loss to the agent. This reflection led them to wonder whether men were right in thinking these actions duties, i.e. whether they thought so truly. Then, having failed to find indirect advantages of these actions which would more than compensate for the direct loss, i.e. such advantages as are found in what we call prudent actions, they drew the conclusion that these actions cannot really be duties at all, and that therefore what may roughly be described as the moral convictions which they and others held in ordinary life were one gigantic mistake or illusion. Finally, they clinched this conclusion by offering something which they represented as an account of the origin of justice, but which is really an account of how they and others came to make the mistake of thinking these actions just, i.e. right.

This is the theory which on Plato's own showing he wants to refute. It is a theory about certain actions, and, on his own showing, what he has to maintain is the opposite theory about these same actions. But how, if our language is to be accurate, should these actions be referred to? Should they be referred to as *just,* i.e. right, actions, or should they be referred to as those actions which in ordinary life we *think* just, i.e. right? The difference, though at first it may seem unimportant, is really vital. In the unquestioning attitude of ordinary life we must either be *knowing* that certain actions are right or not knowing that they are right, but doing something else for which '*thinking* them right' is perhaps the least unsatisfactory phrase. There is no possibility of what might be suggested as a third alternative, viz. that our activity is one of thinking, which in instances where we are thinking truly is also one of knowing. For, as Plato realized, to think truly is not to know, and to discover that in some particular case we were thinking truly is not to discover that in doing so we were knowing. Moreover, when we are what is described as reflecting on the activity involved in our unquestioning attitude of mind, we are inevitably thinking of it as having a certain definite character, and, in so thinking of it, we must inevitably be implying either that the activity is one of knowing or that it is not. For we must think of this attitude either as one of thinking, or as one of knowing, and if we think of it as one of thinking, we imply that it is not one of knowing, and *vice versa.* In fact, however we think of the activity, we are committed one way or the other. Now the Sophists clearly implied that this unquestioning attitude is one of thinking and not one of knowing; for it would not have been sense to maintain that those actions which in ordinary life we know to be right are really not right. Their theory, then, must be expressed by saying that those actions which in ordinary life we think, and so do not know, to be right are not really right. Consequently Plato also, since he regards this as the theory to be refuted, is implying that in ordinary life we think, and do not know, that certain actions are right, and that, to this extent, he agrees with the Sophists. And for this reason, if we are to state accurately the problem which he is setting himself, we must represent it as referring not to *just* actions but to those actions which he and others in ordinary life *think* just.

It is clear then that when Plato states through the medium of Glaucon and Adeimantus the problem which he has to solve, he is guilty of an inaccuracy, which, though it may easily escape notice, is important. For Glaucon and Adeimantus persistently refer to the actions of which they ask Socrates to reconsider the profitableness as just and unjust actions, whereas they should have referred to them as the actions which men in ordinary life think just and unjust.

I shall now take it as established that when we judge from Plato's own statement of his problem, worked out as it is by reference to the Sophists, we have to allow that he is presupposing that ordinarily we do not know but think that certain actions are right and that he is thinking of his task as that of having to vindicate the truth of these thoughts against the Sophists' objection. And this is what must be really meant when it is said that Plato's object is to vindicate *morality* against the Sophistic view of it, for here 'morality' can only be a loose phrase for our ordinary moral thoughts or convictions.

Glaucon and Adeimantus, however, do not simply ask Socrates to refute the Sophistic view; they ask him to do so in a particular way, which they imply to be the only way possible, viz. by showing that if we go deeper than the Sophists and consider not merely the gains and losses of which they take account, viz. gains and losses really due to the reputation for doing what men think just and unjust, but also those which these actions directly bring to the man's own soul, it will become obvious that it is by doing what we think just that we shall really gain. And so far as the rest of the *Republic* is an attempt to satisfy this request, this must be what it is an attempt to show.

Now on a first reading of the *Republic,* it is not likely to strike us that there is anything peculiar or unnatural about this part of the request. Just because Plato takes for granted that this is the only way to refute the Sophists, we are apt in reading him to do the same, especially as our attention is likely to be fully taken up by the effort to follow Plato's thought. But if we can manage to consider Plato's endeavour to refute the Sophists with detachment, what strikes us most is not his dissent from their view concerning the comparative profitableness of the actions which men think just and unjust—great, of course, as his dissent is—but the identity of principle underlying the position of both. The Sophists in reaching their conclusion were presupposing that for an action to be really just, it must be advantageous; for it was solely on this ground that they concluded that what we ordinarily think just is not really just. And what in the end most strikes us is that at no stage in the *Republic* does Plato take the line, or even suggest as a possibility, that the very presupposition of the Sophists' arguments is false, and that therefore the question whether some action which men think just will be profitable to the agent has really nothing to do with the question whether it is right, so that Thrasymachus may enlarge as much as he pleases on the losses incurred by doing the actions we think just without getting any nearer to showing that it is a mere mistake to think them just. Plato, on the contrary, instead of urging that the Sophistic contention that men lose by doing what they think just is simply irrelevant to the question whether these actions are just, throughout treats this contention with the utmost seriousness; and he implies that unless the Sophists can be met on their own ground by being shown that, in spite of appearances to the contrary, these actions will really be for the good of the agent, their conclusion that men's moral convictions are mere conventions must be allowed to stand. He therefore, equally with the Sophists, is implying that it is impossible for any action to be really just, i.e. a duty, unless it is for the advantage of the agent.

This presupposition, however, as soon as we consider it, strikes us as a paradox. For though we may find ourselves quite unable to state what it is that does render an action a duty, we ordinarily think that, whatever it is, it is not conduciveness to our advantage; and we also think that though an action which is a duty may be advantageous it need not be so. And while we may not be surprised to find the presupposition in the Sophists, whose moral convictions are represented as at least shallow, we are surprised to find it in Plato, whose moral earnestness is that of a prophet. At first, no doubt, we may try to mitigate our surprise by emphasizing the superior character of the advantages which Plato had in mind. But to do this does not really help. For after all, whatever be meant by the 'superiority' of the advantages of which Plato was thinking, it is simply as advantages that Plato uses them to show that the actions from which they follow are right.

Yet the presupposition cannot simply be dismissed as obviously untrue. For one thing, any view of Plato's is entitled to respect. For another, there appear to be moments in which we find the presupposition in ourselves. There appear to be moments in which, feeling acutely the weight of our responsibilities, we say to ourselves, 'Why *should* I do all these actions, since after all it is others and not I who will gain by doing them?'.

Moreover, there at least seems to be the same presupposition in the mind of those preachers whose method of exhortation consists in appeal to rewards. When, for instance, they commend a certain mode of life on the ground that it will bring about a peace of mind which the pursuit of worldly things cannot yield, they appear to be giving a resulting gain as the reason why we ought to do certain actions, and therefore to be implying that in general it is advantageousness to ourselves which renders an action one which we are bound to do. In fact the only difference between the view of such preachers and that of the Sophists seems to be that the former, in view of their theological beliefs, think that the various actions which we think right will have certain specific rewards the existence of which the Sophists would deny. And the identity of principle underlying their view becomes obvious if the preacher goes on to maintain, as some have done, that if he were to cease to believe in heaven, he would cease to believe in right and wrong. Again, among philosophers, Plato is far from being alone in presupposing that an action, to be right, must be for the good or advantage of the agent. To go no further afield than a commentator on Plato, we may cite Cook Wilson, whose claim to respect no one in Oxford will deny, and who was, to my mind, one of the acutest of thinkers. In lecturing on the *Republic* he used to insist that when men begin to reflect on morality they not only demand, but also have the right to demand, that any action which is right must justify its claim to be right by being shown to be for their own good; and he used to maintain that Plato took the right and only way of justifying our moral convictions, by showing that the actions which we think right are for the good of the society of which we are members, and that at the same time the good of that society *is* our good, as becomes obvious when the nature of our good is properly understood.

Moreover Plato, if he has been rightly interpreted, does not stand alone among the historical philosophers in presupposing the existence of a necessary connexion between duty and interest. At least Butler, whose thoughtfulness is incontestable, is with him. In fact in this matter he seems at first sight only distinguished from Plato by going further. In a well-known passage in the eleventh *Sermon,* after stating that religion always addresses itself to self-love when reason presides in a man, he says: 'Let it be allowed, though virtue or moral rectitude does indeed consist in affection to and pursuit of what is right and good, as such; yet that when we sit down in a cool hour, we can neither justify to ourselves this or any other pursuit, till we are convinced that it will be for our happiness, or at least not contrary to it.'

Here, if we take the phrase 'justify an action to ourselves' in its natural sense of come to know that we ought to do the action by apprehending a reason why we ought to do it, we seem to have to allow that Butler is maintaining that in the last resort there is one, and only one, reason why we ought to do anything whatever, viz. the conduciveness of the action to our happiness or advantage. And if this is right, Butler is not simply presupposing but definitely asserting a necessary connexion between duty and interest, and going further than Plato by maintaining that it is actually conduciveness to the agent's interest which renders an action right.

Nevertheless, when we seriously face the view that unless an action be advantageous, it cannot really be a duty, we are forced both to abandon it and also to allow that even if it were true, it would not enable us to vindicate the truth of our ordinary moral convictions.

It is easy to see that if we persist in maintaining that an action, to be right, must be advantageous, we cannot stop short of maintaining that it is precisely advantageousness and nothing else which renders an action right. It is impossible to rest in the intermediate position that, though it is something other than advantageousness which renders an action right, nevertheless an action cannot really be right unless it be advantageous. For if it be held that an action is rendered a duty by the possession of some other characteristic, then the only chance of showing that a right action must necessarily be advantageous must consist either in showing that actions having this other characteristic must necessarily be advantageous or in showing that the very fact that we are bound to do some action, irrespectively of what renders us bound to do it, necessitates that we shall gain by doing it. But the former alternative is not possible. By 'an action' in this context must be meant an activity by which a man brings certain things about. And if the characteristic of an action which renders it right does not consist in its bringing about an advantage to the agent, which we may symbolize by 'an *X*', it must consist in bringing about something of a different kind, which we may symbolize by 'a *Y*', say, for the sake of argument, an advantage to a friend, or an improvement in someone's character. There can, however, be no means of showing that when we bring about something of one kind, e.g. a *Y*, we must necessarily bring about something of a different kind, e.g. an *X*. The nature of an action as being the bringing about a *Y* cannot require, i.e. necessitate, it to be also the bringing about an *X*, i.e. to have an *X* as its consequence; and whether bringing about a *Y* in any particular case will bring about an *X* will depend not only on the nature of the act as being the bringing about a *Y*, but also on the nature of the agent and of the special circumstances in which the act is done. It may be objected that we could avoid the necessity of having to admit this on one condition, viz. that we knew the existence of a Divine Being who would intervene, where necessary, with rewards. But this knowledge would give the required conclusion only on one condition, viz. that this knowledge was really the knowledge that the fact of being bound to do some action itself necessitated the existence of such a Being as a consequence. For if it were the knowledge of the existence of such a Being based on other grounds, it would not enable us to know that the very fact that some action was the bringing about a *Y itself* necessitated that it would also be the bringing about an *X*, i.e. some advantage to the agent. No doubt if we could successfully maintain not only that an action's being the bringing about a *Y* necessitated its being a duty, but also that an action's being a duty necessitated as a consequence the existence of a Being who would reward it, we could show that an action's being the bringing about a *Y* necessitated its being rewarded. But to maintain this is really to fall back on the second alternative; and this alternative will, on consideration, turn out no more tenable than the first. It cannot successfully be maintained that the very fact that some action is a duty necessitates, not that the agent will *deserve* to gain—a conclusion which it is of course easy to draw, but that he *will* gain, unless it can be shown that this very fact necessitates, as a consequence, the existence of a being who will, if necessary, reward it. And this obviously cannot be done. . . .

We are therefore forced to allow that in order to maintain that for an action to be right, it must be advantageous, we have to maintain that advantageousness is what renders an action right. But this is obviously something which no one is going to maintain, if he considers it seriously. For he will be involved in maintaining not only that it is a duty to do whatever is for our advantage, but that this is our only duty. And the fatal objection to maintaining this is simply that no one actually thinks it.

Moreover, as it is easy to see, if we were to maintain this, our doing so, so far from helping us, would render it impossible for us, to vindicate the truth of our ordinary moral convictions. For wherever in ordinary life we think of some particular action as a duty, we are not simply thinking of it as right, but also thinking of its rightness as constituted by the possession of some definite characteristic other than that of being advantageous to the agent. For we think of the action as a particular action *of a certain kind*, the nature of which is indicated by general words contained in the phrase by which we refer to the action, e.g. '*fulfilling the promise* which we made to X yesterday', or '*looking after* our *parents*'. And we do not think of the action as right *blindly*, i.e. irrespectively of the special character which we think the act to possess; rather we think of it as being right in virtue of possessing a particular characteristic of the kind indicated by the phrase by which we refer to it. Thus in thinking of our keeping our promise to *X* as a duty, we are thinking of the action as rendered a duty by its being the keeping of our promise. This is obvious because we should never, for instance, think of using as an illustration of an action which we think right, telling X what we think of him, or meeting him in London, even though we thought that if we thought of these actions in certain other aspects we should think them right. Consequently if we were to maintain that conduciveness to the agent's advantage is what renders an action right, we should have to allow that any of our ordinary moral convictions, so far from being capable of vindication, is simply a mistake, as being really the conviction that some particular action is rendered a duty by its possession of some characteristic which is not that of being advantageous.

The general moral is obvious. Certain arguments, which would ordinarily be referred to as arguments designed to prove that doing what is right will be for the good of the agent, turn out to be attempts to prove that the actions which in ordinary life we think right will be for the good of the agent. There is really no need to consider in detail whether these arguments are successful; for even if they are successful, they will do nothing to prove what they are intended to prove, viz. that the moral convictions of our ordinary life are true. Further the attempts arise simply out of a presupposition which on reflection anyone is bound to abandon, viz. that conduciveness to personal advantage is what renders an action a duty. What Plato should have said to the Sophists is: 'You may be right in maintaining that in our ordinary unquestioning frame of mind we do not know, but only think, that certain actions are right. These thoughts or convictions may or may not be true. But they cannot be false for the reason which you give. You do nothing whatever to show that they are false by urging that the actions in question are disadvantageous; and I should do nothing to show that they are true, if I were to show that these actions are after all advantageous. Your real mistake lies in presupposing throughout that advantageousness is what renders an action a duty. If you will only reflect you will abandon his presupposition altogether, and then you yourself will withdraw your arguments.'

I next propose to contend that there is also to be found . . . in Plato . . . , besides this attempt to show that actions which we *think* right will be for our good, another attempt which [he does not distinguish] from it and which *is* accurately described as an attempt to prove that *right* actions will be for our good. I also propose to ask what is the idea which led them to make the attempt, and to consider whether it is tenable.

When Plato raises the question 'What is justice?' he does not mean by the question 'What do we *mean* by the terms 'justice' and 'just', or, in our language, 'duty' and 'right'?', as we might ask 'What do we *mean* by the term 'optimism', or again, by the phrase 'living thing'?'. And as a matter of fact if he had meant this, he would have been raising what was only verbally, and not really, a question at all, in that any attempt to ask it would have implied that the answer was already known and that therefore there was nothing to ask. He means 'What is the characteristic the possession of which by an action necessitates that the action is just, i.e. an act which it is our duty, or which we ought, to do?' In short he means 'What renders a just or right action, just or right?'

Now this question really means 'What is the characteristic common to particular just acts which renders them just?' And for anyone even to *ask* this question is to imply that he already *knows* what particular actions are just. For even to *ask* 'What is the character common to certain things?' is to imply that we already *know* what the things are of which we are wanting to find the common character. Equally, of course, any attempt to *answer* the question has the same implication. For such an attempt can only consist in considering the particular actions which we know to be just and attempting to discover what is the characteristic common to them all, the vague apprehension of which has led us to apprehend them to be just. Plato therefore, both in representing Socrates as raising with his hearers the question 'What is justice?' and also in representing them all as attempting to answer it, is implying, whether he is aware that he is doing so or not, that they all know what particular acts are, and what particular acts are not, just. If on the contrary what he had presupposed was that the members of the dialogue think, instead of knowing, that certain actions are just, his question—whether he had expressed it thus or not—would really have been, not 'What *is* justice?', but 'What do we *think* that justice is?'; or, more clearly, not 'What renders an act just?' but 'What do we think renders an act just?'. But in that case an answer, whatever its character, would have thrown no light on the question 'What is justice?'; and apart from this, he is plainly not asking 'What do we *think* that justice is?'.

As has been pointed out, however, the view which Plato attributes to the Sophists presupposes that ordinary mankind, which of course includes the members of the dialogue, only thinks and does not know that certain actions are just. Therefore, when Plato introduces this view as requiring refutation and, in doing so, represents the members of the dialogue as not questioning the presupposition, he ought in consistency to have made someone point out that in view of the acceptance of this presupposition Socrates' original question 'What is justice?' required to be amended to the question 'What do we think that justice is?'. But Plato does not do so. In the present context the significant fact is that even after he has introduced the view of the Sophists he still represents the question to be answered as being 'What is justice?', and therefore still implies that the members of the dialogue know what is just in particular. Even in making Glaucon and Adeimantus ask Socrates to refute the Sophists, what he, inconsistently, makes them ask Socrates to exhibit the nature of is not the acts which men think just but just acts. And when Plato in the fourth book goes on to give Socrates' answer, which, of course, is intended to express the truth, he in the same way represents Socrates as offering, and the others as accepting, an account of the nature of *just* acts, viz. that they consist in conferring those benefits on society which a man's nature renders him best suited to confer, and then makes Socrates argue in detail that it is *just* action which will be profitable. In doing so he is of course implying, inconsistently with the implication of his treatment of the Sophists' view, that the members of the dialogue, and therefore also mankind in ordinary life, *know* what is just in particular. For in the end the statement 'Justice is conferring certain benefits on society' can only mean that conferring these benefits is the characteristic the vague apprehension of which in certain actions leads us to know or apprehend them to be just; and the acceptance of this statement by the members of the dialogue must be understood as expressing their recognition that this characteristic is the common character of the particular acts which they already know to be just.

It therefore must be allowed that, although to do so is inconsistent with his view of the way in which the Sophistic theory has to be refuted, Plato is in the fourth book (and of course the same admission must be made about the eighth and ninth) endeavouring to prove that *just,* i.e. *right,* action, will be for the good or advantage of the agent.

Given that this is what Plato wants to prove in the fourth book, the general nature of what he conceives to be the proof is obvious. His idea is that if we start with the knowledge of what right actions consist in, viz., to put it shortly, serving the state, and then consider what the effects of these and other actions will be by taking into account not only the circumstances in which we are placed, but also the various desires of the human soul and the varying amounts of satisfaction to which the realization of these objects will give rise, it will be obvious that it is by doing what is right that, at any rate in the long run, we shall become happy.

Now a particular proof of this kind, such as Plato's, naturally provokes two comments. The first is that there is no need to consider its success in detail, since we know on general grounds that it must fail. For it can only be shown that actions characterized by being the bringing about things of one kind, in this case benefits to society, will always have as their consequence things of another kind, in this case elements of happiness in the agent, provided that we can prove, as Plato makes no attempt to do, the existence of a Being who will intervene to introduce suitable rewards where they are needed. The second is that though the establishment of this conclusion, whether with or without the help of theological arguments, would be of the greatest benefit to us, since we should all be better off if we knew it to be true, yet it differs from the establishment of the corresponding conclusion against the Sophists in that it would throw no light whatever on the question 'What is our duty in detail, and why?'. And this second comment naturally raises the question which seems to be the important one to ask in this connexion, viz. '*Why* did Plato think it important to prove that right action would benefit the agent?'.

The explanation obviously cannot be simply, or even mainly, that the combination in Plato of a desire to do what is right and of a desire to become happy led him to try to satisfy himself that by doing what is right he would be, so to say, having it both ways. The main explanation must lie in a quite different direction. There is no escaping the conclusion that when Plato sets himself to consider not what *should,* but what *actually does* as a matter of fact, lead a man to act, when he is acting deliberately, and not merely in consequence of an impulse, he answers 'The desire for some good to himself and that only'. In other words we have to allow that, according to Plato, a man pursues whatever he pursues simply as a good to himself, i.e. really as something which will give him satisfaction, or, as perhaps we ought to say, as an element in what will render him happy. In the *Republic* this view comes to light in the sixth book. He there speaks of τὸ ἀγαθόν as that which every soul pursues and for the sake of which it does all it does, divining that it is something but being perplexed and unable to grasp adequately what it is; and he goes on to say of things that are good (τὰ ἀγαθά) that while many are ready to do and to obtain and to be what only *seems* just, even if it is not, no one is content with obtaining what *seems* good, but endeavours to obtain what is *really* good. It might be objected that these statements do not bear out the view which is attributed to Plato, since Plato certainly did not mean by an ἀγαθόν a source of satisfaction or happiness to oneself. But to this the answer is that wherever Plato uses the term ἀγαθά (goods) elsewhere in the *Republic* and in other dialogues, such as the *Philebus,* the context always shows that he means by a good a good to oneself, and, this being so, he must really be meaning by an ἀγαθόν, a source of satisfaction, or perhaps, more generally, a source of happiness. The view, however, emerges most clearly in the Gorgias, where Plato, in order to show that rhetoricians and tyrants do not do what they really wish to do, maintains that in all actions alike, and even when we kill a man or despoil him of his goods we do what we do because we think it will be better for us to do so.

Now if we grant, as we must, that Plato thought this, we can find in the admission a natural explanation of Plato's desire to prove that just action will be advantageous. For plainly he passionately wanted men to do what is right, and if he thought that it was only desire of some good to themselves which moved them in all deliberate action, it would be natural, and indeed necessary, for him to think that if men are to be induced to do what is just, the only way to induce them is to convince them that thereby they will gain or become better off.

I propose now to take it as established (I) that . . . Plato . . . [is] really endeavouring to prove that right actions, in the strict sense of 'right actions', will be for the agent's advantage; (2) that [his] reason for doing so lies in the conviction that even where we know some action to be right, we shall not do it unless we think that it will be for our advantage; and (3) that behind this conviction lies the conviction of which it is really a corollary, viz. the conviction that desire for some good to oneself is the only motive of deliberate action.

But are these convictions true? For if it can be shown that they are not, then at least Plato's . . . reason for trying to prove the advantageousness of right action will have disappeared.

The conviction that even where we know some action to be right, we shall not do it unless we think we shall be the better off for doing it, of course, strikes us as a paradox. At first no doubt we are apt to mis-state the paradox. We are apt to say that the conviction, implying as it does that we only act out of self-interest, really implies that it is impossible for us to do anything which we ought to do at all, since if we did some action out of self-interest we could not have done anything which was a duty. But to say this is to make the mistake of thinking that the motive with which we do an action can possibly have something to do with its rightness or wrongness. To be morally bound is to be morally bound to *do* something, i.e. to bring something about; and even if it be only from the lowest of motives that we have brought about something which we ought to have brought about, we have still done something which we ought to have done. The fact that I have given *A* credit in order to spite his rival *B*, or again, in order to secure future favours from *A*, has, as we see when we reflect, no bearing whatever on the question whether I ought to have given *A* credit. The real paradox inherent in the conviction lies in its implication that there is no such thing as moral goodness. If I gave *A* credit solely to obtain future favours, and even if I gave him credit either thinking or knowing that I ought to do so, but in no way directly or indirectly influenced by my either so thinking or knowing, then even though it has to be allowed that I did something which I was morally bound to do, it has to be admitted that there was no moral goodness whatever about my action. And the conviction in question is really what is ordinarily called the doctrine that morality needs a sanction, i.e. really the doctrine that, to stimulate a man into doing some action, it is not merely insufficient but even useless to convince him that he is morally bound to do it, and that, instead, we have to appeal to his desire to become better off.

BRIAN MEDLIN

Ultimate Principles and Ethical Egoism*

I believe that it is now pretty generally accepted by professional philosophers that ultimate ethical principles must be arbitrary. One cannot derive conclusions about what should be merely from accounts of what is the case; one cannot decide how people ought to behave merely from one's knowledge of how they do behave.

* Brian Medlin, "Ultimate Principles and Ethical Egoism," *Australasian Journal of Philosophy*, 35 (1957), 111–118. Reprinted by permission of the author and the editor of the *Australasian Journal of Philosophy*.

To arrive at a conclusion in ethics one must have at least one ethical premiss. This premiss, if it be in turn a conclusion, must be the conclusion of an argument containing at least one ethical premiss. And so we can go back, indefinitely but not for ever. Sooner or later, we must come to at least one ethical premiss which is not deduced but baldly asserted. Here we must be a-rational; neither rational nor irrational, for here there is no room for reason even to go wrong.

But the triumph of Hume in ethics has been a limited one. What appears quite natural to a handful of specialists appears quite monstrous to the majority of decent intelligent men. At any rate, it has been my experience that people who are normally rational resist the above account of the logic of moral language, not by argument—for that can't be done—but by tooth and nail. And they resist from the best motives. They see the philosopher wantonly unravelling the whole fabric of morality. If our ultimate principles are arbitrary, they say, if those principles came out of thin air, then anyone can hold any principle he pleases. Unless moral assertions are statements of fact about the world and either true or false, we can't claim that any man is wrong, whatever his principles may be, whatever his behaviour. We have to surrender the luxury of calling one another scoundrels. That this anxiety flourishes because its roots are in confusion is evident when we consider that we don't call people scoundrels, anyhow, for being mistaken about their facts. Fools, perhaps, but that's another matter. Nevertheless, it doesn't become us to be high-up. The layman's uneasiness, however irrational it may be, is very natural and he must be reassured.

People cling to objectivist theories of morality from moral motives. It's a very queer thing that by doing so they often thwart their own purposes. There are evil opinions abroad, as anyone who walks abroad knows. The one we meet with most often, whether in pub or parlour, is the doctrine that everyone should look after himself. However refreshing he may find it after the high-minded pomposities of this morning's editorial, the good fellow knows this doctrine is wrong and he wants to knock it down. But while he believes that moral language is used to make statements either true or false, the best he can do is to claim that what the egoist says is false. Unfortunately, the egoist can claim that it's true. And since the supposed fact in question between them is not a publicly ascertainable one, their disagreement can never be resolved. And it is here that even good fellows waver, when they find they have no refutation available. The egoist's word seems as reliable as their own. Some begin half to believe that perhaps it is possible to supply an egoistic basis for conventional morality, some that it may be impossible to supply any other basis. I'm not going to try to prop up our conventional morality, which I fear to be a task beyond my strength, but in what follows I do want to refute the doctrine of ethical egoism. I want to resolve this disagreement by showing that what the egoist says is inconsistent. It is true that there are moral disagreements which can never be resolved, but this isn't one of them. The proper objection to the man who says 'Everyone should look after his own interests regardless of the interests of others' is not that he isn't speaking the truth, but simply that he isn't speaking.

We should first make two distinctions. This done, ethical egoism will lose much of its plausibility.

UNIVERSAL AND INDIVIDUAL EGOISM

Universal egoism maintains that everyone (including the speaker) ought to look after his own interests and to disregard those of other people except in so far as their interests contribute towards his own.

Individual egoism is the attitude that the egoist is going to look after himself and no one else. The egoist cannot promulgate that he is going to look after himself. He can't even preach that he *should* look after himself and preach this alone. When he tries to convince me that he should look after himself, he is attempting so to dispose me that I shall approve when he drinks my beer and steals Tom's wife. I cannot approve of his looking after himself and himself alone without so far approving of his achieving his happiness, regardless of the happiness of myself and others. So that when he sets out to persuade me that he should look after himself regardless of others, he must also set out to persuade me that I should look after him regardless of myself and others. Very small chance he has! And if the individual egoist cannot promulgate his doctrine without enlarging it, what he has is no doctrine at all.

A person enjoying such an attitude may believe that other people are fools not to look after themselves. Yet he himself would be a fool to tell them so. If he did tell them, though, he wouldn't consider that he was giving them *moral* advice. Persuasion to the effect that one should ignore the claims of morality because morality doesn't pay, to the effect that one has insufficient selfish motive and, therefore, insufficient motive for moral behaviour is not moral persuasion. For this reason I doubt that we should call the individual egoist's attitude an ethical one. And I don't doubt this in the way someone may doubt whether to call the ethical standards of Satan "ethical" standards. A malign morality is none the less a morality for being malign. But the attitude we're considering is one of mere contempt for all moral considerations whatsoever. An indifference to morals may be wicked, but it is not a perverse morality. So far as I am aware, most egoists imagine that they are putting forward a doctrine in ethics, though there may be a few who are prepared to proclaim themselves individual egoists. If the good fellow wants to know how he should justify conventional morality to an individual egoist, the answer is that he shouldn't and can't. Buy your car elsewhere, blackguard him whenever you meet, and let it go at that.

CATEGORICAL AND HYPOTHETICAL EGOISM

Categorical egoism is the doctrine that we all ought to observe our own interests, *because that is what we ought to do.* For the categorical egoist the egoistic dogma is the ultimate principle in ethics.

The hypothetical egoist, on the other hand, maintains that we all ought to observe our own interests, because . . . if we want such and such an end, we must do so and so (look after ourselves). The hypothetical egoist is not a real egoist at all. He is very likely an unwitting utilitarian who believes mistakenly that the general happiness will be increased if each man looks wisely to his own. Of course, a man may believe that egoism is enjoined on us by God and he may therefore promulgate the doctrine and observe it in his conduct, not in the hope of achieving thereby a remote end, but simply in order to obey God. But neither is *he* a real egoist. He believes, ultimately, that we should obey God, even should God command us to altruism.

An ethical egoist will have to maintain the doctrine in both its universal and categorical forms. Should he retreat to hypothetical egoism he is no longer an egoist. Should he retreat to individual egoism his doctrine, while logically impregnable, is no longer ethical, no longer even a doctrine. He may wish to quarrel with this and if so, I submit peacefully. Let him call himself what he will, it makes no difference. I'm a philosopher, not a ratcatcher, and I don't see it as my job to dig vermin out of such burrows as individual egoism.

Obviously something strange goes on as soon as the ethical egoist tries to promulgate his doctrine. What is he doing when he urges upon his audience that they should each observe his own interests and those interests alone? Is he not acting contrary to the egoistic principle? It cannot be to his advantage to convince them, for seizing always their own advantage they will impair his. Surely if he does believe what he says, he should try to persuade them otherwise. Not perhaps that they should devote themselves to his interests, for they'd hardly swallow that; but that everyone should devote himself to the service of others. But is not to believe that someone should act in a certain way to try to persuade him to do so? Of course, we don't always try to persuade people to act as we think they should act. We may be lazy, for instance. But in so far as we believe that Tom should do so and so, we have a tendency to induce him to do so and so. Does it make sense to say: "Of course you should do this, but for goodness' sake don't"? Only where we mean: "You should do this for certain reasons, but here are even more persuasive reasons for not doing it." If the egoist believes ultimately that others should mind themselves alone, then, he must persuade them accordingly. If he doesn't persuade them, he is no universal egoist. It certainly makes sense to say: "I know very well that Tom should act in such and such a way. But I know also that it's not to my advantage that he should so act. So I'd better dissuade him from it." And this is just what the egoist must say, if he is to consider his own advantage and disregard everyone else's. That is, he must behave as an individual egoist, if he is to be an egoist at all.

He may want to make two kinds of objection here:

1. That it will not be to his disadvantage to promulgate the doctrine, provided that his audience fully understand what is to their ultimate

advantage. This objection can be developed in a number of ways, but I think that it will always be possible to push the egoist into either individual or hypothetical egoism.

2. That it is to the egoist's advantage to preach the doctrine if the pleasure he gets out of doing this more than pays for the injuries he must endure at the hands of his converts. It is hard to believe that many people would be satisfied with a doctrine which they could only consistently promulgate in very special circumstances. Besides, this looks suspiciously like individual egoism in disguise.

I shall say no more on these two points because I want to advance a further criticism which seems to me at once fatal and irrefutable.

Now it is time to show the anxious layman that we have means of dealing with ethical egoism which are denied him; and denied him by just that objectivism which he thinks essential to morality. For the very fact that our ultimate principles must be arbitrary means they can't be anything we please. Just because they come out of thin air they can't come out of hot air. Because these principles are not propositions about matters of fact and cannot be deduced from propositions about matters of fact, they must be the fruit of our own attitudes. We assert them largely to modify the attitudes of our fellows but by asserting them we express our own desires and purposes. This means that we cannot use moral language cavalierly. Evidently, we cannot say something like 'All human desires and purposes are bad.' This would be to express our own desires and purposes, thereby committing a kind of absurdity. Nor, I shall argue, can we say 'Everyone should observe his own interests regardless of the interests of others.'

Remembering that the principle is meant to be both universal and categorical, let us ask what kind of attitude the egoist is expressing. Wouldn't that attitude be equally well expressed by the conjunction of an infinite number of avowals thus?—

I want myself to come out on top	&	I don't care about Tom, Dick, Harry . . .
and		and
I want Tom to come out on top	&	I don't care about myself, Dick, Harry . . .
and		and
I want Dick to come out on top	&	I don't care about myself, Tom, Harry . . .
and		and
I want Harry to come out on top	&	I don't care about myself, Dick, Tom . . .
etc.		etc.

From this analysis it is obvious that the principle expressing such an attitude must be inconsistent.

But now the egoist may claim that he hasn't been properly understood. When he says 'Everyone should look after himself and himself alone,' he means 'Let each man do what he wants regardless of what anyone else wants.' The egoist may claim that what he values is merely that he and Tom and Dick and Harry should each do what he wants and not care about what anyone else may want and that this doesn't involve his principle in any inconsistency. Nor need it. But even if it doesn't, he's no better off. Just what does he value? Is it the well-being of himself, Tom, Dick and Harry or merely their going on in a certain way regardless of whether or not this is going to promote their well-being? When he urges Tom, say, to do what he wants, is he appealing to Tom's self-interest? If so, his attitude can be expressed thus:

I want myself to be happy	&	I want myself not to care about Tom, Dick, Harry . . .
and		
I want Tom to be happy		

We need go no further to see that the principle expressing such an attitude must be inconsistent. I have made this kind of move already. What concerns me now is the alternative position the egoist must take up to be safe from it. If the egoist values merely that people should go on in a certain way, regardless of whether or not this is going to promote their well-being, then he is not appealing to the self-interest of his audience when he urges them to regard their own interests. If Tom has any regard for himself at all, the egoist's blandishments will leave him cold. Further, the egoist doesn't even have his own interest in mind when he says that, like everyone else, he should look after himself. A funny kind of egoism this turns out to be.

Perhaps now, claiming that he is indeed appealing to the self-interest of his audience, the egoist may attempt to counter the objection of the previous paragraph. He may move into 'Let each man do what he wants and let each man disregard what others want when their desires clash with his own.' Now his attitude may be expressed thus:

I want everyone to be happy	&	I want everyone to disregard the happiness of others when their happiness clashes with his own.

The egoist may claim justly that a man can have such an attitude and also that in a certain kind of world such a man could get what he wanted. Our objection to the egoist has been that his desires are incompatible. And this is still so. If he and Tom and Dick and Harry did go on as he recommends by saying 'Let each man disregard the happiness of others, when their happiness conflicts with his own,' then assuredly they'd all be completely miserable. Yet he wants them to be happy. He is attempting to counter this by saying that it is merely a fact about the world that they'd make one another miserable by going on as he recommends. The world could conceivably have been different. For this reason, he says, this principle is not inconsistent. This argument may not seem very compelling, but I advance it on the egoist's behalf because I'm interested in the reply to it. For now we don't even need to tell him that the world isn't in fact like that. (What it's like makes no difference.) Now we can point out to him that he is arguing not as an egoist but as a utilitarian. He has slipped into hypothetical egoism to save his principle from inconsistency. If the world were such that we always made ourselves and others happy by doing one another down, then we could find good utilitarian reasons for urging that we should do one another down.

If, then, he is to save his principle, the egoist must do one of two things. He must give up the claim that he is appealing to the self-interest of his audience, that he has even his own interest in mind. Or he must admit that, in the conjunction on page 397, although 'I want everyone to be happy' refers to ends, nevertheless 'I want everyone to disregard the happiness of others when their happiness conflicts with his own' can refer only to means. That is, his so-called ultimate principle is really compounded of a principle and a moral rule subordinate to that principle. That is, he is really a utilitarian who is urging everyone to go on in a certain way so that everyone may be happy. A utilitarian, what's more, who is ludicrously mistaken about the nature of the world. Things being as they are, his moral rule is a very bad one. Things being as they are, it can only be deduced from his principle by means of an empirical premiss which is manifestly false. Good fellows don't need to fear him. They may rest easy that the world is and must be on their side and the best thing they can do is be good.

It may be worth pointing out that objections similar to those I have brought against the egoist can be made to the altruist. The man who holds that the principle 'Let everyone observe the interests of others' is both universal and categorical can be compelled to choose between two alternatives, equally repugnant. He must give up the claim that he is concerned for the well-being of himself and others. Or he must admit that, though 'I want everyone to be happy' refers to ends, nevertheless 'I want everyone to disregard his own happines when it conflicts with the happiness of others' can refer only to means.

I have said from time to time that the egoistic principle is inconsistent. I have not said it is contradictory. This for the reason that we can, without contradiction, express inconsistent desires and purposes. To do so is not to say anything like 'Goliath was ten feet tall and not ten feet tall.' Don't we all want to eat our cake and have it too? And when we say we do we aren't asserting a contradiction. We are not asserting a contradiction whether we be making an avowal of our attitudes or stating a fact about them. We all have conflicting motives. As a utilitarian exuding benevolence I want the man who mows my landlord's grass to be happy, but as a slug-a-bed I should like to see him scourged. None of this, however, can do the egoist any good. For we assert our ultimate principles not only to express our own attitudes but also to induce similar attitudes in others, to dispose them to conduct themselves as we wish. In so far as their desires conflict, people don't know what to do. And, therefore, no expression of incompatible desires can ever serve for an ultimate principle of human conduct.

W. D. FALK

Morality, Self, and Others*

I

In: And how can you say that I never had a moral education? As a child, I was taught that one ought not to maltreat other children, ought to share one's sweets with them, ought to keep tidy and clean; as an adolescent, that one ought to keep one's word, to work, to save, to leave off drink, not to waste the best years of one's life, to let reason govern one's emotions and actions. Nor did I simply learn that one is *called upon* to act in these ways by paternal authority and social custom on pain of censure. I learned to appreciate that one *ought* to do these things *on their merits,* and that what one ought to do on its merits does not depend on the requests or enjoinders of anyone. The facts in the case themselves make one liable, as a reflective person, to act in these ways of one's own accord: they provide one with choice-supporting reasons sufficient to determine one if one knows them and takes diligent account of them.

Out: I know you were taught all this. But why did your teacher say that you ought to act in these ways?

In: Why? For very cogent reasons. My tutor was a student of the Ancients. The moral man, "the man of practical wisdom," he kept quoting Aristotle, "is the man who knows how to deliberate well about what is good and useful for himself." And surely, he would say, you can see for yourself: if you don't act sociably, who will act sociably towards you? Uncleanliness breeds disease. Without work, how are you to live? Without savings, what about your future? Drink leaves one a wreck. Indulging one's sorrows makes them worse. The wasted years, one day you will regret them when it is too late. People who cannot govern themselves are helpless before fortune, without the aid and comfort of inner strength.

Out: And so you think that you had a moral education? Let me tell you, you never even made a start. For what were you taught? That there are things that you ought to do or to avoid on your own account. But one does not learn about morality that way. What one *morally* ought to do is what one ought to do on account of others, or for the sake of some good state of things in general. Now had you been taught to appreciate that you ought to keep clean so as to be pleasing to others, and that you ought to do what moral custom requires for the sake of the general good, then, and then only, would you have learned the rudiments of moral duty.

In: Very well, my upbringing was too narrow. One would hardly be a human being if the good of others, or of society at large, could not weigh with one as a cogent reason for doing what will promote it. So one has not fully learned about living like a rational and moral being unless one has learned to appreciate that one ought to do things out of regard for others, and not only out of regard for oneself.

Out: No, you have still not got my point. I am saying that only insofar as you ought to do things—no matter whether for yourself or for others—for the sake of others, is the reason a moral reason and the ought a moral ought. Reasons of self-regard are not moral reasons at all, and you can forget about them in the reckoning of your *moral* obligations.

In: But this seems artificial. A moral education surely should teach one all about the principles of orderly living and the reasons which tell in

* Reprinted from *Morality and the Language of Conduct,* edited by Hector-Neri Castañeda and George Nakhnikian, pp. 25–47, by permission of The Wayne State University Press. Copyright © 1963. The Wayne State University Press. Parts 4, 5, and 6 are here omitted.

their favor. And if there are also perfectly good personal reasons which tell in their favor, why suppress them? To be sure, in talking to people in ordinary life, we do no such thing. If they say "Why ought I to act sociably?" we say "For the general good as well as your own." If they say "Why ought I to be provident?" we say "For your own good as well as that of others." In short, we offer mixed reasons, and none of these reasons can be spared. One ought not to lie because this is a good social rule, and equally because the habit of evasiveness is destructive of oneself as a person. And one ought not to take to drink or indulge one's sorrows, or waste the best years of one's life primarily out of proper regard for oneself, much as there may be other-regarding reasons as well. If morality were all social service, and one had no moral responsibilities towards oneself or towards others, the moral inconveniences of life would be far less than they are. So I don't see the point of saying "But one has no *moral* commitment to do anything except insofar as one ought to do it on account of others." To say this seems like encouraging people not to bother about doing things insofar as they ought to do them only for personal reasons, as after all this is not a moral ought.

Out: But one does not speak of a moral duty to do things for one's own sake. If one ought to save in order to provide for one's own future, one regards this as a precept not of morals but of prudence. It would be different if one ought to save in order to provide for one's dependents. Moral commitments are those which one has as a moral being, and what makes one a moral being is that one has commitments towards others and does not evade them.

In: Not everyone will agree that as a moral being one has only commitments towards others or that only such commitments are properly "moral." The Greeks, for example, took a wider view. For Plato the equivalent of a moral being was the just or right-living person, and of a moral commitment the right and just course—the one which the right-living person would be led to take. And this right-living person was one who would keep himself in good shape as a sane and self-possessed being, and who would do whatever good and sufficient reasons directed him to do. This is why for Plato and the Greeks temperance and prudence were no less among the just man's commitments than paying his debts and not willfully harming others, and why the one was not treated any less as a moral commitment than the other. The Greeks placed the essence of man as a moral being in his capacity to direct himself on rational grounds; and his commitments as a moral being were therefore all those which he seriously incurred as a properly self-directing being.

Out: Citing the Greeks only shows how distant their concept of morality is from ours. We will not call every rational commitment "moral" or equate the moral with the rational man.

In: This is broadly so, although not entirely. Our concept of morality vacillates between the Greek and the Christian tradition. We associate "moral" with "social" commitment, and the "morally good man" with the "selfless man." But we also speak of man as a "moral agent," of his "moral freedom" and "moral powers"; and here we refer to his whole capacity of self-direction by good and sufficient reasons. One may speak without strain of a personal and social ethic, and refer to the negligent disregard of oneself as a vice, and a sign of moral defect. We call the improvident man "morally weak," and we call the man who can resist drink in company on account of his health or who sticks to his vocation in adversity a man of "moral strength and character." There is certainly little difference in the qualities needed to live up to a social or a personal ought. It takes self-denial to provide for one's future, moral courage to stick to one's vocation. One may show one's mettle as a moral agent here no less than in selfless care for others. There are contemporary moralists who call "moral" any "authentic" commitment of a self-governing person, whether its grounds are social or personal. What justifies them is the broader use of the term which is also part of our language and tradition.

Out: And how eccentric this use is. Our very concept of a moral being is inseparable from the notion of submission of self to a good other than one's own. It is not conceivable that a man should have moral duties on a desert island, devoid of man or beast. Would one say that he still had a moral duty to do what was good for him? You may as well go on and say that if a shipwrecked fellow arrived to share his vegetables, it might be his moral duty to let him starve rather than starve himself.

In: The good of others need not always have the overriding claim on one, if this is what you mean. One could say to a good-hearted and weak-willed person, "For your own sake, you ought to stop neglecting your future, even if this hurts others." This would not be a typically "moral" ought, but one may be giving sound moral advice.

Out: And so, if beneficence had the better of this person, you should call him morally irresponsible and blameworthy. On your showing, he has evaded a moral commitment, and for such evasions one is held morally responsible and liable to censure. But surely, even if I granted your case, one would not call him blameworthy and a morally bad man; as indeed in any case where a person fails to do what his own good requires we do not call him morally bad, but only imprudent, unwise, rash. It is quite a different offense to be slack about brushing one's teeth, than to be negligent about providing dentures for others. And this is so precisely because the second is a moral offense and the first is not and because one is blameworthy for the one and not for the other.

In: I agree that there is a difference. One is only called morally bad and is held answerable to *others* for neglecting what one ought to do out of regard for them. And this is understandable enough. After all, insofar as one fails to do only what one's own good requires, the failing is no one's concern but one's own. But then I should not say that such self-neglect was in no sense morally irresponsible and blameworthy. If it does not call for blame by others, it still calls for self-reproach. A rational person is responsible to himself for not being evasive about anything that he is convinced that he really ought to do. And the lack of moral strength and courage in personal matters, although commonly viewed as an amicable vice, is an amicable vice only in the estimation of others since it is not directly a threat to them.

However, we are not making headway. You find it repugnant to call a commitment "moral" unless its grounds are social and unless its non-observance makes one liable not only to social censure but also to self-reproach; and so be it. Perhaps our disagreement is only verbal, and despite some misgivings, I am ready to settle for your usage. Let us only speak of a moral ought where one ought to do things on account of others. But let us not be misled. For it still does not follow that if one ought to do things on one's own account, this ought may not still be otherwise functioning *like* a moral ought.

Out: How could it be like a moral ought if it is not a moral ought?

In: Because when one thinks of a moral ought, one thinks not only that its grounds are social but also that it has a special force and cogency. A moral ought commits one in all seriousness and in every way, without leaving any reasonable option to act otherwise. Your view comes to saying that if an ought is to be moral it must satisfy two conditions: it must seriously bind one in every way, and it must do so for other-regarding reasons. On your showing, a personal ought cannot be moral, as it cannot satisfy one of these conditions simply by having personal grounds. But it may still satisfy the other condition, and be as cogently binding and action-guiding in its force and function as a moral ought. This is why I can only accept your usage with one proviso: that one may also say that there are other than strictly moral commitments which a right-living person may have to reckon with no less than his strictly moral ones.

Out: Surely you don't expect me to fall for this. When I say "Don't count the purely personal ought as moral" I am not saying "Count it as well, but call it by another name." My point is precisely that it does not function like a moral ought at all. Personal reasons do not commit one to do anything with the same cogency as social reasons. In fact, in calling them reasons of prudence or expediency, we deprecate them. We regard them as inferior, and often disreputable, guides to action. So I won't let you reduce my position to triviality. That only the social commitments are essentially moral must be taken as implying that only they have the characteristic moral force.

In: I thought that this was at the back of our discussion all along. It usually is so with people who are so insistent on your usage, although part of the trouble is that one can never be sure. First one is told that a moral ought is one that commits one on other-regarding grounds and that a personal ought is not a moral ought *for this reason.* But then comes the further suggestion that it is not only different from a moral ought in this way, but is also otherwise inferior. It gives directives, but directives of a somehow shady kind. One way or other, the idea is that a commitment that has personal grounds is either not properly a commitment at all, or, if one in any way, then one that belongs in some limbo of disrepute. But your argument so far has done nothing to prove this point. From your language rule, it only follows that the personal ought must be unlike a moral ought in one essential respect, but not, except by way of confusion, that it must be therefore also unlike a moral ought in other respects too. You might as well say "Surely a lay-analyst is not a doctor," as one is not a doctor without a medical degree, and take this to be proof that a lay-analyst cannot otherwise cure like a doctor either. "No lay-analyst is a doctor" is strictly and trivially true in one way, and may be misleading and tendentiously false in another. And the same with "No personal ought is a *moral* ought." Your language rule makes this strictly and trivially true; but it does not go to show that a personal ought cannot otherwise be *like* a moral ought by being seriously committing or by taking precedence in a conscientious calculus of action-guiding considerations. My point is that, even if this were so, your appeal to usage cannot settle this matter. Logical grammar can decree that only social reasons are properly called "moral." But it cannot decide what reasons can, or cannot, be seriously committing for human beings.

Out: But what I am saying seems substantially true. What one ought to do on account of others is the prototype of the categorically binding ought. Personal reasons have not got the binding cogency of other-regarding reasons, and one deprecates them as inferior and disreputable.

In: And there is some truth in this. Personal and social reasons are not on the same footing in the economy of action-guiding considerations. Personal reasons are very commonly less thoroughly committing, they are often inferior reasons, and not rarely discreditable. But why this is so is a different matter and has not yet been touched on in any way. What is more, personal reasons need not always be in this inferior position. They are often not intrinsically discreditable, and become inferior guides to action only where there are other reasons in the case deserving of prior consideration. Take someone concerned for his health, or future, or self-respect. Surely these are respectable aspirations and there may be things which he ought to do on account of them without violating other claims. His health requires that he be temperate, his self-respect that he live without evasion. Would it not then be positively remiss of him not to act in these ways? If he did not, one would say that he had failed to do what a man in his position really ought to have done, and precisely for the reason which he had. And, if one can say this, what remains of the blemish?

This is why it remains perplexing to me why commitments on personal grounds should be excluded from the orbit of moral teaching, and why modern moralists, unlike the Ancients, should disdain to mention them as an integral part of the moral life. For they may also be cogent and sometimes overridingly cogent commitments to action. And if they are not the whole of morals, why not count them as part of them? For it also seems natural to say that to teach someone all about morality is to teach him about all the valid directives for action; about all those things which he might not otherwise do readily but which, for good and compelling reasons in the nature in the case, he ought to do and would have to break himself into doing whether for the sake of others or his own.

There is, I agree, one tendency to say that the moral man acts in accordance with precepts of selflessness. But there is also another tendency to say that he is the man to organize his life in accordance with all valid precepts. Our disagreement has exhibited the kind of shuttle-service between rival considerations better known as the dialectic of a problem. It may be that this shuttle-service is maintained by a cleft in the very concept of morality. This concept may have grown from conflicting or only partially overlapping observations, which are not fully reconciled in ordinary thinking.

Out: If this is so, I would have to be shown, for common sense still seems to me right in its disparagement of personal reasons.

In: Very well, then we shall have to consider why personal reasons should function as a less cogent guide to action than social ones. I shall admit that in more ways than one the personal ought presents a special case, but not that it presents a case for disparagement except in special contexts. After this, the question of whether the personal ought is properly called moral or not will appear less important, partly because it will have become plainer why there is a question. Nor shall I try to offer a ruling on this point. With a background of discourse as intricate and full of nuance as in this case, discretion is the better part of valor, and clarification is a safer bet than decision.

2

Whenever one remarks that clearly there are things which one ought to avoid or do if only for one's own sake, someone is sure to say, "No doubt; but any such ought is only a precept of prudence or expediency." It is a textbook cliché against Hobbes that his account of morality comes to just this. And this is said as if it were an obvious truth and enough to discredit all such precepts in one go. This assumes a great deal and settles nothing.

What it assumes is this: that everything that one ever does for one's own sake, one does as a matter of prudence *or* expediency; that there is no difference between these two; that morality always differs from prudence as a scent differs from a bad smell; and that everyone knows how so and why.

None of this will do.

In the first place, not everything done for oneself is done for reasons of prudence. That one ought to insure one's house, save for one's old age, not put all one's money into one venture, are precepts of prudence. But it is not a precept of prudence, though it may be a good precept, that someone ought to undergo a dangerous operation as a long shot to restoring his health rather than linger under a disability forever after.

The point is that prudence is only one way of looking after oneself. To act prudently is to play safe, for near-certain gains at small risks. But some good things one cannot get in this way. To get them at all one has to gamble, taking the risk of not getting them even so, or of coming to harm in the process. If one values them enough, one will do better by oneself to throw prudence to the winds, to play for high stakes, knowing full well the risk and the price of failure. Explorers, artists, scientists, mountaineers are types who may serve themselves better by this course. So will most people at some juncture. Thus, if someone values security, then that he ought to save in order to be secure is a precept of prudence. But that someone ought to stick to his vocation when his heart is in it enough to make it worth risking security or health or life itself is not a precept of *prudence,* but of *courage.*

One says sometimes, "I ought to save, as I *want* to be prudent," but sometimes "as I *ought* to be prudent." One may also decide that in one's own best interests one ought to be prudent rather than daring, or daring rather than prudent, as the case may be. Now, that one ought to do something as it would be prudent is a dictate of prudence. But that one really ought to be prudent, in one's own best interests, would not be a dictate of prudence again. One then ought to play safe in order to serve oneself *best* and not in order to serve oneself *safely.*

A dictate of prudence where one wants to be prudent but ought to be courageous in one's own best interests is a dictate of timidity. A dictate of courage, where one feels reckless but ought to be prudent, is a dictate of foolhardiness. Both will then plainly be morally imperfect precepts. But there is nothing obviously imperfect about a dictate of prudence where one ought to be prudent, or a dictate of courage where one ought to be daring. Such precepts seem near-moral enough to allow one to call the habit of acting on them a virtue. The Ancients considered both prudence and courage as moral virtues. Oddly enough, in our time, one is more ready to view courage on one's own behalf as a moral virtue than prudence. It needs the reminder that precepts of self-protection may be precepts of courage as well as of prudence for one to see that any precept of self-protection may have a moral flavor. I think that the dim view which we take of prudence corresponds to a belief that to be daring is harder than to be level-headed, a belief most likely justified within our own insurance-minded culture. But such belief would have seemed strange to Bishop Butler and the fashionable eighteenth-century gentlemen to whom he addressed himself. Prudence in Butler's time, as throughout the ancient world, was not yet the cheap commodity which it is with us; and the price of virtue varies with the market.

There are other precepts of self-protection which are not "just a matter of prudence" either. That one ought not to take to drugs or drink, indulge oneself in one's sorrows, waste one's talents, commit suicide just in the despair of the moment, are precepts made of sterner stuff. One wants to say, "Surely, it is more than just a matter of prudence that one ought to avoid these things." And rightly so. The effect on oneself of taking to drugs or drink, or of any of the others, is not conjectural, but quite certain. To avoid them is therefore more than a matter of *taking no risks.*

Sometimes, when one looks down a precipice, one feels drawn to jump. If one refrains, it will hardly be said of one, "How prudent he is, he takes no chances." The avoidance of excesses of all kinds in one's own best interests is in this class. The habit of avoiding them the Greeks called temperance, a virtue distinct from prudence.

Another error is to equate the prudent with the expedient, and, again, the expedient with everything that is for one's own good. To save may be prudent; but whether it is expedient or convenient to start now is another matter. With a lot of money to spare at the moment it will be expedient; otherwise it will not. But it may be prudent all the same. Again, one marries in the hope of finding happiness; but marriage in this hope is not a marriage of convenience. The point is that reasons of expediency are reasons of a special sort: reasons for doing something on the ground that it is incidentally at hand to serve one's purpose, or because it serves a purpose quite incidental to the purpose for which one would normally be doing this thing. One marries for reasons of expediency when one marries for money, but not when in hope of finding happiness. Hobbes said that "men never act except with a view to some good to themselves." This would be quite different from saying that "they never act except with a view to what is expedient."

There is also this difference between the prudent and the expedient: one can speak of "rules of prudence," but less well of "rules of expediency." The expedient is what happens to serve. It is not therefore easily bottled in rules.

The word "prudence" is used too freely in still one more context. When one wishes to justify the social virtues to people, a traditional and inviting move is to refer them, among other things at least, to their own good. "You ought to hold the peace, be honest, share with others." "Why?" "Because an order in which such practices were universal is of vital concern to you; and your one hope of helping to make such an order is in doing your share." The classical formulation of this standard move is Hooker's, quoted with approval by Locke: "If I cannot but wish to receive good . . . how should I look to have any part of my desire herein satisfied, unless I myself be careful to satisfy the like desire: my desire therefore to be loved of my equals in nature, as much as possible may be, imposes upon me a *natural duty* of bearing to themward fully the like affection."

Now, it is said again, "So defended, the social duties come to no more than precepts of prudence"; and this goes with the veiled suggestion that it is morally improper to use this defense. But, even if so defended, the social duties are not necessarily reduced purely to precepts of prudence. For they may be recommended in this way either as mere *rules* or as *principles* of self-protection; and as principles they would be misdescribed as mere precepts of prudence. The distinction is this: When one says, "People ought to practice the social virtues, if only for their own benefit," one may be saying, "They ought to practice them for this reason as a *rule,* i.e., normally, as much as each time this is likely to be for their own good." Or one may be saying, "They ought to practice them for this reason not merely as a rule but as a *matter of principle,* i.e., every time, whether at that time this is likely to be for their good or not." And one might defend the adoption of this principle by saying, "Because your best, even if slim, hope of contributing to a society fit for you to live in lies in adding to the number of principled people who will do their share each time, without special regard for their good at that time."

Now this seems to me a precept of courage rather than one of prudence. The game of attempting by one's actions to make society a place fit for one to live in is a gamble worth the risk only because of the known price of not attempting it. This gamble is a root condition of social living. One is sure to give hostages to fortune, but again, what other hope has one got? Hence, if a man practiced the social virtues, thinking that he ought to as a matter of principle, and on these grounds, one will praise him for his *wisdom,* his firm grasp of vital issues, his steadfastness, his courage. But one will not necessarily congratulate him on his prudence. For many times the prudent course might have been otherwise. It may be wise to persist in being honest with cheats, or forbearing with the aggressive, or helpful to those slow to require helpfulness; but it might have been more prudent to persist for no longer than there was requital, or not even to start before requital was assured.

Now would it be a moral precept or not that, if only out of proper care for oneself, one ought to act on principles of wisdom and courage? That one ought to risk life in order to gain it? And, assuming a society of men acting fixedly on these principles but no others, would it or would it not contain men of moral virtue? One might as well ask, "Is a ski an article of footwear?" There is no more of a straight answer here than there. One may say, "Not quite"; and the point of saying this needs going into. But it would be more misleading to say, "Not at all." For it is part of the meaning of "moral precept" that it prescribes what a man would do in his wisdom—if he were to consider things widely, looking past the immediate concerns of self and giving essentials due weight before incidentals. As it is also part of what is meant by one's moral capacities that one can live by such considerations, it becomes fruitless after a time to press the point whether such precepts are properly called moral.

There are then varieties of the personal ought, differing in the considerations on which they are based and the qualities needed to follow them; and they all seem at least akin to a "moral" ought in their action-guiding force and function. But I grant that one does not want to speak of more than a kinship, and the point of this needs considering. One's hesitancy derives from various sources which have to be traced one by one.

Some of the hesitancy comes from contexts where one can say disparagingly, "He did this *only* for reasons of prudence, *only* for reasons of expediency, *only* for himself." This plainly applies sometimes, but it does not apply always. One would hardly say of someone without dependents, "He thought that he ought to save, but *only* for reasons of prudence"; or of someone, "He thought that he ought to have the carpenter in along with the plumber, but *only* for reasons of expediency or convenience"; or "He thought that he ought to become a doctor, but *only* because the career would suit him." "Only" has no point here. Why else should a man without dependents save, except to be prudent? Why else should anyone have the carpenter in along with the plumber, except for convenience? What better reason is there normally for choosing a career than that it will suit one? On the other hand, there is point in saying, "He held the peace only because it was prudent," "He saved only because it was convenient," "He practices the social virtues only for self-protection." It is plain why "only" applies here and is disparaging. One says "only" because something is done for the wrong or for not quite the right reason—done for *one* reason where there is *another* and nearer reason for doing it anyway. Personal reasons are often in this position, and then they are disparaged as inferior. One saves "only" because it is expedient, if one ought to have saved anyway for reasons of prudence. One holds the peace "only" because it was prudent when one ought to have done so anyway as a matter of principle and even if it had not been prudent. And one practices the social virtues "only" for self-protection when one does not *also* practice them for the general good.

The last case is different from the others. Plainly, one ought to practice the social virtues as principles of general good. But on none but perhaps pure Christian principles would it hold, or necessarily hold, that one ought to practice them on this ground unconditionally, however great the provocation to oneself. The case for the social virtues is weakened when the social environment becomes hostile and intractable by peaceable means; it is correspondingly strengthened where they can also be justified as wise principles of self-protection. That someone practices forbearance "only" as a wise principle of self-protection is not therefore to say that he practices it for a reason which is neither here nor there; but rather for a reason which falls short of all the reason there is. This was, in effect, the view of the old Natural Law moralists—Hooker, Grotius, Pufendorf: the social virtues derive joint support from our natural concern for our own good and for that of society. Hobbes streamlined this account by denying the second, which provoked subsequent moralists to deny the first. Both Hobbes's sophistical toughness and the well-bred innocence of the academic moralists since are distorted visions which are less convincing than the unsqueamish common sense of the philosophers and divines of earlier times.

3

So far we have met no reason for deprecating every personal ought. Men often have cause to be temperate, courageous, wise for their own good. This is often the only, or the nearest, reason why they should. It is then pointless to go on complaining, "But they still only act so for their own sakes." "Only" is a dangerous word.

Even so one feels that somehow a commitment that has only personal grounds is morally inferior. "One ought to risk one's life in order to gain it" seems near-moral enough. But compare it with "One ought to risk one's life in order to save others." This still seems different. And this is so not only because the one has a personal reason and the other has not, but also because where the reason is social rather than personal, the ought itself feels different—more binding, more relentless, and more properly called "moral" for this reason. The real inferiority of the personal ought seems here to lie in a lack of formal stringency.

There are such differences of stringency between "I ought to save, as I *want* to provide for my future" and "I ought to save, as I *ought* to provide for my children." The first prescribes saving as a means to an end which one *is* seeking; the second as a means to an end which in turn one *ought* to seek. The first therefore commits one formally less than the second. It leaves one at liberty to escape the commitment by renouncing the ultimate end, which the second does not. One may, as Kant did, call the first ought hypothetical and non-moral, and the second categorical and moral on account of this difference. The distinction is made to rest on a formal difference of the binding force and not at all on any material difference in the justifying grounds. The formally "moral" commitment is to an ultimate end or rule of life and to what one ought to do on account of it in any particular case.

Now the personal ought comes more typically as non-moral and the social ought as moral in form. One says, "You don't *want* to make your misery worse, so you ought not to dwell on it"; "You *want* to secure your future, so you ought to be prudent and save." One might also say "You *want* to provide for your children, so you ought to save"; and then formally this too would be a non-moral ought although its grounds are other-regarding. But this is the less typical case. One is often more grudging about the needs of others than one's own. So there is here less occasion for saying, "You ought to do this on account of an end which you *are* seeking"; and more for saying, "You ought to do it on account of an end which in turn you *ought* to seek."

This typical difference between the personal and the social ought raises two questions: one, whether it is an inherent feature of the personal ought to be never more than non-moral in form; the other, whether, even if this were so, it would be any the worse as a possibly serious commitment. Both of these positions have been taken. One's own good one always seeks. It is not therefore among the ends which one ever ought to seek in the absence of a sufficient inclination. But with the good of others, or the avoidance of harm to them, it is different. Here are ends which one does not always seek, but ought to seek all the same: ends which one may still have reason for seeking on their own account; which one would be led to seek on a diligently comprehending and imaginative review of them (of what doing good, or harm, inherently amount to). Only the social ought, therefore, may bind one to the choice of the final end as well as of the means, while the personal ought binds one only to the means on account of an end which one wants already. The personal ought is therefore only non-moral in form, and "only" once again signifies a defect. But all this is misleading. One does not always seek one's own good as much as one has reasonable ground for seeking it, and about this I shall say more later. But even supposing that one did, then all precepts of self-regard would prescribe what one ought to do consistently with an already desired end. But they would not therefore be negligible or improper all the time.

It is true that what one ought to do consistently with a desired end need not be what one really ought to do at all. The end, or the means towards it, may prove undesirable on further scrutiny either by reason of what it is in itself or of the special circumstances of the case. I ought to save as I wish for security, and there is nothing inherently wrong with the end or the means, and so far so good. But I also ought to support my mother, and I cannot do both. Then maybe I ought not to do *all told* what otherwise I ought to have done. But in this case, the precept of prudence would have been less than "only" non-moral. It would have been invalid all told, and counter-moral altogether. But surely not every case is like this.

For often there is nothing wrong with the things which one cares for on one's own behalf, and one really does care for them. Even if one had the abstract option to give them up, one has no serious wish to do so. One often does care for one's life or health or career or the regard of others, and one often *may* without violating other claims. And one always *may* care, if one does, for one's peace of mind or self-respect. And so what one ought to do as far as these ends go one really ought to do. As one wants to live, one really ought to look after one's health. As one wants to be liked by others, one really ought to keep a civil tongue. As one wants to live after one's own fashion, one really ought to stick to one's vocation in adversity. As one wants to be able to respect oneself or, in Hume's phrase, "bear one's own survey," one really ought to conduct oneself as one thinks that one has good reasons for doing. All these precepts tell one what one ought to do consistently with a personal end which one actually has at heart; and where they hold after scrutiny, they hold no less validly and conclusively than any fully "moral" precept. The conscientious man would have to take notice of them no less than of the others. They deserve to be called "semi-moral" at least.

I keep allowing that a distinction remains. "I ought to work hard, as I *want* to succeed" is still a different kind of commitment from "I ought to work hard as I *ought* to provide for others." The difference is partly in the end, personal in the one case, impersonal in the other. But this quite apart, there is another reason for the difference. The second ought has a quality of sternness which is lacking from the first, and which is a product of its *form,* not of its *content.* For the second is an ought twice over. It says that one ought to take steps for an end which one ought to pursue ultimately. The first is an ought only once; it says that one ought to take steps for an end with regard to which one is at liberty as far as it goes. So the second ought subjects one to a regimen which is complete. It commits one *through and through,* whereas the semi-moral ought does not. And this through-and-throughness gives to the moral ought its notoriously stern flavor. It makes it more imposing and often more onerous. One is having one's socks pulled up all over. And additional qualities are required of one for appreciating it and acting on it: not only forethought and consistency, but also the ability to appreciate an end as committing by reason of its own nature, which, among other things, requires sympathetic understanding and imagination. No wonder that a moral ought inspires those confronted with it with awe. The semi-moral ought cannot compete with this, though when it comes to the precepts of wisdom and courage on one's own behalf they come near enough.

However, having given the formally moral ought its due, I want to add that respect for it should be no reason for slighting the other. For in the first place, and as a reassurance to those who regard lack of onerousness as a defect, though the semi-moral ought is not so bad, it may be bad enough. How hard it is to pull up one's socks does not necessarily depend on their number; two commodious socks may respond more readily than one shrunken one. One semi-moral and one moral case may serve as examples. If one really *wants* to do a thing and do it well, one ought to take trouble. And if one really *ought* to do good to the sick, one ought to telephone and inquire how they are getting on. The first requires a lot: putting oneself into harness, forgoing all sorts of things which one would rather do, particularly at that moment, coping with aches and pains and anxieties, playing the endless game of snakes and ladders with achievement, and yet going on, nursing one's purpose. The second, though in form a commitment through and through, requires nothing but getting up and dialing a number. It may need a great deal not to put things off, not to dwell on one's miseries, not to spend improvidently, all simply because one really ought not to in one's own best interest. The ought that lays down the law on these things may be little imposing in form. But such is the bulk of the stuff which compounds the "moral" inconveniences of ordinary life. And one also measures oneself and others by the show that is made on this front.

But then it is not the lack of onerousness as much as that of formal stringency that is felt to discredit the semi-moral ought. It still is not binding like the moral ought, simply as it is not committing through and through. Moreover, its very subservience to an end which is only desired seems something amiss, as if a man should rather act always for the sake of ends which he ultimately ought to seek, and not just of ends which he happens to be seeking even if nothing is wrong with them.

This sense of guilt about the non-obligatory rests partly on excessive zeal for original sin. What the natural man in one desires never can be quite as it should. It is always "Tell me what you want to do, and I shall tell you what you ought to do instead." But there is also a failure to see that not every semi-moral commitment is renounceable at will. Not every situation need confront one with a commitment through and through, and it is improper to demand that it should or to deplore that it does not.

When one ought to do a thing on account of some desired end, then one need not always be at liberty to escape the commitment by renouncing the end. It depends on whether one is free to give up the end itself, and this is not always so. One says of some ends, "If you want to seek it you may, and if you don't want to you need not." There is here no reason against seeking the end, nor reason enough to tell one to seek it in the absence of a desire for it. And one is free to escape a commitment on account of such an end simply by giving up the end. But in the case of other ends one will say, "If you want to seek it you may, but if you do not want to you still ought to all the same." Again there is no reason against seeking the end if one wants to, but here there would be still reason for seeking it even if one did not want to. A commitment on account of such an end one may not escape at will as one is not here free to give up the end. It is arguable whether commitments on personal grounds are not often in this position. One ought to be temperate as one wants to preserve one's health. And although this is a semi-moral ought as far as it goes, one need not be free to get out of it at will. For even if one ceased to care about the end, one might still here have reasonable ground for caring, and ought to care all the same.

An ought of this kind commits one on account of an end which one seeks as well as ought to seek. And this makes it like an ought through and through, but still not quite. There can be ends which one seeks and ought to seek. But insofar as one *is* seeking such an end, it is strained to say that one also *ought* to seek it at the same time. One would rather say that if one were not seeking it already, then one ought to be seeking it all the same. This is why, if someone is perfectly willing about an end, a commitment on account of this end would still not for him have the form of a commitment through and through; and this although it is potentially such a commitment and would turn into one as soon as he ceased to be readily inclined towards the end.

The point is that ought applies only where there is a case for pulling one's socks up. The same action may be viewed in otherwise the same circumstances either as one which one ought to do, or as one which one wants to and may do, according to the psychological starting point. One normally wants to have one's breakfast, and one would find it improper to have it put before one with the remark, "You ought to eat this morning." "Why ought I? Don't I eat every morning anyway?" But if one were convalescent, the remark would be in place. Nor would one say to a notoriously indulgent parent, "You ought not to be harsh with your children" (though one might wonder whether he *may* be so indulgent). The remark applies to a parent bad at controlling his temper. If I resolved to become an early riser and succeeded, I might report in retrospect, "For the first month it was a duty, but afterwards it ceased to be a duty and became a habit, if not a pleasure."

None of this should be surprising. Ought is an action-guiding concept. It expresses the notion that one is liable to direction by reasons in the case which would motivate one if one gave them due consideration. And one cannot be *liable* to direction by reasons except in a matter of doing what one is not fully motivated to do already. This is why it cannot be an obligation for one to do what one wants to do anyway, much as it might become an obligation for one to do it if one ceased to want to. This is also why, when one really wants to do something, the natural question to ask is not, "And *ought* I to do this thing?" but rather, "And *may* I do it?" or "Would there be anything wrong with it?" or "Ought I perhaps *not* to do it?" One looks for possible reasons against, not for possible reasons for. And what point would there be in doing anything more? When one really wants to do something, one already has, *for* doing it, all the reason one needs. And this is also why one only says "You ought to" to others when one takes it that there is a case for changing their present frame of mind. But to wonder whether one ought to (as distinct from wondering whether one may, or perhaps ought not to) where one already wants to would be like wondering whether to sit down when seated; and to say "You ought to" to someone quite ready to, would be like advising a sitting man to take a seat. *There is no ought for those blessed with wants which are not wrong.*

One may object: "But surely one can say that everyone ought to do good, and if there were benevolent people this would not make this false." And this is correct, but no refutation. What raises a problem are general statements like "People ought to do good," "One ought to be tolerant." But one may make a general statement without having to specify all the conditions when it shall or shall not hold. One says in general, "Butter will melt in the sun"; and if someone interjected, "But *not* when one has just melted it on the kitchen stove," this would be no rebuttal. "*This* butter will melt in the sun," when I am bringing it dripping from the kitchen, would be different. This particular butter is not *liable* to melt, even though it remains true that butter is. The same with "People ought to do good." This is a general statement, and one need not state the obvious: that it will not apply to someone whose heart needs no melting as it is soft already. Nor does one use "one ought to" directively to people, except for general purposes of propaganda. "I ought to" and "you ought to" are in a logically different class.

One makes general ought-statements about standard ends and practices towards which people commonly have no sufficient inclination. These ought-statements apply particularly to doing things for others, and less so to doing things for oneself. And this alone could explain why one normally does not say that people ought to care for their own good. For the question of whether they *ought* to does not here normally arise. They can be trusted with a modicum of well adjustment towards this end—they seek it, and, within limits, they may seek it. Hence, what one ought to do on account of one's own good is commonly a commitment on account of a desired end, much as it might also turn into a commitment through and through with a loss of immediate interest in the end. Nor could one reasonably hope that such commitments were more imposing in form than they are. On the contrary, one may say that the less imposing the ought, the better designed for living the man.

W. E. H. LECKY

The Psychological Egoists*

According to these writers we are governed exclusively by our own interest.[1] Pleasure, they

* From W. E. H. Lecky, *History of European Morals from Augustus to Charlemagne* (New York: George Braziller, 1955), Vol. I, pp. 7–11.

[1] 'I conceive that when a man deliberates whether he shall do a thing or not do it, he does nothing else but consider whether it be better for himself to do it or not to do it.'—Hobbes *On Liberty and Necessity*. 'Good and evil are names that signify our appetities and aversions.'—Ibid. *Leviathan*, part i. ch. xvi. 'Obligation is the necessity of doing or omitting any action in order to be happy.'—Gay's dissertation prefixed to King's *Origin of Evil*, p. 36. 'The only reason or motive by which individuals can possibly be induced to the practice of virtue, must be the feeling immediate or the prospect of future private happiness.'—Brown *On the Characteristics*, p. 159. 'En tout temps, en tout lieu, tant en matière de morale qu'en matière d'esprit, c'est l'intérêt personnel qui dicte le jugement des particuliers, et l'intérêt général qui dicte celui des nations. . . .Tout homme ne prend dans ses jugements conseil que de son intérêt.'—['In all times, at all places, as much in moral as in spiritual matters, it is personal interest that dictates judgments of individuals, and the general interest that of nations . . . Each man is guided in the judgments only by his own interest.']—Helvétius *De l'Esprit*, discours ii. 'Nature has placed mankind under the governance of two sovereign masters, pain and pleasure. It is for them alone to point out what we ought to do, as well as to determine what we shall do. . . . The principle of utility recognises this subjection, and assumes it for the foundation of that system, the object of which is to rear the fabric of felicity by the hands of reason and of law Systems which attempt to question it, deal in sounds instead of sense, in caprice instead of reason, in darkness instead of light.'—Bentham's *Principles of Morals and Legislation*, ch. i. 'By the principle of utility is meant that principle which approves or disapproves of every action whatsoever, according to the tendency which it appears to have to augment or diminish the happiness of the party whose interest is in question.—Ibid. 'Je regarde l'amour éclairé de nous-mêmes comme le principe de tout sacrifice moral.'—['I look upon enlightened self-interest as the fundamental principle of all moral sacrifice.']—D'Alembert quoted by D. Stewart, *Active and Moral Powers*, vol. i. p. 220.

assure us, is the only good,[2] and moral good and moral evil mean nothing more than our voluntary conformity to a law that will bring it to us.[3] To love good simply as good, is impossible.[4] When we speak of the goodness of God, we mean only His goodness to us.[5] Reverence is nothing more than our conviction, that one who has power to do us both good and harm, will only do us good.[6] The pleasures of piety arise from the belief that we are about to receive pleasure, and the pains of piety from the belief that we are about to suffer pain from the Deity.[7] Our very affections, according to some of these writers, are all forms of self-love. Thus charity springs partly from our desire to obtain the esteem of others, partly from the expectation that the favours we have bestowed will be reciprocated, and partly, too, from the gratification of the sense of power, by the proof that we can satisfy not only our own desires but also the desires of others.[8] Pity is an emotion arising from a vivid realisation of sorrow that may befall ourselves, suggested by the sight of the sorrows of others. We pity especially those who have not deserved calamity, because we consider ourselves to belong to that category; and the spectacle of suffering against which no forethought could provide, reminds us most forcibly of what may happen to ourselves.[9] Friendship is

[2] 'Pleasure is in itself a good; nay, even setting aside immunity from pain, the only good; pain is in itself an evil, and, indeed, without exception, the only evil, or else the words good and evil have no meaning.'—Bentham's *Principles of Morals and Legislation,* ch. x.

[3] 'Good and evil are nothing but pleasure and pain, or that which occasions or procures pleasure or pain to us. Moral good and evil then is only the conformity or disagreement of our voluntary actions to some law whereby good or evil is drawn on us by the will and power of the law maker, which good and evil, pleasure or pain, attending our observance or breach of the law by the decree of the law maker, is that we call reward or punishment.'—Locke's *Essay,* book ii. ch. xxviii. 'Take away pleasures and pains, not only happiness, but justice, and duty, and obligation, and virtue, all of which have been so elaborately held up to view as independent of them, are so many empty sounds.'—Bentham's *Springs of Action,* ch. i. § 15.

[4] 'Il lui est aussi impossible d'aimer le bien pour le bien, que d'aimer le mal pour le mal.'—['It is just as impossible for him to love good for its own sake as it is to love evil for its own sake.']—Helvétius *De l'Esprit,* disc. ii ch. v.

[5] 'Even the goodness which we apprehend in God Almighty, is his goodness to us.'—Hobbes *On Human Nature,* ch. vii. § 3. So Waterland, 'To love God is in effect the same thing as to love happiness, eternal happiness; and the love of happiness is still the love of ourselves.'—*Third Sermon on Self-love.*

[6] 'Reverence is the conception we have concerning another, that he hath the power to do unto us both good and hurt, but not the will to do us hurt.'—Hobbes *On Human Nature,* ch. viii. § 7.

[7] 'The pleasures of piety are the pleasures that accompany the belief of a man's being in the acquisition, or in possession of the goodwill or favour of the Supreme Being; and as a fruit of it, of his being in the way of enjoying pleasures to be received by God's special appointment either in this life or in a life to come.'—Bentham's *Principles of Morals and Legislation,* ch. v. 'The pains of piety are the pains that accompany the belief of a man's being obnoxious to the displeasure of the Supreme Being, and in consequence to certain pains to be inflicted by His especial appointment, either in this life or in a life to come. These may be also called the pains of religion.'—Ibid.

[8] 'There can be no greater argument to a man of his own power, than to find himself able not only to accomplish his own desires, but also to assist other men in theirs; and this is that conception wherein consisteth charity.'—Hobbes *On Hum. Nat.* ch. ix. § 17. 'No man giveth but with intention of good to himself, because gift is voluntary; and of all voluntary acts, the object to every man is his own good.'—Hobbes' *Leviathan,* part i. ch. xv. 'Dream not that men will move their little finger to serve you, unless their advantage in so doing be obvious to them. Men never did so, and never will while human nature is made of its present materials.'—Bentham's *Deontology,* vol. ii. p. 133.

[9] 'Pity is imagination or fiction of future calamity to ourselves, proceeding from the sense of another man's calamity. But when it lighteth on such as we think have not deserved the same, the compassion is greater, because there then appeareth more probability that the same may happen to us; for the evil that happeneth to an innocent man may happen to every man.'—Hobbes *On Hum. Nat.* ch. ix. § 10. 'La pitié est souvent un sentiment de nos propres maux dans les maux d'autrui. C'est une habile prévoyance des malheurs où nous pouvons tomber. Nous donnons des secours aux autres pour les engager à nous en donner en de semblables occasions, et ces services que nous leur rendons sont, à proprement parler des biens que nous nous faisons à nous-mêmes par avance.'—['Pity is often a perception of our own troubles in the troubles of others. It is an astute prescience of the misfortunes into which we might fall. We help others in order to commit them to helping us under similar circumstances; and these services we render them are, properly speaking, services we render to ourselves in advance.']—La Rochefoucauld, *Maximes,* 264. Butler has remarked that if Hobbes' account were true, the most fearful would be the most compassionate nature; but this is perhaps not quite just, for Hobbes' notion of pity implies the union of two not absolutely identical, though nearly allied, influences, timidity and imagination. The theory of Adam Smith, though closely connected with, differs totally in consequences from that of Hobbes on this point. He says, 'When I condole with you for the loss of your son, in order to enter into your grief, I do not consider what I, a person of such a character and profession, should suffer if I had a son, and if that son should die—I consider what I should suffer if I was really you. I not only change circumstances with you, but I change persons and characters. My grief, therefore, is entirely upon your account. . . . A man may sympathise with a

the sense of the need of the person befriended.[10]

From such a conception of human nature it is easy to divine what system of morals must flow. No character, feeling, or action is naturally better than others, and as long as men are in a savage condition, morality has no existence. Fortunately, however, we are all dependent for many of our pleasures upon others. Co-operation and organisation are essential to our happiness, and these are impossible without some restraint being placed upon our appetites. Laws are enacted to secure this restraint, and being sustained by rewards and punishments, they make it the interest of the individual to regard that of the community. . . .

woman in child-bed, though it is impossible he should conceive himself suffering her pains in his own proper person and character.'—*Moral Sentiments*, part vii. ch. i. § 3.

[10] Ce que les hommes ont nommé amitié n'est qu' une société, qu'un ménagement réciproque d'intérêts et qu'un échange de bons offices. Ce n'est enfin qu'un commerce où l'amour-propre se propose toujours quelque chose à gagner.'—['What men have called "friendship" is but an "association", a reciprocal management of interests, an exchange of good offices. It is, finally, nothing but a form of commerce where self-interest always expects to gain'.]—La Rochefoucauld, *Max.* 83. See this idea developed at large in Helvétius.

BERNARD DE MANDEVILLE

An Inquiry into the Origin of Moral Virtue*

All untaught animals are only solicitous of pleasing themselves, and naturally follow the bent of their own inclinations, without considering the good or harm that from their being pleased will accrue to others. This is the reason that, in the wild state of nature, those creatures are fittest to live peaceably together in great numbers, that discover the least of understanding, and have the fewest appetites to gratify; and consequently no species of animals is, without the curb of government, less capable of agreeing long together in multitudes than that of man; yet such are his qualities, whether good or bad, I shall not determine, that no creature besides himself can ever be made sociable: but, being an extraordinarily selfish and headstrong, as well as cunning animal, however he may be subdued by superior strength, it is impossible by force alone to make him tractable, and receive the improvements he is capable of.

The chief thing therefore, which lawgivers and other wise men, that have laboured for the establishment of society, have endeavoured, has been to make the people they were to govern believe, that it was more beneficial for every body to conquer than indulge his appetites, and much better to mind the public than what seemed his private interest. As this has always been a very difficult task, so no wit or eloquence has been left untried to compass it; and the moralists and philosophers of all ages employed their utmost skill to prove the truth of so useful an assertion. But, whether mankind would have ever believed it or not, it is not likely that any body could have persuaded them to disapprove of their natural inclinations, or prefer the good of others to their own, if, at the same time, he had not showed them an equivalent to be enjoyed as a reward for the violence, which, by so doing, they of necessity must commit upon themselves. Those that have undertaken to civilize mankind were not ignorant of this; but being unable to give so many real rewards as would satisfy all persons for every individual action, they were forced to contrive an imaginary one, that, as a general equivalent for the trouble of self-denial, should serve on all

* First printed in the second edition of Mandeville's *The Fable of the Bees, or Private Vices, Public Benefits, &c.*, London, 1723.

occasions, and without costing any thing either to themselves or others, be yet a most acceptable recompense to the receivers.

They thoroughly examined all the strength and frailities of our nature, and observing that none were either so savage as not to be charmed with praise, or so despicable as patiently to bear contempt, justly concluded that flattery must be the most powerful argument that could be used to human creatures. Making use of this bewitching engine, they extolled the excellency of our nature above other animals, and setting forth with unbounded praises the wonders of our sagacity and vastness of understanding, bestowed a thousand encomiums on the rationality of our souls, by the help of which we were capable of performing the most noble achievements. Having, by this artful way of flattery, insinuated themselves into the hearts of men, they began to instruct them in the notions of honour and shame; representing the one as the worst of all evils, and the other as the highest good to which mortals could aspire: which being done, they laid before them how unbecoming it was the dignity of such sublime creatures to be solicitous about gratifying their appetites, which they had in common with brutes, and at the same time unmindful of those higher qualities that gave them the preeminence over all visible beings. They indeed confessed, that those impulses of nature were very pressing; that it was troublesome to resist, and very difficult wholly to subdue them. But this they only used as an argument to demonstrate how glorious the conquest of them was on the one hand and how scandalous on the other not to attempt it.

To introduce, moreover, an emulation amongst men, they divided the whole species into two classes, vastly differing from one another: the one consisted of abject, low-minded people, that always hunting after immediate enjoyment, were wholly incapable of self-denial, and without regard to the good of others, had no higher aim than their private advantage; such as being enslaved by voluptuousness, yielded without resistance to every gross desire, and made no use of their rational faculties but to heighten their sensual pleasure. These wild grovelling wretches, they said, were the dross of their kind, and having only the shape of men, differed from brutes in nothing but their outward figure. But the other class was made up of lofty high-spirited creatures, that free from sordid selfishness, esteemed the improvements of the mind to be their fairest possessions; and, setting a true value upon themselves, took no delight but in embellishing that part in which their excellency consisted; such as despising whatever they had in common with irrational creatures, opposed by the help of reason their most violent inclinations; and making a continual war with themselves, to promote the peace of others, aimed at no less than the public welfare and the conquest of their own passion.

> Fortior est qui se quam qui fortissima Vincit
> Moenia . . .[1]

These they called the true representatives of their sublime species, exceeding in worth the first class by more degrees than that itself was superior to the beasts of the field.

As in all animals that are not too imperfect to discover pride, we find that the finest and such as are the most beautiful and valuable of their kind have generally the greatest share of it; so in man, the most perfect of animals, it is so inseparable from his very essence (how cunningly soever some may learn to hide or disguise it) that without it the compound he is made of would want one of the chiefest ingredients; which, if we consider, it is hardly to be doubted but lessons and remonstrances, so skilfully adapted to the good opinion man has of himself as those I have mentioned, must, if scattered amongst a multitude, not only gain the assent of most of them as to the speculative part, but likewise induce several, especially the fiercest, most resolute, and best among them to endure a thousand inconveniences and undergo as many hardships, that they may have the pleasure of counting themselves men of the second class and consquently appropriating to themselves all the excellencies they have heard of it.

From what has been said, we ought to expect, in the first place, that the heroes who took such extraordinary pains to master some of their natural appetites and preferred the good of others to any visible interest of their own would not recede an inch from the fine notions they had received concerning the dignity of rational creatures; and having ever the authority of the gov-

[1] The man who conquers himself is stronger than the one who conquers the strongest states. [Cf. *Proverbs*, 16:32.]

ernment on their side, with all imaginable vigour assert the esteem that was due to those of the second class, as well as their superiority over the rest of their kind. In the second, that those who wanted a sufficient stock of either pride or resolution to buoy them up in mortifying of what was dearest to them, followed the sensual dictates of nature, would yet be ashamed of confessing themselves to be those despicable wretches that belonged to the inferior class and were generally reckoned to be so little removed from brutes; and that therefore, in their own defence, they would say as others did, and hiding their own imperfections as well as they could, cry up self-denial and public spiritedness as much as any: for it is highly probable, that some of them, convinced by the real proofs of fortitude and self-conquest they had seen, would admire in others what they found wanting in themselves, others be afraid of the resolution and prowess of those of the second class, and that all of them were kept in awe by the power of their rulers; wherefore it is reasonable to think, that none of them (whatever they thought in themselves) would dare openly contradict what by everybody else was thought criminal to doubt of.

This was (or at least might have been) the manner after which savage man was broke; from whence it is evident, that the first rudiments of morality broached by skilful politicians to render men useful to each other, as well as tractable, were chiefly contrived, that the ambitious might reap the more benefit from and govern vast numbers of them with the greater ease and security. This foundation of politics being once laid, it is impossible that man should long remain uncivilized: for even those who only strove to gratify their appetites, being continually crossed by others of the same stamp, could not but observe, that whenever they checked their inclinations or but followed them with more circumspection, they avoided a world of troubles and often escaped many of the calamities that generally attended the too eager pursuit after pleasure.

First, they received, as well as others, the benefit of those actions that were done for the good of the whole society and consequently could not forbear wishing well to those of the superior class that performed them. Secondly, the more intent they were in seeking their own advantage, without regard to others, the more they were hourly convinced that none stood so much in their way as those that were most like themselves.

It being the interest then of the very worst of them, more than any, to preach up public-spiritedness, that they might reap the fruits of the labour and self-denial of others, and at the same time indulge their own appetites with less disturbance, they agreed with the rest to call everything, which, without regard to the public, man should commit to gratify any of his appetites, VICE; if in that action there could be observed the least prospect that it might either be injurious to any of the society or ever render himself less serviceable to others: and to give the name of VIRTUE to every performance, by which man, contrary to the impulse of nature, should endeavour the benefit of others or the conquest of his own passions out of a rational ambition of being good.

It shall be objected that no society was ever any ways civilized before the major part had agreed upon some worship or other of an overruling power and consequently that the notions of good and evil and the distinction between virtue and vice were never the contrivance of politicians, but the pure effect of religion. Before I answer this objection, I must repeat what I have said already, that in this inquiry into the origin of moral virtue, I speak neither of Jews or Christians, but man in his state of nature and ignorance of the true Deity; and then I affirm, that the idolatrous superstitions of all other nations and the pitiful notions they had of the Supreme Being, were incapable of exciting man to virtue and good for nothing but to awe and amuse a rude and unthinking multitude. It is evident from history that in all considerable societies, how stupid or ridiculous soever people's received notions have been as to the deities they worshipped, human nature has ever exerted itself in all its branches and that there is no earthly wisdom or moral virtue, but at one time or other men have excelled in it in all monarchies and commonwealths, that for riches and power have been any ways remarkable.

The Egyptians, not satisfied with having deified all the ugly monsters they could think on, were so silly as to adore the onions of their own sowing; yet at the same time their country was the most famous nursery of arts and sciences in the world and themselves more eminently skilled in the deepest mysteries of nature than any nation has been since.

No states or kingdoms under heaven have yielded more or greater patterns in all sorts of moral virtues than the Greek and Roman empires, more especially the latter; and yet how loose, absurd and ridiculous were their sentiments as to sacred matters? For without reflecting on the extravagant number of their deities, if we only consider the infamous stories they fathered upon them, it is not to be denied but that their religion, far from teaching men the conquest of their passions and the way to virtue, seemed rather contrived to justify their appetites and encourage their vices. But if we would know what made them excel in fortitude, courage, and magnanimity, we must cast our eyes on the pomp of their triumphs, the magnificence of their monuments and arches; their trophies, statues, and inscriptions; the variety of their military crowns, their honours decreed to the dead, public encomiums on the living, and other imaginary rewards they bestowed on men of merit; and we shall find that what carried so many of them to the utmost pitch of self-denial was nothing but their policy in making use of the most effectual means that human pride could be flattered with.

It is visible, then, that it was not any heathen religion or other idolatrous superstition that first put man upon crossing his appetites and subduing his dearest inclinations, but the skilful management of wary politicians; and the nearer we search into human nature, the more we shall be convinced that the moral virtues are the political offspring which flattery begot upon pride.

There is no man, of what capacity or penetration soever, that is wholly proof against the witchcraft of flattery, if artfully performed and suited to his abilities. Children and fools will swallow personal praise, but those that are more cunning, must be managed with much greater circumspection; and the more general the flattery is, the less it is suspected by those it is levelled at. What you say in commendation of a whole town is received with pleasure by all the inhabitants: speak in commendation of letters in general, and every man of learning will think himself in particular obliged to you. You may safely praise the employment a man is of or the country he was born in because you give him an opportunity of screening the joy he feels upon his own account under the esteem which he pretends to have for others.

It is common among cunning men that understand the power which flattery has upon pride, when they are afraid they shall be imposed upon, to enlarge, though much against their conscience, upon the honour, fair dealing, and integrity of the family, country, or sometimes the profession of him they suspect; because they know that men often will change their resolution and act against their inclination, that they may have the pleasure of continuing to appear in the opinion of some what they are conscious not to be in reality. Thus sagacious moralists draw men like angels, in hopes that the pride at least of some will put them upon copying after the beautiful originals which they are represented to be.

When the incomparable Sir Richard Steele, in the usual elegance of his easy style, dwells on the praises of his sublime species, and with all the embellishments of rhetoric sets forth the excellency of human nature, it is impossible not to be charmed with his happy turns of thought and the politeness of his expressions. But though I have been often moved by the force of his eloquence and ready to swallow the ingenious sophistry with pleasure, yet I could never be so serious, but, reflecting on his artful encomiums, I thought on the tricks made use of by the women that would teach children to be mannerly. When an awkward girl before she can either speak or go begins after many entreaties to make the first rude essays of curtesying, the nurse falls in an ecstacy of praise; "There is a delicate curtesy! O fine Miss! there is a pretty lady! Mama! Miss can make a better curtsey than her sister Molly!" The same is echoed over by the maids, whilst Mama almost hugs the child to pieces; only Miss Molly, who being four years older, knows how to make a very handsome curtesy, wonders at the perverseness of their judgment, and swelling with indignation, is ready to cry at the injustice that is done her, till, being whispered in the ear that it is only to please the baby and that she is a woman, she grows proud at being let into the secret, and rejoicing at the superiority of her understanding, repeats what has been said with large additions and insults over the weakness of her sister, whom all this while she fancies to be the only bubble among them. These extravagant praises would by anyone above the capacity of an infant be called fulsome flatteries, and, if you will, abominable lies; yet experience teaches us that by the help of such gross encomiums young misses will be brought to make pretty curtesies and behave themselves womanly much sooner, and with less trouble, than they would without them. It is the same with boys, whom they will strive to persuade that all fine gentlemen do as they are bid and that none but beggar boys are rude or dirty their clothes; nay, as soon as the wild brat with his untaught fist begins to fumble for his hat, the mother, to make him pull it off, tells him before he is two years old that he is a man; and if he repeats that action when she desires him, he is presently a captain, a lord mayor, a king, or something higher if she can think of it, till egged on by the force of praise, the little urchin endeavors to imitate man as well as he can and strains all his faculties to appear what his shallow noddle imagines he is believed to be.

The meanest wretch puts an inestimable value upon himself, and the highest wish of the ambitious man is to have all the world, as to that particular, of his opinion: so that the most insatiable thirst after fame that ever hero was inspired with was never more than an ungovernable greediness to engross the esteem and admiration of others in future ages as well as his own; and (what mortification soever this truth might be to the second thoughts of an Alexander or a Caesar) the great recompense in view, for which the most exalted minds have with so much alacrity sacrificed their quiet, health, sensual pleasures, and every inch of themselves, has never been anything else but the breath of man, the aerial coin of praise. Who can forbear laughing when he thinks on all the great men that have been so serious on the subject of that Macedonian madman, his capacious soul, that mighty heart, in one corner of which, according to Lorenzo Gratian, the world was so commodiously lodged that in the whole there was room for six more? Who can forbear laughing, I say, when he compares the fine things that have been said of Alexander with the end he proposed to himself from his vast exploits to be proved from his own mouth; when the vast pains he took to pass the Hydaspes forced him to cry out, Oh ye Athenians, could you believe what dangers I expose myself to, to be praised by you! To define then the reward of glory in the amplest manner, the most that can be said of it is that it consists in a superlative felicity which a man, who is conscious of having performed a noble action, enjoys in self-love, whilst he is thinking on the applause he expects of others.

But here I shall be told that besides the noisy toils of war and public bustle of the ambitious there are noble and generous actions that are performed in silence; that virtue being its own reward, those who are really good have a satisfaction in their consciousness of being so, which is all the recompense they expect from the most worthy performances; that among the heathens there have been men, who, when they did good to others, were so far from coveting thanks and applause, that they took all imaginable care to be forever concealed from those on whom they bestowed their benefits, and consequently that pride has no hand in spurring man on to the highest pitch of self-denial.

In answer to this I say that it is impossible to judge of a man's performance, unless we are thoroughly acquainted with the principle and motive from which he acts. Pity, though it is the most gentle and the least mischievous of all our passions, is yet as much a frailty of our nature as anger, pride, or fear. The weakest minds have generally the greatest share of it, for which reason none are more compassionate than women and children. It must be owned that of all our weaknesses, it is the most amiable and bears the greatest resemblance to virtue; nay, without a considerable mixture of it, the society could hardly subsist: but as it is an impulse of nature that consults neither the public interest nor our own reason, it may produce evil as well as good. It has helped to destroy the honour of virgins and corrupted the integrity of judges; and whoever acts from it as a principle, what good soever he may bring to the society, has nothing to boast of, but that he has indulged a passion that has happened to be beneficial to the public. There is no merit in saving an innocent babe ready to drop into the fire: the action is neither good nor bad, and what benefit soever the infant received, we only obliged ourselves; for to have seen it fall, and not strove to hinder it, would have caused a pain, which self-preservation compelled us to prevent: Nor has a rich prodigal, that happens to be of a commiserating temper and loves to gratify his passions, greater virtue to boast of when he relieves an object of compassion with what to himself is a trifle.

But such men, as without complying with any

weakness of their own, can part from what they value themselves and from no other motive but their love to goodness perform a worthy action in silence: such men, I confess, have acquired more refined notions of virtue than those I have hitherto spoke of; yet even in these (with which the world has yet never swarmed) we may discover no small symptoms of pride, and the humblest man alive must confess that the reward of a virtuous action, which is the satisfaction that ensues upon it, consists in a certain pleasure he procures to himself by contemplating on his own worth: which pleasure, together with the occasion of it, are as certain signs of pride as looking pale and trembling at any imminent danger are the symptoms of fear.

If the too scrupulous reader should at first view condemn these notions concerning the origin of moral virtue and think them perhaps offensive to Christianity, I hope he will forbear his censures when he shall consider that nothing can render the unsearchable depth of the Divine Wisdom more conspicuous than that man, whom Providence had designed for society, should not only by his own frailties and imperfections be led into the road to temporal happiness, but likewise receive, from a seeming necessity of natural causes, a tincture of that knowledge, in which he was afterwards to be made perfect by the true religion, to his eternal welfare.

JOSEPH BUTLER

Sermon Eleven—Upon the Love of Our Neighbour*

And if there be any other commandment, it is briefly comprehended in this saying, namely, Thou shalt love thy neighbour as thyself.—Rom. 13:9

It is commonly observed that there is a disposition in men to complain of the viciousness and corruption of the age in which they live, as greater than that of former ones; which is usually followed with this further observation that mankind has been in that respect much the same in all times. Now, not to determine whether this last be not contradicted by the accounts of history, thus much can scarce be doubted—that vice and folly take different turns, and some particular kinds of it are more open and avowed in some ages than in others; and I suppose it may be spoken of as very much the distinction of the present to profess a contracted spirit and greater regards to self-interest than appears to have been done formerly. Upon this account it seems worth while to inquire whether private interest is likely to be promoted in proportion to the degree in which self-love engrosses us, and prevails over all other principles, or whether the contracted affection may not possibly be so prevalent as to disappoint itself, and even contradict its own end, private good.

And since, further, there is generally thought to be some peculiar kind of contrariety between self-love and the love of our neighbour, between the pursuit of public and of private good, insomuch that when you are recommending one of these, you are supposed to be speaking against the other; and from hence arises a secret prejudice against and frequently open scorn of all talk of public spirit and real good-will to our fellow creatures; it will be necessary to inquire what respect benevolence hath to self-love, and the pursuit of private interest to the pursuit of public; or whether there be anything of that peculiar inconsistency and contrariety between them, over and above what there is between self-love and other passions and particular affections, and their respective pursuits.

These inquiries, it is hoped, may be favorably attended to; for there shall be all possible conces-

* From Joseph Butler, *Fifteen Sermons upon Human Nature.* First printed in 1726. Second edition, London, 1729.

sions made to the favorite passion, which hath so much allowed to it, and whose cause is so universally pleaded: it shall be treated with the utmost tenderness and concern for its interests.

In order to this, as well as to determine the forementioned questions, it will be necessary to consider the nature, the object, and end of that self-love, as distinguished from other principles or affections in the mind and their respective objects.

Every man hath a general desire of his own happiness; and likewise a variety of particular affections, passions, and appetites, to particular external objects. The former proceeds from, or is, self-love, and seems inseparable from all sensible creatures, who can reflect upon themselves and their own interest or happiness, so as to have that interest an object to their minds: what is to be said of the latter is, that they proceed from, or together make up, that particular nature, according to which man is made. The object the former pursues is somewhat internal, our own happiness, enjoyment, satisfaction; whether we have or have not a distinct particular perception what it is, or wherein it consists: the objects of the latter are this or that particular external thing, which the affections tend towards, and of which it hath always a particular idea or perception. The principle we call self-love never seeks anything external for the sake of the thing, but only as a means of happiness or good: particular affections rest in the external things themselves. One belongs to man as a reasonable creature reflecting upon his own interest or happiness: the other, though quite distinct from reason, are as much a part of human nature.

That all particular appetites and passions are towards *external things themselves,* distinct from the *pleasure arising from them,* is manifested from hence, that there could not be this pleasure, were it not for that prior suitableness between the object and the passion: there could be no enjoyment or delight for one thing more than another, from eating food more than from swallowing a stone, if there were not an affection or appetite to one thing more than another.

Every particular affection, even the love of our neighbour, is as really our own affection, as self-love; and the pleasure arising from its gratification is as much my own pleasure, as the pleasure self-love would have from knowing I myself should be happy some time hence, would be my own pleasure. And if, because every particular affection is a man's own, and the pleasure arising from its gratification his own pleasure, or pleasure to himself, such particular affection must be called self-love. According to this way of speaking, no creature whatever can possibly act but merely from self-love; and every action and every affection whatever is to be resolved up into this one principle. But then this is not the language of mankind: or, if it were, we should want words to express the difference between the principle of an action, proceeding from cool consideration that it will be to my own advantage; and an action, suppose of revenge, or of friendship by which a man runs upon certain ruin, to do evil or good to another. It is manifest the principles of these actions are totally different, and so want different words to be distinguished by: all that they agree in is, that they both proceed from, and are done to gratify an inclination in a man's self. But the principle or inclination in one case is self-love; in the other, hatred, or love of another. There is then a distinction between the cool principle of self-love, or general desire of our own happiness, as one part of our nature, and one principle of action; and the particular affections towards particular external objects, as another principle of action. How much soever, therefore, is to be allowed to self-love, yet it cannot be allowed to be the whole of our inward constitution; because, you see, there are other parts or principles which come into it.

Further, private happiness or good is all which self-love can make us desire or be concerned about. In having this consists its gratification; it is an affection to ourselves—a regard to our own interest, happiness, and private good: and in the proportion a man hath this, he is interested, or a lover of himself. Let this be kept in mind, because there is commonly, as I shall presently have occasion to observe, another sense put upon these words. On the other hand, particular affections tend towards particular external things; these are their objects; having these is their end; in this consists their gratification: no matter whether it be, or be not, upon the whole, our interest or happiness. An action, done from the former of these principles, is called an interested action. An action, proceeding from any of the latter, has its denomination of passionate, ambitious, friendly, revengeful, or any other, from the particular appetite or affection from which it proceeds.

Thus self-love, as one part of human nature, and the several particular principles as the other part, are themselves, their objects, and ends, stated and shown.

From hence it will be easy to see how far, and in what ways, each of these can contribute and be subservient to the private good of the individual. Happiness does not consist in self-love. The desire of happiness is no more the thing itself, than the desire of riches is the possession or enjoyment of them. People may love themselves with the most entire and unbounded affection, and yet be extremely miserable. Neither can self-love any way help them out, but by setting them on work to get rid of the causes of their misery, to gain or make use of those objects which are by nature adapted to afford satisfaction. Happiness or satisfaction consists only in the enjoyment of those objects which are by nature suited to our several particular appetites, passions, and affections. So that if self-love wholly engrosses us and leaves no room for any other principle, there can be absolutely no such thing at all as happiness or enjoyment of any kind whatever; since happiness consists in the gratification of particular passions, which supposes the having of them. Self-love then does not constitute *this* or *that* to be our interest or good; but our interest or good being constituted by nature and supposed self-love, only puts us upon obtaining and securing it. Therefore, if it be possible that self-love may prevail and exert itself in a degree or manner which is not subservient to this end, then it will not follow that our interest will be promoted in proportion to the degree in which that principle engrosses us, and prevails over others. Nay, further, the private and contracted affection, when it is not subservient to this end, private good, may, for anything that appears, have a direct contrary tendency and effect. And if we will consider the matter, we shall see that it often really has. Disengagement is absolutely necessary to enjoyment; and a person may have so steady and fixed an eye upon his own interest, whatever he places it in, as may hinder him from attending to many gratifications within his reach, which others have their minds free and open to. Over-fondness for a child is not generally thought to be for its advantage; and, if there be any guess to be from appearances, surely that character we call *selfish* is not the most promising for happiness. Such a temper may plainly be, and exert itself in a degree and manner which may give unnecessary and useless solicitude and anxiety, in a degree and manner which may prevent obtaining the means and materials of enjoyment, as well as the making use of them. Immoderate self-love does very ill consult its own interest; and how much soever a paradox it may appear, it is certainly true, that, even from self-love, we should endeavour to get over all inordinate regard to, and consideration of, ourselves. Every one of our passions and affections hath its natural stint and bound, which may easily be exceeded; whereas our enjoyments can possibly be but in a determinate measure and degree. Therefore such excess of the affection, since it cannot procure any enjoyment, must in all cases be useless, but is generally attended with inconveniences, and often is down-right pain and misery. This holds as much with regard to self-love as to all other affections. The natural degree of it, so far as it sets us on work to gain and make use of the materials of satisfaction, may be to our real advantage; but beyond or beside this, it is in several respects an inconvenience and disadvantage. Thus it appears that private interest is so far from being likely to be promoted in proportion to the degree in which self-love engrosses us, and prevails over all other principles, that *the contracted affection may be so prevalent as to disappoint itself and even contradict its own end, private good.*

"But who, except the most sordidly covetous, ever thought there was any rivalship between the love of greatness, honour, power, or between sensual appetites, and self-love? No; there is a perfect harmony between them. It is by means of these particular appetites and affections that self-love is gratified in enjoyment, happiness, and satisfaction. The competition and rivalship is between self-love and the love of our neighbour. That affection which leads us out of ourselves, makes us regardless of our own interest, and substitute that of another in its stead." Whether then there be any peculiar competition and contrariety in this case, shall now be considered.

Self-love and interestedness was stated to consist in or be an affection to ourselves, a regard to our own private good: it is, therefore, distinct from benevolence, which is an affection to the good of our fellow creatures. But that benevolence is distinct from, that is, not the same thing with self-love, is no reason for its being looked upon with any peculiar suspicion, because every principle whatever, by means of which self-love is gratified, is distinct from it. And all things, which are distinct from each other, are equally so. A man has an affection or aversion to another: that one of these tends to, and is gratified by doing good, that the other tends to, and is gratified by doing harm, does not in the least alter the respect which either one or the other of these inward feelings has to self-love. We use the word *property* so as to exclude any other persons having an interest in that, of which we say a particular man has the property: and we often use the word *selfish* so as to exclude in the same manner all regards to the good of others. But the cases are not parallel: for though that exclusion is really part of the idea of property, yet such positive exclusion, or bringing this peculiar disregard to the good of others into the idea of self-love, is in reality adding to the idea, or changing it from what it was before stated to consist in, namely, in an affection to ourselves. This being the whole idea of self-love, it can no otherwise exclude good-will or love of others, than merely by not including it, no otherwise than it excludes love of arts, or reputation, or of anything else. Neither, on the other hand, does benevolence, any more than love of art or of reputation, exclude self-love. Love of our neighbour, then has just the same respect to, is no more distant from self-love, than hatred of our neighbour, or than love and hatred of anything else. Thus the principles, from which men rush upon certain ruin for the destruction of an enemy, and for the preservation of a friend, have the same respect to the private affection, are equally interested, or equally disinterested: and it is of no avail, whether they are said to be one or the other. Therefore, to those who are shocked to hear virtue spoken of as disinterested, it may be allowed, that it is indeed absurd to speak thus of it; unless hatred, several particular instances of vice, and all the common affections and aversions in mankind are acknowledged to be disinterested too. Is there any less inconsistence between the love of inanimate things, or of creatures merely sensitive, and self-love, than between self-love, and the love of our neighbour? Is desire of, and delight in the happiness of another any more a diminution of self-love, than desire of and delight in the esteem of another? They are both equally desire of and delight in somewhat external to ourselves: either both or neither are so. The object of self-love is expressed in the term self: and every appetite of sense, and every particular affection of the heart, are equally interested or disinterested, because the objects of them all are equally self or somewhat else. Whatever ridicule, therefore, the mention of a disinterested principle or action may be supposed to lie open to, must, upon the matter being thus stated, relate to ambition, and every appetite and particular affection, as much as to benevolence. And indeed all the ridicule, and all the grave perplexity, of which this subject hath had its full share, is merely from words. The most intelligible way of speaking of it seems to be this: that self-love, and the actions done in consequence of it, (for these will presently appear to be the same as to this question) are interested; that particular affections towards external objects, and the actions done in consequence of those affections, are not so. But every one is at liberty to use words as he pleases. All that is here insisted upon is, that ambition, revenge, benevolence, all particular passions whatever, and the actions they produce, are equally interested or disinterested.

Thus it appears, that there is no peculiar contrariety between self-love and benevolence; no greater competition between these, than between any other particular affections and self-love. This relates to the affections themselves. Let us now see whether there be any peculiar contrariety between the respective courses of life which these affections lead to; whether there be any greater competition between the pursuit of private and of public good, than between any other particular pursuits and that of private good.

There seems no other reason to suspect that there is any such peculiar contrariety, but only that the course of action which benevolence leads to, has a more direct tendency to promote the good of others, than that course of action, which love of reputation, suppose, or any other particular affection, leads to. But that any affection tends to the happiness of another, does not hinder its tending to one's own happiness too. That others enjoy the benefit of the air and the light of the sun, does not hinder but that these are as much one's own private advantage now, as they would be if we had the property of them exclusive of all others. So a pursuit which tends to promote the good of another, yet may have as great tendency to promote private interest, as a pursuit which does not tend to the good of another at all, or which is mischievous to him. All particular affections whatever, resentment, benevolence, love of the arts, equally lead to a course of action for their own gratification, *i. e.*, the gratification of ourselves: and the gratification of each gives delight: so far, then, it is manifest they have all the same respect to private interest. Now, take into consideration further, concerning these three pursuits, that the end of the first is the harm; of the second, the good of another; of the last, somewhat indifferent: and is there any necessity, that these additional considerations should alter the respect which we before saw these three pursuits had to private interest; or render any one of them less conducive to it than any other? Thus, one man's affection is to honour, as his end; in order to obtain which, he thinks no pains too great. Suppose another, with such a singularity of mind, as to have the same affection to public good, as his end, which he endeavours with the same labour to obtain. In case of success, surely the man of benevolence hath as great enjoyment as the man of ambition; they both equally having the end, their affections, in the same degree, tended to; but in case of disappointment, the benevolent man has clearly the advantage; since endeavouring to do good, considered as a virtuous pursuit, is gratified by its own consciousness, *i. e.*, is in a degree its own reward.

And as to these two, or benevolence and any other particular passions whatever, considered in a further view, is forming a general temper, which more or less disposes us for enjoyment of all the common blessings of life, distinct from their own gratification: is benevolence less the temper of tranquility and freedom, than ambition or covetousness? Does the benevolent man appear less easy with himself, from his love to his neighbour? Does he less relish his being? Is there any peculiar gloom seated on his face? Is his mind less open to entertainment, or to any particular gratification? Nothing is more manifest, than that being in good humour, which is benevolence whilst it last, is itself the temper of satisfaction and enjoyment.

Suppose, then, a man sitting down to consider how he might become most easy to himself, and attain the greatest pleasure he could; all that which is his real natural happiness; this can only consist in the enjoyment of those objects which are by nature adapted to our several faculties. These particular enjoyments make up the sum total of our happiness; and they are supposed to arise from riches, honours, and the gratification of sensual appetites. Be it so: yet none profess themselves so completely happy in these enjoyments, but that there is room left in the mind for others, if they were presented to them. Nay, these, as much as they engage us, are not thought so high, but that human nature is capable even of greater. Now there have been persons in all ages, who have professed that they found satisfaction in the exercise of charity, in the love of their neighbour, in endeavouring to promote the happiness of all they had to do with, and in the pursuit of what is just, and right, and good, as the general bent of their mind and end of their life; and that doing an action of baseness or cruelty, would be as great violence to *their* self, as much breaking in upon their nature, as any external force. Persons of this character would add, if they might be heard, that they consider themselves as acting in the view of an infinite Being, who is in a much higher sense the object of reverence and of love, than all the world besides; and, therefore, they could have no more enjoyment from a wicked action done under his eye, than the persons to whom they are making their apology could, if all mankind were the spectators of it; and that the satisfaction of approving themselves to his unerring judgment, to whom they thus refer all their actions, is a more continued settled satisfaction than any this world can afford; as also that they have, no less than others, a mind free and open to all the common innocent gratifications of it such as they are. And, if we go no further, does there appear any absurdity in this? Will any one take upon him to say, that a man cannot find his account in this general course of life, as much as in the most unbounded ambition, or the excesses of pleasure? Or that such a person has not consulted so well for himself, for the satisfaction and peace of his own mind, as the ambitious or dissolute man? And though the consideration, that God himself will in the end justify their taste, and support their cause, is not formally to be insisted upon here; yet thus much comes in, that all enjoyments whatever are much more clear and unmixed, from the assurance that they will end well. Is it certain, then, that there is nothing in these pretensions to happiness, especially when there are not wanting persons, who have supported themselves with satisfactions of this kind in sickness, poverty, disgrace, and in the very pangs of death? whereas, it is manifest all other enjoyments fail in these circumstances. This surely looks suspicious of having somewhat in it. Self-love, methinks, should be alarmed. May she not possibly pass over greater pleasures, than those she is so wholly taken up with?

The short of the matter is no more than this. Happiness consists in the gratification of certain affections, appetites, passions, with objects which are by nature adapted to them. Self-love may indeed set us on work to gratify these: but happiness or enjoyment has no immediate connexion with self-love, but arises from such gratification alone. Love of our neighbour is one of those affections. This, considered as a virtuous principle, is gratified by a consciousness of endeavouring to promote the good of others: but considered as a natural affection, its gratification consists in the actual accomplishment of this endeavour. Now, indulgence or gratification of this affection, whether in that consciousness, or this accomplishment, has the same respect to interest, as indulgence of any other affection; they equally proceed from, or do not proceed from, self-love; they equally include or equally exclude, this principle. Thus it appears, that "benevolence and the pursuit of public good have at least as great respect to self-love and the pursuit of private good, as any other particular passions, and their respective pursuits."

Neither is covetousness, whether as a temper or pursuit, any exception to this. For if by covetousness is meant the desire and pursuit of riches for their own sake, without any regard to or consideration of the uses of them; this hath as little to do with self-love, as benevolence hath. But by this word is usually meant, not such madness and total distraction of mind, but immoderate affection to and pursuit of riches as possessions, in order to some further end; namely, satisfaction, interest, or good. This, therefore, is not a particular affection, or particular pursuit, but it is the general principle of self-love, and the general pursuit of our own interest; for which reason, the word *selfish* is by every one appropriated to this temper and pursuit. Now, as it is ridiculous to assert that self-love and the love of our neighbour are the same; so neither is it asserted that following these different affections hath the same tendency and respect to our own interest. The comparison is not between self-love and the love of our neighbour; between pursuit of our own interest, and the interest of others; but between the several particular affections in human nature towards external objects, as one part of the comparison; and the one particular affection to the good of our neighbour, as the one part of it: and it has been shown, that all these have the same respect to self-love and private interest.

There is indeed frequently an inconsistence, or interfering between self-love or private interest, and the several particular appetites, passions, affections, or the pursuits they lead to. But this competition or interfering is merely accidental, and happens much oftener between pride, revenge, sensual gratifications, and private interest, than between private interest and benevolence. For nothing is more common than to see men give themselves up to a passion or an affection to their known prejudice and ruin, and in direct contradiction to manifest and real interest, and the loudest calls of self-love: whereas the seeming competitions and interfering between benevolence and private interest, relate much more to the materials or means of enjoyment, than to enjoyment itself. There is often an interfering in the former, where there is none in the latter. Thus, as to riches: so much money as a man gives away, so much less will remain in his possession. Here is a real interfering. But though a man cannot possibly give without lessening his fortune, yet there are multitudes might give without lessening their own enjoyment; because they may have more than they can turn to any real use or advantage to themselves. Thus, the more thought and time any one employs about the interests and good of others, he must necessarily have less to attend his own; but he may have so ready and large a supply of his own wants, that such thought might be really useless to himself, though of great service and assistance to others.

The general mistake, that there is some greater inconsistence between endeavouring to promote the good of another and self-interest, than between self-interest and pursuing anything else, seems, as hath already been hinted to arise from our notions of property; and to be carried on by this property's being supposed to be itself our happiness or good. People are so very much taken up with this one subject, that they seem from it to have formed a general way of thinking, which they apply to other things that they have nothing to do with. Hence, in a confused and slight way, it might well be taken for granted, that another's having no interest in an affection (*i. e.*, his good not being the object of it) renders, as one may speak, the proprietor's interest in it greater; and that if another had an interest in it, this would render his less, or occasion that such affection could not be so friendly to self-love, or conducive to private good, as an affection or pursuit which has not a regard to the good of another. This, I say, might be taken for granted, whilst it was not attended to, that the object of every particular affection is equally somewhat external to ourselves: and whether it be the good of another person, or whether it be any other external thing, makes no alteration with regard to its being one's own affection, and the gratification of it one's own private enjoyment. And so far as it is taken for granted, that barely having the means and materials of enjoyment is what constitutes interest and happiness; that our interest and good consists in possessions themselves, in having the property of riches, houses, lands, gardens, not in the enjoyment of them; so far it will even more strongly be taken for granted, in the way already explained, that an affection's conducing to the good of another, must even necessarily occasion it to conduce less to private good, if not to be positively detrimental to it. For, if property and happiness are one and the same thing, as by increasing the property of another, you lessen your own property, so by promoting the happiness of another, you must lessen your own happiness. But whatever occasioned the mistake, I hope it has been fully proved to be one; as it has been proved, that there is no peculiar rivalship or competition between self-love and benevolence; that as there may be a competition between these two, so there may also between any particular affection whatever and self-love; that every particular affection, benevolence among the rest, is subservient to self-love, by being the instrument of private enjoyment; and that in one respect benevolence contributes more to private interest, *i. e.*, enjoyment or satisfaction, than any other of the particular common affections, as it is in a degree its own gratification.

And to all these things may be added, that religion, from whence arises our strongest obligation to benevolence, is so far from disowning the principle of self-love, that it often addresses itself to that very principle, and always to the mind in that state when reason presides; and there can no access be had to the understanding, but by convincing men, that the course of life we would persuade them to is not contrary to their interest. It may be allowed, without any prejudice to the cause of virtue and religion, that our ideas of happiness and misery are, of all our ideas, the nearest and most important to us; that they will, nay, if you please, that they ought to prevail over those of order, and beauty, and harmony, and proportion, if there should ever be, as it is impossible there ever should be, any inconsistency between them; though these last, too, as expressing the fitness of action, are real as truth itself. Let it be allowed, though virtue or moral rectitude does indeed consist in affection to and pursuit of what is right and good, as such; yet that, when we sit down in a cool hour, we can neither justify to ourselves this or any other pursuit, till we are convinced that it will be for our happiness, or at least not contrary to it.

AUSTIN DUNCAN-JONES

Selfishness and Egoism*

Butler's discussions of selfishness are directed against two distinct, and incompatible, errors: one characteristic of philosophers, the other of men of the world.

He wished to give an account of human nature, and its virtuous and vicious dispositions, which would refute both the teaching of psychological egoists, such as Hobbes, who held that every action is necessarily selfish, and the assumptions of less sophisticated people, who supposed that good conduct and self-interested conduct must be antithetical, and virtue must imply self-denial. He relies on two main contentions: (1) that a correct analysis of the notion of a selfish or "interested" action shows that it applies to some actions only, not to all; (2) that it shows also that the class of actions which are good or virtuous and the class of those which are selfish or interested are not mutually exclusive, but overlap to a considerable extent.

The theory of universal selfishness, known as psychological egoism, and in one of its forms as psychological hedonism, seems to have a perennial life. It has often been refuted by philosophers, and Butler's is the classic refutation of it. Yet it flourishes still, and is felt by many people to have the force of an axiom, whose denial is absurd. There is no doubt that, as Butler made plain, its plausibility rests partly on confusions about the meaning of words. These confusions we must now try to remove.

The theory of universal selfishness seems to rest on two supports. (1) Every action of mine is prompted by motives or desires or impulses which are *my* motives, not someone else's. This fact might also be expressed by saying that "whenever I act I am always pursuing my own ends, or seeking to satisfy my own desires". And from this statement we might pass to the statement "I am always pursuing something for myself, or seeking my own satisfaction". Here is what seems like a proper description of a man acting selfishly, and if the description applies to all actions of all men it follows that all men in all their actions are selfish.

(2) It might be added—though Butler does not develop the point—that for this conclusion we can find some empirical evidence. There is no doubt that men sometimes act hypocritically, and affect to be disinterested when they are not. And they sometimes deceive themselves in supposing that they are disinterested. If we have some antecedent reason for believing in universal selfishness, the existence of hypocritical and self-deceived action will confirm the hypothesis. It will show that the appearance of disinterested action is reconcilable with the reality of selfish action, and will make it easier to suppose that in other cases also the appearance of disinterestedness is illusory.

But the empirical evidence is not enough to prove universal sefishness unsupported by some antecedent presumption in its favour. To Butler it seemed obvious that from principle (1) it could not follow that men always act selfishly. But it will be as well to see what sort of grounds there are for accepting principle (1), and what exactly this principle amounts to.

On the face of it, there may be exceptions to the generalisation that every action of mine is prompted by motives of mine. For example, I may be hypnotised, and perform some action at the suggestion of the hypnotist which I should never have performed unhypnotised. Let us imagine for the moment that the vulgar conception of hypnotism is true, according to which a hyp-

* From Austin Duncan-Jones, *Butler's Moral Philosophy* (Harmondsworth: Penguin Books, 1952), pp. 95–98. Reprinted by permission of Penguin Books, Ltd.

notist is a sort of magician, who by suitable spells can bind the will of others independently of any previous readiness to co-operate on their part. If that were true, we should surely have to admit that people's actions were sometimes prompted by someone else's motives or desires, not their own. We cannot be certain that such a dependence of one man's actions on another man's will never exists, and therefore we cannot be certain that a man's actions are always, without any exception, prompted by his own desires or motives.

It may be replied that performances produced in the magically hypnotic way could not properly be called 'actions', in the sense in which moralists use the word, any more than the convulsions produced by an electric shock, or blinking in response to a dazzling light. Only what results in some way from the will or desires of the agent can be an action. If we imagine that a hypnotist might arbitrarily induce his subject to behave in ways repugnant to him when unhypnotised, there are, it might be said, two possibilities. He might generate in his subject desires or impulses never previously felt, or he might bring about bodily movements and utterances directly, as though by giving an electric shock. But if the first alternative is realised, the statement that the subject's actions are prompted by motives of his own remains true: while if the second alternative is realised, the subject's performances are not actions at all, so that the generalisation is still unaffected.

All this could be put more precisely, but enough has perhaps been said to explain the axiomatic certainty which seems to belong to the statement that a man's actions must be prompted by his own motives. When a case, real or imaginary, is produced in which it appears that a man acts from no motive or desire of his own, we may at once classify his performance as not properly an action. Alternatively, we may retain the right to call his performance an action by postulating a desire or motive on the subject's part in spite of appearances. In short, the generalisation that all my actions spring from *my* desires or motives proves to be a disguised tautology, which must be true, given the accepted meaning of the word 'action'. In an undisguised form, it would appear as the statement 'every performance which springs from a motive of mine is a performance which springs from a motive of mine'. And this tautology cannot support the conclusion that all my performances spring from selfish motives.

Psychological egoists would claim that every action is prompted, not merely by a motive of the agent's own, but by a motive of a particular kind. . . .

FRANK C. SHARP

The Case of Abe Lincoln and the Drowning Piglets*

. . . The man we call altruistic commonly derives a certain satisfaction from helping others, and feels uneasy and dissatisfied when he injures them or leaves them in the lurch; what more obvious than the suggestion that it is the attainment of this satisfaction or the avoidance of this dissatisfaction which supplies the motive of his action?

Abraham Lincoln (in reality one of the most altruistic of men) once expressed this theory of the will in the course of a famous incident, one version of which reads as follows:

"Mr. Lincoln once remarked to a fellow-passenger on an old-time mud-coach that all men were prompted by selfishness in doing good. His fellow-passenger was antagonizing this position when they were passing over a corduroy bridge that spanned a slough. As they crossed this bridge they espied an old razor-backed sow on the bank making a terrible noise because her pigs had got into the slough and were in danger of drowning. As the old coach began to climb the hill, Mr. Lincoln called out, 'Driver,

* From Frank C. Sharp, *Ethics* (New York: Appleton-Century, 1928), pp. 74–76.

can't you stop just a moment?' Then Mr. Lincoln jumped out, ran back, and lifted the little pigs out of the mud and water and placed them on the bank. When he returned, his companion remarked: 'Now, Abe, where does selfishness come in on this little episode?' 'Why, bless your soul, Ed, that was the very essence of selfishness. I should have had no peace of mind all day had I gone on and left that suffering old sow worrying over those pigs. I did it to get peace of mind, don't you see?' "[1]

The fallacy of this explanation, however, is very easy to expose. The attainment of every desire, of whatever sort, tends to arouse a feeling of satisfaction. There is, for example, the desire to know certain facts, whether these refer to the size of the great star Betelgeuze in the constellation of Orion, or the status of the young man who calls so assiduously on the girl next door. When the knowledge comes, satisfaction is normally felt. But the rise into consciousness of this satisfaction is due to the existence of the desire; and the object of the desire, therefore, was not the satisfaction, but the satisfaction was rather the consequence of the preëxisting desire. This statement of course holds equally for dissatisfaction, from its weakest form as a vague feeling of uneasiness to its most massive and intense manifestations as sorrow or grief. Each is the sign of an aversion from a state of things which now is, or which is expected to come into existence. If there had been no such aversion there would have been no feeling.[2]

All this applies to altruism. As with all other desires, attainment brings, or tends to bring satisfaction or joy; failure normally brings dissatisfaction, and in extreme cases sorrow. But the satisfaction could never have been obtained, dissatisfaction would never have come, if the desire for the realization of the other person's welfare had not been there in the first place. Therefore when a man's peace of mind is interfered with by the sufferings of another he must have at least some amount, whether great or small, of direct desire for their good and aversion from their harm.

It is possible for people possessed of only a small measure of altruism so to manipulate their altruistic desires as to use them as a means for the promotion of personal pleasure. They may carefully avoid scenes likely to call for any large amount of sacrifice; and when fairly caught, so that escape is out of the question, they may meet the situation by turning the attention in another direction; like the man who always rode in the street car with his eyes closed, because he could not bear to see ladies standing when he had a seat. But this is no more than we can do with our egoistic desires. The man who is without deep, long-sighted egoism, who is possessed of no capacity to adopt as an end of action a good for himself somewhat remote in time, may handle his desires for personal good with strict reference to the interests of that immediate future which we commonly call the present. A spendthrift, for example, may be driven by his fears into giving a moment's attention to his ebbing assets. But when the thought of the impending crash becomes quite unendurable he may drive it from his mind by rushing into a new debauch. The fact that we may use our altruistic endowment for the sake of our own "present" pleasure no more proves its non-existence than the fact that we may do precisely the same thing with our desire for the welfare of our next year's self proves that no such thing exists as regard for our more remote personal future . . .

[1] Quoted from the Springfield (Ill.) *Monitor* in the *Outlook*, Vol. 56, p. 1059.

[2] *Cf.* James, *Principles of Psychology*, Vol. II, pp. 555–558.

Suggestions for Further Reading

PART 1. REASON AND RELIGIOUS FAITH

Virtually all of the important writings on the ontological argument from St. Anselm to the present have recently been brought together in one volume, *The Ontological Argument,* edited by Alvin Plantinga, with an introduction by Richard Taylor (New York: Doubleday Anchor Books: 1965).

For recent versions and defenses of the arguments of St. Thomas Aquinas, see G. H. Joyce, The *Principles of Natural Theology* (New York: Longmans, Green, 1951), and D. J. B. Hawkins, *The Essentials of Theism* (New York: Sheed and Ward, 1949).

A classic statement and defense of the argument from design is found in William Paley's *Evidences of the Existence and Attributes of the Deity* (1802). See also the discussion in John Stuart Mill's "Theism" in his *Three Essays on Religion* (1875). David Hume's writings on religion have been gathered together in a useful volume with an excellent introductory essay by Richard Wolheim, *David Hume on Religion* (Meridian Books, 1964).

For the problem of evil see *God and Evil,* edited by Nelson Pike (Englewood Cliffs, N.J.: Prentice-Hall, 1964) and the helpful bibliography contained therein.

For contemporary discussions of the meaning of religious statements, verification, falsifiability, and related problems, see the following two excellent collections: *New Essays in Philosophical Theology,* edited by Antony Flew and Alasdair MacIntyre (New York: Macmillan, 1955), and *Faith and Logic,* edited by Basil Mitchell (London: Allen and Unwin, 1957). See also Alasdair MacIntyre's "The Logical Status of Religious Belief," in *Metaphysical Beliefs* (London: S. C. M. Press, 1957).

For sympathetic discussions of religious mysticism, see W. R. Inge, *Mysticism in Religion* (Chicago: University of Chicago Press, 1948), and W. T. Stace, *Mysticism and Philosophy* (Philadelphia: Lippincott, 1960). For an unsympathetic discussion based on psychological analysis, see J. H. Leuba, *The Psychology of Religious Mysticism* (New York: Harcourt, Brace, and World, 1925).

For discussions of the religious significance of drugs, consult the footnote references in Huston Smith's article above. For views opposed to William James's on the reasonableness of beliefs based on no adequate evidence, see W. K. Clifford's "The Ethics of Belief" in his *Lectures and Essays,* Vol. II (London: Macmillan, 1879). The classic statement of "agnosticism" (that in the absence of evidence belief should be suspended) is T. H. Huxley's in his *Essays upon Controversial Questions* (1889).

Many of the topics in Part 1 are discussed in two recent important books: John Hick's *Faith and Knowledge* (Ithaca, N.Y.: Cornell University Press, 1957), a book sympathetic to religious belief; and Wallace I. Matson's *The Existence of God* (Ithaca, N.Y.: Cornell University Press, 1965), a book written from the agnostic point of view.

PART 2. HUMAN KNOWLEDGE: ITS GROUNDS AND LIMITS

For general introductions to the problems of epistemology (the theory of knowledge), the following books are recommended: A. J. Ayer, *The Problem of Knowledge* (Baltimore; Penguin Books, 1956); R. M. Chisholm, *Theory of Knowledge* (Englewood Cliffs, N.J.: Prentice-Hall, forthcoming, 1966); John Hospers, *Introduction to Philosophical Analysis* (Englewood Cliffs, N.J.: Prentice-Hall, 1953), Chap. 2, 3, 6; Bertrand Russell, *The Problems of Philosophy* (London: Oxford University Press, 1912); C. H. Whiteley, *An Introduction to Metaphysics* (London: Methuen, 1949), Chap. 6, 7; A. D. Woozley, *Theory of Knowledge* (London: Hutchinson's University Library, 1949).

For general accounts of the period from Descartes through Kant in histories of philosophy, see Frederick Copleston, S. J., *A History of Philosophy* (Westminster, Maryland: Westminster Press, 1960), Vol. IV, V, VI; and Frank Thilly and Ledger Wood, *A History of Philosophy,* 3rd ed. (New York: Holt, 1957).

Norman Kemp Smith has written valuable commentaries on Descartes, Hume, and Kant: *Studies in the Cartesian Philosophy* (London, 1902), *New Studies in the Philosophy of Descartes* (London, 1953), *The Philosophy of David Hume* (London, 1941), and *A Commentary to Kant's 'Critique of Pure Reason'* (London, 1918).

The following are also valuable studies of individual philosophers: G. J. Warnock, *Berkeley* (Baltimore: Penguin Books, 1953); A. H. Basson, *David Hume* (Baltimore: Penguin Books, 1958); and S. Körner, *Kant* (Baltimore: Penguin Books, 1955).

Classical expositions of phenomenalism are John Stuart Mill's *An Examination of Sir William Hamilton's Philosophy* (London, 1872) and Karl Pearson's *The Grammar of Science* (London, 1892).

For an illuminating discussion of the kind of argument used in Berkeley's first dialogue, see A. J. Ayer, *The Foundations of Empirical Knowledge,* Chap. 1. Ayer is criticized in turn by J. L. Austin in *Sense and Sensibilia* (New York: Oxford University Press, 1964).

Additional statements of pragmatism are found in William James, *Pragmatism* (New York: Longmans, Green, 1907), and John Dewey, *Reconstruction in Philosophy* (New York: Henry Holt, 1920). W. B. Gallie's *Peirce and Pragmatism* (Baltimore: Penguin Books, 1952) is a helpful commentary.

PART 3. MIND AND ITS PLACE IN NATURE

A very valuable recent collection of articles on the mind-body problem by philosophers of all persuasions is *Dimensions of Mind,* edited by Sidney Hook (New York: New York University Press, 1960). Another useful anthology is *Body, Mind, and Death,* edited by Antony Flew (New York: Macmillan, 1964).

Descartes's *Meditations* are published with the complete *Objections and Replies* in *The Philosophical Works of Descartes* (Cambridge: Cambridge University Press, 1934; and New York: Dover Publications, 1955), as well as in several other editions. Descartes's views on the relation between mind and body are also found in *On the Passions of the Soul* (1630). For an account of Gassendi's own positive views see *The Philosophy of Gassendi* by G. S. Brett (New York, 1908).

Among twentieth-century works defending interactionism are John Laird's *Our Minds and Their Bodies* (London: Oxford University Press, 1925) and J. B. Pratt's *Matter and Spirit* (New York: Macmillan, 1926).

C. J. Ducasse's conceptions of mind and the prospects of its survival of the death of the body are spelled out in more detail in his book, *A Critical Examination of the Belief in a Life after Death* (Springfield, Illinois: Charles C Thomas, 1961). See also his *Nature, Mind, and Death* (La Salle, Illinois: Open Court, 1951), Chap. 20 and 21; and H. H. Price, "Personal Identity and Survival" (London: Society for Psychical Research, 1958). For the case against survival, see Corliss Lamont, *The Illusion of Immortality* (New York: G. P. Putnam's, 1935) and C. Cohen, *The Other Side of Death* (London: The Pioneer Press, 1922).

J. J. C. Smart's *Philosophy and Scientific Realism* (London: Routledge & Kegan Paul; New York: Humanities Press) is a recent statement and defense of "the identity theory." Classic statements of the other form of materialism (epiphenomenalism) are found in T. H. Huxley's "On the Hypothesis That Animals Are Automata and Its History" in *Methods and Results* (London and New York: Appleton, 1874), and in Shadworth Hodgson, *The Metaphysics of Experience* (London: Longmans, Green, 1898), Vol. II. Epiphenomenalism finds expression in the form of a beautiful parable in George Santayana's "Normal Madness," in *Dialogues in Limbo* (New York: Scribners, 1926).

PART 4. DETERMINISM, FREEDOM, AND RESPONSIBILITY

Three very valuable symposia on these subjects have appeared in recent years: *Determinism and Freedom in the Age of Modern Science,* edited by Sidney Hook (New York: New York University Press, 1958); *Free Will,* edited by Sidney Morgenbesser and James Walsh (Englewood Cliffs, N.J.: Prentice-Hall, 1962); and *Freedom and the Will,* edited by D. F. Pears (London: Macmillan; New York: St. Martin's Press, 1963). Most of the essays in the latter originated as talks in the Third Programme of the British Broadcasting Corporation.

The reconciling determinist position is defended in Thomas Hobbes's *Leviathan* (1651), Chap. 21; in John Locke's *Essay Concerning Human Understanding,* Book II, Chap. 21; in David Hume's *Treatise of Human Nature,* Book II, Part III; and in John Stuart Mill's *System of Logic* (1843), Book VI, Chap. 2. Recent influential arguments for the theory are found in Chapter 7 of Moritz Schlick's *Problems of Ethics* (Englewood Cliffs, N.J.: Prentice-Hall, 1939); in Chapter 14 of Charles L. Stevenson's *Ethics and Language* (New Haven: Yale University Press, 1944), in R. B. Hobart's "Free-Will as Involving Determinism and Inconceivable without It," *Mind,* 1934; and in Frederick Vivian, *Human Freedom and Responsibility* (London: Chatto & Windus, 1964).

Deterministic theories of a relatively non-reconciling kind are found in Baruch Spinoza's *Ethics,* Part III; in *System of Nature* by Baron D'Holbach (1770); and in essays by Paul Edwards and John Hospers in the Sidney Hook anthology mentioned above. See also the speeches of the great American criminal lawyer Clarence Darrow, in *Attorney for the Damned,* edited by Arthur Weinberg (New York: Simon and Schuster, 1957), especially Part One.

Indeterminist theories are defended in Henri Bergson, *Time and Free Will* (New York: Macmillan, 1921); Isaiah Berlin, *Historical Inevitability* (London: Oxford University Press, 1954); Roderick M. Chisholm, *Human Freedom and the Self,* The Lindley Lecture, University of Kansas, 1964; Stuart Hampshire, *Thought and Action* (New York: Viking Press, 1960); William James, "The Dilemma of Determinism," first published in 1884 and now widely anthologized; Charles S. Peirce, "The Doctrine of Necessity Examined," reprinted in *The Philosophy of Peirce,* edited by J. Buchler (New York: Harcourt, Brace, 1950); Thomas Reid, *Essays on the Powers of the Human Mind* (1812), Vol. III; and Jean-Paul Sartre, *Being and Nothingness* (New York: Philosophical Library, 1956). C. A. Campbell's theory, outlined in his selection in this book, is worked out in greater detail in his *Skepticism and Construction* (London: Allen and Unwin, 1931), and *On Selfhood and Godhood* (London: Allen and Unwin; New York: Macmillan, 1957), Lecture IX.

PART 5. RESPONSIBILITY, BLAME, AND PUNISHMENT

For a large and unusually complete collection of readings on criminal punishment and other problems concerning responsibility in law and morals, see Herbert Morris (editor), *Freedom and Responsibility* (Stanford, Calif.: Stanford University Press, 1961). Excellent general discussions of the topics of this and the preceding section are also found in Richard B. Brandt, *Ethical Theory* (Englewood Cliffs, N.J.: Prentice-Hall, 1959), Chap. 18–20; and in John Hospers, *Human Conduct* (Harcourt, Brace, & World, 1961), Chap. 9 and 10.

For a general account of Aristotle's ethics, see W. D. Ross, *Aristotle* (New York: Meridian Books, 1959), Chap. 7. An excellent analysis of Aristotle's theory of personal responsibility against the background of centuries of Greek thought on the subject is found in Arthur W. H. Adkins, *Merit and Responsibility* (Oxford: Clarendon Press, 1960), Chap. 15.

Classical scources of the utilitarian theory of punishment are Jeremy Bentham, *An Introduction to the Principles of Morals and Legislation* (Oxford: Basil Blackwell, 1948) and *The Rationale of Punishment* (1830). See also the Marquis de Beccaria, *An Essay on Crimes and Punishments* (Albany: W. C. Lettle, 1872), first published in 1764; Hastings Rashdall, *Theory of Good and Evil* (Oxford: Clarendon Press, 1924), Vol. I, Chap. 9; and H. Wechsler and J. Michael, "A Rationale of the Law of Homicide," *Columbia Law Review,* 1937.

Views similar to those of Butler's Erewhonian "malcontents" are expressed in Plato's *Protagoras* (324–325), *Gorgias* (479–480 and 525–526), and *Republic* (380); in Robert Owen, *Letters to the Human Race* (London, 1850), and in Leo Tolstoy, *What I Believe* (Oxford Centenary Edition, 1933), Vol. II. See also Tolstoy's novel *Resurrection.* For recent versions of the view that all crime is sickness, see Benjamin Karpman, "Criminality, Insanity, and the Law," *Journal of Criminal Law and Criminology* (1939), and *The Criminal Mind,* by Philip Q. Roche, M.D. (New York: Grove Press, 1958). For the contrary view, that only some criminals are mentally ill, see Paul Schilder, *Psychoanalysis, Man, and Society* (New York: Norton, 1951).

For the moralistic (Kantian) version of the retributive theory, see Josef Kohler, *Philosophy of Law* (Boston: Boston Book Co., 1914), and Rudolf Stammler, *The Theory of Justice* (New York: Macmillan, 1925). The leading American Kantian was Francis Wharton. See his *A Treatise on Criminal Law,* 8th ed. (Philadelphia, 1880).

The main source of Hegel's theory of punishment is *Hegel's Philosophy of Right,* translated by T. M. Knox (Oxford, 1953), especially sections 90–104. An excellent critique of retributivism is found in Chapter I of A. C. Ewing's *The Morality of Punishment* (London: Kegan Paul, 1929). Ewing's book is probably the best book-length treatment of the philosophy of punishment written in this century.

For discussions sympathetic to the view that vengeance is a legitimate function of criminal punishment, see James Fitzjames Stephen, *History of the Criminal Law* (1883), Vol. I, p. 478, and Vol. II, pp. 81–82 *et passim;* and G. de Tarde, *Penal Philosophy* (Boston: Little, Brown and Co., 1912).

A developed theory of the sort suggested by the Mabbott and Rawls selections is to be found in S. I. Benn and R. S. Peters, *Social Principles and the Democratic State* (London: Allen and Unwin, 1959), Chap. 8.

For discussions of blame and blameworthiness, see Chapter 18 of Richard Brandt's *Ethical Theory,* and consult the footnote references in Elizabeth Beardsley's article included here.

PART 6. SELF LOVE AND THE CLAIMS OF MORALITY

For commentaries on Plato's *Republic,* see A. E. Taylor, *Plato, the Man and His Work* (New York: Humanities Press, 1927), Chap. XI; and R. C. Cross and A. D. Woozley, *Plato's Republic, A Philosophical Commentary* (London: Macmillan, 1964).

For various answers to, and discussions of, the question "Why Should I Be Moral?" see the following: Kurt Baier, *The Moral Point of View* (Ithaca, N.Y.: Cornell University Press, 1958), Chap. 11, 12; F. H. Bradley, *Ethical Studies* (Oxford, 1876), Essay II; John Hospers, *Human Conduct* (New York: Harcourt, Brace & World, 1961), Chap. 4; Frank C. Sharp, *Ethics* (New York: Appleton-Century, 1928), Chap. 22, 23.

Other discussions of ethical egoism are contained in Richard C. Brandt, *Ethical Theory,* Chap. 14; G. E. Moore, *Principia Ethica* (Cambridge: Cambridge University Press, 1903), Chap. III C; James B. Pratt, *Reason in the Art of Living* (New York: Macmillan, 1949), Chap. 10; Moritz Schlick, *Problems of Ethics* (Englewood Cliffs, N.J.: Prentice-Hall, 1939), Chap. 3; and Henry Sidgwick, *The Methods of Ethics,* 7th ed. (New York and London: Macmillan, 1907), Book II.

Philosophical works arguing against psychological egoism are legion. Among the best of these are: C. D. Broad, "Egoism as a Theory of Human Motives" in *Ethics and the History of Philosophy* (New York: Humanities Press, 1952); Lucius Garvin, *A Modern Introduction to Ethics* (Boston: Houghton Mifflin, 1953), Chap. 2; William James, *The Principles of Psychology* (New York: Henry Holt, 1890), Vol. II, Chap. XXVI; Hastings Rashdall, *The Theory of Good and Evil* (London: Oxford University Press, 1924), Vol. I, Chap. 2; and Henry Sidgwick, *Methods of Ethics,* Book I, Chap. 4.

Even if the a priori arguments for psychological egoism are all fallacious, there may yet be empirical evidence for egoism derived from psychological learning theory, argues Michael Anthony Slote in his suggestive article "An Empirical Basis for Psychological Egoism," *Journal of Philosophy,* Vol. 61, 1964.